Selected Writings, Volume 1

Okwui
Enwezor

Selected Writings

VOLUME 1

Toward a New African Art Discourse

Edited by Terry Smith

DUKE UNIVERSITY PRESS
Durham and London
2025

© 2025 Duke University Press
All rights reserved

Printed in the United States of America
on acid-free paper ∞

Project Editor: Lisa Lawley
Designed by A. Mattson Gallagher

Typeset in Portrait Text, Real Head Pro,
and Source Serif 4 Caption
by Westchester Publishing Services

Library of Congress
Cataloging-in-Publication Data
Names: Enwezor, Okwui, author. | Smith, Terry
(Terry E.), editor.
Title: Selected writings, volume 1. Toward a
new African art discourse / Okwui Enwezor;
edited by Terry Smith.
Other titles: Toward a new African art discourse
Description: Durham : Duke University Press,
2025. | Includes bibliographical references
and index.
Identifiers: LCCN 2024042941 (print)
LCCN 2024042942 (ebook)
ISBN 9781478031529 (paperback)
ISBN 9781478028314 (hardcover)
ISBN 9781478060536 (ebook)
Subjects: LCSH: Arts, African. | Arts, American. |
Arts and society. | Arts–Political aspects–
Africa. | Arts–Political aspects–United States. |
Postcolonialism and the arts. | African diaspora
in art. | Curatorship–Political aspects.
Classification: LCC NX587 .E58 2025 vol.1
(print) | LCC NX587 (ebook) |
DDC 700.96–dc23/eng/20241230
LC record available at https://lccn.loc.
gov/2024042941
LC ebook record available at https://lccn.loc.
gov/2024042942

Cover art: Okwui Enwezor, Kassel, Germany,
March 2002. Photo by Sabine Simon/ullstein
bild via Getty Images.

Published in cooperation with The Africa
Institute and Sharjah Art Foundation

SHARJAH ART FOUNDATION

Contents

Illustrations

Foreword

Hoor Al Qasimi,
President and Director, Sharjah Art Foundation

These two volumes of selected writings by the late Okwui Enwezor are one of the outcomes of the multiyear research project and curatorial initiative Thinking Historically in the Present. Coming together as a constellation of discursive and aesthetic experimentations centered around the thirtieth anniversary of the Sharjah Biennial, the volumes reflect, commemorate, and reaffirm Enwezor's influential thinking on the contemporary arts. My first encounter with Enwezor's line of inquiry was at Documenta11 in 2002, the many platforms of which reframed the experience of globalization and contemporary arts beyond the purview of Western colonial epistemologies. At the twilight of a century haunted by cultural wars and new global realities after the attacks of 9/11, Enwezor's corpus of work inspired curatorial models that abandon the nation and its ideology as a condition of human experience and its expression, emphasizing instead experiences of hybridity, multimodality, and creolization.

I extended Enwezor's exhibition making by questioning the Sharjah Biennial's existing embrace of the national-pavilion curatorial model, as had been established during its inauguration in 1993. Having grown up in Sharjah with the local biennial, first as a visitor and then as a participating artist, I curated the Biennial in 2003 by overhauling this existing model and brought together artists, practicing locally and globally, to propose new art modalities and solidarities, outside the prevailing status quo of national or ideological identities. The sixth edition of the Sharjah Biennial then paved the way for the consequent experimentation with the biennial format and for the founding of the Sharjah Art Foundation in 2009. This consolidated a permanent space in Sharjah as a non-Western center for the circulation of people and ideas, a place that could grow into a critical alternative to entrenched institutional thought.

In 2018 I invited Enwezor to curate the thirtieth edition of the Sharjah Biennial as an extended lens into this history of the Biennial and the evolution of his pedagogy. He wrote to me about his ideas for the Biennial in an email on October 26, 2018:

> I see the Sharjah Biennial and by extension, Sharjah Art Foundation as a product of a certain historical development, as a model with which to deal with the disruptive power of artistic multilingualism, but also as a horizon, a horizon of possibility, to conceive another theoretical space for thinking historically in the present. With that, I have said it and with further thinking to be done, my provisional idea is to use thinking historically in the present as the basis to develop Biennale 30. However, I'm not interested in doing just another middling contemporary art exhibition that just disappears. I want to engage your entire institution.

Before his passing, we agreed that given the personal and reflective nature of the fifteenth edition of the Biennial and the twenty years since its curatorial shift, I would curate and stage the concept of Thinking Historically in the Present through a contextual interpretation. The edition served as a vantage point for the Biennial to reflect on its cultural heritage and historical influence, the artistic possibilities it has enabled, and its role in linking Sharjah to transnational intellectual and artistic discourses. It took root in the three editions of the March Meeting from 2021 to 2023, Sharjah's annual convening of artists, practitioners, and thinkers, which occurs in addition to the Biennial exhibition of more than 150 artists, as well as performance, film, music, and publishing initiatives. Together, these projects and works pay tribute to postcolonial subjectivity, underrepresentation and auto-archival practices, the body as a repository of memories, processes of creolization and hybridization, the restitution of museumized objects, the racializing gaze, transgenerational continuities, global modernisms, Indigeneity, and decolonization in contemporary cultural practices. Not confined to the Sharjah Art Foundation, it also included discreet overlaps with our extended cultural network, such as with the sites of the Africa Institute and the Sharjah Architecture Triennial as well as the towns and cities of the Sharjah Emirate. Initiating relationships to Hamriyah, Al Dhaid, Kalba, and Khorfakkan through the biennial form, it echoed Enwezor's sentiments of bringing the civic engine of art to places where art is rarely seen—as he did when using the Electric Workshops in Johannesburg as the major venue for his 1997 exhibition, *Trade Routes*, the title of the 2nd Johannesburg Biennale.

In this joint collaborative project of the Sharjah Art Foundation, the Africa Institute, and Duke University Press, under the editorial leadership of Terry Smith, we deploy scholarship and cultural critique to highlight the necessary relationship between the arts. Readers are invited to journey through the evolution of Enwezor's thoughts, from 1993 through 2019, with one volume dedicated to Enwezor's body of work on the African arts, and the other his writing on postcolonial subjectivity. The selection of texts pays due heed to Enwezor's intellectual project and to his influences on exhibition spaces and curatorial models from non-Western and nonhegemonic perspectives. It brings together a selection of his most important writings, interviews with and reviews of the work of leading artists, and collaborative texts with peers.

The Sharjah Art Foundation, the Africa Institute, and Duke University Press are delighted to have initiated this collaboration that brings the subjects and visions of Enwezor's substantive practice to a wider audience. I would like to thank everyone involved in the realization of this publication; the editor, Terry Smith; and the Enwezor Estate for providing us with access and rights to the publication of these important texts. I have no doubt that these two volumes of selected writings by Enwezor will make his work more accessible and provide a vital contribution to the fields of visual culture and to the representational politics of contemporary art in cultural institutions, platforms, and organizations.

Advisory Editors' Preface

Salah M. Hassan and Chika Okeke-Agulu

By the time our dear brother and colleague Okwui Enwezor died in March 2019 at fifty-five, he was a peerless presence and voice in the world of contemporary art. During a career that lasted only twenty-five years, he led the way, more than any other curator and critic, in reordering not just the landscape of contemporary art but also the ways we talk and write about it. The clarity and tenacity of his vision were remarkable, compelling, urgent, and necessary, and Terry Smith has made this utterly evident in this two-volume anthology of Okwui's important writings.

Okwui relished long-form articles and texts. However, he did not publish a single-authored monograph or a collection of his writings in his lifetime, but not because he could not stay with his subject matter in the sustained manner such publications require, or did not see the need for gathering his ideas in such a way that allowed for greater appreciation of the threads and lines connecting his prodigious and wide-ranging scholarship. In fact, he liked to talk with much enthusiasm about his rolling plans for collections of his writings on topics like African artists and the archive, photography, film, and the postcolonial condition, but he would change the topic when pressed for a schedule or timeline. In this, he was Okwui the procrastinator. But as his illness took its toll in what would be his last years, it became clear that we needed to make concrete plans for one or more anthologies of his published and unpublished writings in his absence. And when Okwui conveyed to us his wish to have Terry Smith serve as the editor of his published writings, we could not imagine a better choice. Not only had Smith established a sure reputation as a leading scholar and theorist of contemporary art's global contexts, but he was among the very few scholars who helped bring Okwui's work to the attention of academic art history and criticism in the United States. Moreover, he identified with the critical interventions Okwui made through his exhibitions and writings; in turn, Okwui counted him as a veritable intellectual ally, and their many collaborations testified to their mutual respect and admiration. With this two-volume anthology, Smith delivers what we believe will be an enduring collection of Okwui's most important texts. With his magisterial introductory essays, Smith illuminates the originality and progression of Okwui's ideas as critic and scholar, which we who witnessed their making from the closest range possible find truly refreshing.

Given his stellar record of accomplishments as a curator, critic, academic, and museum director, Okwui's unlikely journey from what were the margins of the art world to what would be its multiple nodal points is at once remarkable and telling. Years after leaving Nigeria as a young man in search of America's attractive opportunities, he realized, as did many among his generation of Africans who made similar journeys out of the continent, that to secure a place at the table, you must have the agentive power and confidence to fight for it. We still recall the clarity of the vision he articulated in his invitation to us and a few others working in Africa, Europe, and the United States in late 1993 to start a new journal through which we might, as he put it, redraw the boundaries of African art. That publication, *Nka: Journal of Contemporary African Art*, stands today as one of Okwui's most enduring intellectual legacies, and it was in the journal's pages that, from the onset, he insistently made the case for African and African diaspora artists' place in the global arena, but also for a rigorous critical discourse on their work.

Even so, Okwui was profoundly aware of the tough task he set for himself, all the more because of, in the first instance, pervasive resistance by the old guard Africanists to his call for reassessment of who and what constituted contemporary African art; and, second, the resounding lack of meaningful interest on the part of Western institutions in these artists and their work. The assertive and vigorous tone of his early writings on individual artists and groups, or on such art fields as African photography, is indicative of the seriousness with which he embarked on his critical enterprise. While it would take years for the full impact of his mission—along with the network of peers he mobilized through the journal and his curatorial work—to be manifest in scholarship and museums, the singularity of his voice as a commentator and theorist of contemporary art was groundbreaking. To track, across the two volumes of this anthology, Okwui's investment in anticolonial, postcolonial, diasporic, and global dimensions of contemporary African art and its intersections with the art worlds of the Global South and North is to witness the making of what has since become a veritably international art discourse in which African and Black artists now figure prominently. They testify, moreover, to the uniqueness and substance of his engagement with the politics of representation and with the long shadow that the age of systematic enslavement of Africans and the colonization of Africa has cast on contemporary art, its institutions, and the knowledge economy.

Allied with Okwui's insistence on the value and urgency of a vigorous critical discourse in support of the important yet largely ignored work of African and Black artists is his view of curating as groundwork scholarship needed for the emergence and consolidation of this vital field of contemporary art. Each exhibition, for him, was an opportunity to showcase the art and artists he identified with; even more important, it served for him as an occasion to engage deeply with existing and new ideas, theories, and critical discourses on his subject. As much as he was peerless—even legendary—in putting up a good show, with impeccably installed artworks, and in engaging collaboratively with his artists, he put as much value on the substantial introductory essay, convinced that curating is first and foremost scholarly and intellectual work. The reader of this anthology, we hope, will appreciate the vigor and sophistication of Okwui's critical and theoretical reflections on art, photography, and film in the service of exhibitions such as the 2nd Johannesburg Biennale (1997), *The Short Century* (2001), Documenta11 (2002), *Archive Fever* (2008), the 56th Venice Biennale (2015), and *Postwar* (2016), as well as the revelatory and insightful exploration of the work of individual artists. In fact, we cannot think of anyone, past or present, with a comparable record of sustained deployment of the art exhibition as an instrument and site of consequential and critical knowledge production.

In his last years, Okwui had several new and ongoing projects, despite his advancing illness. One of these was curating the 15th Sharjah Biennial, which the president of the Sharjah Art Foundation, our dear friend and colleague Sheikha Hoor Al Qasimi, had invited him to curate. As usual, Okwui planned to use the Biennial as the occasion to present the work of important artists from the Global South who explore the multiple contexts and histories of what he called the *postcolonial constellation* but also as a venue for convening new and existing scholarship on the subject. While he did not live to realize the Biennial, he entrusted its curation to Al Qasimi, who successfully delivered a momentous exhibition and program and gave her unflinching support for this anthology as part of the publications associated with the Biennial. We are truly grateful to her for giving Okwui the opportunity of conceiving the Biennial to articulate the artistic and exhibitionary manifestation of the idea of the postcolonial constellation that served as a theoretical armature for his late scholarship. While Okwui thought of the Biennial and the publication of an anthology of his writings as separate projects entrusted to us (his estate and circle of friends), conjoining these projects, as has happened, affirms the fundamental relationship between his scholarly and curatorial work. The resulting institutional and financial support of the Sharjah Art Foundation and its sister organization, the Africa Institute, eliminated what might have been multiyear delays in securing the requisite funding for major, dare we say hefty, publications such as these two volumes.

Acknowledgments

The editor wishes to thank in particular two long-term collaborators with Okwui Enwezor: Chika Okeke-Agulu, his literary executor, and Salah M. Hassan, director of the Africa Institute, for their sustained support of this project and acute advice in their role as advisory editors.

I also thank Hoor Al Qasimi, president and director of the Sharjah Art Foundation, for her commitment to this project and generous support of it.

Thanks to Okwui Enwezor's family, in particular his daughter Uchenna and sister Maureen.

I thank Ilhan Ozan for providing initial research assistance and for compiling the bibliography.

I am grateful to Octavio Zaya for permission to reprint a text coauthored with Okwui Enwezor.

For their advice and encouragement, I thank Louise Neri, Molly Nesbit, Ute Meta Bauer, Nancy Condee, Ulrich Wilmes, Damian Lentini, James Meyer, and the many who offered expressions of support during the March 15 Meeting of the Sharjah Art Foundation in 2023.

At the Africa Institute, I thank in particular Sataan Al-Hassan for his shepherding of the project and Reem Elbadawi for her outstanding work on securing the illustrations and permissions.

At the Sharjah Art Foundation, I thank Maria Mumtaz and Ahmad Makia.

At Duke University Press, I thank chief editor Ken Wissoker for his unstinting support of the project from the beginning, Ryan Kendall for managing the project through the publication process, project editor Lisa Lawley, and the external readers for helpful reports.

Every reasonable effort has been made to secure all permissions for the use of each image. For granting permission to reproduce images of their work, I thank the artists. For supplying the images, I thank the following: Artimage, London; ADAGP, Paris; Agence photographique de la Réunion des Musées Nationaux et du Grand Palais RMNGP, Paris; Allan Sekula Studio, Los Angeles; Autograph, London; Cendrine du Welz; Centro de Documentação e Formação Fotográfica, Maputo, Mozambique; Clark Art Institute Library, Williamstown, MA; David Goldblatt Estate; Design and Artists Copyright Society, London; documenta archiv, Kassel; Etienne Bol; Fatimah Tuggar and BintaZarah Studios; Galerie Chantal Crousel, Paris; Awa Diarra Gaye; Getty Images Middle East, Dubai; Goodman Gallery, Johannesburg, Cape Town, London; Haupt and Binder, Berlin; Hauser and Wirth, London; Helene Smuts; IMO DARA, London; Jack Shainman Gallery, New York; Janine Zagel; Jean Marc Patras, Paris; The Jean Pigozzi African Art Collection, Geneva; Lyle Ashton Harris Studio, New York; MAGNIN-A, Paris; Maker Studio, Johannesburg; the Metropolitan Museum of Art, New York; Musée du quai Branly–Jacques Chirac, Paris; Museum of Modern Art, New York; Otobong Nkanga Studio; Paula Cooper Gallery, New York; Queens Museum, Queens, New York; Revue Noire, Paris; Roman Mensing Fotografie, Münster; Ruth and Marvin Sackner Archive of Concrete and Visual Poetry, Miami; Scala Archives, Florence; Selma Feriani Gallery, Tunis; Sprüth Magers, Berlin; Shirin Neshat Studio, New York; the Solomon R. Guggenheim Foundation, New York; Stephan Köhler, chairman of Kulturforum Sud-Nord, Hamburg and Cotonou; Verwertungsgesellschaft Bild-Kunst, Bonn; Video Data Bank, School of the Art Institute of Chicago, Chicago; and William Kentridge Studio, Johannesburg.

Introduction

Okwui Enwezor's Diasporic Imagination

Terry Smith

Okwui Enwezor was born in Calabar, Nigeria, on October 23, 1963, and was buried there, in the family plot, shortly after he died in a Munich hospital on March 15, 2019, surrounded by members of his family, his partner, and some close friends. Between these plainly stated dates and facts occurred times of tumult and confrontation leavened by communality, as well as much hard work, many pleasures, occasional moments of peace, and, through all this, in a growing arc, a certain magnificence.

Enwezor's extraordinarily productive career is seen by many today as one trajectory among those traced by the "star curators" who emerged in the 1990s to set the agendas through which the global expansiveness of contemporary art is to be seen. Exhibitions such as the 2nd Johannesburg Biennale, titled *Trade Routes: History and Geography* (1997), *The Short Century: Independence and Liberation Movements in Africa, 1945–1994* (2001), Documenta11 (2002), the 56th Venice Biennale, titled *All the World's Futures* (2015), and *Postwar: Art between the Pacific and the Atlantic, 1945–1965* (2016), curated by brilliant teams under his artistic direction, fit this bill. Yet they also exceed it because, while they shared much with the exhibitions of his fellow curators in their pacing of aesthetic pleasures, their introduction of lesser-known artists, and their highlighting of new kinds of art, they also took on a larger task: to manifest, viscerally, for each viewer, the ways in which artists experienced the geopolitical transformations that have occurred throughout the world since World War II. Enwezor had no doubt that these experiences, in all their contradictions, had been at the heart of what it was to become modern and that they continued to be crucial to what it is to participate fully in contemporary life. Nor did he doubt that artists, along with certain thinkers, were at the forefront of registering these experiences and that exhibitions were a primary medium for sharing, and augmenting, their insights.

His grasp of these experiences was shaped by his own life, as a child of civil war in Nigeria (1967–70), as a student there (at the Government College, Afikpo, 1974–79), and, after moving to the United States in 1982, as a student of political science at New Jersey City University, from which he graduated in 1987. Enwezor received no formal training as an artist, art historian, or curator. A young poet living in the Bronx and Brooklyn during the late 1980s, he founded, with sculptor Nari Ward, Akadibia (Igbo for "hand of the seer"), an East Village–based group of poets, artists, writers, and activists committed to finding a voice for an "African imaginary" in that vital scene. *Nka* ("Art" in Igbo) was launched in 1994 as their intervention into the New York art world and into broader debates about creativity and identity. The essays in these two volumes are the outcome of his subsequent career as a critic, curator, educator, and thinker active around the world, including his final years as a museum director in Germany. His insights came from the critical, historical perspective that he took toward the ways of the world, the analytical grounding that underscored his practice in each of these fields. His essays as collected here reveal the emergence, the growth, and then the deepening of that understanding. It was exercised through a profession of writing that matched the ambition of his curatorial practice and was inseparable from it.

Enwezor is best known for curating large-scale exhibitions. Several are now recognized by his peers, scholars, and informed publics as landmarks in the history of art in general, and his own contribution is ranked as equaling, for the subsequent generation of curators, that of his predecessor Harald Szeemann. Yet his achievements as an art critic, art historian (especially of photography, particularly African), theorist of postcolonialism, and university-based public educator have received less acknowledgment. In a 2013 lecture to the British Association of Art Historians, he identified his "own particular area of competence" as "contemporary art and contemporary African art through my work as a curator and writer, but also as a director of a museum and of several major biennials and international exhibitions, and as the dean of a college of art."[1] Except for the last, educational administration, a topic on which he did not publish, the essays in these volumes have been selected to bring out this multiplicity.

Redrawing the Boundaries

All Enwezor's activities served a clearly stated, proudly held, combative agenda: to renew African art—its practice, its theorization, its reception, its institutionalization, and the writing of its histories (to use Michel Foucault's word, its discourse). By African, he meant art made on the continent but also that made by members of its diaspora, especially African American artists and Black artists in Britain, the Caribbean, and Europe. *The diasporic imagination* was a phrase he often used to mark the nature and scope of the psychosocial field within which contemporary African art was being made. Well versed in current theorizations of postmodernity, he constantly sought to ground them in the experience of the midcentury struggles for independence, and those against the legacies of slavery. He drew deeply on the theorizations of postcoloniality that emerged from those experiences. For him, these struggles were the most important drivers of modern history and continued to shape the contemporary present. They were, he believed, decisive for artists of the diaspora.

In his editorial to the inaugural issue of *Nka: Journal of Contemporary African Art*, Enwezor introduces himself as "a writer and poet" and as the "publisher/editor" of the journal. Titled "Redrawing the Boundaries: Towards a New African Art Discourse," the essay sets out, in no uncertain terms, the quest that he would pursue for the rest of his life, one that would inform every aspect of his work, no matter its ostensible topic.[2] The first chapter in this volume, it was one of Enwezor's first essays to appear in print, in 1994.[3] Launching in Brooklyn, New York, a journal devoted to African art, Enwezor begins precisely—and presciently—from inside this apparent contradiction. Close to the heart of power, provoked by a vacuum within it. "One of the problematic aspects of visiting museums, art galleries, and other sites of cultural valuation, in Europe and in the United States," he begins, "is the pervasive absence in these highly policed environments, of art by contemporary African artists."[4] The reasons were everywhere evident. He rages against attitudes such as those expressed by Susan Vogel when she writes that "contact with the West has been the determining influence . . . for African art in the 20th century."[5] William Rubin's (in)famous 1984 exhibition at the Museum of Modern Art, New York, *"Primitivism" in 20th Century Art: Affinity of the Tribal and the Modern*, is slammed for dressing itself up as a "primitivist cultural festival." He is furious about the utter failure, in the West, to recognize that, in fact, the reverse had been taking place since "1906," alluding to Pablo Picasso's transformatory importation of African masks into his *Les Demoiselles d'Avignon*, routinely regarded as the breakthrough moment of twentieth-century modernism. He condemns in equal terms appeals by African artists and writers to "racial essentialism."[6] Instead, if "an artist like [El] Anatsui is insistent on representing African history via a multiplicity of signifiers such as Nsibidi and Uli symbols and ideograms, Akan and Adinkra symbols, Nok and Benin references, it is to say not only that the old European paradigms of representing history are grossly adequate, but also incapable of speaking with any resounding meaning to the malaise of our present ethical and philosophical consciousness."[7] Such speaking, he avers, is the primary purpose of art, of criticism, and of curating. An intense struggle to realize this worldly purpose was indeed taking place in "the field of contemporary African art"—a field that very much includes the artists of the diaspora—giving it, he insists, "an agency, a force, a vibrancy and equally a tension that is unequalled in any other regions of the world."[8]

Although he concludes the editorial with a gesture toward openness, saying, "We have no agendas. Nor do we speak for any special interests," the foregoing words make his determination clear. As does his direct characterization of the goals of *Nka*:

> At *Nka*, the artist who embodies the vision necessary to confront the complexities that face us in an age of change and ferment, yet is also able to carry us beyond established boundaries to other sites of significance and interest is one with whom we share a great affinity. We cherish those great examples of art and writing that harbor the highest degree of imaginative integrity; work that takes risks; that helps open doors once thought forever lost to mediocrity. *Nka* seeks and will support those forms of expression that arise out of the fulcrum of both individual and collective experiences. Work that is transformative, transgressive, visionary, curious, passionate, partisan, idiosyncratic, plainspoken, idiomatic, experimental, difficult, and open.

More specifically, he goes on to say, *Nka* would, "out of necessity," seek "to violate, destabilize, dislocate and unseat all the deep-rooted prejudices, and rote assumptions that pass themselves off as contemporary African art history." It would both "mine and work away from the received wisdom of postmodernist forms to modes of criticality." Finally, it "recognizes that any work that aspires to reach its fullest potential is done not in tiny pockets of imposed isolation or anonymity, but amongst people, in short amongst all humanity. Such work recognizes the necessity of contacts and bridges, and what they teach—like Wole Soyinka so clearly articulated in his poem *Ujamaa*—that 'earth is all people.'"9 The new African art discourse, Enwezor fervently believed, would be based in locality and dislocation, would reach across cultures despite the evident barriers against so doing, and would address the world, whether it was ready or not. These values, and this attitude, would reverberate throughout his subsequent twenty-five years.

Enwezor did not simply issue rhetorical calls for the renewal of African art discourse. As a critic, he did the journeyman work that the profession demands: visit studios, conduct interviews, participate in roundtables, write reviews (in *Frieze*, *Artforum*), found journals (*Nka*), get involved in debates, write catalog essays, promote the artists you admire, join their cohort, become its spokesperson. His founding and long-sustained editing of *Nka* (with Salah Hassan and Chika Okeke-Agulu) is the major, and ongoing, testimony to this enterprise. The essays on Frank Bowling, Georges Adéagbo, Ellen Gallagher, Lorna Simpson, Lynette Yiadom-Boakye, Glenn Ligon, Steve McQueen, Jean-Michel Basquiat, John Akomfrah, and Nari Ward in these volumes represent a small sample from the sixty profiles of individual artists that Enwezor produced. In their insistence that cohorts of African, African American, and Black British artists are making art of aesthetic value and social import that parallels, even eclipses, that of their more celebrated contemporaries, his writings on artists are unabashedly canon building. The more general essays in these volumes frequently mention these artists, along with Isaac Julien, Chris Ofili, Julie Mehretu, and several others. As criticism, they adopt Charles Baudelaire's call for writing on art to be "partial, passionate, and political."10 In its insightful evocations of artistic intent and lucid descriptions of how artworks work, as well as in the distinctive oratory that roundly registers the significance of this art, Enwezor's art criticism evolved to match that of many more celebrated writers on contemporary art. The conferral, by the College Art Association in 2006, of the Frank Jewett Mather Award, the major US-based honor in this field, affirms this judgment.

Among artistic mediums, Enwezor was drawn most to the study of photography. He was acutely aware of how important the documentary qualities of photographs were to the liberation movements in Africa, particularly the struggles against apartheid in South Africa. Images from those troubled times were a subject of research throughout his career. They were the basis of his first significant exhibition, *In/Sight: African Photographers, 1940 to the Present*, at the Guggenheim Museum, New York, in 1996. His introduction, with cocurator Octavio Zaya, is chapter 5 in this volume. His essay for *Snap Judgments: New Positions in Contemporary African Photography* (2006) concludes this volume (chapter 15). These essays, and several others in both volumes, demonstrate his keen interest in photography's expansion from documentary necessity to the transmediality required of it by the complexities of contemporary life. Enwezor traces photography as a performative practice, as an archive of social and personal memories, as a theater of sexualities, and as a precipitating medium for moving-image installations that explore these potentials.

For each of his "landmark" exhibitions—the 2nd Johannesburg Biennale: *Trade Routes: History and Geography* (1997), *The Short Century: Independence and Liberation Movements in Africa, 1945–1994* (2001), Documenta11 (2002), *Intense Proximity* (2012), the 56th Venice Biennale, titled *All the World's Futures* (2015), and *Postwar: Art between the Pacific and the Atlantic, 1945–1965* (2016)—Enwezor wrote catalog essays that are themselves landmarks in thinking about their topics. All are included in these volumes. In the early 2000s, based on his experiences in curating the first three of these exhibitions and reflecting on the proliferation of large-scale exhibitions that aimed to survey what was then called *global contemporary art*, he wrote the definitive essay on this phenomenon: "Mega-exhibitions and the Antinomies of a Transnational Global Form" (2002, chapter 13).

Breakthrough curating of this kind inevitably stirred controversy. Among those aroused by the writings and exhibitions featured in this volume, I note three. Setting the right ratio between local interests and international developments—in which everything is inherently complex, contested, and fluid—is a perennial problem for biennials. Better, it is an irresolvable problematic that attracts and frustrates all concerned, in unequal measure. Such dynamics may be found everywhere in contemporary art and are necessary to its worldliness. The organizers of the first Johannesburg Biennale in 1995 invited curators from several countries to make national exhibitions on the condition that they include South African artists. Rejecting this as a provincializing transposition of Venice's national pavilions to a peripheral city, Enwezor's second iteration, *Trade Routes: History and Geography* (1997), showed the work of 160 artists from sixty-three countries, including thirty-five South Africans. His introduction to the catalog is chapter 6 in this volume. He insisted on the priority of postnationalist perspectives as a response to what he saw as the current situation in both South Africa and the world at large: "The basis of *Trade Routes* was the idea of exchange, the flow of commodities, the flow of history, of contestation, of the range of ideas transmitted via the trade routes that opened after [Vasco] da Gama found South Africa. I wanted to use South Africa as a point of departure to reconnect South Africa, which had been separated from the rest of the continent during apartheid. I wanted to make part of the exhibition reflect on this history of transition, which we can say came to an end in 1994."[11] *Trade Routes* attracted criticism from some of its international visitors for celebrating postnationalism in a country that, in the immediate postapartheid period, was struggling to rebuild itself as a nation, and for imposing the most advanced models of the international mega-exhibition in a city that had been isolated by sanctions for decades and had just begun to build an arts infrastructure. Indeed, sessions of the Truth and Reconciliation Commission were being held in the same city at the same time.[12] Asked whether South Africa was ready for such an internationalist exhibition, Enwezor was unapologetic, responding that "on one level South Africa wants to be global while not taking responsibility for what an international practice could mean in terms of diluting its sense of particularity. . . . At the same time, even though this exhibition is one that the country is not really ready for, it is only possible to make such an exhibition in a place like South Africa."[13] He went on to praise works by Andries Botha and Santu Mofokeng in the Biennale (both illustrated in this volume) as among the few to fully manifest the nuances of this fraught situation. And to him, for all their differences, the Biennale and the Truth and Reconciliation Commission shared the same discursive space—an idea he was to elaborate in the "platforms" of Documenta11, notably Platform 2, "Experiments with Truth: Transitional Justice and the Processes of Truth and Reconciliation," held in New Delhi in 2001.[14]

During these years, Enwezor was hyperalert to the challenges of representing African identity. In a review of africa95, a festival of exhibitions relating to the continent staged in London that year, he savaged the efforts of their curators, Black and white alike, for indulging in false positivity and stereotyping.[15] In related writings, he was particularly critical of white South African artists, such as Penny Siopis, Pippa Skotnes, and Candice Breitz, whose work at the time appropriated pseudoethnographic tourist postcards of Black Africans (in his description, "near-naked African women in a state of colonial arrest") and altered them to highlight the racist voyeurism of this popular form.[16] To Enwezor, this imposed a false, Western feminist presumption that the artists' and the subjects' shared status as women somehow overrode vastly different experiences resulting from race and class difference. In South Africa in particular, it served to assuage white liberal guilt by creating an imagery of a "Rainbow Nation." Focusing on the psychological dimensions of this imagery, as did much of his writing at the time, Enwezor acknowledges that the fantasy of creating a "Rainbow Nation" was deeply shared by many South Africans, both Black and white. He does not pretend that these dilemmas are readily resolvable, if at all. He concludes with reference to poet Aimé Césaire's call for a Black heterogeneity.[17]

In the conclusion to his essay introducing Platform 5 of Documenta11, the exhibition at Kassel (chapter 11 in this volume), Enwezor set out what he hoped the project might achieve:

> The collected result in the form of a series of volumes and the exhibition is placed at the dialectical intersection of contemporary art and culture. Such an intersection equally marks the liminal limits out of which the postcolonial, post-Cold War, post-ideological, transnational, deterritorialized, diasporic, global world has been written. This dialectical enterprise attempts to establish concrete and imaginative links with the various projects of modernity. Their impact, as well as their material and symbolic ordering, is woven through the procedures of translation, interpretation, subversion, hybridization, creolization, displacement, and reassemblage. What emerges in this transformation in different parts of the world produces a critical ordering of intellectual and artistic networks of the globalizing world. The exhibition as a diagnostic toolbox actively seeks to stage the relationships, conjunctions, and disjunctions between different realities: between artists, institutions, disciplines, genres, generations, processes, forms, media, activities; between identity and subjectification. Linked together the exhibition counterpoises the supposed purity and autonomy of the art object against a rethinking of modernity based in ideas of transculturality and extraterritoriality. Thus, the exhibition project of the fifth Platform is less a receptacle of commodity-objects than a container of a plurality of voices, a material reflection on a series of disparate and interconnected actions and processes.[18]

This is a succinct summary of the underlying goal of each of his large-scale exhibitions and of his hopes for mega-exhibitions more generally. Due to expectations built up over time, and the extraordinary resources available to them, the Venice Biennale and Documenta are felt to have special responsibilities in this regard. They are, in a word, meta-exhibitions, expected to take on a wider perspective toward contemporary art and to other contemporary art exhibitions, for which they are models.

Enwezor's Documenta11 attracted criticism for hubris and overreach, a standard complaint in prepandemic times. More specific were the evaluations of its inclusion of several artists whose inspiration came largely from places outside Europe and the United States, "non-Western" versus "the West," in the parlance of those times. The message seemed obvious: not only had the art of the Rest of the World arrived in Europe, but it was also now setting the agenda for art everywhere, and that agenda was one of critical globality. A sure measure that this message got through was the trouble that many commentators took—after noting the Nigerian origins but New York base of the artistic director and similar profiles among the curatorial team—to count the birthplaces of the artists involved and then go on to chart where they now lived and worked. A *New York Times* report entitled "Documenta 11: The Retro-Ethno-Techno Exhibition: The Silence Is Broken" pointed out that "most of the show's Third World participants live in Europe or America and have frequently lent an exotic touch to international exhibitions."[19] Thomas McEvilley's "rough count" gave twenty-five from the United States, thirty-four from Europe, six from the former USSR, fourteen from Africa, sixteen from Asia, and nine from Latin America. Australian Aboriginal artist Destiny Deacon seems to have been ignored. As well, "some artist collectives are not counted because of ambiguities."[20] While most conceded that the representation from forty-five countries was unprecedented, this caviling over origins expresses concern about exactly the world changes that Enwezor highlighted in his introduction and his team constantly emphasized in their commentaries: most of these artists are members of diasporas—like Enwezor himself, their artistic imaginations were shaped by situations of travail. A more pertinent set of figures are provided by Ruth E. Iskin. Noting that the first Documenta included no artists from outside the West, she went on to observe that "the second (1959) included 3%; in documenta 11 (2002), 22% of the participants were artists living in non-Western countries and 43% were born in such countries."[21] Indeed, she credits Documenta11 with "establishing its own canon," one that "differs significantly from any Western canon of contemporary art."[22] Beyond these numbers, however, as reading the texts in these volumes will quickly show, a more interesting debate about the nature of the "non-Western" representation was taking place.[23]

The Postcolonial Constellation

In several of his most important essays, Enwezor's exceptional grasp of the key developments in global contemporary art is matched with a similarly insightful analysis of the current geopolitical situation, especially of its

implications for the ongoing struggle against old and new kinds of colonization. These ideas arrive at their most complete expression in "The Postcolonial Constellation: Contemporary Art in a State of Permanent Transition"
(2003), chapter 12 in this volume.[24] He calls on us to reject the view that the
end of the Cold War meant that economist globalization led by Western
multinational companies and their political allies would inevitably achieve total
world economic, political, and cultural hegemony, that it would eradicate national and cultural differences, disable critique, and dominate artistic possibility.
On the contrary, he urged, these globalizing forces were themselves elements
within a larger, more complex set of "geopolitical power arrangements" that
were "constellated round the norms of the postcolonial, those based on discontinuous, aleatory forms, on creolization, hybridization, and so forth, all of
these tendencies operating with a specific, cosmopolitan accent."[25] Typically,
he referenced Martinican philosopher Édouard Glissant's *Caribbean Discourse*,
rather than any European or US author, to support this claim.[26]

In such complex conditions, he argued, "the legacy of the Western historical avant-garde seems inadequate to the job of producing a unified theory
of contemporary art," not least because "the structure of contemporary art's
relationship to history is more transversal, asynchronous, and asystematic in
nature" than was modern art's relationship to modernity.[27] He highlighted
five "effects" of the postcolonial constellation on curators, artists, and art
worlds everywhere: first, the messy proliferation of exhibitionary forms (from
blockbusters to biennials) and their constant mutation; second, the fraught
and contradictory experiences of decolonization and of nation building that
have obliged us to think about identity and tradition as operating in more
layered, antinomic ways; third, the impact of heterogeneous art practices
on the logic of the museum, which has managed to absorb many but not
all of them; while, fourth, culture everywhere has been heavily mediated,
indeed mediatized, turned into a provider of spectacular experiences. The
fifth element, the most powerful, is the globalization of economies and cultures, and the digital revolution that has fused cultures with economies.
The net outcome, he avers, is a state of *permanent transition*, in which the
adjacency of difference, or "intense proximity," prevails as the most definitive contemporary experience.[28] Inevitably, this is the world that artists and
curators are called on to reimagine.

These ideas are rehearsed in two other key essays from the late
1990s in which the concept of diaspora is developed in a rich and relevant
way: "Travel Notes, Living, Working, and Travelling in a Restless World"
(1997) and "A Question of Place: Revisions, Reassessments, Diaspora" (1997).

"Between Worlds: Postmodernism and African Artists in the Western Metropolis" (1995–96) tests the relevance of postmodern thinking to the independent development of a diasporic imagination. These essays constitute chapters 6, 7, and 9 in this volume.

Enwezor's essays from the late 1990s and early 2000s stake out the early phases of a shift in perspective, one that is marked by the division of the essays into two volumes. While this has been done mainly for practical and chronological reasons, a change in his outlook can be discerned. It is less a matter of his adopting a different point of view than of expanding one that was realizing some of its initial purposes and needed to grow to face current challenges. By 2000 the metropolitan versus provincialist dynamics that framed his struggles to secure appropriate recognition by the New York art world of the achievement of African artists were being superseded by changes in the two fundamentals of his project. On the world historical, geopolitical scale, neoliberal globalization—a yet more totalizing kind of colonialism—was emergent as the dominant world picture, seemingly in all aspects of contemporary life. Yet, at the same time, African art discourse, alongside much other contemporary art practice and theory, was actively, and successfully, renewing itself by following its urge to globality, to a postnational cosmopolitanism—or, we preferred, a "worldliness" (*mondialité*)—within which localities were positioning themselves. This occurred in critical opposition to the top-down globalization everywhere apparent (including the upper reaches of an eager art market).

The first of these two volumes is centered around Enwezor's quest to renew African art discourse, to rewrite its histories and to insist on its contemporary relevance, in New York, in Africa, and then throughout the world. Its companion volume shows how this discourse became a vital component in the global discourse of contemporary art, not least because of his indefatigable efforts.

The essays presented in these two volumes have been lightly edited to use US spelling and punctuation and to correct some errors in names and other typos. In addition, a few small grammatical errors (for example, subject-verb agreement) were corrected where this could be done without changing the meaning or rephrasing the text, and the citation style has been updated and standardized. No changes affecting meaning or wording were made, and terms reflecting the usage of the time have been left as is (the published usage of African-American, African American, or black is retained, as are Enwezor's pronoun choices). As many of the original illustrations as possible have been found and reproduced. In a few cases, to assist readers who may be unfamiliar with the artists or the exhibitions discussed in the text, appropriate illustrations have been added to essays that were originally published unillustrated. All changes of this kind are noted in the brief paragraphs introducing each chapter.

A comprehensive bibliography of Okwui Enwezor's published writings concludes this volume (and the second). It was prepared by Ilhan Ozan as an essential component of the research for this project. It should be consulted for full references to the texts in these volumes and to gain a broader sense of the scope and depth of Okwui's enterprise, not least how he and the artists he admired grappled with the world's most pressing questions.

Okwui and I met while members of the curatorial team for *Global Conceptualism: Points of Origin, 1950s–1980s*, curated by Luiz Camnitzer, Jane Farver, and Rachel Weiss for the Queens Museum in 1999. At my invitation, he became a visiting professor at the University of Pittsburgh from 2003 to 2006, a highlight being the conference that we, with Nancy Condee, convened in 2004, which led to our jointly edited book *Antinomies of Art and Culture: Modernity, Postmodernity, Contemporaneity* (Duke University Press, 2008). He invited me to participate in some of his exhibitions, not least the second Bienal de Sevilla (2007) and *Postwar: Art between the Pacific and the Atlantic, 1945 to 1965* (2016), and in several other projects. We shared much of our work in progress. This constant contact enriched my thinking, and my life, immeasurably. During what turned out to be his fatal illness, we often discussed the fact that, despite his voluminous published writings (over a million words, I was to discover), there was no one place where a reader might go to gain a sense of the evolution of his main concerns and of the comprehensiveness of his thought. He asked me to bring such a place into being. Our hope is that these volumes will take you there.

NOTES

1   Okwui Enwezor, "From the Editor," *Nka: Journal of Contemporary African Art*, no. 33 (Fall 2013): 5. The contributions to the commemorative issue of *Nka* touch on these several aspects of his life and work: see *Nka: Journal of Contemporary African Art*, no. 48 (May 2021), https://read.dukeupress.edu/nka/issue/2021/48.

2   Okwui Enwezor, "Redrawing the Boundaries: Towards a New African Art Discourse," *Nka: Journal of Contemporary African Art*, no. 1 (Fall–Winter 1994): 3–7.

3   A draft curriculum vitae among Enwezor's papers lists a 1992 portfolio essay on the New York photographer Ross Bennett Lewis titled "Between Character and Essence: The Photographs of Ross Bennett Lewis," with no

evidence that it was published. His poem "Tombs and Flowers" appeared in the *Portable Lower East Side* 10, no. 1 (1993), 68–70. In parallel with his articles for *Nka*, an article titled "The Skoto Gallery of Contemporary African Art," was published in *African Profiles International*, June–July 1994: 38–39, which may have been a review of works by two Nigerian artists, Ben Ajaero and Obiora Anidi, shown at the Gallery in September through November of 1993.

4 Enwezor, "Redrawing the Boundaries," 3.

5 Susan Vogel, introduction to *Africa Explores: Twentieth Century African Art*, edited by Susan Vogel (New York: Center for African Art, 1991), 14. Enwezor italicized "determining influence" in his citation of this sentence.

6 Enwezor, "Redrawing the Boundaries," 6.

7 Enwezor, "Redrawing the Boundaries," 5.

8 Enwezor, "Redrawing the Boundaries," 7.

9 Enwezor, "Redrawing the Boundaries," 7.

10 Charles Baudelaire, *Art in Paris, 1845–1862: Salons and Other Exhibitions*, trans. Jonathan Mayne (London: Phaidon, 1981), 44.

11 Okwui Enwezor, "A Conversation with Okwui Enwezor," interview by Carol Becker, *Art Journal* 61, no. 2 (Summer 2002): 13.

12 See Okwui Enwezor, "The Second Johannesburg Biennale," interview by Carol Becker, *Art Journal* 57, no. 2 (Summer 1998): 101–7.

13 Okwui Enwezor, "Interview with Okwui Enwezor," interview by Carol Becker, *Art Journal* 57, no. 2 (Summer 1998): 102. These challenges are explored in Anthony Gardner and Charles Green, "Okwui Enwezor's 2nd Johannesburg Biennale: Curating in Times of Crisis," *documenta studies*, no. 8 (March 2020), https://documenta-studien.de/media/1/documenta_studies__8_Anthony _Gardner___Charles_Green.pdf.

14 Okwui Enwezor, Carlos Basualdo, Ute Meta Bauer, Susanne Ghez, Sarat Maharaj, Mark Nash, and Octavio Zaya, eds., *Experiments with Truth: Transitional Justice and the Processes of Truth and Reconciliation* (Ostfildern-Ruit, Germany: Hatje Cantz, 2002).

15 Okwui Enwezor, "Occupied Territories: Power, Access, and African Art," *Frieze*, no. 26 (January–February 1996): 37–41. Also published in *Glendora Review: African Quarterly on the Arts* 1, no. 3 (1996): 29–34.

16 Okwui Enwezor, "Reframing the Black Subject: Ideology and Fantasy in Contemporary South African Representation," *Third Text* 11, no. 40 (Autumn 1997): 28.

17 Enwezor, "Reframing the Black Subject," 34–39. He was to modify his views of the subsequent achievements of these artists, including their work, in several exhibitions and articles.

18   Okwui Enwezor, "The Black Box," in *Documenta 11, Platform 5 (Exhibition)*, edited by Okwui Enwezor, Carlos Basualdo, Ute Meta Bauer, Susanne Ghez, Sarat Maharaj, Mark Nash, and Octavio Zaya (Ostfildern-Ruit, Germany: Hatje Cantz, 2002), 55. For a fascinating discussion of the exhibition design of Platform 5, see Mark Nash and Wilfried Kuehn, "Exhibition Staging: Notes and Queries," *Platform 6, Documenta11*, posted April 29, 2021, https://www .documenta-platform6.de/exhibition-staging-notes-and-queries/. On the same site, I offer an extended review of the exhibition; see Terry Smith, "Exhibiting the Postcolonial Constellation," https://www.documenta-platform6 .de/exhibiting-the-postcolonial-constellation/, posted April 29, 2021.

19   David Galloway, "Documenta 11: The Retro-Ethno-Techno Exhibition: The Silence Is Broken," *New York Times*, June 15, 2002, https://www .nytimes.com/2002/06/15/style/IHT-documenta-11the-retroethnotechno -exhibition-the-silence-is-broken.html.

20   Thomas McEvilley, "Documenta 11," *Frieze*, September 9, 2002, https://frieze .com/article/documenta-11-1. Fourteen artists are missing in this count.

21   Ruth E. Iskin, *Re-envisioning the Contemporary Art Canon: Perspectives in a Global World* (Abingdon, UK: Routledge, 2017), 9. The subsequent documenta, no. 12 in 2007, rated even better, as Iskin goes on to note on the same page that "46% of the artists were living in non-Western countries and 56% were born outside the West." Iskin, *Re-envisioning the Contemporary Art Canon*, 9.

22   Iskin, *Re-envisioning the Contemporary Art Canon*, 26.

23   For a range of views, see Massimiliano Gioni, "Review: Documenta 11," *Flash Art*, no. 225 (July–September 2002): 106–7; Rasheed Araeen, "In the Heart of the Black Box," *Art Monthly*, no. 259 (September 2002): 17; Sylvester Okwunodu-Ogbechie, "Ordering the Universe: Documenta 11 and the Apotheosis of the Occidental Gaze," *Art Journal* 64, no. 1 (Spring 2005): 80–89; and Anthony Gardner and Charles Green, "Post-north? Documenta 11 and the Challenges of the 'Global' Exhibition," *OnCurating* 33 (2017): 109–21.

24   Okwui Enwezor, "The Postcolonial Constellation: Contemporary Art in a State of Permanent Transition," *Research in African Literatures* 34, no. 4 (Winter 2003): 57–82. Also published in *Antinomies of Art and Culture: Modernity, Postmodernity, Contemporaneity*, ed. Terry Smith, Okwui Enwezor, and Nancy Condee (Durham, NC: Duke University Press, 2008), 207–34. Subsequent citations are from this version.

25   Enwezor, "Postcolonial Constellation," 208–9. Documenta11 had already shown what this constellation looks like when artists respond to its demands.

26   Édouard Glissant, *Caribbean Discourse: Selected Essays*, ed. J. Michael Dash (Charlottesville: University Press of Virginia, 1989).

27   Enwezor, "Postcolonial Constellation," 222.

28   Enwezor, "Postcolonial Constellation," 222–28.

Redrawing the Boundaries 1

Toward a New African Art Discourse

The editorial to *Nka: Journal of Contemporary African Art*, no. 1 (Fall–Winter 1994): 3–7. The author's note reads: "Okwui Enwezor is a writer and a poet. He is the publisher/editor of *Nka: Journal of Contemporary African Art*."

ONE OF THE PROBLEMATIC ASPECTS of visiting museums, art galleries, and other sites of cultural valuation in Europe and the United States is the pervasive absence in these highly policed environments of art by contemporary African artists. Not only are the works of these artists (many of whom have been working for the past half century) conspicuously absent from the museum and gallery environment, they've also been accorded little attention or significance in academic art historical practices, university curriculums, the print media, or other organs of such reportage.

Needless to say, various shallow and historically untenable positions are ventured by many in the West, a priori to any contact (at least in a sufficient and meaningful context) with this art. The most enduring myth of all such attempts at historicization is the specious assertion by many in Western art establishments that there is really no such thing as modern art from Africa. For Africa—so the argument goes—the term *modern* or *contemporary* is either an aberration or oxymoronic, and necessarily disinherited from all assumptions of continuity and dynamism. This epistemological bias (which also is one of visuality) all but eliminates any real chance to begin to

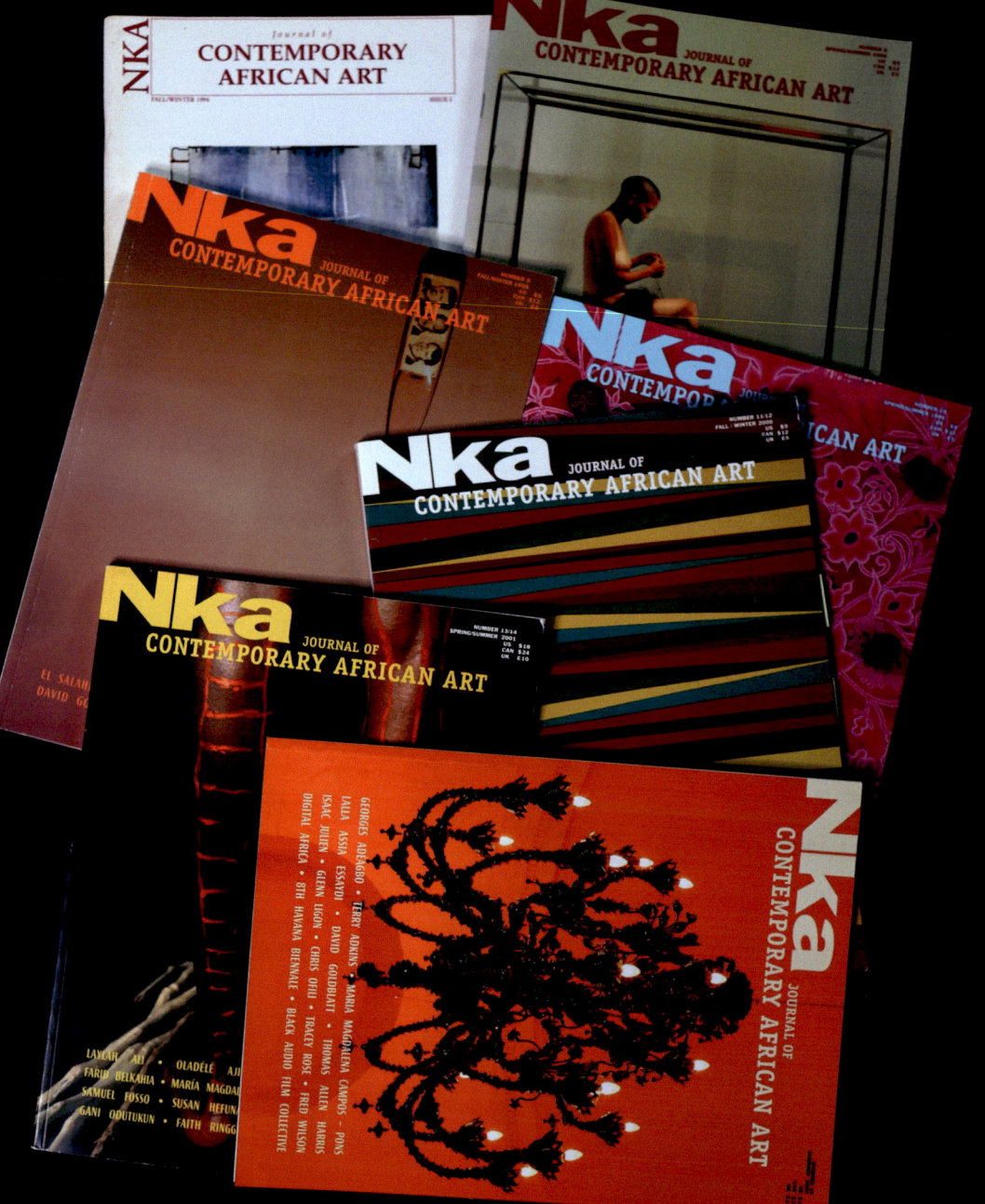

de-exoticize contemporary African art products. And so we are conditioned to take as given the qualifier "Western influenced," as part and parcel of how contemporary African art may be read, understood, and enjoyed, but never do we import into the space of Western modernism a qualifier like "African influenced"—a qualifier which, if used, is potentially distressing to the idea of a wholly autonomous, uninflected Western art historical hierarchy. Perhaps the most astounding statement along this line of thinking in recent memory can be found in the opening lines of Susan Vogel's catalog introduction to *Africa Explores: 20th Century African Art*; here Vogel unabashedly delights in telling her audience that "contact with the West has been the *determining experience*—though certainly not the only influence—for African art in 20th century art."[1]

The implications of this kind of systemic obscuring of historical facts surely titillate a plethora of oppositional desires within many of us, who daily fail to recognize ourselves in the kind of pictures painted to represent the face of twentieth-century African art history. It is the rupture between such nonsense, the obfuscation and anxiety it evokes, and the reality of present constructs that begins to gnaw at our most conflicted view of the grand narratives of twentieth-century art, and its many different currents and moments. To dislodge the obvious bigotry wedged into Vogel's statement requires a little more force than has been allowed in contesting various representations of twentieth-century African cultural practices and histories. But one sees nothing that is particularly unique in Vogel's statement. After all, it has been the fundamental basis for training artists and art historians in the West, for as long as one cares to chart.

The long history of misinformation which inhabits texts like Vogel's is a disgraceful one. Rarely, if at all, in such critiques and discourses do we find African art placed as part of the contiguous critical nexus of revolutionary practices that has up to date confounded and thrilled the processes and highly nuanced modes of transposing into a concrete arena all the elusive stuff of the psyche and unconscious imagination. Except, of course, when it is dressed up in the guise of a primitivist cultural festival, like William Rubin's felicitous attempt at comparative anthropology: *"Primitivism" in 20th Century Art: Affinity of the Tribal and the Modern* at New York's Museum of Modern Art in 1984. A rather curious title, which more or less betrays the ambiguousness and disingenuousness of Euro-American accounts of the formulations of twentieth-century art. The question really is, whose "primitivism" are we talking about here? For if indeed *"Primitivism" in 20th Century Art* denotes only an affinity, as suggested by the exhibition and the critical pedagogy which spawned it, then [Pablo] Picasso, [Paul] Klee, [Constantin] Brancusi, [Georges] Braque, [Amedeo] Modigliani, even [Henri] Matisse, must be its illegitimate children. For nowhere are the sins of their progenitor more apparent than in the sort of artistic "miscegenation" that has informed Western art practices from "1906" onward.

The legacy bequeathed to the West by Africa, while sometimes grudgingly acknowledged, is still an exchange that is by and large unequal. To this day, that legacy still stands at the core of all approaches to ways of seeing, and composing, and in the crucial shifts from art as object to subject to presence. And this presence cuts across the spectrum of all forms of art: from the visual to the performing arts. Yet what we run up against when studying the arts are various forms of cover-ups through evasions and disingenuous rhetorical markers. Meanwhile, the issue at hand is how to remedy and reverse this century-old narrative that has effectively transformed itself almost into "History." The kind of history that not only has appropriated, co-opted, and pillaged entire legacies, but has also confined their viability and understanding to ethnological and anthropological curio cabinets of natural history museums' dioramas. Out of sight, and conveniently dead.

To follow the thread that will lead us to the source of such narratives is one which has been sufficiently explored both in anticolonialist and neocolonialist writings, as well as in the current crop of multicultural discourses on art and culture. Furthermore, a cursory inspection of any university curriculum reveals a curious gap, all the more so for what they lack in the histories, analyses, theories, and practices of modern twentieth-century art than for what they teach. Therefore, the entrenched pejorative viewing of contemporary art from Africa is based mainly on such denial, especially with an art whose complexities, multiple identities, and hermeneutic rigor defy and confound European stereotypes and dissembling racist in-jokes. Thus Africa is rendered as a *National Geographic* phenomenon. And through such a construction, an ignorant public's base, theme-park appetite for the esoteric is constantly indulged and fed an ever-widening array of stereotypes, with the fiction of a primitivist and premodern Africa. An Africa, without artistic or cultural mobility, embalmed and ancient as a mummy encased in an airtight glass vitrine.

One sees no reason for such constructions, except for the enormous profits to be gained in such trafficking (here, it would be pertinent to point to the cottage industry and speculations that have mushroomed around "traditional" African art objects as prime emblems). The exoticization of contemporary African cultural products has also evolved into a burgeoning and highly speculative postmodernist industry (*Africa Hoy*, *Magiciens de la terre*, *Africa Explores*). It seems that to acknowledge such a "beast" as contemporary or modern African art, which is not so amenable to such exoticization, is to destabilize whole agendas, industries, careers, and, as the critic Olu Oguibe has argued, "a world-view carefully and painstakingly fabricated over several centuries."[2] Such an acknowledgment inevitably undermines, usurps, and subverts notions of the esoteric on which Western narration of Africa feeds. As we all know, the quest of such narration inexorably relies on its ability to unearth the exotic, the primordial, the morbidly regressive; elements which clearly do not reside in the art itself, but which live instead as mere figments in hallucinatory imaginations. Obviously, this is not to dismiss a lot of credible and painstaking work that has been done by non-Africans in this field, but only to state that these studies remain anything but conclusive, or impervious to criticism, particularly in light of their conjectural deliberations and hasty conclusions.

Beyond Estrangement and the Trope of the Other

Such conjectures immediately make their entrance when we are faced with such thinly disguised operative, but nonetheless meaningless, appendages as exotic, ritualistic, tribal, naive, urban, functional, untutored, extinct, premodern, etc., as distinguishing elements and spirits possessing the "prone body" of art by contemporary African artists. The power of such art usually is viewed as emanating, not from the consequences or the specificities of its present circumstance, but from a benign antiquity, both remote and unreachable—at once frozen and evocative. By being African, this art is thereby consigned to some remote realm in the early morning of human evolution. This is most celebrated, even promoted, by many of its decoders as its supreme attribute: the savage body uncorrupted, and shielded from the ravages of modernity.

But the primary danger might not lie in the fiction of such abstruse valorization. The danger necessarily resides in the acceptance, by any African artist, of the unwieldy yoke of the "Other." The "Other" as a perpetual outsider hovering at the margins of historical consciousness. The "Other" as a body estranged from and unfamiliar with modernity. The "Other": a body whose erased, barely discernible features, and whose mythologized absence in relevant art historical discourses, are seen positively as presupposing purity, hence immunity, from the corrupt and agitated "Center" represented by Europe.

Unfortunately, much current critical theory has relied on the binaries of Center/Periphery, Self/Other, Black/White, High/Low, Male/Female, and Colonizer/Colonized agglomerations as an insightful means of dealing with the problematics of whatever lies outside the hegemonic, white male supremacist superstructure. One's ambivalence toward such readings is magnified given their origin in European dialectical and philosophical culture. The trope of the "Other" has been so clearly constructed and articulated via these unique sets of perspectives that we need only look at a list of some of the most widely quoted theorists to see how often it yields names from French poststructuralism and the Frankfurt school. I will venture that the dominance of this group of highly influential European writers already problematizes any autonomous and critical unreading of Eurocentric monoculturalism. (As someone appropriately put it, you cannot destroy the master's house with the master's tools.) Thereby, regardless of the pretenses of postmodernist critique, and its false solidarity with so-called outsider cultures, the mise-en-scène of its grand project of cultural synthesis or hybridity is primarily based on the cannibalism and voracity of colonial appropriation. And, one might also add, destruction of the evidence. Here, I call on B. Ruby Rich's apt reading of this tendency in which she argues that "when postmodernism became the fashion, few voices pointed out that its strategies of pastiche, appropriation, and hybridity were precisely those of subcultural and Third World survival, folk art, and artistic production; rather, with the term in place, the aesthetics were *whitewashed* and annexed, maintaining rather than dissolving the barriers between these disparate worlds."[3]

Clearly, Rich's observation not only implicates the work that came out of Euro-American intellectual and philosophical traditions of the past half century, but more importantly, it implicates much of the dominant strategies of postmodernist discourses, based more on binary oppositions than on equal relationships. Undeniably, there is much that is valuable in many of those writings, and one cannot be so dismissive of their critical rigor and provocative insights. But to quote and adopt endlessly the frames of reference adopted by these critiques (many of which have neither the understanding nor interest in non-European cultural practices) is to court erasure in cultural/historical narration.

For one may well ask, where within the pages of such postmodernist deconstructions do we discern the authoritative voice of the subject of such deconstructions? And if we were to hear this voice, to whose tune is it dancing? Such questions are inevitably important, if only to reveal how inadequate many paradigms governing the study of contemporary African cultural practices really are. Clearly, we have to readdress the methodologies with which to study this field. In a world easily ruled by demarcations, based on cultural geography, the imperatives of fictional characterization begin to outweigh the exigencies of factual analysis, particularly when given agency by institutions with powerful mandates to colonize, segregate, and marginalize. We come to a fork in the road and realize how such paradigms, in reality, have little to do with how African artists actually view their practice. Just as Western artists and other cultural workers are not overly consumed with the opinion of Africans as to Western artistic failures and triumphs. In the end, the idea of such carved-in-stone delineations as First/Third World, Center/Periphery, Black/White, and High/Low dichotomies ring false, and certainly exist only in the heads of those who devised them. There are too many complex dynamics attending to the varieties of cultural production in Africa, and in fact throughout the world, to allow for the erection of such suffocating enclosures.

The so-called rupture in official boundaries, the hybridization of cultures, and transnational migrations by artists from one cultural site to another were perhaps viewed as postmodernism's most promising project. But viewed up close it has failed on that count. Within the corpus of postmodernism, old habits die very hard. They remain Euro-tradition bound and insular; dispensing (at least pretending to) patronage through condescending, patronizing, and appropriative gestures to other cultures. In its smugness, it inherited the same bad habits and the prodigious voracity of its modernist precursor. In postmodernism, poses and images are everything: meaning almost nil. At middle age, it has become the repository of occidentalist self-referentiality, and not for one minute sees its role as being transgressive or progressive, but rather as the reigning status quo rehashing the same tried and failed formulas (only now masked in a taxonomic global whole cloth).

Cast into this narrow frame that is narcissistically self-referential, Eurocentric hegemonic philosophy brings to the table of modernist art discourse the hubris of officialdom, not only as the modulator, but also as the ultimate arbiter of taste and value. But what is even more apparent is that despite their power, pull, and influence, mainstream Western institutions are no less cultural ghettos than any other institutions that operate outside their inscribed boundaries of relevance precisely because their policies of selection are exclusionary, restrictive, parochial, discriminatory, narrow, and flagrantly marked by hard-core ethnocentrism. It is, then, hardly a revelation to say that there is nothing irrelevant or marginal at all about those aspects of cultural production that operate—wittingly or unwittingly—outside the parameters of those high-walled, viciously policed boundaries. In the end, the terms *periphery* and *margin* are clearly anachronistic, and simply do not describe the functions of those structures that have over the years persuasively offered us alternative perspectives of what constitutes relevance and excellence in the arts. The current debates engendered by the continuous canonical hegemony of Eurocentric discourses must acknowledge this fact. Subsequently, the focus need not be so obsessively engaged with usurping that perceived center—in a bid to replace one form of domination with another—but rather to begin to depopulate it of all its arrogant assumptions and its myths of universalism.

Disruptions: African Artists and the Writing of History

Perhaps this shift might then return us to a deeper and more meaningful contemplation of all the different strategies of social meaning artists from different cultures carry into the often contentious sites of representation and identity. And the role of artists themselves in dealing with not just medium, or the intertextuality of mediums, but also the multiplicity of issues now unleashed within the space of re/presentation. Increasingly, artists themselves, not just museums, curators, or critics, are beginning to understand the need to redefine the argument and the spaces conducive for this dialogic view of art productions, through the interrogation of the suspect practice of museology and other art historical apparatuses. The recent upsurge in text-based and performative art, the sort embodied in the works of Fred Wilson, Ouattara, El Anatsui, Lorna Simpson, Glenn Ligon, etc., is no mere accident. Artists, particularly those outside the occidental axis, are now seeking ways of reformulating the age-old questions of identity and systems of representation, though not just in terms of binary oppositions or relations. If, for example, an artist like Anatsui is insistent on representing African history via a multiplicity of signifiers such as Nsibidi and Uli symbols and ideograms, Akan and Adinkra symbols, Nok and Benin references, it is to say that the old European paradigms of representing history are not only grossly inadequate, but also incapable of speaking with any resounding meaning to the malaise of our present ethical and philosophical consciousness. The pretend mode of hiding the so-called Other in the margins of history so as to magnify the significance of the Self is one that simply belongs in the junk heap of history, for human cultural memory thoroughly transcends such a hectoring gaze.

My sense of how this interrogation can function as an agent of revolutionary change, particularly in rethinking art historical practices, is sometimes mitigated by how institutional artistic valuation is irrevocably allied and anchored to economic systems of value, rather than cultural value. Michele Wallace's argument is quite correct when she says, "It appears that the only reason black artists aren't as widely accepted as black writers (and this is far from widely enough) is because shifts in art historical judgments result in extraordinary economic contingencies."[4] Wallace's statement, proffered on behalf of African-American artists, can equally be applied to illustrate the predicament faced by African artists.

Since artistic and economic values are not mutually exclusive in this institutionalized world, to obtain passage into the boardrooms of those systems is not only synonymous with but also contingent on how much each artist's work is traded for, as well as what shade of hue, rather than what shade of depth, that artist and his/her work carries. Without minimizing the economic hardships that attend to the reality of the artist's vocation, many artists, unfortunately, still waste valuable time craving the attention, sanction, and validation of such regimes. They look on those bodies endlessly as vectors of that light that gives soul to all meaningful creative energies. Many artists are well aware of, and cannot so easily overlook, the economic and career advantages that come with the legitimizing sanction of those bodies. But the question is, In the absence of a restrictive parochialism and knee-jerk reflexivity, at what cost does an artist historically shunned and excluded from those systems obtain passage? And if the artist refuses the comforts those systems provide, how does a decolonized space (which might eschew implosive insularity, yet insist on the specificity of its various modes of reception and transmission) adequately serve him/her? And with what currency are the products of such a market bought or sold? Some of these questions engage a situation that is in the process of reducing our responses, values, and meanings about what art is and isn't into reflexive and stifling dogmas. Indeed, many have had to tailor and mold their artistic visions to meet the exigencies of those systems that appear to make life in the arts possible. Under the prevailing circumstances, that kind of option is one that might even warrant sympathy and understanding. But long term, it is a strategy that is clearly counterproductive and emasculating.

Whatever the case may be, the protocols of all creative practices, especially among African artists, should recognize that such incongruous terms as *margin/center, modernity/contemporaneity*, are less about places and civilizations than about time and its entire dimensions. Yet we must also agree that to renarrate and restrategize our means of approaching these issues, the radical ethos that will guide the building of any autonomous discourse of contemporary African art and culture will also have to recognize the plurality of other discourses, within and outside its own borders. In this bid for renarration, we must keep open-ended the social, philosophical, and aesthetic constructions that make up the borders of our contemporary cultural histories, its theories and practices and its speculations and reifications. We must remain wary and suspicious of any totalizing centrism that dismisses and excludes viewpoints that might not necessarily cohere with our dominant assumptions about what might be deemed authentically "African." To disavow racial essentialism is not to weaken but rather to strengthen and magnify the many ideological shifts that make present-day Africa the breeding ground and site of the most far-reaching and diverse cultural and artistic activity. It is this approach that permits us to meditate on the divergent notions, modulations, and frequencies that best describe the ongoing work of contemporary African cultural producers. It allows us the opportunity to reject simplistic and sweeping definitions that violate multiple readings of Africa's variegated cultural spaces.

Therefore, the essential nature of this discourse need not be concerned with facile categories, nor should it be tailored to fit prefabricated molds of what some might consider to be an "authentic" African viewpoint. In a world of cross-pollination of ideas, movement between and within cultures, perception and reality, one can no more speak of authentic African art than one can speak of authentic Asian or European art. Every contact between peoples, regardless of claims made for innovation and superiority— while not necessarily enriching to either culture—irremediably alters [the] native topography [of both cultures]. It ushers in new possibilities of continuity, stretching preexisting forms, in order to communicate more clearly and effectively the issues and values of its time and epoch. In this vein, Africa has assimilated, incorporated, and influenced cultures with far-reaching and lasting consequences. No one can, then, reasonably expect more or less from today's African artists, grappling with issues of their time and epoch. None of these artists need toe any imposed stylistic line in order to address effectively the crisis of our present collective consciousness.

Building Frames of Reference

As the millennium draws to a close, for many non-Western artists the logic of modernity is no longer configured along the line of the avant-garde as the prevailing zeitgeist or as progress and change. For many (even in the West), modernity has come to mean a peculiar condition. The condition many times bespeaks dislocation and rootlessness, displacement and dispersal, alienation and exile, even in the familiar rooms of home. More than breaking down boundaries, modernity, it appears, has constructed them. Dwindling economic means and political instability have evolved a phenomenon of migrancy, forcing many artists into exile, turning them into cultural nomads (to borrow a term from Achille Bonito Oliva). Though used in a positive sense to signify the emergence of a global art culture, cultural nomadism clearly means different things to different people. For Western artists, it means an unlimited license to ransack, appropriate, and expropriate other cultures' artistic legacies. For many artists from Africa, it is quite a different matter. While Western artists are commended and encouraged for such nomadism (consider the hoopla around Philip Taaffe's appropriation of Arab and Islamic motifs and iconography, or Francesco Clemente's never-ending attachment to Hindu erotic art as examples), it is decried in African artists as a loss of their "authentic" African selfhood. Bound and pressed by this strain of censorship, many have embarked on alternative means of self-identification and representation. Like a masker, their work is highly subversive and elusive; fluid, indeterminate, and transgressive. Their work inhabits frames of reference that confound, disparage, dislocate, and defeat all attempts to render them either homogeneous or devoid of complexity.

While these laudatory projects are going on, they have nonetheless been met with hostility, resistance, suppression, and intransigence from dominant Western economic and sociopolitical structures. The resurgence of fascism, racism, and virulent nationalism throughout the countries of Europe bears this out. From the Balkans to the countries of the former Soviet Union, from Germany to France to England, the dissonant chords of xenophobia and hatred have placed various exiles in direct physical danger. Difference, used as official target practice by neoconservatives (which in reality is not neo at all), is magnified as either criminal or a present and imminent danger, to be curbed or exterminated. Ultimately, the powerless immigrant populations become the first scapegoats and casualties of this loathing generated from fear of "outsiders": Turks and Africans in Germany, Arabs and Africans in France, Asians and Africans in England. All these in what is being celebrated as the high moment of cultural nomadism.

Defining the Contemporary

For African artists, the events described above are particularly portentous, for within Africa itself have risen many highly policed borders. In fact, ethnocentrism and religious difference remain among the most potent destructive forces, sometimes far superseding the ravages of economic and natural disasters. Parasitic state structures have all but destroyed any meaningful forum for iconoclasm and dissent. Terror is an institutional reality in the daily lives of those artists and intellectuals willing to oppose such structures: whether in the guise of apartheid terrorism (presently being dismantled), or [Hosni] Mubarak's state police battling the Islamic fundamentalists, or the brutality of Nigeria's military regime. As I write this, over a hundred thousand men, women, and children lie slaughtered on the streets of many Rwandan cities, in an orgy of fratricidal bloodletting between the Hutus and the Tutsis. Tomorrow there will more. Be it in Rwanda or any other region of ethnic disputations. We live, it seems, in a constant state of flux and agitations, with impending catastrophes visibly moving the earth beneath our feet. On and on, from one country to another. So much so that even within our own countries and cultures, we remain perpetually in exile. Adrift in an ever-widening existential sea of nihilism, discontent, and ennui.

In this cacophony, the dominant notion of an Africa impeded only by outside meddling and colonization (though they remain prime emblems) becomes a bit untenable and begins to unravel at the seams—destabilizing the constructed fiction of a continent devoid of any complexity; a continent malleable to easy prescriptions.

The problems are many. And we must all tread carefully. The polarities that exist in many different African societies give rise to a real dilemma. This dilemma lies not just in how we make art and the names we give art, but also in how we historicize art. It lies in the spaces we are willing (against impossible odds) to give art as an enabling and empowering reality in our daily lives. It raises questions about the definition of "contemporary African art." What and who does it cover? What and who does it include or exclude? Is it wise to see in the present practices, from Egypt to Algeria, Zaire to Senegal,

Nigeria to Zimbabwe, Sudan to Kenya, a monolithic trajectory? What are the methodologies that will facilitate the study of contemporary cultures in Africa? And if identified, who will lead it? Where is the unifying ground between, say, the art of Pretoria and that of Soweto? Is contemporary African art that which only mimics a Pan-Africanist ideology, or that which assiduously kowtows to Euro-modernist syncretism? Or that which leaves and makes room for individual visions and expressions regardless of how much they stray from our notions of its manifest philosophies and ideologies? Indeed, there's no one answer. They are all of the above and none. But more importantly, they point to the difficulties in trying to construct and inscribe single categories or linearities. Still, as anyone vaguely familiar with Africa or with the human desire to forge futures [knows], the one thing that is clearly apparent from these questions is the welter of voices, oppositions, ideas, desires, positions, and dichotomies clamoring to be heard, nurtured, and fed. They give the field of contemporary African art an agency, a force, a vibrancy, and equally a tension that is unequaled in any other regions of the world.

If, out of crisis and history, the emotive force of art can be harvested and shaped, in that alone Africa is deeply endowed. Her various cultural producers are no less willing and able to meet the challenges presented by the constant shifts in the boundaries of what is modern and contemporary, their effects and resonances within different communities and centers. In fact, such projects are already well underway. Starting from the colonial period to the postindependence period, which saw many projects of reclamations and decentering among young African artists and academies striving for a quest for artistic autonomy, to the present struggles. Today more art is being created in such abundant quantities, and across the divide of disciplines and media, that it is almost impossible to keep up with contemporary cultural production in a country like Nigeria, talk less of the entire continent from east to west, and north to south. Yet we have only been able to apprehend in spates the enormity and size of art practices in Africa. In view of these developments this publication will diligently work toward building the kind of forum necessary to help unite and engage the different spectrums of African viewpoints on twentieth-century cultural practices.

At *Nka*, the artist who embodies the vision necessary to confront the complexities that face us in an age of change and ferment, yet is also able to carry us beyond established boundaries to other sites of significance and interest, is one with whom we share great affinity. We cherish those great examples of art and writing that harbor the highest degree of imaginative integrity; work that takes risks; that helps open doors once thought forever lost to mediocrity. *Nka* seeks and will support those forms of expression that arise out of the fulcrum of both individual and collective experiences. Work that is transformative, transgressive, visionary, curious, passionate, partisan, idiosyncratic, plainspoken, idiomatic, experimental, difficult, and open. We seek the kind of work that out of necessity seeks to violate, destabilize, dislocate, and unseat all the deep-rooted prejudices and rote assumptions that pass themselves off as contemporary African art history. These kinds of art also mine and work away from the received wisdom of postmodernist forms to modes of criticality. Yet *Nka* also recognizes that any work that aspires to reach its fullest potential is done not in tiny pockets of imposed isolation or anonymity, but among people, in short among all humanity. Such work recognizes the necessity of contacts and bridges, and what they teach—and like Wole Soyinka so clearly articulated in his poem "Ujamaa"—that "earth is all people."[5]

Nevertheless, it appears, *Nka* will have to work diligently to realize this vision, with a highly supportive network of contributors: artists, critics, scholars, writers, etc. While soliciting material for this issue, it slowly became apparent—albeit painfully—that much work still needs to be done in this field. The paucity of critical practitioners in support of this field magnifies even more the absence and invisibility of this articulate art in museums, galleries, and the media. I am well aware of how a situation like the one just described can erode confidence in and infringe on a project like the one *Nka* has embarked on. But *Nka* has also received all sorts of support from so many different people, which makes this enterprise particularly gratifying. If we harbor any ambitions, it is the commitment to stay the course. To stay engaged in this fertile soil with hidden and exquisite riches yet to be farmed with adequate coverage and critical examination. We hope to help build a better link between artists, critics, institutions, and the public. To provide a discursive platform of exchange capable of giving weight and meaning to the substance of our work, visions, and desires. This of course requires the responsibility of our readers to read more, see more, and leave no stone unturned in searching out the disparate bodies of writing and art available on and by African artists.

We have no agendas. Nor do we speak for any special interests. In fact, *Nka* is open and receptive to other streams of practice, though its focus remains staunchly committed to contemporary African art and artists. We invite participation from all interested parties: artists, writers, critics, scholars, etc.; anybody willing to invest a critical intelligence and open-minded analysis in the discourse. There is no better time to enter the fray, so send us your commentaries, reviews, articles, essays, portfolios, studies, or whatever project that can adequately speak to the mission outlined above. We look forward to your readership, as well as participation.

NOTES

1   Susan Vogel, introduction to *Africa Explores: 20th Century African Art*, ed. Susan Vogel (New York: Center for African Art, 1991), 14. Italics added.

2   Olu Oguibe, "In the Heart of Darkness," Africa special issue, *Third Text: Third World Perspectives on Contemporary Art and Culture* 7, no. 23 (Summer 1993): 8.

3   B. Ruby Rich, "Dissed and Disconnected: Notes on Present Ills and Future Dreams," *Transition*, no. 62 (1993): 36. Italics added.

4   Michele Wallace, "Modernism, Postmodernism and the Problem of the Visual in Afro-American Culture," in *Out There: Marginalization and Contemporary Cultures*, ed. Russell Ferguson, Martha Gever, Trinh T. Minh-ha, and Cornel West (New York: New Museum of Contemporary Art; Cambridge, MA: MIT Press, 1990), 41.

5   [*Ed. note: Ujamaa*, the Swahili word for "fraternity," was the catchword for the socialist program of social and economic development advanced in Tanzania by President Julius Nyerere after the country achieved independence in 1961.]

The Ruined City **2**

Desolation, Rapture, and Georges Adéagbo

Published in *Nka: Journal of Contemporary African Art*, no. 4 (Spring 1996): 14–17, this reflection on the implications of the work of Benin artist Georges Adéagbo is one of twenty-one articles Okwui Enwezor wrote between 1994 and 2016 for the journal he founded and coedited with Salah Hassan and Chika Okeke-Agulu. Four of these articles were his own editorials, while another, in fall 2014, was a joint reflection, "*Nka* at 20," no. 35 (Fall 2014): 4–5. He reviewed shows by Leonardo Drew, Madame Costello, Toyce Anderson, Yinka Shonibare, and Stan Douglas, as well as significant exhibitions in London, New York, and Venice where the work of African or diaspora artists was shown. Interviews with Ouattara, Frank Bowling, Touhami Ennadre, El Anatsui, and Thelma Golden were conducted. A volatile roundtable discussion with several African American artists in New York, titled "African American Artists on Issues of Museums and Representation of African American Art," led by Enwezor, appears in the second issue of *Nka* (Spring/Summer 1995): 34–41. This chapter responds to Adéagbo's installation as part of the exhibition *Big City: Artists from Africa*, shown at the Serpentine Gallery, London, as part of Africa '95 (also styled africa95), a nationwide festival. In his article "Occupied Territories: Power, Access and African Art," in *Frieze*, no. 26 (January–February 1996): 37–41, Enwezor excoriates the festival for treating the diversity of Africa as if it were a country and for ignoring artists of the African diaspora.

And when, in the city in which I loved you
Even my most excellent song goes unanswered

Li-Young Lee, "The City in Which I Loved You" (1990)

IN NEW YORK, December is the cruelest month, "mixing memory and desire."[1] Here, in the 4 p.m. sunsets, spring's eternal recrudescence seems so far away. I mount the broken sidewalk that takes me down the vacant, bleak, unjoyful backstreets of New York's Lower East Side. The sharp, salty wind, blistering in its measures of intensity, and bone-chilling wintry frost have necessitated that my wool-corseted head stay buried beneath the heavy and uncomfortable pile of so much clothing. Falteringly, in the fading light, I trudge along, lone figure trawling a devastated landscape, sidestepping small eddies of putrid water and piles of uncollected garbage: acrid with modern waste and metropolitan overconsumption. The buildings are bulks of massed shadows. Their broken windows and gutted interiors (firebombed for profit or warmth?) make me think of the pictures I have seen of Beirut. But what Beirut once represented to many along the eastern coast of the Mediterranean, as the lone archipelago of European "refinement and taste" and desire in the peculiar disjunction of the Middle East, seems so completely absent in the Lower East Side's Third World ambience; a living paradox in the towering edifice of high capitalism. Up in Harlem the sliding scale of life expectancy cracks the odometer backward, in a downward spiral that surpasses even Calcutta's.

Companioned by these ghosts that weave themselves around the narrative and glut of modern obsolescence, in this "storied, buttressed, scavenged, policed city I call home, in which I am a guest," I can't help thinking of Georges Adéagbo.[2] Adéagbo makes artworks, or, as it were, masterful installations that accrue from the devastation and sadness evident in the twin histories of cities like Beirut and New York. Cities plunged into decay and confusion, pallid with hunger and death, terror and tragedy. For now, I want to speak of nothing else, not even the weather, but to think only of the frontiers into which Adéagbo's work leads me.

Out there, where the frontiers end, roads are erased. Where silence begins. I go forward slowly and I people the night with stars, with speech, with the breathing of distant water waiting for me where the dawn appears.

Octavio Paz, "Prologue" (1966)

Georges Adéagbo makes stranger music than this. And inasmuch as I am enthralled by Paz's music, it is to Adéagbo that I listen tonight. To his scatological compositions, his incomprehensible jouissance in the midst of the fin-de-siècle's disconsolate mood. My surprisingly keen senses, sharpened by this insistent music playing in my inner ear, cannot help rousing the dust of memory, specifically the memory of my last encounter with his installation: *Art and Evolution* (1995), in London's Serpentine Gallery last October. The controlled chaos Adéagbo assembled here thoroughly reveals both an

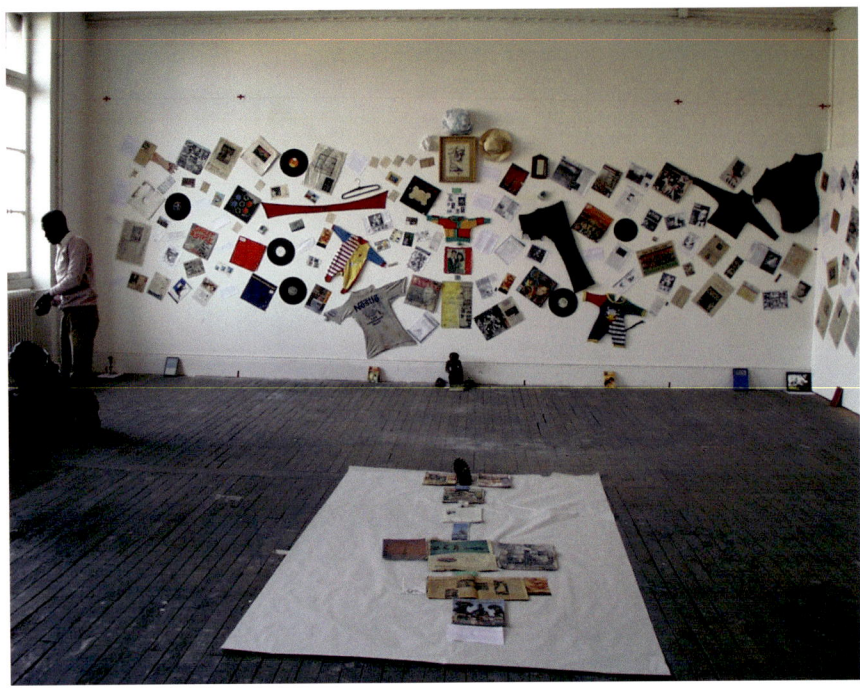

2.1 Georges Adéagbo, *Art and Evolution*, 1995.
Mixed-media installation, originally at
Serpentine Gallery, London; this iteration
(detail), Limoges, 1999. © Georges Adéagbo,
ADAGP, Paris, 2025. Photograph: Stephan
Köhler.

impudent iconoclasm, an idiosyncratic and quirky brilliance. Made out of
a dizzying assortment of carefully chosen, sorted, and arranged detritus
gathered from urban environments, this epic commentary on waste and
transcendence, mutation and ossification, stands in stark contradiction to
the lush arcadian vista of Kensington Gardens that a viewer glimpses as she
looks out through the gallery's glass-paned double doors. What ardor, this
awkward, disjunctive, yet well-organized agglomeration, pitched to the cadence of a different kind of music which insists on feeding the scrawny fires
of desire, a longing for a kind of artistic process free of cant.

Adéagbo is a forty-seven-year-old artist from the Republic of Benin.
Initially trained as a lawyer in France, he started making these installations
in 1973, two years after his return to Benin. For the past twenty-two years
he has, without interruption, kept up a daily ritual that takes him plung-
ing into the streets of Cotonou in search of discarded objects, out of which

he crafts artworks of such melancholic brilliance, poetry, magic, and tragic beauty. The pictures (I find that Adéagbo's work functions most effectively pictorially, rather than as assemblages) which he paints out of these iconic detritus illuminate his uncanny method through the narrative trope of left-overs, the leavings of the orgy of modernity, on whose decimated corpulence we see the corporeal body laid bare; shocked and disembodied.

No place on earth could be more representative of this condition than present-day Africa. An Africa where the idea of progress has today become so perverted and is predicated on the perpetual "newness" of things. An Africa in which history is lived almost like a bad dream, then recycled and discarded according to the logic of what may be deemed a current style. In such a climate, it is not a surprise for work like Adéagbo's to be easily misunderstood. Or for it to be read as so much solipsistic nonsense, as postmodern schizophrenia, as the autistic ramblings of a madman, a character delivered flesh and blood from any of Ayi Kwei Armah's existential novels. Read through this impulse, the dominant attitude toward such work is to ignore its internal logic and engage it as nonart. Or better yet, to say, like some critics have recently insisted, that Africans don't regard such work as art is an obviously patronizing dismissal, even though bricolage, as both process and method, is nothing new to contemporary art.

This inevitably leads me to consider the contingent and the fluctuating patterns (like tributaries run wild in a riverbed) of Adéagbo's work; the ritual and daily dismantling, reassemblage, and reinvention of the same installation on street corners in Cotonou. This acute postmodernity bears the same aspects of and the impermanence of an Africa marketplace. The analogy (by no means a facile delectation) leads one through different sets of questions, but even more, to muse on the coding of what is today construed as postmodern, and how African cultural producers participate in its debates. For me, Adéagbo's work anticipates these debates (which certain critical quarters undoubtedly will inveigh against as a misalliance) by means of its transcription, translation, and transformation of a cultural sphere into an aesthetic one. Thus the cultural space (the marketplace) represents a shifting, unfixed universe which the aesthetic space (Adéagbo's installations) encounters and rerenders allegorically.

Here, I stop to think of Balogun and Jankara Markets in Lagos, Ochanja Market in Onitsha, Ariaria Market in Aba. In those arenas, daily, occurs a vast changing installation. The African marketplace: as pure contingency, as a perpetual site of accumulation and consumption, dissipation and collocation, mercantile exchange and cultural entropy is the same sensibility which Adéagbo's installations both suggest and replicate. One can, for instance, look at the heather-gray sweatshirt bearing the imprint of the Swiss multinational Nestlé and see it as a hybridized product logo or sign, as a kind of emblematic metonym of pop culture which Africa participates in. One might equally use the opportunity the presence of the sweatshirt in *Art and Evolution* insinuates to meditate on the relationship between mineral wealth among many other natural resources and colonialism; the crisscrossing of objects of value and the disposable materials that are returned back to the "Third World" as equal exchange. The aforementioned, particularly, lends keen insight on the nature of international multinational capital and exploitation. Or one may look at the covert reference to natural produce from Africa, particularly cocoa, which arrives daily at Nestlé's plants at a pittance. All these in the end might not have anything to do with Adéagbo's interest in his choice of material, but it does offer an opportunity for multiple readings and interpretations which all "serious" art suggests to a wide variety of audiences or in this case to a critic.

As a figure whose enormous influence I have no doubt will one day be recognized, it is not difficult to see how much his influence already permeates the practices of certain young African artists. We see it in the funky sculptural assemblages of Romuald Hazoumè. Paris-based Bili Bidjocka cites him as a conceptual influence. Still, it is Adéagbo's rawness that sets him apart from the formal refinement of Hazoumè's and Bidjocka's work.

Among other international artists, I can think of no contemporary artist, with the possible exceptions of David Hammons, Joseph Beuys, Nari Ward, and Mo Edoga, able to confront the dilemma of modernism's entanglement with structures of power and cultural capital, investitured in the unique object, playing with the ghosts of identity and of social sedimentation, with such acuity and vision. And fewer artists are able to change the way one thinks about art, as Adéagbo has for me. Seeing his work was a delight, even as it taxed certain preconceptions and prejudices I carry about the vexed relationship of the bricoleur to contemporary cultural production. I must confess the reason for my initial reticence is that Adéagbo's installations all too perversely refuse to declare their knowledge or function. But why should they? In fact, they cannot. They are petrified objects, with this insistent latency deeply enjoined in an organic simulacrum. The installations move no further than the limited attention span of the audience's wandering gaze, which Adéagbo assaults with his peculiar information overload; "the irony is their excess of reality."[3] This, though, is a deceptive ploy, for what he is presenting us is not just a portrait of our beleaguered selves but a mirror into which we can peer to glimpse the sordidness of our existence, of our culture of regression, of "our worlds that have failed."[4]

Translucidity, suspense, fragility, obsolescence: thus the insistence on writing, the insistence of the letter (fringed on the edges), of the mirror and the watch—these are the lost and distant signs of a transcendence that vanished into the quotidian.

Jean Baudrillard, "On Seduction" (1988)

What really thrills about Adéagbo's kind of work is its continuous elaboration of the idea of art as a quest for self-knowledge and fulfillment. Another thrill is the clarity of his painstakingly graded oddities, so exquisite, like the passage of an Indian raga, they shatter the silence of the gallery space as the organizing framework for certain forms of cultural knowledge. Since he makes his work out of what the world and other people have abandoned and rejected, the measure of his work's rigor is not in the spectacle that it offers, but in that which it withdraws and refuses: the monstrous fallacy of an Eden. Hence, Adéagbo's work is about lost innocence. If there is an Eden, it seemed long ago overgrown, and now drowns in rubbish, with monstrosities that transport in their furious eddies the discarded dreams of our consumerist desires. Here: the dismembered limbs of a child's doll, there: a man's forlorn coat hanging on the wall, surrogate and host calling attention to the body's diminishment, its absence, its incommensurability. (Where has the body gone?) Then there are the newspaper and magazine stories chronicling the perpetual state of that body at rest (death?). These are images with which to set the world on fire. But no one lights the match. Adéagbo mediates these scenes of disaster (a miniaturist's vaunted haunt) through the wordplays with which he marks, decorates, and desecrates each transient fragment torn from reality. His ciphers are like love poems sent out to a fallen world, and to us, the soiled angels who must inhabit its ruined cities: desolate and enraptured. What heady hope!

This is the vital scene Adéagbo chose to reenact in the east gallery of the Serpentine in the group exhibition *Big City* as part of the festival Africa '95. To me, *Art and Evolution*, 1995, his contribution to this madness, is a world unto its own, an odd appendage that demands a more exacting interpretation separate and apart from the concerns of the convoluted pretensions of *Big City*. Yet, unlike, say, the epic *L'Archeology*, 1994, or *Histoire de France*, 1992, this particular work seemed to me perhaps the most contemplative and sedate of all of Adéagbo's creations. Where in the past his installations functioned along the logic of their propensity toward aggressivity in the streets, buttressed against the ordered world that surrounds them, here one senses something lost in the process of their translocation into the formal geometry of the modernist cube. But only to a certain degree is his energy attenuated. Instead, his ironic postmodernity, in a surprising reversal, comports itself well in the gallery space. The installation works on viewers slowly. As one approaches, it begins to cast its spell through the exacting and overwhelming detail of the materials deployed across the expanse of the floor and walls, like a surging sea. This vastness finds its form not in the indeterminate sprawl of the carefully sorted "debris" but in the welter of connective tissues that make the work's strength manifest in its embrace of the paradoxical. The material objects suggest, along with their mysterious and opulent mise-en-scènes, a flooded acropolis of memories, the sort Hasan 'Abdallah insisted "will ignite in bitter sugar."[5]

"What memory does the sea have of her lover?" wrote Christopher Okigbo.[6] This is the question one must insistently demand of this piece. What memories does it bear, if any? What knowledge does it confer? Needless to say, despite its declarative intent, the deeper meaning of Adéagbo's work is in its artful conundrum and renunciation. His objects leave not so much memories as they leave an index, a faint and pliant trace of each chosen object's prior cultural, political, economic, and social meaning. Here they tell their own submerged stories. Like carapaced fetishes they are worlds envisioned, not seen, almost unknowable. Too many images, pictures, memories spill from this terrible pile; within them are the scratched and warped vinyl records with their tide of garbled voices and droning nostalgia; the faces printed on T-shirts and magazines seem shocked as they stare out to us, nailed on the cross of silence, they can't speak. Their commentaries circumscribe the boundaries of closure. The world of the frozen images (even as they fix us with their insincere smiles) is muteness like the doll's severed head or the kitsch masks and wood reliefs made for tourist consumption as "African art." They lead us to eternal dead ends. The rest, as Toni Morrison once wrote, is "just weather."[7] They float, inseparable from their intermingled histories and events—a vast archive of ambivalence and desire, stasis and entropy—as if from a dream. They tease and make wobbly the architecture of the mind. They beguile us. They abandon us, evoking as much as they repress.

Tomorrow, Georges Adéagbo will return to preside over this hoard in his tireless beginnings that have no end in sight.

Epigraphs: Li-Young Lee, "The City in Which I Love You," in *The City in Which I Love You* (Brockport, NY: BOA Editions, 1990), 51; Octavio Paz, "Prologue," in *Early Poems, 1935–1955* (New York: New Directions, 1973), 3; Jean Baudrillard, *Selected Writings*, ed. Mark Poster (Stanford, CA: Stanford University Press, 1988), 155.

1 T. S. Eliot, "The Waste Land," in *The Waste Land and Other Poems* (New York: Harcourt, Brace and World, 1962), 29.

2 Li-Young Lee, "The City in Which I Love You," in *The City in Which I Love You* (Brockport, NY: BOA Editions, 1990), 51.

3 Jean Baudrillard, *Selected Writings*, ed. Mark Poster (Stanford, CA: Stanford University Press, 1988), 155.

4 Christopher Okigbo, "Lament of the Silent Sisters," in *Labyrinths* (New York: Africana, 1971), 41.

5 Hasan 'Abdallah, "I Remember Having Loved," in *Modern Arabic Poetry*, ed. Salma Khadra Jayyusi (New York: Columbia University Press, 1987), 113.

6 Christopher Okigbo, "Lament of the Drums III," in *Labyrinths*, 47.

7 Toni Morrison, *Beloved* (New York: Alfred Knopf, 1987), 275.

The Body in Question

Whose Body? *Black Male: Representations of
Masculinity in Contemporary American Art*

The exhibition *Black Male: Representations of Masculinity in Contemporary American Art* was cu-
rated by Thelma Golden and shown at the Whitney Museum of American Art, New York, from
November 10, 1994, to March 5, 1995, before traveling to the Hammer Museum, Los Angeles.
This review was published in *Third Text* 9, no. 31 (June 1995): 67–70.

DESPITE THE PRETENSES OF MUSEUMS, criticality and sensitivity are
ideas that seem extraneous to the way they fashion exhibitions built around
the problematic subjects of race, gender, and sexuality. And when all three
problematics are conflated under one roof, controversy seems a more willful option, often to exploit, for crass gain, the inherent tensions that have
plagued and polarized the American body politic along the highly differentiated boundaries of race, gender, and class. This, clearly, is the case with *Black
Male: Representations of Masculinity in Contemporary American Art*, recently on
view at the Whitney Museum of American Art in New York. Curated by
Thelma Golden and built up as an investigation of racialized imaging and
viewing endemic to art production specifically and culture dissemination in
general within American culture, *Black Male . . .* rather comes off as anachronistic and too easily digestible. There is a familiarity in the exhibition's
obsessive gaze on the "black" male body that parallels (perhaps unwittingly)
the kind of uncomfortable voyeurism which objectifies, fetishizes, and marginalizes that body as the locus of spectacle. This spectacularization—which

also plays with slavery's auction-block legacy—mines the libidinal excesses of the feral predator on which mass media representations of "black" masculinity constantly feed. This media-produced viewing, which also corrodes our knowledge of this subject, has been an emblem, as well as a constraint, which invites the most intrusive of gazes.

For many African American men, to live in America is to live alongside a legacy and within a naturalized habitat in which the intersections of race and masculinity constantly collide to form models of representation deeply encoded in structures of myth so entrenched and pervasive they seem almost impossible to contain and defuse. Even more troubling is how these structures erect and operate the most deterministic and prejudicial visual history—a tragic opera—in which the "black" male body becomes an icon that catalyzes white fear and desire. Charting the genealogy of this almost psychosexual drama whereby the "black" male body represents the exegesis of the exotic object in popular imagination, John Akomfrah writes about it as "a body burdened by an excess of signs; a body literally framed as a figure of torment and bliss, of dangerous knowing and celebrations."[1]

Still we search for that body, looking for that moment when its explosive potentiality will overwhelm and overthrow visual tropes that constrict its ability to form a sense of subjective agency. We wait (forever) for the time when this potentiality will return us back to the curve of a discourse that does not particularize and essentialize that body only as a sign and embodiment of transgressive possibilities. The transformation of the subject (the "Black Male") was what drew me initially to Golden's project. As one of the specimens being studied, I felt excited, yet nervous. I felt troubled by the idea, but nevertheless hopeful that a meaningful praxis between the complexity the subject obviously represents and institutional myopia regarding the said subject can be manageably negotiated, to bring about a more pointed insight, an involved interrogation; in short, a meaningful articulation of our complicated relationship to what he represents in the contemporary imagination.

But here, within the Whitney's white walls, within this emporium that represents the reactionary side of American high culture—its pretensions and aspirations—the body in question looks unrecognizable even to itself. Insistently sited within a kind of temporal abyss, we come upon it as perpetual fragments; we see it as diminished, disembodied, and homeless. And in this abject homelessness, it lies wasted, consumed, and ravished; its psyche is ransacked.

"Origins trouble the voyager much," wrote Arthur Nortje in his poem "Waiting."[2] And as we wait for *Black Male . . .* to reveal itself, much troubles this viewer in regard to the origins of the images which the exhibition proffers, and the excessive burden they impose. In Golden's incessant reliance on mostly postmodernist strategies of production, the complex reality of the subject is not only diluted, but also compromised. It is not that individual artworks do not resonate powerfully; some of them do. But as a coherent body of incisive analysis, many come up well short of expectation. Additionally, many come burdened with claims of high political content and authority, which, when relied on too much, strike one as one-note sermons. As veterans of political art know, polemicism does not always translate into a powerfully engaging art practice. It is on this basis that one would quarrel with Golden's curatorial projection of this exhibition around the thesis of "radical" art being one that is invested, and always intercut, with visible politicality. The insinuation of this thesis also brings *Black Male . . .* down to something reducible and knowable only through the art's political intent.

From this perspective, Carl Pope's *From the Trophy Collection of the Indianapolis Police Department and the Office of the Marion County Sheriff's Department* (1993) and Gary Simmons's *Lineup* (1993), depicting police killings of African American men and the criminalization of "black" masculinity respectively, come close to such a confluence. Still, the two installations in their investigations operate too much through language purloined from the discourse of the public rather than the private sphere. What would have added to the weight of those two moments is a view of how families, in the privacy of their loss and pain, grieve and mourn for these lost bodies. The question really is, How does the black world represent what Greg Tate so poignantly named as "the deepest well of tragedy and spirituality on the planet"?[3]

But Golden never really pursues this. Her gaze never relinquishes its focus on the "black" male body. Ah! This body of ours so easily bought and commodified for its virile investibility; for its high pleasure quotient in mass cultural mythmaking games, as both icon and menace, sign of degenerate criminality and aberrant promiscuity. Is it then a surprise that many people who have seen this exhibition find it difficult to recognize themselves or their communities in this exercise in postmodernist incongruity? Some felt cheated, or as the poet/playwright Carl Hancock Rux put it to me: disempowered. Even before Golden dreamed up her project, Rux, who feels deeply about the subject, had fiercely, and with much intelligence, contested and enunciated "the endangered black male" paradigm which this show so shamelessly traffics in. In his poem "Save the Animals," Rux writes:

But everybody grabs the shovel to dig our graves
and keeps on laughing
keeps on ignoring
keeps on moving.[4]

These words, which exist just on this side of the tragic, find resonance every day in many African American communities. The metaphor of the "black" male as an endangered species, as a body perceived only in parts, a body that is never whole, further points to its anomalous status and homelessness within dominant cultural discourses and networks. Reflecting on this, Andrew Ross writes in one of the essays in the exhibition's accompanying catalog: "The evacuation of young black males from the public sphere has proceeded on every front. As dropouts from the educational system, as victims of suicides, homicides and the penal system, as casualties of the incredible shrinking welfare state, as fatalities of the crack economy, and the AIDS emergency; and as targets of new and more virulent forms of racism, the social obsolescence of the black male youth has been quite systematic."[5] The metaphor of the "black male" as an endangered species, as a body perceived only in parts, a body that is never whole, further points to its anomalous status and homelessness within the fields of representation and dominant cultural discourses. The dominance of the picture which Ross painted begins to worry the nerves. In the show's crowded ambience (twenty-nine artists and seventy artworks stuffed into one floor), many of the artworks came off as either not salient enough or having outworn their allotted span of transgressiveness. Clearly, many of the images have been cast out in very shallow water and can barely float. They run the gamut, from the peripherally illuminating (Adrian Piper's *I Embody*, 1975) to the absurd (Nayland Blake's *Invisible Man*, 1993). In fact, what this exhibition lacked in congruent sufficiency, depth, and power, it more than made up with a surfeit of inconsequential images. Robert Mapplethorpe's inclusion in this show was emblematic of its curatorial and ideological redundancies. His tireless appetite for the potent and "authentic" virility (and obedience?) of "black" gay men has been so exhaustively documented that here they failed to elicit or register any new insight. Instead, they came off looking more like flabby icons of a bygone moment of one white man's obsession, fear, desire, and ultimate loathing of a runaway and untamable black masculinity.

But, of course, one learns to accept Golden's proposal about the power of images to give voice to those thoughts that forever lurk beneath the facade of civil sociability. The evidence, if accepted, was all there, laid out before our very eyes in a quasi-contestatory gesture, out of which we were all supposed to deconstruct the intricately woven kelp from which images such as Mapplethorpe's evolved. And so, for balance, she presented us with Lyle Ashton Harris as the antithesis to Mapplethorpe's studio portraiture. Harris's photographs were posed as a counterdiscourse, albeit with a little rouge. Harris uses his sequence of photographs, *Constructs* (1989), to investigate the nature of masculinity. In questioning assumptions about what masculinity is or is not, he interjects and projects his own body into the combat zone and multivalent site of "black" masculine identity, definition, and determinacy, partly to reclaim subject status for that body, which an anonymous or paid studio model all too easily surrenders. His theatrical poses, as an effete gender-bending provocateur, challenge the viewer's own ground, as they shift emphasis from mere playacting to an embodiment of another kind of masculine ideal frequently excluded in discussions of African American masculinity.

Few artists in this exhibition can match Lorna Simpson's complicated rendering of masculinity as an indeterminate and unfixed space; as an index of shifting meanings. In her *Gestures/Reenactments* (1985) Simpson works to emancipate the "black male" figure from the prison-like box within which it is confined. Her poetic metaphors, intensity, and critical intelligence clearly stand out, glowingly and poignantly so. Her work is successful because it recognizes that to explore the difficult terrain of "black" masculinity, it first has to be unbound from its stereotypical posture of the tough menace and his promiscuous alter ego. She recognizes that viewers have to be powerfully challenged to move farther and deeper, not into the body, but into the psyche, where identities are ultimately formed and defined. Through this photograph augmented with text, she points us less to that figure in the foreground as an iconic beacon than to how language forms and discloses intent.

If language is the tool that drives ideologies of racial gerrymandering in American history, then violence manifests its clearest intent. Mel Chin's *Night Rap* (1993)—a black police baton with a microphone attached to its front end—conveys a sense of radical phallic potency in its shiny erectness, as well as a compelling sense of menace that potency touches off. This very simple minimalist piece has the kind of resonance which the exhibition's overall premise lacked. In its insidious and lethal simplicity we know and recognize the object well—whether absorbing its indiscriminate blows or running from it. Through this weapon we come to understand how certain tools and instruments function in relation to groups. The microphone attachment raises questions about surveillance or as simply a naked symbol of intimidation, power, and coercion. Juxtaposed next to a grainy still of the

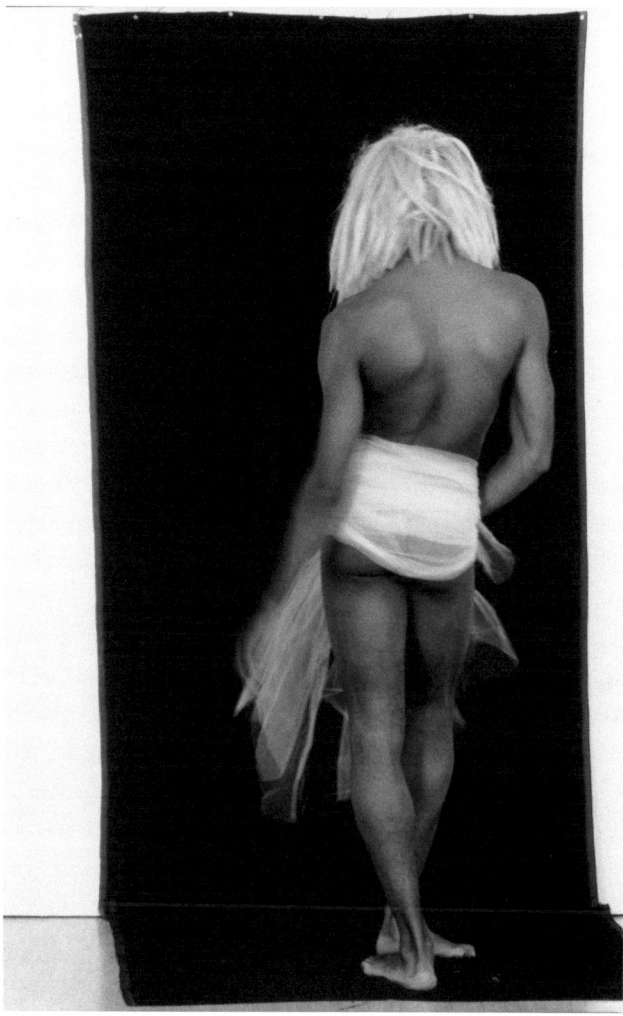

3.1 Lyle Ashton Harris, *Constructs #11*, 1989. Gelatin silver print, 183 × 123 cm. © Lyle Ashton Harris.

Rodney King beating which Danny Tisdale has readapted and worked into his series chronicling *20th Century Black Men* (1991), this sculpture became explosive and frightening in its lurid accuracy. This time, video technology has become the subverting force: the watcher becomes the watched.

Despite some of these high moments, which included works by Alison Saar, Carrie Mae Weems, Renee Cox, and sometimes Andres Serrano's not-always-edifying photographs of homeless African American men, one went through the exhibition searching for the middle ground that could have transformed the curation from its overt capitulation to postmodern theory into a rigorously worked-out critique that raised fresh and compelling questions. Unfortunately, Golden's indiscriminate ethnographic zeal left out much that could have benefited *Black Male . . .* and more.

What impact, for instance, would Mel Edwards's *Lynch Fragments* series (1963–ongoing) have had in an exhibition of this nature? Or better yet, the aesthetic economy and beauty of Leonardo Drew's poetically elegiac and austere sculptures and installations. What about such artists as Faith Ringgold, Howardena Pindell, even Jacob Lawrence (after all, Leon Golub was represented), and so many other artists left out in an exhibition that might never happen again?

Many of these questions remain unanswered. Add to this the fact that this anthropological survey was structured in the true spirit of the current vogue that focuses on the body as a volatile site of political activity, where issues of gender, race, and sexuality, together with their proximate causes, are endlessly staged and played out, and you have a winner. Who wins and who loses? Certainly, the Whitney has won a major bonanza and more feathers for its alleged multicultural cap.

However laudable—and Golden certainly deserves praise for her spirit and energy—her project remained a reformist restatement on an essentially overvalorized subject. Future treatment of this subject matter certainly requires a much more evolved, complex, and complicated visual and historical analysis. Nothing short of that will placate the sense of alienation, ambivalence, and nihilism which currently prowls the riven psyche of a group so incredibly demonized and misrepresented in our contemporary milieu. The grounds for an appropriate discourse on the subject need redefining. The failures of *Black Male . . .* might be a good place to start such a redefinition.

NOTES

1   John Akomfrah, "On the Borderline," *Ten 8*, vol. 11, no. 1 (Spring 1991): 51.

2   Arthur Nortje, "Waiting," in *Dead Roots: Collected Poems*, African Writers Series (Oxford: Heineman, 1973), 90.

3   Greg Tate, "He Is Truly Free Who Is Free from the Need to Be Free: A Survey and Consideration of Black Male Genius," in *Black Male: Representations of Masculinity in Contemporary American Art*, ed. Thelma Golden (New York: Whitney Museum of American Art, 1994), 113.

4   Carl Hancock Rux, "Save the Animals," in *Aloud: Voices from the Nuyorican Poets Café*, ed. Miguel Algalin and Bob Holman (New York: Henry Holt), 130.

5   Andrew Ross, "The Gangsta and the Diva," in Golden, *Black Male*, 162.

A review of her exhibition at the Mary Boone Gallery, New York, published in the London-based international art magazine *Frieze*, no. 28 (May 1996): 74–75, this is one of several short articles for that publication written between January 1996 and October 1998, with an outlier on art schools published in September 2006. Other articles reviewed shows by Antoinette Murdoch, William Kentridge, and Jean-Michel Basquiat, as well as exhibitions of African art in Dakar, London, and New York. During this period Okwui Enwezor also wrote short art critical essays for *Flash Art International* (on artists such as Yinka Shonibare and, with Octavio Zaya, on exhibitions of African art).

UNTIL RIRKRIT TIRAVANIJA RIDES BACK into town and unpacks his cooking utensils, Ellen Gallagher is the current darling of the New York art world. In these identity-and-alterity-saturated times of one-penny operettas, the fact that she is not a conceptual artist but a painter makes this an even more interesting love affair. Take a painting like *Totentanz* (1995), marked out by chalky horizontal blocks of glued-down paper that resemble a brick wall, into which she has packed notions of femininity and race by incising a ghostly, looming shape that mimics a head, the curve of a woman's body, and an urn or trophy, and you will understand why she's raised such a ruckus since appearing in the last Whitney Biennial.

Because innocence and joy are not appealing ingredients in the art world, and because Gallagher is an African American woman who makes gorgeous abstract works of deceptively calm, pleasurable sea surfaces, one

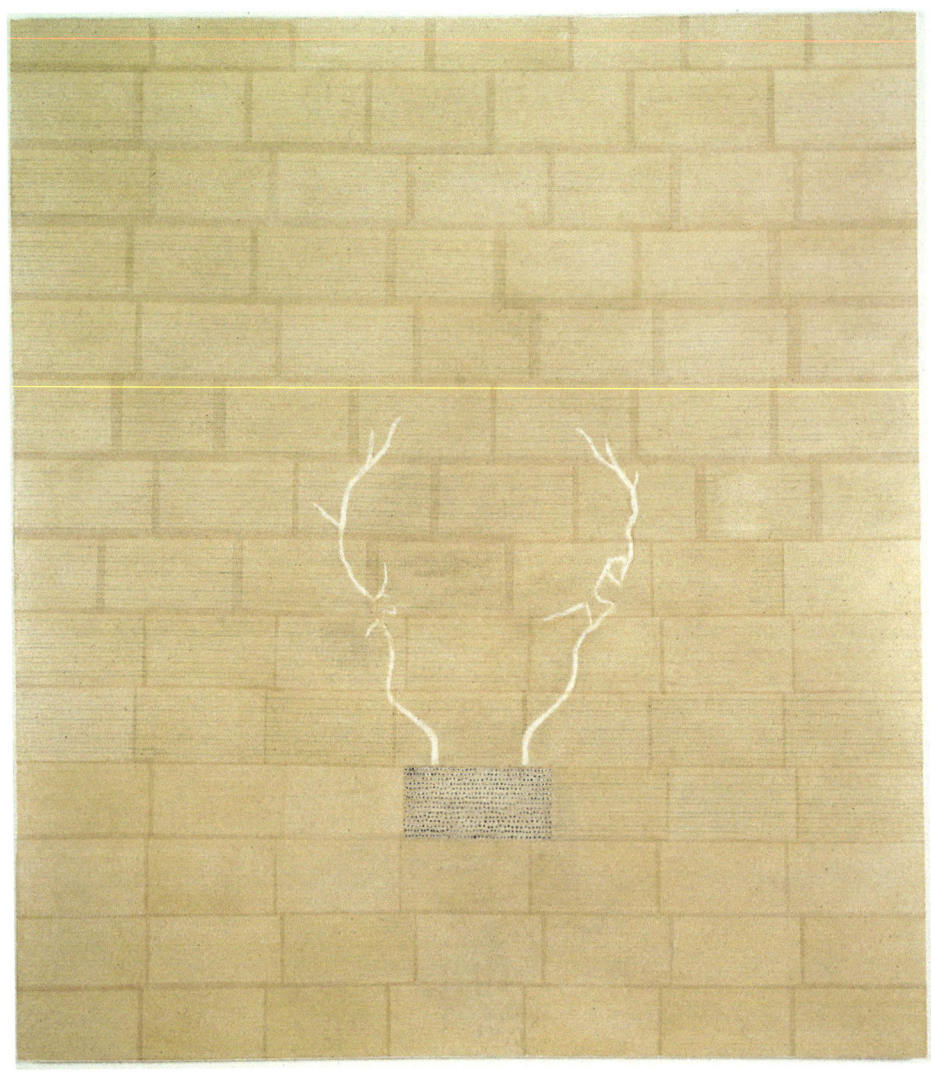

4.1 Ellen Gallagher, *Totentanz*, 1995. Oil, pencil, and paper on canvas, 213.4 × 183.8 cm. © Ellen Gallagher. Courtesy of the artist and Hauser and Wirth.

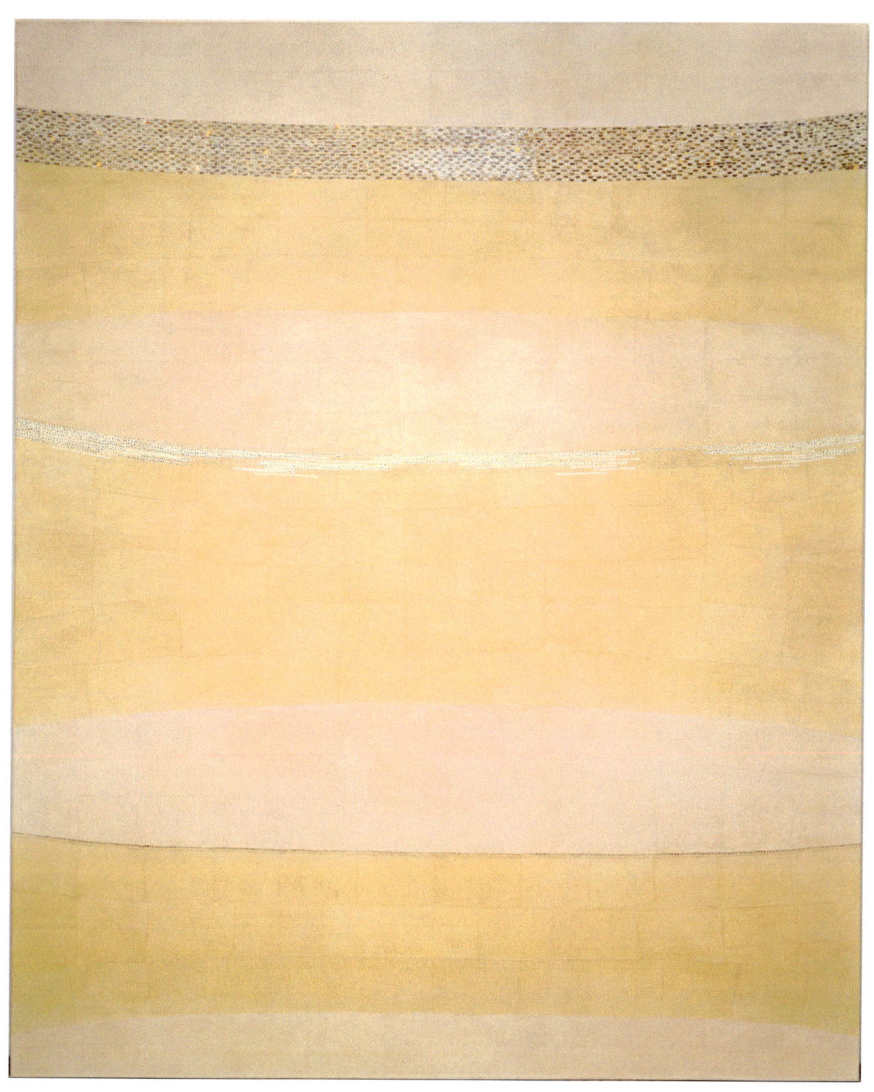

4.2 Ellen Gallagher, *Oh! Susanna*, 1995. Oil, pencil, and paper on canvas, 304.8 × 243.8 cm. Museum of Modern Art, New York. © Ellen Gallagher. Courtesy of the artist and Hauser and Wirth.

gets nervous. Beneath this, though, lies a more discordant purpose that purportedly carries the kind of political content (read: race) and outward signs of otherness that many feel lacking in painting today. In fact, I can tell you a few things about Black artists and abstraction in the history of art in this country . . .

As has been suggested previously in writing on Gallagher, two icons—fat-lipped minstrels and bug-eyed coons with buckwheat hair—are compulsively insinuated into her work, as well as into our field of vision, less to assault us with shrill didacticism than as rueful reminders of how Black pain is usually treasured material for cheap jokes by second-rate comics. In the new works, these two icons have been joined by a third: a red-lipped, blond-haired woman, a parody of a Caucasian socialite, in *Oh! Susanna* (1995). Gallagher's employment of racist stereotypes that spawned a whole cottage industry in the entertainment revues of yore reminds me of one of Carrie Mae Weems's photographic installations. In the work, Weems asks: "What are three things you can't give a black man?" to which she answers, "A fat lip, a black eye, and a job."

Weems's work points to another impossibility, which is the potential lack of seriousness the art world accords to the work of African American artists unless they have some angst-driven flag, tethered to the pole of *difference*, to unfurl. Perhaps that's the prime reason why many people in my art orbit seem to have quickly concluded that Gallagher is being set up for a hard fall. Of course, there is no evidence of such a conspiracy, only what they refer to as *instinct*. Instinct is usually confirmed when you discuss art in very close quarters to race in America. The odds are that critics will more likely fall silent, treating such a matter as a novelty and less as a radical manifestation of paradigmatic currency.

Such declamations notwithstanding, what makes Gallagher's work so satisfying in the end is its sophistication and her confidence in putting forward a proposition that mixes formalism with goofiness. A charmer, she seems to want to elicit laughter from her audience, despite the fact that pain accompanies her happy-go-lucky mark making. Paintings such as *Delirious Hem* (1995) and *Wild Kingdom* (1995), both of which, in their iconographies, implicitly refer to femininity and race, have such a tender beauty. They seem ready to vanish before your very eyes, as if they were never there in the first place. Each work is laid out by carefully gluing down, across the expanse of fairly large canvases, reams of ruled notepaper torn from the pages of a schoolbook. In *Elephant Bones* (1995) they form a grid of continuous, repeating bands of faint blue lines that are sometimes interspersed and supplemented by her own irregular dotted lines. This gives a feeling of topography, only instead of landscape, she incises minute coffee-bean-shaped figures that trail off like ant shit. Those in the know say these shapes represent mouths or something of that kind. I must confess, it wasn't evident to me when I last looked at the piece.

Acknowledging her obvious debt to Agnes Martin, Gallagher takes Martin's humane, less distancing minimalism, with its unaffected, spare, undulating bareness and intense radiance, and supplants it by inflecting her own reading of minimalism with a topical irony and wit. *DY-NO-mite* (1995), which refers to the insouciant exclamations of a popular character in the 1970s sitcom *Good Times*, evinces this radical humor and wide-awakeness to social and cultural history which minimalism seemed incapable of.

Gallagher's sexy, lean, and muscular paintings are truly accomplished. If the history which her work tackles often fails to register, it is only because it has been rendered almost microscopically and obliquely—a savvy move. In fact, the best way to see why her paintings have caused such a brouhaha is to get very close to them, magnifying glass in hand. Only then will you begin to see in precise detail the atlas that makes up the cultural and historical landscape she is cataloging and unpacking on the site of abstraction. The affinity to mapping (which in some sense reminds me of Guillermo Kuitca's work) reveals a process whereby cultural totems are abstractly and faintly delineated for heightened effect, bringing her work quite close to the whispery conditions of today.

Colonial Imaginary, Tropes of Disruption   5

History, Culture, and Representation in the Works of African Photographers

Written with Octavio Zaya, this essay introduced the catalog of the exhibition *In/Sight: African Photographers, 1940 to the Present*, shown at the Solomon R. Guggenheim Museum, New York, from May to September 1996. Curated by Okwui Enwezor and Zaya, along with Clare Bell and Danielle Tilkin, the exhibition presented the work of thirty photographers, most of whose work was seen for the first time by local viewers. The catalog included other contributions by Enwezor and Zaya, as well as essays by Bell and Olu Oguibe. This essay appeared on pages 17–47.

TO MOUNT AN EXPLORATION of African photographers, living or dead, exiled or residing on the continent, is to initiate an investigation of daunting magnitude. Equally, it means entering the terrain of transnational debates on questions of Africanity and issues of boundaries, race, culture, and politics, debates that are at once problematic and enriching. It also entails highlighting new insights on modern and postcolonial African identities and experiences, which may in turn lead to the uncovering of forgotten photographic material.

In pursuing this exploratory activity, it is practically impossible to examine African art and history of any period without taking into account Western anthropology's complicity in constructing and framing a natural history of critical intransigencies and visual codes, as well as the specific means through which the West has apprehended, consumed, and interpreted the African continent as a site of both scientific inquiry and popular entertainment. In building the framework through which this encounter has been accessed and codified as unimpeachable knowledge, photography has often been allied with anthropology. Such codification is exemplified by the tens of millions of postcards produced in the nineteenth century to sate Europe's appetite for exotic, colonized peoples as specimens of curiosity inciting a lurid benevolence. This ethnographic sensibility, which inspired Western artistic, cultural, and scientific pursuits in the past, seems inexhaustible today, as it continuously feeds the commercial hungers of popular entertainment, particularly in movies and pulp fiction. No continent meets the demands of these entertainments better than Africa. Looking toward the more distant past, the movies *Tarzan*, *King Solomon's Mines*, and *Birth of a Nation* come to mind, and a cursory examination of blockbusters made in the past fifteen years yields such examples as *Indiana Jones*, *Out of Africa*, *Congo*, *Ace Ventura*, and *The Gods Must Be Crazy*. Such movies indicate that Africa remains a territory of the Western imagination, often crudely constructed as an aberrant human domain or as a comical screen on which the visuals of such imagination can be projected. In movie footage and also in literature, Africa has been made completely invisible, obscured and masked, screened from our consciousness, and elided from the world's memory banks. For example, Africa is a void, a deep black hole that young Charles Marlow, in Joseph Conrad's novella *Heart of Darkness* (1902), hankered after to quell his passion for maps and the glories of exploration. Says Marlow:

> Now when I was a little chap I had a passion for maps. I would look for hours at South America, or Africa, or Australia, and lose myself in all the glories of exploration. At that time there were many *blank spaces* on the earth, and when I saw one that looked particularly inviting on a map (but they all look that) I would put my finger on it and say, "When I grow up I will go there." . . . But there was one yet—the biggest, the most blank, so to speak—that I had a hankering after. . . . It had ceased to be a blank space of delightful mystery—a white patch for a boy to dream gloriously over. It had become a place of darkness.[1]

Marlow was seized by the giddy urge to possess and own, to occupy and have the power of sanction and legislation, and to impose his will and mastery over territories, territories that could only exist as *blank spaces*. Today, Marlow's passion and hankering might be read as a deformity, but his desire was very much in tune with late nineteenth-century reasoning, a time of explorers, missionaries, and mad scientists. Just as Marlow's attitude reflected the reasoning of even the most enlightened people of the period, *Heart of Darkness* set the contemporary literary tone for the early twentieth century's perception of Africa: Africa as a tangle of bad dreams, hallucinations, disease, madness, and moral decrepitude, Africa as a place where the mind wilts in the humid frenzy of incomprehensibility and cruelty. Of course, Conrad (who himself actually embarked on Marlow's journey to the Congo) as a fiction writer took the liberty to conjure up images that would adequately frighten the European mind and thus reinforce the idea of Africa as a no-man's-land filled with evil, from which only the strongest could emerge unscathed.

The specific ways through which spurious Western agents have constructed a dense catalog of knowledge about Africa, in the process distorting its rich and long historical and cultural traditions, are telling. Such distortions, as Nicolas Monti notes in his remarkable book *Africa Then: Photographs, 1840-1918*, "formed the romantic myth in which the European bourgeoisie tried for the last time to manifest two opposing values: freedom and power."[2] Ultimately, what the European powers that conquered, colonized, and exploited Africa produced is a rendering of the continent as an amoral, primitive, and marginal site of dark, brooding forces, misery, and pestilence, a place that both cripples and fervidly arouses the imagination of the traveler, explorer, missionary, bounty hunter, and colonist. Indeed, it is a matter of quite some contradiction that Africa is also often promoted in the West as the cradle of civilization, an Eden where the last vestiges of a primeval paradise—with its lowland savannahs, misty peaks of mysterious mountain ranges, evergreen valleys, and thundering waterfalls—can be glimpsed from safari trails and game parks. There, in a pure state of nature, purged of any kind of native mediation, the spirit soars, the "heart of darkness" collapses and gives way to untrammeled beauty, awe, and innocence. It is out of such invocations that many Europeans have embarked on trips to Africa. One famous example is the French poet Arthur Rimbaud, who, before abandoning poetry and setting out on his exploration of Africa, declared with fanfare and fantasy in 1873 that he was quitting Europe for odd climates that "will tan me." Above all, he craved freedom from a corrupt France, which was terrorized by the Catholic Church. He ran away "to swim, to trample the grass, to hunt, above all to smoke; to drink liquors strong as boiling metal." He continued, "I shall come back, with limbs of iron, my skin dark, my eye furious." What strange desires these were, desires that only the most fictional places on earth could fulfill. Of course, the Africa of Rimbaud's imagination became, upon his arrival, a place whose peoples he regarded as "stupid and savage."[3] Fifty years later, André Breton and his surrealist cohorts, in their love for delinquency and juvenile rebellion, celebrated Rimbaud, in the first *Manifesto of Surreal-*

ism (1924), as "a Surrealist in the practice of life and elsewhere."[4] The irony of Rimbaud's racist impulse, and the fact that he ended up in Aden (Yemen) and Harar (in what is now Ethiopia) as a gunrunner and slave smuggler, was obviously lost on them.

As a result of the errant experiences and accounts of many such individuals from the West, Africa has remained a foil for Europe's civilizing tendencies and delusions of superiority, "a place of negations at once remote and vaguely familiar, in comparison with which Europe's own state of spiritual grace will be manifest."[5] Let us eavesdrop on Rudyard Kipling focusing his imagination on two vast territories: India, the subcontinent where he was stationed, and Africa, the continent where he was born. He writes in "The White Man's Burden" (1899):

> Take up the White Man's burden—
> Send forth the best ye breed—
> Go bind your sons to exile
> To serve your captives' need;
> To wait in heavy harness
> On fluttered folk and wild—
> Your new-caught, sullen peoples,
> Half devil and half child.[6]

In this last line, "Half devil and half child," Kipling, like his contemporary Conrad, provides us a peek into the binary code that not only gave impetus to but also defined and justified colonial subjugation. Beginning at the end of the eighteenth century, after Napoleon's invasion of Egypt, a massive effort was made by European powers to open up the African hinterland for trade and also for the pursuit of Christian missionary activities. The contest between the French and British for the control of trade from the Red Sea led to the opening of the Suez Canal in 1869. In his essay "The Power of Speech," V. Y. Mudimbe notes that "the more carefully one studies the history of missions in Africa, the more difficult it becomes not to identify it with cultural propaganda, patriotic motivations, and commercial interests, since the missions' program is indeed more complex than the simple transmission of the Christian faith."[7] As part of Europe's conquest of Africa, missionaries and explorers came, followed by photographers, anthropologists, and various other experts, under the guise of these firmly established scenarios and motivations. African self-images grounded in centuries of civilization would be condemned by the European scientific and intellectual communities as heathen, unclean, primitive, and savage. Georg Wilhelm Friedrich Hegel, in *Philosophy of History* (1840), writes that Africa "is no historical part of the world; it has no movement or development to exhibit. Historical movements in it—that is in its northern part—belong to the Asiatic or European world."[8] This prejudice was developed later by Count Arthur de Gobineau and others. Its refutation would become the lifelong quest of the Senegalese historian and anthropologist Cheikh Anta Diop. According to Diop's writings, the invention of the savage meant equally the invention of a master who must tame and guide him. Such notions would pave the way for Europe's final assault on and subdivision of the entire continent into colonies.

On February 23, 1885, at the Berlin Conference, under the auspices of Otto von Bismarck, fourteen European nations redrew the map of Africa, dividing the continent between themselves and conferring the right to explore, prospect, and draw subboundaries as they saw fit, as long as these activities did not interfere with the territorial claims of other member nations. This mad drive, for it can be called nothing else, set in motion what is known historically as the "Scramble for Africa." After the rush was over, only three African countries, Ethiopia (Abyssinia), Liberia, and Morocco, maintained their standing as independent states.

The brutal and total annexation and occupation of Africa lasted for less than a hundred years. But it left an indelible mark in its notion of African national identities, since such identities were more or less figments of the colonial imagination. Borders were drawn indiscriminately by the European powers without any consideration of the location of specific cultures when the cartographers arrived. Beginning in the 1920s, attempts to reverse the course of this territorial violence were made, thereby challenging European hegemony and political and cultural authority. These protestations, which gained momentum from the 1930s, laid the foundation for a protracted battle for independence. The first independent states to come out of this struggle were Egypt, under Gamal Abdel Nasser in 1954, and Ghana, under Kwame Nkrumah in 1957. These two figures helped usher in a new postcolonial era, but, more importantly, they almost single-handedly defined the ideological positions of Pan-Arab unity and Pan-African unity.

Although African nations won independence, Western stereotypes and misconceptions about Africans persisted. It is pertinent to illustrate the kind of image of the African that has survived for generations in the West, since photographic representation is essentially about the image and its construction as a visual analogue. Returning to *Heart of Darkness*, in a passage characterized by both racism and the most implacable earnestness,

Conrad enacts a deliberately false description, as if to write a summation of the Western perception of the image of the African savage:

> And between whiles I had to look after the savage who was fireman. He was an improved specimen; he could fire up a vertical boiler. He was there below me, and, upon my word, to look at him was as edifying as seeing a dog in a parody of breeches and a feather hat, walking on his hind legs. A few months of training had done for that really fine chap. He squinted at the steam gauge and at the water gauge with an evident effort of intrepidity—and he had filed teeth, too, the poor devil, and the wool of his pate shaved into queer patterns, and three ornamental scars on each of his cheeks. He ought to have been clapping his hands and stamping his feet on the bank, instead of which he was hard at work, a thrall to strange witchcraft, full of improving knowledge.[9]

It is the person and context of the above description that are the subjects of this exhibition. While we cannot redeem such distortions, the works in the exhibition provide a different account of that African landscape and history, difficult as they may be to (re)present in two dimensions. Over the course of its encroachment in Africa, no medium has been more instrumental in creating a great deal of the visual fictions of the African continent than photography. Yet, ironically, in attempting to defuse the power of these historicist fictions, we must rely on photography and its vast array of signs, which also stand at the juncture of this refutation.

Photography and the World as Image

In its more than 150 years of existence, photography has left us a deep and startling archive of human identity, its memories, presences, and absences. In a sense, what it has deposited in our care, for our gaze to linger on, are the traces and imprints of vanished moments, while it leaves unaccounted the motivations behind the making of individual photographs. As a supplement, referent, or index, the photograph invokes the perception of a presence on a flat surface. Yet the photograph in reality documents the absence of the subject represented. Drawing on this apparent contradiction, Roland Barthes writes that "the Photograph is pure contingency and can be nothing else."[10] Moreover, photography's prodigious ability to inhale and disseminate so much information multiplies this false sensation of the inscription of presence, thus frustrating efforts to categorize the medium's meaning as a stand-in for visual and/or experiential truth.

As we gather together the stories or pictures created through photography, we must, however, insist on the necessary contingency of all historical accounts, particularly in the case of modern African history, as we scan its progression across the scarred pages of the legacy of European colonialism. An empirical doubt must arise when we are confronted with the "veracity" of certain data—historical records and accounts, and images, especially photographs—built around Africa. In pausing on the issue of photography as an instrument furthering certain historicist fictions, charting and inscribing a visual palimpsest of the West's perceptions about otherness, we must question what is often seen as photographic truth and the notion of photographic images as stable, fixed information. Can decontextualized images be facts contained within an unembellished history? Can they represent an empirical record of experience or serve as objective stand-ins for history?

For photographs to have any meaning beyond their functions as memento mori and as instruments of evidence and record, we must acknowledge another stabilizing factor: the gaze, that which Gordon Bleach has aptly termed "the negotiated space of viewing."[11] When we take on Africa as the subject and African photographers as the interlocutors in this "negotiated space of viewing," the difficulty of interpreting what has been encoded as visual truth arises. Because there is now no prior existence of a language per se with which to discuss photographic activity in Africa (although photography in Africa is no different from that in any other region of the world), what is revealed in interpreting the gaze or the field of vision is its implicit contest for the power of ownership. We must raise the question that has often encircled theoretical investigations into the nature of photography: Who owns the image? Is it the property of the photographer or the viewer, whose prejudices and habits of viewing disturb the field of recognition, thereby unsettling the still waters of the photographic image, its codes and (mis)representations, and its disintegration as a unitary embodiment of the subject represented, particularly when the clues left behind are optical rather than experiential? Bleach poses this problem as a "disorientation: the powers and dis/pleasures of how it feels to (be) look(ed at) are integral to an account of the subject of vision."[12]

In considering the work of the thirty photographers selected, who were all born in Africa but may have lived within or outside the continent, and who are diverse in nationality, ethnicity, race, and religion, we are attempting to explore the critical issues that underpin their practices, identities, and experiences as Africans. In one way or another, Africa as seen through this exhibition is not a monolithic supposition, nor is it merely an idea that can be bent to our wishes and desires. Consequently, all the participating photographers touch on the nodes of these demands. They speak from positions that allow us to explore their various cultural and artistic imperatives, while opening up avenues to examine the dynamic relationship between past and present, history and memory, time and space, origin and authenticity, desire and ambivalence, and ethnic and sexual identity. However, what is truly enriching, thrilling, and even vexing is the diversity of approaches, disciplines, and strategies that the artists have brought to photographic practice. They invite us to call on the processes and resources of cultural, social, and personal transformation as they are unraveled within African realities and within experiences of relocation and diaspora.

Several photographers represented anticipated such issues that defined and at times unsettled aspects of the African experience. Their responses to our request to submit personal statements for this catalog, as well as other writings by them, have been central to our formulations and interpretations. The artists' individual subjectivities and attitudes about representation are also mapped on the metaterritory of the exhibition site. Santu Mofokeng of South Africa, for instance, writes that in the context of apartheid, "I had a rationale for documenting the lives of black people in the South Africa of yore, but, now that things have changed, it has become more difficult to legitimize my role as a documentary photographer in the traditional sense. As I get more intimate with my subjects, I find I cannot represent them in any meaningful way. I see my role becoming one of questioning rather than documenting. The projects I have undertaken recently are about the politics of representation."[13] Nigerian-born Rotimi Fani-Kayode, one of the most promising young African photographers until his untimely death in December 1989, wrote, "As an African working in a western medium, I try to bring out the spiritual dimension in my pictures so that concepts of *reality* become ambiguous and are opened to reinterpretation."[14] Fani-Kayode wished to repossess "the exploitative mythologizing of Black virility" and "the vulgar objectification of Africa . . . to reappropriate such images and to transform them ritualistically into images of our own creation."[15]

These critical positions are an important part of the emerging discourse about contemporary cultural production within an African context. However, though many issues have been raised in this regard, much work remains unearthed or unexhibited. There are structures that historically have staked claim to, appropriated, restricted, and controlled the access, diffusion, circulation, and representation of African art, from London to Paris to Zurich, which have also affected African photography. So how do we address questions of representation, self-imaging, and artistic freedom when those initiatives are counteracted by stronger economic imperatives, and when the contingencies of social and epistemological control are made to bend to the influence of power and access? The answer at the moment is that there is little that can be done until the scholarly and historical import of these primary materials is made public. Hence, this exhibition is necessary.

Signs of Disaffection: Photographic Truth, Technology, and Ethnography

Once seen as both a novelty and a scientific breakthrough, photography has quietly been assimilated into the realm of tradition. It no longer suffices to discuss photographic activity solely on the basis of its mimetic capabilities. Before the invention of photography, painting served this documentary function. And just as photography supplanted narrative painting, cinema and television in turn have attenuated photography's formerly exclusive claim to the infinite reproduction and dissemination of the image. Today, video, digitized images accessed via computer, and CD-ROMs occupy this terrain.

Nevertheless, photography remains one of the most enduring and focused instruments of documentation, regardless of its fragmentary constitution, falsehoods, and mise-en-scènes. Its allure and seductiveness still conscript our gaze, turn us into voyeurs, and utterly redefine our status as observers. Today, the aforementioned technologies have set up new kinds of visual fields that convert the retina to an active sensorium of bodily experiences, where codes of photographic meaning constantly seem to be turned into instruments of subversion. Through this enmeshment, a relationship is established in which the very status of the image can be not only altered and made contingent but also proliferated through myriad networks, modes of production, and multiple routes of delivery. However, it is important for us not to become engulfed by the latter visual fictions no matter how seductive and apparently stale they may seem.

With the advent of new imaging techniques, photography has crossed the boundaries set up by Walter Benjamin in his essay "The Work of Art in the Age of Mechanical Reproduction" (1936), an illuminating reading of the potential effects of the productivist economy and the reproducibility of photographic images on the ways that art is traditionally valued.[16] It is not that formerly dominant modes of visualization have changed or that their meanings have been obviated; rather, what it is that images recount and conduct within the field of vision has shifted perceptibly. Jonathan Crary elucidates this shift when he writes, "If these images can be said to refer to anything, it is to millions of bits of electronic mathematical data. Increasingly, visuality will be situated on a cybernetic and electromagnetic terrain where abstract visual and linguistic elements coincide and are consumed, circulated, and exchanged globally."[17] In this proliferation, it is the subject of the encounter in the electromagnetic terrain that poses the greatest challenge to the reading of the photographic index as a document of experience. Crary grasps this dilemma and invests it with a set of questions that pierces the skin of what has been termed the discursive space of photography: "What is the relation between the dematerialized digital imagery of the present and [that of] the so-called age of mechanical reproduction? . . . How is the body . . . becoming a component of new machines, economies, apparatuses, whether social, libidinal, or technological? In what ways is subjectivity becoming a precarious condition of interface between rationalized systems of exchange and networks of information?"[18]

The questions raised by Crary bear particular relevance in how we image and consume the idea of Africa in that "interface between rationalized systems of exchange and networks of information." As technology changes, so do the possible ramifications for our relationship to material culture and visual information. If we suppose that visual information is now available as cartographic inscriptions both coupling and delinking digital codes, does it yield access to a new kind of vision and a new and renovated subject no longer bound up with the fetishism and voyeurism of traditional photography, particularly that type prevalent within the discipline of ethnography?

From the mid-nineteenth century on, with the growth of colonialism and territorial expansion, a commodification and categorization of those peoples perceived to be different was practiced by Westerners. As a documentary tool, photography was important in providing lasting evidence of the fieldwork of anthropologists, the discoveries of explorers, and the results of scientific studies. The intense imagination of the West's ethnographic lens is revealed, for example, in the orientalist fantasies of paintings by Eugène Delacroix and of French photographic *scène et type* postcards that turn the bodies of nude Algerian women into objects intended purely for the erotic pleasure of the colonial gaze. Following Malek Alloula's seminal study of *scène et type* postcards, *The Colonial Harem* (1986), Salah Hassan writes, in an astute interrogation of orientalism, that "Delacroix's painting [*Women of Algiers*] and the postcards were part of the visual tradition built on preconceived notions essential to Western images and perceptions of Oriental women."[19] Even for the naive Western consumer, to comprehend the subject as framed by the ethnographic lens is to participate in the decapitation or cannibalization of the subject, as the grossly misrepresented African body is consummately fed to the passions of a false imagination, working in consort with the notion of scientific inquiry.

In nineteenth-century studies, subjects could be put through all sorts of bizarre apparatuses in order to display and quantify their encoded gestalts. Physiognomy revealed the body as an avatar containing knowledge available only to science, which could be documented as evidentiary truth by the analytical mechanism of photography. Anthropometric photography was particularly useful in this exercise, because in providing measurements it purportedly gave "objective" interpretations and records of the body as a specimen or type. Brian Street writes that "the nineteenth-century focus on the physical and visual features of cultural variety gave to photography a particular role in 'the formation of a particular discourse of race which was located in the conceptualization of the body as the object of anthropological knowledge.' . . . Anthropological interpretation of the body was conceptualized through 'physiognomy'—the belief that the facial and bodily features indicate specific mental and moral characteristics."[20] Today, even within the "enlightened" corridors of postmodern discourse, the question of difference is still based less on the existence of a multiplicity of identities than it is on the equating of difference with race and otherness. Ethnography still replicates and enters into the service of power. According to Crary, "Problems of vision then, as now, were fundamentally questions about the body and the operation of social power," in the guise of benevolent scientific investigations.[21]

What, then, are the purposes of the purported meaning of photographs? What forms of knowledge do they expose? For whom and for what? How can we trust or be sure of what is being proffered as a form of representation when it is invested with a knowledge beyond mere incident? Elizabeth Edwards writes:

> Central to the nature of the photograph and its interpretive dilemmas is its insistent dislocation of time and space. . . . Closely related to temporal dislocation in a photographic context is spatial dislocation. In the creation of an image, photographic technology frames the world. Camera angle, range of lens, type of film and the chosen moment of exposure further dictate and shape the moment. Exposure is an ap-

posite term, for it carries not only technical meaning, but describes that moment "exposed" to historical scrutiny. The photograph contains and constrains within its own boundaries, excluding all else, a microcosmic analogue of the framing of space which is knowledge.[22]

These fraught questions come into play in Barthes's critique of Richard Avedon's objectifying portrait of William Casby (1963). In the picture in question, a tightly cropped, straight-on view of the face of an aged African American man, Avedon took pains to excise all obtrusive details that might have inflected a different context to the reading of Casby's portrait by zeroing in on the most delectable detail, the mask. Barthes follows Italo Calvino's use of the word *mask* to "designate what makes a face into the product of a society and of its history."[23] The photograph is modified by an important linguistic signifier, the title that reads *William Casby, Born a Slave*. Clearly, this is less a portrait than a sociological and anthropological study. The title points to the limitations of the photograph as a carrier of truth, for the portrait of Casby needs the stabilizing factor of language employed not for clarification or as a source of knowledge but solely for the viewer's delectation. In Barthes's context, Casby's picture purports to tell us the essential truths of photography's "assuming a mask" in order to signify, when in reality it is feeding us information about the otherness of the subject. The photograph seeks to reveal Casby's difference from the rest of society. He is an endangered, dying breed, a monster who must be preserved, even if the process of preservation is essentially false. Indeed, the photographic meaning of Avedon's project might have been completely lost to the viewer without this signpost, the title that points to an irredeemable otherness. Avedon was thus able to create by means of his camera, linguistic modification, and position of power as an objective observer a sample or fragment of a "'type', the abstract essence of human variation . . . perceived to be an observable reality."[24] The temptation is to consume this image as if it represented a form of knowledge more profound than its trashy voyeurism. We are tempted to use this inevitable detail to represent the whole, to allow the specific and incomplete to stand for generalities, and to allow one image to become "a symbol for wider truths, at the risk of stereotyping and misrepresentation."[25]

Here, then, is Barthes's interesting reading of Avedon's image. Seeing the mask as a "difficult region" of photography, he goes on to elaborate that "society . . . mistrusts pure meaning: It wants meaning, but at the same time it wants this meaning to be surrounded by a noise. . . . Hence the photograph whose meaning . . . is too impressive is quickly deflected; we consume it aesthetically, not politically."[26] Are we to assume, then, that Avedon's title, which Barthes ignored in his commentary, was purely incidental and not a calculated titillation serving to reveal to the photographer's audience a different kind of essence lurking beneath the mask? No, Casby's portrait was constructed precisely because Avedon wished it to be consumed both aesthetically and ethnographically. The portrait was made for the picture gallery or for the coffee-table book. To put Avedon's portrait side by side with those of his African contemporaries, such as Seydou Keïta or Cornélius Yao Augustt Azaglo, delimits the mask and calls it into question. The projects of these two great portrait photographers from Africa undress—in part through the dialogue that existed between sitter and photographer—the pretense of excavating a deeper meaning from the subject, a meaning that ethnographic framing assumes as its lens pans across the body of the othered subject.

We can name in our aid three important technical elements in the interesting contest of power that ethnographic authority employs in solidifying its scientific foundation: camera placement and lens angle, the position of the photographer in relationship to the subject, and the "natural" environment selected by the photographer to enact the subject's authenticity. Elaborating on this technique and framing of authenticity, Edwards writes, "The 'real' or the 'natural' or 'authentic' and the elements selected to represent that reality, depend on the status of the objects concerned within the overall classification of knowledge and the representation of those objects in a way which will be understood as 'real' by the viewer."[27] In examining the entire spectrum in which photography worked in collusion with ethnography and anthropology to both frame and undermine our knowledge of Africa, Edwards continues, "In anthropology 'significant' structures of a culture are observed, the fragments of informants recorded and the final work born of synthesis and then generalization; the fragments become molded to a unifying account of 'culture.' So, in photography, the specific moment becomes representative of the whole and the general."[28]

For the ethnographer, the African subject functions and exists in this delimited terrain to better yield access to the kind of knowledge that the pseudoscience of nineteenth-century phrenology skillfully appropriated. It is not the subject depicted who is really of interest but what he or she is supposed or ought to represent, what the body type reveals. Stripped of the most rudimentary of human attributes, of speech, choice, and subjectivity, the subject might as well be a piece of dead wood. In this case, the African subject—who neither signifies nor embodies consciousness—is beyond redemption and is, in Conrad's words, "a thrall to strange witchcraft, full of improving knowledge."

Negritude, Pan-Africanism, and Postcolonial African Identity

The emergence of the concept of negritude in the late 1930s, in particular as a dialectical framework in the development of African and Caribbean post-colonial literary discourse, is also pertinent to the broad discussions that flow from this exhibition. The first appearance of the term *négritude* was in the startling epic poem by the great poet Aimé Césaire of Martinique. In *"Cahier d'un retour au pays natal"* ("Notebook of a Return to the Native Land"), published in 1939, Césaire set down the psychic and temporal order that would come to define this very important branch of modernism. He writes simultaneously out of righteous scorn and penetrating irony:

> oh friendly light
> oh fresh source of light
> those who have invented neither powder nor compass
> those who could harness neither steam nor electricity
> those who explored neither the seas nor the sky but those
> without whom the earth would not be the earth
> gibbosity all the more beneficent as the bare earth even more earth
> silo where that which is earthiest about earth ferments and ripens
> my negritude is not a stone, its deafness hurled against the clamor
>   of the day
> my negritude is not a leukoma of dead liquid over the earth's
>   dead eye
> my negritude is neither tower nor cathedral
> it takes root in the red flesh of the soil
> it takes root in the ardent flesh of the sky
> it breaks through the opaque prostration with its upright
>   patience[29]

Though Césaire originated the word, its conceptualization and subsequent growth as a cultural movement were not his alone. The Senegalese statesman, poet, and essayist Léopold Sédar Senghor was Césaire's partner in giving negritude its stamp and urgency in the tepid dawning of fascism under the gray skies of Europe. Negritude's founding in Paris shortly before World War II was based on a fundamentally modernist vision intermixed with the ideal of an originary essence of African identity. This ideal, however, relates more to Senghor's beliefs, which were rooted in a kind of archaic revisionism, than to Césaire's more fragmentary, indeterminate Caribbean syncretism. The dates of negritude's emergence coincide more or less with the earliest works in this exhibition. This connection is not coincidental.

As negritude's tenets were taking hold (mostly among young franco-phone African and Caribbean intellectuals in Paris such as Léon Damas, David Diop, René Depestre, Frantz Fanon, and Tchicaya U Tam'si), the irreversible changes that would eventually inaugurate the struggle for the end of colonialism were being forged by the Pan-African ideology of Nkrumah and the "scientific socialism" supported by anglophone intellectuals who rejected Senghor's negritude and *Africanité* as essentialist particularism, both emotional and regressive. At a writers' conference in 1962 in Kampala, Uganda, the young Wole Soyinka (who in 1986 was named Nobel laureate in literature) of Nigeria retorted with disdain, while discussing negritude, that "a tiger does not go about asserting its tigritude."[30] A few years later, in 1966, poet Christopher Okigbo rejected an award he had won in Senegal on the grounds that it was based on the absurdity of race and ancestry. Benin's minister of culture, philosopher Paulin Hountondji, criticized Senghor's position because he avoided political issues and was "engaged in the systematic elaboration of 'artificial cultural problems.'"[31] The points of these attacks are to be found in Senghor's unshifting position vis-à-vis *Africanité*, negritude, and the past. Often, his beliefs seem dangerously close to the ideas of nineteenth-century scientific anthropology, which privileged notions of originary essence. For example, Senghor emphasized the past at the expense of the present. He wrote, "There is no question of reviving the past, of living in a *Negro-African museum*; the question is to inspire this world, *here and now*, with the values of our past."[32] Another bombshell that had intellectuals scrambling to the lectern for a rebuttal is this assertion: "The Negro is a man of nature. . . . He lives off the soil and with the soil, in and by the Cosmos. . . . [He is] sensual, a being with open senses, with no intermediary between subject and object, himself at once subject and object."[33] The "Negro-African museum" evoked by Senghor's words is at once a recombined theory of essentialism and a recapitulation of Gobineau.

Negritude's rejection by many African intellectuals on the grounds that it was revisionist and regressive seems to be confirmed in the photographs made by Joseph Moïse Agbodjelou, Mama Casset, Salla Casset, Meïssa Gaye, and Keïta in the same period. Nowhere in their works do we detect the sitters' desires to live in that so-called Negro-African museum. In fact, what we see is their reluctance to be confined in such a natural-history or ethnographic setting. Looking at the majestic portraits of the worldly and sophisticated men and women who frequented the studios of these photographers, we find the unique intersection and cross-referencing of notions of tradition and modernity. Even Senghor himself sat for a portrait by Salla Casset. These photographs produced just before World War II and thereafter contest Senghor's *Africanité*, an ideal rooted in an almost incontestable, primal authenticity, which was drawn from the powerful residues of oratory and represented by the griot and traditional folklore.

The interpretation we may draw from this vehement cultural and ideological dispute is that the African self-image in the late 1930s and the 1940s was already being radically transformed. The subjects of these photographs are the electorate who would cast the decisive vote for independence and initiate the radical break with colonialism. Indeed, the subjects of these portraits are African, but they are not contained by the questionable episteme of ethnographic delectation and otherization. Their subjectivities and desires in a modern and modernizing Africa conflict with the Senghorian interpretation of an originary African essence. For if, as he argued, tradition was the mother of the primal essence, then technology no doubt should have represented its antithesis and negation, an incendiary apparatus imported from the West to deracinate and desacralize tradition's deeply planted taproot. But technology in the modern world was never the antithesis or negation of tradition. What simply happened, as James Clifford notes, was that "after the Second World War, colonial relations would be pervasively contested. . . . Peoples long spoken for by Western ethnographers, administrators, and missionaries began to speak and act more powerfully for themselves on a global stage. It was increasingly difficult to keep them in their (traditional) places. Distinct ways of life once destined to merge into 'the modern world' reasserted their difference, in novel ways."[34]

Before World War II interfered with the drive for self-governance, Africa's sense of itself was changing. Like James VanDerZee in Harlem, New York, and Richard Samuel Roberts in South Carolina, Mama Casset, Salla Casset, and Gaye had already established studios in Dakar and Saint-Louis, Senegal, that catered to the elite and common folk of those cities. They methodically documented an important milieu in that negotiated space bridging the gap between colonial and postcolonial identity, between the self and the other, between modernity and tradition. Keïta set up a studio in Bamako, Mali, at the end of the 1940s, largely continuing the same kind of portrait work, but with a lyrical, modernist sensibility that is as fresh today as when his photographs were made. The aforementioned photographers' popularity as the preeminent image makers of their time is attested to by the presence of their works in many family collections. Encountering their

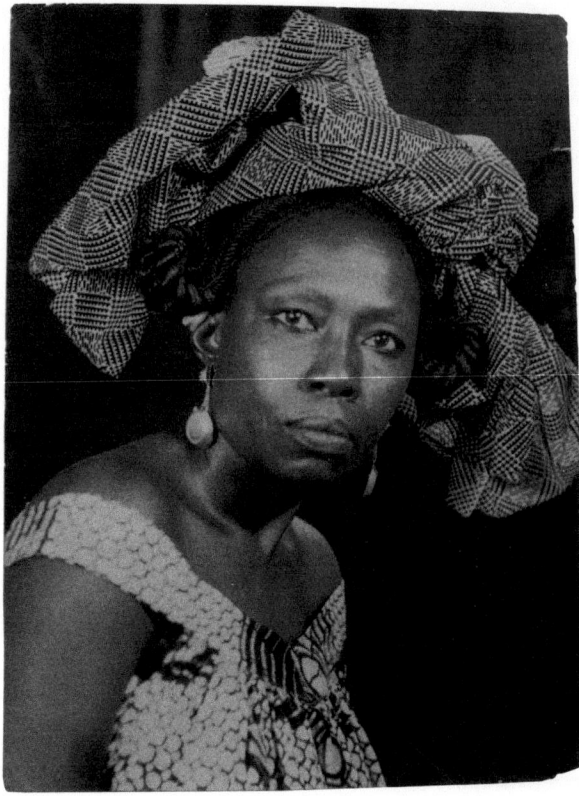

5.1 (*this page*) Meïssa Gaye, *Untitled*, 1941. Gelatin silver print, 18 × 13.1 cm. Collection of Awa Diarra Gaye.

5.2 (*opposite*) Salla Casset, *Les Coépouses*, ca. 1950. Gelatin silver print, 12.9 × 18 cm. Collection of Awa Diarra Gaye.

work today, we feel ourselves deeply embedded in a site of recognition, in a temporal zone between the pathos of loss and rejuvenation. Their photographs chart an ontological space, a period of modern history that has remained largely neglected.

The existence of photographs of the 1940s provides us with an insight into the diverse and complex sensibilities that made up the face of Africa as it entered a new era. The images give us access to vivid, but by no means complete, visual records of a continent gripped by, yet emerging from, the political, economic, social, and cultural structures imposed by colonialism. Given their incompleteness, these photographs represent only a part of that visual history created and documented by Africans. Many of them, such as the cache of photographs borrowed for this exhibition from little-known family archives in Senegal, are difficult to trace and hard to locate. They nevertheless exist. This vast archive of images staged for posterity remains a crucial testimony. Today, the photographs reside scattered and buried in

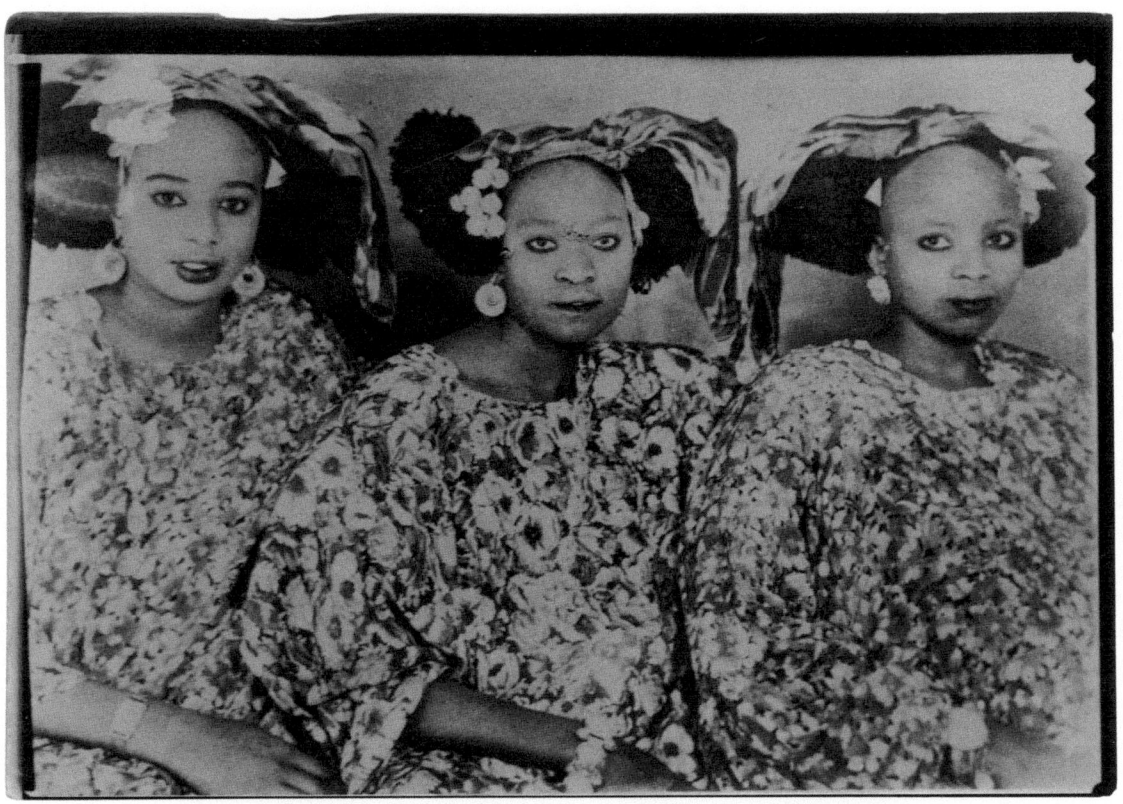

colonial archives, obscure private albums, and commercial business records that have either been abandoned, neglected, or totally forgotten. This hoard remains for historians and archivists to retrieve, catalog, interpret, and preserve for future generations.

The present exhibition constitutes part of that effort. In examining issues of modern and contemporary African representation and identity, and the interpretation and dissemination of history, it calls attention to a continent whose long historical traditions have crossed, touched, and influenced all the consequential byways of human history. That Africa has long been disparaged by innuendo and misrepresentation, its contribution to history eluding comprehension and appreciation over the years, in part accounts for the selection of photographs in the exhibition. We have passed over images of wretchedness and misery, of disasters, genocide, war, hunger, and dictators—plentiful elsewhere—in order to celebrate Africa, to throw its artistic modernity and contemporaneity into sharp relief.

In presenting African visions, the exhibition also suggests how their staging testifies against the dominant notions, preconceptions, and normative codings entrenched in modernist iconography. What we seek to reveal is a whole transactional flow that refutes both Senghorian negritude's salvage paradigms and a complacent Western historicity of morbidly inscribed ethnographic yearnings, lusts, prejudices, appropriations, and corrosive violence. The exhibition presents an African subjectivity from east to west, from north to south, emerging out of the entire continent's multiracial, multiethnic, multilinguistic, and multireligious realities. The continent was also caught up in the dystopic upheavals of modernity, whose currency—from Pablo Picasso's and Georges Braque's cubist pastiches to Henri Matisse's orientalism and Breton's surrealism—was built on a syncretic practice of quoting, renovating, and discarding disparate elements refined across cultural borders. In crossing those borders, signs of authenticity disintegrate, disparaging all claims to an originary essence or purity.

Clifford thoroughly challenges "such claims to purity" and essence as they have persistently marked and circumscribed African representation. He writes that such claims (which, in any case, simultaneously represent negritude's and Western ethnography's attitudes) "are always subverted by the need to stage authenticity *in opposition to* external, often dominating alternatives."[35] It is by no means an exaggeration when Clifford notes that something happens "whenever marginal peoples come into a historical or ethnographic space that has been defined by the Western imagination. 'Entering the modern world,' their distinct histories quickly vanish."[36] But he goes further in amending and supplementing this view of quickly vanishing cultures by contesting a cultural reading based on the preservation of "endangered authenticities." Thus, he suggests that "geopolitical questions must now be asked of every inventive poetics of reality." But "Whose reality? Whose new world?" he asks.[37]

Africa is no different from other places in the shifting, indeterminate landscape of current world conditions, in which every process of cultural texturing goes through a combinative loop of excisions and additions to contradict the persistent ethnographic dramatization of otherness. From the sense of "impurity" and "inauthenticity," we observe that when "intervening in an interconnected world, one is always, to varying degrees, 'inauthentic': caught between cultures, implicated in others. Because discourse in global power systems . . . elaborated vis-à-vis . . . a sense of difference or distinctness can never be located solely in the continuity of a culture or tradition. Identity is conjunctural, not essential."[38] In a global system under rapid transformation, "who has the authority to speak for a group's identity or authenticity? What are the essential elements and boundaries of a culture? How do self and other clash and converse in the encounters of ethnography, travel, modern interethnic relations?"[39] Here, purity becomes incapable of performing even a metonymic duty, embedded as it is with inauthenticities.

Portraiture, Reality, and Representation

Prior to the period of independence, those representations of Africa's social reality available in the West were the work of European photographers. The ubiquity of these photographs produced in mass numbers as souvenirs obscures the existence and availability of work by African photographers who were active in the colonies as early as the 1860s. A. C. Gomes, for instance, established a studio in Zanzibar in 1868 and opened a branch in Dar es Salaam later on; N. Walwin Holm started his business in Accra in 1883 and was, in 1897, the first African photographer inducted as a member into the Royal Photographic Society of Great Britain. Other photographers active during the later part of the nineteenth century were George S. A. Da Costa (in Lagos from 1895), E. C. Dias (in Zanzibar in the 1890s), and F. R. C. Lutterodt (of Ghana, who worked in Accra, Cameroon, Gabon, and Fernando Po in the 1890s). Many other names are currently lost to history.

The material available on these photographers suggests that they were not (either thematically or historically) linked to the decline and the disintegration of European colonial dominance. Nor could we say that they were involved in any way in the destructuring of European hegemony in African existence. Since very little early photography by Africans is available publicly, it would be difficult to claim their production as the embodiment of some counterdiscursive "native" sensibility in an insurgent photographic practice that could have overthrown the imperialist mechanisms of European invincibility and superiority. Within artistic practice, the reclamation of African subjectivity, in any kind of considered manner, existed within the practice of painting, in what Olu Oguibe identifies as a reverse appropriation in the work of the Nigerian painter Aina Onabolu, who was working in Lagos during the early 1900s and in Paris in the 1920s.[40] Kobena Mercer identifies the same process at work in Mama Casset's portraits of the 1920s and 1930s. He writes, "Whereas the depiction of Africans in prevailing idioms of photojournalism tends to imply a vertical axis which literally looks down upon the subject, thereby cast into a condition of pathos and abjection, Mama Casset's portraits are often set on a diagonal whereby the women he portrays seem to lean out of the frame to look straight out to the viewer, with a self-assured bearing that evidences an interaction conducted on equal footing."[41] This positioning and sense of confrontation coincide with the reflective discourses advanced by the African liberation struggle, discourses that affected the work of the portraitists represented in the exhibition. Thus, the period of independence, which began roughly at the end of World War II and ended in the early 1970s, was not a period of amnesia, tabula rasa, and newborn Africanity, but a time of sociopolitical resurrection, reassessment, and transformation. The temptation to search for some sort of "natural" or "pure" state of African photography emerging from this period is great. To proceed from such an assumption, which anticipates an allegedly original photography and an "other" photography, would overlook and mar the very existence and repercussions of the colonial enterprise. On the other hand, it conforms to the idea of an imagined "difference" that marks borders around those "other" cultural practices, isolating and fetishizing them. This kind of paternalistic identification thus separates the viewer from African cultural production and from the social conditions that have shaped its forms. At the same time, it reaffirms the imaginary unity of Western photography and the myth of its own distinctiveness, authenticity, and superiority.

Likewise, in assuming the illusion of an allegedly universal photographic language, we may be reinforcing the systematic process and hegemonic position of Western projection, identification, and appropriation. Too often, many Western critics, curators, and scholars, instructed and trained within the theoretical frame of Western photography, seem predisposed to applying their presuppositions to non-European photographers or artists, thus ignoring or dismissing specific sociocultural situations and ideological conditions that inform artistic practice in other regions of the world.

Kwame Anthony Appiah discusses an instance of Western projection in his revealing *In My Father's House: Africa in the Philosophy of Culture*: "The French colonial project, by contrast with the British, entailed the evolution of francophone Africans; its aim was to produce a more homogeneous francophone elite. Schools did not teach in 'native' languages, and the French did not assign substantial powers to revamped precolonial administrations. You might suppose, therefore, that the French project of creating a class of black *'evolués'* had laid firmer foundations for the postcolonial state."[42] Appiah also asserts that "the majority of French colonies have chosen to stay connected to France, and all but Guinée . . . have accepted varying degrees of 'neocolonial' supervision by the metropole," either culturally, militarily, or economically. And, in most cases, the colonial languages of the British, French, and Portuguese remained the languages of government after independence, according to Appiah, "for the obvious reason that the choice of any other indigenous language would have favored a single linguistic group." These arrangements and policies might have been the only compromising response to the fact that not even the new states with the smallest populations were ethnically homogeneous: "The new states brought together peoples who spoke different languages, had different religious traditions and notions of property, and were politically (and, in particular, hierarchically) integrated to different—often radically different—degrees."[43]

Ironically, in this period that promised African independence from Europe, the liberation struggle was formulated through many visions and schemes that were ideologically, culturally, and politically articulated within European history and philosophical traditions. Both Senghor's *Africanité* and Nkrumah's "scientific socialism" were nothing more than Eurocentric ideas projected and presented either as Africa's own self-conception (in the case of the former) or as a universal and globalized paradigm that unequivocally occluded African historicity and its concrete political and cultural existence (in the latter). If the former internalized and ontologized racism, as Tsenay Serequeberhan pointedly evidences in his piercing analysis of Senghor in his book *The Hermeneutics of African Philosophy: Horizon and Discourse* (1994), the latter, by employing the abstract and universalizing language of Marxist-Leninist idealism, subordinates African existence to the terrain of a homogenized historicity determined by the "historical logic" of the international hegemonic power of the Western proletariat and of European modernity.

Other writers, statesmen, and intellectuals associated with the African liberation struggle, such as Césaire, Amílcar Cabral, and Fanon, focused instead on establishing an African political tradition grounded in African historicity. They articulated a critique exposing the contrast between the unfulfilled promises and ideals of African "independence" and the political realities of the new states. Aware that newly independent African countries were still connected to colonial attitudes and values, they enunciated a notion of liberation as a process of reclaiming African history.[44] The "return to the source" established by Cabral as the basic direction for the movement he directed in the 1960s in Guinea-Bissau is not, however, a return to tradition in stasis; nor is it engaged, as Serequeberhan explains, "in an antiquarian quest for an already existing authentic past." On the contrary, in "returning," the "Westernized native" brings with him "the European cultural baggage that constitutes his person," absorbing the European values into a "new synthesis." Serequeberhan elucidates, "In this dialectic European culture/history is recognized as a particular and *specific* disclosure of existence, aspects of which are retained or rejected in terms of the lived historicity and the practical requirements of the history that is being reclaimed."[45]

The works of photographers like Agbodjelou (working in what is now Benin), Augustt Azaglo (Côte d'Ivoire), Mama Casset (Senegal), Salla Casset (Senegal), Gaye (Senegal), Keïta (Mali), Moumoune Koné (Mali), Boufjala Kouyaté (Mali), and Youssouf Traoré (Mali) are instilled with the euphoria and the disappointment, the pride and the insecurity, the confidence and the contradictions of this period of transformation. Even if none of these photographers directly problematized cultural, political, and social issues of colonialism and postcolonialism, they employed narrative means that contribute to unraveling the issues under discussion and to situating them within the specific historical and ideological framework of the African experience of this period. Taken as a collection of disparate images and aspects of traditional and modern forms and effects, these photographs reveal African societies in flux. Even Agbodjelou's traditional and more luxurious portraits of weddings and other political, cultural, and religious ceremonies offer tradition as something alive, not sealed in the antiquity of a "reconstructed" culture.

In general terms, the portraits by these photographers are descriptions of individuals as much as they are inscriptions of social identities. Although most of them are frontal poses of individuals and groups in the photographers' studios, the portraits expose as much as they hide from view through the complexity and sophistication of representation. Set as they are within a historical model of photographic configuration, these portraits are not necessarily telling any "truth" about their subjects, but, as products of signification, they are claiming a specific presence in representation. Portrait photography, in general, creates the illusion of fixed, immutable presences in images rendered as real bodies. When we pose, we either imagine what people see when they look at us and then try to act out this image, or we want to look like someone else and imitate that appearance. We imitate what we think the observer sees, or what we see in someone else, or what we wish to see in ourselves. This process of reconfiguration and acting out of an ideal is what is so fascinating in the character studies of African studio portraiture. It evidences not only a social transformation but a structural and ideological one, in which the complex negotiations of individual desires and identities are mapped and conceptualized.

Probing how the subject inserts itself into this matrix, Peggy Phelan, following Jacques Lacan, asserts, "Like a good correspondence, the model's reply to the inquiry of the photographer is based on the quality of the photographer's question. Portrait photography is the record of the model's self-inquiry, an inquiry framed and directed by the photographer's attempt to discover what he sees. Models imitate the image they believe photographers see through the camera lens. Photographers develop the image as they touch the shutter; models perform what they believe that image looks like. And spectators see again what they do and do not look like."[46] As is the case with all portraits, those by these African photographers vacillate between glamorizing the sitters and uncritically reflecting their projections and desires. These portraits do not only render reality; they penetrate and evaluate it. These portraits are archetypes, models for the way their sitters wanted to appear. The portrait is, therefore, the outcome of an elaborate constitutive process. As John Tagg writes, "We cannot quantify the realism of a representation simply through a comparison of the representation with a 'reality' somehow known prior to its realisation. The reality of the realist representation does not correspond in any direct or simple way to anything present to us 'before' representation. It is, rather, the product of a complex process involving the motivated and selective employment of determinate *means of representation*."[47]

While reminiscing on that transitional period of the late 1940s, Keïta comments that, by then, "men in town began to dress in European style. They were influenced by France. But not everybody had the means to dress like that. In the studio I had three different European outfits, with tie, shirt, shoes, and hat . . . everything. And also accessories—fountain pen, plastic flowers, radio, telephone—which I had available for the clients." Most of Keïta's pictures depict individuals in traditional African clothing, but the variety, elegance, or origin of these clothes (already cultural inscriptions in themselves) is not precisely what these portraits emphasize; what they reveal is their own sociocultural value as signifiers of status and their functional role in the construction and transformation of identity.

Keïta also recognizes that he helped his models to find ways to look their best. In his studio, he displayed samples of his photographs so customers could choose how they wanted to look. "I suggested a position which was better suited to them, and in effect I determined the good position," Keïta admits. His clients were as conscious of their poses as of their dress and accessories. All elements amount to the construction of solemn images composed as signs of wealth, beauty, and elegance, which act—with the complicity of the photographer—as surrogates for the essences of their subjects.

The clients and subjects of portraiture by Salla Casset, Gaye, and Keïta are primarily family members and friends, civil servants, bureaucrats, society ladies, and well-to-do people. Confirming his own position as a sought-after

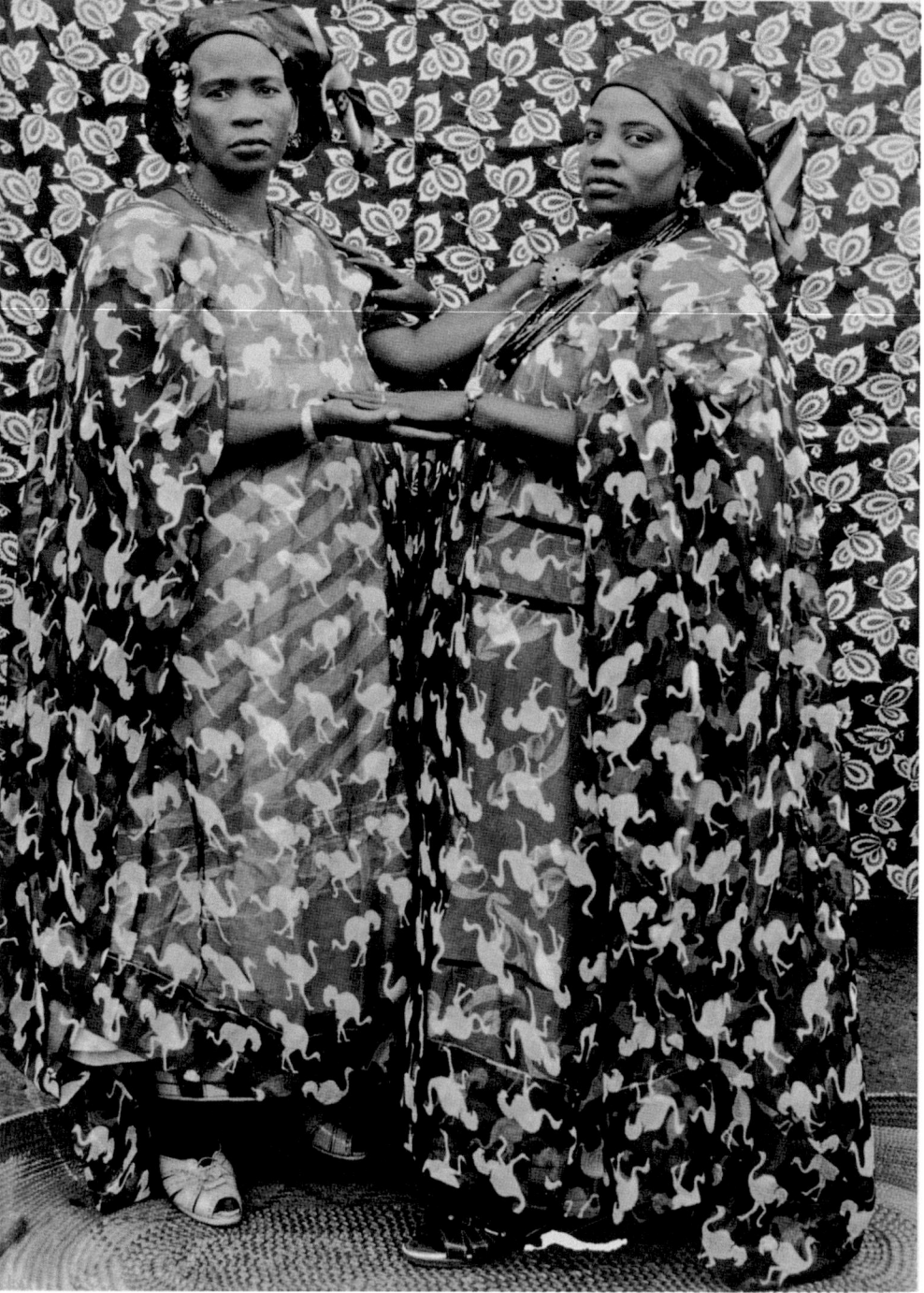

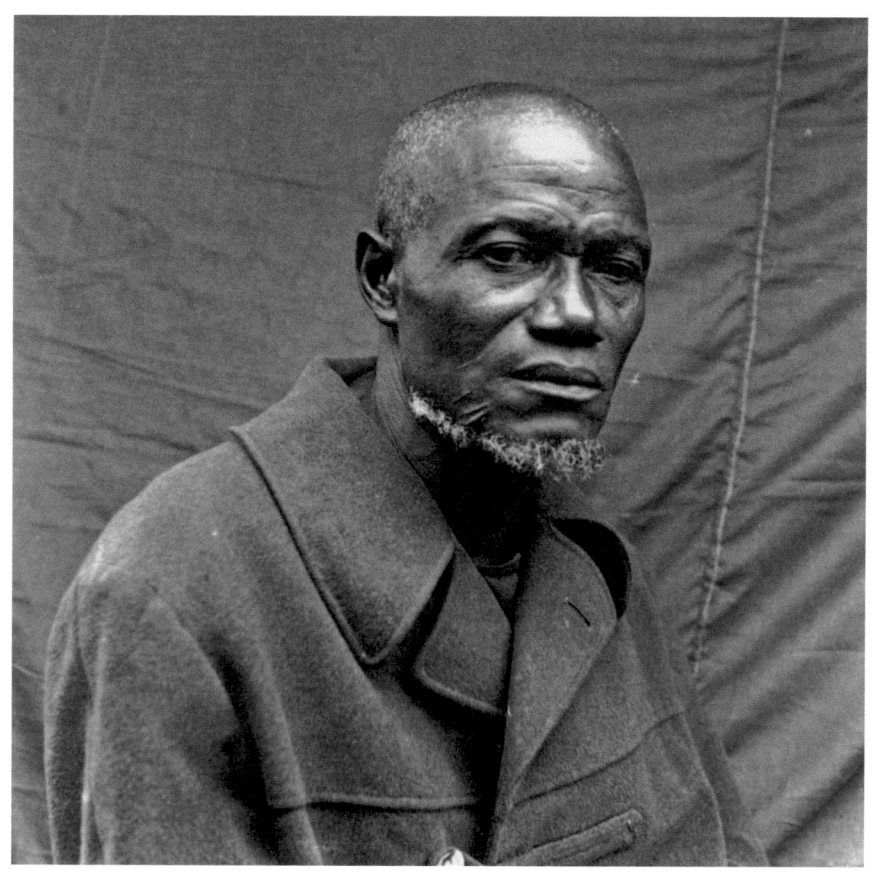

5.3 (*opposite*) Seydou Keïta, *Untitled*, 1957–59.
Gelatin silver print, 35.5 × 25.5 cm. © Seydou
Keïta/SKPEAC. Courtesy of Jean Pigozzi
Collection of African Art, Geneva.

5.4 (*this page*) Cornélius Yao Augustt Azaglo,
Untitled, Pangnergakaha, 1964. Gelatin silver
print, 25.4 × 25.4 cm. © Cornélius Yao Augustt
Azaglo. Courtesy of Revue Noire, Paris.

photographer, Keïta comments, "Even our first president of the Republic [of Mali] came."[48] Most of the photographs, whether taken inside or outside the studio, place the models against plain or patterned backgrounds. In most cases, the backgrounds isolate the model with accessories and props; particularly in Keïta's majestic photographs, they may blend with the subject's clothes, emphasizing the faces. Despite the realism and purported individuality and particularities of these portraits, the generic solid or decorative backgrounds and the props give them an abstract quality. Certainly, Casset, Gaye, and Keïta were not trying to create or document a taxonomy of social types, but the generic character of such elements seems to counteract the subjectivity of individual models.

Portraiture in Africa recorded how models wanted to be remembered, or inventoried their past; sitters could then witness their own (or somebody else's) transformation as well as the disappearance over time of customs and cultural symbols. While the portrait, as a memento mori, could suggest a pathos to the model in its reminder of mortality, it could also be put to societal uses. Much of the most stimulating work of Augustt Azaglo, for instance, consists of portraits made for identity cards in the mid-1960s. They are technically as sharp and clear as Keïta's, but stylistically straightforward and uncomplicated. Augustt's portraits, of the poor, workers, job-seeking rural people, and others, make up a much broader social sampling than Keïta's. The head-on stare of Augustt's models evokes a cross between the mug shot, documentary photo, and old-fashioned studio portrait, although the portraits themselves assert an unusually modern quality.

Portraits also have religious functions in different African cultures. In a continent where technology is always narrated as being at loggerheads with tradition, photography—from the moment it was conscripted into service to create funerary objects—has been renovating and supplementing an existing tradition. Within this context, the portrait, in addition to being a presence in the world, carries great symbolic value, for it is said to represent the spirit of the subject, as an index, a pure trace of the body. In various African cultures, photographic portraits have been appropriated so that the images are perceived, almost literally, as surrogates for the body. Families cherish them. They protect and guard them against evil spells and ill will. Their codes and meanings, their aspect of liminality between the realms of the seen and the imagined, are invested, almost, with the potency of magic. Christian Metz writes about photography having the character of death. Photography, he notes, "is a cut inside the referent, it cuts off a piece of it, a fragment, a part object, for a long immobile travel of no return."[49] While this scenario essays photography as a fascinating outtake of immobility, we would argue the opposite, that the portrait as the object of an elaborate funerary enterprise exists in a rather complex metaphysical location, where it is subsumed within many traditional codes. Rather than being fixed in the immobility of death, the deceased's portrait is rescued from that still ether of abjection by the performative surrogacy enacted by the synecdoche of metaphysical transference.

Thus, in various contexts, the portrait's meaning in Africa possesses its own distinct codes, its own play of signifiers. It enters into the service of myth and fetishism when its perceived opticality is turned into a rich and complex field of signs invested with ritualistic meaning. In eastern Nigeria, among the Igbos, the portrait has come to occupy the realm of the immanent. After a person dies, his or her portrait is usually placed on a bed and addressed by mourners as if it were the live person. In such moments of private communication, the portrait serves as a totemic symbol that banishes the death and projects more than a likeness. It also serves as an aid for eternalization, fixing the subject within the temporal space of remembrance.

Another example of the portrait as part of the accoutrements of funerary ritual is found in Ethiopia. In the 1880s, photography was, according to Richard Pankhurst, "assimilated into the country's traditional structures."[50] Prior to this assimilation, it had been customary for mourners in funeral processions to display the effigy of the deceased along with his personal belongings. This tradition was transformed with the introduction of photography. Pankhurst writes that "with the advent of the camera such articles tended to be supplemented—and the effigy even replaced—by photographic portraits of the departed which mourners held high above their heads, while they wailed, ritualistically, and perhaps recounted episodes of the deceased's life and achievement."[51] Another example of portraits used as objects of ritual performance can also be found in *ibeji*, the Yoruba cult of twins, which Oguibe discusses in this catalog.

The works of Samuel Fosso of the Central African Republic enter another type of photographic performative space by drawing on concepts of mimicry and by expanding, enacting, and theatricalizing the relationships between and limitations of identity and representation. Fosso's self-portraits suggest that in the transformative atmosphere of the 1970s (a period that, as a result of the legacy of colonialism and neocolonialism, was still entangled in struggles for independence, social upheavals, civil wars, and revolutions), African male subjectivity was located in disguise and displacement, in the negotiated space between the construction and dissolution of identity. Much

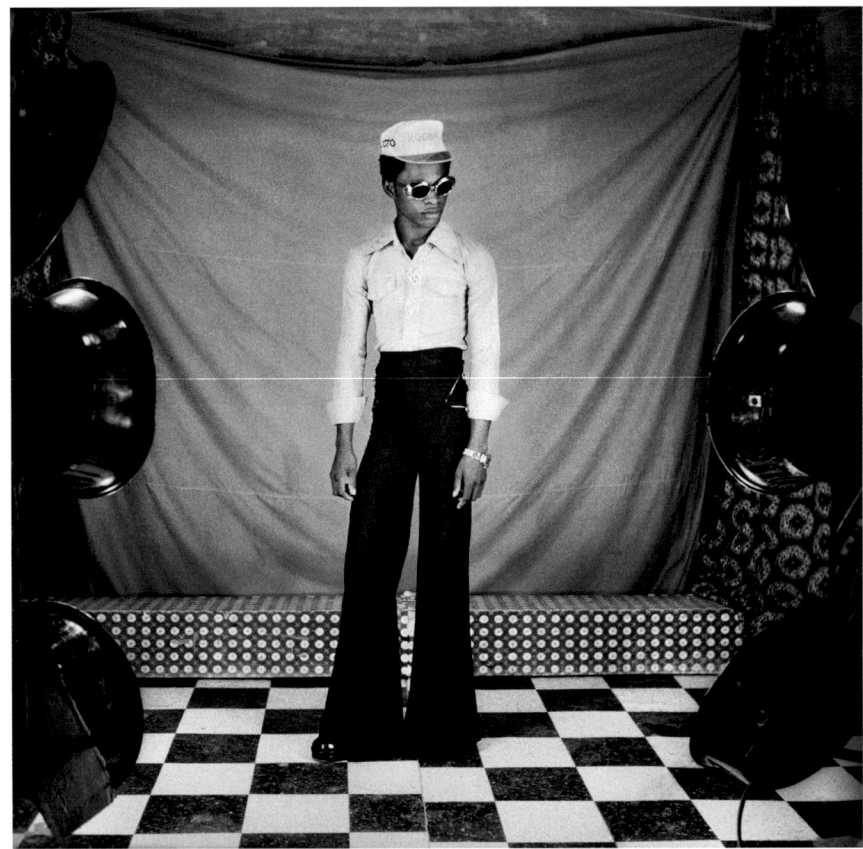

5.5 Samuel Fosso, *Untitled*, from the *70's Lifestyle* series, 1974–78. Gelatin silver print, 100×100 cm. Courtesy of Jean Marc Patras, Paris.

in the same manner that Cindy Sherman would later analyze stereotypes of women, in 1974 Fosso started a large series of self-portraits picturing himself disguised as different and easily recognizable "types" in which the presumed "reality" they refer to is interestingly absent, as if they were anonymous characters. In Fosso's work, these characters are like reliquaries in the theater of the imagination. The photograph has lost the naivete that, to some degree, commanded the composition and aesthetic decisions of earlier portraitists, who were still somehow allied with the "reality" of their subjects. Fosso openly undertakes and absorbs photography as a degeneration of that reality, as a corruption of any stable representation.

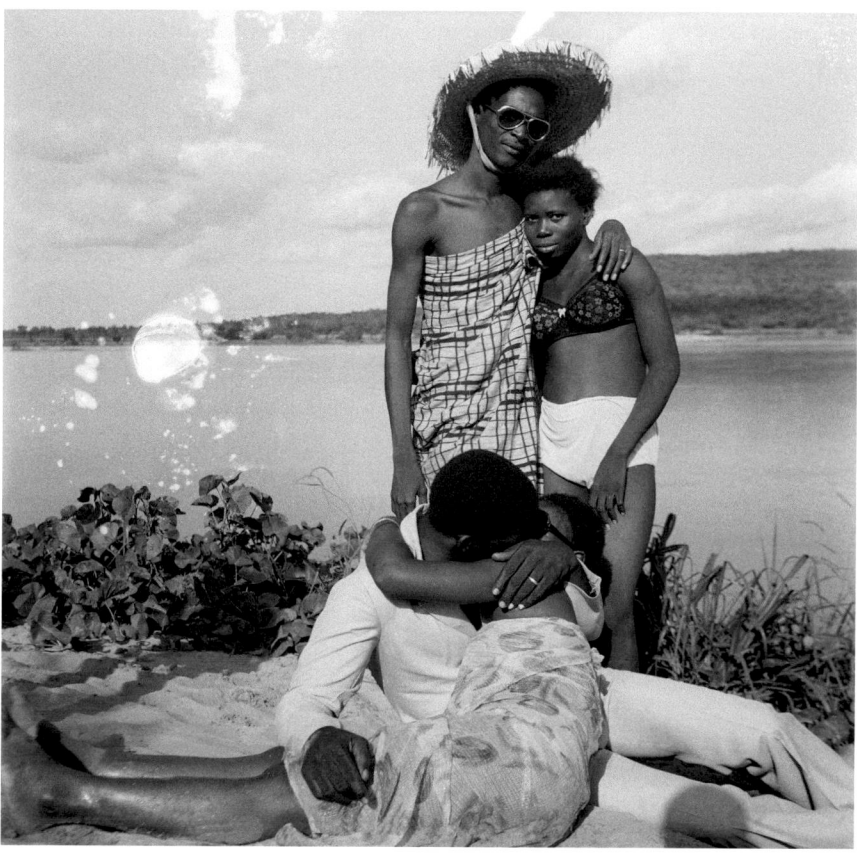

5.6 Malick Sidibé, *Les retrouvailles au bord du fleuve Niger*, 1974. Gelatin silver print, 50×60 cm. © Malick Sidibé. Courtesy of Magnin-A Gallery, Paris.

Social Narratives

In addition to the buoyant economies and political shiftings after independence, some African countries were marked by declining living conditions for rural populations, increasing dependency on Western trade practices and controls, an intensification in the looting of archaeological sites, a general squandering of African cultural patrimony, and the deceptions, confusions, and displacements related to the sociopolitical experience of many African cities. During the 1960s and 1970s, all of these problems were still caught in a web of uncertainties and the domination of the colonial powers. Thus, while some cities (like Bamako) prospered as a result of their relationship with and aid from Western nations (France and the United

States), others (like Maputo, Mozambique) were the victims of the impe-rial (Portuguese) refusal to give up power without violence. In very general terms, these contrasting economic and political realities gave rise to oppos-ing social experiences—one of tranquility and leisure, the other of war and devastation—which, in turn, guided many African photographers toward social issues and engaged them in the voluptuous, traumatic extremes of the African metropole.

Malick Sidibé of Mali focused his attention on the young metropoli-tan youth of Bamako who gathered and partied at city clubs, which were named after their favorite idols, such as the Spoutniks, Wild Cats, and Beatles. Even though Sidibé saw himself as a practitioner of photo-reportage, his 1970s series of photographs gives us a privileged, private vision of then-contemporary conventions and artifices of young Malian metropolitans, as they danced the twist or the jerk, or moved to the beat of Cuban music. These photographs convey neither the casual character nor the fluency and naturalness of photo-reportage. An insider, Sidibé had the confidence of his subjects, who commissioned him to record their activities. Most of these photographs were posed, stylistically framed to accommodate Sidibé's inter-est in social interaction. This is particularly clear in the series of photographs Sidibé shot by the Niger River, ten kilometers from Bamako, depicting the Sunday activities of the young. While they may have been self-conscious subjects for Sidibé's documentary lens, they were also the inspiration for his artistic achievement.

Ricardo Rangel's photographs are more stirring and emotionally charged than Sidibé's, as was Maputo in comparison to Bamako. Mozam-bique's war of liberation was particularly long, lasting throughout the sec-ond half of the 1960s and the 1970s. The country became independent in 1975, only to face a horrifying guerrilla war launched first under the instiga-tion of the racist, illegal regime of Ian Smith in Rhodesia (now Zimbabwe) and later, after Zimbabwe's independence in 1980, fed by Pretoria's apartheid terrorists. The enduring and devastating consequences of these prolonged conflicts are recorded in the poignant and contrasting realities captured by Rangel over his lengthy career. His photographs, however, are not just docu-ments of an agonizing period of isolation, poverty, and social downfall, but the subjective vision of a talented photojournalist critically engaged with his country's liberation from colonialism.

Although it seems that his photographs preserve the character of photo-reportage (piercing across all sections of Mozambique's social fabric, excavating Maputo's underbelly while the war of independence raged

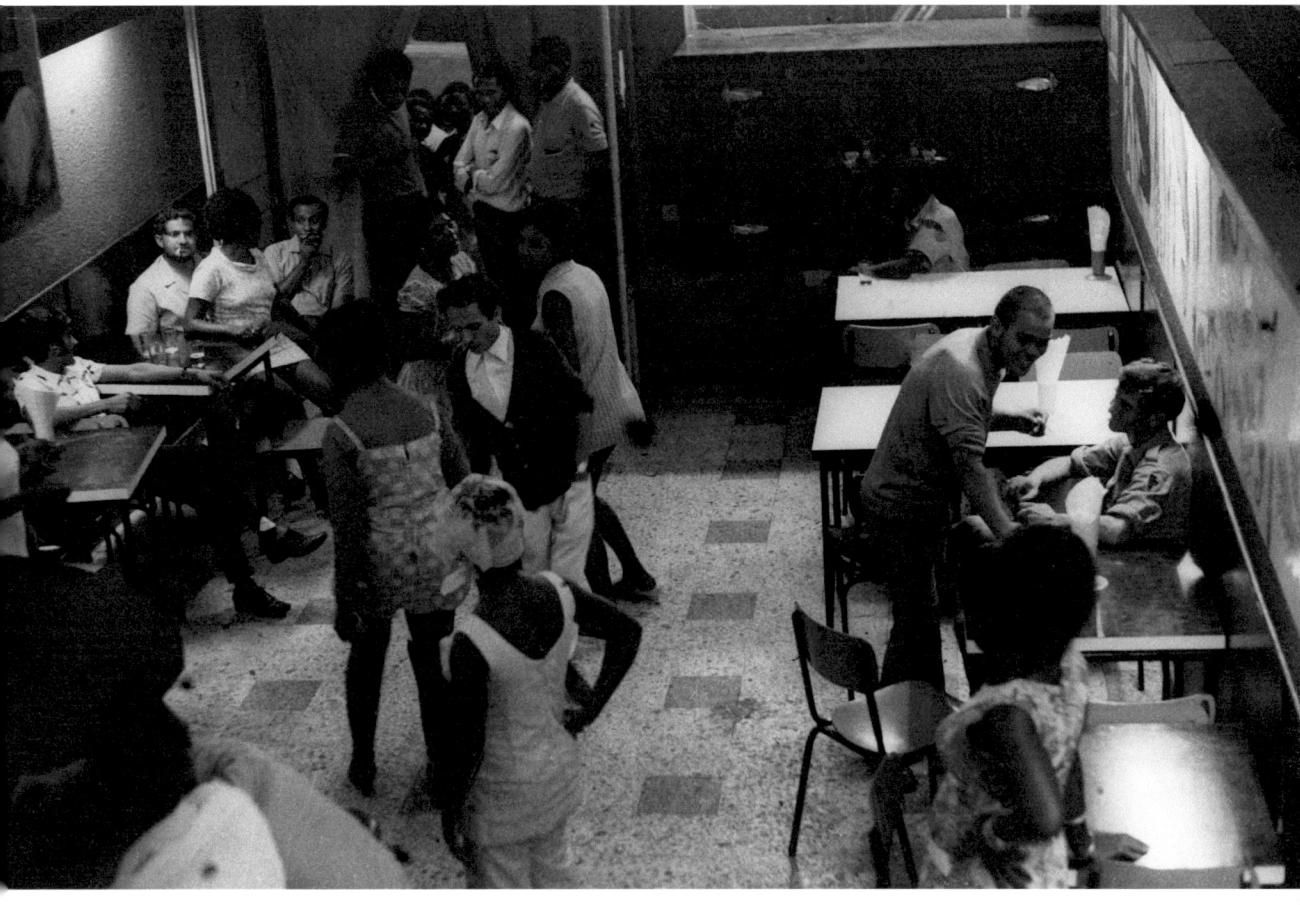

5.7 Ricardo Rangel, *Lourenço Marques—Rua Araújo*, from *Our Nightly Bread* series, 1960–70. Gelatin silver print, 31.14×49.34 cm. Courtesy of Afronova Gallery, private collection of Henri Vergon. Courtesy of Centro de Documentação e Formação Fotográfica, Republic of Mozambique.

outside), Rangel imbued his varied subjects with that same kind of sensitivity and transcendence found in the work of other socially concerned photographers such as David Goldblatt, Santu Mofokeng, and Nabil Boutros. Rangel's celebrated photographs of the prostitutes—women without names, jovial and sad, nameless women with their wigs and provocative clothes—who were a familiar feature of the bars and corners of Maputo's Araujo Street express their mixed emotions through an incommensurable subjectivity, while simultaneously conveying an impenetrable feminine identity.

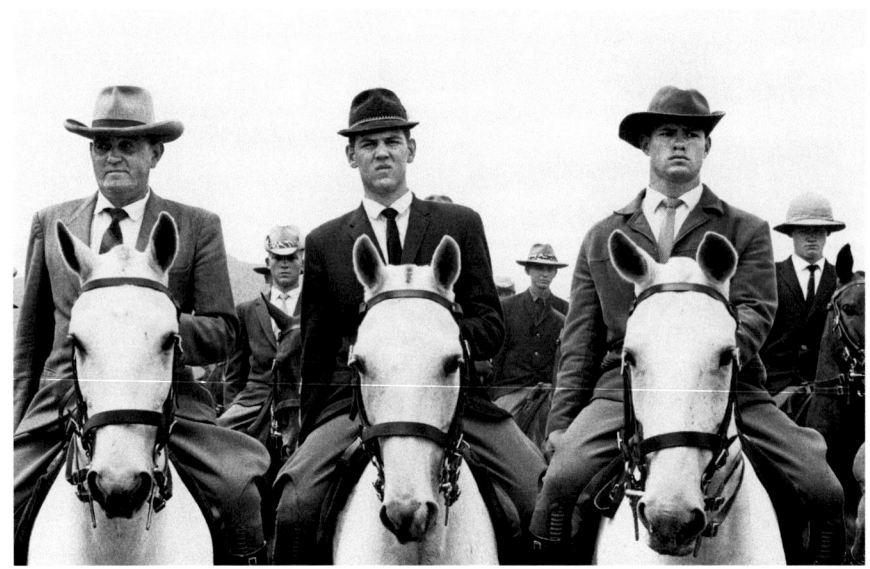

5.8 David Goldblatt, *The Commando of National Party Stalwarts Which Escorted Prime Minister and National Party Leader Hendrik Verwoerd and His Wife Betsie to the Party's 50th Anniversary Celebrations at de Wildt, Transvaal, 1964*, 1964. Gelatin silver print on fiber-based paper, 30×40 cm. Courtesy of the artist.

The increasing interest over the decades in documenting the varieties and contradictions of African reality is most apparent in photography in South Africa, although it is certainly strongly evident in work from Guinea and Mali as well. Today, those extraordinary achievements can be seen in the works of internationally recognized photographers such as Goldblatt and the *Drum* magazine contributors Bob Gosani, Peter Magubane, and Jürgen Schadeberg. Their photographs not only capture various lifestyles of South Africa in the 1950s and 1960s, but also the political upheavals that brought apartheid to the world's attention. The work of Mofokeng, who was trained by Goldblatt, comes out of this tradition, expanding it to encompass the artist's interests in the discourses of representation.

Goldblatt's pictures are commanding photographic essays. They expose the many aspects and faces of an immeasurable South Africa: its landscapes and people, its mines and small towns, its complacency and repressed joy. Little in these images hints at a social urgency, for Goldblatt did not *document* South Africa per se. Rather, he was looking for what he describes as "something of what a man is and is becoming in all the particularity of himself and his bricks and bit of earth and of this place and to contain all this in a photograph."[52] He was hunting for revelations, essences of his country's core, extraordinarily clear, quintessential details, at once recorded by and existing apart from the picture. His 1960s series devoted to Afrikaners is remarkable precisely because it grasps that "something." These photographs show not only the faces of apartheid, its leaders and henchmen, its intimacies and "innocence"; they also bare its very soul, the aspect of its lurking terror.

Mofokeng uses techniques from straight documentary photography to address the politics of representation, in an exploration of his place in South Africa's polarized society. Thus, he positions himself as a witness who brings to his images social awareness, formal refinement, and aesthetic complexity. By means of this successful combination, he effects contrasting and highly lyrical compositions that resist both explicit political interpretation and a reduction to purely formal terms. Mofokeng is not interested in bold statements or in individualities. What his photographs made throughout the 1980s convey are the common threads, the familiar contexts, and the shared experiences of blacks in the townships of South Africa, through the artist's poetic sensibility as one who shares their reality yet is aware of his own potential to intrude or misrepresent. None of these pictures is a contrived narrative; none of these images is clichéd. As Walker Evans might have commented, "It is prime vision combined with quality of feeling, no less."[53]

Like Goldblatt and Mofokeng, Egyptian-born Boutros combines in his photographs the impelling forces of two allegedly opposing photographic traditions: one related to the aesthetic and formal tenets of painting, the other focused on recording the factual world. The former quality in Boutros's photographs stems from the fact that he started his artistic career as a painter. Evident in his work—from refined portraits to desert landscapes to nocturnal views of Cairo—is his interest in creating narrative structures and character studies that are capable of transcending their details, of rendering the essence of Egypt. His photographs conjure the sensuality and perfection of form, which is infused with a quasi-visceral quality. The result is an almost abstract association, an "air," that, as Boutros's work reminds us, is precisely what Barthes called *animula*, "that exorbitant thing which induces from body to soul."[54]

Although seemingly removed from this urge to document the process of Africa's liberation from European systems of reference, Mody Sory Diallo's almost abstract photographs of 1994 show the walls of the infamous Camp

Boiro, where those who dissented from [Ahmed] Sékou Touré's Marxist-Leninist dictatorship in Guinea were detained and tortured. The subjects of these pictures are not the walls themselves, but the erased presence of those who inscribed on them words and symbolic signs of their resilience. This commemorative drive impels Diallo's current goal of creating an agency to collect and archive existing political and cultural images in order to preserve the fragmented memory of his homeland.

The North African Paradigm

If it has seemed throughout this analysis that photographers from sub-Saharan Africa have focused mainly on the human form, its social context, and how it is represented, a review of their North African colleagues suggests other distinctive concerns. Historically, along with economic impediments, Islamic prescriptions could explain the fact that in Egypt, for instance, even though photography was introduced in the first half of the nineteenth century, most photographers were either Westerners or Christian Armenians until very recently. The Islamic aniconic mandate, the prohibition against realistic representations of the body, was strictly observed and was, therefore, a very strong inhibitor of photography's acceptance. In 1839, when the first photographs arrived in Egypt, the Khedive exclaimed, "This is the work of the Devil!"[55] But we may find a similar response even in Germany. In his essay "A Short History of Photography," Walter Benjamin quotes the denunciation published by the *Leipziger Stadtanzeiger* around the same time: "To try to catch transient reflected images is not merely something that is impossible but, as a thorough German investigation has shown, the very desire to do so is blasphemy. Man is created in the image of God and God's image cannot be captured by any human machine. Only the divine artist, divinely inspired, may be allowed, in a moment of solemnity, at the higher call of his genius, to dare to reproduce the divine-human features, but never by means of a mechanical aid."[56] Thus, these variances in the work of North African photographers have not resulted from specific cultural differences alone. The tendency toward abstraction and the interest in a more lyrical, sometimes metaphysical, approach can be understood as the desire to escape the stereotypes that orientalism imposed on photographic representations of the Arab world.

In the case of writer and photographer Mohammed Dib, photography is a projection onto a presence, and a present, that is the future of a time past. As an artifice against death, photography, like writing for Dib, suspends time to capture the fleeting moment, to give it an eternal present. There is nothing in

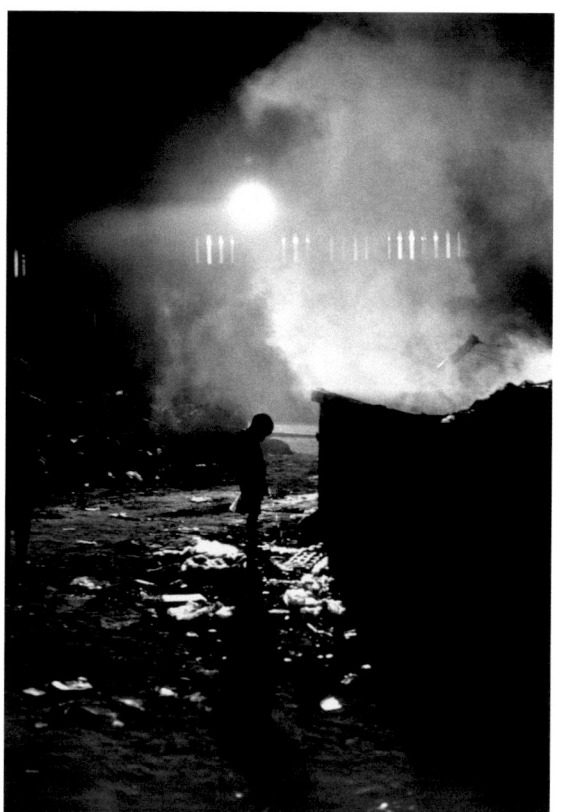 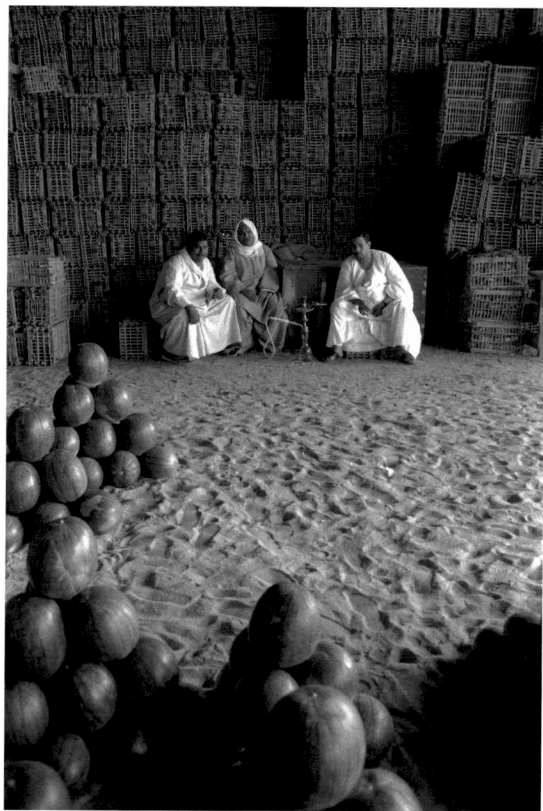

5.9 (*above left*) Santu Mofokeng, *Near Maponya's Discount Store, Dube, Soweto*, ca. 1987. Gelatin silver print, 37.2 × 25 cm. © Santu Mofokeng Foundation. Image courtesy of Lunetta Bartz, MAKER, Johannesburg.

5.10 (*above right*) Nabil Boutros, *Old Vegetable and Fruit Market—Cairo*, 1990. Gelatin silver print, 34.2 × 25.6 cm. © Nabil Boutros.

his images that is imprecise or tentative. On the contrary, as in a poem, everything serves a purpose and is strictly irreplaceable. In his pictures of anonymous people and architectural compositions made in Algeria during the 1940s, Dib did not search for a truth, but for the impasses of the everlasting.

Although time is not the main impetus for the photographs of Kamel Dridi (Tunisia), Lamia Naji (Morocco), and Touhami Ennadre (Morocco), their works procure for themselves presence and meaning through a sense of time. In striving to capture the transience of light, Dridi searches for what Michket Krifa aptly describes as "the magic moments of chiaroscuro's offerings."[57] In Dridi's sensual photographs, these offerings are the radiating presences of light within the shadows of mosques and other interiors. The transitory, however, is best illustrated in Dridi's fugitive images of a praying woman, the 1978 series depicting his mother. In them, that shared desire to look at, to verify, and to give resolution to reality remains unsettled, always immanent but never completely gratified. At most, the viewer is left impassive in that indeterminate predicament of the transitory, somewhere perhaps between the promise of the future and death.

Working in the 1990s, Naji devotes her photographic practice to the unraveling of light within darkness. For her, they are inseparable. In confronting darkness, she may cast on it those uncertain features of herself that she may suspect she has, or her most obscure desires. This transference provides an opportunity to liberate light within the scene of its concurrence with darkness and to allow for the possibility of discerning the difference between darkness and its projections. Each photograph becomes, consequently, a spiritual quest for discovery, an opening to self-knowledge.

Inspired to take pictures at the time of his mother's death, Ennadre has embarked on a quest beyond that which prompted Barthes to write *Camera Lucida*; Ennadre's concern is not the preservation of a photographic memory, the ensnaring of a fleeting presence, or the restitution of that which has been lost. It is true that Ennadre recognizes that his work "is simply a kind of witness to this person [his mother] I once knew."[58] In his photographs, nevertheless, this witnessing is experienced as a traumatic event, an encounter with a supreme moment, or an ultimate experience, in which the space between life and death dissolves, erasing any trace of time, that purloining agent. Through a great variety of subjects, Ennadre has always presented his images within the experience of that moment of collusion between life and death. Perhaps his 1982 pictures of a stillborn baby exemplify this borderline with the most startling and potent evidence. François Aubral asserts that Ennadre is fascinated with "the moment of truth in which death is already there and life has just ceased to be."[59] The overwhelming darkness in these works, perhaps not paradoxically, is what gives presence to them and grants life to that powerful moment of transition.

By contrast, the world of Jellel Gasteli—who, like Ennadre, is based in Paris—is one of light, the incomparable light of his childhood in Tunisia. At its most blinding, light in his work not only transfers an atmospheric effect, but also creates a softly geometric abstract environment. The redundant, disembodied quality of his light suggests the opposing qualities that Krifa mentions in relation to Dridi's light. Gasteli does not use light to emotional effect, but its resplendence and its texture allude, not to the visual images themselves, but to what they insinuate. In his *White Series* (*Série blanche*) of the 1980s and 1990s, the repeated theme functions as an element in a plot; a means of restitution and memory of his childhood, it evokes narrative without offering a culminating visual image. In his work, the vanished past and its restitution by means of photography may remain mysterious, but they are never implausible.

Imaginary Territories, Symbolic Homes

It has been argued that the exemplary site of postmodern consciousness is rooted in exile and diaspora, where boundaries are repeatedly effaced and defaced. The twentieth century is seen as the embodiment of the age of mass immigration, refugees, and displaced people. Exile and diaspora carry debilitating connotations: romanticism and loss, ambivalence and desire, memory and estrangement, myths of authenticity and origin. For many, the process of crossing boundaries is hardly an appealing option. In his essay "Reflections on Exile," Edward Said notes that "exile is strangely compelling to think about but terrible to experience." He sees its manifestation, especially within the violent erasures organized and orchestrated by modern warfare, imperialism, and the quasi-theological ambitions of totalitarian rulers, as an "unhealable rift forced between a human being and a native place, between the self and its true home: its essential sadness can never be surmounted."[60]

Many African artists seem caught in this insurmountable vector, hemmed in by a constant state of emergency. In addition to physical destabilization, they endure a daily fight against erasure by the subjective practices and representations of their new symbolic homes, while attempting to hold on to the frayed and wilting memories of imaginary territories considered to be original homes. The Africa of the twentieth century eludes fictions of origin. Where on the map might we locate Zarina Bhimji, a Ugandan artist

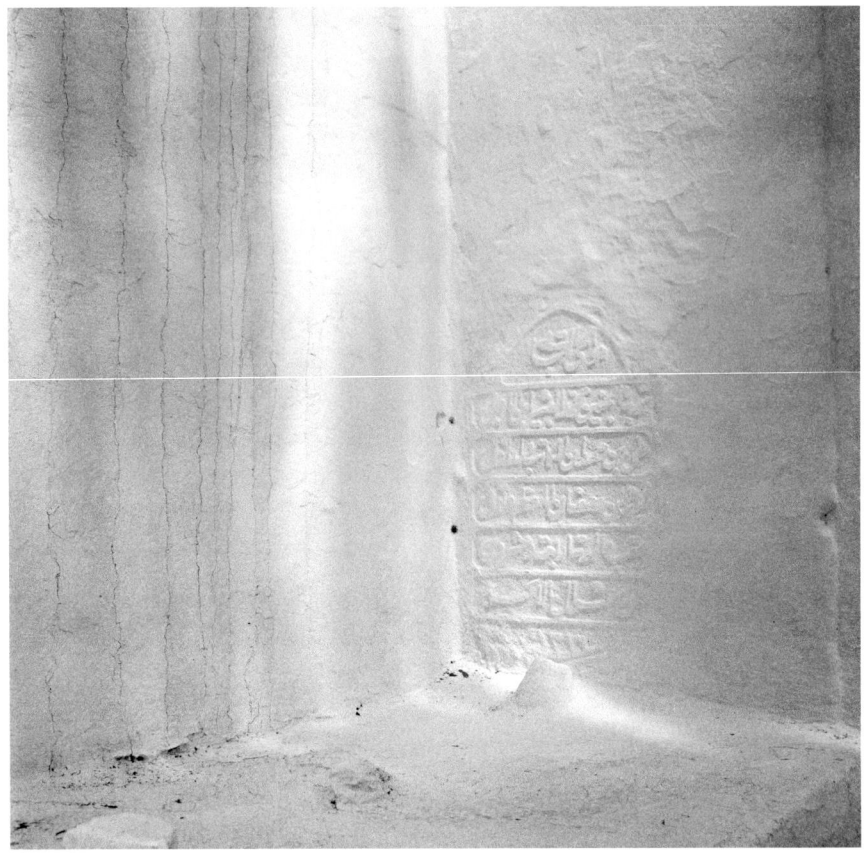

5.11 Jellel Gasteli, *Untitled (Blanche No. I)*, *Série Blanche*, 1996. Pigment inkjet print on Hahnemühle digital fine art paper, 120 × 120 cm. Courtesy of Selma Feriani Gallery and the artist.

of Asian origin who lives in London? Or Bleach, a Zimbabwean of British origin living in the United States, or Iké Udé, Oladélé Ajiboyé Bamgboyé, and Fani-Kayode, three relocated Nigerian artists who grew up in the United States, Scotland, and England, respectively? Or even Goldblatt, whose parents, escaping from czarist oppression in Russia, settled in apartheid South Africa? Or those North African artists who live in the dreary shadows of France's return to racial essentialism? Such are the actively lived contradictions of the African experience. They raise difficult questions about the notion of origin and authenticity, revealing the bald fictions of essentialism. Beyond the pale of their recollected histories, all these artists bear the scar of exile in the sense of living a double consciousness.

If home is the palace of memory, Udé reconstitutes its faded forms by building, via the all-pervasive archive, a critique of its representations. The archive, of course, is suitably useful to photography. In *Uses of Evidence* (1996), Udé co-opts its character to query two opposing values and perspectives: representation and knowledge. In his installation, which literally mimics the exterior and interior of a physical structure, he sets up a dichotomy between what is represented and revealed as knowledge on the outside, and what is hidden or made nonexistent on the inside. However, this suppressed and willfully concealed information, as Udé argues, must be made available to a fruitful examination of the erasures and misrepresentations built into ethnographic practices. In developing the work, he has considered how the images could potentially contradict and supplement that commonly accepted knowledge.

In this sense, we may view *Uses of Evidence* as a manifestation of both a physical and a psychological construct. In the installation, the exterior shows photographic murals of Tarzan, wildlife, and frenzied crowds of "natives" in states of dispossession, display, and distress. Culled from media sources and quasi-scholarly documentary materials, these appropriated images serve as useful reminders of how Africa is recollected through the lens of the West. In the interior, he creates a hushed melancholic ambience, a hermetically sealed world where he installs images from private family albums and archives. The portraits represent loved ones and friends in the context of their contemporary realities. This wallpapered interior, inaccessible to us except through cutouts that metaphorically suggest picture frames, evokes a kind of terrible beauty, a world filled with sweet sorrow, loss, and memories. On the one hand, the interior's configuration alludes to the questions of idealization that Sigmund Freud links to his conceptualization of love. On the other hand, the exterior accentuates those moments of ambivalence that Julia Kristeva denotes as the abject. *Uses of Evidence* explores how the disparate materials (though divided into two fenced-off groups) converge to define the same subject, opening up dangerous chasms for both oppositionality and romanticization. Udé mediates this potential conflict by building into his work a critique that questions assumptions and memories of Africa.

Bamgboyé, on the other hand, obviates the role of the appropriationist in the self-portraits, interiors, and landscapes he renders as videos, light boxes, and photographs, which are constituted out of performance and props standing as repositories for cultural symbols and stereotypes. Out of memory and identity, both blurred by cultural relocation, Bamgboyé presents himself in

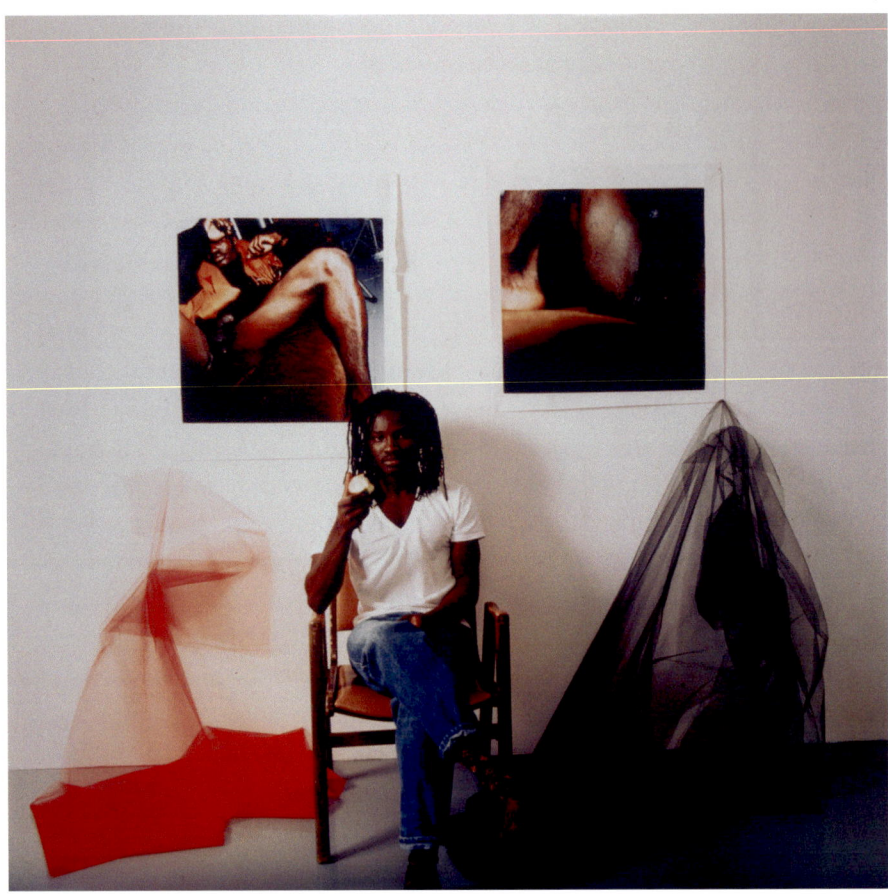

5.12 Oladélé Ajiboyé Bamgboyé, *Puncture*,
1994. Silver dye bleach print, 79.7 × 79.7 cm.
Courtesy of Solomon R. Guggenheim Museum, New York. Gift of the artist, 1996.

his substantiality in his photographs. He departs from the traditional literal
representation of self-portraiture in a truer assault on the real, to rediscover
himself and to establish some sort of intersubjective relationship with the
viewer, by which the emotional and the speculative can be bridged. In this
way, Bamgboyé avoids fetishization and availability as object, deconstructing the sexual codes projected on the African male body and demythicizing
his own role as photographer and sitter, as can be seen in the image from the
1994 *Puncture* series showing a wound in the genital area. Bamgboyé refuses
to idealize himself in many of his light boxes, trying not so much to enthrall

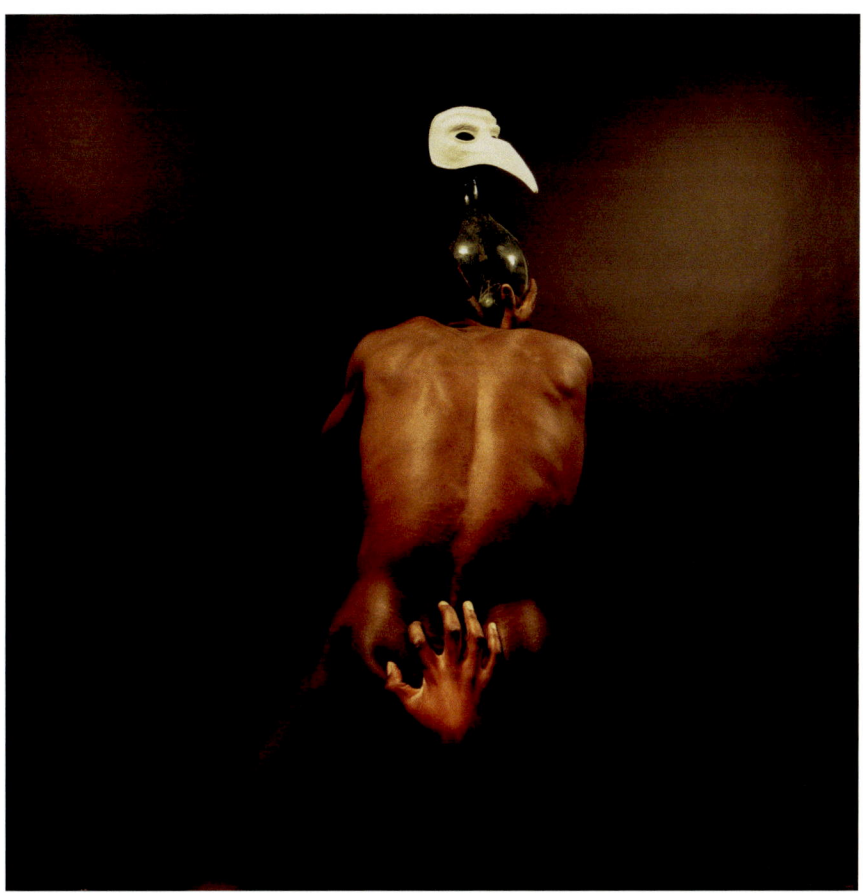

5.13 Rotimi Fani-Kayode, *Untitled (Every Moment Counts II)*, ca. 1989. Chromogenic print, 62.7×60.6 cm. Courtesy of Solomon R. Guggenheim Museum, New York. Purchased with funds contributed by the Photography Council, 2017.

the real, but rather seeking, like Francis Bacon, to render the reality of the subject beyond its circumstantial characteristics, so as to keep no more than its biting essence. Bamgboyé concedes to Ludwig Wittgenstein's comment, "We need friction. Away from the smooth ground!"[61]

Friction is precisely what Fani-Kayode suggested in the last series of photographs that he made before his death in 1989. These beautiful color photographs are informed by Fani-Kayode's attention to the fact that "the great Yoruba civilisations of the past, like so many other non-European cultures, are still consigned by the West to the museums of *primitive* art and culture" and that "the Europeans, faced with the dogged survival of alien cultures, and as mercantile as ever they were in the days of the Trade, are now trying to sell our culture as a consumer product." Fani-Kayode was also conscious of his own potential complicity in sanctioning such a consumerist role. He wanted to avoid any acquiescence to the "reconstructed ethnicity" that accentuates the classification of collectible and tourist art objects into stereotypical ethnic categories. He outlined a territory in which he could "reappropriate such images and transform them ritualistically" into contemporary images of his own creation. This complex, fabricated territory makes the established assumptions about black-male representation counterfeit by averting a single, obvious meaning or point of reference from which the viewer may activate the systematic routines of projection, identification, and appropriation.[62] Fani-Kayode used masks and indecipherable signs and symbols of Yoruba cosmology not to promote an artificial recuperation of precolonial tradition, but to complicate and diffuse the viewer's experience of the work, creating some kind of cultural and sexual friction. In this sense, we can understand Fani-Kayode's practice as parallel to "the Osogbo artists in Yorubaland who themselves have resisted the cultural subversions of neocolonialism and who celebrate the rich, secret world of our ancestors."[63]

Bleach positions his work in the theoretical, but by no means impractical, problematic of the camera as truth teller and calls into question the camera's stable order. He turns the camera's versatility against itself, subverting its existence as an apparatus for encoding on the two-dimensional a visible, material object in space. Bleach's carefully orchestrated photographs of his 1991 *ˢCRYPT* series, in which the process of their production determines the end product, are supported by photography's two constants of time and space. Within a fixed time, he performed repeated traversings of a self-determined triangular space, which become, in the photographs, residual marks. Because of the long exposure and the split-second intrusions of his body in the viewfinder, his repeated walks were evidenced on the film only by the coding of the intense flashlight he carried as he moved his body through the space.

The calligraphic, squiggly emanations that float on the surface of his photographs are like agitated maps, visual and mental palimpsests. The making of these photographs draws from a series of relationships between time and space, inscriptions and erasures, presences and absences, constructions and deconstructions, coding and decoding, all of which are staged over and over. What we encounter in the space (observable as a result of the arc of light and the large-format camera's long exposure) has little to do with the transposition of a physical referent onto our plane of vision. What is revealed is only the referent's echo, a self-portrait turned into signs, like EKG patterns, a map of the body's insubstantiality. As a lost form, the body's absence becomes a suggestion supported by time and tremulously held in a space littered with the ghostly forms of other worlds and imaginary land-scapes, which slowly disintegrate into memory.

In Bhimji's work, the human body (taxed by racial innuendo and embroiled in the Logos of mutation and difference) is encountered as a vast archive, abstracted and absorbed by mechanisms of social, scientific, and legal control. In the places she photographs, access is barred to all but the most privileged. By entering and photographing in these territories, she calls attention to issues of representation and their relationship to sites of power. She reveals how collected information, translated as knowledge, is vetted and organized, sorted and regimented, activities that often omit the unsavory. Bhimji's orientation contests these processes, opening them to new probings and determinations.

Bhimji brings a peculiarly nineteenth-century sensibility to her photographs of human-body parts and membranes collected and sealed in formaldehyde. Yet it could be argued that her work departs radically from the objectification of abjection, disease, and abnormality that Victorian photography cast onto its studies of human anatomy. The elaborate stagings of her photographs, whether taken in hospital wards, doctors' offices, or pathology laboratories, or as part of her study of eugenics, comprise a Foucauldian reading of photography's fascination with the human body as a site of disintegration and degeneracy. Her focus questions the terms of the body's depiction, while also bringing to attention its violation in moments of ritualistic violence, mutilation, distortion, and dislocation. Bhimji's morbidly sensuous color photographs of hospital wards and laboratories transport the viewer to forbidden worlds, places of sorrow, loneliness, and terror, or exile and dislocation. We go to the spaces in which she works either to get well or to die. Visiting them is an incommensurate experience, which Bhimji's work throws sharply into relief. We find ourselves cast afloat on a sea of abandonment, where we are always incomplete and where time defeats every facility of consciousness.

As the twentieth century draws to a close, and the world becomes engulfed in an end-of-millennium anxiety that also looks toward the future, does Africa, in spite of the marginalizing imperatives of its past history, share in this outlook? Can we indeed mark the end of the influence of Western ontologizations about Africa, at least within the grid of representation? The answer to these questions is a resounding yes. On a political and social level, the dissolution of colonialism in many parts of Africa in the 1950s and the subsequent emergence of the postcolonial states provided the first opportunity for its reversal. Second, the recovery of a subjective African awareness of its own responsibility as a key voice—speaking not only out of its past but its contemporary realities—within the shaping of world culture has been very important. With a multiplicity of cultural specificities and identities, Africa thus reengages these fraught questions with new knowledge and self-images. Indeed, this exhibition, with its diverse voices and aesthetic philosophies, reveals avenues to that transcendence. The work of the thirty photographers in the exhibition bears testimony to this endeavor and to the means through which African subjectivity can be freed and detangled from Western epistemological constructs and colonial structures.

Looking at the diverse works through an ostensibly Western gaze, we are struck by their forceful, though not necessarily conscious, intentionality. Written across the photographic images is the inherent problematization of that gaze, which tends to place the African subject in a matrix encoded within ethnographic memory. On the most fundamental level, this disjuncture between what the African photographer sees and what the ethnographic lens remembers lies at the core of the exhibition. This contest, in which the African subject is limned across the phantasmagoric screen occupied by the respective positions of the spectacle and spectator, challenges how viewers—Western and non-Western alike—will grapple with the images in this exhibition. Of great importance is how the viewer's perception might possibly be enmeshed with that ethnographic memory. Kaja Silverman notes that these processes of enmeshment and the production of stereotypes or otherness by projecting and distancing provide "the imperative to get back to those images that provide the fantasmic grounding for all of our fantasies and object choices."[64] Whatever the fantasies and desires of the viewer engaging these images may be, the intentions of both the photographers and the complexity of their radical visions delimit these choices while challenging and opening new critical perspectives from which we may reexamine our relationships to Africa, its history, and its identities.

1   Joseph Conrad, *Heart of Darkness* (New York: Dover Books, 1990), 5–6. Emphasis added.

2   Nicolas Monti, "Introduction: Another Place, Another Time," in Nicolas Monti, ed., *Africa Then: Photographs, 1840–1918* (London: Thames and Hudson, 1987), 4.

3   Arthur Rimbaud, *A Season in Hell/The Illuminations*, trans. Enid Rhodes Peschel (New York: Oxford University Press, 1973). [*Ed. note:* Quotations are taken from Rimbaud's poem "Bad Blood" (page 49), with "stupid" and "savage" being remarks in two letters of Rimbaud, dated February 21, 1891, and September 10, 1884, respectively, both cited in Peschel's introduction (page 18).]

4   [*Ed. note:* André Breton, *Manifestoes of Surrealism*, trans. Richard Seaver and Helen R. Lane (Ann Arbor: University of Michigan Press, 1969), 27.]

5   Chinua Achebe, "An Image of Africa: Racism in Conrad's *Heart of Darkness*," in *Hopes and Impediments: Selected Essays* (New York: Doubleday, 1989), 3.

6   Rudyard Kipling, *A Choice of Kipling's Verse*, comp. T. S. Eliot (New York: Anchor Books, 1962), 143, quoted in Tsenay Serequeberhan, "African Philosophy: The Point in Question," in *African Philosophy: The Essential Readings*, ed. Tsenay Serequeberhan (New York: Paragon House, 1991), 4.

7   V. Y. Mudimbe, "The Power of Speech," in *The Invention of Africa: Gnosis, Philosophy, and the Order of Knowledge* (Bloomington: Indiana University Press, 1988), 45.

8   [*Ed. note:* George Wilhelm Frederick Hegel, *The Philosophy of History* (London: Kegan Paul, Trench, Trübner and Co., 1892–96; New York: Dover Publications, 1956), 99,] quoted in Serequeberhan, "African Philosophy," 6.

9   Conrad, *Heart of Darkness*, 33.

10   Roland Barthes, *Camera Lucida*, trans. Richard Howard (New York: Hill and Wang, 1981), 28.

11   Gordon Bleach, "Home Movies," *Nka: Journal of Contemporary African Art*, no. 3 (Fall/Winter 1995): 43.

12   Bleach, "Home Movies," 43.

13   Santu Mofokeng, 1995 statement originally submitted for this exhibition.

14   Rotimi Fani-Kayode, "Traces of Ecstasy," in *Critical Decade: Black British Photography in the 80s*, ed. David A. Bailey and Stuart Hall, Ten.8 photobook series, vol. 2, no. 3 (Birmingham, UK: Ten.8, 1992), 68.

15   Fani-Kayode, "Traces of Ecstasy," 68.

16 [*Ed. note:* Walter Benjamin, "The Work of Art in the Age of Mechanical Reproduction" (1936) in Walter Benjamin, *Illuminations*, ed. Hannah Arendt, trans. Harry Zohn (London: Jonathan Cape, 1970), 219–53; see also "The Work of Art in the Age of Its Technological Reproducibility; Second Version," in Walter Benjamin, *The Work of Art in the Age of Its Technological Reproducibility and Other Writings on Media*, ed. Michael W. Jennings, Bridget Doherty, and Thomas Y. Levin (Cambridge, MA: Harvard University Press), 19–55.]

17 Jonathan Crary, *Techniques of the Observer: On Vision and Modernity in the Nineteenth Century* (Cambridge, MA: MIT Press, 1990), 2.

18 Crary, *Techniques of the Observer*, 2.

19 Salah Hassan, "The Installations of Houria Niati," *Nka: Journal of Contemporary African Art*, no. 3 (Fall/Winter 1995): 53. [*Ed. note:* Malek Alloula, *The Colonial Harem* (Minneapolis: University of Minnesota Press, 1986).]

20 Brian Street, "British Popular Anthropology: Exhibiting and Photographing the Other," in *Anthropology and Photography, 1860–1920*, ed. Elizabeth Edwards (New Haven, CT: Yale University Press, 1992), 130.

21 Crary, *Techniques of the Observer*, 3.

22 Elizabeth Edwards, introduction to Edwards, *Anthropology and Photography*, 7.

23 Barthes, *Camera Lucida*, 34. See illustration on page 35 of Barthes's book.

24 Edwards, introduction, 7.

25 Edwards, introduction, 7.

26 Barthes, *Camera Lucida*, 36.

27 Edwards, introduction, 7.

28 Edwards, introduction, 8.

29 Aimé Césaire, "Notebook of a Return to the Native Land," in *The Collected Poetry*, trans. Clayton Eshleman and Annette Smith (Berkeley: University of California Press, 1983), 69.

30 [*Ed. note:* Wole Soyinka, quoted in Janheinz Jahn, *Neo-African Literature: A History of Black Writing* (New York: Grove Press, 1969), 265–66.]

31 Hountondji quoted in Tsenay Serequeberhan, *The Hermeneutics of African Philosophy: Horizon and Discourse* (New York: Routledge, 1994), 40.

32 Senghor quoted in Serequeberhan, *Hermeneutics of African Philosophy*, 44. Emphasis added to *Negro-African museum*.

33 Senghor quoted in Serequeberhan, *Hermeneutics of African Philosophy*, 44.

34 James Clifford, *The Predicament of Culture: Twentieth-Century Ethnography, Literature, and Art* (Cambridge, MA: Harvard University Press, 1988), 6.

35 Clifford, *Predicament of Culture*, 12.

36   Clifford, *Predicament of Culture*, 5.

37   Clifford, *Predicament of Culture*, 6.

38   Clifford, *Predicament of Culture*, 11.

39   Clifford, *Predicament of Culture*, 8.

40   Olu Oguibe, "Reverse Appropriation as Nationalism in Early Modern African Art," paper presented at the conference Cultural Responses to Colonialism, Reynalda House, Museum of American Art, Winston-Salem, NC, April 27, 1996.

41   Kobena Mercer, "Home from Home: Portraits from Places In Between," in *Self Evident* (Birmingham, UK: Ikon Gallery, 1995), n.p.

42   Kwame Anthony Appiah, *In My Father's House: Africa in the Philosophy of Culture* (New York: Oxford University Press, 1992), 166.

43   Appiah, *In My Father's House*, 166, 166, 161.

44   For a more specific and thorough analysis on the writing and ideas of these authors and ideologues, see Serequeberhan, *Hermeneutics of African Philosophy*.

45   Serequeberhan, *Hermeneutics of African Philosophy*, 108–9.

46   Peggy Phelan, *Unmarked: The Politics of Performance* (London: Routledge, 1993), 36.

47   John Tagg, *The Burden of Representation: Essays on Photography and Histories* (Minneapolis: University of Minnesota Press, 1993), 154–55.

48   All quotations from Seydou Keïta, "Seydou Keïta (Portfolio)," interview with Andre Magnin, *African Arts* (Los Angeles) 28, no. 4 (Fall 1995): 90–95.

49   Christian Metz, "Photography and Fetish," in *The Critical Image: Essays on Contemporary Photography*, ed. Carol Squiers (London: Lawrence and Wishart, 1990), 158.

50   Richard Pankhurst, "The Political Image: The Impact of the Camera in an Ancient Independent African State," in Edwards, *Anthropology and Photography*, 234.

51   Pankhurst, "Political Image," 234.

52   David Goldblatt, *Some Afrikaners Photographed* (Cape Town, South Africa: Murray Crawford, 1975), 7.

53   [*Ed. note:* Wall Label written by Evans for the exhibition *Walker Evans: American Photographs* (New York: Museum of Modern Art, 1956), cited by James R. Mellow, *Walker Evans* (New York: Basic Books, 1999), 553.]

54   Barthes, *Camera Lucida*, 109.

55   [*Ed. note:* Khedive quoted in Nicolas Monti, ed., *Africa Then: Photographs, 1840-1918* (London: Thames and Hudson, 1987), 7.]

56   Quoted in Tagg, *Burden of Representation*, 41.

57   Michket Krifa, in Dridi Kamel, *Les offrandes de l'ombre* (n.p.: Editions Eric Koehler, 1995), 7.

58   [*Ed. note:* Ennadre cited in Gordon Beach, "Review: François Aubral, ed., *Touhame Ennadre: Black Light*," *Nka: Journal of Contemporary African Art*, no. 8 (Spring/Summer 1998): 68.]

59   François Aubral, "Lumieres noires," *Deja-vu*, no. 12 (Tokyo, January 1, 1993). Unpublished English translation quoted in Nancy Spector, "Touhami Ennadre: The Trace of Time," in *Vital: Three Contemporary African Artists*, ed. Cyprien Tokoudagbar (Liverpool: Tate Gallery Liverpool, 1995), 26, 28n8.

60   Edward Said, "Reflections on Exile," *Granta* 13 (September 1, 1984), https:// granta .com /reflections-on -exile/. Also in *Out There: Marginalization and Contemporary Cultures*, ed. Russell Ferguson, Martha Gever, Trinh T. Minh-ha, and Cornel West (New York: New Museum of Contemporary Art; Cambridge, MA: MIT Press, 1990), 357.

61   [*Ed. note:* Ludwig Wittgenstein, *Philosophical Investigations*, part I, section 107, rev. 4th ed., ed. P. M. S. Hacker and Joachim Schulte (Malden, MA: Wiley Blackwell, 2009), cxxv.]

62   For a more thorough analysis of Fani-Kayode's photographs, see Octavio Zaya, "On Three Counts I Am an Outsider," *Nka: Journal of Contemporary African Art*, no. 4 (Spring/Summer 1996): 24–72.

63   All quotations from Fani-Kayode, "Traces of Ecstasy," 68–69.

64   Kaja Silverman, *The Threshold of the Visible World* (New York: Routledge, 1996), 181.

Travel Notes

6

Living, Working, and Traveling
in a Restless World

Okwui Enwezor was artistic director of *Trade Routes: History and Geography*, the 2nd Johannesburg Biennale, showing from October to December 1997. He was curator with Octavio Zaya of a thematic section, "Alternating Currents," as well as "Projects" throughout the spaces. He led a curatorial team who staged their own sections: "Graft" (Colin Richards), "Important and Exportant" (Gerardo Mosquera), "Life's Little Necessities" (Kellie Jones), "Hong Kong, Etc." (Hou Hanru), and "Transversions" (Yu Yeon Kim), while Mahen Bonetti curated a film program. This essay served as the introduction to the catalog, *Trade Routes: History and Geography; 2nd Johannesburg Biennale*, edited by Matthew de Bord and Roy Bester (Johannesburg: Greater Johannesburg Metropolitan Council, 1997), 7–12. These pages in the original publication were not illustrated; illustrations are of works that Enwezor referred to during interviews about the exhibition, such as "The Second Johannesburg Biennale," interview by Carol Becker, *Art Journal* 57, no. 2 (Summer 1998): 101–7, and "Reflections," in Joost Bosland and Sophie Perryer, eds., *Trade Routes Revisited: A Project Marking the 15th Anniversary of the Second Johannesburg Biennale–1997–2012* (Cape Town: Stevenson, 2012), 11–17.

1

THE TITLE OF THIS ESSAY, as well as the general subject of the 2nd Johannesburg Biennale, owes something to the restless, contingent histories of people who in the last half of the twentieth century have gathered at the edge of events, under a common heading called *globalization*. Such histories neither proceed from what Marshall McLuhan, in the 1960s, gave the name "global village," nor from any sense of a new world economic order. While

McLuhan makes valuable points, his thesis suggests a gathering of common interests in a mediatized exchange system of information and images which today, in many quarters globally, remains only faintly and marginally hopeful. On the other hand, any legitimately "new" world economic order carries a seed of the old that invariably suggests the familiar hegemonic attitudes severely under attack today. It would appear that one can't endorse globalization without borrowing from the antecedent rhetorics of colonialist exploitation. A difficult double bind that a Western media critic, such as McLuhan, could not have anticipated.

The ideas solicited by the contingent histories to which I have alluded lean precariously on the analysis of a period that could be seen as marking certain epistemological closures. Such closures, whether philosophical, ideological, cultural, or political, bear testimony to the debates, contestations, interrogations, and resistance of Western epistemological and ontological concepts of the world carried over from the period of European enlightenment. The closures are variously announced in the guise of teleological proclamations, such as "the death of the author," "the end of history," "the end of ideology," "postmodernism," "postcolonialism," and other posts- and ends of something. I have little faith in such pronouncements. Yet, despite their incompleteness, the questions they raise provide metaphors for issues with which this project will attempt to grapple.

Trade Routes: History and Geography is sited around the axial vector of economic globalization. It is an attempt to elaborate the full measure of its debates, particularly those that rise out of the analysis of modernity as a circulatory system of exchange and site of translation, as transnational/ cultural transactions that do not always arrive in neatly tied packages, as the South African–born British critic Sarat Maharaj wonderfully put it. In this manner, all journeys are not only incomplete, they form part of the vast ways the world is encountered and translated. This project, then, comes at a time when the entire notion of history is being constantly questioned and revisited. Hence, the elaboration of the debates in which the Biennale is necessarily enmeshed could be seen as a kind of open network of exchange involving different levels of cultural significations, translations, transcriptions, phenomenological and social encounters, mobility of ideas, contestations of political methodologies, etc. My interest in globalization, and what the critic Saskia Sassen would term its strategic agents, is to respond to the evolving nature of contemporary culture today as transmitted from a very limited enclosure of Eurocentrism. This response further narrows in a strip of territory we all refer to as contemporary art in the age of hyperconsumerism, ethnographic travel, cultural tourism, the Hollywoodization of mass culture. This necessitates attention to exploring the emergent forms of practice and conditions in the evolving culture of the image within contemporary art today; from the real to the hyperreal, from various aspects of social portraiture to fugitive acts of aesthetic decomposition and transgression.

Within the amalgam of interconnected perspectives claiming space in these articulations, where de-reified concepts of art and decommodified ideas of culture are explored, arise possible ways of reinventing questions of culture in the age of globalization. Rather than insert the works of invited artists into these discussions as illustrative mechanisms, I hope the astute meditations and explorations of the artists could serve as primers for mapping new incarnations of the world and synchronously organized futures. Such mappings provide the key impetus of this curatorial endeavor where responsibilities are shared, while leaving room for individual curatorial maps to be drawn. I hope this will be visible in the choices of the curators with whom I am collaborating on this project. My inclination has always been to furnish my co-collaborators with a broad granite surface from which they can hew blocks of resilient and vital expenditure of compelling intellectual thought. My exhortation to them was to look beyond the givens of history. In return, I have received not just thoughtfully curated exhibitions, but resourceful guidance that has seen me straying into and staying within a constricted narrow thinking.

In the end, the works presented in all six exhibitions of the Biennale give compelling testimony to the complex issues of globalization. Though highly selective, the works do not in any self-conscious manner situate themselves within discussions often raised by limited pronouncements and terms such as *zeitgeist* or *avant-garde*. The "cutting edge" here is measured by the degree to which artists pose durable questions. Even if the works of the artists are pivoted on crucial aesthetic challenges of contemporary practices, they nonetheless do not subordinate themselves to investigations of formal problems. The artists could be seen as operating on the highest levels of the investigations of the philosophical, political, phenomenological, and social processes of our time. They speak about culture in a time when culture is a beleaguered and contested notion. They speak about history in a period when history is no longer submitted to only one notion of authority. They puzzle over complex and troubling political narratives in the chaotic midst of war and senseless destruction of cities and slaughter of innocent people.

Ours is a fascinating time that is filled with despair and what Edward Said, in speaking about displacement and exile, has referred to as

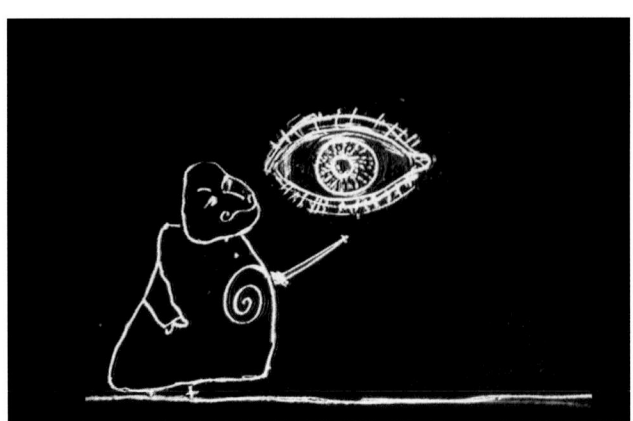

6.1 William Kentridge, still from *Ubu Tells the Truth*, 1997. 35mm color film, 8 mins. Courtesy of the artist and Goodman Gallery, Johannesburg and Cape Town.

the theological ambitions of dictators.[1] Said makes us aware that under the conditions of exile and displacement, "Home" as a sign of stability is no longer easily sustainable. Our cities and lives have been transformed by the ever-changing direction of the compass as populations drift and masses of people are submitted to the most horrific methods of genocide, starvation, and cruelty. Ours is a fascinating world of plentiful material comfort and economic triumphs, yet many countries and their inhabitants are so beggared that their very existence makes mockery of the idea of sovereign national states and subjects.

By what right, then, do people practice art under such clearly traumatic situations? Perhaps a more apt question ought to be: By what right must people cease to find critical expression in the troubling narratives and celebrations of their milieus? Might we also add that the boundary of modernity is not just a site of translation but, more clearly, one of trauma? Such questions, for decades, have also been repeatedly asked here in South Africa, and for very good reasons. For most of this century, South Africa has had to confront its own tormenting demons. In fact, it is a wounded country, scarred by a terrible political process of racial domination and exclusion. When we examine South Africa's history, we find, like in many other places of trauma, that it is through the critical practice of culture that history is not only brought alive and given urgency but is, most importantly, a vital way that societies humanize and define their common interests, even if those interests rest on the daily reality of unbridgeable differences. South Africa's contemporary art scene forms a part of the contradictions and complexities of our modern culture, in the sense that it is postnational and variegated. It is both a settled and a settler nation, based on immigration, economic

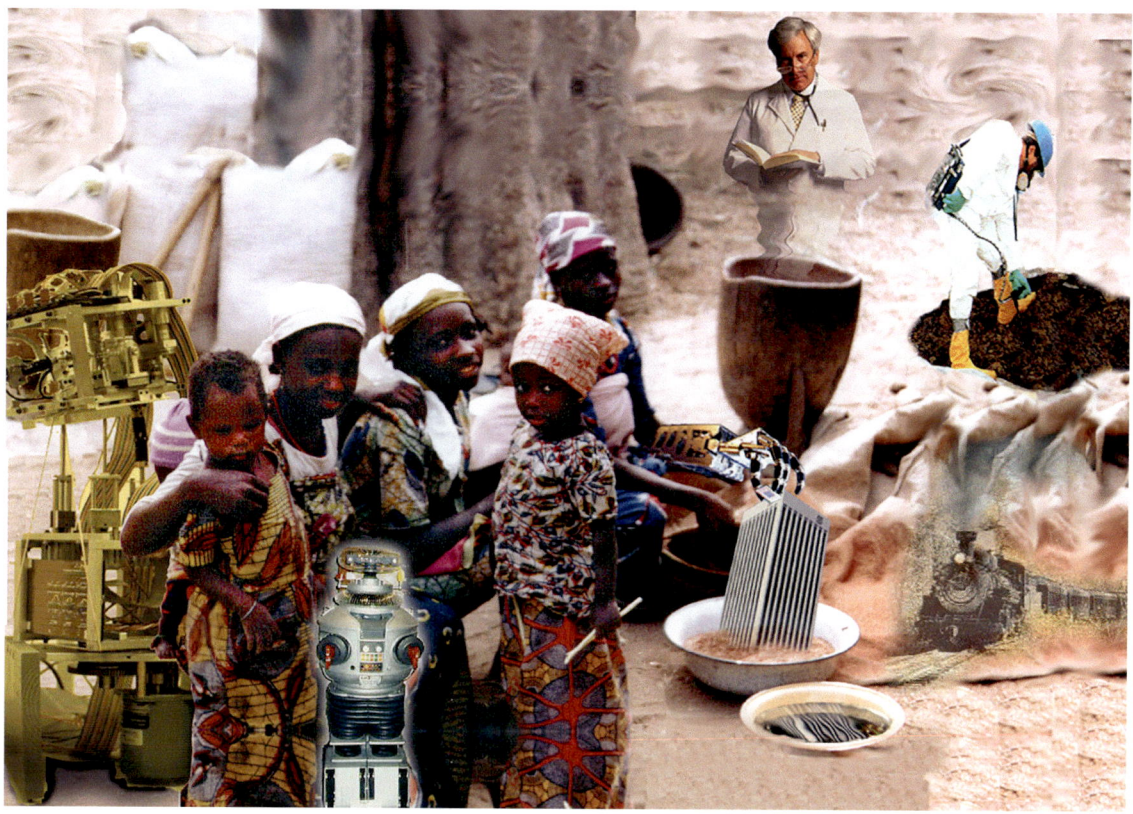

6.2 Fatimah Tuggar, *Village Spells*, 1996. Computer montage (inkjet on vinyl), 90 × 125 cm. Courtesy of BintaZarah Studios.

indenture, and various clashing forms of cultural performance and languages. South Africa's population is equally hybrid, European, Asian, and African. As such, this country forms a microcosm of that critical address defined as globalization. So, in many ways, its very locality already provides more than the metaphorical impetus for this Biennale. However, it is still important to position this project on a broader platform which exceeds the concerns found daily here.

Today it is evident that the world is quickly changing. The question then is whether this unprecedented flurry of activities and events called *globalization*—some of which disguise, mask, even obliterate the contentious nature with which certain epistemological concepts have been received

6.3 (*right*) Andries Botha, *Home*, 1997. Galvanized sheeting, wood, artificial grass and flowers, laminated lead panels, fluorescent lighting, cotton paper, hair, rubber, and latex, Height 3×4×5 m. Exterior view. Courtesy of the artist.

6.4 (*below*) Andries Botha, *Home*, 1997. Galvanized sheeting, lead panels, fluorescent lighting, air-conditioning. Interior view. Courtesy of the artist.

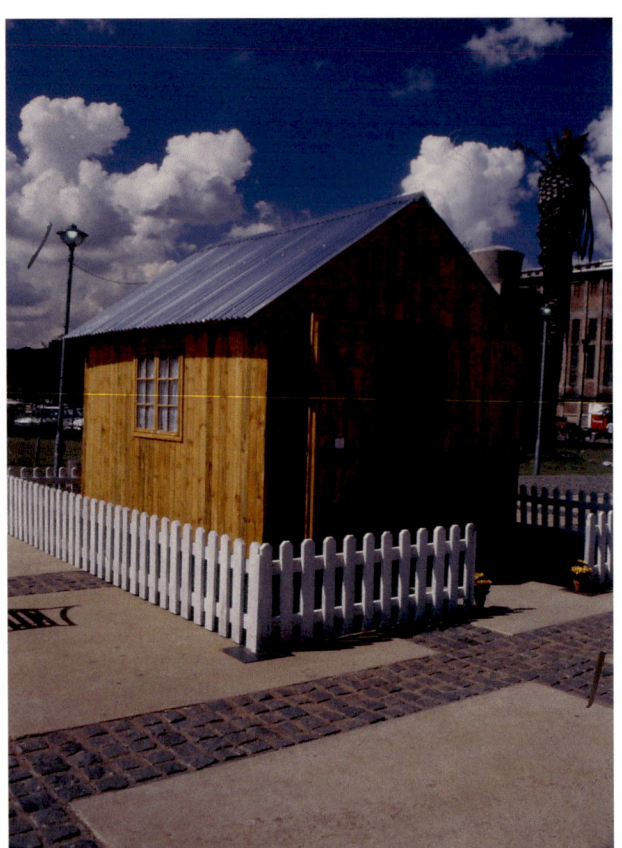

within particular paradigms of the local—leads not to transformation but to displacement. The news of all these events cuts across the borders of technology, political and social upheavals, economic expansionism, ecological disasters, and many spatial disfigurations that accentuate the demise of the apocalyptic rhetoric of the Cold War. Clustered around these issues are several geopolitical changes, beginning with the fall of the Berlin Wall, the collapse of the Soviet Empire, the termination of apartheid in South Africa, the return of the PLO in Gaza, and the dusk of the age of empire and demise of classical colonialism following Hong Kong's handover to the Chinese.

Joining these recent, momentous historical events is the prior history of struggles against domination, colonialism, and dictatorships in Africa, Asia, Latin America, and the Caribbean. In very salient ways, many of these struggles form a long chain of contestations of the historical interpretations of the world, often concentrated around the hegemony of Western imperialism. Whatever form these interpretive exercises take, my aim is not to validate one-dimensional, pitched struggles based only on oppositionality. The aim here is to investigate the cross-layering of discourses that describe issues of globalization. My main concern is neither to be encyclopedic nor to recant the loose terms often used to discuss globalization.

Following many critical analyses, the end of the Soviet hegemony in eastern Europe and fall of the Berlin Wall proclaimed not just the end of the most visible structures (perhaps, even a semiotic sign) of the Cold War years—from nuclear proliferation to détente, along with the spread of ideologies that pitched the world into two opposing camps—but the end of a historical phase of modernity constituted by the epic struggle between liberal democracy and communism, on one hand, and free-market capitalism and Marxist socialism, on the other. Though this may be true, the history which encapsulates what we are witnessing today, at the tail end of the twentieth century, has firm roots in a historical process which began with the expansionist policies of several European countries (Spain, France, Portugal, Holland, England) and early multinationals (the Dutch East India and British East India Companies) from the mid-fifteenth century.

The confluence of the Atlantic and Indian Oceans at the Cape of Good Hope in South Africa—charted by Bartolomeu Dias in 1488 and rounded in 1497 by Vasco da Gama to open up a sea route to India—marks the tangible geographic site around which globalization will be discussed in this context. The occasion for the expansionist policies of the above-named European nations could be seen to have begun in earnest here, together with [Christopher] Columbus's arrival in the Americas, in a bid to open up an alternative, broader, and more efficient route to the East. This search was based on the idea of connecting not only distant worlds, but also on the notion of using such connections for greater global economic mobility and leverage, which would serve to consolidate the powers of the monarchies and the emergent merchant classes of Europe. This rise in trade, and the charting and annexation of distant overseas territories, equally coincided with an increase in scientific discovery, as well as with extensive patronage for the arts from the Catholic Church and the new merchant classes. Thus, what is diligently read and interpreted as the Age of Enlightenment and progress in Europe bore a contrary truth elsewhere. For many peoples and territories, it was the beginning of the fraught encounters—with colonization, displacement, uprootings, and sociopolitical and economic decline.

The Age of Europe thus portended the inverse for Africa, Asia, and the Americas—a negative Age of Decline and Defensiveness. The Age of Exploration and marvelous maritime achievements associated with the European discovery of the Americas, as well as the exploration of the hinterlands of Africa, coincided with the decline of the thriving cultures of Mesoamerica. It opened up routes of trade in human cargo, spices, tea, ivory, precious metals, silk (all of which sound no different from the listings found today in the stock and commodity exchanges in New York, Chicago, London, and Paris). Nonetheless, such transnational and transterritorial trading worked beyond the economic exploitation of natural resources and labor. It equally assumed a concrete position in the most consequential exploration of the meaning of identity: questions of origin, new concepts of ethnicity, and home. It meant that the Age of Enlightenment was inextricably bound to the problematic as well as productive moments of reterritorialized, expressive practices of culture (religion, music, art, linguistics), often formed under the brutal colonial contexts of slavery and indenture.

Moreover, colonization and displacement worked in ways that created entirely new archetypes, peoples, communities, and cultures. Such complex mixtures of societies, cultural expressions, racial identities, and social procedures provided enduring, though tenebrous, testimonies to the processes of globalization. Ought we not agree, then, that exploration of such testimonies breathes new life into the manner in which the discourses of globalization need to be discussed today? Indeed, such frankness captures the idea that the word *diaspora*, forged through migration, displacement, and exile, coincides more with new figurations of globalization than ever before. It puts at the heart of our discussion, at the tumultuous end point of modernity, such easily evaded notions as identity, hybridity, place, and placelessness, nationality, and home. It gives us access into those forms of public speech that tie in with the ways people have been dispersed and gathered, have dwelled and migrated into various modes of social formations and cultural reterritorializations, as well as the ways in which such discussions have been embodied and debated in multicultural agendas and postcolonial revisions.

This is the task that the 2nd Johannesburg Biennale has set for itself. The general concept of *Trade Routes: History and Geography* aims to examine this history of globalization, by exploring how economic imperatives of the past five hundred years have produced resilient cultural fusions and disjunctions. The Biennale directs its attention toward the production of meaning by looking to the social, political, and cultural procedures in operation today, in a highly globalized and technologized period of the twentieth century. The purpose of the Biennale is to give critical significance to those modes of contestation, analysis, exploration, and interpretation with which contemporary artists contend and to contemplate the shifts that have led to the redefinition of our senses of society. The sense of the world which the Biennale hopes to engage—perhaps even to inaugurate—emerges from the sociopolitical procedures of a world in conflict with itself. Yet the sustaining principles which attend these meditations exceed those attachments to the propagandistic methodologies of nationalism and racism. Or those tendentious divisions operative in the narrow dichotomies of inside/outside, native/alien, self/other, straight/gay, citizen/noncitizen, East/West, North/South.

It will be important to maintain that this project remains one about its relationship to all the issues and questions raised above. Hence, the series of exhibitions—which includes a film program and an interdisciplinary conference—will examine the capacity of art to sponsor extensive and broad discussions of culture, philosophy, aesthetics, and technology at the end of the twentieth century. The exhibitions, in varying degrees, will explore how culture and space have been historically displaced through colonization, migration, and technology. In turn, they will also engage, by emphasizing how innovative practices have led to redefinitions and reinventions of our notions of expression, with shifts in the language and discourses of art. Of particular interest is how such redefinitions and reinventions have produced new temporalities and complex cultural cuttings across race, nationality, and gender. To bring about pointed discussions around these issues, we will privilege works and artists who address both explicitly and conceptually new readings and renderings of citizenship and nationality, nations and nationalism, exile, immigration, technology, the city, indeterminacy, hybridity, while exploring the tensions between the local and global.

2

Organizing a project such as this requires processes of thinking, analyzing, discussing, defining, and redefining one's attitudes and positions toward contemporary art and culture at large. I have from the beginning believed that what all this entails—in terms of producing a provocative and legible set of initiatives, under which contemporary art, artists, and intellectuals could gather—would be nothing less than questions driven by intellectual probings, in which certain failures of faith intervene. Such failures are part of the tools of building honest critical work, and besides, they direct one to faults and cracks that exist within one's reasoned position. My perspectives have been enriched and broadened by moments of contact, which in the discipline of anthropology will address the rather problematic connotation of doing "fieldwork." Like anthropological practices, every fieldwork necessitates forms of travel and invariably involves informants, i.e., those personalities who reveal to us knowledges we may otherwise not be privy to. In the sort of curatorial work I have been asked to undertake, such a gathering of information is called *research*, and despite globalization and the connectedness provided by cybernetic networks of information, one still needs to travel, literally, to visit artists' studios, attend exhibitions, and converse with experts in many different disciplines in order to untangle and open new questions about contemporary art and culture as practiced in many parts of the world.

My travels, in the course of these preparations, have made me more acutely aware of incompletenesses and contingencies evident in the work of artists today. Each in turn reveals itself as a parable for living, working, and traveling in a moment and a physical world that is restless to the extreme. They sketch anxious orientations and disfigured maps, where between destinations, nations lapse into obsolete entities (Yugoslavia, the Soviet Union, Zaire). Others cling on, in mutual ethnic hatred (Somalia, Afghanistan, Bosnia), or split (Czech/Slovakia). Others remain deferred with respect to the resolution of old conflicts (Ireland, the Koreas, Taiwan), and yet others fold, enveloped by more powerful entities (Hong Kong, East Germany). As can be seen from these anxious maps, the world we inhabit today makes no pretense toward any idea of coherence or settledness. It is one in constant upheaval, redefinition, and change.

As we travel, then, we must also pay attention to how such changes challenge our positions as settled, coherent national subjects. For if one is settled and coherent, what becomes of the citizen whose country lapses, like some archaic law whose tenure had run out, in the middle of the night as he/

she slips between the borders of the old nation and the time zone of a more stable, prosperous territory? Rendered stateless, all the information in his/her passport also lapses. One thus becomes not only stateless, but also devoid of identity. Certainly, erstwhile citizens of Zaire must surely find this a moment of astonishing modernity, in which nations not only lapse but the concept of home becomes tenuous, incomprehensible. There is nothing incomprehensible, however, about this lapse of the figure of the nation, nor the temporal fissure into which one's identity momentarily drops; it introduces the very idea that the concept of the nation is always durational and contingent.

As I have traveled, I have also lived the anxious moments of cities in perpetual upheaval, cities which have known little respite from cycles of violence and parricide (Brazzaville, Kinshasa, Lima, Jerusalem, Gaza, Paris, London, Kabul). In the course of this journey, I have traced absurdly circuitous routes to emerge in the ruins of a city as an archaeological artifact of modernity (La Habana, Cuba). My understanding of postcolonialism was not only broadened, but staunchly revised, when I had to learn, from a group of artists named Struth (Ostrich) that Norway is a postcolonial nation (Oslo). I was to learn such contradictory things as: the old Norwegian language is in fact the new language; new Norwegian, a more authentic Norwegian free of the taint of colonial contact with Sweden and Denmark, is truly the old Norwegian. Such indeterminate histories were the tools with which I discovered, not without irony or sober bewilderment, my foreignness.

In many areas of the world where such absolute notions as citizenship and nationality form the deadly methods of xenophobic exclusion, the idea of the postnational subject becomes more the norm. This is particularly evident in those spaces in which immense aggregates of human communities circulate in the complex vectors of class, race, gender, ideology, religious beliefs, commodity, and labor. Though these and many more experiences form part of the fragments of my own personal witnessing in the conveyor belt of global travel, there is in fact nothing unique about them. They are part of the legacies of a fraught modernity in which many people actively live. They also define a period in history in which the entire world and its peoples live in a moment of transition.

3

Stories intersect and intervene, opening emphatically into connected and disparate social realities. Today these transnational movements across territories and cultures, between identities and social formations, have come to shape that space we give names like *nation, city, community, home.* Or they unfold in how contemporary events of memory, the past, the bonds of language, family, honor, and belonging are written.

In the course of this journey, many stories offer themselves. London, England: June 1996. A feverish city, and a nation gripped by the convulsive excitement of the European Cup. I, like many visitors to this fabled city, the seat of empire, am caught in the mass bewilderment of a moment we neither share in nor fully comprehend. Here I was to learn that England, Scotland, and Wales do not so much belong together as express themselves as divided along tribal lines and language. A prominent feature of this division is a piece of cloth—the flag, the nation's talisman. Throughout the city it inspires desire, hope, and pride. It appears in all forms—on T-shirts, beer mugs, buttons, hats, jerseys, posters; in magazines; or painted on faces and bodies. But, most prominently, it appears as a single, huge, billowing canvas in which its constituents wrap themselves. The wild reveries which this moment of national identification produces have consequences beyond mere celebrations of national pride or victory. Such celebrations form ways in which the nation as emblem is performed. However, there is a kind of sectarian rhetoric that such performances support, which oftentimes explodes into xenophobia, and in turn produces geographies of exclusion whose methods of enforcement sometimes resort to the most senseless violence.

Violence and xenophobia: these have again become familiar motifs; the double engines that drive the performance of the nation, the double axes which defend a nation's prerogatives. On this count the events of the European Cup did proffer a valuable insight, particularly how sports—beyond providing a context for a kind of homosocial battle—also illustrate the fissure of space into an imaginary contest for the Fatherland. In these situations of pitched battle, players and teams assume war attitudes, while their fans develop the most discriminatory support positions on a nearby home front in the stands, and further in front of televisions. At this time, during the semifinal match between Germany and England, the atmosphere was already electric in the crowded trains in the London Underground. The drunk crowds sang ancient battle songs and waved the Union Jack as the train hurtled toward Wembley Stadium. It was not lost on me—an Igbo, Nigerian-born, New York–based Johannesburg resident, latterly an American citizen—that I am now witness to what James Clifford had so aptly called "ethnographic surrealism."[2]

Meanwhile, in the stadium, the Germans waved their black, yellow, and red flags and taunted the English. There, in that arena, one sensed that this was no ordinary football game, but a contest between nations and everything they have come to represent in the late twentieth century: honor, virility, home, family, patriotism. I was mesmerized by how the various symbols and sentiments woven into them often come to disfigure any form of articulate national speech. Suffice it to say that England fell to the Germans. What followed this defeat was an astonishing orgy of violence. Shops were trashed, cars overturned and set aflame, and an innocent Russian youth, who "looked German," was stabbed in Hyde Park by a gang of frustrated British fans, one of whom dejectedly provided this parting shot: "The Germans will never be my mates."

It would seem that such pronouncements and the punishment visited on the Russian youth rested not only on loyalty to the nation, but also on the assumption that the nation becomes coherent when it knows its enemies. Lord Tebbit's "cricket test" provides a dreadful example of such trials of loyalty. Based on his thesis, in which he attempted to make a distinction between a truly "English" fan and an immigrant, he assumed that such differentiation could be made purely on an atavistic conception of origin. Thus, during a national match between the English cricket team and a West Indian team, any West Indian resident of Hackney *or* Brixton becomes the object of suspicion, the enemy within, for he could never be trusted to root for his now-adopted country. This method of understanding one's enemy lately has become the means through which the tribe's prerogatives are solidified and executed. Writ large amid the deafening echo of the war chant at Wembley, how does the West Indian immigrant, already marked by suspicion, reconcile his divided loyalty between a "native" country, with its ambient illusions, memories, and sentiments, and his "adopted" country, now supposedly spelling "home"? The difficulty of choosing between an originary identity and the more fluid, negotiable one inherited through migration puts the notion of the coherent nation at great risk.

This incident in London is in fact neither new nor necessarily unique. As I was thinking about it, and many other such incidents, it brought to mind the same issues that surrounded the South African Springbok Rugby team campaign against the New Zealand All Blacks during a tour in 1981. This tour was particularly interesting because it took place during a period of growing economic and political sanctions and cultural boycott against the apartheid regime in South Africa. In order to legitimize its racist policy of exclusion through a legislative agenda of white supremacy, the South African government sought different ways to break the stranglehold of international indignation that had condemned its method of prequalifying who is and isn't a citizen of South Africa. The New Zealand tour was thus a perfect opportunity to display those symbols of the nation without which the country remained a renegade, pariah state, with no recognition except in small, contrarian pockets of the world community. It was under the atmosphere of international outcry, condemnation, and protest that the Springboks arrived in Christchurch. Either through naivete or blind arrogance, the regime could never understand the formidable forces of ordinary people and political organizations marshaled against them. And despite warnings of the impending disaster, the tour was commenced. Laid bare before a hostile international audience, the team, also riven by internal divisions involving the all-white team and its lone colored player, put on a tough face and went out onto the field to wrestle with their own claims as recognized national subjects, fighting the fight for the nation's honor, prestige, and legitimacy. But it was not to be.

The issue which the failure of this tour raises isn't how much loyalty preserves the figure of the nation, but how its blindness could equally put it at risk. It leads to the question of: What kind of imperatives bring the nation into being? What is it exactly about the nation, over which we struggle so much, that compels us to risk universal condemnation to secure its premise? And beyond sports, what manner of representation (cultural or otherwise) propels the nation's persistent hunger for incarnation? If a consensus could be reached, beyond the divisiveness, in which people lay claim to the values of their collective past, which images of the national culture survive, and which ones are cast overboard? It is within these tight confines, as well as in that which lies beyond the certain boundaries of the nation's stalwart image and incarnation, that many today inhabit the contradictions of being both citizen and immigrant. But how do such ambivalent positions produce subjectivity? How do they shape intersubjective forms of cultural representation? And who are the prime audiences for such unsettled performative texts?

I want to take this opportunity to move closer to home, which is not a home at all, but a vast, complicated imaginary geography that carries an often oversimplified term called "Africa." Since Africa is not a nation, at least to my understanding, what exactly do we designate as "African" when we invoke that complex space?

I have written that within new, layered cultural formations, one is at once particular and global. Particular and global because the way we resist the sort of impinging narratives practiced daily as figurations of the African imaginary is contingent on the unconditional ways we recognize the transcultural and transnational nature of today's Africa. This particularity and global-ity relates to the political and economic circumstances visible in the way the metropolis unpeels other layers of critical address, based on inventive cultural performances that cut across issues of origin and authenticity. They recognize that globalism has always been vigorously multicultural and counternorma-tive, despite the tendency to injudiciously elide the cracks and sharp edges that define its contours. However, I would like to caution that this situation of indeterminacy is not necessarily a cause for celebration in quarters where the hunger for home supersedes the lure of international fraternity.

Thus, in practice, as well as intellectually, this project sits precari-ously between the disjunctive spaces of home and exile. My main concern is how to explore what "home" means in this context, without excessively illustrating the concept. I want to maintain an open-ended position between the polarities of the national imperative and that of individual prerogative, arguing along the way that belonging is almost always a matter of choice, never coerced. Thus, in the current belligerent stance toward immigration, it is important for conscientious curators and institutions to become more attentive to these issues and to confront these political questions, with-out which the practice of art is not possible. Ours should not be a world in which discussions of art merely rest on outmoded debates over formal and aesthetic methodologies, or on soft-fisted gestures toward so-called Third World societies. The demand of the late twentieth century is about expand-ing the forums within which serious critical debates about culture could be convened, and with meaningful contributions from areas traditionally, but unnecessarily, excluded from participation.

These issues, and many more, tie in with the economic questions already suggested by the concept of *Trade Routes*. To ignore them will be to do so at our own peril. We face today a situation in which mass migration, based on worsening economic realities in many sections of the world (em-bodied in the internal shifts of the labor force from rural to urban areas, or in vociferously defended inter/national immigration legislations), has de-ferred the time of the nation, if not defeated its implementation. We need to address how this mass convergence of cultures and disaffected polities outside the apodictic loop of the globalized, multinational market economy confers a certain air of illegitimacy to the global village rhetoric. Today these excluded cultures and polities—masses of economic refugees, asylum seek-ers, unemployed and laid-off workers, exiles, and guest workers—compel the global economy and its various institutions, as well as governments, to address this crisis. Already the tension created by this volatile confrontation has led to very explosive situations in the cities of Europe, where rising unemployment has led to increasingly racist, violent, neofascist bands who terrorize immigrants and attack their properties.

4

Since contemporary art, especially in the West, has operated throughout this century on the same hegemonic principles as the traditional economic sector, it is my wish for this Biennale not to reduce the qualitative contributions of invited artists by privileging only those who come from affluent countries. It is a fact that major industrial countries of Europe and North America spend disproportionately large sums of money to circulate the products of their contemporary art markets. This has had the unfortunate effect of excluding a large number of valuable artistic practices outside the most important international forums for contemporary art. The 2nd Johannesburg Biennale stands on the principle of building new "contact zones" for productive and lasting exchanges between artists and intellectuals, across cultures, economic positions, and political affiliations. In light of these, I have, while preparing this project, chosen to forgo any attachment to the concept of nationality as a criterion for invitations extended to artists. As such, there will be no national pavilions, nor have I proposed to the artists and curators involved in this Biennale any initiative that may be misconstrued as privileging ideas about national culture.

In my proposition, belonging proceeds from a much broader frame, acknowledging individual situations. Often, it makes critical accommodation for various ways of being, thinking, working, and dwelling in a world where the notion of borders has been soundly problematized. The artists we have invited are members of this broad affiliation. They are part of that mobile, itinerant group whom Homi Bhabha has described as the "tribe of interpreters of such metaphors [as home and exile]—the translators of the dissemination of texts and discourses across cultures—who perform act[s] of secular interpretation" of our fascinating world.[3] Moreover, the tangled routes these artists have traveled to arrive in South Africa speak not only of the daily practice of what a contemporary artist is today; they unpeel all those connotations we associate with diaspora, lucidly described in Clifford's remarkable new book, *Routes*, as "that exemplary community of the transnational moment, made up of . . . domains of shared and discrepant meanings, adjacent maps and histories, a broad, complex fraternity that hinges on nonabsolutist ways of practicing citizenship."[4]

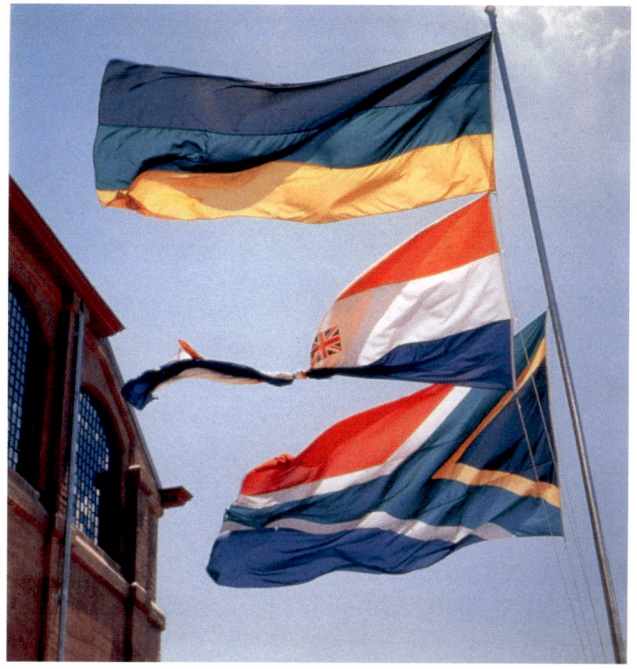

6.5 Hans Haacke, *The Vindication of Dulcie September*, 1997. Flags (cloth, steel, text, photograph), dimensions variable. Courtesy of the artist and Paula Cooper Galley, New York. © Hans Haacke/VG Bild-Kunst, Bonn 2023.

However incomplete the above descriptions of the new global citizen may be, they propose the partial ways of encountering and articulating cultures in the late twentieth century. They are for me liminal figurations of the transitory space we all inhabit in today's globalized and technologized environment. But more importantly, they narrate a sense of openness in the ways we figure identity in the furious ebb and flow of global migration. Here identity no longer signals what we are or how we define, refine, reify, and contest who we are and where we come from. It has become an ideological problem we struggle to solve. And despite its difficulties, it remains a fascinating object of the transcultural, transterritorial, and transnational narrative of the human enterprise. I end here because there is no one way of embodying what this human enterprise is, except to say that it has become increasingly messy. Here identity—stitched into the migratory patterns through which people have traveled, secured, conquered, and settled—spreads outward into that narrative space of not just being, but also becoming. Globalization thus ceases to be a reductive activity of economic consolidation and efficient distribution of labor and capital. These motifs describe a more fascinating modernity than has been properly allowed in broader cultural discussions. Far from being aberrations, they instead suggest partial ways of living, working, and traveling in a restless world of social, political, economic, and cultural transformation like no other in human history.

NOTES

1   [*Ed. note:* In his essay "Reflections on Exile," Said described our age as characterized by "modern warfare, imperialism and the quasi-theological ambitions of dictators." Edward Said, "Reflections on Exile," *Granta* 13 (September 1, 1984), https://granta.com/reflections-on-exile/.]

2   [*Ed. note:* See James Clifford, "On Ethnographic Surrealism," *Comparative Studies in Society and History* 23, no. 4 (Oct. 1981): 539–64.]

3   Homi K. Bhabha, "DissemiNation: Time, Narrative, and the Margins of the Modern Nation," in *Nation and Narration*, edited by Homi K. Bhabha (London: Routledge, 1990), 293.

4   This description of ethnic diasporas is that of Katching Tölölan in the introductory editorial of his journal. Katching Tölölan, *Diaspora*1, no. 1 (1991), 5. It is cited by James Clifford in his essay "Diasporas," *Cultural Anthropology* 9, no. 3 (August 1994), reprinted in Clifford's *Routes: Travel and Translation in the Late Twentieth Century* (Cambridge, MA: Harvard University Press, 1997), 245.

Revisions, Reassessments, Diaspora

A contribution to *Transforming the Crown: African, Asian, and Caribbean Artists in Britain, 1966–1996*, edited by Mora J. Beauchamp-Byrd and M. Franklin Sirmans (New York: Franklin H. Williams Caribbean Cultural Center/African Diaspora Institute, 1997), 80–88. This volume accompanied an exhibition of the same title, which was shown at the publishers' venue and at the Studio Museum in Harlem and the Bronx Museum of the Arts between October 1997 and March 1998.

You must be from my country
I see it by the tick
of your soul around the eyelashes
and besides you dance when you are sad
you must be from my country . . .

Tchicaya U Tam'si, *Epitomé* (1962)

Origins—they are dim in time, colossally
locked in the terrible mountain, buried in seaslime,
or vaporized, being volatile. What purpose
has the traveler now, whose connection is cut
with the whale, the wolf, or the albatross?
what does your small mouth
tell of supernovas or of chromosomes?

Arthur Nortje, "Night Ferry" (1967)

To reconstitute the discourse of cultural difference demands not simply a change of cultural contents. . . . It requires a radical revision of the social temporality in which emergent histories may be written, the articulation of the "sign" in which cultural identities may be inscribed.

Homi Bhabha, *The Location of Culture* (1994)

ACCORDING TO POPULAR PERCEPTION, both within the Western metropolitan psyche and in the critical strategies of postcolonial discourse, the daydream of a diasporic community is always lodged in an imaginary locale, in an elsewhere, far from the articulate inscription of native utterance. It is usually symbolically invested, and ceaselessly organized outside the principalities of any originary geography. For to conceive of a diasporic community is always to invest in its antithesis: the homeland, all the more desubstantialized by distance and absence. It is to enter into correspondence with, and to piece and stitch together, a community adorned with all manners of emblematic gestures (fantastical, illusory, allegorical, ornamental, ostentatious) and significations ruled by contingencies that speak to the desire for self-preservation as well as self-reinvention. The formation of a diaspora could be articulated as the quintessential journey into *becoming*; a process marked by incessant regroupings, re-creations, and reiterations. Together these stressed actions strive to open up new spaces of discursive and performative postcolonial consciousness. To glimpse the communities where such events take place, one inevitably initiates a journey into the heart of the Western metropolis in order to link up with the rest of the wandering tribes screened from the consciousness of the unwelcoming, rooted communities of Europe and North America.

It is from such moments of both utter ambivalence and recuperative action that Gayatri Spivak writes that "in postcoloniality, every metropolitan [diasporic] definition is dislodged. The general mode for the postcolonial is citation, reinscription, rerouting [and rewriting] the historical."[1] The creation of a substantial African diaspora commenced shortly after World War II, when large contingents of workers and ex-soldiers from the colonies were recruited to join in the rebuilding effort of the devastated "mother" country after the war. Enticed by the promise of French citizenship and metropolitan Parisian life, many Africans migrated as students, making Paris the hub of expatriate African culture in Europe. Years later, buoyed by a fiercely revisionist right-wing xenophobia, they would become a prime area of contestation over French citizenship and the question of immigration.

Roland Barthes, on encountering a photograph in *Paris-Match* of "a young Negro in French uniform saluting, with his eyes uplifted, probably fixed on the tricolour," would muse a decade later in the epilogue to his collection of essays *Mythologies* that the image represented what he termed a *myth*. Barthes, anticipating the crisis which the image already represents, goes further to locate this semiological defect in a kind of irreconcilable hybridity. According to him, the image seemed to signify the myth that "France is a great Empire, that all her sons, without any color discrimination, faithfully serve under her flag, and that there is no better answer to the detractors of an alleged colonialism than the zeal shown by this Negro in serving his so-called oppressors."[2] And indeed many former colonial subjects accede to the construction of this fiction. Or as Barthes would have it, "myth." The fictive depiction which the image emphasized becomes even more amplified, because as Barthes offers, "myth is speech *stolen and restored*. Only, speech which is restored is no longer quite that which is stolen: when it was brought back, it was not put exactly in its place. It is this brief act of larceny, this moment taken for a surreptitious faking, which gives mythical speech its benumbed look."[3] Today it can no longer be denied that colonial subjection tended to elide the language of the colonized in the original in order to reinscribe it in translation and, through the act of dissimulation, plunge it into the miasma of chaos, degeneracy, waywardness.

Of course, it was Michel Foucault who taught us, in his blistering deconstruction of systems of power, to be wary of this "act of larceny," to distrust authority and its regimes of control, for they can easily appropriate the radical gesture of the oppressed, sublate its forms, and thus neutralize its potentially transgressive impact. Foucault wrote that "discipline produces subjected and practiced bodies. . . . Discipline increases the forces of the body (in economic terms of utility) and diminishes these same forces (in political terms of obedience)."[4] In more than symbolic terms, postwar France achieved those two aims: "in economic terms of utility" and "in political terms of obedience" in relation to its African *guests*. In fact, the Algerian struggle for independence from French colonialization offers a route into how the forces of discipline and subjection become aligned with violent resistance. The import of such resistance, as in all cases of decolonization or political resistance, lies in the rehumanization of the formerly colonized subject; a shift from the position of ex-native to that of modern citizen. Such a possibility fervently calls attention to the fact that colonialism, despite its destructive methodology, neither represented a total annihilation of the colonized's subjective consciousness, nor a mastery over his language and systems of signification. Yet it could be said that the most interesting thing about African identity in the West, in the early postwar years, is that even intellectual prowess could grow turgid under the spell of the kinds of myth which the *Paris-Match* image displayed. Let us listen briefly to a rapturous Léopold Sédar Senghor—poet, essayist, statesman, and spiritual father of the Negritude movement. In one of his characteristically effusive poems, filled with false emotional commiseration with French culture, he writes:

> Oh Lord, dismiss from my memory the France that is not France,
> this mask of pettiness and hate upon the face of France
> This mask of pettiness and hate for which I've only hate—
> but surely I can hate the evil
> For I am greatly fond of France.[5]

Despite Senghor's penchant to wax contradictory on the question of African political and social agency under the yoke of colonialism, his intellectual example nourished the minds of many young African and Caribbean critical thinkers who were already feeling restless in the suffocating ambience of French colonial domination. Between the late 1930s and 1950s, the Negritude writers and poets, led by Senghor and the Martinican poet and dramatist Aimé Césaire, who were published committedly by Alioune Diop under the Presence Africaine imprint, taught us how a project of "radical revision" of colonialist tropes could be initiated and how the "emergent histories" and "cultural identities" of the diaspora could be written and inscribed. Despite this history, today Negritude suffers criticism as a revisionist critical ideology which favored (at least in the case of Senghor and his coterie of race men filled with unrestrained emotion) nostalgic racial essentialism. Still, Negritude's presence in the intellectual atmosphere of Paris before World War II laid the foundation for what is undeniably the first diasporic African intellectual community to emerge during the colonial era. The Negritude movement's oppositional actions, steeped in a utopian, modernist rhetoric, laid the ground for the final fight against colonial domination. This diasporic community comprising African and Caribbean students and intellectuals became united as much by a political commitment to overthrow colonialism and structural racism via a pan-Africanist vision as by a rigorous intellectual disposition comparable to what was going on around them in Paris.

Though the flow of new immigrants and exiles from the former colonies of the West has swollen the ranks of the diasporic community (in New York, Paris, London, Brussels, and Toronto), there is yet to emerge an equivalent in the visual art community anywhere in the West to rival the concentrated energy created by the Negritude writers. Still, the dream of Africa persists in the metropolis as the principal organizing element of diasporan desire, be that as methods of self-fashioning or critical subjectivity, ruled as it is by the double tropes of longing and ambivalence, and at times derangement. One imagines, for example, what the contemporary South African photographer Ernest Cole's daydream must have been in the bleak, impoverished setting of New York's Harlem, between the physical pangs of hunger and the dim prospects of artistic fulfillment.

In the character of those who, for one reason or another, have been expatriated, there is something not quite grasped by the many theories of postcolonialism which hints at some kind of implausible fatalism. This fatalism is, however, to be distinguished from a hopeless romanticism with death, the lacuna of absence, or the farce of martyrdom. It is something more immediate and fundamental: survival, existence, breathing itself. And as such, the restless, engaged diasporan figure is always in a crouch position, ready to do battle with that perennial and persistent shadow projected full on the wall: himself.

It is thus quite apt that Tchicaya U Tam'si and Arthur Nortje should both die respectively in exile in Paris and London, away from the Africa of their imaginations, dreaming of return. Although this Africa, which, for whatever contingencies, they could only conjure in their dreams, had become merely a tissue of fabrications. Never able to surpass the astonishment of rupture and expatriation, nor able to transcend the biting salt of longing, desire, and despair that eats through the very fabric of individual artistic enterprise, the diasporic artist tenaciously lives in a time warp. He paints, sings, writes, and performs what he imagines constitutes the memories of the homeland, often embellishing such memories with tinges of mythology and phantasm. In the diasporic memory, the gardens of the memorized and memorialized homeland burn ever incandescent with lush flowers and foliage that swing in slow; the sun never sets. Yet hardly does the diasporan subject return to inherit this kingdom. One could say that for this figure, return is always a dream deferred.

Distance and absence further the tenuous reality of the diasporan subject. In the web of marginalization, repulsion, and abjection which personifies his/her reality, in the *resettled* community she/he is constantly caught, like a temporarily blinded deer in the harsh glare of modern displacement, between nation and subject. It is an in-between state that spells doom for those who realize instinctively how permanent exile could be, how years literally dissolve, becoming a blur in memory. The demographics of all the great modern Western cities inscribe this succinctly in their impermanence. They confirm it by the cities' constitutions and reconstitutions that map the ever-increasing deliquescence of the diasporic community, its fatal longings and destructive self-enclosure, traced sharply and mapped by the curve of the shifting populations that form new *settlements* and imaginary communities in all the peripheries of the metropolis.

There can be no doubt that writers and artists like U Tam'si and Nortje are residents of these imaginary and wayward communities, communities that take their pride of place among all the other/ed modern nations via the positionality of the stressed absence. "Like neighborhoods that are defined by the population held away from them," U Tam'si and Nortje personify the quintessential twentieth-century subjects, persons whose search for an interior life and whose sense of boundaries are incessantly written over by new emergencies—Bosnia, Russia, Kosovo, Chechnya.[6] They are part of an increasing number of people (artists, laborers, dissidents, intellectuals, cab drivers, ordinary folk) whom we euphemistically refer to as immigrants and who today roam, unrecognized (beyond recognition in fact), on the vast modern boulevards and in the subterranean cells of the Western metropolis. We know them by their accents and by where they congregate to trade news of the imaginary homeland (where everything happens in the past tense), or by their daily struggles to transcend marginality and the disasters that rule their new communities. But do we know in which neighborhoods they live or the content of the desires that nourish their ambitions? Who speaks for these groups? How are the histories of their social formations written? By whom and for what?

I want to reenter this discussion by suggesting that the above constitutes the unaccounted-for motif of existence which has shaped the texture of the life and work of African visual artists in the West during the past fifty years. This discussion necessarily unfolds, like a Chinese fan, around the forms that twentieth-century African literary figures have either described and/or lived. It is in the mode of the critical address, fashioned both for survival and for creating, that they have narrated that incompatible space between longing and consolidation, the double mark of absence and loss. These spaces are often conjured up around patterns of writing and subversion (here one can go back to eighteenth-century London to encounter [Olaudah] Equiano's slave narrative and essays as an abolitionist) or acts of polemical rhetoric (here we think of Negritude in the leftist politics of the Parisian demimonde in the 1930s and 1940s) which are a leitmotif of all diasporic cultural work. We find the evidence of these works' profound enunciations, not through figurative speech or in the mire of syntactic chaos, but through the piercing, allusive methods of self-illumination as they continually "engage with culture as an uneven, incomplete production of meaning and value, often composed of incommensurable demands and practices, produced in the act of social survival."[7]

Diasporic writers, though self-involved, have dealt and puzzled more eloquently over the question with which we today find ourselves preoccupied, more than any group of African intellectuals. Ousmane Sembène, for example, narrated such a process of intense subjectivity in his book *Dock Workers*, an autobiographical story of racism during his years as a labor organizer in the port of Marseilles. We find this, equally, in the almost crude emotionalism of David Diop's poems or in the scatological irony of Yambo Ouologuem. There is no doubt that in such writings, both subtle and exorbitant, the most lucent examples of contemporary African creative agency and subjectivity have made their mark indelibly felt.

And of the figures whom we may retrieve today as subjects of an extended public meditation, U Tam'si and Nortje offer the student of literature some of the most committed writing on the effects of displacement. If there is an opportunity to repudiate what may be myopically invoked as a continental style, it is in the work of these two disparate writers. Cutting, wry, and self-deprecatingly contrary, U Tam'si is a surrealist to the core. He is a poet of silences, of the discrete moment, the oblique public laughter, the discontinuous. His work moves in avid declensions and explores the most obscure places (public and private) without any obstructive flourish to investigate the lugubrious, lonely, existential geographies where the immigrant African subject whiles away his time dreaming of the homeland and return. U Tam'si's imagery evokes the glazy atmosphere of detachment which speaks to the absurdity of diasporic metropolitan life.

In his epic cycle of poems, *Epitomé*, U Tam'si's Congolese protagonist is one of those millions lost in the shifting cyclone of the urban sprawl—the Parisian conurbation—a sprawl teeming with so many lives and cultures, which often makes the bodies that move through the dreamingly slow, unfolding space of the modern city seem opaque and indistinguishable. But it is the moment of dissonance that gives the modern city its sharp edge and doubtless character as a swallower of dreams and consciousness. In *Epitomé*, one is able to glimpse those little interruptions, those "inventions that vanish before the light dispersed" that are the patterns of imagination available to the subaltern subject in the modern city's setting.[8] His protagonist's space is that of the clandestine glance, that gaze that plays on the screen of verisimilitude. It is a look that searches among the disembarking throngs—be it in the Paris metro, New York subway, or London underground—for little epiphanies, a face of recognition with the twitch around the eyelashes, that signals for him a memory of the homeland. And just when one finds that face, it plays only momentarily, disappearing again into the mass of bodies that weave in and out of that intersection between subject and nation, race and identity, victim and oppressor. It is a blur to the seeing eye yet sharply illumined by the remembering mind.

The process of imagining and memorizing scenes of one's past can be related to the character that photography assumes as a supplement, but that memory replays serially. Though unlike memory, which has available to its mise-en-scènes a surplus of images on which to replay and make various frozen moments unfold cinematically, photography on the other hand memorializes, freezes, and entraps the remembered scenes. Utilizing these two dimensions and activities (one phenomenological and the other mechanical), the exile embraces fictions (myths) that remain just that, until they are retrieved from some disused, dusty, sealed box or some other submerged archive. These two processes propose synchronous sites at which the artistic and cultural activities of the diaspora cross: a past that is dead and a present with an unimaginable future that is constantly shadowed by what in reality intimates death. Within this frame, one could, perhaps, read in greater detail and see that the high chroma of diasporic representational repertoire still remains lodged in the Freudian slip, sublated between the sandwich of speech and its attendant untranslatability. Here, the diaspora, like time, suffers a constant hunger for incarnation. To sate that hunger, it fashions graven images for its lost and active memories, and signs them with the acute reality of the present.

I am quite sure that the British landscape occupied by the many artists whose works and careers are the subject of this survey exhibition is not at all different from the one confronted by U Tam'si's protagonist. The African artist on arrival in Britain encounters an untrusting and alienating social environment. It could begin at the very moment of disembarkation, on the docks of Wolverhampton, like Uzo Egonu, who arrived in Britain from Nigeria in 1945 at the age of twelve and has since gone on to produce, perhaps, the most consistent and variegated body of postwar painting in England despite the nagging impediments of isolation and critical neglect. Or a different sort of diasporan artist arrives (different, because his/her role has multiplied and shifted emphasis, from one of purely artistic practice to

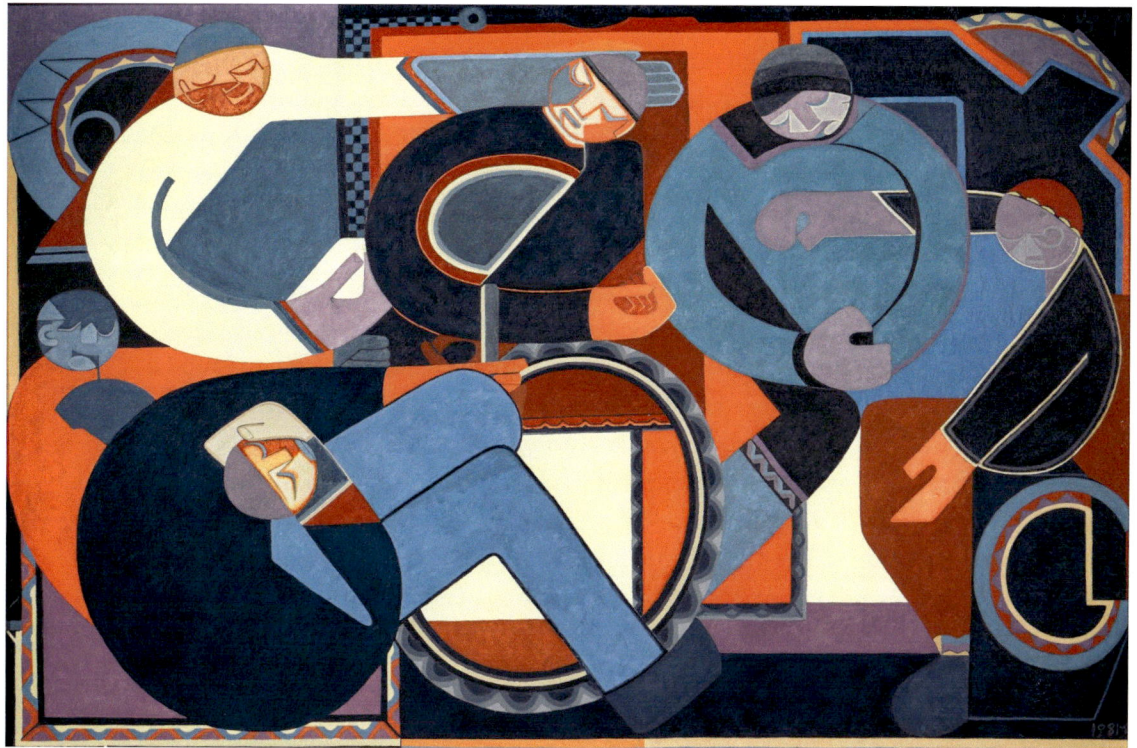

7.1 Uzo Egonu, *Stateless People (an Assembly)*, 1981–82. Oil on canvas, 142×213 cm. Thanks to kó art space, Lagos.

embracing all the difficulties of occupying the sites of scholarship and art production), intent on unpeeling the long-buried records of diasporic artistic achievement. She/he arrives at the airport almost half a century later, with the singular quest to restore to art historical and critical light the incandescent moments of artists like Egonu.

Olu Oguibe came to Thatcherite Britain from Nigeria at the end of the 1980s, as a Foreign Office Scholar to study in London. In the process he obtained the first PhD on an individual modern African artist ever awarded in England for his exhaustive thesis on Egonu's work and career. The telling title of Oguibe's book, *Uzo Egonu: An African Artist in the West*, locates the full meaning of his investigative project, to reveal Egonu fully, apposite his career in the aporia of double consciousness.[9] For to say "Uzo Egonu: An African Artist" is to ignore that crucial marker which qualifies the problematic space that governed both his remarkable artistic achievement and his absence from the tenure it ought to have conferred.

What might have also endeared Egonu to Oguibe, and which would grow to be a preoccupation of the young scholar, was Egonu's deft sensitivity toward an emergent though as yet untapped sense of a diasporan modernist viewpoint. This viewpoint, however, was nestled away from the redundancies of nativist citation, the unrelenting self-referentiality and stylistic falsification bordering on hyperbole and a sensationalistic sentimentality that is so characteristic of artists caught in that perpetual cycle of self-discovery. In Egonu, one evinced a rather different approach: a sophisticated model of thinking that hinged on two, not necessarily irreconcilable methods, on one hand, one which was radically circumspect in its considered intentionality, in its usage of modernism as a central, animating language at the disposal of all avant-garde artists, irrespective of race or origin, and on the other hand, the use of the same modernist language to fiercely interrogate its peripheralization and nominalization of African subjectivity within twentieth-century art.

In the process of writing, Oguibe, who is also an artist, must have learned a few lessons that would enrich the tenor of his own critical perspective and artistic practice. Eschewing the understandable, yet debilitating, postcolonial inclination toward the robust employment of a *usable past* as a paradigm of diasporan subjectivity, Oguibe, on arrival in Britain, recognized that the metropolis is also part of his own space, and its polyglot tongues his necessary inheritance. Rather than disavow the metropolis, he proceeded to lay claim to it; he elected to investigate its curves and trapdoors, its brick walls and insolent stares. In the process he has witnessed a radical transformation in his own cultural idiom, based on precisional thinking and a devastatingly critical and deft deployment of various contemporary registers, despite the great impediments which the metropolis exerts as toll of passage. Finding himself thrown into this situation he neither anticipated nor in the beginning comprehended, his focus became the interrogation of persistent erasure and the denial of agency. Yet his peculiar position finds a comparable echo in the acts of survival evident in the subjective practices of other immigrant communities with whom he finds kinship across the temporization of disaster and social decay as the price of expatriation.

The very term *Black British* makes it obvious that the definition of identity, within the locality of an antagonistic majority culture in which *minorities* are potentially pitted against each other, is not realizable through racial and regional categorization. Yet the employment of a possibly homogenizing signifier like *Black British* for so many ethnically and culturally diverse communities and geographies invites, on the surface, the possible disavowal of the plurality of identities within this body. Despite this danger, one has to admit that this shared responsibility has a political if not cultural merit. As such, a recognizable and potent political signifier becomes all the more needed, to evade the divide-and-conquer strategy of the majority culture. At its most metaphorical and practical, *Black British* is loaded with the oppositional force of transcendence in which African, Caribbean, and Asian identities could conceivably collaborate for a concerted and engaged political attitude toward cultural production.

It is within this political and sociocultural pastiche of diaspora that the African artist or immigrant finds an extended network of other diasporas loosely linked into a community which attempts a recognition of commonality among people who are bound to constructs which often are not only nonexistent within their particular cartographies, but also are plotted to empower. This kinship, which has adopted strategies of political action and a commitment to fight racial oppression and exploitation, as well as an investment in the re-creation of community, becomes the space where the postmodern and the postcolonial intersect. At this crossroads, they form complex layers of difference that both transcend and repudiate constructions of "otherness." It makes the diasporic space the quintessential late twentieth-century space, a space in which the terms of modern immigration, exile, loss, nation, subject, and citizen are negotiated and reinvented for various uses. It is from within the understanding of this struggle that Bhabha writes so penetratingly and convincingly that "culture as a strategy of survival is both transnational and translational. It is transnational because contemporary postcolonial discourses are rooted in specific histories of cultural displacement, whether they are the 'middle passage' of slavery and indenture, the 'voyage out' of the civilizing mission, the fraught accommodation of Third World migration to the West after the Second World War, or the traffic of economic and political refugees within and outside the Third World. . . . The transnational dimension of cultural transformation—migration, diaspora, displacement, relocation—makes the process of cultural translation a complex form of signification."[10]

We find this complexity so persuasively noted and administered in the photographic tableaux of Rotimi Fani-Kayode. In Fani-Kayode's work, loaded with symbolism, the moment of transcendence is opened up not through the recuperative effort, but in his ability to mine the tension that holds in tensile balance the suspended, diasporic worlds of the postmodern and postcolonial spaces he occupied. His work poses an ontological challenge to the referential order, that disturbance which Barthes theorized in his eponymous *Camera Lucida* as the *punctum*.[11] By creating mise-en-scènes of concealment and disclosure, Fani-Kayode narrated his artistic project from the complementary positions of his sexual, cultural, and racial identity, and not in some reductively imagined site of crisis that conflates "otherness" with difference.

In conclusion, it would be fruitful to note that the demand for the iteration of cultural identity within the conventional whole cloth of neither/nor division still echoes unambivalently in those long, winding corridors, dimly lit by the shadows of excess and the abject, which the "other" of the occidental imagination occupies. Of course, conventional wisdom, neglecting the obvious, would hold that the cornerstone of African diasporic art is located at the foundation of oppositionality and insipid nostalgic hankering. But that is obviously false, whether it is used to describe the virtuosity of Egonu's painterly gestures or to damn the work of younger artists like Lubaina Himid, Folake Shoga, Yinka Shonibare, Maud Sulter, Zarina Bhimji, Oladélé Bamgboyé, etc. The work of this younger generation, whether amplified by didactic systems of thought and practice, or exploring more conventional formal concerns, is always enlivened by a complexity as varied as the spaces they occupy in terms of their racial, cultural, and sexual identifications.

Despite debates to the contrary, by now it ought to be quite ridiculous to begin a discussion on the question of cultural identity of the "other" by perpetuating the same paradigms of lack which have persistently enfolded the body and subjectivity of the disrecognized figure of the subalternate, by asking that same old question: "Can the subaltern speak?" Indeed, yet do the subaltern speak, but no longer in the muffled tones of glossolalia, or in the inconsistent speech of hybridity writ large in the patterns of inarticulateness. Throughout Britain, and for almost a century now, the subaltern has been speaking. Artists in this exhibition bear vivid testimony to that effect. The challenge today could then be reposed thus: "Can the subaltern be heard?" and if so, to whom does she/he speak?

NOTES

Epigraphs: Tchicaya U Tam'si, *Epitomé* (Tunis: P. J. Oswald, 1962), in *A Selection of African Poetry*, ed. K. E. Senanu and T. Vincent (Burnt Mill, Harlow: Longman Group, 1976), 143; Arthur Nortje, "Night Ferry" (1967), in Arthur Nortje, *The Country of the Heart: Love Poems from South Africa*, ed.

P. R. Anderson (Bellevue, South Africa: Jacana, 2004), 14; Homi Bhabha, *The Location of Culture* (London: Routledge, 1994), 246.

1   Gayatri Chakravorty Spivak, "Reading the Satanic Verses," in *Outside in the Teaching Machine* (New York: Routledge, 1993), 217.

2   Roland Barthes, "Myth Today," in *Mythologies*, trans. Annette Lavers (New York: Noonday, 1972), 116.

3   Barthes, *Mythologies*, 125.

4   Michel Foucault, *Discipline and Punish: The Birth of the Prison*, trans. Alan Sheridan (New York: Vintage Books, 1977), 138.

5   Léopold Sédar Senghor, "Prayer for Peace," in *The Negritude Poets*, trans. Ellen Conroy Kennedy (New York: Thunder's Mouth, 1989), 138.

6   Toni Morrison, "Unspeakable Things Unspoken: The Afro-American Presence in American Literature," quoted in Homi Bhabha, *The Location of Culture* (London: Routledge, 1994), 198.

7   Bhabha, *Location of Culture*, 172.

8   Octavio Paz, "Prologue," in *Early Poems, 1935–1955* (New York: New Directions, 1973), 3.

9   [*Ed. note:* Olu Oguibe, *Uzo Egonu: An African Artist in the West* (London: Third Text Publishers, 1995).]

10   Bhabha, *Location of Culture*, 172.

11   [*Ed. note:* Roland Barthes, *Camera Lucida: Reflections on Photography,* trans. Richard Howard (New York: Hill and Wang, 1981), 42, 43–46, 39.]

A Few Notes on "African" Conceptualism

A contribution to the catalog for *Global Conceptualism: Points of Origin, 1950s–1980s*, shown at the Queens Museum of Art, New York, in April 1999. The catalog was edited by the exhibition's curators, Jane Farver, Luis Camnitzer, and Rachel Weiss, and published by the museum, with this essay at pages 108–17. Enwezor was a member of a curatorial team invited to present works showing the emergence of conceptualist practices in their regions. Other members were Reiko Tomii (Japan), Claude Gintz (Europe), László Beke (eastern Europe), Mari Carmen Ramírez (Latin America), Peter Wollen (North America), Terry Smith (Australia and New Zealand), Margarita Tupitsyn (Soviet Union), Sung Wan-kyung (South Korea), Gao Minglu (China), and Apinan Poshyananda (South and Southeast Asia). Between December 1999 and November 2000, the exhibition traveled from the Queens Museum to the Walker Art Center, Minneapolis, and the Miami Art Museum.

Is There Such a Thing as African Conceptualism?

THE TERM *CONCEPTUAL ART* has been so institutionalized that it has come to occupy a narrow strip of territory encompassing only discourses flowing out of very specific practices. Most of these practices are connected to or subsumed within the artistic discourses of postwar western Europe and the United States. Moreover, the established meanings of these activities have often proceeded from the idea that what makes such art conceptual begins with the notion of the dematerialization of the object, as well as the privileging of language-based art, institutional critique, the nonvisual, and on the litany goes. My intention here is neither to rehearse this litany nor simply to displace its firmly rooted meanings, but to add to it and, where possible, to enlarge its constricted art historical certitude. Hence, what would it mean, this late in the day, to nominate as "conceptualist" something that acts like, looks like, and resembles those practices, but whose chief concerns may lie elsewhere? Such is the question one must pose for anything called *African conceptualism*.

Given the complex perceptual issues that are its fundamental organizing principles, conceptual art, as elaborated in the United States and western Europe, would seem to exclude Africa. Such an exclusion would, of course, be in line with the already prevailing disqualification of African aesthetic thought from the broader argument of modernism. Despite the different experiences of modernity globally, this art historical conceit remains firmly entrenched in different institutional and epistemological operations. Thus, the notion of pleading a particular area's case for inclusion remains a fraught one. There has still not been a way to remedy that neglect, and here will not be the venue to do so.

It is crucial to state this from the outset, because our assignment as curators for this exhibition is to locate the particular point at which the attitude called *conceptualism* made its first appearance in different areas of the world. If the claim for conceptual art has always been made in reference to its relationship to the dominant language of modernism, and if its institutional valorization has situated it as the most significant artistic breakthrough of the twentieth century after cubism, then it must be allowed that this shift is deeply engrained in the earlier opportunity which African sculptural objects offered the early modernists to escape the convoluted mise-en-scènes of impressionism and classical European art. This is an old story, but worth reiterating. Indeed, how does Africa participate in this exercise in constructive revisionism at the core of which resides the idea of the avant-garde, with so clear a history located in the metropolitan identity of the Western city?

To ask this invites a series of other questions. To wit: What is conceptual art as applied to the conditions that exist in Africa? So identified, would these artistic practices, which might also be "corroded" and "contaminated" by other cultural and political/ideological principles, alter the definition, indeed the material and intellectual manifestation, of what is or is not conceptual art? Would conceptualism in Africa, like its Euro–North American counterpart, constitute [so] significant [a] shift within the dominant institutional framework as to posit a new language or paradigm? If so, what specific labels were applied to this shift, how were they received and discussed? Do these labels constitute a movement in which many artists participated?

Quite simply, is there such a thing as conceptual art in Africa, or is it just a term imported as part of a neocolonial enterprise of modernist art history? Most importantly, in deciding what is conceptual in Africa, whose model of thought and what methods of distinction should be applied in dismissing or admitting works, attitudes, actions, and propositions?

These are vexing questions, yet pursuing them is key to broadening the place of African modernity within the larger discussions of twentieth-century art. One way to address these questions is to ignore all preset rules. But a more promising strategy is to set up a critical correspondence between the disjunctive temporalities of the African imaginary and the highly differentiated space of Western institutional and epistemological reflections on modern art.

Conceptual art, as commonly understood, attempted a fundamental restructuring of the viewer's relationship to the art object. First, its critique of systems of representation and presentation pitched art making toward the dematerialization of the object, thereby placing less value on the perceptual codes through which art is traditionally received. This strategy sought to challenge the autonomous value placed on objects, which value is, in turn, connected to cultural ways of looking. Second, conceptual art privileged linguistic, informational, and philosophical systems over materialist modes of production, making communication, performance, documentation, process, actions, and the world outside the studio part of the intensive phenomenology of process. It should be added, however, that this understanding of conceptual art—in view of alternative information that has since become available—is only a partial account. Still, there is a reality—hegemonic or not—that is not so easily evaded.

My task, then, is to examine how this understanding of conceptualism relates or corresponds to the fundamental philosophical questions of African systems of signification. And we find that in classical African art, conceptualism would seem oxymoronic. While many African cultures produced exquisite objects, many of which clearly permitted early Western modernists to explore different forms of representation through spatial disembodiment, it bears remarking that African objects were never ends in themselves, nor did they acquire any form of autonomy as sculpture through their objecthood. While in Western art the cycle of art is completed in the aesthetic realm of display, in African traditions this finale is achieved through a desublimination strategy that perpetually displaces the object and places greater significance on nonvisual codes and performative actions, particularly through linguistic puns and aphoristic utterances. By repeatedly making contingent the status of the object as an autonomous signifier, the artwork functions within a fluid system of exchanges and relationships among object, artist, and audience.

In African art, two things are constantly in operation: the work and the idea of the work. These are not autonomous systems. One needs the other and vice versa. A paraphrase of an Igbo idea will clarify this relationship: where there is something standing which can be seen, there is something else standing next to it which cannot be seen but which accompanies the object. In its material basis, African art is object bound, but in its meaning and intention, it is paradoxically anti-object and antiperceptual, bound by the many ways of conveying ideas whereby speech or oral communication is highly valued. The work of an artist such as Frédéric Bruly Bouabré is an extension of this idea. And if Bouabré sought to put his words and ideas on paper, there is a clear ideological motivation for doing so. Yet evidence of the dematerialized object does not in itself mean that the object is not valued or that the culture of visual memory is deadened by the weight of sight. I certainly cannot identify a self-reflexivity in which artists deliberately sought to remove their work from functioning on the visual level. More to the point, in African art there is an interpellation of the object and language.

While the argument laid out so far would seem to ground conceptualism in the classical art of Africa, contemporary practice is actually a much trickier and even contradictory enterprise. The conceptual work of the Senegalese group Laboratoire Agit-Art and the South African artists included in this exhibition was never directed at maintaining a relationship with older African philosophical systems, as in Bouabré's case. In many ways, they deploy the same conceptualist strategies prevalent in the West. The reason for this perhaps is their shared relationship with concepts of modernity. But this is where the comparison ends, since the motivations supporting each strategy were different and the results sought were widely divergent. Malcolm Payne, for example, resorted to conceptualist tactics—dematerialization, language works, and a process he calls "confusion acts"—as a response to political conditions under apartheid. In African conceptualism, it is crucial to acknowledge the role of politics and responses to political institutions by artists operating under dictatorships.

As far as I can tell, there has never existed anything that can be definitively declared a conceptual "movement" in Africa, at least one in which everybody agrees as to its parameters. A sustained investigation has yielded only a few artists, and in the case of Laboratoire Agit-Art, a single group. Hence, conceptualism in Africa is a practice associated with scattered, isolated, and solitary examples and never blossomed into a full-fledged artistic discourse. Along with the received definitions of conceptualism as propagated by the Euro–North American axis, the mid-1960s has often been "universally" accepted as its point of periodization and entrance into "art world" currency. For the artists considered here, the conceptualist moment begins in the early 1970s.

Laboratoire Agit-Art: Excavating the Social and the Political in the Postcolony

The 1960s was the moment of Africa's emergence, a decade of incredible political, social, and cultural ferment. As many countries agitated for and gained independence from years of debilitating colonial domination by Europe, it is fair to say that they shared a political context connected to the processes of decolonization and the struggle against Western hegemonic influence. Throughout Africa, the urgent political and ideological questions of the postindependent nation-state, accelerated and pressurized by rapid urbanization, gave rise to new concepts of identity and the individual. Linked to this sociopolitical complexity was the tense relationship between ideas of modernity and a nationalistic sense of tradition and culture. At one end of the continent, a Pan-Africanist notion of modernity, led by Ghana's first prime minister, Kwame Nkrumah, and armed with scientific socialism, became a ready-made context from which the significant reformulation of Africanism was proposed. In North Africa, the Suez Canal crisis launched Gamal Abdel Nasser's Pan-Arab movement. Nasser's aim, like Nkrumah's in Ghana, was to rally unity against Western imperialism.

But by the mid-1970s, the political transformation that swept the colonial powers out of Africa was in crisis. The prospects of, and euphoria over, the social and political reconstruction of the independent countries had dimmed considerably as a series of dictatorships and repressive regimes entered the scene. It is within this troubled era of the postcolony that the most significant expression of avant-gardism, and a practice that can be labeled *conceptual*, would emerge.

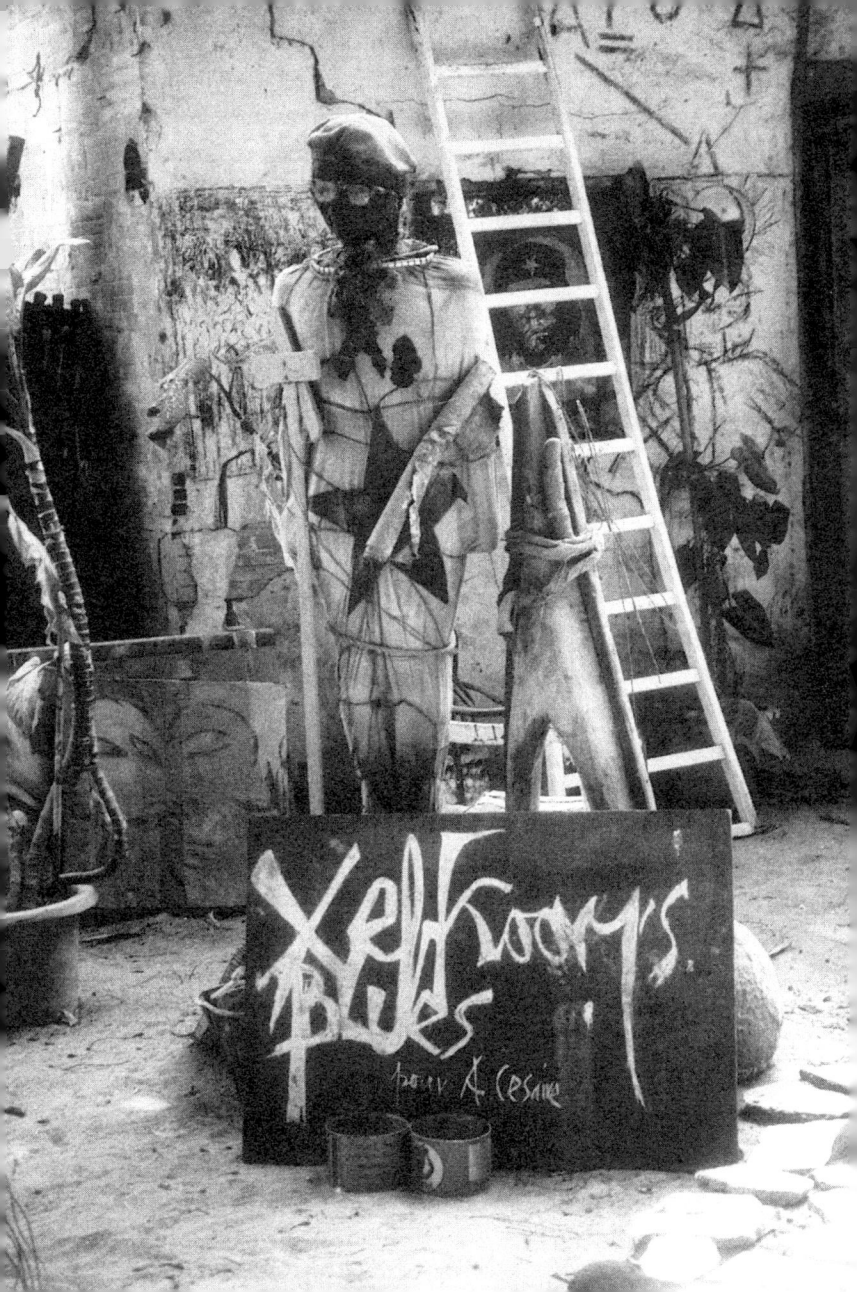

The Dakar-based Laboratoire Agit-Art was founded in 1973–74 by an interdisciplinary group of artists, writers, filmmakers, performance artists, and musicians. Laboratoire's aim was to transform the nature of artistic practice from a formalist, object-bound sensibility to practices based on experimentation and agitation, process rather than product, ephemerality rather than permanence, political and social ideas rather than aesthetic. Audience participation was of paramount importance to the group's work, which privileged communicative acts over the embodied object. Neither utopian nor self-referential, Laboratoire grounded its actions in the immediate sociopolitical situation.

Whether or not the group was aware of similar practices in the West, Laboratoire's position on art after the object is supremely consistent with Lucy Lippard's assertion that conceptual art was "emerging from two directions: art as idea and art as action."[1] In this sense, according to Ima Ebong, Laboratoire Agit-Art

> has attempted nothing less than a reshaping of both the language of Senegalese art and the terms on which artistic production occurs in that country. . . . The group engages aspects of Western modernism, but it concerns itself with the conceptual ideologies of the avant-garde rather than with Modernist formalism. Its tactics of provocation and agitation in keeping with its name, suggest a connection with the Western anti-art performance aesthetic. These artists work outside the government-sponsored system of galleries and museums, distancing their collaborative creations from the painting on canvas, an art form subject to a deeply rooted system of commodity control.[2]

An important precursor to Laboratoire Agit-Art can be found in the work of Nigerian musician, performer, political activist, and social iconoclast Fela Aníkúlápó Kuti. From the mid-1960s, Fela's relentless critique of the postcolonial state and his challenge to the corrupt political order were exemplary links to the strategies later adopted by the group. Throughout his career, which included founding a political party and running for president in 1979 (before being disqualified by the military regime), Fela never made a distinction between his music, lifestyle, and political resistance. Revered by the public and constantly censored by the government, in the early 1970s Fela declared his complex of buildings in Lagos—living quarters, a nightclub, and a recording studio—an independent territory, which he named Kalakuta

Republic. All actions, he stated (especially as related to drugs and sex), were legal in his republic, and all applicable Nigerian laws declared null and void.

In 1977 two members of Laboratoire Agit-Art, El Hadji Sy and Issa Samb (aka Joe Ouakam), visited Kalakuta Republic. According to Issa, they were drawn by Fela's courage and his avant-gardism, which went well beyond mere aesthetic reaction.[3] Laboratoire's focus on the impermanent, contingent character of actions informed by a critique of institutional power "corresponds in great part to this notion of the socialization of an aesthetic, in the form of an activist avant-garde that inserts itself within the wider cultural discourse of Senegal but refuses to follow its institutional and formal criteria."[4] This aggressively contextual relationship to regimes of legitimation and power distinguishes Laboratoire Agit-Art from many other African groups of the same period which were operating within a proto-modernist framework directed at recovering lost origins, rather than problematizing the meaning of "origin" in the broader analysis of contemporary culture in the postcolony.

Signs and Systems: Frédéric Bruly Bouabré

While the practices of Laboratoire Agit-Art were concerned with communication through the "socialization of an aesthetic" and activism against the postcolonial state, Frédéric Bruly Bouabré's work is embedded in the traditional conceptual issues of classical African art. His interest in signs and systems, language and symbology, subjectification over representation, vision over sight, classification, documentation, lists, codification, etymology, archival practices, and experimentation with written text as opposed to the production of images—all are related to his attentive transcription of the oral culture of his people, the Bété.

Bouabré was born in 1923 in Zépréguhé, Ivory Coast. Originally a translator and colonial informant for Western anthropologists and ethnographers, in 1948 he was convinced by a vision to abandon this work and dedicate himself to recording, transcribing, and translating the rapidly disappearing oral culture of the Bété. According to the dictates of his vision, Bouabré christened himself Sheik Nadro (One Who Does Not Forget), and his activities shifted completely and permanently to that of taxonomist and artist. Language, for Bouabré, is the supreme tool for preserving memory and reconstructing history, and also serves as a model of representation through which ideas and the everyday life of a dynamic society can be explored and explained. This commitment to instrumentalizing language ultimately led to his invention of a Bété alphabet. His quest, it seems, is to

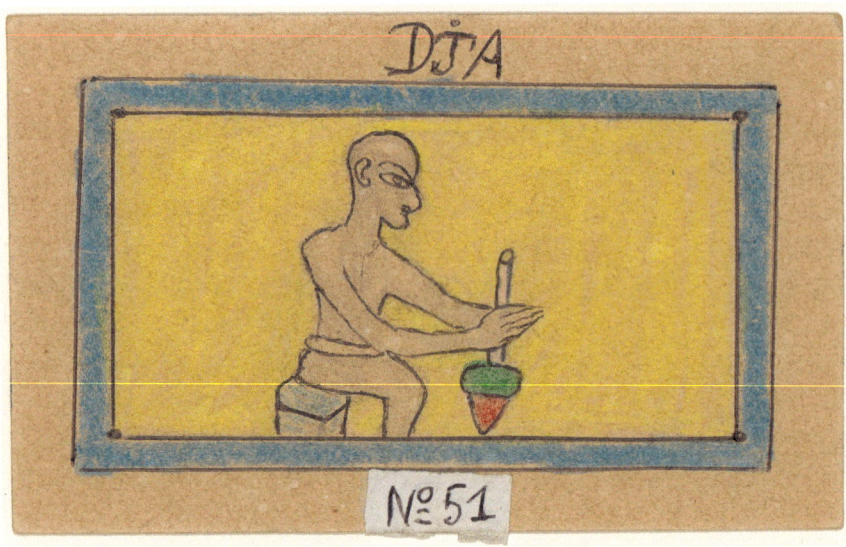

8.2 Frédéric Bruly Bouabré, *DJA N° 51*, from *Alphabet Bété*, 1990. Colored pencil, pencil, and ballpoint pen on board, 9.8 × 14.9 cm. Jean Pigozzi African Art Collection, Geneva. Gift of Jean Pigozzi. Digital Image © 2023, Museum of Modern Art, New York / Scala, Florence.

make transparent the meanings buried in obscure phenomena, to make them available as source material for the writing of history. Bouabré is a decipherer of dreams, of images that hover at the edge of consciousness. He is equally a cosmologist of signs and numbers, a taxonomist of ethnographic knowledge, a recorder of his people's history.

In Bouabré's work, there is a cabalistic attention to the structure of numbers and words, their multiple associative meanings and permutations used to delve into the murky depths of the unconscious. He proposes theories and explanations, constructs maps, compiles indexes, writes compendia. He has created a pictographic alphabet of more than 450 characters, dedicated to excavating and preserving the disappearing oral history of his people. Bouabré's unique narrative form, composed on Tarot-like cards, often combines text and image in a detailed elaboration of complex systems of communication.

However, Bouabré does not only make images in the quasi-naive form that has led many to view him as some kind of mystic of the primeval African world, or as an untutored curiosity. For almost fifty years, he has produced an astonishing array of books on classical African systems of representation, for instance, *Le langage des symboles africains dans les musées* (The language of African symbols in the museum, 1975), *Le calendrier du "monde noir" d'origine (Bété)* (*The calendar of the "Black World" of [Bété] origin*, 1982), *Le musée du visage africain* (*The museum of the African face*, 1975), etc. But the singular character of his work lies in his sensitivity to the most mundane elements. For example, he sees in discarded leaves of kola nuts and orange rinds signs and meanings that could be transposed to readable visual propositions. As an archivist and deconstructionist, he has studied the staggering meanings of scarifications on African faces, revealing them to be as much a linguistic form as a communal rite of passage.

The Language Project of Rachid Koraïchi

Born in Algeria but now living in exile in Tunisia, Rachid Koraïchi has relentlessly produced works in which he utilizes the Arabic script to delineate urgent political questions. Like the classical forms of Islamic art, Koraïchi's art is devotional but resistant to ideological fundamentalism. Spare and austere, his works are rendered on expansive sheets of paper, fields of black text on white laid out in alternating vertical and horizontal bands that surge, deviate, retreat, invert, detour, and veer all over the page like a musical score. The structure of Koraïchi's work is both graphic and calligraphic, expository and nonsensical, what Abdel Kebir Khatibi characterized as the "metamorphosis of the visible . . . these transmutations, these translations from one sign system to another, one image to another . . . a spatial paradigm oriented towards all languages, from pictographs to a form of writing resembling ideographs, by way of Arabic graphic (here exquisite), whether it be legible or illegible, whether it be inverted or even rove in all directions . . . as if seeking escape from the confines of the unframed images."[5]

Yet Koraïchi's art is not to be reduced to writing alone. His investment in signs and symbols means also that he has worked assiduously to decompose the script, to turn its cursive elegance into personal codes and concrete poetry. It would appear that with this decomposition, Koraïchi writes on the margins of his own psychic exposition, sublimating his public political concern into the limits of the individual voice. His program is often both romantic and grand, as in his banners of gold-decorated texts that may seem like propaganda productions. Or it can be caustic and pensive, tough and combative, melancholic and mournful, as in his responses to political injustice and exile.

Throughout a career that has spanned at least three decades, Koraïchi has set out a rigorous intellectual program from which he simultaneously

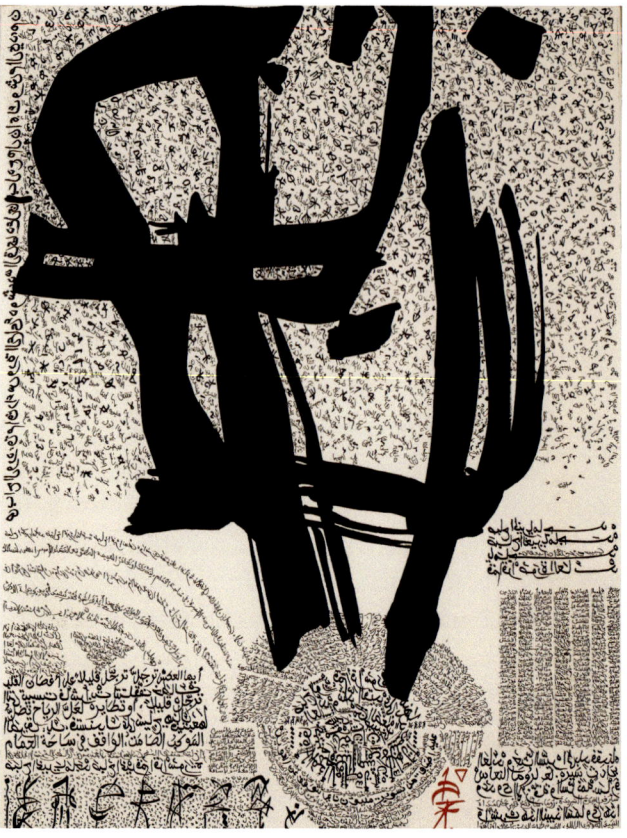

8.3 Rachid Koraïchi, *A Nation in Exile: Hymne Gravé*, 1981, etching, 76 × 56 cm, edition of twenty-five. Published in *A Nation in Exile* (Amman: Darat al Funun, Abdul Hameed Shoman Foundation, 1997). © Rachid Koraïchi. Courtesy of the artist and October Gallery, London.

works inside and outside the parameters of institutional authority. His drawings and writings, at once lyrical and iconoclastic, borrow from classical Islamic texts and the work of contemporary writers and poets. His attentiveness to language as the repository of individual and collective action is manifested in his adoption of both traditional lyrics and subversive political rhetoric to critique the repressive regimes of his region. Yet Koraïchi is not a heretic, nor is he interested in that ugly, stereotypical image of Islam as fundamentalist, obdurate to new forms of discourse. He comes from a tradition of "enlightened Islam," which in recent years has begun to gather steam in many Islamic countries where the subject of Islam's ethical humanism is vigorously debated.

Still, in encountering Koraïchi's work in the realm of contemporary art, how do we resist the temptation to read it as decorative motif and not language? Because non-Roman-derived script may be confused with the decorative (what I will call the recourse to the sign as calligraphy), it is often difficult to assess the proper place of art that works inside its formal basis. In the context of this exhibition, then, Koraïchi's work is somewhat of a paradox. It raises the question of what to do with works which, if we strictly adhere to the judgment of classical conceptual matrices in Europe and the United States, both understand and deracinate that judgment. This stems from the fact that what may be appreciated as conceptual in Islamic art— especially in its relationship to text (calligraphy) and language (discourse) as the fundamental basis of both representation and signification—is more in tune with the tradition of, as opposed to rebellion against, the material- ized image. But if the meaning of the sign is contained in the text, in the sublimity of language rather than in the image—particularly with regard to the Islamic aniconic mandate, which sublimates the representation of the human form into rapturous devotional songs and words of the Prophet—how can we then characterize the work of an artist such as Koraïchi, an artist who seemingly has obeyed this rule as conceptual, when the very problem- atic conceptualism sets for itself is an insistent philosophical and anarchic program intent on destroying such authority? First it would be important to understand that the reading of works by artists like Koraïchi presents a problem not only within this context, but also for the larger context of that rigid body known as the Western canon.

The rendering of "pure conceptualism" in the reductive vocabulary of institutional critique and language systems as the procedural condition of understanding art after the image must then also contend with works like Koraïchi's. His attitude from the beginning has been both political and personal, often veering far from hard resistance to celebratory, incantatory poetry. Over the years he has worked in collaboration with some of the most brilliant contemporary Arab writers of his generation, including the great Palestinian poet Mahmoud Darwish. His work with literature favors delicate and complex meditations over reactive protest. Yet it is clear that Koraïchi's work is set along the edges of a corpus of art and writing that not only compares with the Western canon, but also without which what we call the history of the West would not be possible.

South Africa

Until the official end of apartheid in 1994, South Africa suffered under an often violently enforced system of racial segregation and was for years cul- turally isolated from the rest of the world. The work of the South African artists in this exhibition—Willem Boshoff, Malcolm Payne, and Kendell

8.4 Willem Boshoff, page from *Kykafrikaans*, 1980. Soft-cover book, ninety-five A4 pages, an anthology of concrete poems published by Pannevis Publishers, Johannesburg, 1980. Courtesy of Willem Boshoff and Ruth and Marvin Sackner Archive of Concrete and Visual Poetry, Miami.

Geers—must therefore be considered in the light of this unique history. The reason for such an examination is not to fetishize what is obvious about South Africa's historical memory and its exile from the rest of Africa, but because of the ways in which the work of these artists critically implicates and interrogates that history.

Willem Boshoff's conceptual practice is an elaborate effort dedicated to the study of ignorance, that is, pushing to the point of dissolution the idea that the world is knowable. Imprisoned by South African authorities for his refusal to serve in the military (the micrographic work *Kleinpen II* was produced in prison as a way to maintain mental equilibrium), Boshoff considers rational knowledge a useless mechanism for mapping its revelation. Described as an orthodox conceptualist, in the sense that he keeps, in Gerardo Mosquera's apt phrase, a clean concentration on language, Boshoff finds in obscure and obsolete words a way to construct a map that denies sight but empowers knowledge.[6]

Boshoff compiles extensive dictionaries and encyclopedias of names, words, plants. The laborious exactitude of his compositions, collocations, and accumulations does not operate on the thrill of esotericism, but on the recognition of the vastness of the world and the ideological systems that circumscribe it. Paradoxically, Boshoff insists he is not interested in teaching: "I write dictionaries of words that I hope nobody will understand."[7] The very invention of these dictionaries, far from reanimating interest in what they seek to represent or reveal, is first intended as a detour, a way of denying the rationalist's persistent will to knowledge. Mosquera has characterized this process as a kind of imaginary travel: the artist in his room, ruminating, chewing over, constructing and deconstructing, calculating, as "he stages the relations between words, meanings, and visual and tactile images, and discusses language and its material base and representation. . . . Possessed by insomnia . . . he navigates dictionaries, and tries to open routes through the oceans of language."[8] Here language becomes buried in language, referring only to itself.

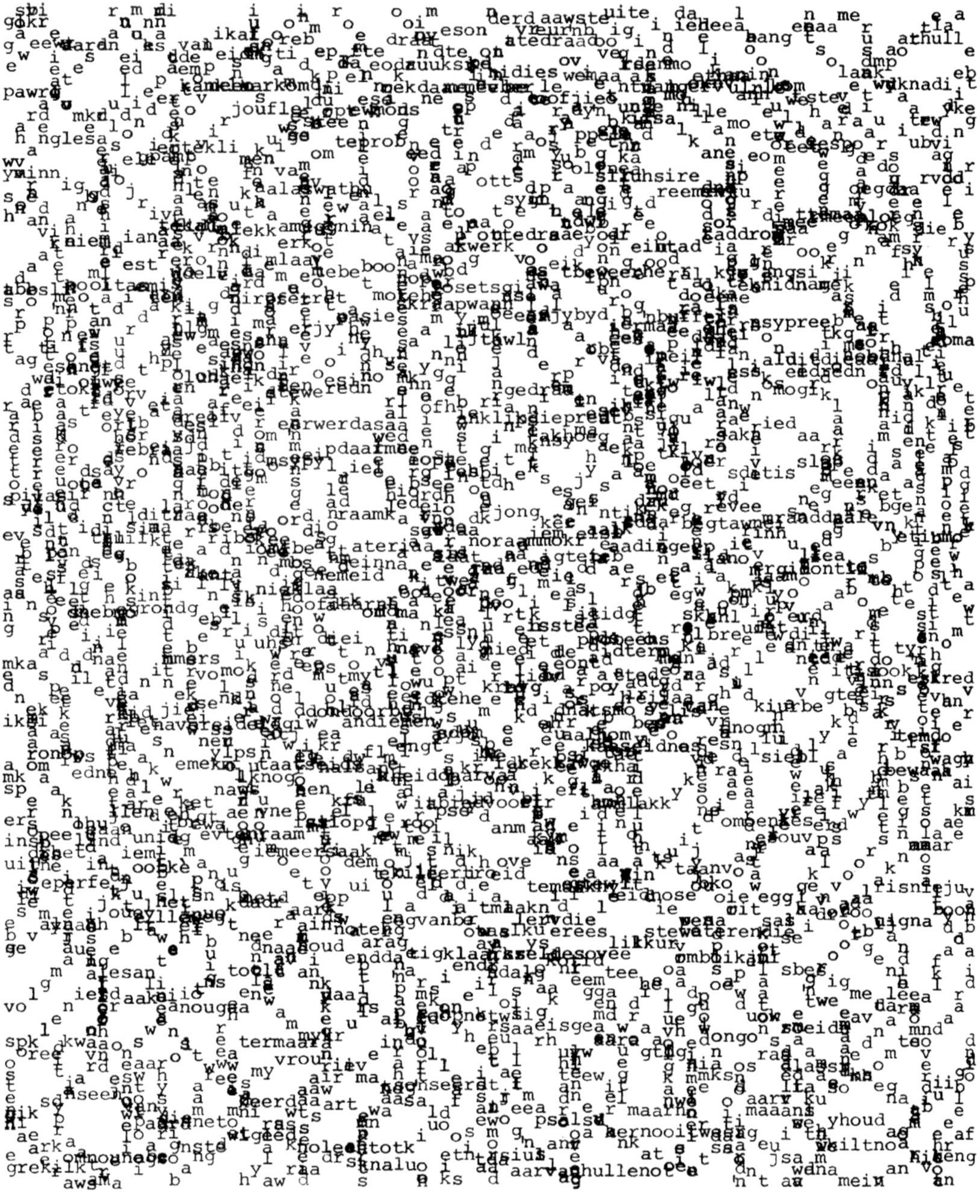

But Boshoff is not content to leave things as they are. He seeks other strategies for making available what words represent, how their semantic meaning might be reconstituted. His study of linguistics and Wittgensteinian philosophy led him to explore other ways of rendering words into pulsating signs, resulting in *Kykafrikaans* (1980), a serial work of concrete poetry and his most sustained inquiry into the nature of words and obsolescence.

If Boshoff, like Bouabré, keeps a clean concentration on language, Malcolm Payne's very complex and critical work keeps a clean concentration on the political and subversive. Here the political functions not on a literal level, but as an act of contamination. Rather than responding to an oppressive regime via the clichéd fist-and-guns of the revolutionary artist, Payne engages in acts of subterfuge by penetrating ideological spaces, "carefully contrived confusion . . . [as] the only weapon to keep my creative impetus vaguely alive."[9] This struggle to maintain creative independence has typically been perceived as anarchic. For the 1973 Aquarius Art Festival in Durban, for instance, he proposed to explode underwater a huge quantity of red dye as part of the festivities marking the Afrikaner celebration of Blood River Day, during which they commemorate their defeat of the Zulus. According to Payne, "The idea was further nuanced to include the ultimate irony, to sell the idea to the organizers, explaining to them that they could achieve for themselves and followers an enhanced spiritual and religious experience if the river ran red."[10] The organizers rejected the proposal.

Of all the African work included in this exhibition, Payne's early projects seem conclusively conceptual, in their orientation and rejection of the material base of what he called "an overdose of Greenbergian and late Caro modernism."[11] This he endured as a student at St. Martin's School of Art in London in 1973. Partly because of his early exposure to the critical discourse of Western conceptualism, and his contact with the work of artists like [Joseph] Beuys, the practices of Art & Language, and others who were seeking broader spaces for their ideational propositions, Payne sought ways to transpose some of their theories to the situation in his own country.

Upon his return to a South African art scene still in thrall to Clement Greenberg, Payne turned increasingly to performance, using endurance as a metaphor for the individual's quest to transcend the political and intellectual fragmentation imposed by apartheid. Payne was among the first young artists to explore systems of representation of the self, and the state's overwhelming control over defining that self. Identity as an intense site of

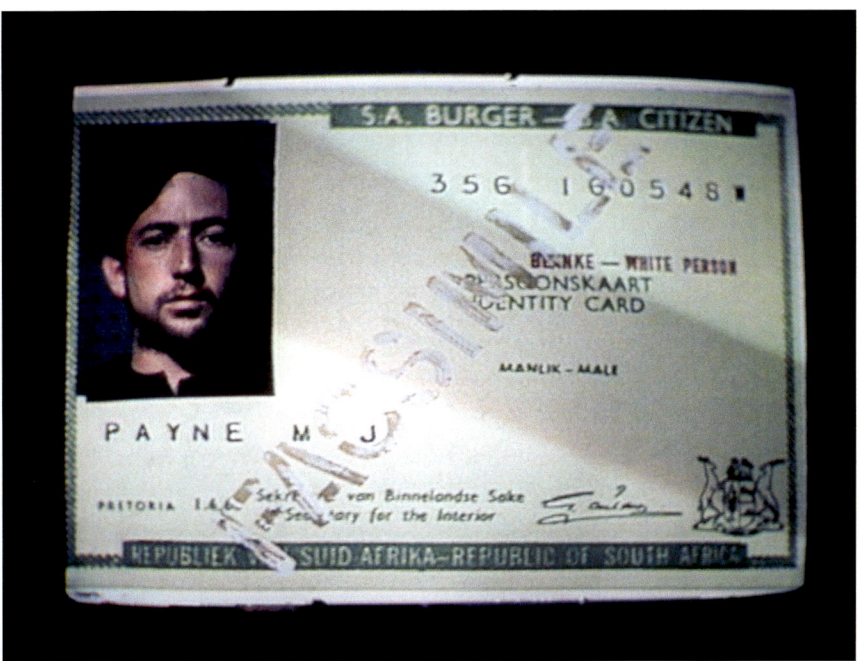

8.5 Malcolm Payne, *Past, Present, Future, 1973,*
1973. Still from videotape, included in the exhibition *Global Conceptualism: Points of Origin,
1950s–1980s* (1999), Queens Museum, New York.
Image courtesy of Queens Museum. Videotape collection of the artist.

subjectification thus became a basis for resistance. Appropriating the tools
of surveillance, Payne began to meld video, slide projections, photographs,
and facsimiles of his body and face into a conceptually sophisticated practice, the goal of which was to deny the state's final right of adjudication in
the construction of identity. Payne's intense meditation on the political possibility of subversion laid the groundwork for many artists who would delve
into similar questions twenty years later.

One such artist is Kendell Geers. Following Payne's stellar example,
Geers has channeled his provocative and vigilant sensibility into an art that
acts as an incendiary device within systems of representation. If art is activity, then Geers has made his own existence the signal vector of its convergence, completely blurring the distinction between his life and art, and, by
extension, self-regulation and institutional administration. Hence, Geers's
art is an activity located not inside the solitude of the studio but in the rough-
and-tumble world of actions, of political, social, and cultural engagement. In

1995 Geers was invited to exhibit his work at the Johannesburg Art Gallery, the institutional showcase of South African art, its classical architectural design by Edwin Lutyens a reminder of the country's ugly and continuing colonial domination. Rather than making anything that might be construed as an object or merit consideration as an artwork, Geers offered *Title Withheld (Boycott)*, in which he emptied an entire room within the museum of its contents. With this attack on the institution (and, by extension, some of his fellow artists), Geers asserted that art could refuse and resist the ideology of museological practice. Thus, the seemingly empty room questioned the pervasive modernist hunger for market-oriented postcolonial objects. As an amplification of this debate, *Title Withheld (Boycott)* returns us to the vault of the museum, to its ethnographic storage rooms and holding docks, where art and cultural objects await dispersal into the myriad networks of institutional recontextualization. It is precisely what has been cleared and evacuated from the gallery's walls that is the subject of this intensely aware intervention.

Moving away from Geers's long-standing relationship with the traditions of the modernist avant-garde (an example is his alteration of his birthday to May 1968 as a gesture of solidarity with the students who initiated the summer of civil disobedience in Europe), we return to his position via postmodernism as it neatly converges on the question of identity. In *Untitled (ANC, AVF, AWB, CP, DP, IFP, NP, PAC, SACP)* (1993–94), a work whose genesis is directly linked to the political chaos and violence that ravaged South Africa in the months leading to the country's first democratic elections, Geers staged an elaborate set of political actions in the wake of the murder of a member of the Inkatha Freedom Party. On July 19, 1993, the day of the killing, in defense of the political rights of the individual within an intolerant political culture, Geers decided to join all the official parties of South Africa. He would comment that, in this way, it would be impossible to lose. Of course, this response to the institutionalization of politics through party affiliation is an ironic one, for it is the very basis of belonging that produces the kind of rigid fetishization of identity that continues to plague his country with violence. By joining all these parties—culminating on February 7, 1994, when the ultra-right-wing Afrikaner Weerstands beweging (AWB) issued him an identity card—Geers sought not only to claim all these false identities, but to mark them as suspect beyond measure.

As we begin to sift through the material that accompanies this exhibition, we will find that new networks and connections will emerge, some

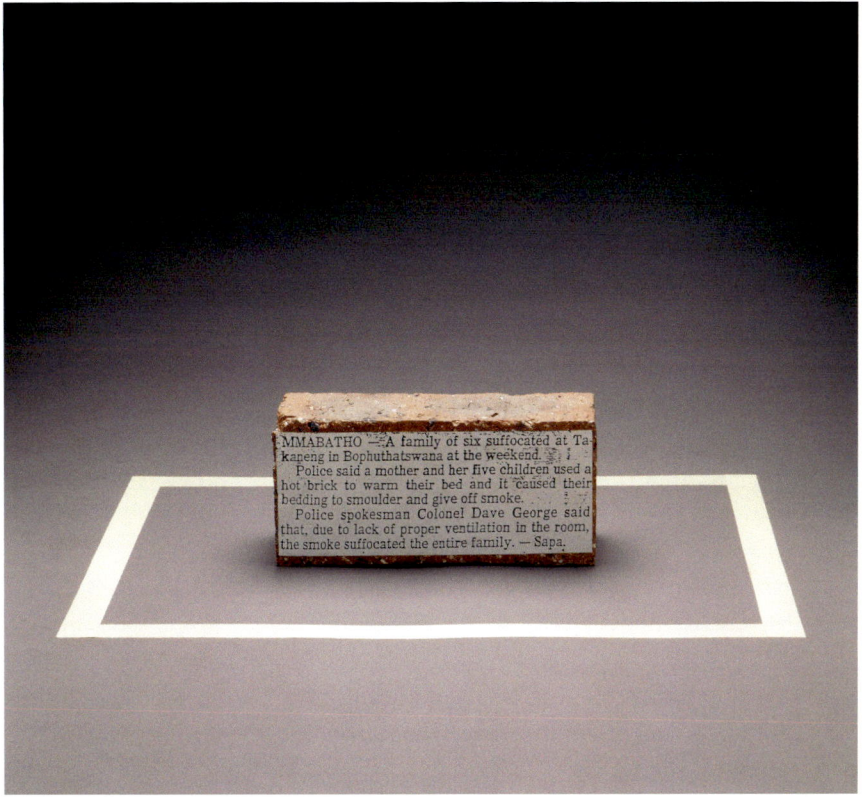

8.6. Kendell Geers, *Brick,* 1988. Xerox on
brick, tape, 10 × 22 × 17 cm. Private collection.
© Kendell Geers. Courtesy of the artist.

familiar, some obscure. In this way, *Global Conceptualism: Points of Origin* will
have accomplished its goal of illuminating the forces that propelled artists
to find a detour and, in effect, change the ground rules regulating art production and the very language of art itself. At their most critically aware,
the African artists considered here have met those challenges, and the richness and acuity of their interventions have left their own indelible mark.
Perhaps now we can begin to embrace other accounts of conceptualism that
do not always adhere to the strict regimes of orthodox conceptual art, but
document the multivalent strategies and diverse motivations behind its
appearance globally. This section on African conceptualism should thus be
seen as a source for future investigation, which no doubt will uncover other
practices that I have overlooked.

1   [*Ed. note:* Lucy Lippard, *Six Years: The Dematerialisation of the Art Object from 1966 to 1972* (1973; repr. Berkeley: University of California Press, 1997), ix.]

2   Ima Ebong, "Negritude: Between Mask and Flag, Senegalese Cultural Ideology and the 'Ecole de Dakar,'" in *Africa Explores: 20th Century African Art*, ed. Susan Vogel (New York: Center for African Art, 1991), 198.

3   Issa Samb, interview by the author, Dakar, April 1998.

4   Clémentine Deliss, "7 + 7 = 1: Seven Stories, Seven Stages, One Exhibition," in *Seven Stories about Modern Art in Africa*, ed. Clémentine Deliss (Paris: Flammarion, 1995), 19.

5   Abdel Kebir Khatibi, in Mahmoud Darwish, Rachid Koraïchi, Hassan Massoudy, and Abdel Kebir Khatibi, *A Nation in Exile* (Amman: Darat al Funun, Abdul Hameed Shoman Foundation, 1997). [*Ed. note:* These remarks paraphrase Khatibi's main argument in his essay in his volume.]

6   [*Ed. note:* Gerardo Mosquera, "Important and Exportant," in *Trade Routes: History and Geography—2nd Johannesburg Biennale*, ed. Matthew de Bord and Roy Bester (Johannesburg: Greater Johannesburg Metropolitan Council, 1997), 270.]

7   Quoted in Ashraf Jamal, "Willem Boshoff: Blind Alphabet," in *Object Lessons* (São Paulo: 23rd São Paulo Bienal, 1996), 4. Exhibition pamphlet.

8   Mosquera, "Important and Exportant," 270.

9   Malcolm Payne, "Fault Lines—Breakwater Conference," unpublished speaker's notes for a visual presentation at the Breakwater Conference, Cape Town, 1996.

10 Payne, "Fault Lines."

11 Payne, "Fault Lines."

Between Worlds

Postmodernism and African Artists
in the Western Metropolis

Originally published in *Atlántica: Internacional Revista de las Artes*, no. 12 (Winter 1995–96): 119–33, this essay was republished in *Reading the Contemporary: African Art from Theory to the Marketplace*, edited by Olu Oguibe and Okwui Enwezor (London: Institute for International Visual Arts; Cambridge, MA: MIT Press, 1999), 245–75.

AT THE END OF THE CENTURY, studies of postmodernism and critical writing on questions of identity and artistic production thoroughly distance themselves from the spaces occupied by African artists in the Western metropolis. In the rare cases of contact between what so far has been identified as the "center" and the subaltern, the zones of enunciation are so fraught with gross misreadings and the most miserable translations of work by these artists that it seems nothing could possibly mediate the gap that separates the two worlds. This misapprehension and misrecognition are exacerbated by a gaze that perpetually fixes the cultural production of contemporary African artists, if not in the sites of invisibility and nonexistence, then on the periphery of encounters between the public and contemporary representation. This gaze reduces their artistic expression to either the aberrant production of a denativized imagination or to an inferior mimetic exercise in futility. In addressing the basis for this exclusion of African artists from the sites of normativity and the critical silence that surrounds their practice, my interest lies mostly, though not entirely, in those gaps—between worlds—where the potent signs that these artists carry from different localities are translated and ultimately transfigured through relocation into new imaginary constructs of identity, which their new places of domicile constantly deny them.

As metropolitan African artists, Iké Udé, Bili Bidjocka, Olu Oguibe, and Ouattara occupy such a matrix of elision in relation to the Western postmodernist discourse. Of great interest to me is the variety of approaches, the measure of articulateness that they have employed in delineating boundaries and allegiances, modes of representation and production, which both reincorporate them into and disunite them from specific traditions within the realm of contemporary African cultural production. However, this discussion does not approach their work as disinherited from a progressively elusive sense of a triumphant African modernist ethic that ruptures the neocolonial burden of the unrecuperable other. Nor does it view them as representative or exemplary models of knowledge in contemporary African cultural production, in which their individual aesthetic projects revel. They come together on these pages based on that which they represent in the hegemonic imagination: "African artists," working in the interstices of postcoloniality in the Western metropolitan arena.

As such, I am interested in how their ineluctable presence disturbs, disrupts, and problematizes the postcolonial border; how their existence in the postmodern arena embodies the discontinuity of normative assumptions about originary "authenticity" in their work. Labels, as practicing cultural anthropologists know, are necessary evils. They either illuminate or they misname. The latter—in cases where the status of the sovereign narrator is accorded as the divine right of a hegemonic imperative—quite often outdistances the former, particularly where such labeling is a morphological binary that separates mere nags from thoroughbreds. Fundamentally restated along the linear parameters of the Western modernist canon (much more firmly entrenched since the 1930s, and through the era of Greenbergian American aesthetic nationalism), the pull of hierarchy quite naturally offers the sovereign narrator unprecedented power either to contextualize or dismiss, to dissolve all edges and turn variety into an atrophied body of sameness, until the subject dissolves and vanishes. (The collapse of entire "minority" populations into one body known as "Black British" is but one example of this taxonomic game playing that reductively homogenizes identities while obliterating their disparate and composite social realities.)

If one were to believe the highly efficient Western critical apparatus, as it has existed within the major metropolises of the Western art world, it would seem that no African artist of consequence exists within its sphere of knowledge. To question such views remains, of course, our critical obligation; a clear opportunity for self-fashioning, self-representation, and hermeneutic recovery. On the other hand, in the crude climate of the current multicultural war, such contestation of history through recovery plays differently in the camps of two very self-interested parties. For the neoconservatives, with their antique, crusade-flavored, paleo-Christian fanaticism, placing the marginalized in the oculus of critical knowledge is seen not only as a travesty but also as an assault on received notions of "quality" and, more significantly, as heretical. For the self-serving liberal critical establishment, still clinging to outmoded models of Marxist liberal triumphalism, such knowledge, however truncated, represents an epiphany. It will be important to hold on to these two sets of views, because art historical and critical judgments of art and artists in the West constantly play themselves out in the well-regulated and predictable interstices where Eurocentric hegemonic power-mongering meets and colonizes the contributions of non-Western cultures; those cultures that, in polite euphemism, disappear into the opaque rubric of the "other." But more significantly, because the comets of artists whom critical amnesia wishes to narrate out of history refuse to crash in the arctic wasteland of inconsequence. Under the demanding imperialistic gaze of twentieth-century Western art history, modernism's self-arrogated centrality and exclusionism become the great totems that bear the imprimaturs of this legacy of erasure, which marginalizes as it appropriates. This is an old story, yet it is one that remains relevant if only to remind us of the distasteful task of continuously questioning not only that history but also the ethnographic paradigms that it appends to the subjects it marginalizes.

In developing this text, my main concern is how to resurrect the figure of the metropolitan African artist as she/he presently exists in that less-than-hospitable site. I use the word *resurrect* not only as a means of reframing the marginal status of these artists, but also to examine the constricted cultural and social space under which they have existed for so long. Because nowhere is the ethnographic trope of the "other" more transparent, resilient, and stalwart than in the seemingly plural environment of the Western metropolis. And nowhere have we been called on to mediate on the uses of marginality as a weapon of enclosure and exclusion, and as a critical/structural construct, more than in the site of the Western metropolis. For it is there that the cultures of the so-called margins are more visible, and dangerously more transgressive by the sheer force of their articulation of a difference that the center does not already own. Such transgressiveness, often commodified and reduced to spectacle, to the carnivalesque, makes the marginalized culture more nakedly vulnerable to structures that incessantly sanction its marginality, its co-option, displacement, and dispersement into the center. I am thinking here of those moments of contact when the language of the margin is appropriated and abstracted into the larger body, which denies its specificity and concreteness. This denial comes into sharp conflict with what for a decade has been postmodernism's celebration of the inherent fragmentariness, indeterminacy, contingency, and so-called shifting nature of the subaltern universe. It is in this sense that the postmodern Western metropolis, with its centrifugal pull, has always, in the minds of many marginal communities, represented a site of theft, a port of dispossession. It is there that the margin comes face to face with the real threat of erasure and defacement; of being whitewashed for the intense pleasure of those who have the least interest in understanding the marginal's power to name those moments that live in what Homi Bhabha calls the "wordless barrens" of human desire; a desire that is always denied those who have been deauthorized.[1]

Alongside the multiple events engendered by a currently embattled multicultural discourse and by other subaltern spheres in an allegedly more inclusionist postmodernism, the importance of examining the space that African artists occupy must never be underestimated. In the 1990s—the decade that has followed the ascendancy of postmodernism as a prominent critical tool that recognizes the cultural "rights" of the "other," but has thus far organized itself around the axis of a prime canon—a radical revision of the relationship based on the binary structure of the self/other has occurred. Not only does postmodernism position itself as a corrective to the monocular modernist metanarrative and its privileging hierarchy (a model referred to by Hal Foster as "neo-conservative postmodernism"), it also views its discourse—in historical terms—as one that marks a rupture in modernism's self-centered aggrandizement of the artist as author (Foster names this "post-structural postmodernism").[2] Straddling this conflictive divide, postmodernism thus encodes its position as being the prime vessel through which artistic and metaphysical knowledge and meaning necessarily flow. Metaphorically, as well as literally, it casts itself as a sort of cultural relativist instrument, an all-encompassing apparatus that embodies paradigmatic border interpenetrations; one that mediates between the identity of the marginalized and its cultural dominant, the center.

Within this notion of a transcendental postmodernism, we are told, marginalized cultures will be recuperated and recognized in a decentered renarration of nonhegemonic discourse. Furthermore, the postulation is that at every turn of these historical rearrangements of borders, the concerns of "the other" will be given a "fair hearing." Recognition of difference, cultural hybridity, and the apparent instability of identities within postcontemporary (to borrow an absurdity from Fredric Jameson) spheres of production and representation will indeed become semiological emblems of a postindustrial twenty-first-century culture. If this sounds like a kind of postpsychedelic love-in, the truth is that it is, albeit with a few caveats: the Swamis of this commune are academic all-stars from various French, American, and German academies. However, one must raise a note of caution here. For although, on the surface, the radical proposition of the Western postmodernist project seems reformist and therefore appealing, nothing so far in its overtures—which seem too conclusive, too neatly resolved epistemologically—has given us an inkling, as Olu Oguibe had stated, that its dominant perspective and value system will be loosened from the authoritarian grip of a Western historicism hell-bent on shaping its definition.[3] No matter how seductive, the disinterment and recuperation of the so-called margin into the center must also call for the delocalization and decentering of the center. The summary declaration of decentering history consistently proffered on postmodernism's behalf is simply not enough. Homi Bhabha reminds us of this when he writes that in the early 1980s, as "the conceptual boundaries of the West were being busily reinscribed in a clamor of counter texts—transgressive, semiotic, semanalytic, deconstructionist—none [of these texts] pushed those boundaries to their colonial periphery; *to that limit where the West must face a peculiarly displaced and decentered image of itself.*"[4] Of course, that is hardly surprising, experience having taught us that decentering does not necessarily correlate with equality.

The fact remains, however, and is always implicitly stated, that recognition of difference does not in itself connote inclusion nor acceptance. Or as Charles Merewether pertinently asks, "How in this time of recognition of cultural difference, can we appeal to a universality without losing the particularity of that difference that refuses to return us to the plural same, or the incommensurate or irreducible polarities?"[5] Here, Merewether is enacting a vital scenario, for "difference" as posited and circulated through the clogged arteries of the Western postmodernist discourse is never a conjunctive force that impels fresh relationships, nor does it produce new and honest structures through which novel, unencumbered knowledge and meaning can be received, tested, and shared. "Difference," as the character in Jean-Paul Sartre's novel *Nausea* would have put it, is always located in the limited territory of the colonized "other," who when rehabilitated into the "center," which the West occupies, must remain thankful, until his/her usefulness expires like a transit visa. But as we travelers who wear our badges of difference with unremitting pride on the postmodern bandwagon have repeatedly learned, the expiration of one's visa means the termination of tolerance (an idea that the false premise of a visa naturally disallows).

While Western modernity—and by extension postmodernity—was founded on the totalizing project of the Enlightenment, the mastery of reason over the world of spirit, it nevertheless subsists on superstition, forever inventing ghosts to satisfy the needs and demands of its specious status of singularity. Read thus, "difference" in the mind of Western postmodernism carries the authority of an unimpeachable fact whose continuous elaboration must again and again put to service certain bodies, not as surrogates for this phenomenon, but as representatives of the thing itself. In this charade, the authoritative figure of the subject (very much a romantic illusion of Western empiricism) exits the stage of autonomy onto one of metonym—the body of "difference" rediscovered. It will not, however, be a waste of precious time to argue the point that such an elaboration of "difference," which forces into service certain groups of people, desacralizes Western postmodernism's rhetorical pretensions to plurality. Even Jean-François Lyotard's argument that postmodernism deracinates and destroys modernism's pretensions of singularity as a metanarrative fails in the face of its ontological ellipsis.[6]

Our reading of "difference" within this postmodernism, which Lyotard believes to have finally done in modernism, will not be greatly broadened or enhanced if we insert into its definitional zone Fredric Jameson's most instructive and decided conceptualization of "difference." Jameson's Nietzschean argument is that it is "essential to grasp postmodernism not as a style, but rather as a *cultural dominant*, a conception which allows for the presence and coexistence of a range of features."[7] It may interest the reader to learn that the key moment of entrance into the heterogeneous zones of postmodern culture is predicated on these "different yet subordinate features" being allowed "presence" and "coexistence" within such a culture. In other words, they have first to be granted audience in order to speak the essential truths of their existence. One would have granted Jameson his sly manipulation of the terms of this entrance, if he had not compounded what at first could have been thought a misreading of "difference" by stating that "the postmodern is, however, the force field in which very different kinds of cultural impulses—what Raymond Williams has usefully termed 'residual' and 'emergent' forms of cultural production—must make their way. If we do not achieve some general sense of a cultural dominant, then we fall back into a view of present history as sheer heterogeneity, random difference, a coexistence of a host of distinct forces whose effectivity is undecidable."[8] As revealing and fascinating as Jameson's position might appear, even for such a highly respected critical thinker and theorist, it is not surprising nevertheless. The truth, if anyone still cares about such a metaphysical concept, remains that Western postmodernism in relation to other postmodernisms has always aimed at establishing Jameson's "general sense of a cultural dominant." In less subtle terms, this cultural dominant, in its periodization, inscription, and affectivity, can be read as a culture of conquest. Its hegemony allows the West access to those modes of postmodern culture outside its immediate control while not becoming embroiled in a field that represents "sheer heterogeneity [and] random difference."

It is within this corrupt terrain in which power, co-opted either through the means of production—a manifestation of the efficiency of capital ([Michel] Foucault)—or through the means of representation—technological and digital control over information and images ([Jean] Baudrillard)—is maintained and held by the West that many African cultural producers have pitched their tent. For African artists, the Western metropolis, popularly represented as a plural environment in the contemporary imagination, is nothing but a site of displacement and dispersal, diminishment and disintegration. Additionally, a representational disruption in the material culture under which African artists live and practice also marks the Western metropolis as a site of ambivalence and longing, a site in which their faith in secular humanistic philosophies and in the inviolability of their alleged originary traditions is constantly imperiled, to the point of apostasy. This rupture has created a new migratory space that severely tests the contexts of national and diasporic borders of the new postcolony, which simultaneously speaks to a desire of place and the ambivalence of relocation.

Imprecise signals from the postmodernist establishment further throw these ambivalent social spaces into sharp relief, exposing many gaps in need of resolution. Within the realm of signification, the diasporan desire wears the impassive melancholy of exile. It is a fragmented cultural space, a place of desire that is perpetually in flux; always in the process of "becoming," as Chike Aniakor has referred to it.[9] Add to these the resurgent refusal of the benefits of multiculturalism from hard-line American modernist reactionaries and incurable Eurocentrics (Hilton Kramer, Robert Hughes, Harold Bloom, et al.), and we have a deck fully stacked against artists currently operating under the stained and tattered flag of difference. But these artists are hardly defenseless charity cases; they are far from being the obsequious natives who must wait for invitation to pick at leftover scraps on a dinner table long ago plundered by modernism. Through refusal to be patronized, ventriloquized, dismissed, misnamed, or miscategorized, despite the difficult conditions under which they practice, they transgress the boundaries of "otherness": a colonial condition that a reductive postmodernist thinking constantly attempts to refashion under the polite but alien banner of "difference."

Writing about postmodernism's ineffectual collapse of identities into a kind of crude, hard-edged, and immutable hybridity, Anthony Ilona remarks that "the inclination here is always to seek, in the works of these artists, references to problems of nationhood, corrupt dictatorships, neocolonialism, underdevelopment, and so on; a narrative of crises."[10] Essentially, the mark of difference, as has been repeatedly proposed, becomes quite literally undifferentiated from this "narrative of crises." Within this field of representation lies an epistemic doubt as to the value of the presence of these artists in the postmodern discourse. This doubt, which also elides the composite production and contributions of these artists, is thus carried, circulated, and resold in a structurally encoded language that is disciplined by fear, ignorance, and erasure. Since the implicit and adjunct banner under whose nationalistic desires the "other" must necessarily seek residence is a fictive construction that militates against complexity, artists who refuse sanctuary within its borders must then brace themselves for the accusation of not being "native" enough (a charge that will normally come from Eurocentrics) or for not being "authentic" enough (a reversal that usually comes from Africanists).

These accusations make it particularly difficult to read the careers of these artists as genuine and nonderivative contributions to contemporary representation, as well as profoundly testing the critical academies that determine such matters. Claimed by no community of interest (neither in the West nor within their own cultures), these artists seem to have clearly positioned their practices within a liberatory matrix that is oppositional in nature, while at the same time refusing to allow their strategies to harden into a doctrinaire or post-*histoire* essentialism of the agitated "other." By unflinchingly engaging the entire contemporary art world, they evoke what bell hooks has named the "Oppositional Gaze," that contestatory act whereby subjects of imperialist subjugation assert their right of agency through resistance to structures of domination.[11] By problematizing the simplistic binary of the self/other relationships that tend to split down the middle issues of identity and representation, the presence of these artists marks not only an ontological ellipsis, but also questions assumptions that derive from a reading of such identity formation. And since their status as exiles ill affords them roots in any one culture, it seems a mistake simplistically to collapse the space they occupy into a hybridized one. Their relationship to different modes of representation in and outside the West is far more complicated than the term *hybrid* (a troubling notion that calls up images of miscegenation, mongrelization, impurity, and inauthenticity) can explicate.

Multiplicity: The New Boundaries of Difference

In his essay "The New Politics of Difference," Cornel West writes that the distinctive features of the new cultural politics of difference are to trash the monolithic and homogeneous in the name of diversity, multiplicity, and heterogeneity; to reject the abstract, general, and universal in light of the concrete, specific, and particular; and to historicize, contextualize, and pluralize by highlighting the contingent, provisional, variable, tentative, shifting, and changing.[12]

Since persistent border crossings have in many instances prevented contemporary African artists from becoming types reducible to knowledge formed by a crisis of identity, they represent the contingencies of multiplicity foregrounded by the "new politics of difference" while still remaining anchored to specific contexts that propel them into new territories. In fact, the problem of these artists in the West is due more to their grounded, resolute identities as African artists who do not take their contemporary existence for granted through repeated forays into what Manthia Diawara has dubbed the "Kitsch of Blackness," than in their search for an identity.[13] For them the realm of culture represents a plural universe built from a multiplicity of frames that aspire toward the creation of new territories, toward a kind of new boundary of difference. Though the precise grounds for the enunciation of this new boundary of difference remain theoretical at best, still there are conjunctions of diverse cultural signs, in the form of quotations, appropriations, and reappropriations (which are employed in various degrees) in the work of Udé, Bidjocka, Oguibe, and Ouattara. These devices (which are hardly unique) are used less to seek resolution for a specific artistic transcendence than to disrupt the boundaries, categories, and frames that persistently enclose them in marginal economies of production and representation. Far from the naive simplicity that is generally ascribed to work by African artists—who must be primitivized and exoticized so as to be easily commodified, appropriated, and dismissed—the reality is that the

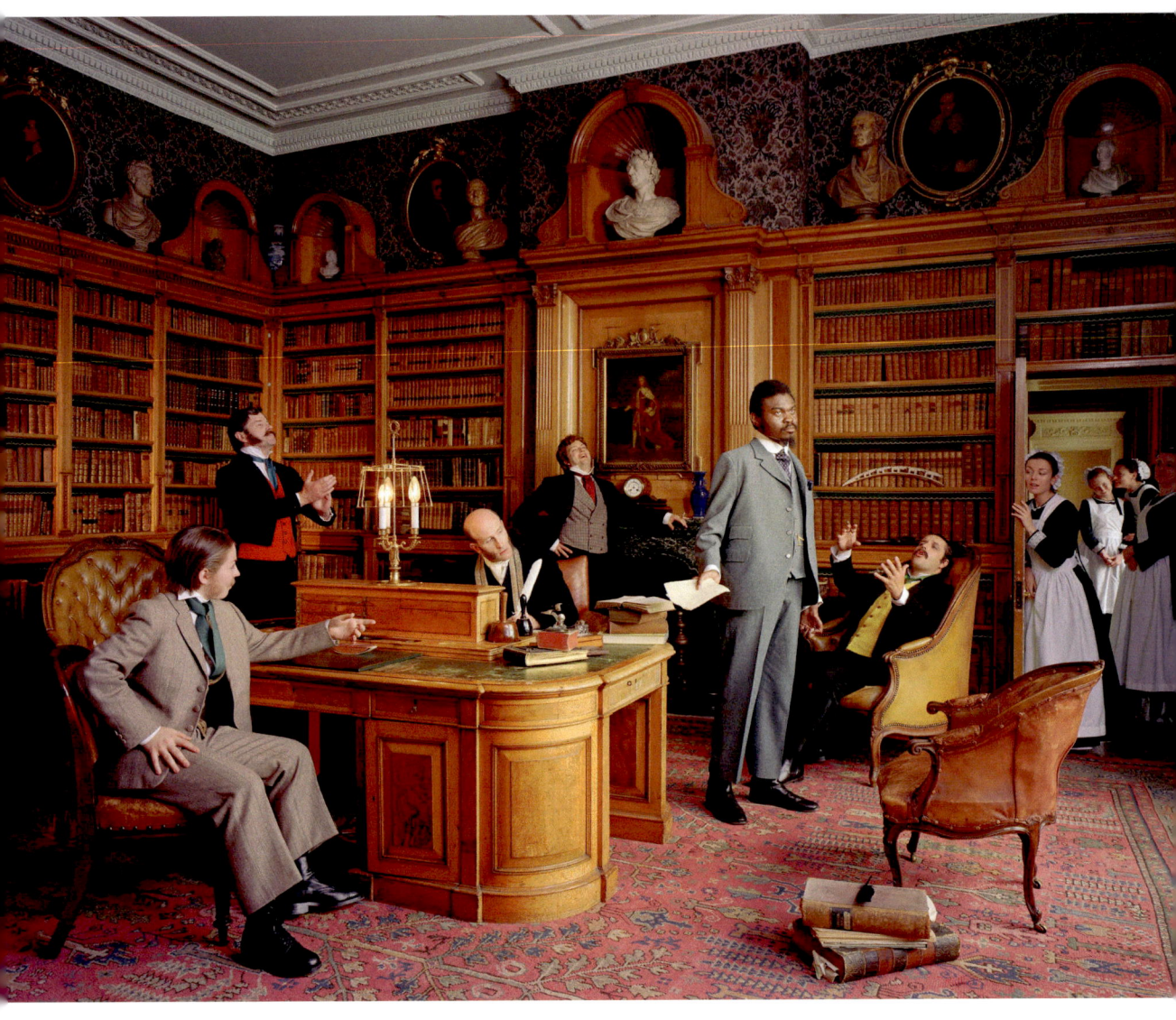

9.1 Yinka Shonibare CBE, *Diary of a Victorian Dandy, 14.00 Hours,* 1998. C-type print, 183×228 cm. ©Yinka Shonibare CBE. Image courtesy of Stephen Friedman Gallery, London. All Rights Reserved, DACS 2025.

work of artists so commodified always carries multiple content and layered meaning. They dislocate the encoded idea of an "authentic" homogeneity, the bastard narrative of a "native" existence that is untouched by a meditative acumen or critical nomenclature.

It is within such an entropic cultural economy (the Foucauldian heterotopia), which parodies and inverts postmodernism's reification of difference, that one obtains the most useful insight into the careers of Udé, Bidjocka, Oguibe, and Ouattara.[14] The work of these four artists and their strategies of production no longer sit easily within the rigid confines that are marked by the dichotomy between tradition and modernity. A different force impels their movement beyond the conscious stream suggested by a post-Kantian reconfiguration of the world.

How, then, may one approach the bold oppositional transgressions of these postmodernist artists in the face of the critical timidity that has been reluctant to recognize how African artists and artists from non-Western centers have reinvigorated the crucial debates with which we will all grapple in the next century? The temptation here will be to draw a map that delineates, in hard-edged, formal routes, such a rehabilitative project, through a labor that relentlessly reproduces the virtues of site of origin and place, and the valorization of difference. The quest, then, calls for an open-ended investigation of each artist, since their vision of the world is simply not reducible to the meager insights that hierarchization and categories allow. By consistently interrogating the spaces that modernism and postmodernism both occupy in the West, through the centrality of an African reality, these artists effectively disable the paradigm of colonial mimicry that can only see in their self-reconstitution the reproduction of the colonial, albeit inferior, ideal rooted in imitation. But one thing is for sure: these are not mimic men. How can they possibly be, when their interventions in the contemporary arena (though unheralded) clearly speak otherwise? To talk, then, of any contemporary representation that entangles itself in the laws of a xenophobic Western art culture, which measures events in tidily marked-out, straight progressions, is not only short-sighted, but also idiotic. If metropolises like Lagos and Bombay represent quintessential postmodern cities, simultaneously existing in that interface between modernity and tradition, between the present and utopia, why then do we still reduce postmodernism to poststructuralist deconstruction, Marxist and feminist theory, Lacanian psychoanalytic themes, and the new discourses of alterity?

Clearly, what can be located and simultaneously experienced within the polymorphous and thriving urban cacophonies of Lagos and Bombay are two crystalline postmodern realities that are built on parallel ideals. The most obvious is the seemingly endless collision of high and low, alien and familiar, abject and serene, the exquisite and the torturously grotesque, a phoenix-like immanence of new cultural juggernauts, a never-ending collage of incongruities. A perfect example, where such collision can be experienced firsthand, is the Jankara Market in Lagos. A sprawling, cacophonous theater of colorful apparels and languages, Jankara Market defies the laws of order. It is a bewildering, exciting environment, a postmodern installation par excellence. In its autonomous existence as a site of cultural and mercantile exchange, where only the laws of the market apply, entire continents converge and are visibly re-created and dissolved under the dizzying pace of its domain. From one stall to another, Italian leather goods jostle for space with Hausa leather goods, freshly arrived electronic goods from Taiwan, Korea, or Hong Kong compete for space with goods from Singapore, Brazil, England, India, Senegal, Ghana, France, Cameroon, and the USA. In one afternoon in this market that operates by its own rules, one touches base with virtually all the continents of the modern world. Even snow from Antarctica is rumored to have been sighted there. It is from this debris of clashing cultures, which first anticipated what has come to be known as postmodernity, that many African artists (especially those of the postindependence generation) find and reprocess materials and ideas for an art that possesses a critically universal language.

For these reasons, in Africa today, postmodernism (whatever it finally comes to stand for) seems particularly relevant. Despite impatience with, and resistance to, its general tenets within the African intellectual world, postmodernism nonetheless is neither misguided nor anathema to the contests that permeate issues of nationality and cultural identity in the late-capitalist economy—more on that continent than anywhere else. Facing history from the privileged perspective of a postcolonial condition, emergent nationalistic desires have produced in Africa a prism out of which emerges a disturbingly bleak picture. However, this picture is not particularly unique to Africa. It is the heritage of the entire modern world in the face of what seems like the triumph of the capitalist ideology. It appears that there is no moment in history that reflects postmodernity—its anxieties, ambivalences, and confusion—better than the present historical moment. We have been witnesses to events by which entire countries have vanished in a matter of minutes, like rabbits in a magician's hat. We have seen their fragments reconstituted into barely coherent entities that are also on collision courses to split apart and replicate more absurd boundaries. Every map one looks at becomes an obsolete relic in the act of looking. New countries appear, old ones fall into decay and inconsequence: a cartographer's nightmare fully realized. Postmodernity, then, is not just an ideology or scheme that accentuates difference and gives it the varnished allure of wholeness; it also becomes the offspring of chaos born out of the desire to reconstruct a different idea of the world. After the fall of communism and the Berlin Wall; after the defeat of apartheid in South Africa; after Tiananmen Square, the Gulf War, Bosnia, Haiti; and in the wake of the obscene decadence of late capitalism, postmodernity places the world, or what remains of its depleted and degraded environment, at perilous crossroads. Which way the world will proceed is a mystery, but we can rest assured that it will have multiple routes. In this sense, Thomas McEvilley's assertion that postmodernism is represented by a multivalency that makes it "multiple-coded" seems more relevant than Charles Jencks's earlier theorization of it as "double-coded."[15]

Indeed, these multiple routes lead us into and away from various sources of cultural production. But most importantly, they lead us to the works of these four African artists. Beyond the interplay of social forces harvested out of the ambivalent spaces of colonialism and postcolonialism; beyond the various interpretive agencies that assume, as no longer given, questions of fixed identities and nationalistic consciousness; beyond all that, what these artists offer us in their works are provocative aesthetic and philosophical propositions. They also offer us insights formed out of highly self-conscious modes of address; an epistemological fracture built out of the relationship between text and meaning that reveals and invalidates the most sinister core of the hegemonic narrator's language.

Troubling the Water

Through astute employment and manipulation of text as a code of interrogation and disturbance, Iké Udé's conceptual photo-text work brings the engagement between the meaning of the text and the reading of the image to its most fundamental friction. This is exemplified by his installation *Cover Girl* (1994), shown at the experimental gallery space Exit Art/The First World in 1994. Nigeria-born, New York–based Udé's exquisite use of the derelict narcissism of the dandy, his theatrical playing out of the roles associated with the margin, his facility in deploying the seemingly banal texts of popular culture, are at once a disputation, a mockery of "proper" behavior, and a disruption of its inherent fallacy. In the multimedia installation, encompassing video, a row of *Ass Prints* hanging along the wall, and a newsstand stocked with cigarettes, chewing gum, and magazines, and further augmented with such implements of beauty rites as lipsticks, combs, powders, perfumes, etc., Udé initiates an ambitious interrogation of modes of representation gleaned from magazine covers that too frequently represent a one-sided idea of beauty.[16] But most importantly, he uses this interrogation not only to excoriate the representation of Africa as the backwater in which the sinister lurks, but also to reclaim her as a "site of beauty." Though not reduced to articulating the dilemma and the diminished possibilities of mass cultural representations and the limits they impose on identity, Udé nevertheless acknowledges that yes, image is complicit in such diminishment. But he also proposes that we delve deeper into the core of the image's most resilient, structured existence through textual construction. It is through literal and metaphoric reading, he insists, that the intricate language of magazine covers reveals itself.

In *Cover Girl*, Udé replicates the very magazines that serve as models for his intervention. Meticulously disguised, he photographed himself in different personas, which he then translated into virtual magazine covers, such as *Vogue, Mademoiselle, Glamour, Town and Country*, and *Harper's Bazaar*. Undoubtedly, many viewers will feel somewhat uncomfortable with the image of Udé made up in drag. But it was not shock value that Udé meant to articulate by hijacking the idealized and glamorized image-machine of magazines. Nor was he pointing to the abject state of living between worlds that drag highlights. Instead, he was aiming to ironize and subvert the whole notion of gender and racial permission, as well as the self-congratulatory narcissism (of which Europeans remain the primary beneficiaries) which many popular-culture magazines celebrate. Far from taking its precedent from the performative space of the Western drag tradition, which carries a kind of repressed sexual content, Udé was instead appropriating and quoting *Adanma*, a contemporary Igbo masquerade performance genre in which men impersonate feminine characters to question and reveal certain truths about gender and difference. Writing on the fascinating exegesis of *Adanma* and the construction and regulation of gender power relations within a given community, Benjamin Hufbauer states that the performance of this masquerade "indicates the desire of Igbo men to connect gender identity and gender politics with masquerades"—which in most Western cultures would be called *theater*.[17] What is also remarkable in Udé's poseur-identity is its level of abjection, its incommensurable irresolution, its ambivalent narrative of displaced desire. Like the racialized construction of difference in Western culture, "gender identity is perceived as dangerously fluid, [and] always in need of stabilisation."[18] Like race in Western culture, in *Adanma*, "through parody, femininity is criticised and then idealised, controlled" in a bid to attenuate feminine power.[19] For Udé, then, impersonation and masquerading—acting out, if you will—replicated from an African context and extended into the rigid borders of Western media empires, are willful political and subversive acts that seek to trouble notions of racial difference as much as gender difference. The will to interrogate becomes a way of de-centralizing the composition of identity through race or gender, making them less idealized and impervious to co-option and control.

In many instances, as presented through this organic installation, the contestation of meanings and affects that Udé brought to his project from the outset was posed from the perspective not only of troubling those borders but also of subverting them. Udé manipulates the signs and codes of propriety and etiquette (crucial *Adanma* strategies), circulated through pop-cultural representations, for his frontal attack on issues of history, identity, and difference. At various points, he is an insouciant socialite involved in the conceit of beauty as a marker of a classist majority imperative. But at others he is an impetuous provocateur, throwing textual bombs at his intended audience—colonizer and colonized alike—by pointing out to them that their ravenous craving for the image of the "other" as exotic object is nothing but cannibalism.

But Udé does not allow this ravenous audience the pleasure of consumption. Peopled with idealized images of beauty, with him as the interlocutor, the magazine covers are not empty spaces for vainglorious enactments of image obsession, but active discursive platforms. All the covers have textual captions that become the activators of *Cover Girl*'s premise. For example, on the cover of *Town and Country*, one particularly telling caption declares, in vivid bold type, that "The Noble Savage Is Dead." The myth of the "Noble Savage" is a projection that officially sanctions all kinds of negative impressions (fear, horror, demonization, and degradation). Thus, declaring the "Noble Savage" dead is a seditious act, a mutiny against hegemonic cultural authority. Not satisfied with the impact of this almost benign declaration on his viewers, Udé dug deeper into the meaning of his refusal, by portraying what might be the reaction to such a declaration, not by mere suggestion, but through assertion on the cover of British *Vogue*. His declaration, "Hysteria over the Death of the Noble Savage," astutely reflects the paradoxical relationship of postmodernism with the desires of the no-longer-other that creates such hysteria, as well as the critique of the British Empire and its vampiric relationship to its former colonies. The fact that this declaration was placed on the cover of British *Vogue* was no mere accident. To comprehend fully what Udé was attempting requires further reading of the cover captions. The most telling pointer of his critique of empire and colonialism lies in Udé's literal burying of the empire's symbolic authority: the Queen. The declaration "The Queen Is Dead: A Song's Reality" not only puns on the punk rant of the British pop group the Smiths, but more importantly, along with "The Noble Savage Is Dead," he is marking the close of two particularly distasteful historical myths: the empire's assured superiority and the "Noble Savage's" assumed inferiority.

The tragedy that besets identity and the longing for an actualized wholeness has come to represent Udé's entire project, especially as revealed through the lens of another magazine cover: *Condé Nast Traveller*. Recalling the violent project of slavery, the erasure of its memory, and the perpetuation of negative representations against those it marked as "different," Udé presented three elliptically shaped diagrams of the interior of slave ships containing their human cargo. The allusion to travel, of course, is a cynical one, which calls into question the involuntary nature of that passage. It is a memory that continues to trouble the waters of the Atlantic as we repeatedly traverse its vast countenance. The consumption of the body of the "Noble Savage" is clearly linked to the violence of his/her co-option as commodity, entertainment, and cheap labor. As with all journeys, that depicted on the cover of *Conde Nast Traveller* is indelibly etched in our historical consciousness; it is one that still remains the seedbed of our discontent and resistance to racial stereotyping. But this journey is not administered and regulated by the image of bliss and release we obtain when we vacation in exotic locales. The image proffers no solace in the matters of self-creation, for no matter how realized, it nonetheless remains anchored to violence. Disturbingly so, because the history of self-creation in a diasporic system seems to be bound up with the violence it seeks to efface. Moreover, if realized, it offers no possibility of return, because identity constantly becomes projected into a temporal vacuum that is bound up in myth. And in many cases, as in the fantasies reproduced by magazines, in delusion. Thus, through the negation of the stereotype ("The Noble Savage Is Dead"), Udé emphatically reveals to his audience that identity, however stabilized, is never a wholly fixed, immutable entity. He insists, as he did through the various personas he assumed on the magazine covers, that it is always assumed and always subtended to any notion of fixity through its denial of permanence in social construction.

Memory, Absence, and Renunciation

Cameroonian-born Bili Bidjocka arrived in Paris as a twelve-year-old in 1974 and has lived there ever since. He has practiced as an artist for more than a decade. Blurring the line between painting and installation, he makes tableaux-like paintings and radiant installations, so delicate in their allusive content that they can be read as apt metaphors for loss and absence, ravishment and renewal. His works possess a quiet, ponderous beauty, reminiscent of art of the most liminal kind. He transposes postminimalist sensibility into reductive, emptied abstractions that have charged, material urgency. Elliptical in nature, Bidjocka's paintings/objects, characterized by empty niches, and long moments of silence, call to mind the submerged and hidden gaps in which many immigrants who reside in industrialized Western countries exist. They further recall the silence shrouding the violence that constantly seeks to obliterate immigrant memories from the social fabric in these countries. Bidjocka's work is suffused with the glow of desire, yet it speaks in a hushed voice. Its narration of identity, if it can be called that, discreetly recollects those figures pushed to the edges of existence within the monstrously afflu-ent Western metropolis. These figures, like the shadows that haunt the bleak precincts of poverty and racist castigation, exist in violently limited bodies.

In these subaltern figures, the "dominant" contemporary imagination can only surmise a lack. It is through this frame of lack, through the trope of marginality, the invocation of its absence, that Bidjocka installs this figure's presence. Eschewing the modernist ideal of representation that is predicated on the image of the figure, what his paintings reveal is the body's corporeality (however diminished), its cognitive potential for transcendence. He uses the metaphor of empty spaces, carved out of the physical surfaces of his work, into which he places such items as a pair of rubber shoes, underwear, a simple long orange dress, plastic roses, and Christmas lights to create a subdued melancholic atmosphere. The clear impression one receives through repeated viewing of these paintings, some of which are placed directly on the floor, is the sense of a memorial or an altar on which memories are propitiated. The absence of the body, for which these uninhabited items come to stand as surrogates, clearly calls in associations with physical and psychic wounds. In one of his many (one can read the meaning of anonymity in this) untitled works of 1992, although the body has disappeared, its indexical presence (the memory of the body) is fully foregrounded. Like an X-ray, the skeletal representation of a pelvis is painted on the monochrome surface of one of the niches, juxtaposed with, and faintly echoed by, a pair of underpants.

The strategy of pairing the pelvic trace with actual underwear (though disembodied) is a rhetorical device through which Bidjocka calls attention to the status of the body as primal presence, even though the painting addresses its absence. Yet the more one looks at Bidjocka's works, the less they seem to adhere to their referents in the material world or to the urgency of their charged meanings in the debased ruins of late-century capitalist economy, where, to paraphrase Oscar Wilde, people know the price of everything and the value of nothing.

This nonrepresentational strategy in Bidjocka's work (quite distinct from abstraction), which can be traced through the phosphorescent halos that envelop the objects he hangs or places in his installations, parallels, on one hand, the fierce brilliance of the Congolese poet Tchicaya U Tam'si and, on the other, the protean diffidence of Joseph Cornell's constructions. Whereas Cornell's aim was to trespass on the grounds of reality through a kind of surrealist and absurdist trope of reconfigured realism, Bidjocka, however, eschews pure representation through the sublation of any kind of identifiable facture that might lead viewers into reading things into his work. Placing an emphasis on art as a vehicle for subversion, Bidjocka not only interrogates the fallacy of racial recognition in the work of an artist, he has also remarked on the sheer impossibility of producing art that has an immediately recognizable identity. In this sense, his work reads as a deliberate effacement of evidence, a romantic penchant for self-deprecation. But sustained looking produces a palpable sense of the consistent accessibility of his objects. It comes as no surprise then that Bidjocka, like Cornell in his tableaux assemblage of surrealist ephemera, returns to the most elemental of forms and shapes: the egg. His installations utilizing eggs arranged in multiple groups, on chastely subdued brownish and whitish grounds that seem lit from within and suffused with possibility, carry the poignant ethereality of a protean world, hidden, yet palpable with life, longing, and desire. This one finds surprising and astonishing, for in the debris of so much loss, an artist like Bidjocka still finds room to dare to transcend the violence of marginality and the strictures placed on identity. The central virtue of such a stance stems less from the Christian metaphor of suffering as transcendence than from a more fundamental humanism, much more clearly articulated by Tchicaya U Tam'si in a line in his epic poem *Epitomé*, where his nameless protagonist insists he must "forget to be a negro so as to forgive."[20] Though this stance has been attacked as the romanticization of suffering embedded in so many exemplary Negritude texts, it still retains the element of refusal and renunciation (whether of misinterpretation or its violent, antecedent erasure) as willful political acts, as signifiers of loss and bereavement, resistance and renewal.

Precariously placed between minimalism's refinement of form and its aesthetic purification and reduction of content (the apotheosis of late-modernist desexualized distance and detachment, which marginalizes as it consumes the viewer's corporal existence), Bili Bidjocka's work relentlessly refuses containment within the familiar register of racial identification. In fact, he has carefully overlaid and effaced all clues to such interpretation. It seems a fugitive act to say the least, since the last thing he wishes for is the premature termination of his interventions through a recourse to racial sentimentalization. Fraught with his tendentious reading, which carries only the most nominal features of political signification (no "narrative of crisis" can be heard here), Bidjocka's work nonetheless leaves spaces wide enough to introduce readings of nationality, indeterminacy, and identity.

Questioning Authority

For Nigeria-born Olu Oguibe: painter, Conceptualist, poet and critic, the realm of politics is consistently inscribed within his personal and professional life. In the mid-1980s, when Oguibe was twenty-two, the great Nigerian novelist and essayist Chinua Achebe fondly dubbed him the "Angry Young Man," perhaps in reaction to his predilection for questioning power and authority through his work.[21] Recognizing the visionary restlessness of Oguibe's mind, Achebe invited him to join the editorial board of *Okike*, one of Africa's leading literary journals. What would be a great compliment for any aspiring artist and writer was, for Oguibe, in the authoritarian environment of Nigeria's military dictatorship, more like a burden. Within this context, artists such as him, with their brutal frankness and iconoclasm, are bound to run into trouble. And he did. Hence, his quick flight out of the country and into exile in England. Oguibe is emblematic of a generation who came of age too quickly. A generation whose lives and careers were steeped in political activism, and whose presence, although sorely needed in their individual countries, has been dispersed and displaced to anonymous cities and towns in the Western hemisphere.

As a cultural producer, much like the poets Christopher Okigbo of Nigeria and Jean-Joseph Rabéarivelo of Madagascar, what Oguibe brings to the metropolitan space in which he practices is a grand melancholic vision. Postmodernist in outlook and sensibility, his continuous interrogations of the metropolitan arena have become emblems for his explorations into the meanings of exile and displacement, of the place of identity in a landscape scrubbed and washed clear of any notion of human community without borders. England, as we all know, embraces a social hierarchy that rigorously maintains and polices such borders. In such a landscape, artists of his intellectual and critical makeup always face the possibility of censure for holding views contrary to official prescription. Again, true to his contestatory nature, Oguibe inevitably ran into trouble, leading to one of the most hotly debated issues of control over an artist's work by a public institution, when the Commonwealth Institute in 1989 censored part of his one-person installation, a multipaneled work, on the grounds that it contained obscenities. He withdrew his work rather than bend to censorship. Such rare integrity is what makes Oguibe unique among many postindependence African artists practicing today. As such, any survey of his work requires a knowledge of these histories. For it is through such knowledge that we can adequately engage his work.

In more than a decade of practice, Oguibe has produced work that is as varied as the media he has employed. His production always seems freighted with the perpetual memory of loss, alienation, abandonment, and the violence of representations projected on the undesirable other. Through refusal to be contained within the domain of an already predetermined boundary that unceremoniously dumps the marginalized into polite ethnic categories, Oguibe, in his own words, aims not only to problematize and transgress all notions of otherness, however embellished by postmodernism's invocation of "difference," but also "to pull up the rungs of hierarchy and trample the hedgerows of race."[22] By producing work that is forever difficult and vigilant rather than celebratory, he embraces, not without romantic implications, Susan Sontag's invocation of the "Artist as Exemplary Sufferer."[23] The wound that the exile bears appears repeatedly in Oguibe's work of the past five years, through a rare and touching vulnerability. The state of displacement and dispersal inherent in the exilic existence is hardly appealing, particularly to those who must live under its unstable banner. Hence his proposal, through a multiplicity of frames and strategies of narration (installations, painting, poetry, critical practice, scholarly work, video, etc.), for public debate on the statue of the exilic body, a body that must remain obedient and contained within its limited status in order to survive in its already constricted borderland of desire and longing.

Oguibe dissociates himself from modernist archetypal heroism, which insistently sought resolution to the problems of representation in purified formal systems that subsumed the presence of other identities lying outside its totalizing gaze. Instead, he employs a highly subjective critical apparatus to interrogate such identities, while still mediating the relationship between the dominant "self" and the marginalized "other," between "citizen" and "alien," "nation" and "subject." Employing the postmodernist autobiographical trope and self-narration in an untitled installation at the Bluecoat Gallery in Liverpool (1994), Oguibe sought to bring notions of identity, usually implemented through self/other, center/periphery, nation/subject relationships, into crisis by hanging and roping off a heavy gilded mirror on the gallery wall. One might also read the gilded frame as Oguibe's meditation on the nature of the masterpiece, fetishized and imbued with supernatural power by both the frame and our gaze. The *Mona Lisa* in the Louvre, encased in bulletproof glass and roped off, an object of great fetish power, comes to mind. However, the power of this "masterpiece," in its movement from one domain to another, must always be renegotiated. By vacating the frame of his masterpiece, Oguibe interrogates its assured place as an emblematic presence, as an all-encompassing visual cultural symbol.

The obvious responses to this installation call up associations with the Duchampian laissez-faire utilitarianism of the ready-made or the Lacanian mirror stage. But in this case, rather than operating through the Lacanian trope of self-cognition whereby the split image becomes reunited in the zone of reflection, a projection of the actualized self, Oguibe uses the mirror to frame the viewer's provisional status within the domain of the all-encompassing totality that the mirror produces. The relocation of the site of interrogation is crucial in reading what he is proposing on the conditions of self/identity as being purely enmeshed only in representation. But the mirror disrupts such an association by constantly reproducing copies that can only be mediated and modified by the viewer's presence, or absence, as the case may be; a copy without a prior trace, always lacking body in its fluctuations. Cast out in such an indeterminate zone, the reproduced image is thus both real and illusionistic. This bisection of the self, a problematic that echoes the travestied binaries of the self/other, citizen/alien paradigm, is not a recapitulation to postmodernist faddism; it clearly carries the suggestion of exilic confusion, which produces the sense of disjunction and disruption more than wholeness or resolution. The mirror thus serves as a simulacral apparatus through which identity's amoebic forms ebb and rise, split and reunite.

It is not, however, lost on this writer that the signifier: the mirror, which attends such production, might in reality be lost, even on the most interested viewer. For however interested, however disciplined or empathetic the viewer, the image itself is not at all contained within the matrix of its production (the mirror) but in a migratory realm, an elsewhere that cannot guarantee the self a determinate form. Thus, Oguibe's proposal to the viewer is that the gaze, which is uncontainable within the frame of the mirror, is just as aberrational as the gaze that fixes the non-European and names him/her the "other," the "alien," the "outcast."

Clearly differentiated from [Jacques] Lacan's mirror stage notion, Oguibe's mirror proffers no easy answers that might lead to a shock of self-recognition or actualization. The mirror image is always regulated through distance and indeterminacy; its roots dissolved and dispersed through many channels that lead everywhere and nowhere. The image's fluctuations run from crisis to tranquility, from memory to amnesia, remembrance to dis-remembrance. In short, what it introduces is the impurity of identity, thereby rendering the mirror merely a simulacral vessel, a reflective veneer beneath which lie much more troubled histories; those histories which when appropriated through language, through the semiotics of "difference," be-come irresolvably mired in both denial and self-production.

Predicated on the above, it seems clear that to survive, marginal communities—where exiles almost inevitably end up—must constantly op-erate in the territory of self-fashioning and production. Another untitled installation, this time at the Savannah Gallery in London (1993), forcefully addresses this condition of constant self-production. More accessible than the mirror installation, this work makes clear the never-resolved, ambivalent status of the marginalized. Appropriating an icon of late-capitalist consum-erism, the shopping cart, he attached to it a miniature Union Jack and piled it with personal belongings, conjuring the severely deprived lives of those who must keep moving lest they become caught in the snares of authority. Through this installation, Oguibe institutes a commentary on the haves and have-nots, on colonialism and the unresolved nature of postcolonialism, on desire and nationality, on what Homi Bhabha calls "culture's in between."[24]

But Oguibe also points us to other locations, to insist that the condi-tions of exile are not necessarily rooted in migrancy, but can also be gleaned in the tenuous status of many Europeans: Gypsies [Romani], Turks, and Bosnians come to mind. For him, Bosnia, especially, represents the ugliness and brutality that the West would rather consign to the tragedies that end-lessly seem to plague places such as Africa and South America. His instal-lation *Requiem* (1993), at the Savannah Gallery, also universalized suffering and the violence of displacement. In this requiem for the children of Bosnia, four white dolls lie on a pedestal draped in black cloth. A sepia portrait of an anonymous young girl completes the memorial. The implication is quite

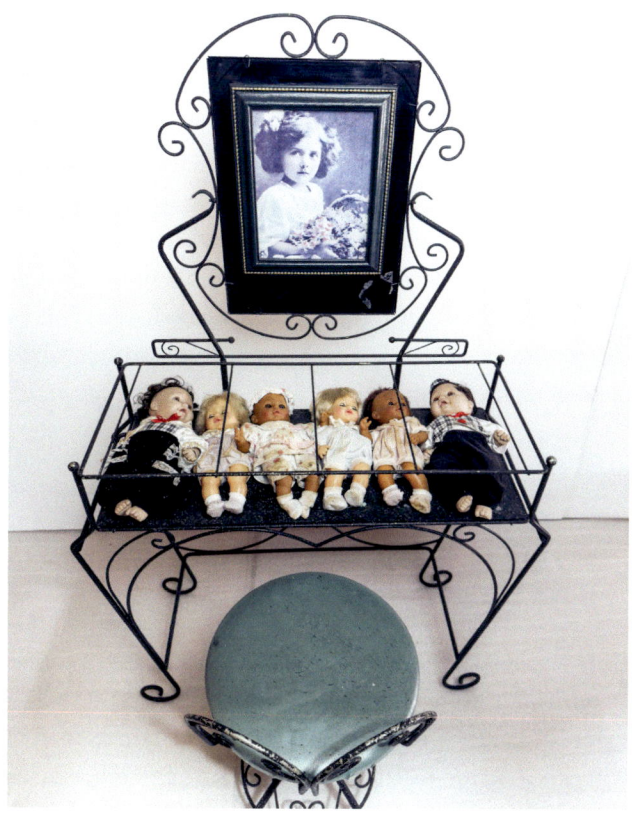

9.2 Olu Oguibe, *Requiem,* 1993. Sculpture assemblage. © Olu Oguibe. Courtesy of the artist.

clear: that Europe's charity is not only to be bestowed on its former subjects in its former colonies. In this installation, Oguibe addresses the fundamental paradox of violence as a tool of political and social emancipation, especially in Europe, under whose titular sky this century's most brutal crimes against humanity took place. Hence, the installations call for a less hypocritical approach in how we deal with the legacy violence that seems to suffuse the relationship between the marginalized and the dominating.

Largely ignored, like many of his contemporaries, Oguibe has nonetheless shown himself to be an artist of exemplary courage, vision, and humanity. He has quite correctly refused to embark on a project of neoprimitive representation, which his peculiarly postmodernist inclination naturally rejects, and for which many critics excoriate him. His refusal, of course, is not predicated on the hubris of poststructuralist obscurantist closure, which concedes nothing through its insistence on the image's indeterminacy or its existence as a mere vessel for provocation. Instead, he attempts to search for a language whereby art of revolutionary nature can move between the realism of aesthetic and social discourse, while still retaining the autonomy of the art object as a signifier of the larger world and without entrapping the art in interpretations that reduce its substance to a vessel for agitprop and self-indulgent victimhood. Though their conceptual nature at times makes Oguibe's installations seem like exercises in impenetrable postmodern obscurantism, their humanistic concerns and referents in the material world bring them down to a personal level, where his audience is able to experience the art as a source of self-reflection and knowledge. This participatory element clearly mediates the distance between postmodernist detachment and the audience's increasing alienation from its language and message.

Alchemical Monumentality

Ivorian-born Ouattara's paintings are performative venues in which African modernist aspiration and postmodernist transcendence converge. This is achieved through neoprimitivist parody, neoexpressionism, and the deconstruction of the sources of modernism, via an ironic postmodernist consciousness. Unlike Udé or Oguibe, Ouattara is not a conscious postmodernist in the sense that the primary aim of his works is to test those boundaries where authority is constantly displaced and dispersed into other systems of knowledge; where the meaning of a social community is raised almost to the pitch of dissonance. But he is a postmodernist in the manner in which he has appropriated its sign of pastiche and composite production, its regulation of disparate cultural values and forms. What emerges is an ecstatic parody of poststructuralist signification. It is in modernist iconography, however, that Ouattara finds the most efficacious uses of the pastiche.

Given that modernism loved structures and surfaces, affect and grandiloquence, almost to the exclusion of other systems, Ouattara appropriates its essential gesture of monumentality. He also adopts its stream-of-consciousness, essentialist view of the artist as wonderworker, as high priest and author. He aims to examine the boundaries of the secular and the religious, alchemy and science, magic and empiricism, popular culture and canonical African classicism; above all, to examine the fundamental questions posed by the dichotomy between tradition and modernity, between Western and non-Western representation. Unlike modernist formalism, which in painting was once said to have been "burnt to a crisp by the phenomenological stare," Ouattara's work seems as if it has been wrung out and turned inside out, then reinvested with a vast array of expressive and subversive signs.[25] In his monumental assemblages, he ranges freely through disparate cultural landscapes and milieux, seamlessly applying a composite representation of various signs and iconographies, from the Iberian Peninsula to Mexico, from Byzantine to Gondar, from Egypt to Mali, pop to expressionism, pop culture to Pan-Africanism, high modernism to postmodernism.

Furthermore, Ouattara manipulates the frictions between modernism and postmodernism in a manner that deflects their literalist imposition of primitivism as the universal emblem of African art. If the postmodernist pastiche and its code of impure forms are veritable marriages of high and low, camp and seriousness, modern and traditional, piety and profanity, reality and simulation, all of which are mediated by technology, Ouattara, like Joseph Beuys, co-opts these categories as sites onto which he can inscribe and encode a relational presence (self/other) through which he makes art that aspires to performance and magic. The danger here would be to lapse into the problematic investigation of Ouattara's work through a frame that baptizes him shaman or native doctor, as many who have written about him have done. Or even through the unsettling trope of the artist as ethnographer, rummaging through the cracks of ancestry to satisfy the demands of the dominant imagination. This would be to limit talk about his work to the spectacle that its stupendous architectonics sometimes produces.

An investigation of this tendency in his work inevitably brings us to his huge tarpaulin paintings of the late 1980s, on which he placed various African sculptural objects and a flotilla of highly conscious primitive effects. The gesture of such mimetic usage of African objects and Western-derived notions of primitivity was akin to camping out, spectacle as closure, the carnivalesque as an attempt at reclamation, through the oculus of a deterritorialized African modernism. Viewed through such a lens, these affects become, via Ouattara's use of them, subversive vessels—his Trojan horse for infiltrating the closed quarters of Western international art.

The demand for an international presence for African artists makes clear that Ouattara's career, more than ever before, needs to be read through the internationality of his practice. There is a clear affinity between his present work and Robert Rauschenberg's early *Combine Paintings*. In their physicality, however, in their pop-cultural graftings and appropriations, and in their illusions of three-dimensionality, Ouattara's paintings/constructions need to be seen in the parallel light of the neoexpressionist movement of the 1980s, from the Italian trans–avant-gardists, such as Sandro Chia, Mimmo Paladino, Francesco Clemente, and Enzo Cucchi, through the New York branch, represented by Jean-Michel Basquiat (a personal friend of Ouattara),

Julian Schnabel, Keith Haring, to the ultimate champions, the postwar German neoexpressionists, Georg Baselitz, Markus Lüpertz, A. R. Penck, and Anselm Kiefer. It is with the Germans that one can identify an international kinship for Ouattara. His primal stick figures, which populate virtual dreamscapes, easily find affinity with A. R. Penck's utilization of such figures in his consciously primitivist schtick. Then there are Kiefer's overwrought, monumental works, whose quotidian emblems can be viewed as repositories of multiple strands of historical narration. Ouattara's engagements with such historical narration, however, come from a much more vast and depopulated landscape.

Kiefer is particularly important in terms of how we frame Ouattara's stature as an international artist who engages global concerns, be it through politics or the politics of representations. Though Ouattara makes his inscriptions in full consciousness of the likes of Penck, Schnabel, Lüpertz, Clemente, and Baselitz, one still understands that they are motivated by a desire that far outweighs the demands and values invested in the idea of "authenticity" and shamanistic function—contra-Africa—necessary for his passage into the realm of "serious" international art practitioners. Here, Kiefer's monumentality and its antinomies of decadence (whether affected or deeply felt and realized, through whispers of vicarious intent that still pervade the debate around his work) bring sharply into focus Ouattara's own insistent play on scale: at once grand and compressed, open and occluded, while overlaying Kiefer's mastery and tradition with his own subjectivity.

Ouattara's *Barouah Adonais* (1992) and *Masada* (1993) can be read as counterpoints to Kiefer's *Your Golden Hair Margarete* (1981) and *Lilith's Daughters* (1991). In his relentless, almost obsessive, referencing of his country's Nazi past, Kiefer plays with the ghosts of a German nationalism run amok, inventoried and bound up in his famous dreary, charred books. On the other hand, Ouattara, though not Jewish, by employing the Kaddish in his work, aims to discredit the kind of authority invested in works like Kiefer's. In trespassing the boundaries of ethnicity through the appropriation of another culture's mourning rituals, Ouattara universalizes history as an experience of shared anguish and destiny. By acknowledging the pain of another's history, he also honors his own memory, Africa's memories, and the wounds suffered through colonialism's destruction of entire cultures and neocolonialism's impingement on identity.

Lately, he has been producing work that takes its signage from architectural fragments of Africa, specifically those of old Mali. By subordinating and enclosing the viewer within its frame, the work addresses one of the most fundamental questions of otherness: from where does its reproduction as a sign of the margin come? By whose authority do we bestow such a status? Ouattara's employment of African architecture as a nationalistic emblem, as a signifier of his cultural past and identity, seems to be saying to the viewer, "In this brief moment of your presence before my work, you are resident within the domain of Africa: her culture, art, philosophy; her entire worldview. In short, everything you carry into this arena is mediated and processed through that singular perspective." This marginalization of the center within its own domain is not a mere accident, but a conscious and tactical opposition, a refusal of "otherness," a deterritorialization of the modernist project, regardless of the consequence. The circumstances of his present works are so powerfully delineated that he has broken and extended the mold and language of painting as an objectified presence. These works no longer perform in accordance to ascribed notions of painting's formalism, its narrative structure of illusion. Rather than being paintings, they are painting-like, objects and structures relocated and painted over.

Ultimately, Ouattara's paintings/constructions erode the absurd premise of the modernist hegemonic view of African painting as naive, unsophisticated, and as less innovative than its Western parallel. In his outsized canvases, he re-creates the square—neither the Greenbergian grid nor Josef Albers's puny experiments with a form that will never contain the world it seeks to colonize—but the town square, the venue where the event between art and life, the sacred and profane, secular and religious, high and low mix to violate absurd boundaries that, in the waning years of the twentieth century, finally seem destined for dispatch into the deep grave of "History."

Postscript

Undeniably, the political ramifications of the invasion by the "other" of the territories that for the entire duration of the twentieth century belonged to those who saw themselves as guardians of advanced art traditions must not be underestimated. And these ramifications are being played out nowhere more than in the spaces, however denied, that many African artists, diasporic or otherwise, are hacking out within postmodernism while the West argues with the rest of the world about the end of "History."

In rereading postmodernism and its relationship to artists such as those represented in this text, we must also turn our attention to the Africanist critical establishment, which thus far sees no benefit in engaging with, or lending its voice to, the ongoing debates around postmodernist and postcolonial discourse. Entrenchment into a dogmatic African essentialism entraps us all, and ignores the real commitment of many artists who wish to see such dogmas dismantled. Manthia Diawara cautions us against an Afrocentric essentialism that obdurately refuses to look to new texts in advancing its arguments, an important point that the Africanist academia must carefully take to heart.[26] Decreeing postmodernist discourse as irrelevant to discourse on contemporary African culture neither advances nor helps the future of African artists in a fragile global economy. Events such as the Venice Biennale, where African artists can only participate as guests of invited European countries, make it imperative that academia be vigorously challenged to open up its doors to new terrains of critical practice. Culture, though predicated on the ideal, the whole, and the pure, is of course never those things. And neither are the artists on whom the mantle of representing culture falls. Therefore, it seems ridiculous constantly to translocate contemporary African artists back to cultural milieux with which they have very little engagement. Nor should the value of their work be contingent on the display of an "authenticity" certified, codified, and ratified by an adjudicating tribunal.

This practice of ratification, which postmodernism processes, reproduces, and fashions into "difference," denies African artists a claim to subjectivity and self-narration. The complexities that enliven the contemporary condition, the contradictory and often aberrant nature of identity and memory, of race and nationality, the reckless interchangeability of either for the other—its metonymic character—within the temporal domain of contemporaneity, make the work of Udé, Bidjocka, Oguibe, and Ouattara ever more uncontainable within one social or artistic milieu. Their presence in the domain of the Western metropolis problematizes the notion of difference as a determining criterion for their inclusion within the pantheon of contemporary cultural producers.

In these widely contested terrains, in which the very notion of "History" as constructed through hegemonic texts seems imperiled, neoconservative and reactionary voices have risen. Weak-willed liberals lacking the courage of their convictions have no doubt conceded the ground to the bulldozing of these cultural storm troopers, whom Jean-Michel Basquiat, were he still alive, would perhaps have called "obnoxious conservatives." Homi K. Bhabha reminds us of the exposure of the liberal flank, an Achilles heel, no doubt, when he writes that the "borderline negotiations of cultural difference often violate liberalism's deep commitment to representing cultural diversity as plural choice."[27] Bhabha further argues that "liberal discourses on multiculturalism experience the fragility of their principles of 'tolerance' when they attempt to withstand the pressure of revision. In addressing the multicultural demand, they encounter the limit of their enshrined notion of 'equal respect.'"[28] While Bhabha's remarks are illuminating and trenchant in their accuracy, the real enemy remains the neoconservatives who would wish for nothing more than a return to the glory days of modernist pathos, its disdain for the culture of the "other," and its delusional self-referentiality predicated on Europe's superiority complex. One doubts very much, however, whether artists such as Udé, Bidjocka, Oguibe, and Ouattara see the necessity to seek the Western establishment's sanction before embarking on an oppositional practice that will either change the rules of the game or shift the "center."

It seems sufficiently apparent in works by many African artists that the exemplar of postmodern representation, under whose leveling authority identity might fall and become contained, is not in itself a closed shop that receives and transmits only those images that are circumstantial to the production of a positivist idea of a given society or culture. Indeed, truly to define postmodernism seems an almost futile act. Its precepts and values seem forever shifting. Its codes, digressions, and constitutions, its analogues and localization within systems whether banal or profound, immanent or dissolved into highly contested critical texts and countertexts, excisions and exclusions, affective or enunciatory, are always in flux. Today, postmodernism would seem even more tailored to Ihab Hassan's insistence on its indeterminacy as "an equivocal concept, a disjunctive category, doubly modified by the impetus of the phenomenon itself and by the shifting perceptions of its 'critics.'"[29] But approached from the perspective of how art made by these artists has functioned within its domains, how it has enlivened and given texture to contemporary representation in the metropolis (one thinks of hip-hop culture here), postmodernism becomes an ethical compass, an apparatus for interrogating both the negative and positive aspects of identity. Or put more precisely, a means of addressing identity's fragility: its temporality. Hence, productively looked at and experienced, the common purpose of a postmodern society is one that is no longer in direct opposition to the modernist project. Instead, postmodernism seeks to bypass modernism by way of its multivalent identities and multiplicity of tongues. In the immediacy of our desires, postmodernity presupposes a shift that is neither utopic nor entropic. It persistently leads us to an elsewhere, to new terrains of possibilities, even if they are places for which we must continually fight and renegotiate, over and over again.

1   [*Ed. note:* At the beginning of his essay "Signs Taken for Wonders," Bhabha refers to "the scenario—played out in the wild and wordless wastes of colonial India, Africa, the Caribbean, of the sudden, fortuitous discovery of the English book." See Homi Bhabha, *The Location of Culture* (1994; repr. Berkeley: University of California Press, 2010), 145.]

2   Hal Foster, *Recodings: Art, Spectacle, Cultural Politics* (Seattle: Bay, 1985), 129.

3   See Olu Oguibe, "A Brief Note on Internationalism," in *Global Visions: Towards a New Internationalism in the Visual Arts*, ed. Jean Fisher (London: Kala Press in association with the Institute of International Visual Arts, 1994), 50–59.

4   Homi K. Bhabha, "The Other Question: Difference, Discrimination, and the Discourse of Colonialism," in *Out There: Marginalization and Contemporary Cultures*, ed. Russell Ferguson, Martha Gever, Trinh T. Minh-ha, and Cornel West (Cambridge, MA: MIT Press; New York: New Museum of Contemporary Art, 1990), 71 (emphasis added).

5   Charles Merewether, "The Promise of Community," in *Africus: Johannesburg Biennale, 28 February–30 April, 1995* (Johannesburg: Greater Johannesburg Transitional Council, 1995), 58.

6   Jean-François Lyotard, *The Postmodern Explained* (Minneapolis: University of Minnesota Press, 1993).

7   Fredric Jameson, *Postmodernism, or, The Cultural Logic of Late Capitalism* (Durham, NC: Duke University Press, 1991), 4 (emphasis added).

8   Jameson, *Postmodernism*, 6.

9   [*Ed. note:* Chike Aniakor cited in Simon Ottenberg, "Olu Oguibe: Angry Young Man, Artist, and Poet," in *New Traditions from Nigeria: Seven Artists of the Nsukka Group*, 85–99, 272–73 (Washington, DC: Smithsonian Institution, 1997), 85.]

10 Anthony Ilona, "Olu Oguibe: Recent Works," *Third Text*, no. 25 (Winter 1993–94): 87.

11 bell hooks, *Black Looks: Race and Representation* (Boston: South End, 1992), 115. The oppositional gaze is employed in this instance as a device of affirmation and for the disempowerment of hegemonic structures of reference, rather than a device of mere resistance or one used for the construction of difference.

12 Cornel West, *Keeping Faith: Philosophy and Race in America* (New York: Routledge, 1993), 3.

13 Manthia Diawara, "Afro-Kitsch," in *Black Popular Culture*, ed. Gina Dent (Seattle: Bay, 1992), 289.

14 Michel Foucault, quoted by Nancy Spector in "Felix Gonzales-Torres: Travelogue," *Parkett*, no. 39 (March 1994): 24.

15 Thomas McEvilley, "Fusion: Hot or Cold?," in *Fusion: West African Artists at the Venice Biennale* (New York: Museum for African Art, 1993), 17; Charles Jencks, *What Is Postmodernism?* (London: Academy Editions, 1986), 29.

16 Attempting to locate the source of anxieties, ambivalence, and phobias about the body and its related activities, Udé produced a group of work entitled *Ass Prints*, which sought to challenge our perceptions of certain bodily functions. He obtained the imprints by asking his "sitters," whose buttocks he had coated with acrylic paint, to sit on a piece of heavy-duty watercolor paper. Each *Ass Print*, obtained just like a fingerprint, was a unique document, serving as an index of that part of the body.

17 Benjamin Hufbauer, "Performing the Feminine: The Adanma Masquerade in Igboland," *TVC: Thresholds: Viewing Culture* 8 (1994): 40–41.

18 Hufbauer, "Performing the Feminine," 40–41.

19 Hufbauer, "Performing the Feminine," 40–41.

20 Tchicaya U Tam'si, *Selected Poems*, trans. Gerald Moore (London: Heinemann, 1970), 71.

21 Chinua Achebe, catalog essay for the exhibition *Statements*, Syrian Club, Lagos, 1989. [*Ed. note:* The catalog for *Statements* is not available. Reference to Olu Oguibe as an "Angry Young Man, Artist, and Poet" is found in the subtitle of chapter 11, which Simon Ottenberg devotes to him in his *New Traditions from Nigeria: Seven Artists of the Nsukka Group* (Washington, DC: Smithsonian Institution, 1997), 223.]

22 Olu Oguibe, "Brief Note on Internationalism," in *Global Visions: Towards a New Internationalism in the Visual Arts*, ed. Jean Fisher (London: Kala Press, 1994), 58.

23 [*Ed. note:* Susan Sontag, "The Artist as Exemplary Sufferer," in *Sufferer against Interpretation* (1966; repr. New York: Dell, 1969), 49–57.]

24 Homi K. Bhabha, "Culture's In Between," *Artforum* 32, no. 1 (September 1993): 167–214. https://www .artforum .com /features /cultures -in -between -2 -229652 /.

25 Peter Schjeldahl, "Susan Rothenberg's *United States*," *Artforum* 32, no. 1 (September 1993): 146–47.

26 Diawara, "Afro-Kitsch."

27 Bhabha, "Culture's In Between."

28 Bhabha, "Culture's In Between."

29 Ihab Hassan, "Pluralism in Postmodern Perspective," *Critical Inquiry* 12, no. 3 (Spring 1986): 508.

Independence and Liberation Movements
in Africa, 1945–1994

The Short Century: Independence and Liberation Movements in Africa, 1945–1994 was an exhibition curated by Okwui Enwezor at the Museum Villa Stuck, Munich, in February to April 2001, before traveling to the House of World Cultures, Berlin; the Museum of Contemporary Art, Chicago; and PS1, Museum of Modern Art, New York, during the subsequent twelve months. It treated its subject as manifest in art, posters, photography, architecture, music, theater, literature, and film, as well as archival texts. The following essay introduced the accompanying book of the same title, edited by Enwezor, and published in Munich by Prestel and Museum Villa Stuck in 2001 (pages 10–16).

Fellow African Freedom Fighters still carrying the burden of Imperialism, pull together. We who have won our freedom stand uncompromisingly behind you in your struggle. Take heart. Unite your forces. Organization and discipline shall command your victory. All Africa shall be free in this, our lifetime. For this mid-twentieth century is Africa's. This decade is the decade of African independence. Forward then to independence. To Independence Now. Tomorrow, the United States of Africa.

Kwame Nkrumah, opening session of the All-African People's Conference (1958)

The Scramble for Africa: 1885

THE STORY OF COLONIALISM IN AFRICA is a well-known one—or so it seems. While contemporary historiography on Africa has often focused on the pathology of violence and official institutional degradation, very little is said today about the structure of colonial violence and its concomitant contribution to the historical view of recent history in Africa. Where to begin?

Berlin, 1885: No single historical event has had as much impact on the shape of modern Africa as the one that took place between November 15, 1884, and February 23, 1885, in Berlin, under the auspices of the German chancellor Otto von Bismarck. The scramble for Africa that precipitated the Berlin Conference, or the Belgian Congo Conference, and the unilateral, quasi-legal document called the Belgian Congo Act that it engendered, illustrates the willingness of the fifteen European nations attending the conference to betray, for profit, the juridical principles at the foundations of their own civil societies.[1] It was at this meeting that Africa's final fate at the hands of the imperial powers of Europe was sealed. To be sure, the colonial enterprise was short, a mere but brutal seventy years (as the history of the Belgian Congo under Leopold II reminds us). Yet it left an indelible mark, whose crude, schematic features remain difficult both to erase and to reconcile with civilized conduct. Any attempt to return to that exemplary scene of uncivil conduct that was Berlin—so masterfully provoked and instigated by King Leopold II of Belgium, a man whose violent actions and gross human rights violations in the Congo have come to symbolize the pernicious and brutal activities of colonial conquest—renders unto European history a dark blot.

It cannot be repeated enough that the territorial violations and abject violence that followed the annexation of most of Africa sprang from a deeply held belief that simple issues of human decency and legal protection do not and cannot apply to subject peoples, especially those deemed in need of civilizing. Despite the flimsy illusion of respectability conveyed by the Belgian Congo Act, the mad race by European powers to occupy desirable swaths of African territory, whether by absurd "legal" treaties or by outright military conquest and occupation, represents one of the most tragic encounters between Europe and Africa since the abolition of slavery in the mid-nineteenth century. The act carved up Africa, like war booty, into five main spheres of influence: British, French, Portuguese, Belgian, and German.

Today, at the conclusion of another historical period, to view the history of the twentieth century from the vantage point of the struggle of subject peoples to regain their independence and liberty is to see up close the intricate and calculating mechanisms in the complex interrelationship of dependence and exploitation, violence and patronization, that bore on the emergence of numerous non-European cultures and nations into modernity. At the conclusion of this millennium, it is quite commonplace to ignore the dramatic processes of decolonization, from India to Indonesia, Ghana to Kenya, Egypt to Jordan, Algeria to Congo, perhaps the most significant events of the twentieth century. Decolonization, and its attendant ideological and philosophical contestation of Western imperialism, does in fact remain one of the most significant events of the twentieth century, much as the abolition of slavery was in the nineteenth century, but very little of what its processes represent—especially in proposing new narratives and subjectivities, identities and nationalities, contemporary and historical forms—has produced a proper understanding of the mutually binding relationship between Europe and its former colonial territories, a relationship manifest in areas of language, culture, politics, law, and other social institutions. Thus, to reexamine and assess what this relationship means with regard to the vast corpus of historical writing dedicated to the study of the twentieth century requires new methods.

It is with this in mind that *The Short Century: Independence and Liberation Movements in Africa, 1945–1994* was initiated. This exhibition and book are an attempt to construct a contemporary "critical biography" of Africa. The exhibition's principal aim is to explore and elaborate on the critical paradigms and ideas related to concepts of modernity, the political and ideological formations of independence and liberation struggles, their impact in the production of self-awareness, new models of cultural expression, dialogues with processes of modernization, and what lies at the heart of modernity itself out of the ruins of colonialism.

Independence Now: Toward a Political and Social Ethic

As long as the black man is among his own, he will have no occasion, except in minor internal conflicts, to experience his being through others. There is of course the moment of "being for others" of which Hegel speaks, but every ontology is made unattainable in a colonized and civilized society.

Frantz Fanon, *Black Skin, White Masks* (1967)

Perhaps there is a need to clarify a central operating principle of this exhibition, namely, to examine the link between independence movements and liberation struggles as methods for achieving African political auton-

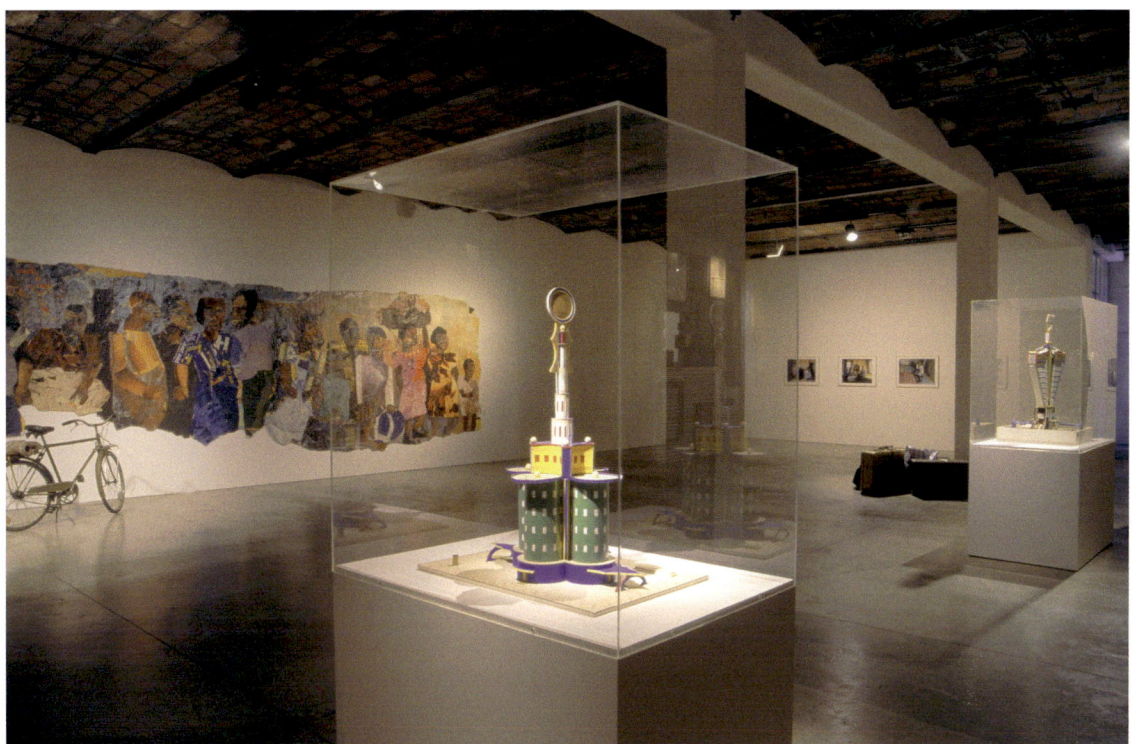

10.1 Installation view of the exhibition *The Short Century: Independence and Liberation Movements in Africa, 1945–1994*, Museum of Modern Art (MoMA) PS1, New York, February 10–May 5, 2002. MoMA PS1 Archives, II.A.1294. Museum of Modern Art Archives, New York. Digital image © 2025, Museum of Modern Art/Scala, Florence.

omy and cultural self-awareness. Independence and liberation on the first level are constitutive of two radical and revolutionary political programs. One, based on the Gandhian notion of nonviolence and civil disobedience (especially in West Africa), adopted a strategy of working within colonial law, albeit by provocatively testing its limits in order to mobilize popular discontent against its oppressive system. Early independence leaders such as Nnamdi Azikiwe, Jomo Kenyatta, and Kwame Nkrumah successfully applied this method, using the editorial platforms of newspapers and publications, public speeches and campaigns, strikes and trade union activities, to disrupt the machinery of colonial economic interests and to undermine its legal authority. Even in cases where this method was the desired approach, however, there was never a guarantee against the use of violence; the Mau Mau insurrection in Kenya in 1952, and the brutal British suppression of it, being a case in point. By the time the Mau Mau challenge of British rule was over, more than fifty thousand Kenyans had been killed, against under twenty losses for the British.

As we will see elsewhere, Kenya was not the exception. Armed struggle constituted the final method in territories such as Algeria, Mozambique, Angola, Zimbabwe, and South Africa, where a mixture of colonial intransigence and inflexibility undermined peaceful negotiations. The Front de liberation nationale (FLN) in Algeria, which began an armed revolt in 1953 against French colonial military violence, not only affected Algeria but had a direct impact on France itself. Algeria represented both a political loss and a psychological crisis for France.

Whatever the method on the road to independence and liberation, these two programs foregrounded the necessity to overthrow the colonial presumption. The central goal was always to wrest the instruments of power from the colonial elite. It also needs to be noted that the Gandhian method of nonviolence was never entirely nonviolent. In Congo, for example, Belgium's need to exact revenge against the charismatic Patrice Lumumba not only led to his assassination in 1961, less than a year after he and his Mouvement national Congolais (MNC) successfully led the nation to independence as her first prime minister, it more crucially undermined the new nation's hard-won independence, setting up a weakened and manipulated President Joseph Kasavubu for Joseph-Désiré Mobutu's coup d'état. The notion of colonial revenge can thus be seen as a subtext of the independence and liberation struggles, whether exacted through imprisonment and exile or through torture and murder.[2]

With the independence of Ghana in 1957, a powerful psychological and ideological force put in place what would become the main political event of the 1960s: what Nkrumah, Ghana's first prime minister, in a 1958 speech at the First All-African People's Conference in Accra, announced as Africa's decade of independence. In 1960 a loud cannon shot was fired across the bow of the political spectrum, in Africa and around the world: not only did seventeen African countries gain independence that year, but the United Nations, on admitting them en masse into the international body, declared that year to be the year of Africa. For the rest of the decade, independence celebrations and solemn ceremonies of the colonial handover of power were as commonplace as the zeal with which citizens of the new nations embraced their new reality.

But what indeed is the reality of independence and liberation? For sure, independence and liberation, in the African context, find critical and philosophical filiation in the fact that both of them announce themselves as political and social movements in the case of Pan-Africanism, and as a philosophy of culture, regeneration, and modern consciousness in the case of Negritude. Across each spectrum there is a synthetic elaboration to clarify the program toward modernity. V. Y. Mudimbe, reading Frantz Fanon and elaborating on the political philosophy of Léopold Sédar Senghor and Nkrumah, two proponents of Negritude and Pan-Africanism, says that "the alienation caused by colonialism constitutes the thesis, the African ideologies of otherness (black personality and Negritude) the antithesis, and political liberation the synthesis."[3] Mudimbe's argument also rests on Jean-Paul Sartre's famous essay "Black Orpheus" (1948), which introduced the postwar French public to the works of the writers of Negritude. For Clayton Eshleman and Annette Smith, "In the framework of Hegel's dialectics, Sartre saw the Negritude movement as the moment of separation, of negativity, that is, like the 'antithesis' following the 'thesis' of the colonial situation and preceding the 'synthesis' in which not only blacks but all oppressed people would unite and triumph over their oppressors."[4] But the Fanonian philosophy of liberation has a particular appeal for Mudimbe. To negotiate the antipathy of colonialism, the colonized must first understand the Manichaean scheme and structure of colonial domination:

> The alienation of colonialism entails both the objective fact of total dependence (economic, political, cultural, and religious) and the subjective process of the self-victimization of the dominated. The colonized internalizes the imposed racial stereotypes, particularly in attitudes toward technology, culture, and language. Black personality and negritude appear as the only means of negating this thesis, and Fanon expounds the antithesis in terms of antiracist symbols. Negritude becomes the intellectual and emotional sign of opposition to the ideology of white superiority. At the same time, it asserts an authenticity which eventually expresses itself as a radical negation: rejection of racial humiliation, rebellion against the rationality of domination, and revolt against the whole colonialist system. This symbolic vio-

lence ultimately turns into nationalism and subsequently leads to a political struggle for liberation.[5]

Against this backdrop, the independence and liberation struggles and revolts represent the twin projects from which the text of African modernity after World War II was fashioned. First, their central aim was the destruction of the inferiority complex imposed by colonialism; second, they attacked the disempowering devices of colonial injustice and economic exploitation; third, they affirmed a political and social vision that recuts the fabric of the modernist dialectic of progress and change; fourth, they described an ethic of modernity and a view of history that puts Africa in the center of all international events; and, fifth, they rejected the anachronism of European cultural superiority and argued for an African critical subjectivity that is both a political ethic and a cultural ideology.

The Cultural Dimension of Decolonization: Modernism, Pan-Africanism, Negritude, and African Art

Our error was not that we fought with the weapons of colonialism—most African politicians, though not all, unfortunately, are anticolonialist—but with the weapons of Europe.

Léopold Sédar Senghor, *On African Socialism* (1964)

Since culture does not just reflect the world in images but actually through those very images conditions a child to see that world in a certain way, the colonial child was made to see the world and where he stands in it as seen and defined by or reflected in the culture of the language of imposition.

Ngũgĩ wa Thiong'o, *Decolonising the Mind* (1986)

As much as the political ideologies, nationalist movements, and other decolonization tropes constitute bases for self-fashioning knowledge, on a cultural level decolonization represents the exemplary scene of ambivalence. This ambivalence is readily perceivable in the complex relationship between colonial discourse and the African interpretation and use of that discourse. *Ambivalence* and *alienation* have been crucial terms employed to describe the relationship of the colonized to the colonial text. As such, the crux of this exhibition concerns, on the one hand, the uses of the normative structure of modernism and, on the other, the uses or nonuses of that structure.

Here, however, we are not concerned with nor unduly exercised by the modernism dispatched by some colonial envoy and assimilated by Africans. The modernism addressed in this exhibition concerns the African systematization, deployment, and usage of modern forms, values, and structure. It may be productive to look closely at how African modernism accomplishes its modernity. To begin with, this modernism is not founded on an ideology of the universal, nor is it based on the recognition and assimilation of an autonomous European modernism, or on the continuity of the epistemic field of artistic territorialization achieved and consecrated by the colonial project.

Paris, 1934: While Europe is in the grips of fascism, amid it lies a marginalized and restless population of Africans and West Indians. One way or the other, the silence will break, because the colonized wish to speak. René Maran's *Batouala* (1921), an anticolonial novel set within an African culturescape, had been published and had won the Goncourt Prize a decade before. The works of African American and West Indian writers such as Langston Hughes, Claude McKay, Countee Cullen, and Jean Toomer, which formed the crux of the Harlem Renaissance, were becoming readily available in Europe and made an impression on Africans living there. Marcus Garvey's "return to Africa" movement provided the political ballast. What the Harlem Renaissance writers and Garvey offered was a view of blackness (Africanness, if you will) that found value and beauty in African culture and history as subjects for their art, much in the same way that African sculpture and religious rituals had penetrated cubism and surrealism.

The Negritude movement—begun by Aimé Césaire, Senghor, Léon Damas, and other African and Caribbean students in Paris in 1934, and one of the key founding moments of African modernism—had absorbed this lesson. Through *L'Etudiant noir*, a small student review founded by Senghor and Damas, the framework that would propel Negritude into the ranks of the Paris intellectual and artistic scene was born. To say that this difficult birth was an event of great importance would be to understate its radical import. Negritude, facing the example of African American writers of the Harlem Renaissance during the Jazz Age, when black culture carried a bit of the charge of the exotic and was desirable, posited a conscious intellectual dramatization of African alterity and insisted on the reality and originality of an African culture in the making of modernity. Thus, African modernism from this instance onward achieved its first synthesis through an act of internal reflexivity on the status and value of African culture. It also constructed for itself a tool for bringing about a structural and philosophical change in the making of modern culture. According to Sartre, "Negritude is the negro's being-in-the-world."[6] This "being-in-the-world" and its arrival in the cultural and literary economy of Europe are not merely a production of bombastic self-regard; its "antiracist racism," as Sartre puts it, is a strategy of subversion and rebellion. Thus, Negritude, as a modernist avant-garde, was based on the construction of an ethic, a field of practice, and on the primacy of African subjectivity and subject matter in order to contradict colonial alienation. It was the same impetus that led Kenyatta to try to demonstrate in his anthropological study *Facing Mount Kenya: The Tribal Life of the Gikuyu* that the Gikuyus as an African people had a conception of society, politics, law, and culture that was as complex and sophisticated as that of any European culture.[7]

Manchester, September 1945: World War II is over. African and West Indian soldiers from the war, along with students and trade unionists, stage a radical congress that demands, among other things, independence and the right of self-determination for Africa and the West Indies. The organizers had made clear the contradiction of colonialism by fighting to help secure freedom for Europe during the war. Organized by George Padmore, Nkrumah, Peter Abrahams, Kenyatta, and many others, the Fifth Pan-African Congress openly contested the European right to rule Africa and other colonies.

Like Negritude, Pan-Africanism situated itself in the field of the subjective. It sprang from the political recognition of an African search for social and cultural equality and autonomy. Where Negritude began as a francophone phenomenon, Pan-Africanism found its strongest appeal among anglophone artists and students. In terms of art and culture, Negritude and Pan-Africanism sought their meaning and viability in relation not to a canon (art history, for example) but to a political and social process (contemporary African society).

If, as Senghor had indicated, Negritude was a humanism and Nkrumah's Pan-Africanism centered on the African personality, one other approach to African modernism is to see in it an awareness by artists, intellectuals, activists, poets and writers, political leaders, and students, a necessity to subvert and destroy European cultural imperialism as the sine qua non of progressive culture. Thus, African modernism arrives at its strongest proposition in relation to its progressive alignment against racism and petty European superiority. Césaire had articulated it best when he stated his case for Negritude, insisting:

my negritude is neither tower nor cathedral
it takes root in the red flesh of the soil
it takes root in the ardent flesh of the sky
it breaks through the opaque prostration with its upright patience.[8]

But Césaire's self-deprecation is not merely a pragmatic strategy; within it lies the prime argument of many Africans for rejecting the construction of a questionable universal subject. We see this rejection of universalism formally embodied in the principle of nonalignment of the Bandung Conference in 1955. African delegates to the conference saw in its ethos a way to begin with a fresh perspective, while not rejecting the West completely. Bandung was a statement and declaration of autonomy. As the old colonial world crumbled, a new order of social, political, and economic relations among nations of the developing world took hold. These relationships in part exemplified a critical response to that which Western modernity could neither properly digest nor outright negate. Thus, we can say that Western modernity's limits expose it to a parallel international dimension of political philosophy. In a sense, the objectification and inscription by the formerly marginalized of a new will to power into a political philosophy of equality and respect for other nations and cultures in the international arena specify for us a new consciousness of modernity as it took hold among the formerly colonized. Thus, rather than pure celebration, Césaire's is an occasion to muse over the process of regeneration:

I say right on! The old negritude
progressively cadavers itself
the horizon breaks, recoils and expands
and through the shredding of clouds the flashing of a sign
the slave ship cracks everywhere. . . .
Its belly convulses and resounds. . . .
The ghastly tapeworm of its cargo gnaws the fetid guts of the
    strange suckling of
the sea![9]

Like the cracking of the slave ship, the relationship of African modernity to Europe's construction of the universal subject is both a critique and modification, a rip in the body of the colonial text. The aesthetics of African artists and writers in the post–World War II period were never founded on a spatial concept to which a proper geography could be ascribed; their aesthetics constituted both an ethic and an imaginary. On this basis the internal cohesion of midcentury African aesthetics is, first, a discourse of an awareness of otherness and, second, a process of regeneration that draws on the particularity of an African perspective. According to Mudimbe, "In literature this position is expressed in three major ways: first, in terms of domestication of political power (Ezekiel Mphahlele, Mongo Beti, and Ousmane Sembène); second, in criticism of colonial life (Chinua Achebe, D. Chraïbi, Ferdinand Oyono); and third, in the celebration of African sources of life (A. Loba, A. Sefrioui, Cheikh Hamidou Kane)."[10]

The crystallization of a powerful political ideology through Pan-Africanism is another moment at which the relationship of power and knowledge between Africa and Europe was reworked. Pan-Africanism in the post–World War II period was never the amelioration of an African cultural order but a field of recognition that sought active political, social, cultural, and economic integration of Africa into the international system. On this level, Pan-Africanism was a more critical and progressive project than Negritude. Pan-Africanism's promotion of the notion of a collective production of a common social space was rooted in the twin ideas of the recognition of the discourse of otherness and the need of regeneration based on that recognition. Mudimbe reminds us that it was in the political essays of early Pan-Africanists such as Nnamdi Azikiwe, in *Renascent Africa* (1937); Nkrumah, in *Towards Colonial Freedom* (1947); Obafemi Awolowo, in *Path toward Nigerian Freedom* (1947); Césaire, in *Discours sur le colonialisme* (1950); and Fanon, in *Peau noire, masques blancs* (1952), "that a clearly progressive awakening gradually affirmed the principles of African nationalism and international integration."[11] "For a number of African intellectuals," he continues, "these works have been, and probably still are, major sources for their cultural autonomy."[12]

Taking Inventory: Decolonizing African Cultural Production

Our books in the colonial schools taught us about the wars of the Gauls, the lives of Joan of Arc and Napoleon, the list of French departments, and the poems of Lamartine and the theater of Molière, as if Africa had never had a history, a past, a geographical existence, or a cultural life. Our students were valued only for their aptitude for this policy of complete cultural assimilation.

Ahmed Sékou Touré, Second Congress of Black Writers and Artists, Rome (1959)

By the early 1960s, the concept of African liberation had gradually shifted from political dogma to the realm of cultural nationalism and liberation. Some of the inherent ambiguity of Negritude in relation to European cultural hegemony was challenged by a more militant discourse. In their searing study of postcolonial literature and critique of the attempt to domesticate African literary production by subsuming it into the European canon, Chinweizu, Onwuchekwa Jemie, and Ihechukwu Madubuike had this to say: "The cultural task in hand is to fend off all foreign domination of African culture, to systematically destroy all encrustations of colonial and slave mentality, to clear the bushes and stake out new foundations for a liberated African modernity. This is a process that must take place in all spheres of African life—in government, industry, family and social life, education, city planning, architecture, arts, entertainment, etc."[13]

A liberated African modernity? The question bears on what this exhibition seeks to demonstrate, namely, that the construction of African modernity in the twentieth century is inextricably bound to the defense and legitimation of all and every sphere of African thought and life. It seems unnecessary, then, to make an argument that does not take the totality of this manifestation (political, social, economic, identity, culture, etc.) into full account. Thus, this exhibition and the book that accompanies it should be understood in light of this totality, which bears on the construction of both a political sphere and a cultural order.

In fact, artists and intellectuals made this analysis the very heart of their discourse—that to constitute a decolonized African aesthetic, one must first make a complete inventory of what needs to be decolonized. The Kenyan novelist, dramatist, and essayist Ngũgĩ wa Thiong'o had exactly such a thing in mind in his equally militant and soberly polemic view of African literature. Ngũgĩ insists that the inventory requires, first, a systematic review of what constitutes African literature, and that part of that review requires the decolonizing of one's mind; a part of which is the rejection of the Africanness of any African literature written in colonial languages. He sees in the language of African literature a means of mediating for an African audience a sense of their own reality. He writes that "language, any language, has a dual character: it is both a means of communication and a carrier of culture."[14] Ngũgĩ goes further, suggesting that only literature written in African languages can qualify as African literature, and describing its method in relation to its capacity to produce and carry a meaningful representation to real life by noting that "language as communication is speech and it imitates the language of real life, that is communication in production."[15]

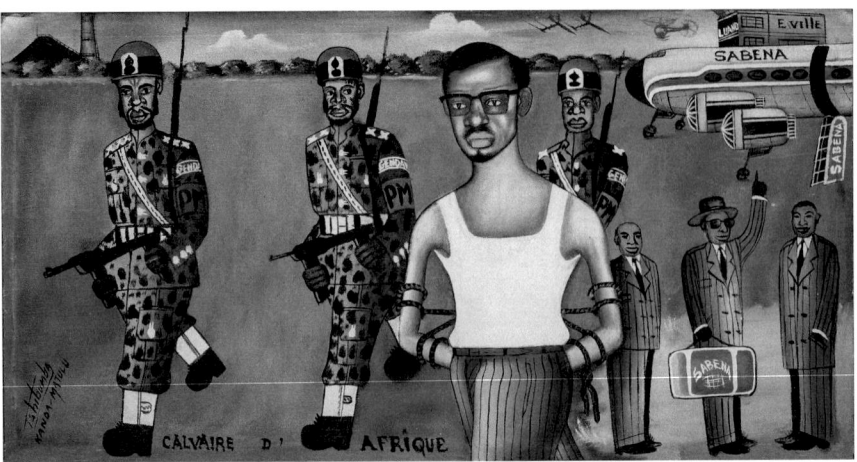

10.2 Tshibumba Kanda Matulu, *African Calvary*, from *The History of Zaïre* series, 1973. Black-and-white oil paint on canvas, 73 × 39 cm. © Coll. Etienne Boll, London.

Ngũgĩ's well-argued position and analysis of the situation of African writing in whatever colonial language could just as easily be transmuted to the situation of visual art. But not all African writers were in agreement that literature written in European languages by Africans is necessarily illegitimate and colonial. Some writers insisted that colonialism was a reality, that to critique it is to recognize it, and that writers and artists must be allowed to work in whatever method allows them the fullest capacity to express their ideas. Chinua Achebe saw the entire relationship of African representation to European languages as one of choice rather than of imposition. Writers, he cautioned, must not be put in positions where they have to choose sides. Wole Soyinka, the Nigerian Nobel laureate, had already made a preemptive strike against a stance like Ngũgĩ's, dispensing with what he saw as the wrongheaded essentialism of such a position, particularly in the philosophy of Negritude. In a famous quip against Negritude's essentialism, Soyinka stated, "A tiger does not proclaim its tigritude."[16] He pointed, in other words, to the pitfalls of relying on genetic codes and false African experience as the prerequisite for an authentic African cultural voice.

Though Soyinka did not need to justify the fact that Yoruba cosmology, religion, epic tradition, poetry, ritual, and language were sources for his dense poetic, literary, and dramatic works, he nonetheless came under attack from Chinweizu, Jemie, and Madubuike, who called themselves *Bolekaja* critics.[17] The *Bolekaja* critics accused Soyinka, J. P. Clark, and Christopher Okigbo of constituting a parade of writers whose works employed African imagery and situation in order to domesticate it within a European modernist literary formalism. They read this as a loss of self-confidence, and a compromise of the radical call for a total break with colonialism. Such debates made their rounds in conferences on African literature, language, and culture throughout the 1960s and 1970s.

In the Fifth Pan-African Congress of 1945, the rallying call was for emancipation, independence, and a drive toward an autonomous African culture; in the First Congress of Negro Writers and Artists in 1956, at the Sorbonne, and the Second Congress in Rome in 1959, the focus was on African culture and history as a theme of a rediscovered past and dignity; at the Conference of African Writers of English Expression, at Makerere University College, Kampala, Uganda, in 1962, the debate concerned the state of African literature in the postindependence period and the role of the writer in nation building. But more than any other discussion, the Makerere University College conference raised an issue that had for a time been skirted: the linguistic tool of African literature, and who its audience was. Within the visual arts, a similar debate was developing among artists in groups such as the Zaria Art Society, who were labeled "Zaria Rebels" for questioning the formalist European curriculum of art education in Nigeria. There was also the multiracial Amadlozi group in South Africa, who sought inspiration in African forms, themes, and history rather than looking toward Europe; and similarly, in Senegal the École de Dakar adapted Senghorian Negritude as a source of inspiration. In 1966 the Senegalese government, under the patronage of President Senghor, organized a landmark Pan-African festival, the Premier Festival Mondial des Arts Nègres, not only to celebrate the culture of Africa and its diaspora but also to examine the remarkable achievements of the previous twenty years. In a sense, the Premier Festival Mondial was an anniversary of the independence movements.

Looking back today at the period between 1945 and 1965, it is clear that there was already in formation an emergent category of discourse that would furnish us with the tools with which to analyze African modernity. That the debates and theories formulated in the period under study in this exhibition have yielded a rich trove of material from which we can begin a proper historical examination of the constitutive models of African creative, intellectual, political, and subjective practices is the great profit of this exhibition. The legacy of this discourse is the ethical, social, political, cultural, historical, and above all the epistemological compass they have fashioned for the study of modern and contemporary African culture. We make the necessary link to the relations between modern and contemporary art in this exhibition with a view of the historical impact of the independence period on the activities and thinking of many African artists working today. What we will encounter in the exhibition, which looks at the totality of all spheres of production in Africa (music, photography, art, literature, theater, film, and architecture), both by Africans and Europeans, is the insistent paradox of all modernities, namely, that they are simultaneously inward looking and totally open to all influence and receptive to rich dialogues.

The exhibition is divided into seven distinct subject areas: art, photography, film, architecture, graphics, theater, and literature. All of these are intimately linked to a wider historical framework. The subjects presented here are distinguished not as categories or paradigms, but as general discursive frames, allowing us to trace developments within each area and wherever possible to draw conclusions on specific topics or operations depending on the context. In no way should a clear line be drawn between each subject; instead, each section operates in mutual determination and entanglement, constantly maintaining a "soft" boundary that could allow critical interpenetrations.

That Africa was a staging ground for some of the most important questions of postwar politics and society, and that these questions made a crucial impact on identity, modernity, freedom, subjectivity, ethics, and culture, can no longer be debated. The more salient question arising from this exhibition is: "What is African and what is Africa to us?" This is, of course, a question neither philosophy nor metaphysics can provide answers to. But suffice it to say that *The Short Century: Independence and Liberation Movements in Africa, 1945-1994* represents an Africa of the imagination, as much as it addresses Africa in the context of her lived experiences and realities.

Conclusion: The Reader

To conclude, I should like to say something about the historical documents—essays, speeches, manifestos, resolutions, pamphlets—that are gathered in this book as an anthology, forming a crucial part of the project that must be seen in relation to its visual dimension. Throughout this text I have argued that the processes of African independence and liberation that began in the period after World War II produced an epistemological change in the Western conception of the universal subject, challenging and transforming

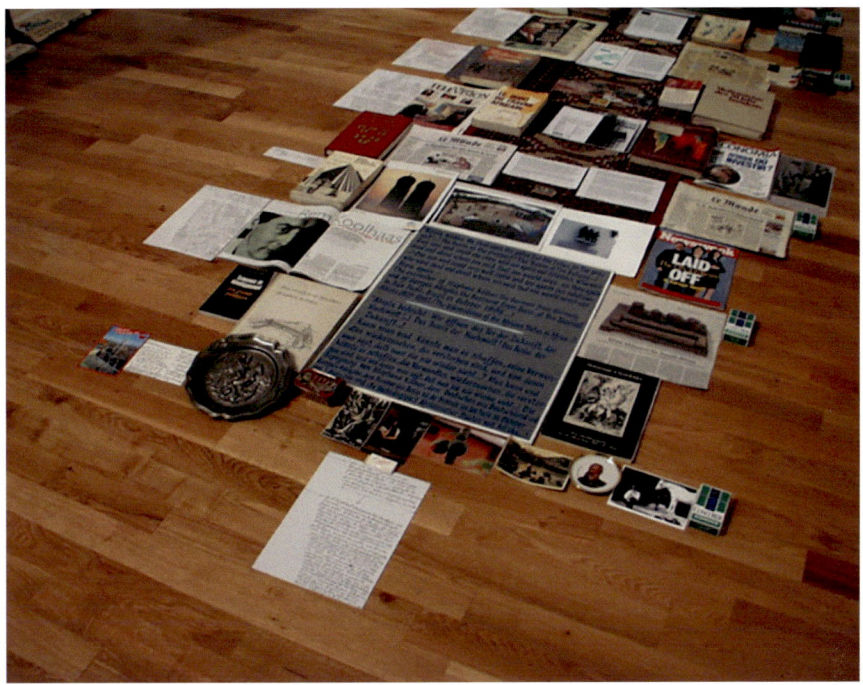

10.3 Georges Adéagbo, *Le Socialisme Africain*
(detail), 2001. Mixed-media installation at
Museum Villa Stuck, Munich, 2001. Courtesy
of the artist, Stephan Köhler, and AGADP,
Paris, 2025.

the ontological limits imposed by European hegemony over African history
and societies. Before the end of World War II, the world was essentially divided
into two spheres: the colonizer and the colonized. This division manifested
itself further into two spatial distinctions: Europe and its colonies. The
critical emergence of new African nations from colonial vassalage and into
nationhood ushered in a fresh context, the narrative of which is inscribed
in a new kind of historical text. This text defined limits to colonial power
and authority, ushering in a world no longer constituted by the Manichaean
scheme of the absolute self and the abject other.

The Reader is divided into two thematic sections. The first, Politics/
Ideology/Ethics, seeks to analyze the questions that concern the discourses
of Pan-Africanism, Pan-Arabism, liberation movements, and African socialism, and their structural and discursive performance in organizing social and
philosophical thoughts. The second section engages culture, as an operation
of subject formation, and the emergence of artistic and literary production.

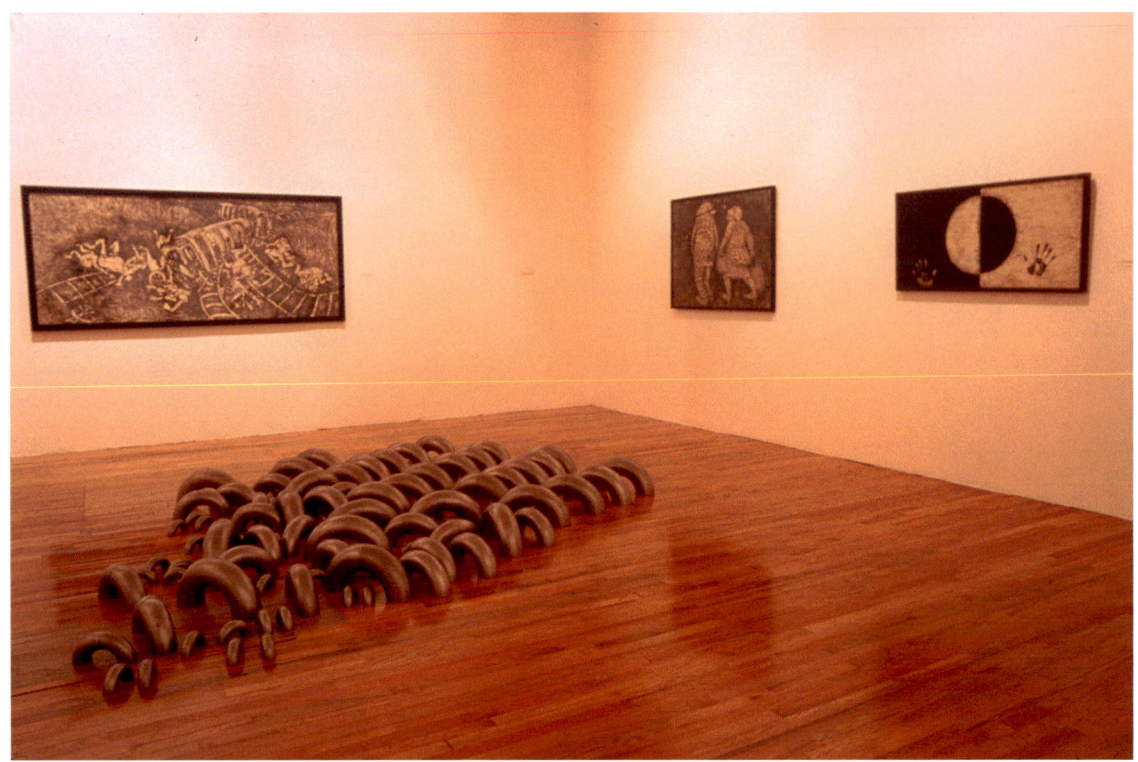

10.4 Installation view of the exhibition *The Short Century: Independence and Liberation Movements in Africa, 1945–1994*, Museum of Modern Art (MoMA) PS1, New York, February 10–May 5, 2002, showing Amir Nour, *Grazing at Shendi*, 1969, metal sculpture, on the floor. Paintings in the background are by Dumile Feni (Mslaba), Lucas Sithole, and Erhabor Ogieva Emokpae. Photograph: Donnelly Marks. Courtesy of MoMA PS1 Archives, II.A.1294, Museum of Modern Art Archives, New York. Digital image © 2025 Museum of Modern Art, New York/Scala, Florence.

This section looks closely at the role of culture in the practice of the everyday and the articulation of popular and individual visions.

With this in mind, any analysis of the tumultuous period of African decolonization must seek to begin with the primary texts and actions of that historical moment. The question for such an enterprise could be posed this way: In what forms and forums were the activities that were the spur for the independence and liberation movements organized? And who were the chief ideologues, theoreticians, and leaders of these nascent movements? The many essays, speeches, manifestos, conference resolutions, and pamphlets gathered in this volume commit themselves to exploring those questions. The Reader recommends itself as one of those rare occasions that allow for a deeper penetration of an important historical project in order better to understand its complexity and heterogeneity. By carefully reading these texts addressing contemporaneous events and attitudes, we become witnesses to the confrontations that shaped the processes of African modernity in the mid-twentieth century, we learn how they were written, and in what arenas they found their audience.

The task here is more than the mere recapitulation of the major themes of decolonization through the critical exegesis of varied intellectual, political, cultural, and theoretical frameworks. The Reader is a signpost for revisiting those themes, focusing on how new interpretations of African modernity were framed and disseminated. More important, we would do well to read the texts in relation to their import in organizing the forms and ideals of the new societies after colonialism. Attached to this purpose is the emergence of ideas of subjectivity and forms of representation that seek to link praxis and theory, ideology and action, emancipation and agency, history and consciousness, race and difference, nationhood and citizenship, identity and society. Many of the texts included here can be read today as documents of their time, while others remain as vivid to political, cultural, philosophical, and literary theories as they were when they were written.

To read Africa in light of these formative and well-argued positions is to emerge on the other side of the present African condition and the unfinished project of decolonization. Yet underlying many of the debates in this volume are contradictions that require forceful argumentation in the formulation of the goals of an African modern consciousness—whether those goals are based on instruments of armed struggle, or on the tension between cultural philosophies and political ideologies, or whether they are allied and subservient to Western democratic traditions and the institutions of global capitalism. On such a platform, the multiple voices in this volume give us an occasion to readapt many forms of historical argument concerning African modernity, especially in relation to the links between European models of political practice, institutions, and artistic and intellectual forms, be they painting, sculpture, the novel, poetry, music, or film, and the modalities of today's African realpolitik.

What one must also search for are the signs of rupture embedded in the very formation of African freedom from European colonization. From this rupture we may be able to glimpse the beginnings of several notions of identity discourse and cultural philosophy, social movements and ideological projects, that became solidified both in popular political agitation and in the founding texts of intellectual developments. In these texts, the discourses and projects take such names as Negritude, Pan-Africanism, black consciousness, Pan-Arabism, the African personality, African socialism, African nationalism, and so on. These critical projects, more than being ideological, posit affirmatively the deep entanglement of Africans in the project of twentieth-century modernity. It will become obvious that the instruments of action with which African independence (political and cultural) was fought test many of the earlier arguments, which often made no links between Africa and what could now be viewed as a historic period of global transition.

Today it seems impossible to believe that the emancipatory project of redefining Africa's relationship to the rest of the world and particularly to Europe—a project championed by a generation of young, determined, radical, and zealous students and trade union members from the 1930s onward—should have happened in the short span of less than twenty-five years. Of course, the groundwork for the radical beginnings of the movements of the 1930s, 1940s, and 1950s had already been laid in the works of writers, historians, and political activists such as Edward Wilmot Blyden, Alexander Crummell, W. E. B. Du Bois, and Herbert Macaulay, and in events such as the formation in 1912 of the liberation movement that became the African National Congress. By the time World War II ended, in fact, the conflagration stoked by the movements of Pan-Africanism (in the anglophone world), Negritude (in the francophone world), and Pan-Arabism (in the Maghreb) meant that the horizon for a new range of actions had broadened significantly.

This book, then, offers a means of accounting for the urgent issues that were placed before the postwar publics of Europe on the one hand and Africa on the other, as parts of a strong critical discourse on colonialism, independence, liberation, autonomy, self-determination, and freedom. These texts, I would argue, must not be read, as we are so often wont to do, as merely discursive and speculative. On the contrary, many of them were manuals for actions linked to praxis and directed toward the production of the subjective through the liberation of the individual. On the next level, the Reader is not simply an anthology for the Africanist or Africanophile; it is compiled as part of the historical record of the twentieth century, as a way to deepen our engagement with forms of historical understanding and narration.

In the context of decolonization, on which many of the texts pivot, the arguments and ideologies are many; the means and methodologies for their realization and integration into the political cultures and structures of the emergent nation-states are diverse and varied. Moreover, they point to the richness that accompanied the debates of this generation of thinkers (African and European alike) in formulating forms of governance and the political ethics of the new societies born in the aftermath of independence and liberation. Despite the variety of positions expressed in the present volume, the main impetus is the instrumentalization of the procedures of an Africanist intellectual space, and through that space a penetration of the question of what it means to be modern, African, and free in a world in which the notion of colonialism is diametrically opposed to that of European democracy, institutions of which not long ago made Africans and others into subject peoples. Whatever we may make of them (especially of those positions that today may seem to us untenable), they remain a strong knot in the tangled web of the modern condition—ciphers for decoding the fractious memory of a time lived in the shadow of subjection and born in the deeply unethical code and moral conduct of colonialism.

NOTES

Epigraphs: Kwame Nkrumah, prime minister of Ghana, speech at the opening session of the All-African People's Conference, Accra, Ghana, December 8, 1958, in Kwame Nkrumah, *Speeches by the Prime Minister of Ghana at the Opening and Closing Sessions of the All-African People's Conference* (Accra: Community Center, 1959), 8; Frantz Fanon, *Black Skin, White Masks* [1952], trans. Charles Lam Markmann (New York: Grove Press, 1967); Léopold Sédar Senghor, "The African Road to Socialism: An Attempt at Definition," in *On African Socialism*, trans. Mercer Cook (New York: Frederick A. Praeger, 1964), 68; Ngũgĩ wa Thiong'o, *Decolonising the Mind: The Politics of Language in African Literature* (London: James Currey; Nairobi: Heinemann, 1986), 17; Ahmed Sékou Touré, "The Political Leader as a Representative of a Culture," lecture delivered at the Second Congress of Black Writers and Artists, Rome, March 25–29, 1959.

1 The countries were represented by Graf Kapnist of Russia, Baron Lambermont and le Comte van der Straten Ponthoz of Belgium, Baron de Courcel of France, Said Pasha of Turkey, the Marquês de Penafiel and M. de

Serpa Pimentel of Portugal, [Ambassador Edoardo] de Launay of Italy, Sir Edward Malet of Great Britain, [Count] Benomar of Spain, Emil da Vind of Denmark, General Baron Bildt of Sweden and Norway, [Count] von Hatzfeldt, Herr Busch, and Herr von Kusserow of Germany, [Count] Széchényi of Austria and Hungary, and Jonkheer van der Hoeven of the Netherlands. J. A. Kasson and H. S. Sanford attended in the capacity of observers for the United States.

2 Recently a "Lumumba Commission" was set up in Belgium to examine the role of the Belgian government in his assassination. The same process of reexamining colonial participation in the torture, kidnapping, and execution of Algerian rebels by French soldiers is currently underway in France. In South Africa, the Truth and Reconciliation Commission has looked into the "gross human rights violations" of the apartheid government. This will suggest that colonial violence during the period of the independence and liberation movements was more the norm than the exception.

3 V. Y. Mudimbe, *The Invention of Africa: Gnosis, Philosophy, and the Order of Knowledge* (Bloomington: Indiana University Press; London: James Currey, 1988), 92.

4 Clayton Eshleman and Annette Smith, in *Aimé Césaire: The Collected Poetry*, trans. Clayton Eshleman and Annette Smith (Berkeley: University of California Press, 1983), 7.

5 Mudimbe, *Invention of Africa*, 93.

6 Jean-Paul Sartre, "Black Orpheus," in *What Is Literature and Other Essays*, trans. Steven Ungar (Cambridge, MA: Harvard University Press, 1988), 314. Sartre's essay originally appeared in French, under the title "*Orphée Noir*," as the introduction to Senghor's 1948 *Anthologie de la nouvelle poésie nègre et malgache de langue française*, the first attempt to bring together a body of literary works exemplifying the spirit of Negritude. But the most radical work of this literature was Césaire's seminal long poem "*Cahier d'un retour au pays natal*" ("Notebook of a Return to the Native Land") of 1938. Debate continues today on when exactly the term Negritude was first used, but the earliest published appearance of it was in Césaire's poem, which includes the lines "My negritude is not a stone, its deafness hurled against the clamor of day / my negritude is not a leukoma of dead liquid over the earth's dead eye / my negritude is neither tower nor cathedral." [*Ed. note:* Césaire, "Notebook of a Return to the Native Land," in Eshleman and Smith, *Aimé Césaire*, 67, 69.]

7 [*Ed. note:* Jomo Kenyatta, *Facing Mount Kenya: The Tribal Life of the Gikuyu* (London: Secker and Warburg, 1938).]

8 Césaire, "Notebook," 67, 69.

9 Césaire, "Notebook," 79.

10   Mudimbe, *Invention of Africa*, 92.

11   Mudimbe, *Invention of Africa*, 90. [*Ed. note:* Mudimbe references Nnamdi
      Azikiwe, *Renascent Africa* [1937] (London: Routledge, 1968); Kwame Nk-
      rumah, *Towards Colonial Freedom: Africa in the Struggle against World Im-
      perialism* [1945] (Accra and London: Guinea Press Ltd, 1962); Obafemi
      Awolowo, *Path towards Nigerian Freedom* (London: Faber and Faber, 1947);
      Aimé Césaire, *Discourse on Colonialism* [1950] (New York: Monthly Review
      Press, 1972); Frantz Fanon, *Black Skin, White Masks* [1952], trans. Charles
      Lam Markmann (New York: Grove Press, 1967).]

12   Mudimbe, *Invention of Africa*, 90.

13   Chinweizu, Onwuchekwa Jemie, and Ihechukwu Madubuike, *Toward the
      Decolonization of African Literature* (Washington, DC: Howard University
      Press, 1983), 1.

14   Ngũgĩ, *Decolonising the Mind*, 13.

15   Ngũgĩ, *Decolonising the Mind*, 13.

16   [*Ed. note:* Wole Soyinka, cited in Janheinz Jahn, *Neo-African Literature: A
      History of Black Writing* (New York: Grove Press, 1969), 265–66.]

17   The word *Bolekaja* roughly translates from the Yoruba as "Come down,
      let's fight," a metaphor adopted by Chinweizu, Jemie, and Madubuike
      for the kind of critical operation they were performing on postcolonial
      literature. In their minds a great deal of this literature was pretentious,
      pompous, and exemplary of what they called "Hopkins disease," a refer-
      ence to the kind of colonial British literature taught in most university
      literature departments in anglophone Africa.

Under the artistic direction of Okwui Enwezor, Documenta11 was presented on five "platforms." Public symposia on key topics in four cities between March 2001 and March 2002–"Democracy Unrealized" (Vienna and Berlin), "Experiments with Truth: Transitional Justice and the Processes of Truth and Reconciliation" (New Delhi), "Créolité and Creolization" (St. Lucia), and "Under Siege: Four African Cities, Freetown, Johannesburg, Kinshasa, and Lagos" (Lagos)– were followed by the exhibition at several venues in Kassel from June to September 2002. His curatorial and co-editorial team consisted of Carlos Basualdo, Ute Meta Bauer, Susanne Ghez, Sarat Maharaj, Mark Nash, and Octavio Zaya. For recent reflections on the exhibition, see the Documenta11 Platform6, accessed September 20, 2024, https://www.documenta-platform6 .de. "The Black Box" is Enwezor's introductory essay to the book *Documenta 11_Platform 5 (Exhibition)* (Ostfildern-Ruit, Germany: Hatje Cantz, 2002), 42–55.

ALTHOUGH PREPARATION AND RESEARCH began nearly four years ago, it is nonetheless permissible to say that the discursive drive of Documenta11 will never see its conclusion in the spectacular spaces filled with art projects that the exhibition offers to visitors to Kassel. The exhibition, despite its ambition, scale, and complexity, and the sheer heterogeneity of the forms, images, and positions that encompass its far-reaching vision, is not to be understood as a terminus for understanding the wide-ranging disciplinary models spelled out in the first four Platforms of conferences, debates, and workshops that preceded it in five locations: in Europe (Vienna and Berlin), Asia (New Delhi), the Americas (St. Lucia), and Africa (Lagos). Built into interlocking constellations of discursive domains, circuits of artistic and knowledge production, and research modules, the parameters that have shaped the organization of this project are to be found in the complex predicaments of contemporary art in a time of profound historical change and global transformation.

The careful examination and analysis of contemporary art, visual culture, and its spectatorial regimes, as well as other material orders of representation, should also be understood in relation to those other changes taking place across disciplinary and cultural boundaries that inform today's artistic procedures. The horizon of Documenta11's project and the full scope that its five Platforms occupy are twofold: first, there is the spatial and temporal dimension; the second is historical and cultural in nature. The full measure of Documenta11's critical procedure, then, is to be sought not only within the optics and visual logic of contemporary art. Thus, the entire scope of the project inverts the logic that the exhibition's centrality is what defines the proper meaning of the artistic and intellectual possibilities of its procedures.

To construct an exhibition, the curator is always confronted with the double displacement of space and time. If the function of the artwork and the story it tells in an exhibition is to be understood primarily through the nature of its presentation, or by calling on the context of the exhibition system to restore the temporal displacement that a work is often pressed into through the empirical logic of one thing standing next to another, this would also mean to establish the artwork's limits as such. Another observation is to see an exhibition as a kind of metalanguage of mediation that constructs a tautological system in which the artwork is bound up in its own self-referentiality through the relationships established between mediums, objects, and systems. This would be particularly true when calling on the work of art to present for scrutiny all its constitutive formal, conceptual, and analytical relations to the language of the exhibition's ideology. Under such a condition there is no life for the artwork outside the system of art, no autonomy outside the framework of an *art exhibition*. The artwork—which, in any case, is understood a priori to be extraterritorial to an exhibition's logic—functions as time spatialized, but only inside the space in which it is corseted, which does not refer to an external world. However, there is another less formal route to penetrate the logic of the exhibition's viewpoint; this is through methods that are manifested in a range of social, political, and cultural networks that have incessantly marked the limit and horizon of global discourse today and that present a different context for working on a project such as Documenta11. As such, this exhibition could be read as an accumulation of passages, a collection of moments, temporal lapses that emerge into spaces that reanimate for a viewing public the endless concatenation of worlds, perspectives, models, countermodels, and thinking that constitute the artistic subject. The description offered above, however, proves inadequate to fully capture the interrogations to which Documenta11 has subjected current contexts of artistic production and reception. As an exhibition project, Documenta11 begins from the sheer side of extraterritoriality: first, by displacing its historical context in Kassel; second, by moving outside the domain of the gallery space to that of the discursive; and, third, by expanding the locus of the disciplinary models that constitute and define the project's intellectual and cultural interest.

In fact, if the larger intellectual and curatorial scope of Documenta11 is to be placed in proper perspective, it is in the idea that there are no overarching conclusions to be reached, no forms of closure, and that no prognosis can be derived from the critical task it set out to examine and question, namely, the idea that the means and approach taken by an exhibition are necessarily fully encrypted into the result of what it displays and the forms it recuperates for artistic posterity. What, then, is the task of this exhibition project if it is not the tacit assumption that it will show the critical orientation of all engaged contemporary forms of visual production (images, objects, architecture, nonimages, etc.) as they are arrayed before us today? In the past, the use of institutional forms of exhibition practice such as Documenta to form a narrative, and from thence to posit a unified vision of art or to draw conclusions about its formal distinctiveness from all other kinds of practice, was central to the understanding of the institutional parameters of modern and contemporary art. In other cases, a different kind of conclusion was sought through critical departures from such a unified vision: this strategy of disarticulating critical art from its institutional support for the most part resides in the history of the avant-garde.

Yet, in a sense, the avant-garde and formalist art share a common assumption in the completeness of their vision, which is to say: to secure the past and maintain tradition, or to depart vigorously from the past and renovate tradition. According to Guy Debord, institutional formalism in the name of tradition and the avant-garde through its lofty invocation of innovation are locked in "the struggle between tradition and innovation, which is the basic principle of the internal development of the culture of historical societies, [and] is predicated entirely on the permanent victory of innovation. Cultural [artistic] innovation is impelled solely, however, by that total historical movement which, by becoming conscious of its totality,

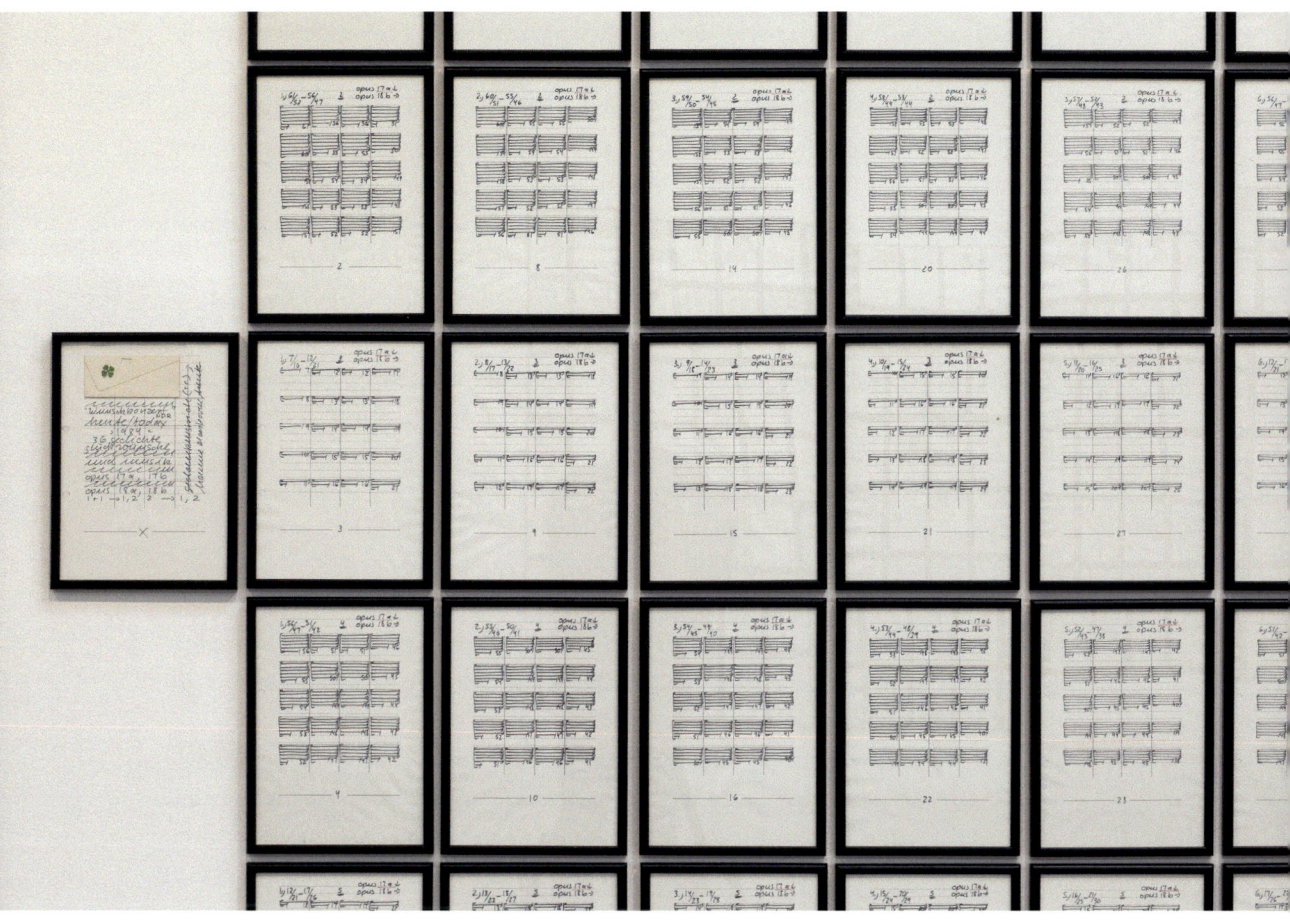

11.1 Hanne Darboven, *Wunschkonzert, Opus 17 a und b, Opus 18 a und b*, 1984. Collage, felt pen on paper, greeting cards, 1,009 sheets, 29.7 × 21 cm each. Shown at Documenta11, Kassel. Courtesy of Sprüth Magers, Berlin and Regen Projects, Los Angeles. © Hanne Darboven Stiftung, Hamburg/VG Bild-Kunst, Bonn 2025. Photograph: Brian Forrest.

tends toward the transcendence of its own cultural presuppositions and hence toward the suppression of all separations."[1]

The five Platforms that form the project of Documentaⅱ share in no such presupposition. If the animating intellectual and artistic quests of past Documentas have been to prove such conclusions were possible, Documentaⅱ places its quest within the epistemological difficulty that marks all attempts to forge one common, universal conception and interpretation of artistic and cultural modernity. We begin with a rather direct questioning of the efficacy of the institutionalized discourses that have attended the dissemination and reception of so-called radical art; especially one that insists on and promulgates the notion that art, especially radical art, in its conflictual relationship to bourgeois society (in spite of all attempts to bring its full measure into the ethical-political space of culture), remains autonomous from all political and social demands. But this is hardly the case today. We are today confronted with a singular predicament; one in which we would ask: What could be Documentaⅱ's spectacular difference if viewed from the refractory shards thrown up by the multiple artistic spaces and knowledge circuits that are the critical hallmarks of today's artistic subjectivity and cultural climate?

At the turn of an already less than promising century, Documenta is confronted by and placed in the challenging situation of declaring what its spectacular difference will be, without shielding its past triumphs and successes from the transhistorical processes that shake the ground of every ontological pronouncement about artistic uniqueness. That spectacular difference proceeds not simply from the difficult-to-sustain notion of art's eternal autonomy from all domains of sociopolitical life, but from the view that art's proliferating forms and methods, histories and departures, conditions of production and canons of institutionalization, call strongly for a forum from which to announce its critical independence from the conservative academic thinking that has taken possession of art's place in life and thought. Therefore, one claim that can be made for Documentaⅱ's spectacular difference is that its critical spaces are not places for the normalization or uniformization of all artistic visions on their way to institutional beatification. Rather, through the continuity and circularity of the nodes of discursivity and debate, location and translation, cultural situations and their localities that are transmitted and perceived through the five Platforms, Documentaⅱ's spaces are to be seen as forums of committed ethical and intellectual reflection on the possibilities of rethinking the historical procedures that are part of its contradictory heritage of grand conclusions.

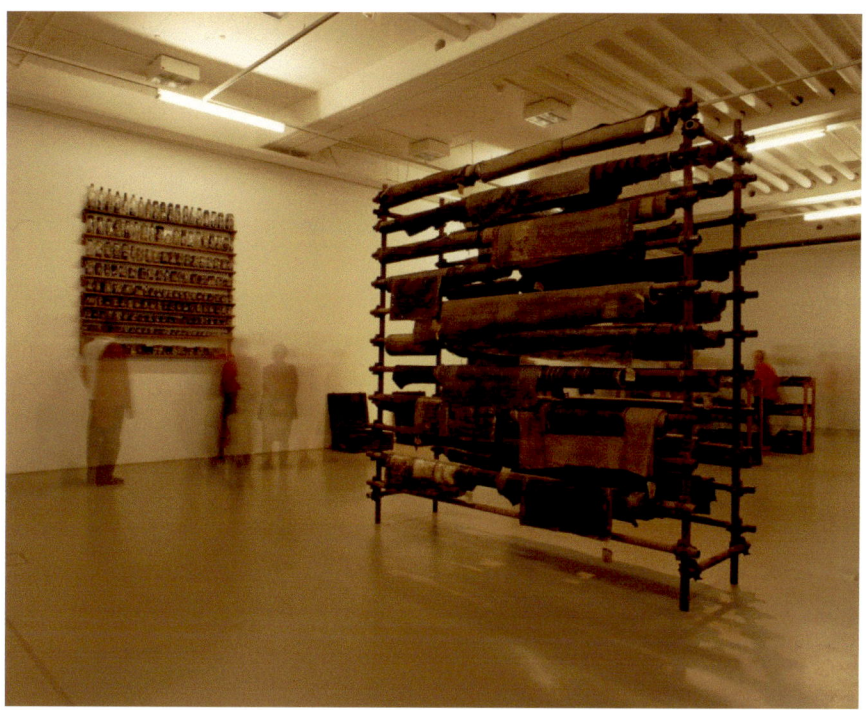

11.2 Chohreh Feyzdjou, *Boutique Product of Chohreh Feyzdjou*, 1973–93. Mixed-media installation at Documenta11, Kassel, 2002. © documenta archiv/Ryszard Kasiewicz photographer.

What Is an Avant-Garde Today?

The Postcolonial Aftermath of Globalization and the Terrible Nearness of Distant Places

One feature of most definitions of *globalization* is the degree to which the term is constantly brought into the phenomenological orbits of spatiality and temporality in order to be disciplined inside the cold logic of the mathematical analysis of capital production and accumulation and economic rationalization (a point made so deftly by Maria Eichhorn's project in the exhibition). Another point about globalization gives rise to the thought that its cumulative effects and processes are to be understood as mediations and representations of spatiality and temporality: globalization is said to abolish great distances, while temporality is at best experienced as uneven.

In his essay "At the Edge of the World: Boundaries, Territoriality, and Sovereignty in Africa," Achille Mbembe makes the case clear by evoking Fernand Braudel's monumental study of capitalism and the world system. Mbembe writes, "If at the center of the discussion on globalization we place the three problems of spatiality, calculability, and temporality in their relations with representation, we find ourselves brought back to two points usually ignored in contemporary discourses, even though Fernand Braudel had called attention to them. The first of these has to do with temporal pluralities, and, we might add, with the subjectivity that makes these temporalities possible and meaningful."[2] Such temporal plurality could be understood, according to Mbembe, by the distinction Braudel drew between "temporalities of long and very long duration, slowly evolving and less slowly evolving situations, rapid and virtually instantaneous deviations, the quickest being the easiest to detect."[3]

Whatever definition or character we invest it with, it is in the postcolonial order that we find the most critical enunciation and radicalization of spatiality and temporality. From the moment the postcolonial enters into the space/time of global calculations and the effects they impose on modern subjectivity, we are confronted not only with the asymmetry and limitations of globalism's materialist assumptions but also with the terrible nearness of distant places that global logic sought to abolish and bring into one domain of deterritorialized rule. Rather than vast distances and unfamiliar places, strange peoples and cultures, postcoloniality embodies the spectacular mediation and representation of nearness as the dominant mode of understanding the present condition of globalization. Postcoloniality, in its demand for full inclusion within the global system and by contesting existing epistemological structures, shatters the narrow focus of Western global optics and fixes its gaze on the wider sphere of the new political, social, and cultural relations that emerged after World War II. The postcolonial today is a world of proximities. It is a world of nearness, not an elsewhere. Neither is it a vulgar state of endless contestations and anomie, chaos and unsustainability, but rather the very space where the tensions that govern all ethical relationships between citizen and subject converge. The postcolonial space

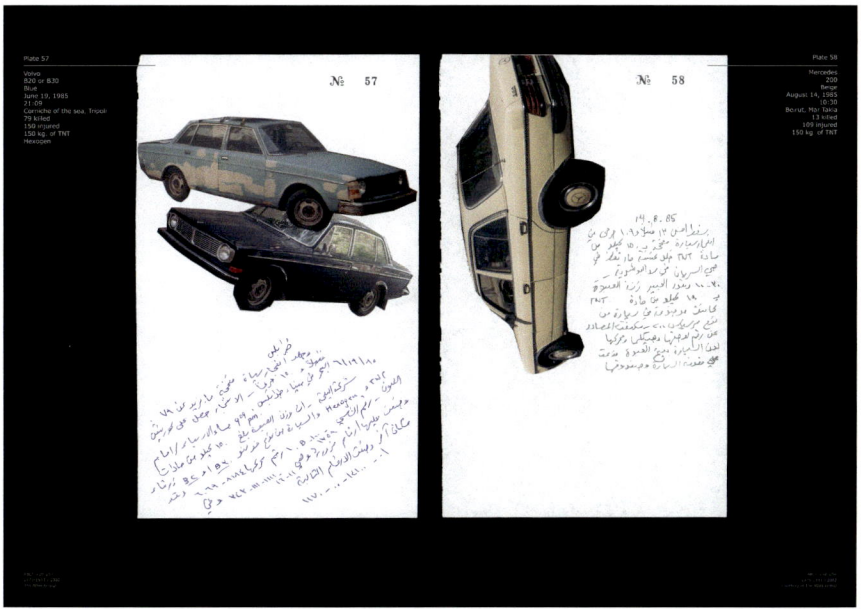

11.3 Walid Raad/The Atlas Group, *Note-book volume 38: Already been in a lake of fire, Plates 57–58*, 1991/2003. Archival ink-jet print mounted on anodized aluminum, 111.8 × 198.8 cm. Shown at Documenta11, Kassel. © Walid Raad. Courtesy of Paula Cooper Gallery, New York.

is the site where experimental cultures emerge to articulate modalities that define the new meaning- and memory-making systems of late modernity.

In the analysis of postcoloniality we witness a double move: first through the liberatory strategy of decolonization. Decolonization—that is to say, liberation from within—as the political order of the postcolonial is not only counternormative and counterhegemonic but also tends toward the reproduction of the universal as the sign of the rupture from imperial governance. Decolonization is also understood here by what Mbembe and Janet Roitman call a "regime of subjectivity," which they describe as "a shared ensemble of imaginary configurations of 'everyday life,' imaginaries which have a material basis; and systems of intelligibility to which people refer in order to construct a more or less clear idea of the causes of phenomena and their effects, to determine the domain of what is possible and feasible, as well as the logics of efficacious action. More generally a regime of subjectivity is an ensemble of ways of living, representing, and experiencing contemporaneousness, while at the same time, inscribing this experience in the mentality, understanding, and language of a historical time."[4] Postcoloniality's second lesson is that it exceeds the borders of the former colonized world to lay claim to the modernized, metropolitan world of empire by making empire's former "other" visible and present at all times, either through the media or through mediatory, spectatorial, and carnivalesque relations of language, communication, images, contact, and resistance within the everyday. Two decades ago, a number of theorists would have called this double move postmodernism's saving grace. But postcoloniality must at all times be distinguished from postmodernism. While postmodernism was preoccupied with relativizing historical transformations and contesting the lapses and prejudices of epistemological grand narratives, postcoloniality does the obverse, seeking instead to sublate and replace all grand narratives through new ethical demands on modes of historical interpretation.

In this regard, it could be said that the history of the avant-garde falls within the epistemological scheme of grand narratives. What, then, is the fate of the avant-garde in this climate of incessant assault on its former conclusions? Seen from this purview, all economic, social, cultural, and political questions that emerged in the past half century, and the vital relations of power that attend their negotiations, have had the distinctive historical impact of abolishing all the claims that the former European avant-gardes made for themselves. Nowhere is this historical termination more visible than in the recent drive by global capitalism to frame a new optics of spatial and temporal totality that forms the project of neoliberalism after the demise of the crudely managed and regulated Soviet Communist system. To understand what constitutes the avant-garde today, one must begin not in the field of contemporary art but in the field of culture and politics, as well as in the economic field governing all relations that have come under the overwhelming hegemony of capital. If the avant-gardes of the past (futurism, Dada, and surrealism, let's say) anticipated a changing order, that of today is to make impermanence, and what the Italian philosopher Giorgio Agamben calls *aterritorality*, the principal order of today's uncertainties, instability, and insecurity.[5] With this order in place, all notions of autonomy which radical art had formerly claimed for itself are abrogated.

Calculating the effects of these uncertainties within the new imperial scheme of "Empire," Michael Hardt and Antonio Negri inform us of the features of a new type of global sovereignty which, in its deterritorialized form, is no longer defined by the conservative borders of the old nation-state scheme. If this Empire is materializing, hegemonizing, and attempting to

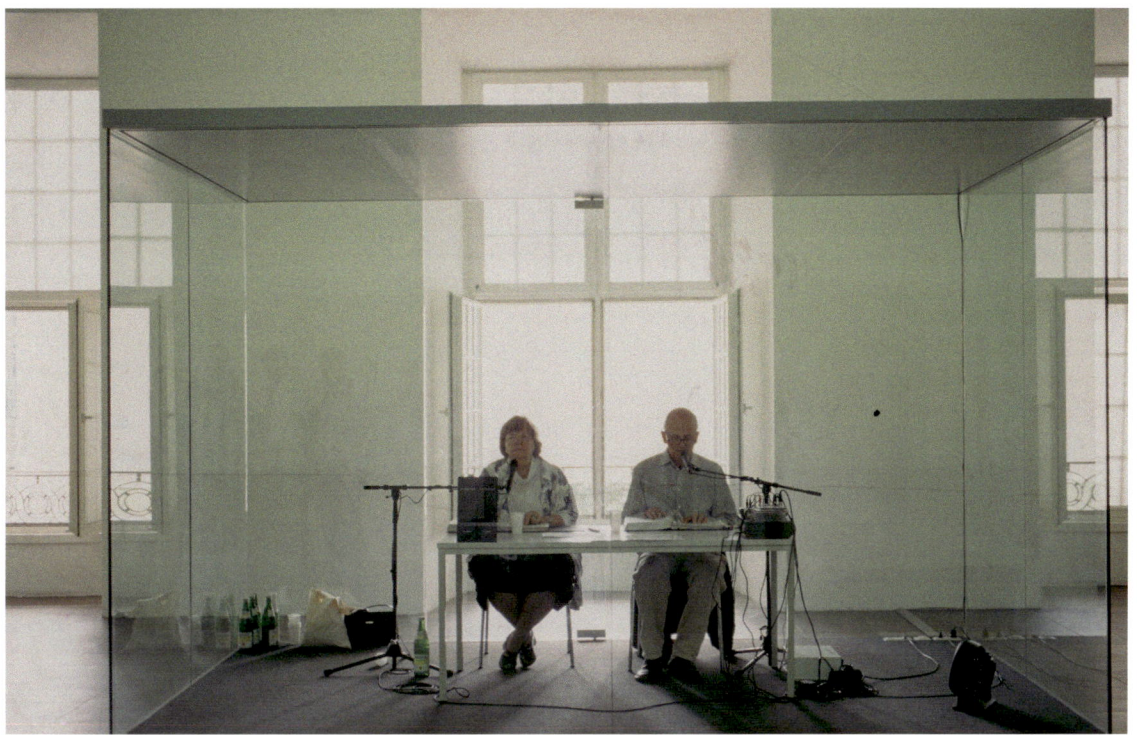

11.4 On Kawara, *One Million Years, [Past]*
9–25, Future [9–25], 2002. Performance, Docu-
menta11, Kassel, 2002. © documenta archiv/
Ryszard Kasiewicz photographer.

regulate all forms of social relations and cultural exchanges, strong, critical
responses to this materialization are contemporary art's weakest point. In
their thesis, Empire is that domain of actions and activities that have come
to replace imperialism; whose scope also harbors the ambition to rule not
just territories, markets, populations, but most fundamentally, social life in
its entirety.[6] Today's avant-garde is so thoroughly disciplined and domesti-
cated within the scheme of Empire that a whole different set of regulatory
and resistance models has to be found to counterbalance Empire's attempt
at totalization. Hardt and Negri call this resistance force, opposed to the
power of Empire, "the Multitude."[7] If Empire's countermodel is to be found
in the pressing, anarchic demands of the multitude, to understand what
sustains it historically returns us yet again to the move by postcoloniality
to define new models of subjectivity. In postcoloniality we are incessantly
offered countermodels through which the displaced—those placed on the

margins of the enjoyment of full global participation—fashion new worlds by producing experimental cultures. By *experimental cultures* I wish to define a set of practices whereby cultures evolving out of imperialism and colonialism, slavery and indenture, compose a collage of reality from the fragments of collapsing space.

Ground Zero or Tabula Rasa: From Margin to Center

But we have precisely chosen to speak of that kind of tabula rasa which characterizes at the outset all decolonization. Its unusual importance is that it constitutes, from the very first day, the minimum demands of the colonized. To tell the truth, the proof of success lies in a whole social structure being changed from the bottom up. The extraordinary importance of change is that it is willed, called for, demanded. The need for this change exists in its crude state, impetuous and compelling, in the consciousness and in the lives of the men and women who are colonized. But the possibility of this change is equally experienced in the form of a terrifying future in the consciousness of another "species" of men and women, the colonizers.

Frantz Fanon, *The Wretched of the Earth* (1963)

As in the early years of decolonization and the liberation struggles of the twentieth century, radical Islam has today come to define (for now) the terms of radical politics in the twenty-first century. Also, following the strategies of the liberation struggles of the past century, the program of political Islam today is based on an agonistic struggle with Westernism: that is, that sphere of global totality that manifests itself through the political, social, economic, cultural, juridical, and spiritual integration achieved via institutions devised and maintained solely to perpetuate the influence of European and North American modes of being. Two chief attributes of this integration are to be seen in the constitution of the first and second phases of modernity: first, in the far-reaching effects of the world system of capitalism and the state form; and, second, in the perpetual interpretation of what a just society ought to be, pursued through the secular vision of democracy as the dominant principle of political participation. The main political rupture of today is properly caught in the resistance struggles being initiated by a host of forces (whether Islamic or secular) in order to prevent their societies from total integration into these two phases of the Western system.

If we are to have a proper analysis by which to interpret the fundamental rationale for such resistance, we must try to understand that processes of integration proper to the idea of Westernism rest somewhat on what Jürgen Habermas calls "boundary-maintaining systems," which are also systems of conceptual appropriation of sociocultural processes schematized in his distinction between society and lifeworld.[8] One way of touching on this distinction is communicated by a view that sees non-Western societies in evolutionary stages of movement toward integration: from tribal to modern society; feudal to technological economy; underdeveloped to developed; theocratic and authoritarian to secular democratic systems of governance. In his classic study of the colonial discourse around Africa, V. Y. Mudimbe writes about the colonial system "as a dichotomizing system [within which] a great number of current paradigmatic oppositions have developed: traditional versus modern; oral versus written and printed; agrarian and customary communities versus urban and industrialized; subsistence economies versus highly productive economies."[9] This evolutionary principle of integration returns us to Braudel's notion of "temporalities of long and very long duration, slowly evolving and less slowly evolving situations." In every stage of this evolutionary scheme, Westernism's insistence on the total adoption and observation of its norms and concepts comes to constitute the only viable idea of social, political, and cultural legitimacy from which all modern subjectivities are seen to emerge. As I shall argue later, the social and political struggles of today have their roots in the flaws inherent in the two concepts on which Westernism is based.

Within the field of art, the concepts of the museum and art history rest on a similar unyielding theology that founds the legitimacy of artistic autonomy, canons, and connoisseurship on the same interpretive pursuit of modernity, which would also formulate the historical and formal understanding of all artistic production for all time. In the specific instance of large-scale international exhibitions, Gerardo Mosquera has proposed the view that Western modernism's theology of values turns into a moment from which to gauge the asymmetry in the relationship between those he calls "curating cultures" and those others who are "curated cultures."[10] In hindsight, the top-down view of curating contemporary art operates similarly within the frame of artistic and canonical integration and totalization that grounds the principle of Westernism as such. The horizon of artistic discourses of the past century, regardless of claims made for the affinities between the tribal and modern, is neatly described by the cleavage that defines the separation between Western artistic universalism and tribal object particularities and peculiarities which also define their marginality. While strong revolutionary claims have been made for the avant-garde within

Westernism, its vision of modernity remains surprisingly conservative and formal. On the other hand, the political and historical vision of the Western avant-garde has remained narrow. The propagators of the avant-garde have done little to constitute a space of self-reflexivity that can understand new relations of artistic modernity not founded on Westernism. The foregoing makes tendentious the claims of radicality often imputed to exhibitions such as Documenta or similar manifestations within the exhibitionary complex of artistic practice today. What one sees, then, in Documenta's historical alliance with institutions of modernism is how immediately it is caught in a double bind in its attempt to negotiate both its radicality and normativity.

The events of September 11, 2001, in the United States have provided us with a metaphor for articulating what is at stake in the radical politics and experimental cultures of today, while opening a space from which culture, qua contemporary art, could theorize an epistemology of nonintegrative discourse. The metaphor of September 11 is to be found in the stark notion of Ground Zero. But what does Ground Zero mean at that moment it is uttered? Where do we now locate the space of Ground Zero? What constitutes its effects on the nature of radical politics and cultural articulations today? Is Ground Zero the space of the kind of antagonistic politics in which the enemy always appears the same, undifferentiated, making his annihilation all the more justifiable? Or is it to be found in the terrible pile of molten steel, soot, broken lives, and scarred, ashen ground of the former World Trade Center in downtown Manhattan? In Gaza, Ramallah, or Jerusalem? In the ruins of Afghan cities? Or is Ground Zero the founding instant of the reckoning to come with Westernism after colonialism?

Let's begin again. It may be said—in the sense of the insecurity, instability, and uncertainties it inspires—that the kind of political violence we are experiencing today may well come to define what we mean when we invoke the notion of Ground Zero. Beyond the symbolic dimension of its funerary representation, the notion of Ground Zero resembles most closely Fanon's powerful evocation of the ground-clearing gesture of tabula rasa, as a beginning in the ethics and politics of constituting a new order of global society moving beyond colonialism as a set of dichotomizing oppositions, and beyond Westernism as the force of modern integration. No contemporary thinker comes closer than Fanon to articulating with such radical accuracy and propinquity the chaos that now proliferates inside the former dead certainties of the imperial project of colonialism and Westernism. These dead certainties are still to be found in the discourses that have equally proliferated to describe the radical spatial and temporal violence

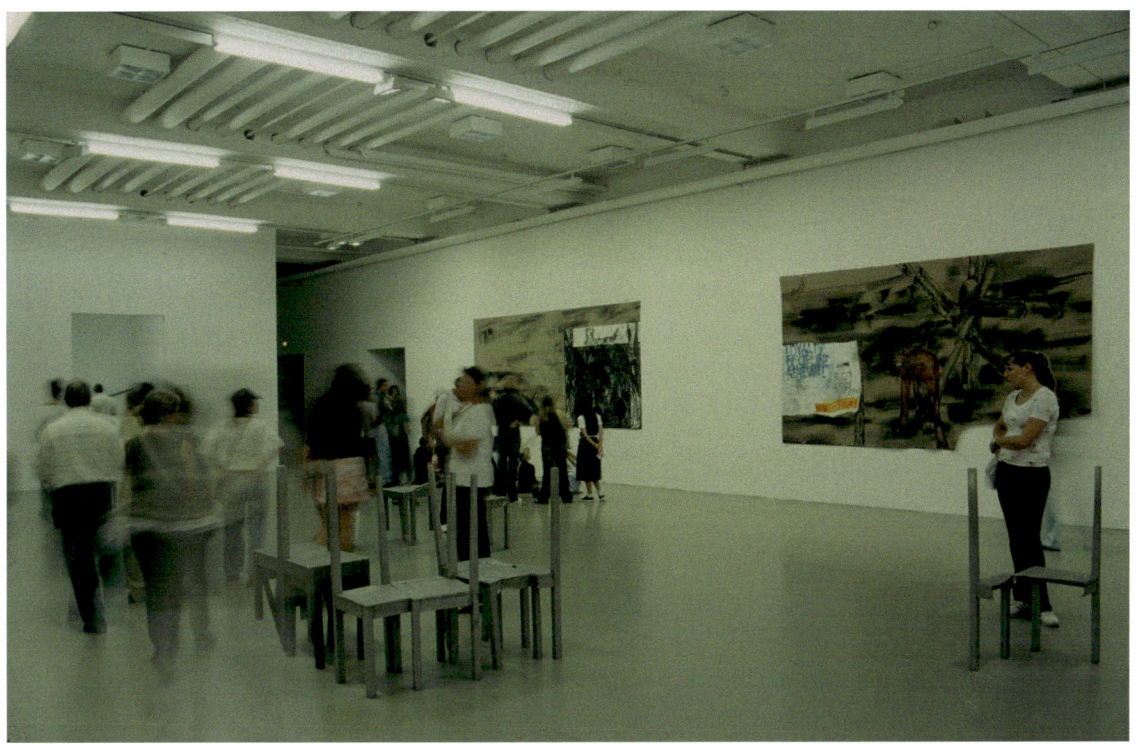

11.5 Doris Salcedo, *6 November 1985*, 2001.
Installation, stainless steel, lead, wood, resin.
Shown at Documenta11, Kassel. © Doris Salcedo
and documenta archiv/Ryszard Kasiewicz
photographer.

of the actions of September 11. Some call it the clash of civilizations, others
the axis of evil, or the battle between good and evil, between the civilized
and uncivilized world; others call it jihad, intifada, liberation, etc. In all the
jingoistic language that mediates this state of affairs, cultural and artistic
responses could, however, posit a radical departure from the system of hegemony that fuels the present struggle. In fact, it was the Iranian president
Mohammad Khatami who called for a dialogue between civilizations. Even
if the void in downtown Manhattan constitutes a sort of apocalyptic vision
of destruction, we must do well not to see its destruction as an apotheosis
and the final chapter in the confrontation between the West and Islam; or in
fact, the West and the rest of the world that is not doing its share in George Bush
the Younger's war on terrorism. September 11, therefore, far from positing a

logical end in the long series of oppositions to Westernism, should perhaps be framed as the instance of the full emergence of the margin to the center.

When Fanon was writing in the 1950s and early 1960s, the Islamic and Arab world in Algeria had risen up in bloody resistance against the brutal force and terror of French colonialism. The Algerian war of liberation, along with other decolonization processes across the southern hemisphere from the 1940s onward, should have taught us a lesson on how to read the history of all future political struggles. Ground Zero as such is not the lacuna in downtown Manhattan out of which the symbolic pillar of blue light that illuminates its empty center is the suture that will restore it to its past. Ground Zero, as the tabula rasa defining global politics and cultural differentiation, points toward that space where the dead certainties of colonialism's dichotomizing oppositions, and Westernism's epistemological concepts for managing and maintaining modernity, have come to a crisis. The emptiness at the center is not a ground but a founding moment for articulating the demands of the multitude that have emerged in the wake of Empire.[11] In the later stage of the Algerian liberation war, Fanon articulated this tension between the multitude and Empire so clearly, a view that completely prefigures fundamentalist Islam's radical transnational enterprise. In terms of strategy, program, and the direction of their assault on the West, the fundamentalist Islamic challenge to the global order is clearly Fanonian. Let us listen to Fanon, writing toward the end of the French/Algerian war:

> The naked truth of decolonization evokes for us the searing bullets and bloodstained knives which emanate from it. For if *the last shall be first*, this will only come to pass after a murderous and decisive struggle between two protagonists. That affirmed intention to place the last at the head of things, and to make them climb at a pace (too quickly, some say) the well-known steps which characterize an organized society, can only triumph if we use all means to turn the scale, including, of course, that of violence.
>
> You do not turn any society, however primitive it may be, upside down with such a program if you have not decided from the very beginning, that is to say from the actual formulation of that program, to overcome all the obstacles that you will come across in so doing. The native who decides to put the program into practice, and to become its moving force, is ready for violence at all times. From birth it is clear to him that this narrow world, strewn with prohibitions, can only be called in question by absolute violence.[12]

Absolute violence seen from Fanon's perspective is not an end in itself but a means for the confrontation to come with the forces of Westernism, today defined by the hegemony of industrial capitalism. In the Islamic world, the Iranian Revolution led by Imam Khomeini clearly marked the opening of this confrontation. The defeat of the occupying Soviet forces by a broad coalition of Islamic mujahideen in Afghanistan in 1989 marks another point in the continuous Islamic battle with Westernism. Similarly, the sanction placed on Salman Rushdie's novel *The Satanic Verses* was clearly a contestation of the Western epistemological avant-gardism out of which the novel emerged.[13] From the foregoing, it seems quite clear that the West had completely underestimated the ferocity of fundamentalist Islam's hostility toward Western hegemony. On the other hand, there is also a clear recognition by forces within Islam (enlightened and fundamentalist alike) that the only force capable of challenging the global political and cultural power of the West is that of Islam as a viable world culture.[14] As such, radical Islam must therefore be properly understood as a serious counterhegemonic opposition, at least on the global political stage. Because radical Islam has often drawn from theories of jihad—which it narrowly interprets from a binary oppositional standpoint of believers and nonbelievers, infidels and good Muslims—it underwrites, through the deployment of excessive violence, a view of Islam as belligerent, warmongering, and violent. By objectifying violence as a means through which to bring about social and cultural transformation in regions where it is a majority culture, and by proposing very little innovative political model for its interaction with the rest of global society, radical Islam risks alienating other blocks of the disaffected global polity if it does not confront a long-standing perception of it as intolerant of difference and coercive and unjust in its juridical procedures. The place of women and religious minorities, the lack of transparency and corruption in its elite, and the lack of political rights and participation of a large segment of its societies further undermine Islam's claim to universalism.

As the battle with the forces of terrorist elements continues apace in Afghanistan and elsewhere—as Palestinians fight Israeli hegemony in the Occupied Territories; as antiglobalization groups battle the police in Genoa, Seattle, Montreal, and other cities in Europe and North America; as protesters in Argentina, Turkey, Nigeria, and all across the developing world engage the pernicious policies of the World Bank and the International Monetary Fund—there is a view today that Ground Zero represents the clear ground from which the margin has moved to the center in order to reconceptualize the key ideological differences of the present global transition.

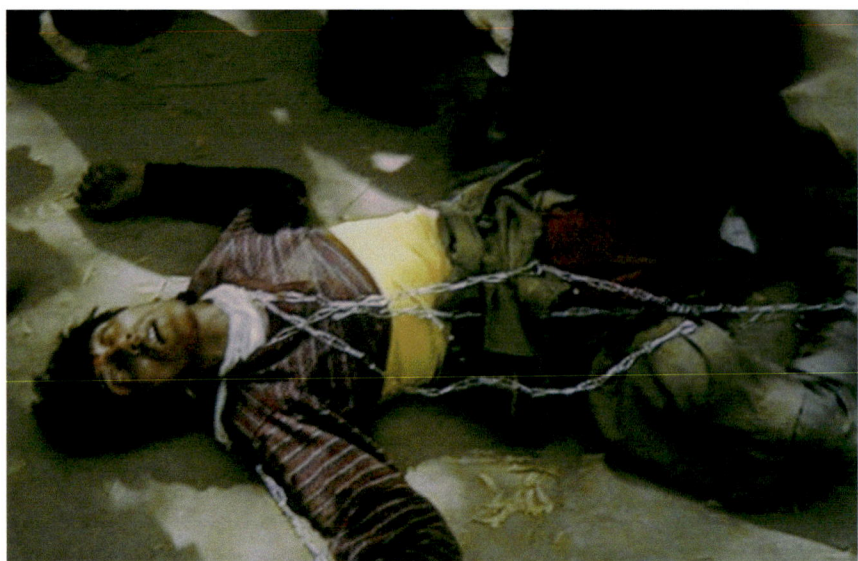

11.6 Amar Kanwar, still image from *A Season Outside*, 1997. Shown at Documenta11, Kassel. Beta SP transferred to DVD, color, sound, and film art, 30 mins. © Amar Kanwar, Haupt and Binder.

Platforms: Five Constellations, Domains of Knowledge and Artistic Production, Circuits of Research

PLATFORM—an open encyclopedia for the analysis of late modernity; a network of relationships; an open form for organizing knowledge; a non-hierarchical model of representation; a compendium of voices, cultural, artistic, and knowledge circuits—

I have briefly sketched the sociocultural-political-historical dimension within which Documenta11 was constituted. "Democracy Unrealized," the first Platform in the five-platform project of Documenta11, opened on March 15, 2001, in Vienna, Austria, exactly six months before the events of September 11. Two months later, on May 7, the second Platform, "Experiments with Truth: Transitional Justice and the Processes of Truth and Reconciliation," opened in New Delhi. The second part and conclusion of "Democracy Unrealized" began on October 9, 2001, in Berlin. Both Platforms, in the serious discursive direction of their respective themes, presaged the discussions that would come to dominate global debate in the wake

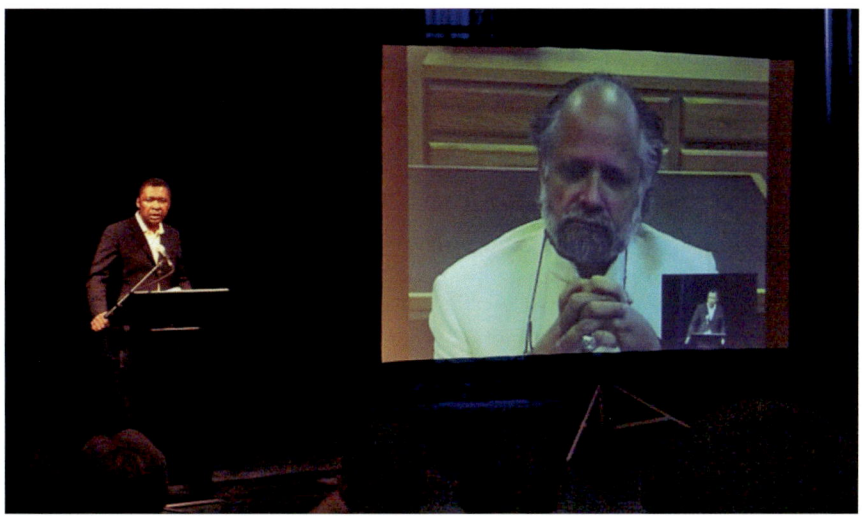

11.7 Okwui Enwezor and Homi Bhabha, "Democracy Unrealized" symposium, Documenta11, Platform1, Berlin, 2001. Photograph: Haupt and Binder, universes.art.

of the destruction of the World Trade Center. The third Platform, "Créolité and Creolization," was organized on the Caribbean Island of St. Lucia in January 2002; and the fourth, "Under Siege: Four African Cities, Freetown, Johannesburg, Kinshasa, and Lagos," was held in Lagos, Nigeria, in March 2002. The fifth Platform, the exhibition, brings the historical space of Documenta in Kassel into the orbit of other domains. The five Platforms define a constellation of disciplinary models that seek to explain and interrogate ongoing historical processes and radical change, spatial and temporal dynamics, as well as fields of actions and ideas, and systems of interpretation and production; all of which significantly enlarge the exhibition format of Documenta11.

Platform1. Democracy Unrealized

The tradition of the oppressed teaches us that "the state of emergency" in which we live is not the exception but the rule. We must attain to a conception of history that is in keeping with this insight. Then we shall clearly realize that it is our task to bring about a real state of emergency, and this will improve our position in the struggle against Fascism.

Walter Benjamin, "Theses on the Philosophy of History" (1940)

There is an illuminating paradox in the political field today, whereby the end of communist universalism has not proven to be democracy's greater profit. Several factors have contributed to the current wave of reassessments of the hegemony of liberal democracy. As Francis Fukuyama pronounced in *The End of History and the Last Man*, first, the end of communism and the triumph of the liberal form of democracy represents a logical conclusion in the distinct political form of the constitutional state whose perfection no longer requires any innovation or change; and, second, liberal democracy is logically tied to capitalism, which is best expressed in the scale and penetration by which global capitalism determines every facet of cultural and political life around the world.[15] This in a sense makes democracy exportable and adaptable to any given context that wants to participate in the global "New World Order." Despite these pronouncements and formulations of democracy from a number of academics and Western politicians, the rise of nationalisms and fundamentalisms of every imaginable kind as responses to the neoliberal globalist onslaught, the widened horizon of notions of citizenship produced by the large-scale displacements and immigration that today are reshaping the face of once stable societies, and, finally, the emergence of the postcolonial state as it grapples with the imperfect legacy of imperialism and colonialism have brought about a structural and epistemological reevaluation of liberal democracy as the best of all possible forms of popular political representation and participation.

The project "Democracy Unrealized" represents a questioning inversion of the theories and institutional policies that have defined the field of democracy as essentially realized. In the series of debates, presentations, and workshops organized within the purview of the project, philosophers, political theorists, historians, activists, and students present imaginative and wide-ranging interpretations and arguments that assert that even if democracy has been the watchword for different kinds of participatory governance and political systems of the past half century, to a large degree it remains a project under constant reinvention. The notion "unrealized" alluded to in the title of the project is a way to interpret the varied modifications that the ethic of democracy and its institutional forms have undergone and continue to undergo today, making democracy a fundamentally unrealizable project, or put another way, a work in progress.

Platform2. Experiments with Truth: Transitional Justice
and the Processes of Truth and Reconciliation

The past two decades have witnessed a series of juridical inquiries and conflicts—as well as political and social assessments all over the world that have considered the nature of state impunity—from which have arisen overwhelming cases of genocide and gross human rights violations. While the expressibility of the law is mostly concerned with the legality of the state, its actions, and the individuals acting within it (a central thesis of the Nuremberg Trials and Adolf Eichmann's trial in Jerusalem), the truth commissions that have recently emerged in the lexicon of the search for answers to genocide and state repression seek to engage the dimension of the cultural, the social, and the political as spaces of collective bargaining within civil society.

What comes after violence and after the collapse of the state? Where does the horizon of culture and civility lie after state impunity and the termination of authoritarian rule and fascism? How are human rights to be fashioned in the wake of the unaccountable power of a radical force that displaces, decapitates, dehumanizes, and destroys? What guarantees these rights? These questions, among many others, converge in ordering the central problematic that structures "Experiments with Truth: Transitional Justice and the Processes of Truth and Reconciliation." The project looks at two normative interpretations of justice and their political, cultural, and social corollary attending the mechanisms of prosecution, testimony, witnessing, political liberalization, and social transformation in the past half century. The second part of the project considers the historical work that has emerged from the study of these commissions and the philosophical and political theories, as well as the artistic and cultural responses that have accompanied their formation.

Across the divide of regions, continents, and national or quasinational denominations, the sheer proliferation of "truth commissions" has made them one of the prime manifestations of our time. On the one hand, the concept of "universal jurisdiction" which indicts perpetrators of violence and war crimes has led to the establishment of an international juridical process of borderless justice, making it possible for the prosecution of offenders regardless of their status and citizenship, as has been made clear in the cases of Augusto Pinochet (Chile) and Slobodan Milosevic (Yugoslavia/Serbia). But the kind of justice that has emerged could hardly be said to be perfect. Oftentimes, its application is quite arbitrary, with political convenience and expediency dictating indictments and prosecutions.

According to Ruti Teitel, "The paradigm of a provisional, hyperpoliticized transitional jurisprudence is linked to a conception of nonideal justice that is imperfect and partial. What is fair and just in extraordinary political circumstances is determined not from an idealized Archimedean point but from the transitional position itself."[16] It is this development which has followed the political deliberations of justice, and which has determined the cases that have spelled out the conceptual and juridical modalities of transitional justice.

On the other hand, the trauma of survivors and victims militates against silence, while the potential destabilizing effects on societies undergoing transition, with minimal state security, have led to the consideration of "truth commissions" as alternative spaces in which to mediate the debilitating structure of trauma and loss. Today each of these two forms—"truth commissions" and transitional justice—has acquired a level of juridical legitimacy that has become part of our contemporary understanding of a human rights–based law. They have further animated the distinction we make between those seen to be perpetrators and those who are victims. Where law and scholarship convene around the aporias of trauma and testimony, works of art and literature have emerged that give form to the remnants of these histories. Whereas each of these cultural fields offers a singular perspective on the limits of witnessing and the limits of representation, the spate of memorials and public commemorations continues to haunt the imagination where the work of artists, architects, writers, filmmakers, museums, and archives has been called to intervene in spaces of representation.

Platform3. Créolité and Creolization

Two points define the theme of this platform. First, in terms of its poetics, *créolité* is to be understood as a critical theory of creole language, literary form, and mode of producing locality. The locality that envelops this language is, of course, the Caribbean. However, this does not capture the entire complexity around which creole is situated, that is, if we extend its geographic character beyond the borders of the Caribbean. But for the moment let us just imagine the Caribbean as the locus of its international projection to other branches of creole linguistics—in Africa, the Indian Ocean islands, South America, and even the United States. The founding text of this critical theory as a literary form is expressed in a manifesto, *Éloge de la créolité/In Praise of Creoleness*, published in 1989 by three Martinican intel-

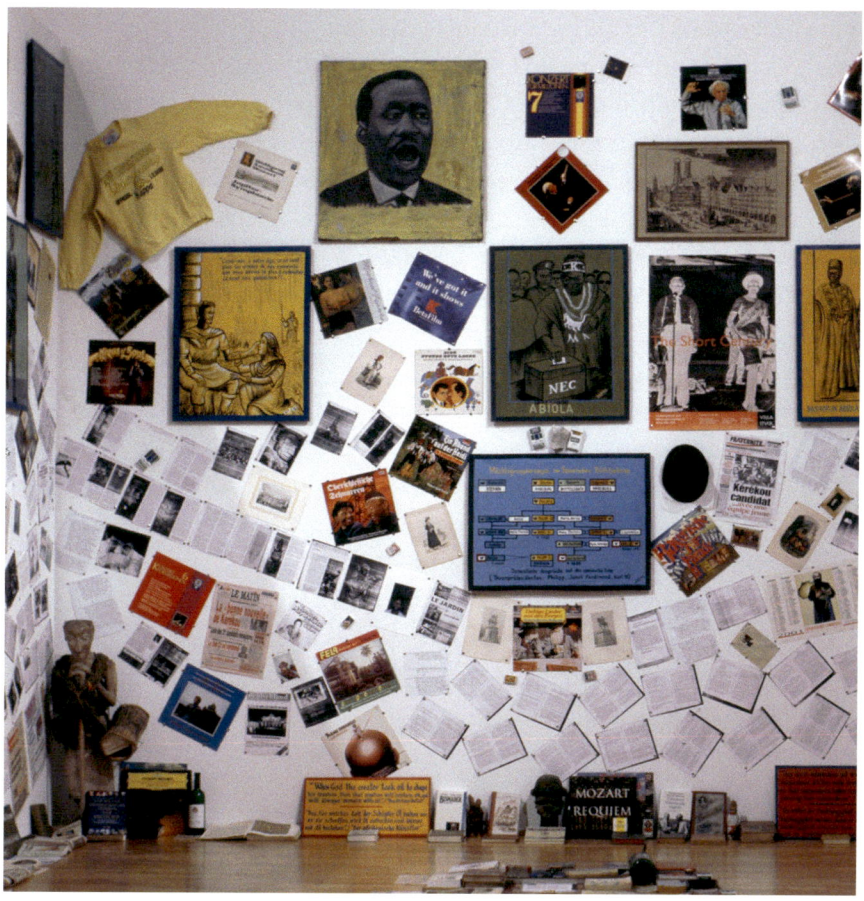

11.8 Georges Adéagbo, *L'explorateur et les explorateurs devant l'histoire de l'exploration . . . !*
Le théatre du monde (detail), 2002. Mixed-media installation. Shown at Documenta11, Kassel.
© Georges Adéagbo, ADAGP, Paris, and VG Bild-Kunst, 2025.

lectuals, Jean Bernabé, Patrick Chamoiseau, and Raphaël Confiant. In their controversial text, the three writers underline their intervention; first, by furnishing it with a name; and, second, by designating its intertextual dimension as "a sort of mental envelope in the middle of which our world will be built in full consciousness of the outer world."[17] In this "mental envelope," the writers conceive of their cultural world as emerging out of the world of colonial domination into one of "*nontotalitarian consciousness of a preserved diversity*."[18] The critical gesture and expression of this diversity is at the heart of the radical discourse of *créolité*, especially as it concerns the question of what it means to live and work from the polycentrism of the Caribbean. In this context Creoleness emerges in the scissions and agglutinations forged in the contact zone of its historical transmission, i.e., "Creoleness [as] the *interactional or transactional aggregate* of Caribbean, European, African, Asian, and Levantine cultural elements, united on the same soil by the yoke of history."[19]

The second part of the thematic is concerned with defining creolization as a process of emergence of a world culture conceived from the perspective of radical cultural and situational flux. More than five hundred years separates us from the first arrival of slaves in the New World. Slavery and colonialism as the Janus-faced projects of European imperialism and the global institutionalization of capitalism today define an array of configurations through which to understand the paradigms of mixing and hybridization that underpin such concepts as modern culture, identity formation, language, ethnicity, and race. Creole societies have their roots in the institutions of slavery and colonialism and mark the intersections where modern subjectivity and historical processes meet. In recent years, through waves of migration and displacements, creolization has emerged as a dominant modality of contemporary living practices, shaping patterns of dwelling that are crossed and differentiated by massive flows of images and cultural symbols expressed through material culture and language.

Equally, the intersections of modern subjectivity and the historical consciousness that it circumscribes are never smooth. They come out of uneven, and often violent, encounters, and in patterns of articulating and signifying norms of cultural heritage, exchange, difference, and resistance strategies seeking to maintain the integrity of nondominant cultures. If globalization has defined and reworked old circuits of capital, creolization represents its strongest cultural counterpoint. While globalization tends toward consolidation and homogenization, creolization moves toward differentiation and dispersal. Creolization's mode is a "signifying system through which . . . a social order is communicated, reproduced, experienced, and explored."[20] In elaborating its discourse, creolization as a process of transformation of cultural givens subtends its critical fashioning in the Caribbean to involve other areas of its historical manifestation in the Indian Ocean islands of Africa, in South America, the United States, Asia, and Europe, and to the global world at large.

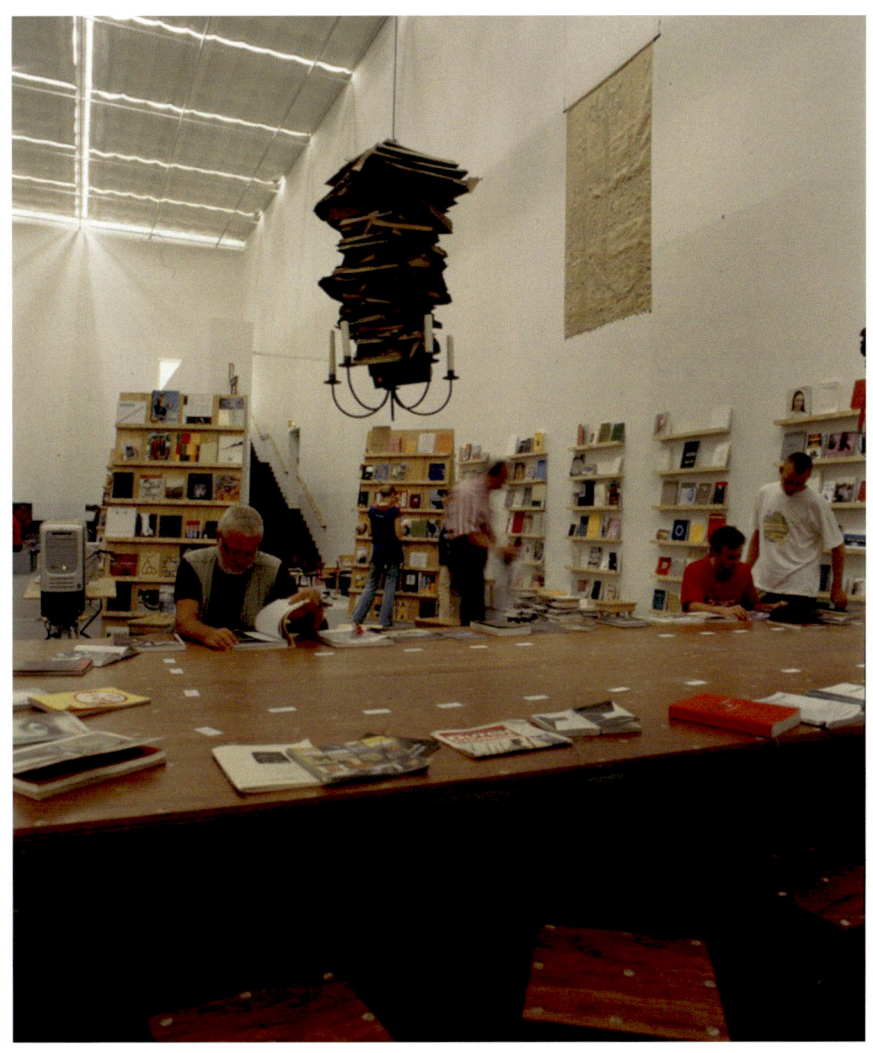

11.9 Meschac Gaba, *Museum of Contemporary African Art: The Library*, 2001. Shown at Documenta11, Kassel. Mixed-media installation. © Meschac Gaba/VG Bild-Kunst, 2025. © documenta archiv/Ryszard Kasiewicz photographer.

Platform4. Under Siege: Four African Cities, Freetown, Johannesburg, Kinshasa, and Lagos

This platform represents an attempt to foreground the dimension of global formations that animate the study of urban systems as a category of spatial relations and ecologies of sustainability from which are derived a set of imperatives toward development and modernization. The loci of this study are the urban systems of four African cities which over the past two decades have witnessed increased population growth, migration, and the pressures of fragile urban governance, and state and economic collapse. That African cities are fragile urban systems is without a doubt; however, the conventional wisdom that describes them as unsustainable, chaotic, and unmanageable fails to understand the inventive dynamism out of which their urban residents have written new texts of resilience, survival, and growth.

In the study of these four cities, a number of issues have emerged. The first is the degree to which informality—sometimes constituting as much as 70 percent of all functioning institutions—has shaped the nature of activities governing many sectors, and also mediates all relations (economic, cultural, social, political, and civic) where the state no longer plays a dominant role. The second issue is premised on a contradiction: one that simultaneously underwrites these urban systems as conurbations of multiple crises and obsolescence, but also as inventive systems of creativity, vitality, and dynamism. The third aspect of the survival strategy of city inhabitants—understood here as coextensive with rural, traditional, indigenous, and familial practices—is the expanded role of women in the production of new types of subjective practices that have consolidated their role as important players in the shaping of urban imaginaries. A fourth point relates to the catastrophic effects of the International Monetary Fund and World Bank Structural Adjustment Program policies of the 1980s across Africa. SAP (as it is popularly known and explicitly translated by Africans in terms of its effects on their lives) overnight destroyed the middle class and dramatically increased poverty, destroyed value, and limited productivity. The fifth conclusion relates to the effects of state collapse (Johannesburg linked to the demise of apartheid, Freetown and Kinshasa with civil conflict, and Lagos with a pernicious dictatorship) on the stability of the cities' urban economies.

Writ large, these four African cities express paradigmatic contexts of intense production of locality (neighborhoods, associations, imaginaries of religion, and circuits of mediatic representations).[21] As any other urban space around the world, African cities are centers for the migration and refuge of increasing numbers of people. As such, they are also the meeting place and battleground for two conflicting worlds of power and impotence, wealth and poverty, corruption and hope, center and periphery. But the issue we want to emphasize is that African cities are not only outlined by these troubling bifurcations. Nor do we wish to reproduce only the images of cities riddled with crime and ethnic violence, the grinding poverty, the overcrowded suburbs and shantytowns, the congested living spaces that are usually lacking essential services and are breeding grounds of disease, the high mortality rate, or the persistent degradation of their environments. These are certainly important issues that need addressing. Yet our attention is also persistently called to focus on the ethical accounting of the dynamics of these cities as hosts of great potentials that challenge the often gloomy, doomsday pictures painted by the popular media. As part of the complexity of the issues at play within these urban conditions, there may be a need to highlight the reality of these cities as vibrant spaces that foster and recapture the possibility for self-constitution.

The foregoing define a field of praxis and intention. They are constitutive of the critical envelope in which we wanted to place the entire paradigmatic operation of Documenta11. It is above all an attempt to shape and assess the common points of fruitful exchanges and the questioning necessary to craft an exhibition project that would project a more complicated picture of contemporary life and thought. Traversing continents and cities, locations and disciplines, practices and institutions, formats and publics, Documenta11's proposition to open up new spaces for critical reflection on contemporary artistic and cultural situations creates for us—in dialectical interaction with heterogeneous, transnational audiences—a public sphere through which to think and analyze seriously the complex network of global knowledge circuits on which interpretations of all cultural processes and research today depend. The shaping of Documenta11's public sphere of multiple relations and intersections was, in part, a recognition of the limits of all models of large-scale international exhibitions that aspire to be global and inclusive, but which wittingly maintain the separation between disciplinary models and publics. Equally, it was to deterritorialize and exacerbate modernism's strategy of differentiation and homogenization, its reification of pure objects of art in relation to value and hierarchy within the artistic canons. But in a larger sense, it expresses the limits of Documenta itself as an institution of important global stature.

It goes without saying that, given the unruly nature of late modernity, and the inadequacy of spaces of agency to interrogate the uneven conditions of global development and governance today, the scope of Documenta11's intellectual and exhibition project needed redefinition and enlargement—that is, if we are to understand the contribution contemporary art and artists can make in shaping the future. Some would argue that art must stay above politics. Such a call is not only perversely conservative but, more importantly, misunderstands the nature of the critical energy that drives the conditions of artistic production, dissemination, and reception across a multiplicity of institutional and noninstitutional frameworks today.

Platform5. Passages through the Construction of an Exhibition

ENCYCLOPEDIA/CONSTRUCTION—emergence of the social and political; the city as a modern manifestation of transnationality, sociality, and transindividuality; the city as an incarnation of a postnational, identitarian model of citizenship—MIRROR/REFLECTION—the domain of spectatorship and the carnivalesque; level of the individual and society; the constitution of the individual as subject, popular sovereignty, difference—

Nearly fifteen years of unrelenting neoconservative attacks have weakened the political and cultural base within which artists have expressed—via modes of popular sovereignty and difference and through an engaged critique and self-reflexivity, especially in the strategies of many artistic positions—the multicultural and postcolonial nature of modern and contemporary culture. Here is not the space to debate the merits or failures of multiculturalism, feminism, or minority rights movements; or to answer back to the pernicious dismissal of postcoloniality that is so prevalent in academic forums, media, and politics. I only wish to remark that contemporary art institutions have often been defined as the most enlightened and liberal of all cultural institutions working on the global stage. In the 1980s, the movements of multiculturalism, feminism, and gay rights forced new debates that sought to decolonize long-standing resistance to reform by major institutions. In the context of the contemporary art sphere, expanded opportunities that came through the discourses of multiculturalism and difference brought about a new visibility in the participation of minorities and women, consequently redrawing the borders of institutional and gallery systems. However, in the 1990s there was a change of course, which slowly and systematically eroded what had been a healthy, vigorous environment of debate. According to Habermas:

04

BINDING-BRAUEREI

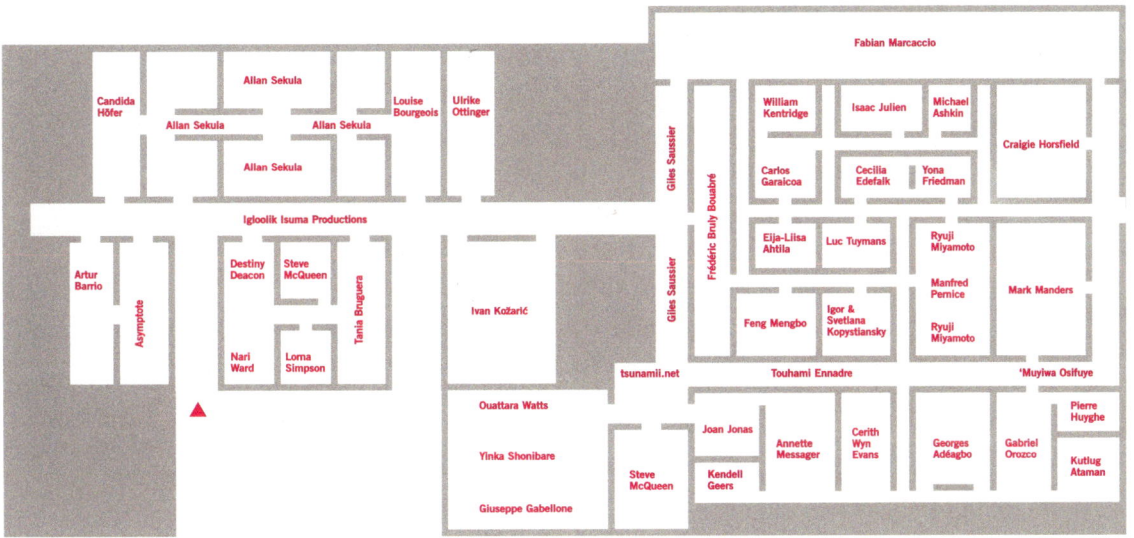

11.10 Map of Binding Brauerei with artists' names, from the exhibition guidebook for Documenta11, Kassel, 2002. © documenta archiv (docA_BI_11documentaA_2002-Binding Brauerei).

At first glance, however, claims to the recognition of collective identities and to equal rights for cultural forms of life are a different matter. Feminists, minorities in multicultural societies, peoples struggling for national independence and formerly colonized regions suing for equality of their cultures on the international stage are all currently fighting for such claims. Does not the recognition of cultural forms of life and traditions that have been marginalized, whether in the context of a majority culture or in a Eurocentric global society, require guarantees of status and survival—in other words, some kind of collective rights that shatter the outmoded self-understanding of the democratic constitutional state, which is tailored to individual rights and in that sense is "liberal"?[22]

But to make an exhibition of art, I would insist on the proposition that spectatorship is central and fundamental to all forms of valuation of the visual content of an exhibition. Spectatorship is that dimension of subjectivity and consciousness that defines the relation of power to acts of cognition and valuation. Spectatorship, which takes the carnivalesque as its mode of enunciation, can only function productively in a democratic, open system. Here I am mostly interested in the kind of democratic spirit whose referent is constituted by the degree to which a plethora of institutions—formal and informal, public and private—rather than mediating all aspects of popular sovereignty, make room within their regimes for the experimental, the imperfect and unfinished. Such recognition connects artistic practice to notions such as community and citizenship. In the democratic system, which is to be distinguished from popular politics, but rather one that promotes agency over pure belief, the demands of citizenship place strong ethical constraints on the artist based on his or her commitment to all "forms-of-life." The practice of art presents the artist with the task of making such commitment.

Therefore, it does not matter whether the artist is an abstract painter, an avant-garde filmmaker, or a "political" provocateur, as the constraint is the same. Giorgio Agamben, from whom I have borrowed the notion "forms-of-life," describes it as "that life which can never be separated from its form, a life in which it's never possible to isolate something such as naked life. A life that cannot be separated from its form is a life for which what is at stake in its way of living is living itself. It defines life—human life—in which the single ways, acts, and processes of having are never simply facts but always and above all possibilities of life, always and above all power."[23] Taken at

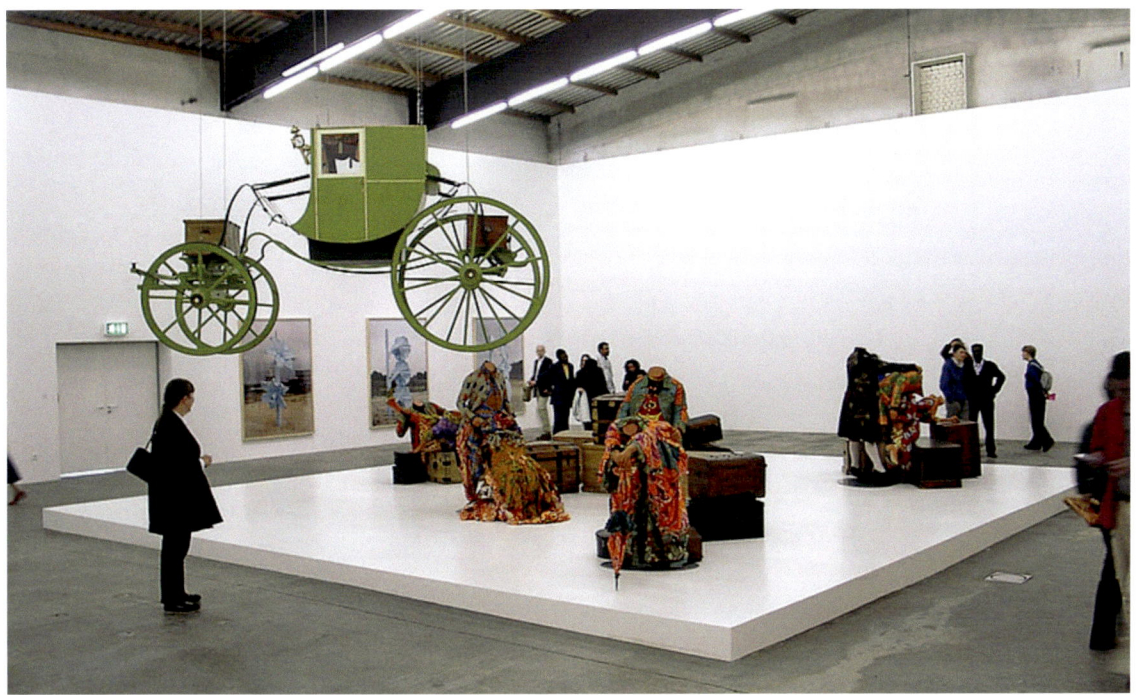

11.11 Yinka Shonibare, *Gallantry and Criminal Conversation*, 2002. Installation, one-horse carriage, suitcase, eleven life-size mannequins, costumes. Dimensions variable. Shown at Documenta11, Kassel. © Yinka Shonibare CBE. All Rights Reserved, DACS 2025.

its most radical interpretation, Agamben's philosophical argument would seem to place the very act of artistic practice that seeks to designate itself as autonomous from all regulative political and social processes in a suture of constraint. The question confronting any artistic practice that designates itself as completely autonomous from political participation within which notions of community and citizenship are constituted—and which also refuses to recognize the conflicts that arise in the relations of power grounding the subjective dimension of spectatorship—is: From what is art autonomous? This obviously cannot be taken to mean that art, through its

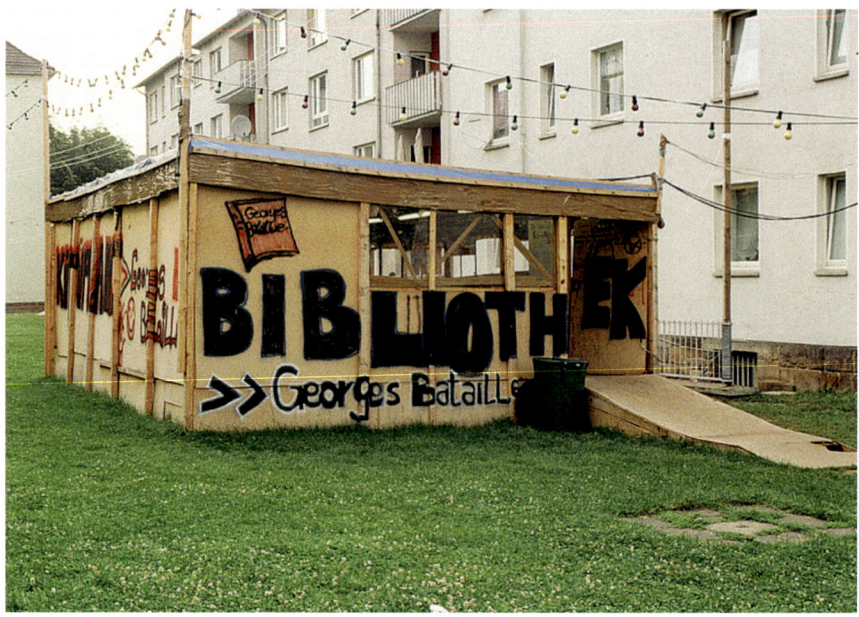

11.12 Thomas Hirschhorn, *Bataille Monument* (*Bibliotek*) [Library], 2002, Documenta11, Kassel, 2002. Photograph: Werner Maschmann. Courtesy of Thomas Hirschhorn/ Gladstone Gallery, New York. © ADAGP, Paris, 2025.

unique institutions and procedures, cannot construct for itself a space from which to engage critically with all domains of sociopolitical life without being integrated within their mechanism.

Afterword

Despite their proliferation, institutions such as museums and large-scale international exhibitions cannot on their own define the legitimacy of contemporary art today; rather, they are caught up in reshaping their own legitimacy as a consequence of their delayed recognition of the complex topos of the new global community. Therefore, from the outset, the project of Documenta11 was conceived not as an exhibition but as a constellation of public spheres. The public sphere of the exhibition gesture, implicit in the historical formation of Documenta, in which art comes to stand for models of representation and narratives of autonomous subjectivity, is rearticulated here as a new understanding in the domain of the discursive rather than the museological. Documenta11's paradigm is shaped by forces that seek to enact the multidisciplinary direction through which artistic practices and processes come most alive, in those circuits of knowledge produced outside the predetermined institutional domain of Westernism, or those situated solely in the sphere of artistic canons.

If the Platforms were a compendium, a constitutive map of contemporary knowledge circuits: art, theory, science, culture, ecology; spatiality and temporality; urban systems, locality, globality; institutional formations (informal and formal), metaterritory, experience—albeit always incomplete, discontinuous, forever requiring qualification, elaboration, and continuous enunciation—then each phase of staging the discursive potentialities of the engagement between artistic practice and social reality, theoretical reflection and political systems, forms-of-life and image economies, advanced technology and local industries, confronts us with a world of vast displacements and deterritorialized understanding of culture. In the process of its composition, the exhibition stands for the rigor, precision, courage, vision, power, freedom, agency, openness, and imagination of the individual statement as it opens to changes wrought by global transformations. These individual statements and sometimes individuated units connect to and overlap with each other. The demands placed on each component and composition require that they each complete, complicate, and reveal that which is deliberately masked, distanced, and effaced in others. The Platforms signify journeys of experience and methods for thinking the global at the height of its own reconstitution. Within their individual formats, there is no need to make a polemic of globalism, multiculturalism, and difference; the wider scope of the project assumes them as already part of the complex weave of tongues, the tide of voices that will activate the final meaning of its dramatization.

The collected result in the form of a series of volumes and the exhibition is placed at the dialectical intersection of contemporary art and culture. Such an intersection equally marks the liminal limits out of which the postcolonial, post–Cold War, postideological, transnational, deterritorialized, diasporic, global world has been written. This dialectical enterprise attempts to establish concrete and imaginative links within the various projects of modernity. Their impact, as well as their material and symbolic ordering, is woven through procedures of translation, interpretation, subversion, hybridization, creolization, displacement, and reassemblage. What emerges in this transformation in different parts of the world produces a critical ordering of intellectual and artistic networks of the globalizing world. The exhibition as a diagnostic toolbox actively seeks to stage the relationships, conjunctions, and disjunctions between different realities: between artists, institutions, disciplines, genres, generations, processes, forms, media, activities; between identity and subjectification. Linked together, the exhibition counterpoises the supposed purity and autonomy of the art object against a rethinking of modernity based on ideas of transculturality and extraterritoriality. Thus, the exhibition project of the fifth Platform is less a receptacle of commodity-objects than a container of a plurality of voices, a material reflection on a series of disparate and interconnected actions and processes.

NOTES

Epigraphs: Frantz Fanon, *The Wretched of the* Earth, trans. Constance Farrington (New York: Grove, 1963), 35–36; Walter Benjamin, "Theses on the Philosophy of History" [1940], in *Illuminations*, ed. Hannah Arendt, trans. Harry Zohn (London: Jonathan Cape, 1979), 259.

1   Guy Debord, *The Society of the Spectacle* (New York: Zone Books, 1999), 130–33.

2   Achille Mbembe, "At the Edge of the World: Boundaries, Territoriality, and Sovereignty in Africa," *Public Culture* 12, no. 1 (Winter 2000): 259.

3   Fernand Braudel, *Civilization and Capitalism: 15th–18th Century*, vol. 3, *The Perspective of the World*, trans. Sian Reynolds (New York: Harper and Row, 1984), 17; paraphrased in Mbembe, "At the Edge," 259.

4   Achille Mbembe and Janet Roitman, "Figures of the Subject in Times of Crisis," *Public Culture* 7, no. 2 (Winter 1995): 324.

5   See Giorgio Agamben, *Means without End: Notes on Politics*, trans. Vincenzo Binetti and Cesare Casarino (Minneapolis: University of Minnesota Press, 2000).

6   Michael Hardt and Antonio Negri, *Empire* (Cambridge, MA: Harvard University Press, 2000), xv.

7   Hardt and Negri, *Empire*, xv.

8   Jürgen Habermas, *The Theory of Communicative Action*, vol. 2, *Lifeworld and System: A Critique of Functionalist Reason*, trans. Thomas McCarthy (Boston: Beacon, 1987), 151.

9   V. Y. Mudimbe, *The Invention of Africa: Gnosis, Philosophy and the Order of Knowledge* (Bloomington: Indiana University Press, 1988), 4.

10   See Gerardo Mosquera, "Some Problems in Transcultural Curating," in *Global Visions: Towards a New Internationalism in the Visual Arts*, ed. Jean Fisher (London: Kala Press in association with the Institute of International Visual Arts, 1994), 133–39.

11   See Hardt and Negri, *Empire*.

12   Fanon, *Wretched of the Earth*, 37. Emphasis added.

13   [*Ed. note:* Salman Rushdie, *The Satanic Verses* (London: Viking Penguin, 1988).]

14   See Akbar S. Ahmed, *Postmodernism and Islam: Predicament and Promise* (London: Routledge, 1992). Ahmed has argued the point that within the "new world order" only two categories of societies exist, those that are imploding and those that are exploding. Imploding societies represent those caught up in underdevelopment, economic helotry, cultural insecurity, social malaise, political fragmentation, and collapse of the state form, and are marked by crises; while exploding cultures are those segments of the industrialized world which he identifies as bubbling with optimism, and have the technological achievements which allow them to continuously expand economically, culturally, and politically. With such asymmetry in place, those societies seen to be imploding offer no alternative to Western global hegemony and are condemned to be ruled by the West. In the case of Islam, Ahmed makes the case that Islamic modernity is caught in the tension in which ideas of both implosion and explosion define the basis of what its societies are undergoing, but also provides it with the tools to adequately respond to Western hegemony.

15   Francis Fukuyama, *The End of History and the Last Man* (New York: Free Press, 1992).

16   Ruti G. Teitel, *Transitional Justice* (Oxford: Oxford University Press, 2000), 234.

17   Jean Bernabé, Patrick Chamoiseau, and Raphaël Confiant, *Éloge de la Créolité/In Praise of Creoleness*, bilingual edition, English trans. Mohamed B. Taleb-Khyar (Paris: Gallimard, 1993), 75.

18   Bernabé, Chamoiseau, and Confiant, *Éloge de la Créolité*, 89.

19   Bernabé, Chamoiseau, and Confiant, *Éloge de la Créolité*, 87.

20   Raymond Williams, quoted in Terry Eagleton, *The Idea of Culture* (Oxford: Blackwell, 2000), 33.

21   For a nuanced discussion of the notion of how "locality" is produced both as an ethos and as an imaginary encapsulation of delocalized formations, see Arjun Appadurai, particularly the chapter "The Production of Locality," in *Modernity at Large: Cultural Dimensions of Globalization* (Minneapolis: University of Minnesota Press, 1966), 178–200.

22   Jürgen Habermas, *The Inclusion of the Other: Studies in Political Theory*, ed. Ciaran Cronin and Pablo De Greiff (Cambridge, MA: MIT Press, 1998), 204–5.

23   Agamben, *Means without End*, 3–4.

The Postcolonial Constellation

Contemporary Art in a State of Permanent Transition

The version of this essay presented here is the first, as published in *Research in African Literatures* 34, no. 4 (Winter 2003): 57–82. A slightly shorter version was published in *Antinomies of Art and Culture: Modernity, Postmodernity, Contemporaneity*, edited by Terry Smith, Okwui Enwezor, and Nancy Condee (Durham, NC: Duke University Press, 2008), 207–34.

The proper task of a history of thought is to define the conditions in which human beings "problematize" what they are, what they do, and the world in which they live.

Michel Foucault, *The History of Sexuality* (1985)

This flood of convergences, publishing itself in the guise of the commonplace. No longer is the latter an accepted generality, suitable and dull—no longer is it deceptively obvious, exploiting common sense—it is, rather, all that is relentlessly and endlessly reiterated by these encounters.

Édouard Glissant, *Poetics of Relation* (1997)

1

IT IS A COMMONPLACE of the current historical thinking about globalization to say: There are no vantage points from which to observe any culture since the very processes of globalization have effectively abolished the temporal and spatial distance that previously separated cultures.[1] Another way this thinking has been expressed is in the idea of globalization as the mode and ultimate structure of singularization, standardization, and homogenization of culture in service of instruments of advanced capitalism and neoliberalism. After such totalization, what remains of the critical forces of production that throughout the modern era have placed a strong check on the submergence of all subjective protocols to the orders of a singular organizing ideology, be it the state or the market? What may immediately follow this spatial and temporal reordering is to ask: If globalization has established, categorically, the proximity of cultures, can the same be said about globalization and art? Here, what marks the critical division between culture and art is that for centuries art as such has waged a fierce battle of independence from all cultural, social, economic, and political influences.

Unlike the apotropaic device of containment and desublimation through which the modern Western imagination perceived other cultures—so as to feed off their strange aura and hence displace their power—the nearness today of those cultures formerly separated by their distance to the objectifying conditions of modernist history calls for new critical appraisals of our contemporary present and its relationship to artistic production. I start with these observations in order to place in proper context the current conditions of production, dissemination, and reception of contemporary art. Contemporary art today is refracted, not just from the specific site of culture and history but, in a more critical sense, from the standpoint of a complex geopolitical configuration that defines all systems of production and relations of exchange as a consequence of globalization after imperialism. It is this geopolitical configuration and its postimperial transformations that situate what I call here *the postcolonial constellation*. The changes wrought by transitions to new forms of governmentality and institutions, [as well as] new domains of living and belonging as people and citizens, cultures, and communities, define the postcolonial matrix that shapes the ethics of subjectivity and creativity today. Whereas classical European thought formulated the realm of subjectivity and creativity as two domains of activity each informed by its own internal cohesion, without an outside, such thought today is consistently questioned by the constant tessellation of the outside and inside, each folding into and opening out to complex communicative tremors and upheavals. Perhaps, then, bringing contemporary art into the context of the geopolitical framework that defines global relations—between the so-called local and the global, center and margin, nation-state and the individual, transnational and diasporic communities, audiences and institutions—offers a perspicacious view of the postcolonial constellation.

The constellation, however, is not made up solely of the dichotomies named above, but also can be understood as a set of arrangements of deeply entangled relations and forces that are founded by discourses of power. Such discourses of power are geopolitical in nature and by extension can be civilizational in their reliance on binary oppositions between cultures, which in a sense are inimical to any transcultural understanding of the present context of cultural production. Geopolitical power arrangements are defined along much the same *ligne Maginot* in the artistic context. With a terrible tear at its core, evidence of such a *ligne Maginot* in the artistic context lends contact between different artistic cultures an air of civilizational distinctions predicated on the tension between the developed and underdeveloped, reactionary and progressive, regressive and advanced, avant-garde and outmoded. Such a discourse, however, is a heritage of classical modernity, which, through these distinctions, furnishes the dialectical and ideological agenda for competition and hegemony often found in the spaces of art and culture.

What follows is a response to my initial assertions that the current artistic context is constelled around the norms of the postcolonial based on the discontinuous, aleatory forms, creolization, hybridization, etc., with a specific cosmopolitan accent. From the outset, the assertions are not relativistic, even if they attempt to displace certain stubborn values that have structured the discourse of Western modernism and determined its power over other modernisms. Édouard Glissant, whose classic work *Caribbean Discourse* made us aware of the tremor at the roots of the postcolonial order, interprets current understanding of global modernity as essentially the phenomenon of creolization of cultures, wherefore he permits us to see in global processes of movement, resettlement, recalibration, changes and shifts, modalities of cultural transformations that by necessity can neither be wholly universal nor essentially particular.[2] Contemporary culture as such, for Glissant, is cross-cultural, reconstituting itself as a "flood of convergences, publishing itself in the guise of the commonplace."[3] In this statement, there is an intimation that instructs our notion of the modern world, one that carries the echo and the guise of the commonplace, the social universe that produces the content of all modern subjectivities—that is, all subjectivities that emerge directly from the convergences and proximities wrought by imperialism and that today direct us to the postcolonial. The current history of modern art sits at the intersection between imperial and postcolonial discourses. Therefore, any critical interest displayed toward exhibition systems that takes as its field of study modern or contemporary art necessarily refers us to the foundational base of modern art history and its roots in imperial discourse, on the one hand, and, on the other, the pressures that postcolonial discourse exerts on its narratives today.

From its inception, the history of modern art has been inextricably bound to the history of its exhibitions both in its commodity function through collectors in the economic sphere and in its iconoclasm evidenced by the assaults on formalism by the historical avant-garde. Both the commodity function of modern art and the avant-garde legacy have played strong legitimizing roles through exhibitions. In fact, it could be said that no significant change in the direction of modern art occurred outside the framework of the public controversies generated by its exhibitions.[4] To phrase it differently, fundamental to the historical understanding of modern art is the important role played through the forum and medium of exhibitions in explicating the trajectory taken by artists, their supporters, critics, and the public in identifying the great shifts that have marked all encounters with modern art and advanced its claim for enlightened singularity among other cultural avatars. For contemporary art, this history is no less true, and the recent phenomenon of the curator in shaping this history has been remarkable. There have occurred, however, a number of remarkable mutations in the growing discourse of exhibitions and in the public representations of art as something wholly autonomous and separate from the sphere of other cultural activities that must be studied very carefully. Exhibitions have evolved from the presentation of singular perspectives of certain types of artistic development to the frightening *Gesamtkunstwerk* evident in mega-exhibitions globally that seem to have overtaken the entire field of contemporary artistic production. If we are to judge correctly the proper role of the curator in this state of affairs, then the exhibition as form, genre, or medium, and as a communicative, dialogical forum of conversations between heterogeneous actors, publics, and objects, needs further probing.

2

Today most exhibitions and curatorial projects of contemporary art have come under increasing scrutiny and attack. More specifically, they have been called into question by two types of commentary. The first type is generalist and speculative in nature. To my thinking, such commentary lacks critical purpose and can, therefore, be dispensed with rather quickly. The response to exhibitions by this type of commentary is sensationalist; and its chief interest is its fascination with contemporary art as novelty, consumed by effects of reification as a pure image and object of exhibitionism, i.e., with spectacle culture. This means that it tends to equate the task of an exhibition with entertainment, fashion, new thrills, and discoveries that seasonally top up the depleted inventory of the "new" exhausted in the previous season. The so-called mega-exhibitions such as Documenta, *biennales*, *triennales*, festivals, along with commercial gallery exhibitions of a certain type, are normally the haunt of this kind of appraisal. Such an appraisal easily grows bored with any exhibition that lacks the usual dosage of concocted outrage and scandal. Impatient with historical exegesis, it contents itself with the phantasmagoric transition between moments of disenchantment and populist renewal of art.

The second type of commentary is largely institutional, divided between academic and museological production: it is one part nostalgic and one part critical. It usually takes the approach of a buttoned-up, mock severity, based, as it is, on a pseudocritical disaffection with what it sees as the consummation achieved between art and spectacle, between the auguries of pop-cultural banality and an atomized avant-garde legacy. For such commentary, art has meaning and cultural value only when it is seen wholly as art and autonomous. That is, any encounter with art must relate to that art scientifically, not culturally, in order to understand the objective conditions of the work in question. To the degree that it reflects the inner logic of the work of art, art's removal from the realm of the social-life world that introduces it as an object of high culture comes with a price imposed by the formal constraints won through its autonomy with regard to any accreted social or ideological baggage. For such critics, the curator's task is to maintain the greatest fidelity to a restrained formal diligence as derived from values inculcated and transmitted by tradition, which can only be interrupted through a necessary disjuncture marked by innovation. The paradox of a disjunctive innovation that simultaneously announces its allegiance and affinity to the very tradition it seeks to displace is a commonplace in the entire history of modernism, especially in the discourse of the avant-garde.

For curators and art historians, the central problematic between art and the avant-garde begins when there is a breach in the supposed eternality of values that flow from antiquity to the present and the autonomy of art that suddenly has to contend with the reality of the secular, democratic public sphere that has been developed through a concatenation of many traditions.[5] This is all the more so when such a breach appears, for instance, in the very conditions of artistic production. One example of such a breach in the concept of art addressed in the very facture of artistic production is what has been called elsewhere the "Duchamp Effect."[6] Another view comes from Walter Benjamin's much-referenced essay "The Work of Art in the Age of Mechanical Reproduction," which announced the changes in the medium of art that transform and question traditional notions of originality and aura.[7] Yet another view is based on a spirit of "mutual" recognition of substantive development in other traditions that then feeds into new models of practice: the most obvious example is the encounter between modern European artists and the African and Oceanic sculptures at the turn of the twentieth century that gave birth to cubism. The Duchamp Effect is the most traditional view, to my thinking, because what it purports to do is delineate the supremacy of the artist: the artist not only as a form giver, but a name giver. It is the artist who decides what an object of art is or what it can be, not simply the progressive, formal transformation of art inside of the medium of art. With Duchamp, it is not tradition, but the artist who not only decides what the work of art is but also controls its narrative. For most of us, this idea found its final culmination in the tautological exercises of conceptual art whereby the physical fabrication of art could ostensibly be replaced with linguistic description. Artistic genius emerges, then, from a subjective critique of tradition by the artist, against all other available data, not from an objective analysis of the fallacy of tradition. For Benjamin, mechanical reproduction expands the field and horizon of art, freeing it from traditional biases of originality and aura.

Let me invoke another example, within the "contact zone" of cultures, that of the confrontation with African and Oceanic sculptures by European artists.[8] What this confrontation did was to transform the pictorial and plastic language of modern European painting and sculpture, hence deeply affecting its tradition. What is astonishing in this story of encounter is the degree to which the artistic challenges posed by so-called primitive art to twentieth-century European modernism have been assimilated and subordinated to modernist totalization. Therein lies the fault line between imperial and postcolonial discourse, for to admit to the paradigmatic breach produced by the encounter between African sculptures and European artists would also be to address the narrative of modern art history. We should also remember that the non-Western objects in question first must shed their utilitarian function and undergo a conversion from ritual objects of magic to reified objects of art. The remarkable import of this conversion is that its historical repercussion has remained mostly consigned to formal aesthetic analysis.

I cite these examples because they are material to our reading and judgment of contemporary art. The entrance into art by historically determined questions in terms of form, content, strategy, cultural difference, etc. establishes a ground from which to view art and the artists' relationship to the institutions of art today. Thus, this breach is visible, because it no longer refers to the eternal past of pure objects or to the aloofness from society necessary for autonomy to have any meaning. In his *Theory of the Avant-Garde*, Peter Bürger makes this point clear: "If the autonomy of art is defined as art's independence from society, there are several ways of understanding that definition. Conceiving of art's apartness from society as its 'nature' means involuntarily adopting the l'art pour l'art concept of art and simultaneously making it impossible to explain this apartness as the product of a historical and social development."[9]

The concept of *l'art pour l'art* as part of the avant-garde formulation of artistic autonomy was described by Benjamin as a *theology of art* that "gave rise to what might be called a negative theology in the form of the idea of 'pure' art, which . . . denied any social function of art."[10] It is based on this denial that Bürger's analysis advances a claim for a socially determined theory that stands at the source of two opposing traditions of art historical thought found among certain practitioners today. Not surprisingly, the two opposing traditions furnish the content of the rivalry discernible in the second type of commentary on curatorial procedures. It is the domain most struggled over by conservative (traditionalist) and liberal (progressive) groups, both of whom have increasingly come to abjure any social function of art, except when it fits certain theories. Two recent examples will demonstrate my point here. In the first, I refer to the recent debate in a roundtable discussion on the state of art criticism published on the occasion of the hundredth-issue anniversary of the influential art journal *October*.[11] I had read this issue of the journal with a heightened sense of alacrity, especially at the predictiveness of the panelists' critique of the state of art criticism today. Though the attack against certain populist types of criticism was indeed cogent and necessary, I could not help but detect a tone of condescension in the voices of the *October* critics who appeared merely concerned, in their irritation, with a certain type of popular criticism identified solely with American-based critics.

The second example highlights the ideological tension within the academy between the progressive ethos represented by *October*'s brand of art history and the conservatism of the traditional museum of modern art as it concerns modernism. In the case of the traditional museum, we can apply a similar scrutiny to a museum like the Tate Modern in London. For at this museum, we recently see so visibly rendered an overarching curatorial over-view, straddling over a large expanse of historical developments in modern art. Central to the Tate Modern's curatorial overview is the relationship be-tween modern art and the European tradition and between contemporary art and its modernist heritage. To demonstrate these relationships and at the same time transform the methodology for rendering them in a public display, the museum needed to move between a synchronic and diachronic ordering of its message. Upon its opening two years ago, much discussion appeared in the press about Tate Modern's "radical" attempt to break with the outmoded chronological emphasis of modernist art history. This break would inaugurate something far more dialectical, hence the discursive ap-proach in the permanent collection's display, which was arranged according to genre, subject matter, and form affinities. In this manner, the history of modern art and the transformations within it would be ready at hand for the general public, particularly if it is demonstrated and relayed to them that a [Claude] Monet landscape, for example, can be understood as an im-mediate ancestor to the stone circle sculptures and mud wall paintings of Richard Long.

Divided into four themes: *Still Life/Object/Real Life*, *Nude/Action/Body*, *History/Memory/Society*, and *Landscape/Matter/Environment*, the *decisive* idea was to break with a conception of modernist historiography long entrenched at the Museum of Modern Art in New York since its founding more than seventy years ago. Never mind that many professional visitors—namely, cu-rators and historians—whispered that the *decisiveness* of the Tate Modern in breaking with the traditional historiography of the modern museum owed more to the lack of depth in its collection of modern art than to any radical attempt to redefine how the history of modern art is to be adjudicated and read publicly. But let me return to the galleries proper and the displays. As mentioned already, one of the most memorable rooms in the new installa-tions that seeks to connect modern and contemporary art, hence the conti-nuity of an uninterrupted tradition, is the one that combines one of Richard Long's typical mud wall paintings and one of Monet's water lilies paintings. What are we to make of this pairing? It certainly shows us that both Monet and Long are deeply interested in nature as a source for their art. The pair-ing could also evoke for the viewer that aspect of spirituality and the meta-physical often connected to nature, as well as in the conception of landscape as genre of art from which artists have often drawn. That this pairing is a curatorial gimmick is not so difficult to see. Yet it is an interesting-enough proposition for the unschooled average museum visitor. For the rest of this exercise in dialectical and discursive historiography, rooms were divided like stage sets into the four themes that read much like a textbook. The chilling unmessiness of art's undisturbed progression in a newly founded museum of "modern" art without contradictions, frictions, resistance, and changes that confound and challenge conventional ideas of modernism (beyond the textbook lessons, which we all know so much by heart) is in itself a historical conceit. Every possible position that could challenge this most undialectical of approaches has been sublated and absorbed into the yawning maws of the Tate Modern's self-authorizing account.

One example, and by far the most troubling, of the curatorial reasoning behind this account will suffice. Typical of cynicism toward any socially and historically determined analysis of the object of discourse in a museum of modern art is a room in the *Nude/Action/Body* section. What this theme suggests is a series of transformations in the manner that the body has been used in modern and contemporary art. The series of passages from *nude* to *action* to *body* suggest an image of contingency, internal shifts in the development and understanding of the human form and subjectivity as it moves from modern to contemporary art. The image that presides over this shift is both corporeal and mechanical, symbolic and functional, artistic and political, from the *nude* as an ideal to the *body* as a desiring machine.

The first gallery serves as a sort of introduction and opens out to an eclectic selection of paintings by Stanley Spencer, John Currin, [Pablo] Picasso, and others. This is not an auspicious introduction. The selection and arrangement of the works in the gallery is striking, but more for its formal sensibility than in authoritatively setting out any radical thesis of the nude and the body. So, we walk through the first gallery into the second gallery, where we come upon two imposing large-scale black-and-white photographic works—one by Craigie Horsfield and the other by John Coplans—facing each other. Horsfield's picture *E. Horsfield (1987)*, 1995, is in the tradition of the classical modernist reclining nudes reminiscent of [Paul] Cézanne's bathers and [Henri] Matisse's odalisques. It is an outstanding ponderous picture, heavy like fruit, with the graded tones of gray lending the mass of flesh a stately presence. Coplans's *Self Portrait (Frieze No. 2, Four Panels)*, 1995, is typical of his performative and fragmentary, multipaneled serial self-portraiture, often representing his flabby, aging body. In a typical Coplans manner, the seriality of the depicted parts reveals a body seemingly laying claim to its own sentient properties. Here it should be said that the position of the contemporary nude, in relation to the classical modernist nude, finds formal echoes in the other. But what distinguishes the contemporary nude from its early modernist antecedents—as far as one can make out—can best be summarized as the difference between the self-conscious subjectivity of the former and the formal idealization of the latter. The former recalls [Gilles] Deleuze and [Félix] Guattari's notion of the desiring machine consumed by expressing itself, while the latter is more a force of nature trapped in classical culture.[12]

But what are we to make of what immediately follows this initial encounter with the body in the next gallery? When we enter this gallery, what do we find? We find a small ethnographic vitrine embedded into one of the walls of the room. To the left of the wall is a discreetly placed LCD monitor playing extracts from two films, one by Marc Allégret and André Gide, *Voyage to the Congo* (1927), and the other an anonymous archival film, *Manners and Customs of Senegal* (1910). The two extracts evince a theme common to travel documentary. Though temporally and spatially apart, we can group these two films within a well-known genre, a system of knowledge that belongs to the discourse of colonial, ethnographic film studies of "primitive" peoples. (We already know much about the Western modernist fascination with "primitive" peoples' bodies, along with their orientalist correlatives, that is to say that the concept of alterity was not only important for Western modernism but was necessary as well as a focus of allegorical differentiation.) But Allégret and Gide's film and the more structurally open archival footage provide us with much to think about with regard to modernism, spectacle, otherness, and degeneracy. In each of the two films, we see the setting of the African village and its social life: villagers self-consciously working on their everyday chores such as grinding grain, tending fires, minding children, or participating in a village festival of dance and song. What is most striking about Allégret and Gide's film, however, is that it mostly highlights nakedness—the nakedness of black African bodies under imperial observation. Here nakedness opposed to the nude yields a structure of critical differentiation between the primitive and the modern, between the savage and the civilized, between nature and culture.

To be sure, the method of the camerawork is to be objective, to show primitive peoples as they are, in their natural space. While this may be the film's purpose, one could still detect that part of its conscious structure is to show the degree to which primitive man is not to be confused with the modern man. If this differentiation lends what we are viewing not exactly a quality of empathy, it "underlines," in the words of James Clifford, "a more disquieting quality of modernism: its taste for appropriating or redeeming otherness, for constituting non-Western arts in its own image, for discovering

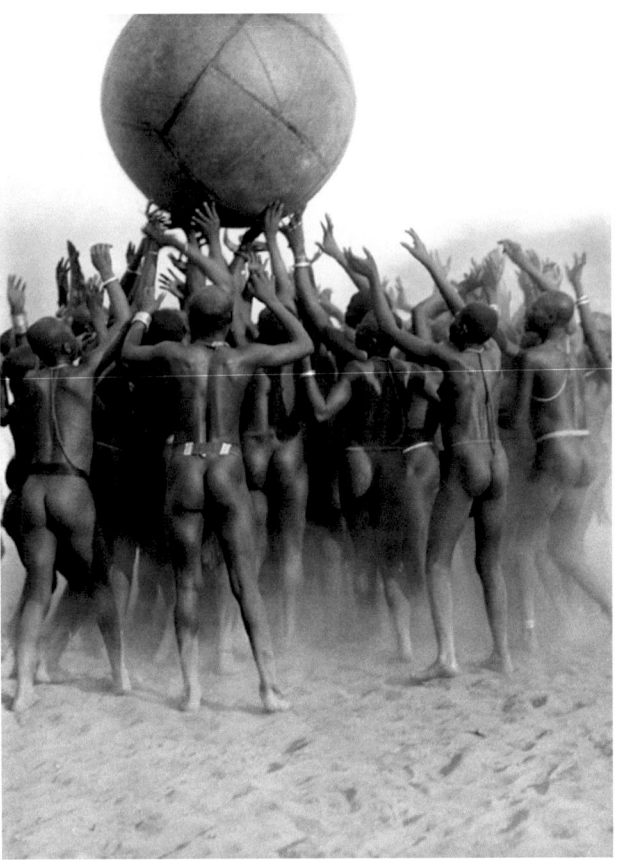

12.1 (*this page*) Marc Allégret and André Gide, still from *Voyage to the Congo*, 1927. 8mm black-and-white-film, 127 mins. Dist. RMN-Grand Palais. © Marc Allégret.

12.2 (*opposite*) Rotimi Fani-Kayode, *Untitled*, 1987–88. Photograph, C-type archival print, 121.9 × 121.9 cm. © Rotimi Fani-Kayode. Courtesy of Autograph, London.

universal, ahistorical 'human' capacities."[13] This observation taken in toto with modernism's relationship to otherness, the primitive and the savage, bears on what the discourse on the nude says concerning the distinction between the nude's formal, aesthetic status within Western modernist art and that of simple nakedness that has no redeeming aesthetic value, commonly found in ethnographic discourse.

If, however, the Tate Modern were an institution working beyond the smug reflex of Western museological authority, it would have found right in its own context the work of artists like Rotimi Fani-Kayode, the Nigerian British photographer whose work—formally and conceptually—involves a long, rigorous excursus into the distinction between the nude and nakedness as it concerns the African body. The analytic content, not to say the formal and aesthetic contradictions that Fani-Kayode's photographic work introduces us to about the black body in contrast to the modernist nude, is

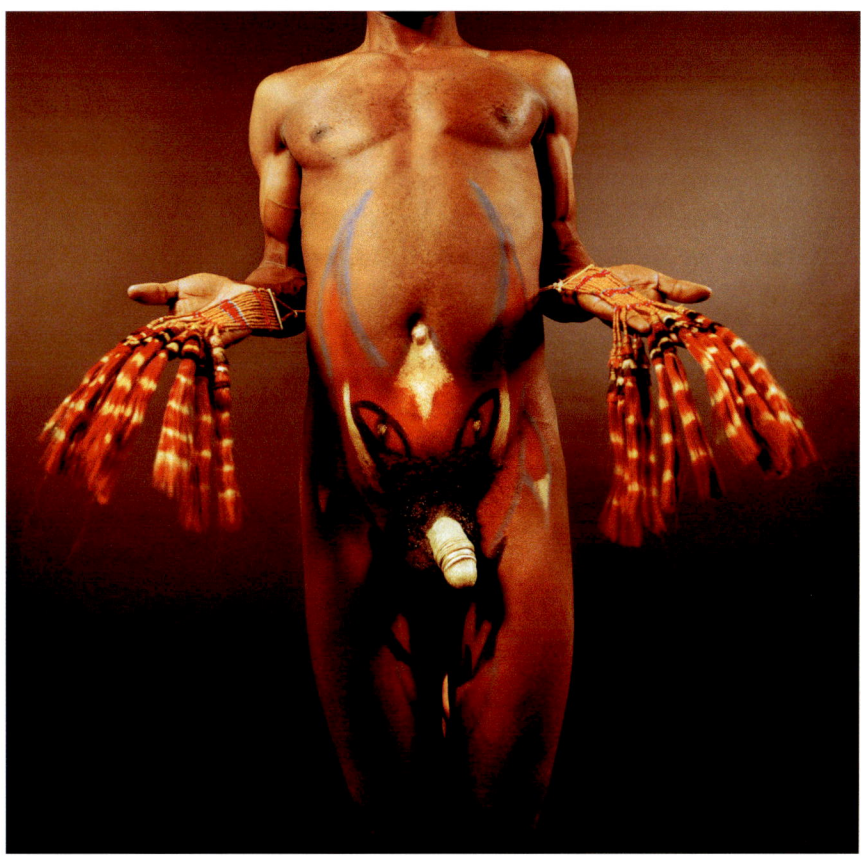

quite telling. More substantial is its awareness of the conflicted relationship
the black body has to Western representation and its museum discourse.[14]
This makes the absence of works like his in the *Nude/Action/Body* section
of the Tate Modern the more glaring. We can substitute Fani-Kayode with
any number of other practitioners, but he is important for my analysis for
the more specific reason of his Africanness, his conceptual usage of that Africanness in his imagery, and his collapse of the fraught idea of nakedness
and the nude in his photographic representation. Fani-Kayode's pictures
also conceive of the black body (in his case the black male body with its homoerotic inferences) as a vessel for idealization, as a desiring and desirable
subject, and as self-conscious in the face of the reduction of the black body
as pure object of ethnographic spectacle. All these critical turns in his work
make the Tate Modern's inattention to strong, critical work on the nude and
the body by artists such as Fani-Kayode all the more troubling, because it is

precisely works like his that have brought to crisis those naturalized conventions of otherness, which throughout the history of modern art have been the stock-in-trade of modernism. Whatever its excuses for excluding some of these artists from its presentation, we should discount the Tate Modern's monologue on the matter of the ethnographic films. Accompanying the extracts, which also manifest a characteristic doublespeak, the label expounds on the matter of the films' presence in the gallery: "European audiences in the early 20th century gained experience of Africa through documentary films. Generally, these conformed to stereotyped notions about African cultures. An ethnographic film of 1910, for instance, concentrates on the skills and customs of the Senegalese, while *Voyage to the Congo*, by filmmaker Marc Allégret and writer André Gide, perpetuates preconceptions about life in the 'bush.' However, the self-awareness displayed by those under scrutiny, glimpsed observing the filmmakers, subverts the supposed objectivity of the film."[15]

The Tate Modern in this supplementary discourse imputes both the manufacture and consumption of the stereotype to some past European documentary films and audiences, which is to say that the business of such stereotypes lies in the past, even if it has now been exhumed before a contemporary European audience for the purposes of explaining modernism's penchant for deracinating the African subject. But if the discourse of the stereotype as implied is now behind us, is its resuscitation an act of mimicry, or is it, as Homi Bhabha has written (in "The Other Question"), an act of anxious repetition of the stereotype that folds back into the logic for excluding African artists in the gallery arrangement?[16] Does the repetition of the stereotype caught, if you will, in a discursive double maneuver posit an awareness of the problem of the stereotype for contemporary transnational audiences, or does the museum's label present us with a more profound question in which the wall text causally explains and masks what is absent in the historical reorganization of the museum's memory cum history? One conclusion can be drawn from this unconvincing explanatory maneuver: more than anything, it entrenches European modernist appropriation and instrumentalization of Africa in its primitivist discourse to which the Tate Modern in the twenty-first century is a logical heir.

Still, as we go deeper into the matter, our investigation has much to yield as we look further into the ethnographic desublimation (an uneasy conjunction, no doubt, between colonialism and modernism) taking place in the museum. Inside the vitrine, we find, casually scattered, postcards with the general title "Postcards from West Africa" (the subject of which relates to that of the two film extracts) and an untitled, undated small, dark figurative sculpture, identified simply as *Standing Figure*. The label informatively tells us of the sculpture's provenance: having come from the collection of Jacob Epstein, which thus conveys to us through the synecdoche of ownership the sculpture's aesthetic aura. What is implied is this: the ownership of such a sculpture by one of Britain's important modernist artists means that he must have appreciated the sculpture first and foremost as a work of art with important aesthetic qualities that recommend it to the modern European sculptor.[17] But if this is so, why then is the sculpture not more properly displayed along with other sculptures installed in the gallery? Or is its namelessness and authorlessness unable to deliver it into the domain of aesthetic judgment necessary for its inclusion as an authoritative work of art?

It is no use speaking about the lyrical beauty and artistic integrity of this powerful sculpture so pointlessly compromised by the rest of the detritus of the colonial knowledge system crammed in the vitrine. The sculpture's presence is not only remote from us, it seems to connote not art, above all not autonomous art, just artifact, or, worse still, evidence. Nearly a hundred years after the initial venture by Western modernists (and I do not care which artist "discovered" what qualities in African or Oceanic art first), it would have been clear enough to the curators at the Tate Modern that in terms of sheer variety of styles, forms, complexity, genres, plastic distinctiveness, stylistic inventiveness and complexity of sculptural language, and conception, no region in the world approaches the depth and breadth of African sculptural traditions. Let's take, for example, the Congo, from where Gide and Allégret gave us the deleterious impressions of their *voyage*, as a point of illustration. In just this single region we find distinct traditions of sculpture such as Yombe, Luba, Mangbetu, Kuba, Teke, Lega, Songye, and Dengese. These traditions of sculpture and many others are as unique as they are historically different in their morphological conception of sculpture. The expressive and conceptual possibilities in the language of artists working within each group have produced sculptural forms of such anthropomorphic variety and complexity, whether of the mask or figure, the statue or relief, that simple comparative study between them yields such an active field of artistic experimentation and invention that many a modernist recognized, understood, and appreciated. But this is not communicated at all in the lugubrious gathering at the museum. It should also be noted that what this installation communicates is neither a history nor even a proper anthropology of modernism; rather, the task of this "historical" instruction is more a convention that has often been repeated in a variety of museums

of modern art. To my thinking, such types of instruction more or less ob-
fuscate rather than enlighten. In fact, along with museum collections, most
Western modernist museology is predicated on the repetition and circulation of disparate apocrypha and objects connected to this obfuscation.[18]

As for the African conception of modernity in this depressing tale
of museology, that would be for another place and time. Meanwhile, what
remains on view inside the rest of the vitrine is not the basis for a system of
knowledge according to which the relationship between Western modernist
artists in correspondence to their African contemporaries exists in the affilia-
tive spirit of mutual influence and recognition. Instead, the vitrine posits a
method, a mode of instruction on what is modern and what is not. In the
method and instruction there are Carl Einstein's well-known book *Negerplastik*, Marcel Griaule's accounts of the Dakar-Djibouti expedition, published
in the journal *Minotaure*, which is contemporary to Michel Leiris's famous
book *L'Afrique fantôme*, all performing a pantomime of the modern opposed
to the primitive that the Tate Modern has now upgraded to the most astonishing form of ethnographic ventriloquism.[19] Having emptied and hol-
lowed out the space of African aesthetic traditions, the rest of the gallery
was filled in—with customary care and reverence—with carefully installed
"autonomous" sculptures by [Constantin] Brancusi and [Alberto] Giacom-
etti and paintings by the German expressionists Karl Schmidt-Rottluff and
Ernst Ludwig Kirchner. A Kirchner painting of a cluster of nude figures
with pale elongated limbs and quasi-cubist, conical, distended midsections
is noteworthy and striking in its anthropomorphic resemblance and formal
correspondence to both the sculpture in the vitrine and what we had been
looking at in the film of the naked Congolese women and children in Gide
and Allégret's film.

Given the large literature on the subject, should we take the Tate
Modern to task by asking whether it could have found African artists from
whatever period to fit into their dialectical scheme? The evidence emphatically suggests they could have. The result is they did not. Not because they
could not, but most likely because they felt no obligation to stray from the
modern museum's traditional curatorial exclusions. This laid open to question the dialectical assumption of the museum's display. However, what was
concretely conveyed was an attitude, a point of view, a sense of sovereign
judgment.

We should nonetheless concede the fact that the Tate Modern is
merely operating on a well-trodden ground. For example, when Werner
Spies reinstalled the galleries of the Centre Pompidou in 1999, he applied

a curatorial flourish to the museum's cache of modernist paintings and sculptures, mixing them with postwar and contemporary art while assigning classical African sculpture and masks a garishly lit vitrine wedged into a hallway-like room. A more serious example of this sort was the Museum of Modern Art's scholarly, superb, and curatorially important and influential *"Primitivism" in 20th Century Art: Affinity of the Tribal and the Modern* exhibition in 1984/85, which treated the African and Oceanic works as it would any highly refined modernist object. But even this treatment of the works as autonomous sculptures was achieved through a sense of reification that all but destroyed the important symbolic power of the objects and the role they played in their social contexts.

In 1989 Jean-Hubert Martin curated Centre Pompidou's still-controversial exhibition *Magiciens de la terre*, which set a different course in its response to the question that has vexed the modernist museum from its earliest inception, namely, the status and place of non-Western art within the history of modernism and contemporary art. To evade this conundrum, Martin elected to eliminate the word *artist* from his exhibition—mindful of the fact that such a designation may be unduly burdened by a Western bias—choosing instead the term *magiciens* as the proper name for the object and image makers invited to present their art. If the MoMA and Centre Pompidou exhibitions—in New York and Paris respectively, two bastions of the history of modern art in the world—responded critically to the controversial and unresolved aesthetic and historical debates within modernist accounts concerning art and artists from other cultures, the Tate Modern, in its own attempt to further the rewriting of modernist reception of the other and non-Western art, proved both unevolved and unreflexive. There is a sense of the entire setup being ahistorical, bearing no semblance to the critical content of what Habermas calls "the philosophical discourse of modernity."[20] After this encounter, I contented myself with looking at the rest of the collection without troubling further with its justifications, its subjugation of historical memory—in fact, its savage act of epistemological and hermeneutic violence.

3

If I have dwelled on elucidating this particular view, it is only to frame what is at stake for artists and curators who step into the historical breach that has opened up today within the context of contemporary art. As regards modernist historiography, that is another matter. But we do know that modernism has many streams that do not all empty into the same basin. Equally evident is the fact that the rising tide of institutional interest in other accounts of artistic production will never lift all the boats into the dialectical position of tradition and continuity so beloved by museums like the Tate Modern. And there is the nub of the current skepticism toward a globalized reception of contemporary artistic practices from far-flung places with little historical proximity to the ideas transmitted from within the legacy of the Western historical avant-garde.

With regard to the complex conditions of production today, the legacy of Western historical avant-garde seems inadequate to do the job of producing a unified theory of contemporary art. Because of its restless, unfixed boundaries, multiplicities, and the state of "permanent transition" within which it is practiced and communicated, contemporary art tends to be much more resistant to global totalization. Yet the past two decades have witnessed an exponential rise in the fortunes of curators, who, with their portmanteau of theories neatly arranged—befitting of their status as the enlightened bureaucrats of modernist totalization—travel the world scouring for new signs of art to fill the historical breach.

Current enthusiasm for deftly packaged multicultural exhibitions aside, there is a sense that such exhibitions are mere responses of convenience and strategy to keep at bay certain social forces that demand greater inclusion that reflects the complexity of societies in which museums exist. To be sure, the responses by museums and academies to the troubling questions of inclusion/exclusion have a historical basis, particularly imperialism and colonialism. The rupture in continuity to which imperialism and colonialism subjected many cultures continues to have contemporary repercussions on matters such as taste and judgment, giving many artists an important dispute as well as capacities for figuring new values of truth within the field of contemporary art. It is the fields of modern and contemporary art that have given us the view of the utter disability of the one true judgment of art, however authoritative such judgment may be.

It has been long recognized that postcolonial processes have increasingly highlighted the problematics of Western judgment over vast cultural fields in the non-Western world. Many curatorial practices today are direct responses to postcolonial critique of Western authority. What I am trying to foreground here is the fact that the conditions of production and reception of contemporary art evince a dramatic multiplication of its systems of articulation to the degree that no singular judgment could contain all its peculiarities.

The curatorial responses to the contestations initiated both by post-colonialism and expanded definitions of art seem directed at assimilating certain historical effects that became clear only in the past three decades, especially in the 1980s and 1990s, and have accelerated since the late 1990s. I will thus delineate five effects that, to me, are the most salient. The effects address not so much the value system of the old world of modernism but the postcolonial conditions of the contemporary world as such. Because modernist formalism has tended to respond to contemporary culture with hostility, the effects I am speaking of are therefore not so much marked by the speed of their transposition into networks and teleologies of organized totality (or as the theology of universal history, as is common with all modernist effects), but rather founded on the impermanent and aleatory. Impermanence here does not mean endless drift and evacuation of specificity; rather, the structure of contemporary art's relationship to history is more transversal, asynchronous, and asystematic in nature, thereby revealing the multiplicity of cultural procedures and countermodels that define contemporary art today.

The first effect is the proliferation and mutation of forms of exhibitions—such as blockbusters, large-scale group or thematic exhibitions, cultural festivals, *biennales*, and the like, all of which have significantly enlarged the knowledge base of contemporary art in museums and culture at large. This enlargement is crucial, because it has created new networks between hitherto separated spheres of contemporary artistic production—both in the everyday engagement with the world and its images, texts, and narratives and what I have called modernism's dead certainties. Even if this phase is still in a developmental stage, it has oriented the transmission of contemporary art discourses toward a deeper confrontation with what Carlos Basualdo has called the "new geographies of culture."[21] Basualdo's "new geographies of culture" confront curatorial and exhibition systems with the fact that all discourses are located; that is, they are formed and begin somewhere, they have a temporal and spatial basis, they are read synchronically and diachronically. Furthermore, the located nature of cultural discourses, with their history of discontinuities and transitions, confronts curatorial practices with the fragility of universalized conceptions of history, culture, and artistic procedures.

The second effect first appeared as an allegory of transformation and transfiguration, then subsequently as a mode of resistance and repetition. It is easy to underestimate today the force of the dissolution of colonialism on art and culture until we realize that, not so long ago—barely half a century—the majority of the globe (covering almost two-thirds of the earth's surface and numbering more than a billion people) consisted of places and peoples without proper political rights. Now, with postcolonialism and the decay of the postcolonial state structure, it is again easy enough to mock the utopian aspirations of self-determination, liberation from colonialism, and political independence that began to see off the imperial discourse that distinctly marked global modernity in its early phase. Similarly, global modernity, in the guise of the modern nation-state that has furnished the political identity of the modern and contemporary artist, intercedes on behalf of a plethora of fictions that found the idea of a national tradition in art and culture. As such, decolonization and national identity represent the bookends of two concomitant projects of late global modernity. On the one hand, decolonization portends to restore sundered traditions to their "proper" pasts, while national identity through the state works assiduously to reinvent and maintain them in the present and for the future. This is what has been called the road map to nation building and modernization. Decolonization, qua the postcolonial, transforms the subject of cultural discourse, while the nation-state reinvents the identity of the artist and transfigures the order of tradition for posterity. If the mode of the post-colonial is resistance and insubordination through transformation, that of the nation is consolidation and repetition through transfiguration. Out of each, the figure of the new becomes the emulsifier for either tradition and restoration, or tradition and continuity. In each, we also can locate the antinomies of the modern and contemporary. No doubt, contemporary issues of curatorial practice are keenly aware of the uses (and make use) of the fictions of a sundered past and tradition to produce narratives of various invented histories of the modern and contemporary.

Nowhere is this discourse more palpable than in the fiery debates centered around cultural identity, such that representation is not merely the name for a manner of practice, but quite literally the name for a political awareness of identity within the field of representation. Therefore, the making of the new in the context of decolonized representation was as much about the coming to being of new relations of cultures and histories, practices and processes, rationalization and transformation, transculturation and assimilation, exchanges and moments of multiple dwelling, as it is about the ways artists are seen to be bound to their national and cultural traditions. Here the political community and cultural community become essentially coterminous. But beyond nationalism and national cultures, decolonization is more than just the forlorn daydream of the postcolonial artist or intellectual, for it has, attached to it, something recognizable in the ideals of modernity: the notion of progress.

The new in art, then, has a self-affirmative content in its postcolonial guise. But how was this view received in the much-lamented art that is derogatively referred to as identity-based or multicultural art? Notice the conflation of the terms *identity* and *multiculturalism*. The weakness of all identity-based discourse, we were told, was in its self-contradiction, in its attempt to conflate the universal and the particular, self and other, into the social site of artistic production. Another analysis sees identity-based practices as presiding over cultural and political grounds that are too reductive and simplistic, specific, and limited, and, because of their incapacity to deal with abstraction, incapable of transcending that specificity that leads to universal culture. Concerning the fragmentation of modernist totalization introduced by postmodernism, art historian Hal Foster posed the following questions: "Is this fragmentation an illusion, an ideology of its own (of political 'crisis,' say, versus historical 'contradiction')? Is it a symptom of a cultural 'schizophrenia' to be deplored? Or is it, finally, the sign of a society in which difference and discontinuity rightly challenge ideas of totality and continuity?"[22]

Are we to then argue, based on Foster's questions (and of course putting aside for the moment that identity-based discourses have been eviscerated), that identity discourse from the standpoint of its oppositionality, contingency, and discontinuity is the specter that haunts modernism? To take it further, was there a false consciousness in the belief that identity-based discourses, along with their multicultural correlatives, in alliance with postmodernism's critique of grand narratives and universal history (including those elaborations on paradigms of asymmetrical power relations unleashed by postcolonial studies), could bring about the possibility of a decentered global cultural order? Certainly, global culture is thoroughly decentered, but its power can hardly be said to be contained. Foster does offer a view that can allow us to think a bit further on this question, through an unsentimental reading of Marxism and cultural ideology, writing of how

> new social forces—women, blacks, other "minorities," gay movements, ecological groups, students . . . —have made clear the unique importance of gender and sexual difference, race and the third world, the "revolt of nature" and the relation of power and knowledge, in such a way that the concept of class, if it is to be retained as such, must be articulated in relation to these terms. In response, theoretical focus

has shifted from class as a subject of history to the cultural constitution of subjectivity, from economic identity to social difference. In short, political struggle is now seen largely as a process of "differential articulation."[23]

No museum or exhibition project, even if it wishes not to address the consequences of this "differential articulation," can remain critically blind to the importance of multicultural and identity-based practices, however wrongheaded and regressive they may appear. One guiding reason for this vigilance among cultural institutions has to do with both the politics of enlightened self-interest and the changing of the cultural and social demographics of many contemporary societies due to large-scale immigrations of the twentieth century and postcolonialism. In the case of the United States and Europe, the civil rights movement, antiracist movements, and the struggle for the protection of minority rights have increased the level of this vigilance. There is also the recognition of the role of the market in the institutionalization of national identity in recent curatorial projects, especially in exhibitions designed to position certain national or geographic contexts of artistic production. What is often elided in the excitation of these new national or geopolitical spaces is the politics of national representation that recommends them through various national funding and promotional boards, cultural foundations, and institutions.[24] Increasingly, curators have become highly dependent on the patronage of such institutions. The critic Benjamin Buchloh, in relation to the neoexpressionist market juggernaut of the late 1970s and 1980s, has analyzed a similar curatorial symptom that trades on the morbid cliché of national identity: "When art emphasizing national identity attempts to enter the international distribution system, the most worn-out historical and geopolitical clichés have to be employed. And thus, we now see the resurrection of such notions as the Nordic versus the Mediterranean, the Teutonic versus the Latin."[25]

The third effect concerns the explosion of and the heterogeneous nature of artistic procedures immediately at variance with the historically conditioned, thereby conventional, understanding of art within the logic of the museum. Such procedures have been theorized, quite correctly, as neo-avant-garde, rather than as a true rupture from their academic obverse. However, it can be said that institutional canniness has often found inventive ways to absorb the energies of even the most insurrectional positions in art. The emergence of new critical forces has all too often become cashiered as another instance in the positivist ideology of advanced art's claim of *engagement* set forth by the institution.

The fourth effect is connected to the mediatization of culture, especially in the transformation of the museum form into an extension of the culture industry of mass entertainment, theatricality, and tourism. The most fitting expression of the passage of museums into the concept of mass culture has been achieved through the fusion of architectural design and the museum's collection whereby the collection and architecture become one fully realized *Gesamtkunstwerk* and are understood as such.[26] Here the fusion of the collection with museum architecture is as much a value-supplying feature as any other purpose, such that out-of-town visitors can either go to visit the Frank Lloyd Wright–designed Guggenheim Museum in New York or Frank Gehry's Guggenheim Bilbao as unique works of art in their own right or they may travel to see the buildings and visit the collections at the same time. Despite their universalist aspirations, most contemporary museums exist with the dark clouds of nationalism or ideologies of civic virtue hovering over them. For even if the aspiration of the museum is not specifically nationalist, in order to attract funding and state support, its discourse in today's competition between global cities is decidedly nationalist in spirit.

Finally, the fifth effect, which I believe ultimately subtends the previous four, is the globalization of economic production and culture, and the technological and digital revolution that has fused them. Two things underscore the points about globalization that make it fascinating in relation to this discussion: its limit and reach. While the compression of time and space is understood as one of the great aspects of this phenomenon of modernity, there still appears within globalization of art and culture a great unevenness for many artists in terms of access.

Having abandoned the strictures of "internationalism," there is now the idea that the globalization of artistic discourses opens the doors to greater understanding of the motivations that shape contemporary art across Europe, North America, Asia, Africa, and South America. Paradoxically, it is globalization that has laid open the myth of a consolidated art world. Rather than a center, what is much in evidence today are networks and cross-hatched systems of production, distribution, transmission, reception, and institutionalization. The development of new multilateral networks of knowledge production—activities that place themselves strategically at the intersection of disciplines and transnational audiences—has obviated the traditional circuits of institutionalized production and reception. These emergent networks are what I believe Basualdo meant by "new geographies of culture." By *emergent*, I wish, especially, to foreground not so much the newness of these territories (many of which in fact have extraterritorial characteristics) but their systematic integration into mobile sites of discourse, which only became more visible due to the advances in information technology as a means of distributing, transmitting, circulating, receiving, and telegraphing of ideas and images.

4

If the foregoing is so far incontestable, the direct question to be asked is this: How does the curator of contemporary art express her intellectual agency within the state of "permanent transition" in which contemporary art exists today? How does the curator work both within canonical thinking and against the grain of that thinking in order to take cognizance of artistic thought that slowly makes itself felt, first in the field of culture, before it appears to be sanctioned by critics and institutions? I do not have specific answers to these questions. But I do have a notion or two about how we may approach them.

From the moment exhibitions of art assumed a critical place in the public domain of social and cultural discourse among political classes—within the bourgeois public sphere that first emerged actively in Europe in the aftermath of the French Revolution (see Habermas[27])—exhibitions have been constituted, pace Foucault, within the field of "a history of thought." The field of a history of thought, however, is a field of institutionalized power and systems of legitimation. Even though institutions of art have moved, inexorably, from the private, courtly domain of the feudal state to the increasingly public domain of the salon of the democratic secular state, fundamental instruments of power were still disproportionately held through patronage by the bourgeois elite in alliance with the aristocracy. Today this process of social differentiation has entered another sphere dominated by capital and contested by forces of the so-called avant-garde. As Pierre Bourdieu writes, "The literary or artistic field is at all times the site of a struggle between the two principles of hierarchization: the heteronomous principle, favorable to those who dominated the field economically and politically (e.g. 'bourgeois art') and the autonomous principle (e.g. 'art for art's sake'), which those of its advocates who are least endowed with specific capital tend to identify with degree of independence from the economy, seeing temporal failure as a sign of election and success as a sign of compromise."[28]

Such a struggle between the strategic utility of failure or success also confronts curators and their judgment. For contemporary artists, the adjudication of success or failure—the principle between academicism and avant-gardism, between tradition and innovation—by curators remains a key factor in public and institutional legitimation. Therefore, historically, the emergence of exhibitions as a cultural activity of public institutions is defined within a general field of knowledge. It is informed and governed by aesthetic criteria, disciplinary and artistic norms that designate the historical relationship of the public to all of art. While all aesthetic criteria, disciplinary and artistic norms, are said to derive from nothing less than the ontological facture of art as an autonomous drive of artistic creativity—hence the universal dimension of our grasp of art's meaning, and supplementarily its history—we do know that the constitutive field of art history is a synthetically elaborated one, that is, a man-made history. Nonetheless, transcategories of art, or works that seek to highlight this synthetic elaboration and as such obviate its foundational principle, still come under the putative influence and exertion of epistemes of historical thought. Even the most radical exhibitions are constituted in this general field of knowledge and define themselves within or against its critical exertion, which is both historical and institutional. Within contemporary art exhibitions, the horizon of art in a dispersed, fragmentary, and asymmetrical state of economic capitalization endemic to all global systems is foreshortened by these historical and institutional forces. And here the radical will of the curator is no less compromised. As such, all exhibition procedures today call for a new kind of assessment grounded in the historical reality of the general field of knowledge. This is all the more so if we view the task of an exhibition and the work of the curator as fundamentally contiguous. And what exactly do exhibitions propose and curators organize if not the alliance of historically and institutionally ordered experience governing the reception and relations of art and its objects, concepts, forms, and ideas by a heterogeneous and culturally diverse public? The avidity with which critics seek to define the task of the curator and the curator's relationship to the one true history of art makes this imperative very necessary.

5

With this in mind, I want to call attention to the fact that all curatorial procedures as grounded in the discursive mechanisms of "the history of art" have an optics, that is to say a lens, a way of looking, seeing, and judging art and its objects, images, texts, events, activities, histories, and the inter-media strategies that define the artwork's public existence through institutions, museums, galleries, exhibitions, criticism, etc. The almost Orwellian dispensation toward constructing a viewpoint that is overarching in terms of its conclusions about certain artistic skills and competencies, concepts, and meaning represents a node within which the discursive field of the postcolonial constellation has been formed, namely, to limit the power, if not necessarily the import, of such judgment. For the judgment from which the "history of art" as a specific discipline of the Western academy oversees all artistic matters tends to surreptitiously adopt and incorporate into its discursive field a bird's-eye, panoptic view of artistic practice, which in turn appropriates and subverts subjective judgment into a sovereign assessment of all artistic production. However, if the curator is not quite the sovereign we have made her out to be, she nonetheless operates (with the unambiguous sanction of historical and imperial precedent) like a viceroy among the nonbelievers to be brought over to the sovereign regard of the great Western tradition. It is the sovereign judgment of art history, with its unremitting dimension of universality and totality, that leads us to question whether it is possible to develop a singular conception of artistic modernity, and whether it is permissible to still retain the idea that the unique, wise, and discriminating judgment of curatorial taste, or what some would ambiguously call *criticality*, ought to remain the reality of how we evaluate contemporary art today. Foucault's call for the problematization of the concept of thought in relation to critical praxis is therefore instructive. The fields of practice in which relations of production, acculturation, assimilation, translation, and interpretation take place confront us immediately with the contingency of the contemporary norm of curatorial procedures that spring from the sovereign world of established categories of art inherited from "the history of art."

Therefore, the museum of modern art as an object of historical thought has a social life, as well as a political dimension, and its function cannot be dissociated from the complex arena of society and culture within which its discourse is imbricated. To that end, then, it is of significant interest to see in the curator a figure who has assumed a position as a producer of certain kinds of thought about art, artists, exhibitions, and ideas and their place among a field of other possible forms of thought that govern the transmission and reception of artistic production; to think reflexively also about museums. Interestingly, it is artists who have interrogated the institution of the museum and its categorical exceptions of greatness with such rigor. Even if "institutional critique" that inaugurated this critical intervention into the discursive spaces of the museum has made itself redundant in light of the parasitic relationship it developed within the institution, it nonetheless opened up a space of critical address that few curators rarely attempt.

Another way of approaching the discourse on curatorial practice is to understand the work of the curator as a mode of practice that leads to particular ways of aligning thought and vision through the separation and juxtaposition of a number of models within the domains of artistic production and public reception. This can tell us a lot and show how the curator reflexively produces an exhibition: allowing the viewer to think, see, appreciate, understand, transform, and translate the visual order of contemporary art into the order of knowledge about the history of art.

Meanwhile, if we were to attempt a definition of the status of the artwork in the current climate of restlessness and epistemological challenges, it would not be a definition, but the artwork understood and recognized as being produced and mobilized in a field of relations.[29] A field of relations places contemporary art and its problematics within the context of historical discourses on modernity. Such a field elucidates the possible challenges of curatorial work today. On such challenges Foucault's splendid definition of the idea of "work" provides a true flash of insight: "that which is susceptible of introducing a meaningful difference in the field of knowledge, albeit with a certain demand placed on the author and the reader, but with the eventual recompense of a certain pleasure, that is to say, of an access to another figure of truth."[30]

Across the line from which the public faces institutions of legitimation, how does one reach this other figure of truth, especially in an exhibition context? With what aesthetic and artistic language does one utter such truth? And in what kind of environment? For which public? How does one define the public of art, particularly given the proliferation of what qualifies as public? Finally, what truth, in the circumstances of the contemporary upheaval of thought, ideas, identities, politics, cultures, histories? The upheaval that today defines our contemporary assessment of events is a historical one, shaped by disaffection with two paradigms of totalization: capitalism and imperialism, and socialism and totalitarianism. If the disaffection with these paradigms did not shift significantly the axis and forces of totalization, it did shape the emergence of new subjectivities and identities. However, the context and the reception of the news of this emergence have crystallized into a figure of thought that is radically enacted in oppositional distinctions made on civilizational and moralistic terms: such as "the clash of civilizations,"[31] "the axis of evil,"[32] the "evil empire."[33] During the late 1980s and early 1990s, the culture wars in the United States were waged equally on these terms, which in time cooled the ardor of those institutions tempted to step beyond the scope of this limiting argument.[34] I will not rehearse here the anguish of these debates, for they are well known. Suffice it to say that my conception of the postcolonial constellation comes out of the recognition made clear by the current upheaval evident in a series of structural, political, and cultural restructurings since after World War II, which include movements of decolonization and the civil rights, feminist, gay/lesbian, and antiracist movements.[35] The postcolonial constellation is the site for the expansion of the definition of what constitutes contemporary culture and its affiliations in other domains of practice, the intersection of historical forces aligned against the hegemonic imperatives of imperial discourse.

In conclusion, I would like to reaffirm the importance of postcolonial history and theory in the understanding of the social and cultural temporality of late modernity. If I recommend the postcolonial prism as the lens that can illuminate our reading of the fraught historical context from which the discourses of modernism and contemporary art emerged, it is only to aim toward the maturity of the understanding of what art history and its supplementary practices can contribute today toward our knowledge of art. Therefore, the postcolonial constellation is an understanding of a particular historical order that configures the relationship between political, social, and cultural realities, artistic spaces, and epistemological histories, not in contest but always in continuous redefinitions.

Acknowledgments

I would like to thank Muna el Fituri-Enwezor for her crucial editorial advice and comments; Terry Smith and Salah Hassan for reading this text with care; and David Wilkins, Phillip Johnson, Carlos Basualdo, Henry Louis Gates, and Iwona Blazwick for inviting me to deliver parts of it as lectures during visits in Pittsburgh, Providence, Buenos Aires, Cambridge, and London.

NOTES

Epigraphs: Michel Foucault, *The History of Sexuality*, vol. 2, *The Uses of Pleasure* (New York: Pantheon, 1985), 10; Édouard Glissant, *Poetics of Relation*, trans. Betsy Wing (Ann Arbor: University of Michigan Press, 1997), 45.

1   Fernand Braudel's discussion of the structural transformation of the flow of capital and culture by distinct temporal manifestations, i.e., the paradigmatic and diagnostic attribute of historical events in relation to their duration. Such flow and unfolding Braudel calls "temporalities of long and very long duration, slowly evolving and less slowly evolving situations, rapid and virtually instantaneous deviations." Fernand Braudel, *Civilization and Capitalism: 15th–18th Century*, vol. 3, *The Perspective of the World*, trans. Sian Reynolds (New York: Harper and Row, 1984), 17, as paraphrased by Achille Mbembe, "At the Edge of the World: Boundaries, Territoriality, and Sovereignty in Africa," *Public Culture* 12, no. 1 (Winter 2000): 259.

2   See Édouard Glissant, *Caribbean Discourse: Selected Essays*, ed. and trans. J. Michael Dash (Charlottesville: University of Virginia Press, 1992). Much like Gilles Deleuze and Félix Guattari with their idea of the rhizome, Glissant employs the prodigious spread of the mangrove forest to describe the processes of multiplications and installations that for him describe the tremor of creolization as a force of historical changes and ruptures brought about by changes in the imperial order. See also Édouard Glissant, *Poetics of Relation*, trans. Betsy Wing (Ann Arbor: University of Michigan Press, 1997).

3   [*Ed. note:* Glissant, *Poetics of Relation*, 45.]

4   Admittedly, the advent of mass culture has all but made mute the ability of exhibitions to be truly seminal in a wider cultural sense in the manner in which the salons of the nineteenth and early twentieth centuries were, or the Armory Show of 1917 in New York. Much of what is known and important about Dada was through its many exhibitions and happenings that helped define it as a new artistic movement. Today the miniscandals of the art world, such as the lawsuit brought against the Contemporary Art Center of Cincinnati upon its exhibition of Robert Mapplethorpe's homoerotic photographs, or the controversy surrounding Chris Ofili's painting of a Madonna with elephant dung used as one of its breasts in the Brooklyn Museum's exhibition *Sensation*, show the degree to which exhibitions of art remain culturally significant in the narratives of art historical writing.

5   The Nobel economist Amartya Sen gives the example of the cross-pollination of ideas between cultures that has continued unabated for two millennia. He distinctly argues the fact that

> what is often called "Western Science" draws on a world heritage. There is a chain of intellectual relations that links Western mathematics and science to a collection of distinctly non-Western practitioners. Even today, when a modern mathematician at, say, Princeton invokes an algorithm to solve a difficult computational problem, she helps to commemorate the contribution of the ninth century Arab mathematician Al-Khwarizmi, from whose name the term "algorithm"

is derived. (The term "algebra" comes from his book, *Aljabr wa al-Muqabalah*.) The decimal system, which evolved in India in the early centuries of the first millennium, arrived in Europe at the end of that millennium, transmitted by the Arabs. Amartya Sen, "Civilizational Imprisonments: How to Misunderstand Everybody in the World," *New Republic*, June 10, 2002, 28–33.

In the arts, a typical typological casting is the importance assigned to influence, and when such a term demonstrably involves relations of power, there occurs a remarkable modification that denotes influence in a singularized incubated form and substitutes it with affinity, as we have seen in the cases involving so-called tribal art and modern art. From scientific to philosophical concepts, translations, economic to cultural exchanges, architecture, art, literature, music, what may appear to many a Western mind as the singular progression of heritage has come through to us via so many paths. Rather than continuity, what above all defines relations of the arts and sciences to tradition is contiguity.

6   See Martha Buskirk and Mignon Nixon, eds., *The Duchamp Effect* (Cambridge, MA: October Books, 1998).

7   Walter Benjamin, "The Work of Art in the Age of Mechanical Reproduction," in *Illuminations: Essays and Reflections* (New York: Schocken, 1969), 217–51.

8   See Mary Louise Pratt, *Imperial Eyes: Travel Writing and Transculturation* (New York: Routledge, 1992); and James Clifford, *Routes: Travel and Translation in the Twentieth Century* (Cambridge, MA: Harvard University Press, 1997), where he especially adapts Pratt's term in a specific treatment of discourses of contact in the art and museum communities. In a related interview Clifford argues that relations between the art of different cultures are often shot through with complex intentions when they meet: "These are perspectives that do not see 'culture contact' as one form progressively, sometimes violently, replacing another. They focus on relational ensembles sustained through processes of cultural borrowing, appropriation, and translation—multidirectional processes." James Clifford, "An Ethnographer in the Field," in *Site-Specificity: The Ethnographic Turn*, vol. 4, ed. Alex Coles (London: Black Dog, 2000), 63.

9   Peter Bürger, *Theory of the Avant-Garde*, trans. Michael Shaw (Minneapolis: University of Minnesota Press, 1984), 35.

10   Benjamin, "Work of Art," 224.

11   See "Obsolescence," special issue, *October*, no. 100 (Spring 2002), particularly the roundtable on art criticism. The composition of the speakers of the roundtable is instructive in the way in which the modes of elision and discrimination that are recurrent in most mainstream institutions and conservative academies pervade even this self-styled progressive intellectual organ. It is, of course, universally known that this journal, despite its

revolutionary claims, remains staunchly and ideologically committed to a defense of modernism as it has been historically elaborated within the European context and updated in postwar American art. There is nothing inherently wrong with such commitment, if it were not its elevation of that discourse to the height of a universal paradigm for the uneven, diachronic experience of modernity. That there is very little acknowledgment of the radical political strategies and the social and cultural transformations developed since the decolonization project of the postwar period outside the West, which have equally shaped the reception of modernism in the work of artists outside of Europe and North America, is a grave error, which cannot now be ignored after a hundred issues of continuous publication.

12   Gilles Deleuze and Félix Guattari, *Anti-Oedipus: Capitalism and Schizophrenia*, trans. Robert Hurley, Mark Seem, and Helen R. Lane (Minneapolis: University of Minnesota Press, 1983).

13   James Clifford, *The Predicament of Culture: Twentieth-Century Ethnography, Literature, and Art* (Cambridge, MA: Harvard University Press, 1983), 193.

14   For a thorough account and brilliant analysis of this issue, see Thelma Golden's groundbreaking exhibition catalog *Black Male: Representations of Masculinity in Contemporary American Art* (New York: Whitney Museum of American Art, 1994).

15   [*Ed. note:* Tate Modern curators, wall label, 2000.]

16   Homi Bhabha, "The Other Question," in *The Location of Culture* (London: Routledge, 1994), 66–84.

17   The appreciation of the "aesthetic" sophistication of so-called primitive sculptures by modern European artists such as Picasso, Matisse, André Derain, and Maurice de Vlaminck has often been cited as one reason for the serious transformation of such sculptures from being merely fetish objects to their being recuperated as serious examples of artistic quality within museums of art.

18   The same holds true for most museums of contemporary art in Europe and the United States. I have often found it curious how exactly identical contemporary museum collections are irrespective of city. The unconscious repetition of the same artists, objects, and chronology both in museums and private collections should make curators less sanguine about the independent role of their judgment in connection with art and artists who may not fit easily in this logocentric logic of seriality.

19   [*Ed. note:* Here Enwezor references Carl Einstein, *NegerPlastik* (Leipzig: Verlag der Weissen Bücher, 1915); Paul Rivet and Georges-Henri Rivière, "La Mission ethnographique et linguistique Dakar-Djibouti," special issue, *Minotaure*, no. 2 (Paris: Alfred Skira, 1933); and Michel Leiris, *L'Afrique fantôme* (Paris: Gallimard, 1934).]

20   Jürgen Habermas, *The Philosophical Discourse of Modernity*, trans. Frederick G. Lawrence (Cambridge, UK: Polity, 1987), offers an extensive development of the discourse of modernity, modernization, and the artistic and aesthetic corollary of modernism, particularly from the point of view of surrealism. Habermas, in his thorough treatment, especially in the opening essay "Modernity's Consciousness of Time and Its Need for Self-Reassurance," pays close attention to Max Weber's contention that the concept of modernity arose out of a peculiarly "Occidental rationalism." According to Habermas, "What Weber depicted was not only the secularization of Western *culture*, but also and especially the development of modern *societies* from the viewpoint of rationalization. The new structures of society were marked by the differentiation of the two functionally intermeshing systems that had taken shape around the organizational cores of the capitalist enterprise and the bureaucratic state apparatus. . . . As that continent of basic concepts bearing Weber's Occidental rationalism sinks down, reason makes known its true identity—it becomes unmasked as the subordinating and at the same time itself subjugated subjectivity, as the will to instrumental mastery" (1, 4).

21   Carlos Basualdo, "New Geographies of Culture," statement written for a flyer accompanying a series of public seminars organized by the Jorge Luis Borges National Library, Buenos Aires, Argentina, 2002.

22   Hal Foster, *Recodings: Art, Spectacle, Cultural Politics* (Seattle: Bay, 1985), 139.

23   Foster, *Recodings*, 139.

24   Some of the most active institutions are extensions of the foreign policy of the given countries. The British Council (UK), AFAA (France), Danish Contemporary Art (Denmark), IFA (Germany), Mondriaan Foundation (the Netherlands), and Japan Foundation (Japan) are perhaps the most well-funded of these national organizations and employ the export of artists and exhibitions as an active tool of cultural diplomacy. These foundations and cultural export institutions often organize curatorial tours in their respective countries, fund artists for overseas projects, support exhibitions in highly visible international cities, and organize and tour exhibitions of art from their national collections to other parts of the world.

25   Benjamin H. D. Buchloh, "Figures of Authority, Ciphers of Regression: Notes on the Return of Representation in European Painting," in *Art after Modernism: Rethinking Representation*, ed. Brian Wallis (New York: New Museum of Contemporary Art; Boston: D. R. Godine, 1984), 123.

26   The Guggenheim Bilbao, designed by Frank Gehry; the Centre Pompidou, Paris, designed by Richard Rogers and Renzo Piano; and the Milwaukee Art Museum, by Santiago Calatrava, are examples of this conjunction whereby the architecture is understood as much as a work of art in its

own right to be enjoyed on its merits independent of function as the collections of art contained within it. The objective reality of this effect is that discreet architecture no longer serves the purpose of the museum as a destination of culture. The clearest example of this tendency is the Guggenheim Museum in Bilbao, Spain. Gehry's phoenix-like sculptural form that rises into view like some mythological creature against the backdrop of the city's postindustrial landscape emphasizes the idea that architecture is as much an object of the spectator's observation as the pieces of art scattered in the cavernous spaces of the museum's interior. No other museum, however, achieves this fusion more thoroughly and with such audacious rhetorical panache than the Jewish Museum by Daniel Libeskind in Berlin. Libeskind's architectural narrative is so forceful and complete that any visit through the museum is nothing less than an architectural guided tour, in which the experience of the displays is always mediated by the stronger narrative of the building.

27 Jürgen Habermas, *The Structural Transformation of the Public Sphere: An Inquiry into a Category of Bourgeois Society* (London: Polity, 1992).

28 Pierre Bourdieu, *The Field of Cultural Production: Essays on Art and Literature*, ed. Randal Johnson (New York: Columbia University Press, 1993), 40.

29 My idea of a field of relations recapitulates Bourdieu's own assessment of the artistic sphere as one enmeshed in a field of activities in which various agents and position takers collaborate in an ever-expansive set of relations that define, conceive, conceptualize, and reformulate norms and methods within the field of cultural production.

30 Michel Foucault, "Des travaux," in *Dits et écrits* (Paris: Gallimard, 1994), 4:367, cited in Paul Rabinow, ed., *Essential Works of Foucault, 1954–1984*, vol. 1, *Ethics: Subjectivity and Truth* (New York: New Press, 1997), xxi.

31 Samuel Huntington, *The Clash of Civilizations and the Remaking of World Order* (New York: Simon and Schuster, 1996).

32 In a speech before the US Congress, President George Bush outlined the new US doctrine of preemption and also laid the policy grounds for the stark distinction between states that belong to the moral universe of the civilized (*sic*) world and those others, especially Iran, Iraq, and North Korea, who exist in the pool of darkness marred by evil intentions against the peaceful, civilized world. See "State of the Union Address," January 2002, https://georgewbush-whitehouse.archives.gov/news/releases/2002/01/20020129–11.html.

33 This is in reference to Ronald Reagan's congressional address that gave us this classic characterization of the Soviet Union, toward the end of the Cold War.

34 Conservative critics such as Hilton Kramer, Allan Bloom, and others made fodder of any cultural form or concept seen to want to relativize the obvious

categorical and empirical truth of the great Western tradition with a cultural insight that deviates from the superiority of the Western canon. Postmodernism, and latterly postcolonial theory, became the easy route to show that the emperor of multiculturalism has no clothes and must be exposed as such with the most strident ideological attacks. Political subjectivity or social awareness of the dimension of multiplicity in any creative work was not only seen as fraudulent but also anti-Western. The culture wars destroyed any vestige of dissent within the intellectual field and exposed the weaknesses of the liberal academy. Part of the terrible legacy of this civilizational discourse is a return to consensual opposition between the left and the right, each pitched in its own historical bivouacs. Today, to speak a measure of truth about art that contradicts the retreat back into the rampant academicism is indeed a dangerous occupational hazard.

35 See my essay "The Black Box," in *Documenta11 Platform 5 (Exhibition)* (Ostfildern-Ruit: Hatje Cantz, 2002), 42–55.

Mega-exhibitions and the Antinomies   13
of a Transnational Global Form

First published in German as "Grossausstellungen und die Antinomien einer transnationalen globalen Form," in *Berliner Thyssen–Vorlesungen zur Ikonologie der Gegenwart*, vol. 1, ed. Gottfried Boehm and Horst Bredekamp (Munich: William Fink, 2002), 94–119, the essay as reproduced here was slightly revised and extended for publication in English in *Manifesta Journal*, no. 2 (Winter 2003–Spring 2004): 6–31. Illustrations are those chosen for the latter publication. In both editions, Enwezor thanked Horst Bredekamp, Gottfried Boehm, Sarat Maharaj, and Andreas Huyssen for their input.

World exhibitions glorify the exchange value of the commodity. They create a framework in which its use value recedes into the background. They open a phantasmagoria which a person enters in order to be distracted. The entertainment industry makes this easier by elevating the person to the level of the commodity.

Walter Benjamin, *The Arcades Project* (1999)

Introduction

IN RECENT YEARS, a new figure of discourse, intended to analyze the impact of global capitalism and media technologies on contemporary culture, has put forward the notion that the conditions of globalization produce new maps, orientations, cultural economies, institutional networks, identities, and social formations, the scale of which not only demarcates the distance between here and there, West and non-West, but also, at a deeper level of penetration, embodies a new vision of global totality and a concept of modernity that dissolves the old paradigms of the nation-state and the ideology of the "center," which now give way to a dispersed regime of rules based on networks, circuits, flows, and interconnections. These rhizomatic movements are said to follow the logic of horizontality, whose disciplinary, spatial, and temporal orders enable the mobility of knowledge, information, culture, capital, and exchange, and are no longer based on domination and control. In the short term, globalization was part of the maturation of a certain kind of liberal ideal, which, because it joined democratic regimes of governance with free-market capitalism, was prematurely proclaimed "the end of history." Underwriting this paradoxical culmination of a modern totalization embodied by the world system—and forestalling any serious doubt about the equity of globalization—was one of the longest sustained periods of economic growth in our history, along with phenomenal technological accomplishments in cybernetics, communication, and genetic encoding, that is to say, in virtually every facet of the scientific system. All this resulted in a cosmopolitanization of global society and identity, which in turn has ensured outstanding growth in consumer culture and entertainment.

Not so long ago, it seemed that everything global was celebrated, though there have always been opposing voices as well. Nonetheless, globalization was supposed to represent the final and full realization of an idea that has been with us ever since the European conquest of the New World, the circumnavigation of the globe, the expansion of trade to previously closed societies, and the founding of colonies based on the then-hyperpower of coercion and pacification—namely, the idea of a truly unified modern world system in which all systems of modern rationalization can at last be properly fused together. For theorists of the benefits of globalization, such phenomena as dispersed regimes of global governance and the multilateralism that emerged after World War II with the creation of the United Nations, the Bretton Woods institutions, treaties on the protection of minorities, the International Court of Justice, etc., tended to represent checks on the power of the state and forces of domination and control (whether by empires or multinationals), as well as the possibility for the developing world to become a partner in the broader critical conversation about the equitable distribution of the global common good. Open borders of exchange were not only thought to protect cultures but were also seen as enabling backward cultures to innovate, to become modern. This was to be achieved through transparency and multilateral negotiations, whether in scientific, biotechnological, economic, political, juridical, or cultural matters. As one might expect, skeptics of globalization tended to see this picture through a completely different set of lenses. To them, globalization was exploitative and disadvantageous to developing economies; it disproportionately concentrated influence in the hands of a very small number of states, which exerted power and control over vast economic, natural, and human resources. Moreover, the skeptics believed that it did damage to fragile ecosystems and was riddled with bad examples of governance, inequality, etc.

How wistfully we now look back on those halcyon days, especially in light of the now-emerging doctrine of American hyperpower. At least it was possible in the past to engage in a productive debate (now perceived as mere illusion) on the merits and demerits of globalization—and such debate may well continue in isolated pockets. But today we face a new kind of menace, namely, the return of institutional power as the authorizing force of contemporary narratives of history, art, culture, and ideas. To say there has been a rupture in the belief that globalization can invest positive content into new paradigm formations in art, culture, and ideas is to be an optimist of a certain mien.

Biennial Fever: Contemporary Art and Globalization

Perhaps it is premature to write the obituary of the global ideal, which throughout the 1990s promised us greater connectivity and enabled a certain proximity between spaces of culture, sites of artistic production, and contexts around shared interests in the new artistic formations taking place in different regions around the world. The vehicle for this critical pursuit was based, first, on a reconceptualization of a nineteenth-century model for displaying cultural heterogeneity and spectacle that was epitomized, during the great period of the Industrial Revolution, by the world exhibition. Second, there was an expansion and extension of the world exhibition model through its proliferation. Today the world exhibition model—for better or for worse—has been readapted in the form of the mega-exhibition, of which biennials are a prime example. What follows is an assessment of the rise of the mega-exhibition model over the past two decades, and a generalized review of how the exhibition systems it gave rise to have financed a way of thinking about contemporary art and globalization at large.

The predominant discourse surrounding globalization—particularly in relation to modern and contemporary art as it is embedded in museums, in large-scale international exhibitions, in the culture industry, etc.—has

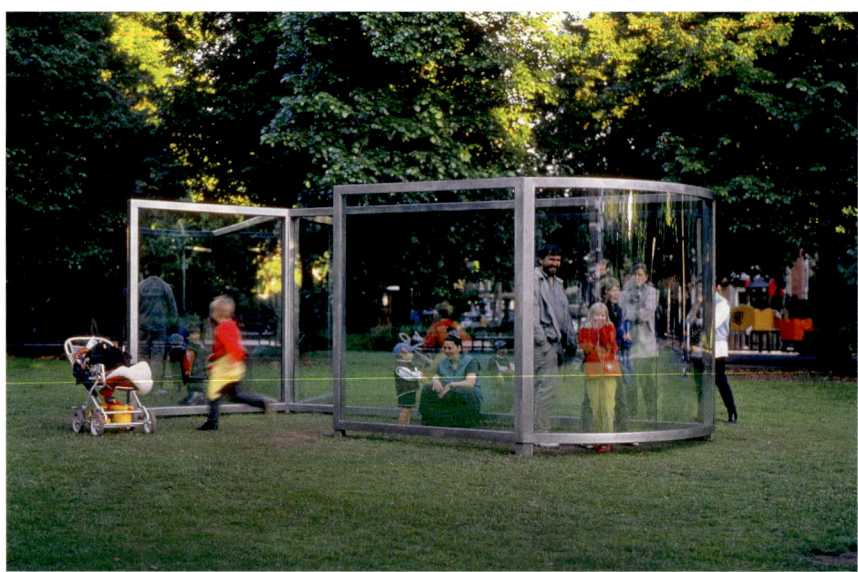

13.1 Dan Graham, *Fun House for Münster*, 1997.
Skulptur Projekte Münster 1997. Pavilion, two-
way mirrored glass, steel, 250 × 500 × 200 cm.
Courtesy of Dan Graham Estate and Marian
Goodman Gallery. © Dan Graham Estate.

increasingly articulated the notion that the conditions of cultural and artistic practice today, as well as the complexity of the institutional discourses
that mediate their circulation and insertion into broader global networks,
face the risk of becoming homogenized and subject to ideological control.[1]
On the other hand, there is the view that sees the globalization of contemporary art as the necessary development of late modernity toward a
sphere of greater inclusion of artistic practices that converge with and extend the historical discourse of modernism. At the nexus of this convergence
and extension is the negotiation of the relationship between the classical
aesthetic language of European high modernism and those other modernisms that offer differential interpretations of what is modern in modern art.

Yet what this discourse has so far not made clear is: To what end? It
is not enough simply to integrate the view of other modernisms into highly
selective Western museological training programs, based as they often are
on expediency rather than on a conviction of real intellectual and historical purpose. It is here that globalization raises further issues. For even in

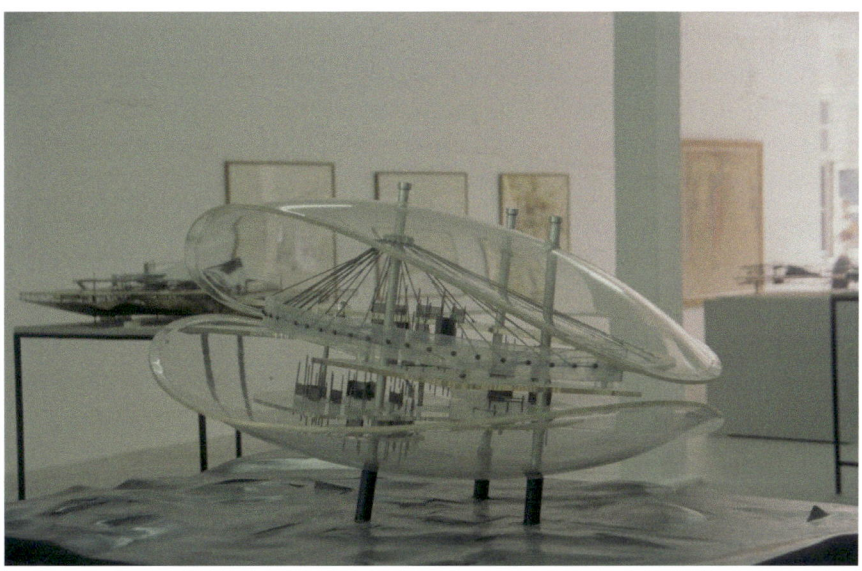

13.2 Constant Nieuwenhuys, *New Babylon: Space Eater, Large Yellow Sector, Drawing, Mobile Ladder Labyrinth,* 1959–74. Exhibition view, Documenta11, Kassel, 2002. © documenta archiv/Ryszard Kasiewicz photographer.

historically based studies, Western modernism still remains uncomfortable with the modernisms of the South. In the past, this discomfort has been addressed by an insistence that modernism is specific—specific, that is, to the European experience—which leads one to ask whether the exuberant celebration of the globalization of art, museums, exhibitions, academies, universities, and their attendant industries does not, in fact, mask something more troubling. What I mean is a return to the cynical absorption and integration of a range of counterhegemonic contemporary practices and cultures—such as would highlight crucial factors of difference, experimental cultures, and recalcitrant notions of art—into an already well-honed system of differentiation, domestication, and homogenization. This, after all, is something most modernist ventures in other areas have tried to do in regard to non-Western societies. If we are to have any meaningful debate about the nature of the venture surrounding globalization and art, we would do well to remind ourselves that the historical transformation currently underway is not simply a fanciful notion that impedes serious thinking about the very nature of art. Rather, this transformation has the potential to dehistoricize, delegitimize, and dismantle the norms of control and domination that underpin many Western modernist claims to uniqueness, and it is already encountering serious resistance. Today antiglobalization has been derisively—often through ideological intentions—constructed as antimodern, nationalist, or anti-Western, or as the rage of an archaic subalternity unable to confront its failures. Conversely, any embrace of the potential of globalization as a way to broaden the space of international participation across a range of cultural, social, and political spheres has been decried as a neoliberal capitalist attempt to assimilate non-Western spaces and subjectivities into the West. Even where the spaces of inclusion are mutually and dialectically embraced across the borders of ethnic, racial, cultural, gender, and sexual difference, the pull and pressure to hold on to the coordinates and demands of certain identifications (be they local, exclusionary, nationalist, fundamentalist, or orthodox) remain strong. To be sure, there is no easy resolution to these oppositions. Still, it is possible to look at the issues, as I shall try to do, from the perspective of a number of structural and philosophical differentiations that will help us understand the current discourse of modernity, contemporary art, and globalization. At least within the sphere of culture, the given doxa of artistic practice and the heterodoxy of forms of globalization (for example, in such areas as film, world music, the strong emergence of national literary traditions, etc.) have continuously called our attention to the broader means through which we can apprehend and appreciate the formidable forms of contemporary art currently being produced across many regions. One example is in the area of film, where the Iranian and Chinese cinemas are currently in full flower.

There are two ways to study the present situation. On the one hand, as I have said, there is a vigorous expansion taking place in regard to museum and exhibition programs, as well as academic curricula, aimed at extending the standard art historical view of modernism and contemporary art and integrating artistic contexts previously considered to be marginal to the intellectual economy of Western modernism. On the other hand, there remains staunch resistance to such a critical rapprochement between Western modernity and the modernities that exist in the so-called developing world of the non-West. Such resistance has made its claims by resorting to what amounts to a theology of modernism propagated from the particular view of the Western avant-garde, but without situating that avant-garde within the larger complex political, cultural, and economic determinations of colonialism and imperialism, which made possible the great expansion of the

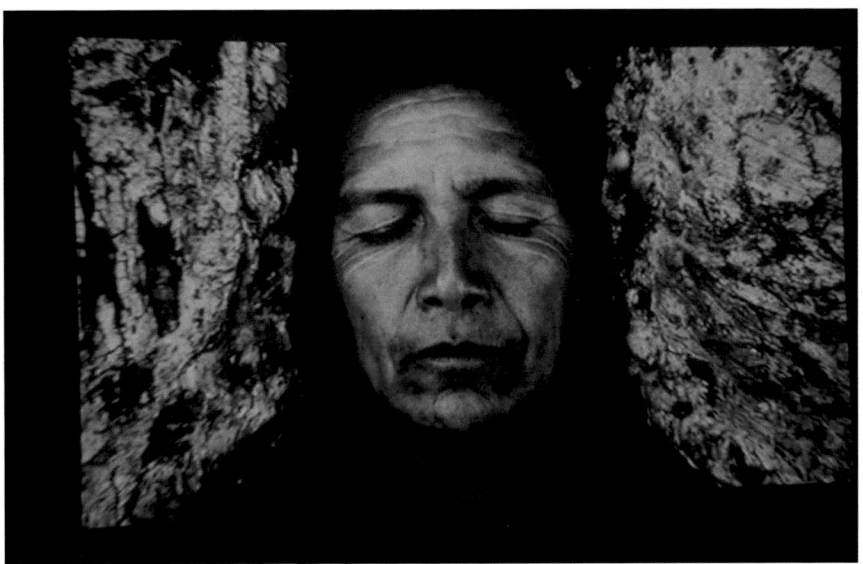

13.3 Shirin Neshat, still from *Tooba*, 2002.
35mm film transferred to DVD, color, sound,
film art. Shown at Documenta11, Kassel, 2002.
© Shirin Neshat.

European economies in the first place. Increasingly, a number of influential historians and journals, through recourse to such notions as medium specificity, postmediumness, artistic autonomy, institutional critique, artistic particularity, and so on, have encouraged this occidentalist reiteration of modernity and art with very little said about the historical conditions around which art was produced and practiced throughout the entire modern period.

Nevertheless (and without making any easy concession as to the value of the global), the discussion is pointless unless we acknowledge that much of what is presented as the fact of globalization—as the historical rupture par excellence—fails to take account of the historical conditions under which the labor of art and culture is manifested outside the developed economies of advanced capitalism. But the presumption that globalization, in alliance with market liberalism and politics, takes us further down the road in our long arduous march toward modernity is, today, kept in check by a number of oppositional activities and critical negotiations that have recently arisen to force new debates about the disciplinary and institutional efficacy of globalization. I shall mention briefly two areas around which these debates are

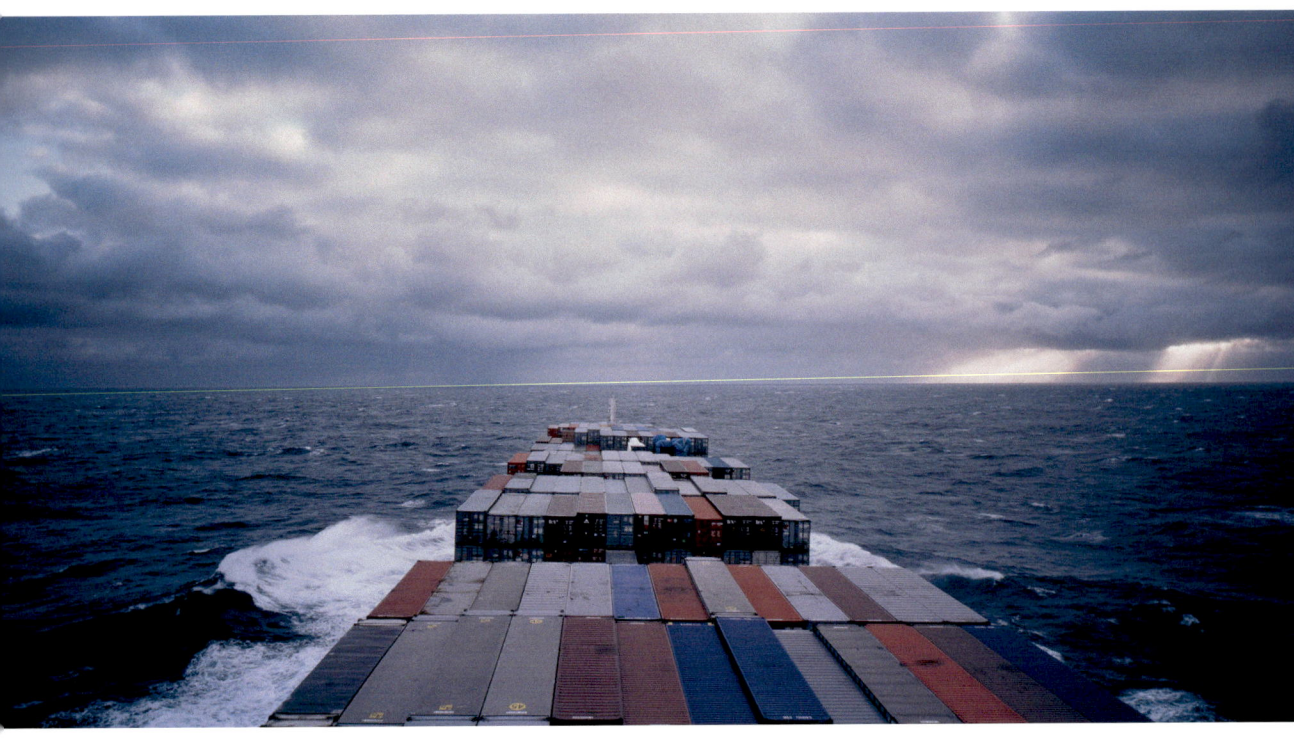

13.4 Allan Sekula, *Panorama. Mid-Atlantic*,
from *Fish Story*, 1989–95. Photographic series with text, shown at Documenta11,
Kassel, 2002. Framed cibachrome print,
62.8×99.6×4.5 cm. Courtesy of Allan Sekula
Studio, Los Angeles.

being waged: one is the domain of cultural and social production of identity;
the other, the political and economic arena of democratic rights, national
sovereignty, and economic self-determination.

For metropolitan audiences, the most visible struggles around globalization often take place in the mediated activities of a loose network of social
movements, labor and environmental organizations, and nongovernmental
organizations (what I shall call the Porto Alegre contingent), and through
antiglobalization scuffles such as those recently witnessed in Genoa, Seattle,
Prague, and Montreal.[2] But there are other views of globalization, ones that
are "Third-Worldist" in their perspective and only nominally antiglobal.[3]
These are more complex and differentiated, in that they are much more
deeply embedded in a historically determined analysis of global regimes and

concern themselves primarily with questions of justice and social, political, and economic agency—none of which, at face value, contradict the positive theories of globalization. This second phalanx of the struggle attacks globalization—in its present form—over its attempt to establish hegemonic control over vast areas and systems of production and knowledge (whereby those whom Michel de Certeau calls "everyday users" are systemically disadvantaged and deprived of the means to assert their agency).[4]

In these debates, therefore, only a cursory examination is needed to see that there is a range of antinomies inscribed within the defining features of globalization, with all its apotropaic promises. Some of these antinomies are historical, based on a disequilibrium of power and material resources, while others are built around careful cultural reflexes that manifest themselves in the form of resistance to the hegemonic power of supranational global forums controlled by the forces of industrial and technological capitalism. One should also note the degree to which resistance from within the institutions of the West to other forms of knowledge inscribes another level of antinomy. Similarly, the imagined community of global culture—as seen from the point of view of new transnational artistic communities, various kinds of global exhibition enterprises, and museums, and telegraphed through networks of global exchange and such reception systems as the media—is no less fraught with these antinomies, saturated as they are with forms of institutional control over vast resources, which constantly obviate the possibility of serious exchange.[5]

But must contemporary culture and art—including both the discursive and the market-oriented sites in which they are produced, reproduced, marketed or exhibited, and received—be subjected to, and compelled to enunciate, the radical shift in paradigm that is increasingly apparent in today's complex systemic delocalizations of capital, labor flows, markets, technologies of communication and mediation (between the net and the self), which globalization is said to have engendered?[6] How do institutions of art integrate the putatively slower critical cultural shifts that arrive in the wake of these transnational, denationalized, and global transformations? Where does the final arbitration about the status of the work of art occur today? What are the criteria for recognizing, within the global mainstream, artists who produce outside the rich circuit of advanced institutions, media, and economic visibility? As for the preceding modernist period, which artists are to be included in the broader discussions of modernism that have yet to be properly developed among museums? The record of museums in both the United States and Europe is not particularly encouraging, especially in view of the burgeoning and ever-diversifying range of options that exist in quite prolix forms—curatorial procedures; museums and exhibition spaces; media, catalog historiography, academic journals, and art magazines; commercial galleries, auction houses, private collections, and other economies of art.

These questions mark a tension in the formation of the global public sphere that mega-exhibitions seem to exemplify. Furthermore, they reveal a space of instability as the contemporary art arena expands, tracing, as it mutates, the complex mechanisms of control and subordination that exist in the domains of various institutional forums of modern art. In the end, if the fact of globalization as often pronounced is the unhinging of the pro-scriptions of institutional modernism by mobilizing new artistic thoughts, histories, practices, and conditions of production from beyond the borders of the West, then we see levered into relief a number of issues that shadow and foreshadow the anxieties of the present artistic context within which there performs a range of actors—curators, exhibitions, museums, collectors, the media, and the market. An awareness of the three-dimensionality of the space of artistic modernity as multifaceted, however imperfectly understood or acknowledged by the dominant teleologies of museums or exhibitions, lies at the heart of Stuart Hall's observation that, because

> contemporary art practices locate themselves within an awareness of the slow decentering of the West, we see the constitution of lateral relations in which the West is an absolutely pivotal, powerful, hege-monic force, but is no longer the only force within which creative energies, cultural flows, and new ideas can be concerted. The world is moving outward and can no longer be structured in terms of the center/periphery relation. It has to be defined in terms of a set of in-tersecting centers, which are both different from and related to one another. . . . Any museum which thinks it can incorporate or grasp the best texts and productions of modern artistic practice, believing the world is still organized on a center/periphery model, simply does not understand the contradictory tensions that are in play.[7]

The problem, though, is that, rather than abolishing the center/periphery opposition, globalization has sharpened and made visible its fault lines. It is my intention to explore some of the underlying problems that arise at the juncture where global capitalism and culture intersect. Here I am primarily concerned with analyzing the nature of the museum and mega-exhibitions today. To do this, I will first focus on three broad areas—the market,

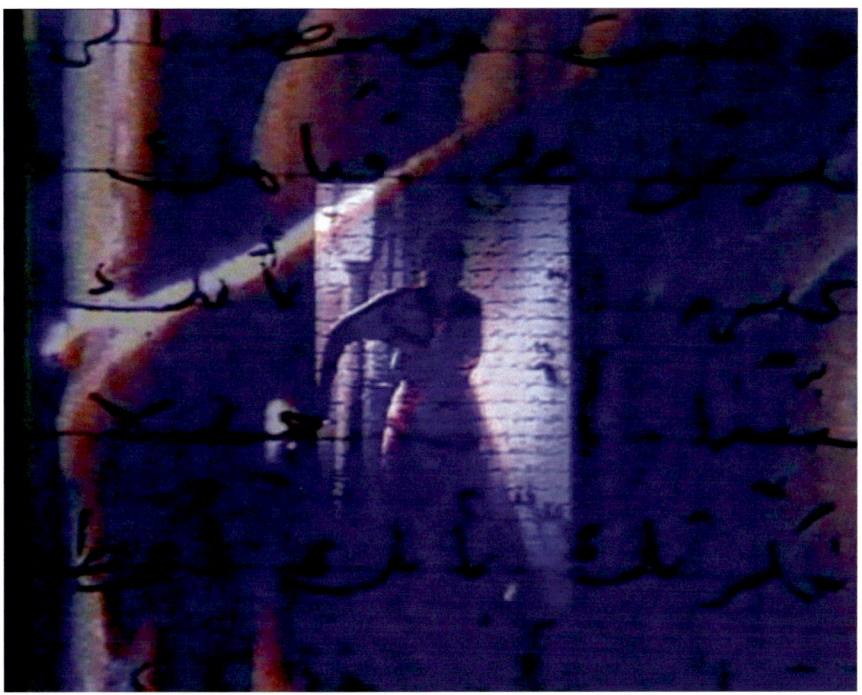

13.5 Mona Hatoum, still from *Measures of Distance*, 1988. Video transferred to DVD, color, sound, 15 min. Shown at Documenta11, Kassel, 2002. © Mona Hatoum. Courtesy of Video Bank, School of the Art Institute of Chicago.

institutions, and the media—in order to show their impact on a range of subsystems within the contemporary artistic framework, for instance, exhibition models, curatorship, artistic practice, and epistemes of contemporary art. This analysis will then fold back to articulate how each of these systems and subsystems exists in the present social, cultural, and political climate within which contemporary art functions. Finally, the remaining part of this essay will be situated within a theoretical reflection on modernity.

Mega-exhibitions and Museums as Transnational Global Forms

Let me begin with a general overview of large-scale international exhibitions of contemporary art and the recent discourses that analyze their present proliferation. In the summer of 1997, I participated in a three-day conference organized by the Rockefeller Foundation and Arts International (both institutions are headquartered in New York). The conference, which was devoted to the rise and proliferation of large-scale international exhibitions such as are embodied in the phenomenon of biennials and other art festivals, was convened with the tacit hope of understanding the critical shifts being initiated internationally by such large-scale exhibition structures and of gauging their global dimension and impact. The gathering took place in a beautiful villa situated on top of a cliff that overlooks the small northern Italian town of Bellagio on Lake Como, with the Italian Alps hovering on the horizon—an edifying place of seclusion for thinking and working through the travails of contemporary art and the alarmingly mutating map (as some might protest) of the international art economy. The very notion of mutation strikes me as highly suggestive of the kind of disorder that overwhelms systems of knowledge that have been the bedrock of Western imperialism when they are confronted by the critical values of other forms of knowledge previously subordinated to imperial authority. I would prefer, however, not to speak of either mutation or disorder, but rather of the transnationalization, translocalization, and denationalization of the international contemporary art world, insofar as biennials and other such exhibitions are concerned. By 1997 their novelty had reached a peak, to the extent that every conceivable cultural context was host to some form or variety of these exhibitions. This was most clearly seen in the diversity of the speakers at the conference: they came from São Paulo, Venice, Istanbul, Dakar, Perth, Pittsburgh, Costa Rica, Havana, Austin, Sydney, Bangkok, Johannesburg, and many other places.

Throughout the conference questions were raised about the pressures of this astronomical growth in exhibitions and the new demands they bring to bear on artists and local cultural and artistic scenes as they become more and more unhinged from the stable ground of local sites (the nation-state) and transformed into increasingly transnational endeavors. In short, what are the contexts of power through which artists who are eager to enter the global scene are being processed? Here I should like to note that such contexts are not only artistic, but political, social, and economic as well; for it is in the context of the global production of artistic identity that we witness a number of strategies employed by artists hoping to leap out of underfunded contexts and into the resource-rich pastures of the global space. In other words, biennials are important proving grounds that attract both institutional and curatorial attention. One consequence of adjustment in artistic strategy by artists in biennials concerns the scale of their work—what I would call the *biennial scale*—often resulting in large, spatially distorted installations, Cinemascope projections, and mural-size paintings and photographs. A curator colleague has characterized such huge works as the artistic version of genetically modified organisms. But for many artists, the anxiety of anonymity and failure in the face of the stiff competition to be included in such exhibitions has meant that, in order for their work to be visible and noticed, the spatial dimensions of their objects and images must be dramatically expanded so as to be commensurate with the global ambitions of the exhibitions themselves. In other words, mega-exhibitions require mega-objects.

Blind to the complex historical and psychological issues at stake, most critics of biennials have vociferously declared such expansions to be the bane of serious art. I would insist, however, that the ever-increasing itinerant phalanx of artistic strategies and curatorial concepts that respond directly to mega-exhibitions is far from naive. On the contrary, they are really quite shrewd, for they represent the realization that the space of the global is a Darwinian universe. The depiction of biennials as an agon of epic struggle may be slightly overstating it. But there is something of this in the destiny toward which all artists strive who join in the agonistic struggle for visibility in the artistic field. Pierre Bourdieu explains it well: "The literary or artistic field is a *field of forces*, but it is also a *field of struggles* tending to transform or conserve this field of forces. The network of objective relations between positions subtends and orients the strategies which the occupants of different positions implement in their struggles to defend or improve their positions (i.e., their position-takings), strategies which depend for their force and form on the position each agent occupies in the power relations (*rapports de force*)."[8]

To reflect seriously on the problematic of the mega-exhibition, then, forms of critical analysis are required that can properly understand the significance of biennials and the attempts they have made to recode the complex dialectics between globalization and the long process of modernization vis-à-vis the market-based economies toward which much of the developing world has set its course ever since the early days of decolonization. Furthermore, such an analysis would seek to comprehend the resulting impact on institutional practices, both Western and non-Western, as contemporary art has expanded into the global scene. In my own close observation of biennials, the circumstances within which they are made provide a remarkable filter for witnessing globalization at work, especially in comparing the funding bases of the haves and have-nots and the access of artists who are well funded by their home countries versus those without funding.

This last point became an important issue that dominated the deliberations of the conference. It extended to the relationships between biennials and globalization and multiculturalism, multiethnic metropolitan identities, local cultures with few cosmopolitan attachments (except in terms of the relations of power and production in the circulatory logic of capital), and, finally, the spatial and temporal disjunctures that lie at the heart of modernity, especially as expressed through various filters of colonial and postcolonial discourse. There were diverse opinions and approaches to curating contemporary art, including those focused on heritage and the ethics of representing the art of very fragile cultures, such as the First Nations peoples of the United States; those specifically concerned with bridging territorial, regional, and cultural worlds, such as the Asia Pacific Triennial in Queensland, Australia; institutions whose mandates concern the representation of the art of minorities in the United States (the Asia Society and Studio Museum); and those representing seemingly independent organizations that organize biennials (using the term in its most generic sense), such as Istanbul, Venice, Johannesburg (for which I was the artistic director), Sydney, Carnegie International, Dakar, Havana, and São Paulo.

Two points emerged in this array of institutions defending, promoting, or historicizing contemporary art. The first is that almost without exception all the organizations were founded more from ideological considerations than artistic ones: local political, social, and economic issues to a large extent determined what form an organization would take. Even with museums, ideology came first, before any mention of art, even if, ultimately, it was art that became the main object in question. But museums, too, convey not only culture, but also civic pride and a sense of belonging to the great tradition of civilized cultures. The second point was that almost all the organizations (with the exception, however, of the Venice Biennale and the Carnegie International) imagined themselves to be furthering an alternative view of what internationalism looks like, and each believed it possessed the historical outlook to bring this about. Of this camp, Istanbul had the most marketable image, billing itself as the bridge between East and West and between Europe and Asia. In the main, the imperative that drove the idealism to build museums and to invent and host biennials was a connection to cosmopolitanism and, to the degree that it made sense, globalism. As such, cosmopolitanism and globalism both furnish positive content in the image-making strategies of cities that believe in the capacity of art to bring economic benefit, cultural capital, civic pride, social cohesion, and global visibility. Consider, for example, the phenomenal success of the Guggenheim

Museum in Bilbao, which opened in 1997, the same year as the conference. In Bilbao, art, architecture, and tourism have been carefully fused and displayed in resplendent, shimmering titanium reflectors as a beacon on a hill for all cities looking to globalize. The success of the Guggenheim Bilbao has led to attempts to replicate its iconicity as a monument to cultural capitalization.

What I have been enumerating so far are the realities, beliefs, and hopes of those who see mega-exhibition spectacles and museums as both transnational mediating systems and forms of civic politics and subjectivity. The conference provided a rare opportunity to discuss the many areas around which contemporary art, exhibitions, museums, and art academies are today being defined. It also afforded a perspective for seeing contemporary art fully captured within a transitional and transnational nexus. Suffice it to say, there were no conclusions drawn or decisions reached at the conference, but there was general agreement about the enormous and growing cost of staging such large-scale exhibitions and building more museums. We also agreed about the need for better cooperation between the dominant organizing institutions, a kind of G7 for biennials, so as not to further dilute the "cachet" of this incredibly ambiguous global brand. We also recognized how important it was to meet again and vowed to do so. And indeed, we have met again and again on the global circuit, as the wild spiral of biennials and other mega-exhibitions has continued to expand. I will not bother to count how many such exhibitions currently exist, but I am sure they run into the hundreds.

Spectacle Culture: Biennials, History, and Modernity

In their expansionist mode, as well as in their insatiable propensity to absorb even the most arcane of artistic grammars and scales of production, biennials not only exemplify important scenes of cultural translation and transnational encounters between artists, art markets, institutions, and various professionals, but have also left a negative impression as agoras of spectacle, and this has come to define the mega-exhibition's relationship to art. While this tendency toward spectacularization and dispersion into the logic of what [Theodor] Adorno and [Max] Horkheimer defined as the culture industry may be true, it nonetheless requires further explication to make obvious the fact that not all biennials function according to the logic of spectacle. Even should they desire this, limitations in economic and institutional circumstances militate against them becoming purveyors of spectacle. In truth, most biennials, particularly those working in and addressing specific artistic contexts, often function as low-budget projects. Within this sort of framework, the works are usually of modest scale, portable, and intimate, while the site-specific works and exhibitions appear rather improvisatory and often compensatory. But to make such distinctions still does not give us a full picture of the reasons behind the exponential growth in large-scale international exhibitions, whose chief characteristic is the heterogeneity of the strategies and objects they assemble.

I would like to examine, briefly, some of the reasons why a new global culture of biennials has emerged at this historic juncture. I will largely bypass discussions that view the biennial as descending from a genus known as the *world exhibition*. Nor will I evoke what is believed to be its earlier ancestor, namely, the so-called *Wunderkammer* collection.[9] My interest is its present historical context: Why biennials?

History and Trauma

If we exclude the Venice Biennale and the Carnegie International in Pittsburgh, most, if not all, large-scale cyclical exhibitions that currently exist within the international framework are largely post–World War II creations. Of these, I am interested in the degree to which the desire to establish such exhibition forums is informed by a response to traumatic historical events and ruptures occasioned by the dissolution of an old order. Documenta and, more recently, South Korea's Gwangju Biennale and the Johannesburg Biennale exemplify such institutions. Their founding closely mirrors political and social transitions in the countries where these exhibitions are situated. In fact, such transitions are central to the identity of each of these exhibitions and were the chief impetus behind their formation. So, in a sense, one can say these exhibitions are commemorative, much in the same way that the building of the Crystal Palace for the Great Exhibition of 1851 in London was meant to commemorate both the rule of Queen Victoria and the international power of Britain during the period of the Industrial Revolution. The Carnegie International in Pittsburgh, even given its "international" gloss, is nothing but a monument to the progressive and modern outlook of Andrew Carnegie. But both the Crystal Palace and the Carnegie International are constituted around a different sort of ideology, namely, the ideology of progress and power.

Trauma, however, peers into something darker and more ambivalent, perhaps even melancholic. In this context, then, the commemorative event assumes symbols of celebration from an entirely different perspective: as a lesson in history and the limits of power. In the case of Documenta, the critical signpost is Germany's post–World War II attempt to rebuild the foundations of its destroyed civil society, as well as the artistic and intellectual frameworks depopulated by the Nazi pogroms that led to the exile and death of many important thinkers and leaders of the avant-garde. Gwangju and Johannesburg were both founded during critical moments in the political and social transitions of South Korea and South Africa, respectively. For South Korea, it was the return to democracy after years of repressive military dictatorship, while for South Africa, the end of apartheid served as the impetus for signifying to the rest of the world that the work of the imagination is a fundamental part of a society in transition, as it moves toward democracy and develops new concepts of global citizenship.

Modernity and Modernization

Recently, while waiting my turn at a barbershop in Brooklyn, New York, I happened to cast a glance at a publicity bill pinned on the salon wall with the heading "Black Inventors." On the chart were listed every conceivable invention, from the toothpick and ironing board to airplane engines, computer hardware and software, and stabilizing instruments for the space shuttle. But the entries that caught my attention were the first four on the list, which read as follows: culture = African; alphabet = African (Egypt); writing = African (Egypt); paper = African. Having lived in the United States for twenty years, I was fairly familiar with the ways in which many African Americans assert their sense of cultural worth in response to Western cultural marginalization. From the days of slavery and through the height of the civil rights movement and the Black Power era, part of the construction of African American cultural worth has involved a battle waged on the ground of the fanciful ideology of origin. Given the basic historical schism between the United States and its black citizens, I was not surprised by the poster, though I was still struck by the deft deployment of its entries, which sought to underline the precondition of social visibility for any knowledge-based society, namely, that one must be not only a consumer of culture, but also a producer and inventor of the norms of modern society. According to the poster's well-told tale, civilization has its roots in a black cultural past, which continues today. And if Africa—having invented culture, the alphabet, writing, and paper—is the primal scene of civilization, then it must also be the basis for the ontological construction of modernity as such, through a range of inventions made possible by culture, the alphabet, writing, and paper. As bombastic as this list may seem, its presumptions are almost identical

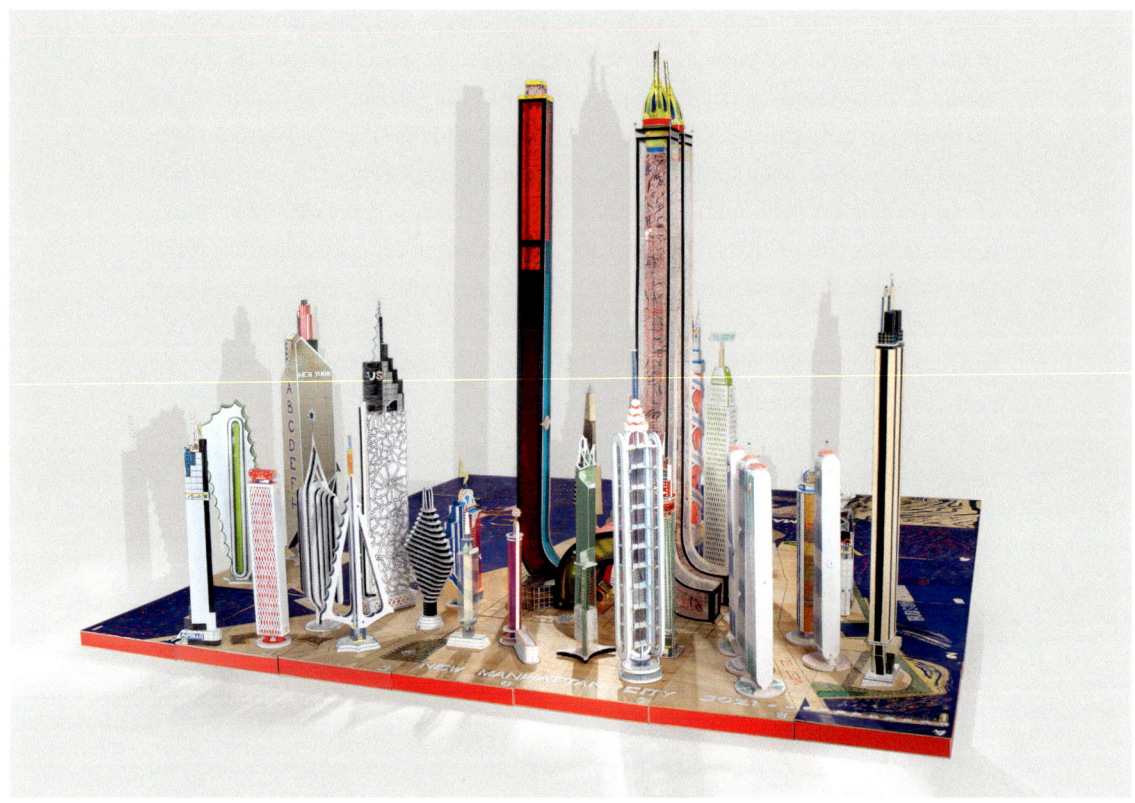

13.6 Bodys Isek Kingelez, *New Manhattan (Manhattan City 3021)*, 2002. Plywood, paper, cardboard, foam board, and mixed materials, 205×300 × 280 cm. Shown at Documenta11, Kassel. ©Bodys Isek Kingelez. Photo ©Maurice Aeschimann. Courtesy of Jean Pigozzi African Art Collection, Geneva.

to the way in which Western subjectivity conceives its own cultural self-understanding. Equally, Western epistemological thought constitutes the dimension of a knowledge-based society as essentially springing from the European imagination. Here, we can say, is an obvious example of one antinomy of global culture, the struggle over cultural legitimation.

It is striking, then, to see, in this ideological struggle to establish the prehistory and history of the modern world, how the text of historical legitimation has been written out of the bitter imposition of indenture, marginalization, and the opposition to it through counterhegemonic strategies. I would, therefore, like to offer the view that one consequence of Western imperialism and colonialism is the degree to which cultures and societies that are seen as marginal to Western culture have written, out of the antagonism of European imperial conquest and hegemony, a complex narrative of other human lifeworlds. Having started with the Brooklyn barbershop, let us stay in the contemporary and cosmopolitan Western realm and look at how this antagonism appears today from the perspective of someone like Jürgen Habermas. In the second volume of his *Theory of Communicative Action*, Habermas offers a most perspicacious view on the question of the institutionally determined sense of culture:

> In advanced Western societies conflicts have developed in the last ten to twenty years that deviate in various respects from the social-welfare-state pattern of institutionalized conflict over distribution. They do not flare up in areas of material reproduction; . . . they are not allayed by compensations that conform to the system. Rather, these new conflicts arise in the areas of cultural production, of social integration, and of socialization; they are carried out in sub-institutional, or at least extraparliamentary, forms of protest; and the deficits that underlie them reflect a reification of communicatively structured domains of action, which cannot be gotten at via the media of money and power. It is not primarily a question of compensations that the social-welfare state can provide, but of protecting and restoring endangered ways of life or of establishing reformed ways of life. In short, the new conflicts do not flare up around problems of distribution but around questions concerning *the grammar of forms of life*.[10]

Through Habermas, then, we may approach the second antinomy as being predicated on cultural plurality, difference, and "questions concerning the grammar of forms of life." We can say that within the broader discourse of regimes of representation, decolonization complicates the classical texts of international and global curatorial work, the art historical work bound to the institutional domains of the museum and the academy and the conception of the ideal public. Decolonization reorients and transforms the priority placed on productive and representational values, as well as the multifarious objects, texts, and images of Western artistic modernity. With decolonization and the emergence of postcolonial states, as well as the dispersion of many postcolonial subjects to far-flung places, a new figure of the modern subject in the global metropolitan circuit became much more visible, challenging, by its mere presence, such enlightenment concepts as *liberté*, *egalité*, and *fraternité*.

For the postcolonial state, modernization and development not only of the superstructure of the state but also of the substructure of culture came to be seen as the best means of escaping peripheralization. Modernity as such, and the desire to modernize, that is, to leave backwardness behind, became a tacit agreement to re-Westernize, to be reintegrated into a neocolonial scheme in the name of progress, institutional development, and access to technology. In light of these two movements, toward modernity and modernization, the significance of certain forms of mega-exhibitions and museums becomes clear. The São Paulo Biennial, founded in 1952, certainly offers one key example, while the Havana Biennial presents a kind of counterreformation logic to the mega-exhibition model. While São Paulo insistently looks toward the example of European modernism, Havana looks toward the revolutionary ideals of state Marxism to address the exclusion of the Third World and, as such, was conceived as a critical third space amid the "prejudices" and "decadence" of Western neoliberalism and modernity. The São Paulo Biennial, which was founded by a member of an Italian immigrant family and modeled after the Venice Biennale, was designed to mediate, for a modernizing Brazil, an idea of progress through the iconography and innovations of the Western artistic avant-gardes, to bring to Brazil historical works of European art so as to reveal Brazil's continuity and contiguity with European culture. This conceit of cultural continuity and contiguity is interesting, insofar as the founder of the biennial wished to present Brazil in the company of advanced visual cultures and thus separate it from other Latin American countries. Havana, on the other hand, was founded in 1984, six years before the collapse of the Soviet Union brought to an end its intricate economic, ideological, and political alliance with the world's other superpower, and against the backdrop of extensive emigration by many Cubans impoverished by the US embargo. Although the Havana Biennial defined itself as an alternative to Western and American power, what was more important was its emotional identification with artists working throughout the so-called Third World. Standing in stark contrast to one another, these two Latin American biennials clearly demonstrate that not all mega-exhibitions follow the same model.

They do, however, offer us a lesson in understanding the function of the mega-exhibition and museum complex, especially in the way they operationalized the discourse of modernity and modernization in relation to use and exchange value and to cultural and political ideology. Even mega-exhibitions in the West are not excluded from instrumentalizing the discourse of modernity and modernization. Though recent examples offer a view into an intricate form of cultural micromanagement, the emergence of global culture in peripheral locations in Europe as suprastate policy is powerfully illustrated by the formation of Manifesta and the development of the "European Cultural Capital" program in which cities bid, as with the Olympic Games, to host the avatars of advanced artistic and curatorial initiatives. The clear impetus for many large-scale international exhibitions, as such, is not necessarily to instill a more complex understanding of artistic movements in local publics through the symbolic use and exchange of forms and ideas of international advanced art, but to propagate a certain will to globality. By so doing, such exhibitions seek to embed the peripheral spaces of cultural production and institutional articulation in the trajectory of international artistic discourse. Modernity and modernization mean, then, the development of greater proximity not only to the institutional patronage of international artistic spheres, but also to acquire and master its language, harvesting its surplus resources, and, ultimately, to position and promote the periphery as a genuine destination of artistic modernity. I shall not speak here of the links to economics, tourism, regional revitalization, nationalism, etc., inasmuch as it is obvious that all these concerns are part of the complex mechanisms at play in the formation of large international exhibitions and the building of new museums.

Enacting the Diasporic Public Sphere: Mobility, Meditation, and Proximity to the West

Even if the desire for modernity and modernization propels some institutions of international contemporary art, it would be misleading to think of them—and, especially, of those that exist outside the context of the large industrial centers of the West—as merely pale imitations (pardon the pun) of the authentic thing as it is constituted within the West. The very notion of proximity to the West, as a strategy enunciated in the dialectical framework of the global relations of power inherent in the development of the discourse of artistic modernity, is a double-edged sword. This sword cuts a swath between the revolutionary and emancipatory portents of the postcolonial critique of master narratives and the nationalist rhetoric of tradition and authenticity. We can, then, quite clearly state that the periphery does not simplistically absorb and internalize what it does not need. Nor does it vitiate its own critical power by becoming subservient to the rules of the center. In the wake of the globalization of culture and art, what the post-colonial response to it has produced is a new kind of space, a discourse of open contestations that spring not merely from resistance but are rather built on an ethics of dissent. Therefore, in its discursive proximity to Western modes of thought, postcolonial theory transforms this dissent into an enabling agent of historical transformation and thus is able to expose certain Western epistemological limits and contradictions.

In his book *Modernity at Large: Cultural Dimensions of Globalization*, Arjun Appadurai put the issue of what I have called *open contestations* in a much more elegant way by telling the story of the circuitous map of global cultural networks through the twin instances of mass mobility and mass mediation as paradigms of globality and locality. He writes:

> As with mediation, so with motion. The story of mass migrations (voluntary and forced) is hardly a new feature of human history. But when it is juxtaposed with the rapid flow of mass-mediated images, scripts, and sensations, we have a new order of instability in the production of modern activities. As Turkish guest workers in Germany watch Turkish films in their German flats, as Koreans in Philadelphia watch the 1988 Olympics in Seoul through satellite feeds from Korea [*sic*], and as Pakistani cab drivers in Chicago listen to cassettes of sermons recorded in mosques in Pakistan or Iran, we see moving images meet deterritorialized viewers. These create diasporic public spheres, phenomena that confound theories that depend on the continued salience of the nation-state as the key arbiter of important social changes. . . . In this sense, both persons and images often meet unpredictably, outside the certainties of home and the cordon sanitaire of local and national media effects. This mobile and unforeseeable relationship between mass-mediated events and migratory audiences defines the core of the link between globalization and the modern.[11]

What exactly does Appadurai mean, then, when he writes about diasporic public spheres? Who and what is the public referred to here? Does not the very concept of diaspora as a historical condition through which global cultural processes are mediated confront us with another antinomy in the dialectic between the tribal and modern, particularly in circumstances where diasporic cultures indigenize themselves on the soil of other entrenched values? Here I return once more to the Brooklyn barbershop poster, but now seen from the purview of its proliferation—not on the occasion of the

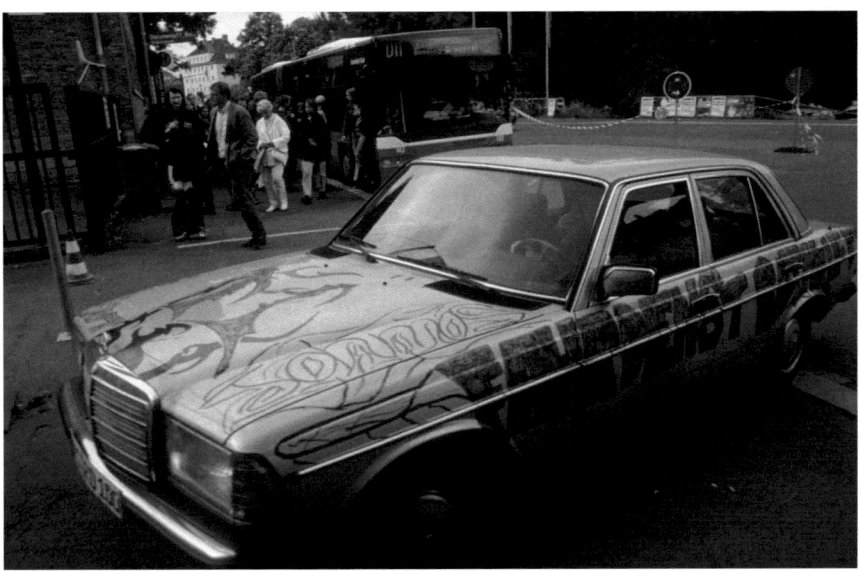

13.7 Thomas Hirschhorn, *Bataille Monument* (*Fahrdienst*) [Driving Service], 2002. Shown at Documenta11, Kassel, 2002. Photograph: Werner Maschmann. Courtesy of Thomas Hirschhorn/Gladstone Gallery, New York. © ADAGP, Paris (2025).

journey out into slavery and indenture, but on the basis of its inscription into and passage through the global scene of cultural translation. Today the Brooklyn barbershop represents the site of another diasporic public sphere, a new transnational locality embedded in networks of knowledge, labor (intellectual and manual), trade, tourism, immigration, technology, and finance. Writ large, the diasporic public sphere articulates the distinctive travelogue of twentieth-century modernity while writing new concepts of translocalization and transnationalization of culture within twenty-first-century globalizing processes. The diasporic public sphere offers the clearest example of what Néstor García Canclini, in his book *Hybrid Cultures*, calls strategies for entering and leaving modernity.[12] This to-and-fro movement predisposes Michel de Certeau's "everyday user" toward the instrumental-ization of his or her own agency.

The diasporic, then, delineates late modernity's transnational, trans-cultural, postcolonial, and global attitudes toward such concepts as identity, culture, nationality, and citizenship. It postulates an open-ended relationship with a variety of institutional productions and private experiences, as well as between models of professional and personal identity. The diasporic, through its twists and turns, from indeterminacy and contingency to indigeneity, shows us, in a paradoxical sense, both the limits of identity discourse and the fate of all *Leitkulturen* in the wake of the mass mobility, not only of people traveling beyond home, nation, race, ethnicity, and continent, but also of all forms of migratory knowledge, cultural iconography, artistic objects, contemporary subjectivities, and the networks of their distribution, mediation, and interpretations.[13]

If I have dwelled on the notion of the diasporic public sphere, it is to show how intertwined it is with the conditions of the global, even when it objectifies the ceaseless contradictions and antagonisms between the two, especially in regard to the issues of centers and peripheries, local and global, national and regional, enlightened and backward, mobility and stasis, citizen and subject, and cosmopolitan and provincial. One visible space where these contradictions and antagonisms are often encountered is the global city, with its social, political, and cultural spheres. As the diasporic public sphere emerges from the spatial and temporal disorientation of the global city, it becomes the space where the problems of translation for culture arise. Avid for a critical incarnation of new forms of experimental productions, cultural translation in the global present confronts us with a way to begin again, where the past is neither a foreign country nor simply the authentic name for origin. We can say, then, that the recent phenomenon of biennials in the periphery should not be bemoaned as a ready-made case of biennial syndrome. Instead, one needs to see in the biennial phenomenon the possibility of a paradigm shift in which we as spectators are able to encounter many experimental cultures, without wholly possessing them.

Spectacle, Spectatorship, and Mega-exhibitions

But what of the critique that biennials and other large-scale exhibitions foster an environment of speculative artistic enterprise and spectacle, and in so doing undercut artistic practice and its critical autonomy from the forces of market, ideology, and media? I will address this critique in two ways: first, through the notion of what I call *strategic globality* and, second, through the notion of spectatorship. I base my argument on a partial reading of Guy Debord's *Society of the Spectacle* and Michel de Certeau's idea of the everyday user, not as a passive consumer and receiver of culture, but as an active participant in it, an agent whose critical engagement with culture makes the complexity of its meaning more focused.[14] Pierre Bourdieu, in

The Field of Cultural Production, imagines culture as a habitus where position takings among users and producers create a strong dialectical framework through which culture makes visible its institutional, ideological, and conceptual practices, among others. Beginning with these assumptions, I would like to address the question of multiculturalism as a moment where the contradictory aspirations of users, agents, producers, institutions, and communities converge.

Before we look at the multicultural bogeyman, let us first examine the question of art exhibitions as spectacle. It has been often argued that the chief value of all institutional forms of mega-exhibitions (biennials, triennials, Documenta, Cultural Capitals, cultural festivals, blockbuster exhibitions of modern and classical European art, ethnographic exhibitions, world fairs, etc.) is grounded in the domain of spectacle and the spectacularization of art and culture through a process of diffusion and the reproduction of excess.[15] While a certain case can be made for this view, I would argue that such exhibitions address themselves not to the ideal viewer, whose senses have already been co-opted and homogenized into the institutional logic of display and transformation, but to a general viewer who represents an unknown demographic in the fragmented network of global cultural exchange. This general spectator I see lined before us in a field of spectatorship that articulates itself, not inside Debord's critique of spectacle qua the delirium of capitalist excess, but in a new instance of spectatorial experience through diffusion and differentiation.

Thus, the general field of spectatorship as an active field of everyday users, agents, producers, and position takings, in the context of recent postcolonial, postimperial discourse, inserts a new spectator whose gaze on the mottled screen of modernity is counterhegemonic and not simply an instance of countercultural positioning. Postcolonial subjective claims (multiculturalism, liberation theology, resistance art, feminist and queer theory, questions of third cinema, anti-apartheid, environmental and ecological movements, rights of indigenous peoples, minority demands, etc.) deviate from the hegemonic concept of spectatorial totality and render it fragmentary, because experiences of looking do not always apprehend this same meaning from what is being looked at or the same meaning from the effects of an image. For example, in the United States, the reading of the videotape of police officers beating Rodney King or the media depictions of the O. J. Simpson murder trial elicited different responses among African Americans and white Americans. This divergence was based, at least in part, on a subtle set of codes embedded in the representations of race and African American masculinity, not whether the depictions were factual or not. So, the question of spectacle is never a universal question, but is mediated, as Debord rightly argues, by extra-spectatorial issues. This brings up all sorts of counterhegemonic conceptions of looking and how ideas of art and culture may be rearticulated and reimagined in the wake of globalization.

Though there have been many celebrations of the death of multiculturalism in the service of a higher, more exemplary *Leitkultur*, we must continue to remind ourselves that what the multicultural paradigm opened up was a space (to return to this term) of open deliberations around what James Clifford has called the "radically asymmetrical relations of power" that have been the rule in most institutional practices.[16] And despite some of the shortcomings of multicultural discourse, its ethical project of citizenship, the recognition of difference, tolerance, and respect for other cultures and forms of living, remains quite salient today, and no more so than in the post–September 11 return to the old asymmetrical discourse of the clash of civilizations. Multiculturalism at its best is inclusive and makes clear the complex cultural and social maps of all globalizing societies. It releases the discourse of art and culture from the false natal bonds of ethnocentrism, while showing powerfully and critically that relations of exchange between cultures are also necessarily adumbrated by strong relations of power. And it is here that multicultural discourse has shown that, when placed at the service of nationalistic identification, power can easily turn into a tool of exclusion and marginalization.

As we rethink the values of the emergent forms of spectatorship that offer new critical insight into the historical condition of globalization, I would like to conclude by invoking—with reference to the political critique of imperialism in Michael Hardt and Antonio Negri's book *Empire*—what a new horizon of spectatorship might mean for nonnationalist art and culture. In *Empire*, Hardt and Negri claim that former domains of relations of social production became untied from the nation-state apparatus and its imperial program. And with this unbundling, a new type of sovereignty, which they have given the name "empire," has emerged. It is a movement that mobilizes the force of critical counterhegemonic movements whose sovereignty supersedes the nation-state's imperial claims to such things as territorial autonomy, self-determination, a view of economic totality, and the ability to regulate economic and cultural life. Empire has no boundaries, no limits, they claim. It encompasses what they call a spatial totality; in other words, it is everywhere.

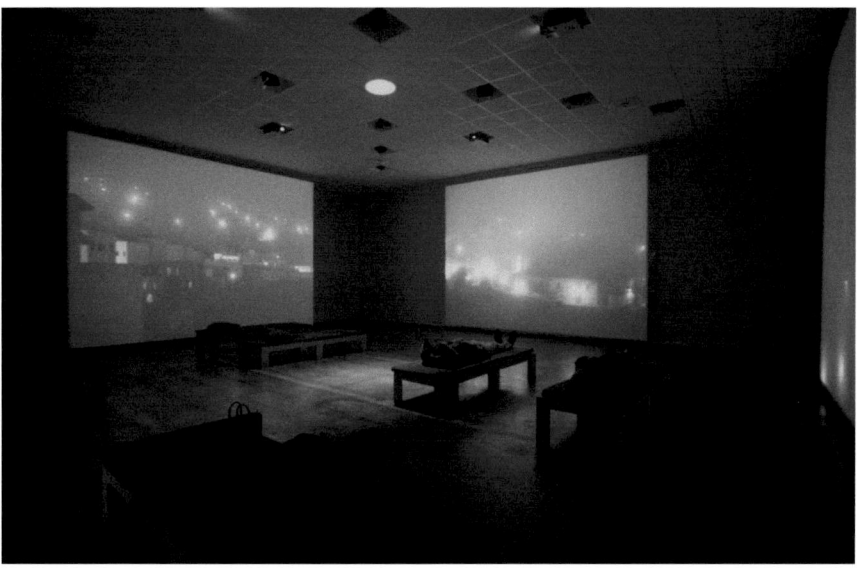

13.8 Craigie Horsfield, *El Hierro Conversation,*
2002. Installation at Documenta11, Kassel,
2002. © documenta archiv/Ryszard Kasiewicz
photographer. © Craigie Horsfield, ADAGP,
France 2025.

If it is true, as this stellar work argues, that "the sovereignty of the
nation-state was the cornerstone of the imperialisms of European powers
constructed throughout the modern era," where can we today situate the
mega-exhibition format, which still functions under the imprimatur of
the nation-state's hegemonic view of culture?[17] While there can be no single
answer to this question, one can, with all due respect to Hardt and Negri,
begin such a discussion by asserting that mega-exhibitions have adopted the
notion of the global from the perspective of imperial and colonial modes of
differentiation and homogenization, absorption and diffusion. They have not
been attentive enough to that differentiated position of general spectatorship that heralded, simultaneously, the twilight of the nation-state and the
dawn of empire. As such, I would claim that Debord's notion of the "society
of spectacle" was only partially attentive to the new sovereign power that
emerged with the dawn of "empire." In Debord's scheme, such a sovereign
power was flattened out by the spectacle-producing effects of capitalism.
Everything, all social life, was seen to be caught in the optical haze of mediation, perpetually ringed by the fearful machines of media absorption. The
logic of the spectacle was, on the one hand, a colonial logic, as Debord rightly

demonstrates, but on the other hand, this reading of the symptomatic logic of imperial discourse did not completely displace it. The society of spectacle, then, was concerned chiefly with a negative dialectic, where the relations of production, circulation, dissemination, reception, and acculturation proper to the European domain of culture find their expression. It did not, however, probe deeply enough into the discrepant categories of spectacle whose energies and modes of articulating their strategic globality within the domains of cosmopolitan networks and relations of social production are strictly anti-imperialist and counterhegemonic. Such strategies of globality introduce to contemporary artistic and cultural circuits new relations of spectatorship whose program of social differentiation, political expression, and cultural specificity reworks the notion of spectacle and constructs it as the site of new relations of power and cultural translation. It is here that I believe that certain cases of mega-exhibitions function, especially when viewed in the light of Mikhail Bakhtin's notion of the carnivalesque. The gap between the spectacle and the carnivalesque is the space, I believe, where certain exhibition practices, as resistance models against the deep depersonalization and acculturation of global capitalism, recapture a new logic for the dissemination and reception of contemporary visual culture today.

NOTES

Epigraph: Walter Benjamin, *The Arcades Project* (Cambridge, MA: Belknap Press of Harvard University Press, 1999), 7.

1   For a more theoretically inflected discussion on the concept of the culture industry, see Theodor Adorno, *The Culture Industry: Selected Essays on Mass Culture* (London: Routledge, 1991), 98–106; see also Theodor Adorno and Max Horkheimer's landmark study of mass culture, *The Dialectic of Enlightenment* (New York: Continuum, 1976), where the notion of the culture industry was first introduced. Here I use the term *culture industry* to denote the mass phenomenon that currently seems to be overtaking the museological presentation of art as traveling blockbuster cultural exhibitions, which can have both a legitimate mass appeal and a specialized appeal to connoisseurs and scholars. The increase in museum attendance across all categories of museological practice appears to bear this out. Following on the heels of the institutional success of art as part of the industry of mass culture and media is the increase in the number of curatorial programs in universities and specialized art academies. Also noteworthy are the almost two decades of expansion that have led to the proliferation of international and local biennials as models of the com-

modity culture of global capitalism and its great appeal to the diffusion of artistic practice, with little to offer in terms of heuristic function or content but merely as pure visuality in relation to mass culture.

2   Surely, Antonio Negri and Michael Hardt, with their recent book *Empire* (Cambridge, MA: Harvard University Press, 2001), have become the most fashionable theorists of this conjunction.

3   Here I am referring to the kind of resistance that is opposed not to globalization per se but only to the current form of globalization, whereby the high technological economies dictate the terms of global trade through the forums they control, such as the International Monetary Fund, the World Bank, and the World Trade Organization, while the developing economies wield little policy leverage in determining their own course. One should note that much of the developing economies' resistance to globalization is not antimarket in principle but is rather opposed to the supranational global institutions' imposition of stringent structural adjustment programs through such agencies as the Bretton Woods institutions.

4   See Michel de Certeau, *The Practice of Everyday Life* (Minneapolis: University of Minnesota Press, 1984).

5   See Benedict Anderson's superb *Imagined Communities: Reflections on the Origin and Spread of Nationalism* (London: Verso, 1996).

6   Manuel Castells, *The Rise of the Network Society*, vol. 1 of *The Information Age: Economy, Society and Culture* (Oxford: Blackwell, 1996), 3.

7   Stuart Hall, "Museums of Modern Art and the End of History," in *Modernity and Difference*, by Stuart Hall and Sarat Maharaj, Annotations 6 (London: Institute of International Visual Arts, 2001), 21.

8   Pierre Bourdieu, *The Field of Cultural Production: Essays on Art and Literature* (New York: Columbia University Press, 1993), 30.

9   For a particularly insightful book on the *Wunderkammer* and spectacle, see Horst Bredekamp, *The Lure of Antiquity and the Cult of the Machine: The Kunstkammer and the Evolution of Nature, Art, and Technology* (Princeton, NJ: Markus Wiener, 1995).

10   Jürgen Habermas, *The Theory of Communicative Action*, vol. 2, *Lifeworld and System: A Critique of Functionalist Reason* (Boston: Beacon, 1987), 192.

11   Arjun Appadurai, *Modernity at Large: Cultural Dimensions of Globalization* (Minneapolis: University of Minnesota Press, 1996), 4. Appadurai's deployment of migratory audiences through the figure of the mobile spectator whose encounter with the objective world is mediated through forums of global technologies closely resembles an observation made by Manuel Castells in regard to subjectivity and modernity. Within conventional narratives of globalization Castells locates "a fundamental split

between abstract, universal instrumentalism, and historically rooted, particularistic identities." From such a split, the coordinates of identity and subjectivity become enmeshed in the polarities between mobility and mediation, a position Castells sees as "a bipolar opposition between the Net and the Self." Castells, *Rise of the Network Society*, 3.

12 See Néstor García Canclini, *Hybrid Cultures: Strategies for Entering and Leaving Modernity* (Minneapolis: University of Minnesota Press, 1995).

13 This refers to a recent controversy in Germany in which a German parliamentarian advocated that in order for immigrants to become full citizens and so assimilate and integrate themselves into the German cultural context, they should, as it were, adopt German culture as the leading culture (*Leitkultur*). This implies, then, that an immigrant's original cultural context, which has hitherto represented values that structure the deepest commitments of his or her identity, should now be suppressed or made secondary so as to be subjugated to the proliferate presence of the German *Leitkultur*.

14 Guy Debord, *The Society of the Spectacle* (Cambridge, MA: Zone Books, 1995).

15 Such a critique, based on what *New Yorker* art critic Peter Schjeldahl calls "festivalism," has been gleefully taken up in the United States. [*Ed. note:* See Peter Schjeldahl, "Festivalism," *New Yorker*, July 5, 1999, 85–86.] Suffice it to say, I find nothing either intellectually useful or historically correct in such an analysis.

16 [*Ed. note:* In his book *Routes: Travel and Translation in the Late Twentieth Century* (Cambridge, MA: Harvard University Press, 1997), 192, Clifford discusses Mary Louise Pratt's famous concept of the "contact zone" and cites a passage in which she defines "contact" by emphasizing "how subjects are constituted in and by their relations to each other. . . . [It stresses] copresence, interaction, interlocking understandings and practices, often within radically asymmetrical relations of power." See Mary Louse Pratt, *Imperial Eyes: Travel and Transculturation* (London: Routledge, 1992), 6–7.]

17 Hardt and Negri, *Empire*, xii.

Repetition and Differentiation 14

Lorna Simpson's Iconography of the Racial Sublime

Written for the midcareer retrospective organized by the American Federation of Arts, this essay appears on pages 102–30 of the book *Lorna Simpson* (New York: Harry N. Abrams, in association with the American Federation of Arts, 2006). The exhibition was shown at the Museum of Contemporary Art, Los Angeles; the Miami Art Museum (now the Pérez Art Museum Miami); and the Whitney Museum of American Art, New York. Enwezor's essay was excerpted as "The American Sublime and the Racial Self, 2006" in *The Sublime*, ed. Simon Morley (Cambridge, MA: MIT Press for Whitechapel Gallery, London, 2010), 193–97. The photographs discussed in the first section of this essay are reproduced in the book *Lorna Simpson*, mentioned above, but were not made available for reproduction in this volume. An earlier essay on Simpson's work, "Social Grace: The Work of Lorna Simpson," appeared in *Third Text* 10, no. 35 (Summer 1996): 43–58.

Fundamentally, the camera is merely a subjective apparatus, an apparatus of subjectivity. I would go so far as to say that the camera is a wholly philosophical product; it is an instrument of cogito.

Georges Didi-Huberman, *Invention of Hysteria* (2003)

Beginnings

IN THE LATE 1970S, Lorna Simpson embarked on a trip of discovery: the discovery of photography, to which she has devoted a quarter century of her illustrious artistic career. At the same time, there was a parallel journey, closely allied with the first, based on an extended series of travels to Europe,

Africa, the Caribbean, and the United States, where she began employing the camera to document her passage through territories that were then just beginning to register their diverse cultural and spatial settings in her pictorial imagery. These two coordinated trips over several summers—across continents, communities, and cultures—give the first indications of Simpson's preternaturally clear artistic motivation. What is immediately striking in the images generated from these trips is not the furtive tentativeness of an amateur. Instead, her photographs exhibit a sense of great visual control and a directness that is neither too intimate nor surreptitious. There is a hint of diffidence that one senses in the photographs, as if she were working around the edges of her subjects. By the same token, the images are utterly devoid of cant and sentimentality. In this clutch of photographic images that form the earliest public manifestation of her practice, the ground was laid for what ultimately became the basis of a photographic argument about the nature of photographic subjectivity and the artist's control over the process of image making.[1] In Italy, Spain, France, Morocco, Mauritania, Algeria, Jamaica, New York, and the American South, Simpson pursued her practice by training herself to see images in everyday events and social rituals, absorbing their import, as well as shaping her observations into photographic meaning, sharply delineating the spatiotemporal connection of her subjects to place.

First Lessons

The images are not timeless, universal signs. They are scorched with emblems and textures of their time and place (both in the garb and coiffure of the subjects). A photograph of two women wearing hijabs and semitransparent veils in the medina of Marrakech is instructive, not least because it is an agitated image. In the image it is clear that the woman at the bottom edge of the left corner may have just become aware of the presence of the photographer. Does the photographer have permission? This oft-repeated question inscribes the social contract between photographer and subject, especially when the cultural context demands it. It seems that this photograph demands an answer congruent with the question. The look in the eyes of the veiled woman, along with the sternness of her furrowed brow, does not signal any invitation. They merely place, for the record, evidence of her disapproval. Yet one cannot know for sure. There is an ambiguity in the exchange of looks between photographer and subject. The struggle for power and control over the scene of representation makes the simple plot of this photograph an ambivalent one.

The encounter with the Moroccan woman is familiar, that is, if we apply an orientalist reading on this scene of differences, with the barely adult Simpson occupying the position of the penetrating Western gaze, that look that pierces and enervates the subject. But here it is the photographer's subjectivity that is at stake. She is being judged, along with the instrument that seemingly authorizes her entrance into the orientalist context. Her subjects do not give ground—the larger looming figure at the central portion of the image has turned from the camera. She either is ignoring the photographer or is oblivious to her presence. She is buried in her thoughts, her tense, invisible body burrowed within the flowing outfit that all but conceals it. But this obliviousness is betrayed by the palpable tension that runs from her hunched shoulders down to the hands hidden inside her outfit, which does indicate a response to the camera's presence. Neither woman collaborates in the slow striptease of the photographic game that frequently strips the "other" naked, turning her into merely an object of desire. This kind of refusal has engendered a multiplicity of critical literature, especially with the advent of the publication of Edward Said's landmark book *Orientalism* in 1978.[2] The two women and the photographer are protagonists in a critical cultural conversation. Here we must see the exchange purely from the point of view of the subjects, whose gaze and body language dominate and seize control of the picture. Simpson must yield ground. She has lost the capacity to maintain the authority of the camera and its ability to invade the space of the other as most street photography tends to do.

In all the images from this trip, the confrontation between the Muslim women and the American girl inscribes a dialectic of power, about who has control over the image. Such struggle for power, for control over representation, has played a formidable role in Simpson's conception of photography and its capacity to enter a judgment of the scene of representation. The critical attitude that accompanies the photographic encounter is further distilled, years later, in Simpson's engagement with American racialized modes of representation and the bodies of black women. Yet, in contradistinction to the uneasy encounter with the Muslim Moroccan women, Simpson's other documentary pictures produced around the same period lack a similar dramatic face-off. In other words, they are not dialectical. These pictures, shot entirely in familiar Western contexts, are not as contested. In Sicily, for example, the images, while clearly competent, are not as arresting. They appear hackneyed, depending as they do on clichés of tourist photography. We have seen such images before in countless establishments—pizza parlors, travel agencies, "Visit Italy" brochures—retailing cheesy Italian exotica. There is the image of robust, dark-haired Italian women full of merriment and so obviously delighted by the presence of the camera. The scene is as it should be: a combination of rustic charm and the simple joy of being alive. Another image is a street scene of a group of dark-suited men gathered in conversation in the middle of the picture. In the central foreground a young boy is playing, his smiling face crinkled in delight at an invisible object to which he has turned his head. In the background, to the right, a matronly woman dressed in black is leading a small child outfitted in ruffled white chiffon into a courtyard, while to the left, in the far background, stands another woman in black and a young girl in white. But the winning charm of the picture is also the true subject of the photograph: he is standing there, like the lover he models himself as, arms akimbo, an unlit cigarette dangling from the corner of his lips. He is a perfect caricature of the local gigolo. These images clearly betray Simpson's absorption of classic postwar street photography modes of observation.

However, in subsequent images taken in New York, there is clearly a sense that Simpson's perception of her own cultural context is far more acute and less dependent on the crutch of touristic exoticism. These images are shot across different settings but are mostly set within the urban milieu. The subjects are middle-class, urban black Americans or immigrants in various ceremonial or ritual contexts, such as families attending a wedding, going to church, or watching a parade on Eastern Parkway in Brooklyn. The ease with which Simpson photographed these events is reciprocated with a similar ease in the manner the subjects present themselves to the camera. One image in particular shows Simpson's debt at this time to the work of the great African American photographer Roy DeCarava, especially his classic book *The Sweet Flypaper of Life* (1955), a collaboration with Langston Hughes.[3] The photograph in question depicts a young black woman in a tiered lace bridesmaid dress clutching a small, white-ribboned bouquet of flowers as she faces the camera. In the image there are four figures posed against the backdrop of a station wagon. The bridesmaid is standing to the left side as she leans slightly forward while supporting the weight of her body with her left hand placed against the car's front door. In the middle is an older woman (also dressed formally in a white lace dress) half sitting inside the car's open back door. She is staring at the camera with a look of bemusement. To her immediate left stands another young woman holding a small child in her arms. The photograph is reminiscent of DeCarava's picture *Graduation, New York* of an extravagantly attired black girl on her way to graduation. Simpson's photograph evokes a similar sense of tenderness. This portrait of a black family displays the sensitivity that is the hallmark of DeCarava's analysis of black life in America, and may perhaps explain the ease one detects in these images. In a way, Simpson was working within her own culture. Notice that she has completely avoided the cliché of urban strife, poverty, and dilapidated neighborhoods in which black subjects are normally portrayed. These, then, are questioning photographs, images that go to the heart of black subjectivity and sense of the self. But are these images adequate to the task demanded by the encounter with the Muslim Moroccan women? We will soon discover the answer to this fundamental question in the decision Simpson makes in the 1980s.

Defamiliarization

Like most beginners in photography, Simpson, who was in her late teens during the period the photographs were taken, worked in the honored documentary tradition. The documentary tradition to which she had initially responded includes both the work of European and American modernists: men and women such as Henri Cartier-Bresson, Walker Evans, Dorothea Lange, Margaret Bourke-White, Consuelo Kanaga, Gordon Parks, Roy De-Carava, Robert Frank, and many others. Such photography, splashy with bravado and social gravitas or cool and distanced, as was the case with Evans, had reached its height with the advent of the witnessing industry procured by photojournalism and perfected in arty style through the invention of the "decisive moment" in the work of the likes of Cartier-Bresson and Robert Capa. This style became indisputably cemented in the public imagination in the postwar years.

Most practitioners who employed the documentary form had great belief in the mediated truth of the image, especially one that was generally concerned with the human condition; with the poetic beauty of the ordinary and the metaphysical power inherent in observed nature. The introduction of the less bulky handheld camera in the 1930s changed the nature of the photographic enterprise. Freed of the encumbrance of the stationary large-format machines of the previous era, photographers became more agile, an advantage afforded by the mobility the portable camera offered. It also changed the nature of documentary photography. As the twentieth century was being rapidly transformed, the documentary photographer was there to record and document it, to preserve, translate, and transmit its ideals of change and progress. This portable camera, in the overwhelming way it was used, and in its attempts to penetrate social conditions, was both a sensitive and an indiscriminate machine. This machine in turn manifested a superficial image-mongering in the gossipy snapshot of the paparazzi. On the other hand, in the ponderous style of "concerned photography," it became a sort of ethical shorthand directed toward the most troubling parts of society.[4] We shall not speak of the nature of this "concern," whether it lacked decorum or was just simply excessive.

Suffice it to say that from its very inception "concerned photography" was troubled and presumptuous. It was ready to be subjected to a radical process of defamiliarization: at once sensational (Diane Arbus), detached, and severely objective (conceptual art). During this period in the 1950s and 1960s, American society was undergoing a profound and radical change. The changes brought about by the civil rights movement, the Vietnam War, and the women's rights movement touched the practice of photography in immeasurable ways, especially as artists became more inclined to deploy its methodologies and images.

Andy Warhol, that cool purveyor of the profound and the mundane, was one of the early contemporary artists to recognize the crucial shift in the practice of photography and the relationship between public images and the defamiliarization from their referent. In *Red Race Riot* (1963), a large silkscreen of repeated images of a news photograph showing the police setting attack dogs on civil rights demonstrators in Birmingham, Alabama, Warhol was able to critique the fundamental flaw inherent in documentary photography, which though attentive to the event was less able in negotiating the signifier/signified relationship reading of the image solicited. *Red Race Riot* indicated a different photographic paradigm, one that turned from the photojournalistic tendency of the documentary as news to the more iconic treatment of photographic images as archives of public memory (from celebrity to the infamous, disasters, and the bizarre).

This shift, which was already clear in the photomontages of the 1920s and in the defamiliarizations of surrealism and Dada, would occur frequently throughout the 1960s in the work of Richard Hamilton, Gerhard Richter, Sigmar Polke, and other pop artists. With conceptual artists such as Bruce Nauman, Ed Ruscha, Eleanor Antin, Adrian Piper, Dan Graham, Gordon Matta-Clark, Robert Smithson, Hans Haacke, and Martha Rosler, photography became a tool of documentation to be dissociated from the "concern" of the documentary practitioner. Photography was an instrument of investigation, a mechanism of critical analysis; its product a series of citations involving systems, experiments, preconceived narratives, "based in daily, lived rhythms or 'real time,'" that were no less true than the so-called unmediated images drawn by "pure" documentary.[5] Photography at this juncture in contemporary art was fundamentally subjective. Simpson entered art school at the climax of the dialectic between the two traditions: one putatively objective and the other brazenly subjective. Needless to say, the latter view had the greater appeal and held more meaning for Simpson. The realization that there was a different photographic possibility would prove pivotal to Simpson's attempt to constitute a new discursive strategy for subsequent work. It was the strip of photographic territory she had to traverse in order to understand that photography was "fundamentally subjective," but also that it was vitally philosophical.

Apostasy

For a young artist still discovering the world of contemporary art, such realization as was manifested through the encounter with multiple photographic tropes was not necessarily reassuring. By the time she enrolled in art school in New York in 1978, Simpson, like the rest who passed through the birth canal of the documentary school, had become an apostate. However, the transformation of her work would come only later, while in graduate school in San Diego. In 1982, after leaving New York for the West Coast, she would become involved in an artistic environment where procedures of working were radically different from those of her beginnings in New York.[6] The art department of the University of California, San Diego, comprised a number of experimental artists, including Allan Kaprow and Eleanor Antin. Owing to the performance- and process-oriented work championed by the faculty, regular attendance at performances was de rigueur.

The activities surrounding contemporary artistic procedures furthered Simpson's ongoing interrogation of photography. She was increasingly engaged with the analysis of the intermedia and temporal relationship between the performative act and the camera. She was in doubt about the adequacy of the documentary method as a way of digging beneath the crust of photographic truth. While the documentary form often proved incisive in the observation of social reality, declaiming on the imperturbable relationship between photographic truth and reality, it still appeared limiting for the kind of work she wanted to pursue. Rather than just recording reality, she wanted to investigate it, to unravel it, to interrogate it, and, if possible, to reenvision reality—in short, to reinvent truth.

What Simpson was most concerned with was not "self-evident" truth. Rather, she was invested in "historical" truth, that is to say, those images calcified like plaque in the social unconscious. Such images needed to be produced, in a similar vein to Cindy Sherman's series *Untitled Film Stills*. To get to her goal, Simpson needed to demonstrate to herself that the camera was not just an instrument designed to probe into the depths of truth (self-evident or historical), one fashioned through apostolic devotion by various industries of the manufactured image. She wanted to reveal it also as a machine that spewed all manner of conventions and clichés, stereotypes that had to be overcome if the camera was truly to become "a wholly philosophical product" in the deconstructive mode. It was then that Simpson began her own quest of defamiliarizing the documentary image by turning to the staged, composed, performative image. She achieved her goal by first discarding the conventions of her documentary past. Working with a sequential, though not necessarily repetitive, relation of images shot in black and white, she inserted clips of language: dialogues and monologues to open up the discursive and narrative possibilities of the work.

The introduction of language in direct relation to the images owes partly to the fact that Simpson wanted to erase the caption that was so necessary for the denotative aspect of documentary practice. Her photographs began then to embody aspects of film stills, where she made the vital link between language and visual form. But this kind of relation had to be wholly invented in Simpson's work. The photographs would bear resemblance to nobody and no event. They would become the event and their own singular semblance. By purging her shadowless images of any allusion to a socially recognizable environment, slicing away all the chiaroscuro detail for severe, empty, monochromatic, evenly lit scenes, she was able to realize the conceptual task that had previously stymied her documentary work.

> I did a lot of documentary photography in college—it's an interesting practice, but as you distribute these photographs, what are you really saying with them? I found conceptual photography took that issue up. Being in California in the '80s was completely the opposite of being on the East coast. Everyone was doing performance. I was at a point with taking photographs that I would think "I'm sick of seeing shows of only documentary work." Yet, I wasn't a performance artist. I like watching people perform but I don't like to be out there, so my entire time was in observation.[7]

The settings of her photographs—which in the beginning alternated between a stark white background or lugubrious black, and later included a

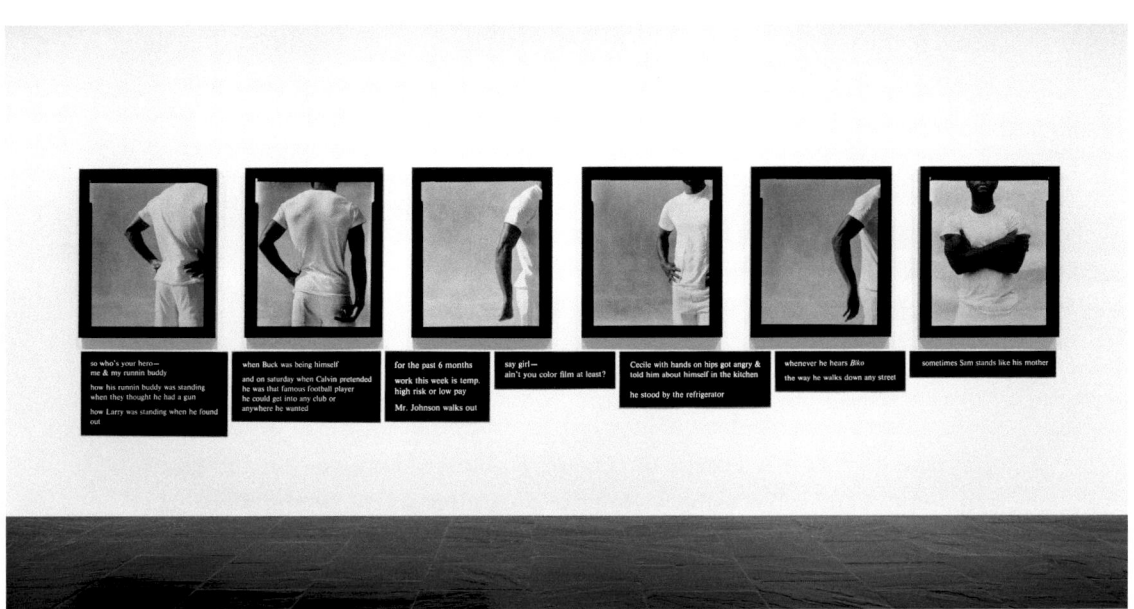

14.1 Lorna Simpson, *Gestures/Reenactments*, 1985. Six silver gelatin prints, seven engraved text plaques, overall 145.1×708 cm, each framed print 122.6×99.7 cm. © Lorna Simpson. Courtesy of the artist and Hauser and Wirth, New York.

brownish-red background after she started working in color with the large-format Polaroid camera—appeared like backdrops for technical or scientific photography. The images have a neutral institutional appearance and tend to isolate the figures from any referential system. When necessary, the backdrops were employed to accentuate depth of field or aided in the establishment of shallow perspective. These were rigorously worked-out systems for depicting scenes of angst, despair, and gestures of resistance.

The very first image that emerged from this new body of work, *Gestures/Reenactments*, encapsulates the first stage of this period of intense experimentation. It is in the nature of the unresolved issues in Simpson's development that the germinal work in her mature practice would be based on the image of the black male figure. Given the fact that in subsequent images Simpson would work exclusively with black female subjects, what is the significance of this appearance of the black male figure in the scene of representation? What becomes immediately clear in this depiction is the appearance of the castration complex. The series of monologues that runs beneath the six panels explores various anxieties that bedevil the black male subject in American culture. In the first panel the monologue runs thus:

So who's your hero—
me & my runnin buddy
How his runnin buddy was standing
when they thought he had a gun
How Larry was standing when he found
out

There is an elegiac quality to these lines that may lead to the interpretation that this is a scene of tragedy and loss, a dissociation and emptying out of the subject. By leaving the lines incomplete, Simpson appears to be calling on viewers to complete the picture, to draw some conclusions about the fate of the "runnin buddy." Standing off the frame, the anonymous male figure clad in white shorts and T-shirt appears as if he had been roused from bed. The mark of resignation in his slightly slackened frame is drawn out by the manner in which he stands, with his hands placed on his hips, scratching his thigh, or with hands folded facing the viewer. The gesture and pose indicate how people often stand when absorbing disturbing news. This work carries the rumor of the depleted black male subject, who is simultaneously feminized (how Larry was standing when he found out) and menacing (when they thought he had a gun).

Because the black male often is portrayed as either too constrained or uncontrollable, the figure in *Gestures/Reenactments* is a cipher of his social condition. The text panels that accompany the work present an essay on that condition. Simpson forces us not just to read the panels; she calls on us to scrutinize their meaning. Hers is an ethical gesture that reaches out beyond the principles of representation and into the zone of historicity. To historicize and theorize sources of black pleasure and denial requires a recoding of the iconic nature of the subject. Consequently, in portraying the subject as a character of sexual ambiguity completely devoid of the armors of masculine toughness yet exorbitantly endowed with such masculinity—so much so he risks death by his mere existence—she points us to the general aporia inherent in his social condition.

The commingling of sexuality and race has since remained an undercurrent of Simpson's work. Where Simpson explores the sexual ambivalence of the black male subject historically in American culture, her contemporaries such as Gary Simmons do so less ambiguously in works like *Line Up*

(1993), while artist and filmmaker Isaac Julien returns us to the scene of ambivalence in the film *Looking for Langston* (1989), as Glenn Ligon would do later in *Notes on the Margin of the Black Book* (1991–93). Each of these works by artists of Simpson's generation shows how generative the figure of the black male subject has been in contemporary visual culture, a theme productively underscored by Thelma Golden in the exhibition *Black Male: Representations of Masculinity in Contemporary American Art* at the Whitney Museum in 1994–95.[8]

Crisis

What crisis? Crisis of race and gender? Or crisis of method? It is both. Let us focus on method first: Simpson's repudiation of her own photographic beginnings has largely remained unexamined in the large critical literature that has accrued around her work. This may be partly owing to the fact that after some early exhibitions at the beginning of the 1980s, she withdrew them from circulation. But to better understand the import of her subsequent work requires a return to the scene of crisis in her work, one that bequeathed her a surplus of new artistic maneuvers.

The abandonment of documentary practice was the first significant crisis in Simpson's understanding of photography, whereby she fell out of love with photographic realism and its apostolic truths. But she fell in love, so to speak, with photography as a shaper of subjectivity, as a moment in praxis in which to enact its vast theoretical promise and historical application. But this crisis was not unique to her alone. Around it was the crisis of representation, race, gender, sexuality, ethnicity, authorship, and authority. It was part of the radical reorientation of the artistic hierarchies that were being dismantled by artists in the 1960s and was occurring on the political front in the wake of decolonization, the Algerian War, the Vietnam War, the civil rights movement, and the revolt of students in May 1968. Simpson's estrangement from documentary realism occurred at that moment in historical recognition when the certainties of the monolithic, hegemonic arrangement of economic and political dominance of Western culture experienced an open revolt. The increasing multicultural dimension of this revolt remains palpable.

Events of the Self

Accompanying these events were the epistemological investigations initiated by artists, many of them utilizing performance and the camera. Whether performing the body or examining the socioeconomic, racial, and sexual codes that surrounded it, in the 1960s, photography, along with video and structuralist films, became one of the preferred methods for recording, documenting, and witnessing the excessive production of subjectivity in contemporary art, making the resulting image the iconographic remainder of the extinguished embers of passionate performances, actions, processes, and analysis (Chris Burden, Ed Ruscha, Carolee Schneemann, Eleanor Antin, Bruce Nauman, Gordon Matta-Clark, Hans Haacke, Valie Export, Adrian Piper, Robert Smithson, Ana Mendieta, Yvonne Rainer, Richard Serra, Cindy Sherman, and Martha Rosler). The photographic support as such was overcome as a supplement, surrogate, index, archive, etc. For these artists, the "camera [became] a wholly philosophical product; it [was] an instrument of cogito."

This turn to the camera to record the tumultuous events of the self, giving rise to a formal analytical procedure in photographic practice, coincided with critical developments in postmodernism, psychoanalysis, and poststructuralism. In contemporary art this focused on the crucial dialectic of the signifier/signified relationship in image making. The conceptual matrix of this induction of postmodernism, psychoanalysis, and poststructuralism and the camera was most productively explored by such artists as Adrian Piper, whose series *Food for the Spirit* pointed clearly to the idea of the self as something sutured from a multiplicity of sources, none of which properly designated a pure, authentic self. Instead, the investigation on which these artists embarked was a larger philosophical quest, one that concerned the possibility of self-knowledge through the restaging of the self by positioning the activity of the investigation in the crack between the signifier/signified dialectic. Piper's and Sherman's critical projects with the camera thoroughly exemplify the crux of the signifier/signified dialectic. To understand Simpson's artistic practice, therefore, we need to invest our interaction with her work by exploring this domain of analysis involved in the recording of the events of the self, whether as surrogate, invented, imagined, or real. To understand how the signifier/signified relationship has functioned in Simpson's photographic production requires taking an inventory of the forms, objects, signs, discourses, and types of images that have emerged in her carefully constructed mise-en-scène.

The American Sublime and the Racial Self

We will see how and why this fresh logic of the photographic instrument held great appeal for Simpson, as was already demonstrated in *Gestures/Reenactments* and subsequently in *Screen 1, Screen 2, Screen 3, Screen 4* (all 1986), and

Completing the Analogy (1987). The turning point in her work lies specifically in the fact that for her generation photographic inquiry became concerned principally with cogito, and it was not necessarily the drive to self-knowledge nor autobiography that compelled this shift. There were larger issues at stake: a whole social body and its pathologies. Let us give this a name: it is the spectacle of the racial self and the gendered body.

Take the example of *Completing the Analogy*, in which a tousle-haired black female garbed in a crinkled cotton gown, her back turned to the viewer, appears to be facing a blackboard in an image in which foreground and background have been erased. The slightly animated pose contrasts dramatically with the text printed on the photograph, which reads:

> HAT IS TO HEAD
> AS DARKNESS IS TO. . . . . SKIN
>
> SCISSORS ARE TO CLOTH
> AS RAZOR IS TO. . . . . SKIN
>
> BOW IS TO ARROW
> AS SHOTGUN IS TO. . . . . SKIN

But insofar as this is concerned with certain practices of dissection, we can more properly locate its aesthetic properties as the ken of the American sublime: race and gender in social discourse. Therefore, to confront Simpson's early photographic work (1985–95) and the elliptical linguistic registers that ring it like a halo, we have to engage how the disquietingly straightforward, pared-down images open the viewer up to a vast epistemic field. It is a field rooted in a particular type of violence. This violence is grounded in methods of subjection and denial. Access to its disclosure therefore requires more than the tacit acknowledgment of its historical base and its temporality.

Over the past century, manifold cultural examinations and artistic investigations have been opening knowledge of this violence to viewers. D. W. Griffith's *The Birth of a Nation* (1915) is a key example of the iconographic violence rooted in the American sublime. Popular media, literature, and countless Hollywood films are saturated with such images. It is never said enough that nothing escapes the racial sublime and the epistemic violence that surrounds it in the American civilization. The scrutiny of the racial sublime constitutes a key philosophical and methodological framework of Simpson's critical project. But what is this violence, and how does it frame

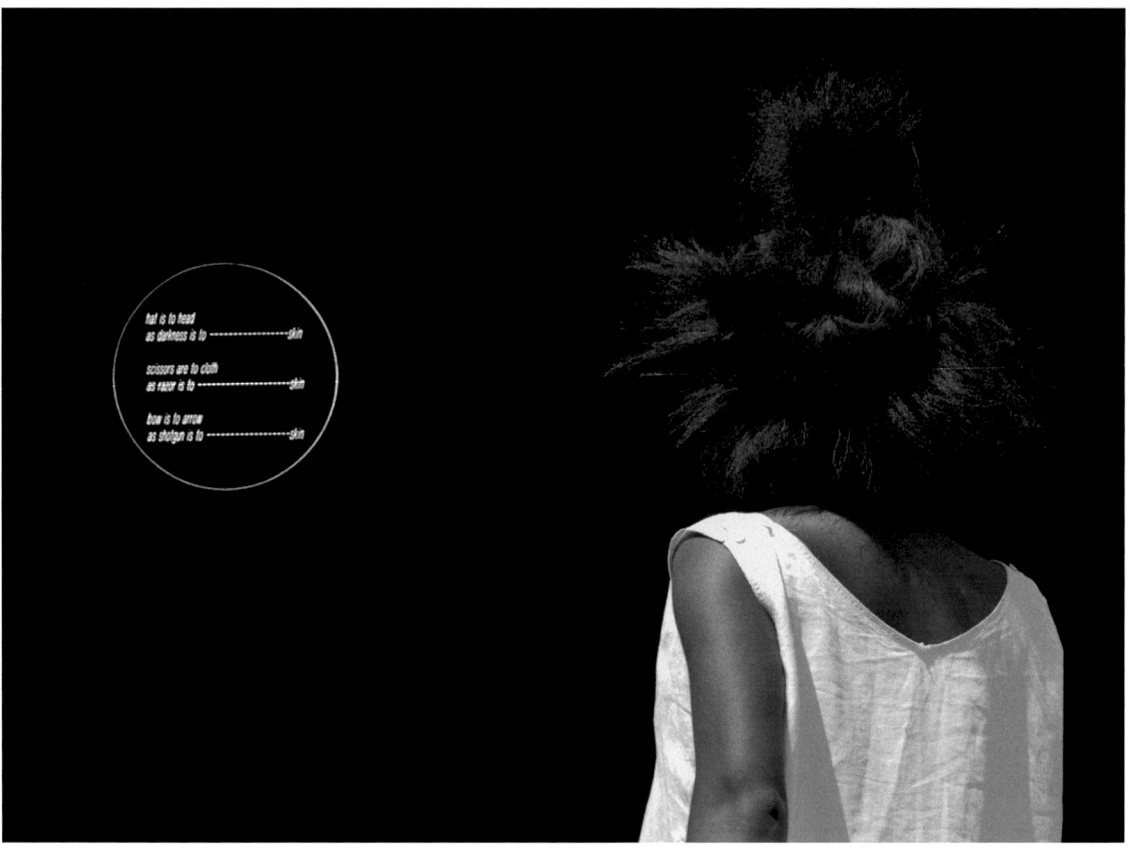

14.2 Lorna Simpson, *Completing the Analogy*, 1987. Silver gelatin print, one engraved plastic plaque, overall 91.4 × 121.9 × 5.1 cm; plaque 25.4 cm in diameter. © Lorna Simpson. Courtesy of the artist and Hauser and Wirth, New York.

her artistic procedures? Or, rather, how has Simpson deployed the dispersed regimes of this violence to explore the limits of the body, the black body mounted on the scaffold and bound up in its suffocating hold? Then there is the female body. And then the black female body. And then . . . Simpson stages her work in the tumultuous events of the racial and gendered self. Perhaps we can see why it is possible to speak here of the double displacement that is evident in all her work, especially in the constant insertion of the photographic subject into the zones of racial and female identification. The first displacement connects to the question of what it is to be black and female. This frame represents the universal and the particular in her line of inquiry. The second displacement is on the narrower subject of what it means to be African American and American simultaneously. This frame is driven by the concepts of diaspora and subalternity; nationality and citizenship. The relay of positions and modes of address also touch on specific formal and methodological issues: the intermedia relationship between photography and film, text and image, speech and narrative. All of these form the backdrop of what this essay seeks to explore.

Rupture, or the Madness of Race

There is in the "mythology of madness" the oft-repeated story of the radical therapy effected by Philippe Pinel when he released the madmen and madwomen from their chains in the Bicêtre and Salpêtrière hospitals in Paris in 1794. Pinel's freeing of the madmen and madwomen was said to have ushered in a revolution in the treatment of madness. Not only did he free these men and women from their literal chains, he simultaneously, through their deincarceration, also freed them from the stigma to which the chain had interminably condemned them beyond repair.

By the same token, Pinel did not so much free the insane from their hellish confinement as much as he released their madness from total censure. In this way he returned them back into the world, or rather, into the social government of the asylum from which the insane had been banished. And in which for centuries scores languished, under lock and key, behind high walls, where no "serene" gaze of rationality and respectability would ever fall on that insolence that represents the ruined human character.

In America, race constitutes its own form of madness, along with its own asylums and governmentalities. From the earliest moment that European colonists arrived on the American shores, race has been the great alloy of a potent social experiment, one that produced slavery and the plantation economy. If the Bicêtre and Salpêtrière hospitals were more than therapeutic zones—being as they were places of seizure—the confinement on the plantation under slavery mobilizes similar senses of capture and stigma. Race in America simultaneously represents the unspeakable and the irrepressible, as well as an epistemological model of biological differentiation that produces a prodigious body of discourse and representation. And like madness in the asylum, it enjoys a particular kind of censure behind the high walls of its own asylum. Except, unlike the asylum, which is ringed by thick, mortared walls and protected by a forbidding gate, the madness of race exists nakedly visible in the tumescent flesh of the American social ideal and is practiced in the open terrain of the cultural landscape.

Toni Morrison has productively explored how the episteme of race as a literary device of social and political differences was constituted. She makes us aware of how the discourse of race suffuses the canons of early and modern American writing, particularly the novels of America's most celebrated writers. She argues that the madness of race, along with its utter naked visibility, is part of the unique character of American literary arts. According to her analysis, a cursory search into American literature reveals the obsessive nature of the racial attitude in what she identifies as the uses of an Africanist presence to elevate the representations of literary whiteness and at the same time ameliorate the lurking sense of a human bond that connects the enslaved and the free. This presence, as it were, stages a discourse, a funnel through which the dialectic between enslavement and freedom could be passed. Morrison came to this insight through close readings of Edgar Allan Poe, Herman Melville, Nathaniel Hawthorne, Harriet Beecher Stowe, William Styron, William Faulkner, Ernest Hemingway, and many others.

My curiosity about the origins and literary uses of this carefully observed, and carefully invented, Africanist presence has become an informal study of what I call *American Africanism*. It is an investigation into the ways in which a nonwhite, African-like (or Africanist) presence or persona was constructed in the United States, and the imaginative uses this fabricated presence served. I am using the term *Africanism* not to suggest the larger body of knowledge on Africa that the philosopher Valentin-Yves Mudimbe means by the term *Africanism*, nor to suggest the varieties and complexities of African people and their descendants who have inhabited this country.[9] Rather, I use it as a term for the denotative and connotative blackness that African peoples have come to signify, as well as the entire range of views, assumptions, readings, and misreadings that accompany Eurocentric learning about these people. As a trope, little restraint has been attached to its uses. As a disabling virus within literary discourse, Africanism has become, in the Eurocentric tradition that American education favors, both a way of talking about and a way of policing matters of class, sexual license, and repression, formations and exercises of power, and meditations on ethics and accountability. Through the simple expedient of demonizing and reifying the range of color on a palette, American Africanism makes it possible to say and not say, to inscribe and erase, to escape and engage, to act out and act on, to historicize and render timeless. It provides a way of contemplating chaos and civilization, desire and fear, and a mechanism for testing the problems and blessings of freedom.[10]

Abolition literature and the slave narrative were direct literary responses to the disjuncture of racial difference. This disjuncture has been well preserved in the American aesthetic imagination, from the vaudeville black face of Al Jolson to President George H. W. Bush's deployment of Willie Horton in an advertisement during his presidential campaign in 1988. During the Black Arts Movement of the 1960s, the disjuncture of race as an artistic paradigm made a return in the form of black nationalism, while in the 1980s it was penetrated by the insight of cultural and postcolonial studies and postmodernism. In contemporary art, a denotative and connotative Africanist presence has been abundantly used by artists—black and white alike—who find in the form of this spectral subject a language for the racial sublime. Simpson, Kara Walker, Glenn Ligon, and Fred Wilson are some of the better-known younger African American artists who have wrung meaning out of the vast Africanist visual archive and who have also departed from the props of black nationalism of the 1960s. They have devised a more nuanced if not always successful philosophical engagement with its imagery. If the madness of race suffused the work of these artists—providing, as their work proved, a topic of serious theoretical and historical reflection—it has not come without misgivings on the part of the critical establishment. As Morrison correctly observed, "When matters of race are located and called attention to in American literature [and art], critical response has tended to be on the order of a humanistic nostrum—or a dismissal mandated by the label 'political.' Excising the political from the life of the mind is a sacrifice that has proven costly."[11]

However, the work of these artists was accompanied by a number of broader theoretical positions. One such position could be found in the work of the Martinican psychiatrist Frantz Fanon, whose book *Black Skin, White Masks* sought to unravel the power of the racial asylum over its inhabitants and administrators.

I want to think through some of the implications of race and madness in connection with the important work Fanon did in the asylum in Blida, Algeria, during the colonial war there in the 1950s. Early in his career Fanon had grasped the link between racism and madness. Similar metaphors used to describe Pinel's historic deincarceration of the insane have been applied to Fanon's work in Blida. In Algeria, Fanon wanted to demonstrate through the case study of asylum inmates interned in colonial jails that racism literally drives the subject insane. In order to offer the inmates effective therapy, he, like Pinel, had to release them from the chain of inferiority imposed by colonial racism.[12]

Fanon's work, then, was a double therapy, dealing with literal madness and colonial racism. Lorna Simpson's interrogation of race in her work has consistently attempted to unravel the underlying madness of the same: the racial sublime, a combination of desire and repression. The racial sublime operates on the prodigious multiplication of social signifiers along with the phantom forms of subjection in everyday life in America. No wonder Cindy Sherman suppressed an early work in which she developed a number of female characters in blackface, adding to the archive. In this series of untitled photographic impersonations produced in 1976, she projected the romance of race back into the scrim of the racial sublime.

But in Simpson's work we will notice that the selfsame racial sublime was not only a romance but was accompanied by the episteme of violence to the black body, which is doubly violent to the black woman's body and psyche. Therein lies the undercurrent that lurks in many of Simpson's images. While the theoretical basis of the intersection of race and gender in Simpson's work is soundly grounded in the broader project of feminism, as her project doubtless is, it still does not obscure the basic premise argued by many African American feminists, such as Michele Wallace and bell hooks, that mainstream feminism has been quite blind to the violence of the racial sublime.[13] Within this terrain Simpson's work has introduced a fundamental dialectic, namely, the relationship between plenitude and negation. The privileging of the black female subject in her photographic projects addresses the question of plenitude, while the insistent refusal of the face of the woman alludes to her negation by the culture at large. In fact, much of Simpson's work proceeds from the establishment of this crucial disjuncture.

The Negation of Portraiture

In all of Simpson's attempts at interrogating forms of hysteria that surround the racial sublime, what the viewer is confronted with time and again is the paradoxical denial of the facade of the stereotypical victim (woman and black, black and woman). That is to say, the superficial characterization via portraiture of the face on which could be read the inscription of racial, gendered, and sexual violence. By denying this access, Simpson reworks the ethical paradigm of the documentary, critically questioning the maudlin sentimentality introduced in early photography of the face as a window into the soul of a subject. The face has been a cheap trick in photography, wherein shallow psychological and morality tales become conventions for reading deep character into nothing but a mask. Proponents of this trick want us to believe in the oracular certainty of the mask, as if a more penetrating insight can be gleaned from the gaze of the subject. By having her models face away from the camera, cropping off the head, and screening the faces, Simpson was constantly performing surgeries and excisions, cutting away the skin of resemblance. In so doing, she was able to abolish the facade and the distraction of the gaze. To address this conundrum she has invented her own countersystem of knowledge that plays on the linguistic nature of everyday speech: tongue twisters, pantomimes, riddles, and puns. The locution is richly American. It is self-knowing and self-effacing speech, an exchange of tongues to fit into areas the gaze may not reach.

For example, in *Twenty Questions (A Sampler)* Simpson uses the nineteenth-century circular device of portraiture to negate the portrait of the subject and thereby deny and eradicate the insolence of the gaze. The subject's face and gaze do not encounter the viewer's. Yet Simpson goes ahead to lead us into the trap, inviting us to make judgments of her character, to cast aspersions, to damn with an epithet, indicate delight, or register horror in the clear rendering of five questions, each related to the will to define who this subject is. The questions run thus: "IS SHE AS PRETTY AS A PICTURE," "OR CLEAR AS CRYSTAL," "OR PURE AS A LILY," "OR BLACK AS COAL," "OR SHARP AS A RAZOR." It is an effective ruse: four identical images of a reversed portrait bust featuring a woman's back, her features obscured and masked by a shock of lush pomaded hair (hair plays a crucial role in the work) that runs down to and conceals her neck, revealing only the naked vulnerable flesh around the shoulder, down to the upper reaches of the back, which is covered by a simple calico chemise.

It is a clinical image, undifferentiated like a police lineup photograph, elements of which she has appropriated from Alphonse Bertillon's infamous machine. As we know, the lineup is an agent of identification and misidentification. Simpson has used and tweaked it, so that the self-repeating image calls on the viewer to decipher the characterological zone into which to confine the subject. Didi-Huberman calls this the "legend of identity and its protocol."[14] The constant use of the lineup by Simpson feeds this legend, yet it assumes an entirely different protocol by the sheer obduracy of the subject's refusal to declare an identity, to reveal herself before the iron law of the legend's damning gaze. This is the function of the negated portrait, to open us up to the original sin fundamental to the miasma of racial hysteria.

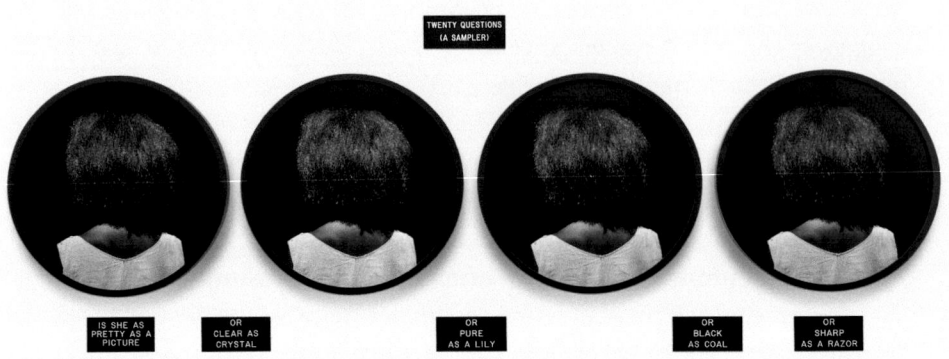

14.3 Lorna Simpson, *Twenty Questions
(a Sampler),* 1986. Four silver gelatin prints,
six engraved plastic plaques, overall
83.8×264.8×1 cm, each framed print 61 cm
diameter × 1 cm. Top plaque 10×25.4×0.3 cm,
five bottom plaques 10.2×20.3×0.2 cm.
© Lorna Simpson. Courtesy of the artist
and Hauser and Wirth, New York.

The Hypocritical Gaze

The gaze is unforgiving. It operates below the surface and under the skin,
even more so with all the scopic devices that clatter around all contemporary
existence. From airport scanning machines, MRI scanners, and Doppler tests
to conventional cameras, these instruments magnify the gaze, leading it
into the deepest recesses of the body. *Looking Devices* (1996), a grid of photographs documenting various examples of binoculars, is a commentary by
Simpson on the prosthetic attachments of the gaze. In this instance, the key

issue for her was the subject of voyeurism. However, today the machines of voyeurism have proliferated. These numbing instruments that suffuse life and in a flash of shattering immobility fix the subject or body into a classification system, into a zone of knowledge, tabulated in a ledger of all-encompassing visibility, have become what must be overcome for us to have bodies. Didi-Huberman might have declared such a system hypocritical, by which one may point to the hypocrisy of the photographic apparatus. Here "it is hypocrisy as method, a ruse of theatrical reason as it presumes to invent truth."[15]

Perhaps the claim that the camera is an instrument of cogito bears examining. To get around the apparent contradiction of such a statement in response to the hypocrisy of the apparatus, it should be added that the camera is equally a blunt instrument. It is the latter understanding, one suspects, that led to Simpson's rethinking of the documentary method by seeking to detach the camera from the body. Which asks the questions: By what method, then, does the camera know the truth of the body? In what way is it an instrument of cogito? In part, Simpson's work has been about resolving this contradiction. By nominating the photographic apparatus as both agent and double agent. By forcing the camera to betray its clandestine undermining of the body, while making it serve the task of inventing an entirely different subjective protocol by theatricalizing the body through the selfsame camera. *Wigs*, a large-scale series of fifty individual photographs of wigs printed on felt, exemplifies the theatricalized body, albeit its surrogate form, disciplined within the grid of scientific rationality. But *Wigs*, despite its impressiveness, is in many ways a transitional work, developed at a point at which Simpson was beginning to erase the trace of the body entirely from her work; suppressing even the corporeal parts on which the marks of gender and race had been bound. Here the absent portrait is being dispersed, broken down into surrogate parts.

Weird Synesthesia: The Speaking Organ and Prophecy

But let us hold on a while longer to the negative dialectic of the portrait—understood from the perspective of the hypocritical instrument—and enumerate other ways it furnished Simpson with her ordnance of philosophical arguments. We know that the details of this argument were established in the postdocumentary images. But the earliest account of it in the refusal of the Muslim Moroccan women was purely serendipitous. Since then, for Simpson, portraiture has served the function of refusal and dissidence, like the Muslim Moroccan women a decade earlier who, though they did not turn away, yet denied Simpson full access to their portraits. Whatever the lessons learned from that earlier encounter, it was properly absorbed, perhaps unconsciously, into the later work. The subject is never fully visible. There is never eye contact. Nor invitation to intimacy. Nor familiarity. It is not a question of the decorum of portrayal or resemblance: the target is the limits of photographic depiction and representation, vision and visibility. The more to underline the hypocrisy of the camera as it presumes to invent truth. The linguistic association is nothing more than the opportunity for Simpson to rubbish the presumption. But it is much more than that, for that would be too easy. In fact, the linguistic connotations unmask the violence inherent in racial hysteria. As such, *Twenty Questions (A Sampler)* manifests an attempt to render the symptom of the hysteria, which is not at all dependent on mere representation but rather is linked to mental images burned into the cerebral cortex.

In 1989 Simpson produced a series of photographs in which she introduced images that may be seen as complete portraits in that the faces are neither turned away nor cropped out of the frame. These images were not a complete concession to portraiture or resemblance; rather, they are informed by the underlying assumption of the insufficiency of visuality alone to explain phenomena. In this case, which is partly experimental, Simpson appears to want to invest the gaze with a new kind of capacity: the capacity of speech. In the portraits that ensued from this experiment, text has been overlaid on the faces, partially obscuring the full identity of the subjects. In *Sounds Like* (1988), *Proof Reading* (1989), and *Easy for Who to Say* (1989), the obliterated eyes or faces are covered by either a single word related to subjectivity or letters related to sentence structures, becoming the speaking gaze. Here the eye/gaze may not be allied with vision, but it certainly is with prophecy. It is literally a speaking organ in a form of weird synesthesia.

In *Easy for Who to Say*, five identically formatted Polaroid photographs are presented in a repeating horizontal line. But we do not see the faces that bear the portraits, since they are not vehicles of recognition. It is already quite clear that these enigmatic images are not portrayals but ciphers. For where the eyes/gaze would have been, Simpson has superimposed five vowels, each representing a word: for example, A = Amnesia; E = Error; I = Indifference; O = Omission; U = Uncivil. In *Sounds Like*, the Polaroid portrait shows a model wearing a white blindfold across her eyes with the lettering

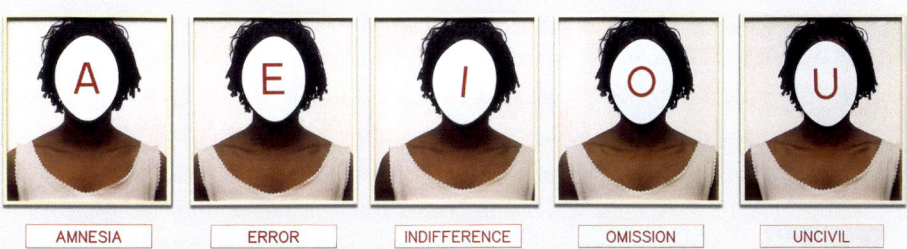

14.4 Lorna Simpson, *Easy for Who to Say*, 1989. Five dye diffusion color Polaroid prints, ten engraved plastic plaques, overall 279.4×72 cm, each framed print 50.8×61 cm. © Lorna Simpson. Courtesy of the artist and Hauser and Wirth, New York.

I-WIT-NESS etched across where the gaze would have been. The work performs the task of bearing witness and inscribes subjectivity simultaneously. Like in *Easy for Who to Say*, each letter and the associated word take on the charge of delineating a mnemonic game; a disturbance perhaps in the experience of the subject. *Proof Reading* similarly engenders associations with ophthalmologic examination. All three works are principally concerned with methods of disclosure whereby the structure of memory is conjoined with the capacity to see, to visualize, and to be visible: to be believed, issues already anticipated in *Waterbearer* (1986).

The degree to which Simpson refuses full disclosure of her photographic subjects' faces is part of her attempt to limit the connotation of autobiography. It is also a denial of the anxious, stereotypical victim, that is to say, the superficial rendering, via portraiture, of the face of the black woman as victim on which could easily be deciphered the inscription of racial violence or sassiness. This matter is adjudicated in *Untitled (2Necklines)* (1989) and *Stereo Styles* (1988). What is in a face if not, as some would argue, the oracular insight gleaned from the gaze of the subject? But with the eyes bound by the glaucoma of nonsight, words become the manner of prophecy. The countermeasure against the hypocrisy of sight.

I suggested earlier that negation is pivotal to Simpson's use of the portrait. To understand the way the liminal figures who inhabit her photographic tables function in relation to representation, we would do well to linger on the nature and status of the photographic portrait: between the portrayed and the depicted, the represented and the documented, the visible and the invisible, the inchoate and the overdetermined. From very early on, the figures appear to have been assigned a rather standard set of outfits befitting their roles as stand-ins for a generic racial and gendered self. The plain smocks, the unadorned studio settings scrubbed of every detail, almost as if the studio were an isolation chamber in an institution. Because the figures are almost always black women, they represent a kind of every black woman. They have no names. No faces. No identity except their biology. But they are made alive to us via their symptoms. Didi-Huberman's keen insight into the work of [Jean-Martin] Charcot and his treatment of hysterics at the Salpêtrière Hospital in Paris is apt in exploring what Simpson is concerned with: "[the symptom of race] . . . in its ever-renewed reification of bodies, in the maintenance and mastery, and even *jouissance*. . . . In this way it fomented a perverse relation . . . constantly asking [itself], in a certain way, the ultimate perverse question: 'Of what corporeal substance is a woman made?' . . . Confronted with this quest, the hysterical body consented to an indefinite reiteration of symptoms, shreds of responses, a maddening reiteration. For a perverse authority, it was titillating. Iconographable."[16]

But is the body of a woman, much less that of a black woman, so easily procured by the machine of iconographic reification? Sherman approaches this question in one way in her send-up of the conventional female stereotypes merchandised in Hollywood cinema, or turns them into tools of historical struggle in the Renaissance portrait styles she pilfered to serve her ends. Simpson approaches it differently. Because she eschews pure portrayal, she arrives at portraiture by way of negation, canceling out the visage; suppressing and obscuring the identity of the sitter. In this way her images resemble no one. The portraits are resemblances of a general kind that are bound up in the limits of race and gender. In these quintessential antiportraits, one is raced and sexed: black and woman.

Indifference: On Not Being Proper Subjects

Because Simpson rarely divulges the full identity of her sitters, the portraits she composes stand not just for a general figuration; they stand for an abiding American Africanism. The models in the photographs are never proper subjects. They are shadow figures, specters, archetypes of the American racial sublime. Here the model is thoroughly dissociated and turned into a figure of indifference. Gilles Deleuze's opening sentence in the first chapter of his *Difference and Repetition* speaks directly to Simpson's method, insofar as the indifference to portraiture is concerned. He writes, "Indifference has two aspects: the undifferentiated abyss, the black nothingness, the indeterminate animal in which everything is dissolved—but also the white nothingness, the once more calm surface upon which float unconnected determinations, like scattered members: a head without a neck, an arm without a shoulder, eyes without brows."[17]

It is quite clear that throughout the construction of the works the artist has been carefully gesturing toward that plenitude that marks the position of the black figure in the American imagination. The black figure is abundant with meaning and has filled to the brim the corpulent estate of the country's artistic legacy. The black figure is a monstrous body: at once threatening and benign, capable of the most horrific actions yet essentially a child. In the carefully chosen texts that accompany the photographs, it is quite clear that the figures we see are struggling to exceed their limits. It is also clear that these are troubled bodies, excessive bodies, subjugated and unmanumitted bodies.

Here we return to the principle of negation, for the Africanist presence is essentially a vehicle of negation and negativity. There is never a surplus that accrues to that figure. It is a disfigured subject, marked by indifference, that suffers the malediction that racism produces; confined in "the undifferentiated abyss, the black nothingness, the indeterminate animal in which everything is dissolved." It is in this sense that Simpson's approach to portraiture opens up the unresolved role of the black figure in a generally racialized society that is steeped and invested in the production of indifference.

Voice and Mime

Much of Simpson's work imbricates language, speech, and text. Language is employed like a lever to pry open the lid of the unconscious. Here text plays a subsidiary role. However, when it approximates speech, it functions like a memory trigger in relation to a visual cue. The text panels also confront the viewer with a fundamental contradiction between the sense of vision and voice as separate forms of knowing: between seeing and speaking. If we are to reconcile this contradiction, then much of Simpson's work is not simply annexed to the text/image relationship, it is fundamentally audiovisual.

Repetition and Differentiation

In *Five Day Forecast* (1988), for example, Simpson deploys a staccato device, a kind of mechanistic action of repetition and differentiation. One feels as if doused with a shower of recriminations. Arranged like a weekday diary— from Monday to Friday—five nearly identical photographs of female figures with arms folded tightly across the body, just below the breast, form a single horizontal line facing the viewer. Above each image, the day of the week is correlated with two words running beneath each image, forming a total of ten such words. A word is repeated and immediately differentiated to signal the shift to a different register of meaning. For instance, we shift from mis-description to misinformation to misidentify, misgauge, and misconstrue. In each case, *mis* is repeated and comes to stand almost like an object. Each repetition functions like a mark of emphasis, ballast for the point of differentiation that announces yet another set of clues. Here, as with the case of portraiture, an object of negation is introduced to indicate the status of the subject's relationship to the narrative. It is a sonic recall attached to a linguistic sign. Language not only involves the voice, it is lashed to the ear. Here the aural landscape and sonic texture of the voice combine to propose the nonconcordance of the figure which constantly slips out of recognition, which falls back into the void, down the abyss.

Memory Knots (1989) and *Guarded Conditions* (1989) are similarly struc-tured, each adopting the same principle: the former is organized by the logic of a journal (a similar arrangement is deployed in *1978-1988* [1990]), the latter like a flowchart of symptoms. Both distill and elucidate in clear terms the chief historical argument—race and gender, memory and amnesia—that runs through much of Simpson's work. *Guarded Conditions* is monumental, slightly larger than human scale. Simpson uses the iconography of the police lineup to high effect in the pose of the model, a big-boned black woman clothed in the signature unadorned white, hospital-issue wrinkled gown, standing with both arms folded behind her back. There are six images in all, comprising a total of eighteen individual prints. Though the arrangement of the images may indicate they are repeated, they are in fact not exactly the same picture all the time, as if mimicking chronometric photography. Above the images, a large sign like an advertising shingle is hung, and beneath runs a band of fevered verbs—skin attacks, sex attacks—repeated like a mantra. But in this case it is more an urgent act of repetition and differentiation than pure denotation. The repetition and differentiation of sex and skin attacks—the inferno of the subject—serve to conjunct the horizon of race and gender discourse as an attack and stain on the subject.

Grain of the Voice

Does the text sponsor the image or vice versa? Is the image part of an imaginary domain, one that has lapsed to the rear of recognition and must now be coaxed back with words? These questions bear on the proper understanding of the artist's enterprise. Simpson's facility with language is not merely technical. It is not part of the compositional technique of a writing course. It is located in discourse, and this is what makes her lines bristle with such authority. The rigor and discipline of her lines are not unlike that pursued in the poet's ardor to stage in language the materiality of speech. The grating sound of words translating terrible deeds against identity; the grain of the voice communicating the infamy of the body. The cadence of the voice (and its voicing), the staccato and cool precision of delivery, makes impossible the eradication of a single line or word. What the reader/viewer experiences is the climax of a radical tension, the meaning of each line, the acerbic brevity of a compositional rigor that recuperates the dispersed subject, that brings her back to historical visibility. Here words are laid on the grounds of each figure or on a separate plaque attached next to or affixed between frames or on the image, like slabs of stone on pavement. Like sentinels demanding recognition, each word sitting on the white sheet or etched on a black plastic rectangle becomes an object, a thing in itself, not merely a sign. This is clear in the arrangement between image and discourse in *Three Seated Figures* (1989) or violence in *Double Negative* (1992).

Each of the text panels sublimates the literal denotative conjunct. In *Double Negative*, a stacked vertical panel of four Polaroid photographs consisting of a single image of a braided hairpiece formed into a circle, there is an ungiving solidity to the appearance of each text panel between the images. The four repeated images suggest a noose, while the verticality of the stack gives the impression of the scaffold. Language and image are used to represent the violence of the Jim Crow mob, bringing to mind the image of the lynched body. Consequently, the relationship between text and image

Prints   Signs of Entry   Marks

her story

each time they looked for proof

14.5 Lorna Simpson, *Three Seated Figures*, 1989. Three dye diffusion color Polaroid prints, five engraved plastic plaques, overall 78.7×239.4×3.5 cm, each framed print 62.9×54 ×3.5 cm, three top plaques 8.3×40.6×0.2 cm, two flanking plaques 25.4×27.3×0.2 cm. © Lorna Simpson. Courtesy of the artist and Hauser and Wirth, New York.

in the work is completely different from the way the caption is used to domesticate photography, which always turns the image into an illustration of something rather than a complement to an event.

Intermezzo: Works from the Mid-1990s

I have been interrogating the extent to which Simpson invested her practice with certain features of American Africanism, in the inferno that is the American racial sublime. Throughout this exercise, we saw how the racial sublime invented a veritable asylum out of the plantation. When we entered the asylum, we saw that it was drenched with the deposits of black female trauma that since the early days of slavery attacked and infested the body, producing a toxic stench. Simpson shows how unbearable this stench had become in representation. But by 1994 she had grown weary of stalking this body. She had become exhausted with attempting to lance the boil of American racial agnosia. Though her contemporary Cindy Sherman would persist and go on, ad infinitum, plying the same impersonation tropes, for Simpson gender and race had become intolerable subjects. She was at the end of her tether.

In 1995 she meticulously began scrubbing her images of the iconography of racial and gendered bodies. She turned instead to what could be called the rumor of the body. She turned to innuendo and insinuation because the female body had slipped from the stage to attend to certain carnal rendezvous and assignations, to the pleasures of the body. Simpson's new work in the spring of 1995 suddenly introduced images in the documentary mode that were completely devoid of figures. Instead, there were photographs of real sites: landscape, cityscape, interior and exterior architecture. She was setting the stage, as it were, for what was to come in her films, in which identity of the female kind would be rendered quite visible and play a crucial role in her exploration of the multiplication of feminine roles and identities.

The works that make up her *Public Sex* images are not in any sense entirely new, being as they were extracts from a larger compendium of images Simpson had built up over the years, stretching back to her early beginnings. So while she had abjured images with any referential—documentary—facture, she did not entirely stop photographing scenes of everyday life or events. During trips to other countries or drives around or outside the city, she had continued all the while photographing architecture and landscapes and depositing the images in a growing archive of notebooks, each image carefully annotated with commentary. The *Public Sex* series grew out of these notebooks. They represent a partial return to her beginnings in documentary, except, where a moat had existed between them, she now constructed a bridge to link them: between that past and the present in order to realize an entirely different view. Rather than explicit image/text disjunction, Simpson abstracted the associative content of each image, setting them up as scenes and vignettes of public encounter and enlivening them with short narratives. There is something self-consciously melodramatic about the works, as if she had placed her visual tongue firmly in cheek. She was employing the implements of the detective story by assuming, in some images, the persona of the private eye or a reporter. The combination of images with snippets of dialogue, some of which identify places, is a far cry from the antiseptic institutional spaces of the previous work. These pieces clearly prefigure Simpson's move into film.

The Clock Tower (1995) shows a hulking view of a tower photographed from a distance and placed dead center in the image. The two clocks embedded on the south and east face of the tower are slightly misaligned (one face reads 8:21 and the other 8:24), recalling Félix González-Torres's elegiac *Untitled (Perfect Lovers)* (1987–90), a sculpture of two out-of-sync generic white clocks. *The Clock Tower* follows the trajectory of a conversation overheard—note again the conjunction of audio and visual, the eavesdropper and the voyeur simultaneously—between two people, man and woman, who work in the same office. (The conversation in *The Clock Tower* presages the hilarious series of pas de deux that will emerge in Simpson's first film, *Call Waiting* [1997].) However, in the present conversation, the two lovers are discussing details of their after-work assignation in the tower where the clocks are. Close reading of the text, along with the cadence, inflections, pauses, and descriptive elements of the unfolding drama, reveals Simpson's keen ear for intrigue, her perspicacious observations of the mundaneness of people's lives and desires; their constant pursuit of dangerous thrills and petty gratifications. From the breathy planning for an illicit meeting by two coworkers who obviously relish the edge of danger associated with doing it right there in the office; to the casual racism that the folks in *The Bed* (1995) have to endure as black people lodging in an upscale hotel; or the homoerotic encounter in *The Park* (1995), where the cruising "sociologist" haunts men's public bathrooms in search of sexual fulfillment on the pretext of some unstated research assignment; or feverish sex in a parked car in the imagined silence of the vaulted space in *The Car* (1995), Simpson, like a detective, places us in the center of a psychosexual game and of dream narratives.

Each of the works' prominent scenes designates both an object and a place. The car, bed, rock, park, clock tower, each acquires an enigmatic fetish character. For example, the scene and narrative of *The Staircase* (1998) seem completely drawn from an element in [Sigmund] Freud's essay "Dream-Work," published in *The Interpretation of Dreams*. In the case of "A Modified Staircase Dream," the patient's oedipal fantasy about his mother is played out in a scene in which he dreamed about repeatedly climbing the stairs while accompanied by his mother.[18] A comparable sexual anxiety and enigmatic tension is illuminated in the chilling silence and empty image of the curvilinear staircase, the form of which, along with the ambient chiaroscuro projecting deep into the nave on the left corner of the image, no doubt mimics the folds of a sexual organ. Nevertheless, the object/place relationship transmits the idea of zones into which inner desires, or places of intimate encounters, are displaced. Again one should note the degree to which Simpson has honed her skills of hearing and observation, skills so evidently natural for cinema.

The soft-focus, woolly, inky surfaces and the moody dramatic lighting that washes over the large expanses of the images convey a sense of film noir.[19] However, the noir genre does not, as some have argued, carry over to the films. Rather than cinema, the structure of films like *Call Waiting* and *Interior/Exterior, Full/Empty* (1997) is drawn from television. It is a classic send-up of daytime soap operas. Simpson's *31* (2002) enlarges this framework, only in this case the tracking of the single female character over a period of thirty-one days is much in the mode of "reality television." Yet *31* draws from the structure of the diary, a method already employed in earlier photographic pieces such as *Five Day Forecast* and *Memory Knots*. Nothing is arbitrary in the planning and execution of Simpson's works. Each tableau or mise-en-scène is carefully planned and continuously edited and pared until the work strikes the right psychic balance and visual impact.

What Does a Woman Want?

Freud's famous question remains a fascinating problem in terms of the psychic and corporeal drives that determine female desire. While Freud never found a satisfactory answer to his inquiry, it was more than compensated for in his theory of the castration complex and penis envy, whereby the absent member, the missing part now inhabited by the lacuna of the feminine sex, indicates the struggle between man and woman; the wish and desire of the female to possess a penis.[20] For Freud, perversions of female sexuality arise from the wish to have the male organ, an organ that, having been castrated, has been folded back and now returns as the erogenous clitoris. Freud seems to suggest that the relationship between men and women is fueled by envy or jealousy. Does the woman wish to castrate every man in sight so as to diminish the wish to reattach the absent member? Joan Copjec makes an important point about the difference between jealousy and envy (a frequent trope in film noir that often leads to murder, which then becomes the raison d'être of the film; this is not altogether different from how it is expressed in Simpson's films). Copjec quotes *Crabb's English Synonyms* as defining them thus: "Jealousy fears to lose what it has; envy is pained at seeing another have that which it wants for itself."[21]

What Does the Black Woman Want?

What this suggests is that in Simpson's work the question of gender that is constantly inscribed hinges on this dialectic between envy and jealousy; between absence and fullness, negation and plenitude; between the oedipal and

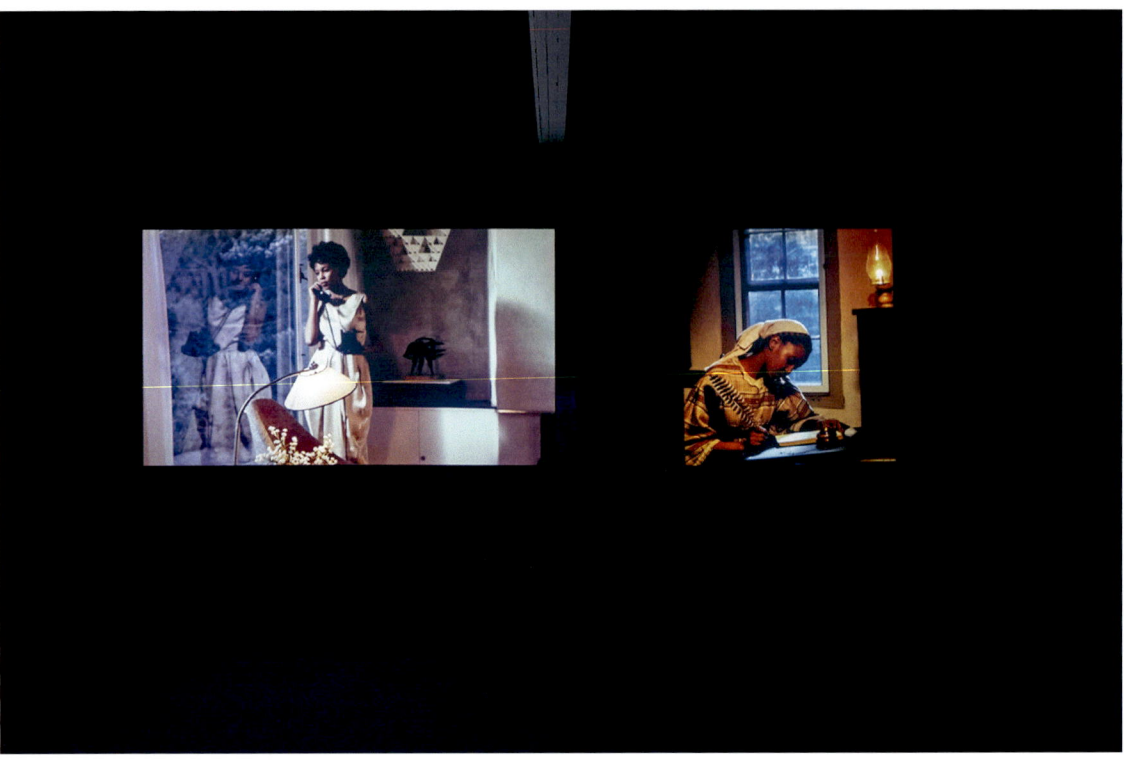

14.6 Lorna Simpson, *Corridor*, 2003. Still from two-channel video installation, color, sound, looped; duration 13:15 min. Installation at Corridor Museum, 2019. © Lorna Simpson. Courtesy of the artist and Hauser and Wirth, New York. Photograph: James Wang.

the castration complexes. *She* (1992), a four-panel, horizontal work showing a sitting woman dressed in a brown suit and buttoned white shirt, implies through the hand gestures in each image that the space of lesbian sexuality has to be included in the dimension of gender that has preoccupied the artist. In the first panel from the left, the sitter lounges laconically with her hands gingerly placed forward on her thighs. The second image that follows is more aggressive; the sitter appears to grasp the crotch (in search of the missing penis?). The third panel is more diffident, as if on finding the member gone, she now wants to cover up her embarrassment, while the fourth and final panel shows her falling back to resignation. If the loss of the penis points toward the development of perversions in the female, as Freud noted, *Suit* (1992), another piece drawn from the same sitting, completes that claim by Freud. But this is questioned by Simpson in the text panel that accompanies the full-length portrait of the woman standing with her right hand on her hip, back turned to the viewer. The text reads:

> AN AVERAGE SIZE
> WOMAN IN AN AVERAGE
> SUIT WITH ILLSUITED
> THOUGHTS

This does specify that the woman's response to sexuality is not passive and can be accompanied by a level of aggressiveness. In *Call Waiting*, Simpson picks up this quarrel again in a series of vignettes showing various characters in a multitude of duplicitous roles, with lovers conversing on the phone, double-crossing and being double-crossed. *Call Waiting* is as much about the search for pleasure and the frustration of desire as it is the locality of the struggle for power between women and men. Simpson positions the woman at the center of this conversation, making her both the protagonist and antagonist in a form of oedipal display of angst between various couples. "What does a woman want?" intones Freud. Fanon recalibrates the question and turns it into "What does the black man want?"[22] It seems we are not yet done with this oedipal quarrel. Fanon is less charitable with the black woman who loves a white man than with the black man who sleeps with a white woman. For him, when the black woman sleeps with the white man, it is a betrayal of the black man, but the black man who sleeps with the white woman is just getting revenge for his castration.[23] With Mayotte Capécia, the black Antillean woman who desires and loves a white man, the weight of an entire discriminatory and misogynist pedagogy, a whole weltanschauung, is brought to bear by Fanon on what he perceives to be her betrayal of the black man.[24] The contradiction is that Fanon ascribes a connotation of inferiority to the black woman's desire, even suggesting that the black woman is the authentic object of the black man's desire. This would mean, then, that the black man is an envious man, whose decapitation fuels his psychosexual frustrations.

Simpson cares not a jot about resolving the problem of the phallus and the way it has weighed negatively on female desire. Neither is she deeply concerned with the pacification of the black male ego. She is most concerned with the fulfillment and enjoyment that black women or women of color (notice that the female characters in *Call Waiting* are either African American or Asian) derive from their sexual empowerment. *Interior/Exterior, Full/Empty*, a seven-channel film shot in black and white, takes up the challenge of elucidating the place of female desire. Filmed in sequences of pairs of women or single female characters engaged in conversation with unseen characters on the phone, each segment of the work makes women—black women—the locus of conversation. The film mediates the absence of the black male from a distance. In the final portion of the sixth segment, two male characters—one black, one Hispanic—appear at the closing of the film and stare directly into the camera, but they are not endowed with speech. They do not speak; their eyes convey through the pantomime of the gaze the incarceration of the male ego. The final segment of the film is shot from a fixed-point perspective against the backdrop of a spring landscape, with a small pond flowing out of a rectangular dam and concrete culvert from which the water is transported serving as the establishing shot. Because the camera stays fixed continually on the landscape, the film takes on the qualities of a stage, a sort of arcadian amphitheater out of which numerous characters—couples—stroll in and out of frame as if in a dream sequence drawn from Akira Kurosawa's great film *Rashomon* (1950), which unfolds as a series of flashbacks. The slow pace of this final wordless segment of *Interior/Exterior, Full/Empty* is as beautifully realized as it is hauntingly ambiguous.

Profile/Profiling

Since the interregnum that marked her shift from photography into film and video, Simpson has maintained a fairly constant interaction between photography and film. Each is used to augment the other, either as an extension of one (stills from films that are stand-alone photographic images) or in the interpretation of the other, or in conjunction. In any case, this has been fairly common practice in recent contemporary art. In 2001 Simpson embarked on a series of small black-and-white portraits shot in profile of single male and female combinations. These portraits are encased in white oval mats and arranged in repeating and alternating directions in an irregular grid formation. Two things are immediately striking in these series of images: the first is the manner in which the figures photographed in profile recall the "racial typologies" of daguerreotypes of African slaves photographed by Louis Agassiz in 1850 in Columbia, South Carolina.[25] Though the profile has a long pictorial history, from Egyptian to Greek and Roman antecedents, and was broadly used for domestic portraiture in eighteenth-century paintings, with the rise of the human sciences in the nineteenth century it was adopted for more pernicious uses as a method for studying and categorizing criminality and racial inferiority. The profile was adapted as a method of study to discern alleged cranial deficiencies and irregularities in the features of criminals or anthropological subjects.[26] Philosopher Giorgio Agamben has engaged these developments in what he describes as the "anthropological machine." In the logic of modern scientific rationality, the anthropological machine "functions by excluding as not (yet) human an already human being from itself, that is, by animalizing the human, by isolating the nonhuman within the human."[27] Profiling thus represents one of the pictorial functions of the anthropological machine. This merged the criminal and racial bodies and brought photography into alliance with anthropometry. For a long spell during the nineteenth century, the reliance on this quack science magnified and extended the capability of the photographic apparatus in shaping the knowledge of "inferior" peoples.

In so doing, the profile portrait plunged from its sentimental perch on the domestic mantel down into the cauldron of the racial and criminal laboratory. Simultaneously, it invented an album of abnormalities and an archive devoted solely to the study of racial types, the multiplication and indiscriminate isolation of the "nonhuman within the human."[28] Between Alphonse Bertillon and Francis Galton—two prominent figures in the usage of anthropometry—the study of the cranial aspects of races and criminals was not only directed toward the biological, each was concerned with their effects on society. This is manifested in their methods and interest in how criminality and race impact the social order. According to Allan Sekula, "Where Bertillon was a compulsive systematizer, Galton was a compulsive quantifier. While Bertillon was concerned primarily with the triumph of social order over social disorder, Galton was concerned primarily with the triumph of established rank over forces of social leveling and decline."[29] Bertillon being French and Galton English, I suppose this indicates the fundamental difference between the composition of French and English class systems. So much for science.

But the science of man in the nineteenth century, especially after the publication of Charles Darwin's *On the Origin of Species* in 1859, was a voracious and insatiable cannibal. Through the anthropological machinery of imperialism, it hunted and consumed in prodigious quantities the body of the other, in order to assure itself that the pseudoscientific interest in racial otherness was not a sublimation of its own carnal abnormality. This brings me to the second point about my understanding of Simpson's idea to use the portrait profile convention, in the contemporary American practice of racial profiling. In these series of works, especially *Men* and *Study* (both 2002), the combination of frontal and profile depictions underscores her intention to alert us to the connection between criminality and race. A similar device exists in Warhol's *America's Most Wanted* (1963).

Simpson's return to the historical exegesis of the black body is by now beyond annotation. It is informed by the constant interruption of aesthetics by ethics. Or rather the knotted relationship between the two, and in light of [Ludwig] Wittgenstein's idea that "ethics and aesthetics are one and the same."[30] Yet it needs stating that the recitation of the travails of the inflamed black body is really beside the point in this work on profiles and profiling. Rather, what Simpson is interested in is the social and cultural devices within which these two subjects are imbricated. The way they each speak to a larger social agenda, whether it be about immigration or terrorism, the uses of profiles and profiling have multiplied.

Shadow Archive

In spite of its contemporary implication or because of it, Simpson addresses contestations that surround racial profiling and the issues they raise by recourse to a Foucauldian archaeology of the history of images of black people drawn from an archive that extends from the 1790s to the 1970s, from historic paintings to Hollywood dramas and blaxploitation films. Inscribed on the framed, demure photographs are the complete or partial titles (employed to magnify both their effect and meaning), drawn from films, paintings, and representations of and by black people, and arranged like a running list of citations or as encyclopedic entries that encode the sophistry of racial science. *Untitled (guess who's coming to dinner)* (2001) is both a title of one work and a subtext for its reading. Interspersed in the frame of this piece are vertical bands of near-identical profile shots of the same young black woman, who is photographed from back to side so as to make prominent by—a slight extension of the neck—the cranial features of her neck and slightly arched back. Arranged facing in and out of the frame, some of the images fill the oval frame or cut off part of the face. In the bottom left and right sides of the photographic panel runs a long vertical list of titles drawn from films and paintings. Whether the viewer remembers the films or paintings is not of interest; instead, what seems to be taking place is the inscription, through the listing of the titles, of a veritable shadow archive, one that is neither explanatory nor expository. Rather, the way the titles open up the space between image and history is epistolary in nature. In this way Simpson remains involved in her extended correspondence with the viewer about the way images signify and what sort of symptoms they point to. *Untitled (guess who's coming to dinner)* addresses the taboo interracial relationship in which Sidney Poitier plays the sensitive, urbane black love interest of a white woman. Needless to say, in the film Poitier has to overcome his blackness through his nonthreatening demeanor (he plays a renowned United Nations doctor) in order to become worthy of his beloved in this romance of race and progressive politics. However, what is ultimately redeemed in the film is neither Poitier's black character nor blackness, but whiteness. These portraits are emotionally loaded and historically acidic even though Simpson adopts the most innocuous form of outmoded imagery to explore the decadent discourse that envelops her subject.

Final Thoughts

I have written elsewhere that the black image is a troubled image; it perturbs the conscience, unsettles the tranquility of settled canons of beauty. Particularly in the museum context, in which the aesthetic authority of art is often arbitrated, the black image is often seen first as an anomaly in the sense that it is foremost a political image before it could ever become a vessel for probing the epistemological fundaments of artistic tradition.[31] A portrait of a black person hanging in a museum is usually disturbing to viewers. Because it has historically resided marginally in the domain of the general imagination, except as a fugitive force—as Toni Morrison clearly shows—this figure is never wholly free of the reflexive assumption that it is outside of the norm of the canons of beauty. Therein lies the great incentive behind Simpson's prodigious complex analysis and usage of the black form in her work. Using a black subject in a work of art is neither a casual act nor innocent. To confer on the black figure an aesthetic and historical value in artistic production is a consciously political act, one that does not in any way diminish the aesthetic value of the intention.

Nothing confirms this more than the manner in which generic blackness has functioned as a trope for negotiating the political and aesthetic in Simpson's work. Ignoring the political conditions of the black subject in art is a self-defeating act of critical bad faith. Along with this, Simpson has shown that the powers of recognition of this figure lie in the attendant compensatory erotic charge it produces. It draws viewers closer, often forcing new modes of recognition and identification. The unremitting monologues on identity and the self, the carefully calibrated discourses on race and gender, the contrapuntal nature of power and social consciousness in her work permit viewers to see the black subject afresh, in modes unfamiliar to their prior experience of it. Simpson asks viewers to engage her subjects not as coincidence but in conjunction with the aesthetic politics of American and Western devalorization of black identity. Her work suggests that politics and aesthetics are formed like Siamese twins. And to extricate their deformed joining requires the most delicate and dexterous surgery. In fact, it requires the complete suspension of belief in the idea that representation has a powerful impact in the formation of opinion about art. The anxiety of castration exhibited constantly by the black male confirms this. We see it in the misogynist acting out that often accompanies his performative public persona in pop culture, especially in sports and hip-hop culture.

The wounded black male figure could after all be recuperated. Simpson permits us to see this in *Cloudscape* (2004), a potent symbol of transcendence and grace. The solitary image of the black male figure whistling and enveloped by fog appears to be a song of departure from the charnel house of the racial sublime. But this does not mean it will disappear completely, since race and masculinity still have social meaning. However, we see that in recent years, the iconographic moorings of Simpson's work are increasingly being cloaked—never concrete nor in full display. Instead, they wear a different sort of covering, a kind of ethical camouflage that does not yield to easy deciphering. For more than twenty-five years Lorna Simpson's work has enriched the archive of American art, investing it with a complexity it has yet to return fully to viewers of contemporary art.

NOTES

Epigraph: Georges Didi-Huberman, *Invention of Hysteria: Charcot and the Photographic Iconography of the Salpêtrière*, trans. Alisa Hartz (Cambridge, MA: MIT Press, 2003), 63.

1   Simpson was twenty when she first exhibited these photographs in New York in 1980 while she was a student at the School of Visual Arts.

2   Edward Said, *Orientalism: Western Conceptions of the Orient* (London: Penguin, 1978). See also Malek Alloula, *The Colonial Harem*, trans. Myrna Godzich and Wlad Godzich (Minneapolis: University of Minnesota Press, 1986).

3   [*Ed. note:* Roy DeCarava and Langston Hughes, *The Sweet Flypaper of Life* (New York: Simon and Schuster, 1955).] In a recent conversation with the author, Simpson cites the seminal influence of this book on her work, particularly the interplay between Langston Hughes's poems and DeCarava's photographs.

4   See Cornell Capa, ed., *The Concerned Photographer* (New York: Grossman, 1968). This classic anthology of documentary photography was the catalog of the exhibition organized by Capa in 1967 at the Riverside Museum. It

introduced another term for documentary work that today may be perceived as tendentious.

5   See Kellie Jones, "(Un)Seen and Overheard: Pictures by Lorna Simpson," in *Lorna Simpson* (London: Phaidon, 2002), 47.

6   The seed of the changes that took place in Simpson's work were already planted in New York before she left for graduate school in San Diego. Simpson's exposure to the work of African American photographers such as Anthony Barboza, who were working experimentally and questioning the uses of photography, supported some of her attempts to formulate a new photographic strategy. At this time, she met Carrie Mae Weems, who had organized a meeting of African American photographers in Just above Midtown, a gallery focused on experimental and "avant-garde" work by black artists. This meeting helped in further clarifying Simpson's own doubts about documentary photography.

7   Ellen Ross, "Conversation: Ellen Ross with Cindy Sherman and Lorna Simpson," *Yard*, no. 1 (Fall 2004): 22.

8   See Thelma Golden, *Black Male: Representations of Masculinity in Contemporary American Art* (New York: Whitney Museum of American Art, 1994). This seminal exhibition and its accompanying book are perhaps the most thorough examination of the fate of the black male subject in visual culture.

9   Valentin-Yves Mudimbe, *The Invention of Africa: Gnosis, Philosophy, and the Order of Knowledge* (Bloomington: Indiana University Press, 1988); Valentin-Yves Mudimbe, *The Idea of Africa: African Systems of Thought* (Bloomington: Indiana University Press, 1994).

10   Toni Morrison, *Playing in the Dark: Whiteness and the Literary Imagination* (New York: Vintage Books, 1992), 6–7.

11   Morrison, *Playing in the Dark*, 12.

12   See Frantz Fanon, *Black Skin, White Masks*, trans. Charles Lam Markham (New York: Grove, 1968). Please consult this work for all references. For additional insight into Fanon's thinking about liberation from colonial racism, see *Wretched of the Earth*, trans. Constance Farrington (New York: Grove, 1968), where Fanon writes, "The truth is that colonialism in its essence was already taking on the aspect of a fertile purveyor for psychiatric hospitals" (249).

13   See Michele Wallace, *Invisibility Blues: From Popular Culture to Theory* (London: Verso, 1990); her reissued classic work *Black Macho and the Myth of the Superwoman* (London: Verso, 1990); and bell hooks, *Ain't I a Woman: Black Women and Feminism* (Boston: South End, 1981).

14   Didi-Huberman, *Invention of Hysteria*, 51.

15   Didi-Huberman, *Invention of Hysteria*, 21.

16 Didi-Huberman, *Invention of Hysteria*, 247.

17 Gilles Deleuze, *Difference and Repetition*, trans. Paul Patton (New York: Columbia University Press, 1994), 28.

18 Sigmund Freud, *The Basic Writings of Sigmund Freud*, ed. and trans. A. A. Brill (New York: Modern Library, 1938), 380.

19 For a discussion of the film noir qualities of this group of works, see Jones, "(Un)Seen and Overheard."

20 Freud, *Basic Writings*, 595.

21 Joan Copjec, *Imagine There's No Woman: Ethics and Sublimation* (Cambridge, MA: MIT Press, 2002), 159.

22 Fanon, "Introduction," in *Black Skin, White Masks*, 2.

23 Fanon, *Black Skin, White Masks*; see the essay "The Man of Color and the White Woman," 63–82.

24 Fanon, *Black Skin, White Masks*; see the essay "The Woman of Color and the White Man," 41–62.

25 Brian Wallis, "Black Bodies, White Science: Louis Agassiz's Slave Daguerreotypes," in *Only Skin Deep: Changing Visions of the American Self*, ed. Coco Fusco and Brian Wallis (New York: International Center of Photography and Harry N. Abrams, 2003), 163–81.

26 See Frank Spencer, "Some Notes on the Attempt to Apply Photography to Anthropometry during the Second Half of the Nineteenth Century," in *Anthropology and Photography, 1860–1920*, ed. Elizabeth Edwards (New Haven, CT: Yale University Press, 1992), 99–107.

27 Giorgio Agamben, *The Open: Man and Animal*, trans. Kevin Attell (Stanford, CA: Stanford University Press, 2004), 37.

28 See Allan Sekula's much-discussed essay "The Body and the Archive," in *The Contest of Meaning: Critical Histories of Photography*, ed. Richard Bolton (Cambridge, MA: MIT Press, 1989), 342–88.

29 Sekula, "Body and the Archive," 364.

30 Ludwig Wittgenstein, *Tractatus Logico-Philosophicus*, quoted in Hal Foster, *Prosthetic Gods* (Cambridge, MA: MIT Press, 2004), 56.

31 See Okwui Enwezor, "Haptic Visions: The Films of Steve McQueen," in *Steve McQueen*, ed. Gerrie van Noord (London: Institute of Contemporary Art in collaboration with the Kunsthalle Zürich, 1999), 37–50.

Snap Judgments

New Positions in Contemporary African Photography

This essay was the major text in the book *Snap Judgments: New Positions in Contemporary African Photography*, co-published by the International Center of Photography, New York, and Steidl Publishers, Göttingen, Germany, in conjunction with the exhibition of the same name shown at the Center from March 10 through May 28, 2006. The exhibition was curated by Okwui Enwezor in his capacity as adjunct curator at the International Center of Photography. Also included was Vanessa Rocco's essay "After *In/Sight*: Ten Years of Exhibiting Contemporary African Photography," which surveyed the impact of Enwezor and Octavio Zaya's 1996 exhibition (see chapter 5).

Part One: The Uses of Afro-Pessimism

TO BEGIN, it is necessary that the reader confront the "idea" of Africa as a substance. But to do so requires us to struggle with a central paradox of this substance, by virtue of the fact that Africa is always perched on a precipice, on the threshold between something and nothingness, between survival and the negativity of life cycles. At the core of our consideration is the unrelentingly grim view of the world Africans occupy. This is the terrain of Afro-pessimism, that impossibility of fathoming another kind of understanding of what Africa stands for in the larger imagination. It could be said without exaggeration that Afro-pessimism is as old as the invention of Africa as the darkest of all places in human history. Afro-pessimism proceeds by first invalidating the historical usefulness of African experience.

This is often based on the belief that "nothing good ever happens in Africa"; that her peoples possess nothing of value for the advancement of humanity. The media is filled with this pernicious objectification. Accompanying this notion are those others that seek to explain Africa's inadequacy. Here, emphasis is placed on the point that the more contact one has with Africa, the better the understanding of the deficiency of its human development index. And therefore, the more obvious the backwardness that plagues the continent and her peoples.[1]

It is always tempting to begin discussions of Africa against this familiar backdrop. Depending on the critic's intellectual disposition, he or she may defend or contest the sins and scandals committed and waged against the continent. As entrenched as Afro-pessimism has been as the dominant way to describe Africa, it has not escaped the careful rebuttal of African intellectuals and artists (following this lead, photography has emerged as fertile ground for this dispute).[2] Some African thinkers take a nuanced and ambivalent position toward the subject, striking a balance between stressing nonessentialism and a critique of problems in African governance.[3] But others may take the tack, like earlier apologists of violence against colonized societies, of justifying the state of things in Africa by completely excoriating her in the harshest, most pitiless terms, as the German philosopher [Georg Wilhelm Friedrich] Hegel, writing in *The Philosophy of History*, famously did at the beginning of the nineteenth century.[4] We all know the caricature and setup: the despotic, corrupt "African Big Man" rules a Potemkin state (a banana republic of some sort), the kind novelist V. S. Naipaul gave us in noxious writings like "The Crocodiles of Yamoussoukro."[5] The British press has recently regaled its readers with the cruel stories of Zimbabwean misanthrope Robert Mugabe and, with no sense of irony, even brought Ian Smith, former racist leader of the now-expired Southern Rhodesia, as expert witness against him.

It is in the nature of the struggle to understand what Africa is and her place among other cultural spaces in history that it excites a lot of passion and sometimes regret. We choose which Africa suits our intentions, or, as it were, inventions.[6] Each of these choices surely will correspond to a "correct" representation. In this way, Africa ceases to exist as a concrete reality. Instead, it becomes phosphorescent like the proverbial will-o'-the-wisp, a dazzling dark ember in the figment of our imaginations.

In thinking about Afro-pessimism and the opaque glass it places on our vision of Africa, we are here primarily concerned with the photographic attributes of its manufacture. Specifically, we are interested in exploring photography's specular and blasphemous enterprise and the visual narratives that drive it, particularly if we are to interrogate the way it shapes images of Africa and uses them to telegraph reports which the global public absorbs as the events of life "over there." Careful consideration of photography's wild hallucinations about "phantom Africa" is not simply about its dimension but also the depth of photographic uses of Afro-pessimism to perpetuate a uniform, fixed, and singular approach to the study of Africa.[7] This approach, given many of its assumptions, tends to offer sweeping impressions whereby spatial and cultural distinctiveness and diversity become one blurry, indistinguishable thing.

Can the photographic event of Afro-pessimism be overcome? And if so, how? To do so, we must look at one major impediment. Most reasonable observers would agree that Africa fares poorly in the lens of the global media industry and the twenty-four-hour news cycle that drives it today. Though the global media is by no means the only agent of this sordid affair, it is infinitely the most saturating. To live in the West is to be intimately acquainted and ruthlessly confronted with the evil eye the media casts on Africa. Africans are turned into specters haunting the photographic imaginary and Western conscience. Entire industries that are dependent on this haunted scene have been sustained by a fiction that has been almost impossible to eradicate. For decades now, the photographic imaginary of Africa has circled the same paradoxical field of representation: either showing us the precarious conditions of life and existence, in which case the African subject always appears at risk, on the margins of life itself, at that intersection where one is forced to negotiate the relationship between man and animal. Or we are confronted with the heartbreaking beauty of its natural world, where man is virtually absent except on the occasion when the landscape is left to the whims of tourists and researchers with dollars and fat grants.

Both Africanists and African scholars have condemned the execrable representations which the media deploy to reduce a landmass ten times the size of Europe into a veritable unknowable. If I, like many others, have become inured to such impressions, it has little to do with wanting to inoculate my sensibility against the depredations that constantly leap at us whenever Africa is, as it were, in the picture. Neither is it apathy toward the African condition, nor the visceral need to shut my cognitive and mental vision against stories of debilitation that accompany much of the reporting. My single and sole reason, after decades of absorbing no other kind of information about the continent, is that these stories are no longer plausible. The disaster-mongering of the media and its concentration on those scenarios (many abstracted from larger and more complex pictures) that make Africa seem less than a nurturing place for any imaginative and fulfilling life stretch credulity. This calls for a kind of counterreporting, one driven by an informed, balanced approach to writing or picturing Africa, which is what the group of artists and photographers in this project are carefully sketching. The works they present do not offer palatable impressions and accounts of Africa; rather, what is important is that they bring to bear on the subject in question a different set of lenses guided by a scrupulous attention to images that form their photographic investigations.

To avoid undue sentimentality, it is important to state that there are reasons for reexamining representations of Africa other than the wish to construct "positive" views and stories. The development of such stories will in itself be a good thing. But that will be the job of an advertising and marketing campaign.[8] The role of intellectuals and artists is another matter. It is their task to provide a different environment for reasonable discourse on Africa and, through such discourse, call into question the prejudicial misrepresentations that characterize the work of thinkers and writers like Hegel, Naipaul, Joseph Conrad, H. Rider Haggard, and many others. The reasons are both ethical and epistemological. To transform the epistemology of Afro-pessimism is to dismantle an entire intellectual edifice and with it a seemingly incorrigible worldview. Ethically, placing the quest for truth above newsworthiness is essential. An ethical commitment to Africa requires the recognition of the complexity of each situation, seeing and writing about what is at hand in any given context as part of a larger world and not merely as a series of disjointed, fragmentary narratives.

An Atlas of Disorder

For more than 150 years, photography has been an intractable ogre in the visual lifeworld of modernity. Photography either sees through the caked layers of life and reality, or it obfuscates them in a relentless production of sentimentality, spectacle, and fragmented rumors of existence. For Roland Barthes, photography's final scenes—often wrought as textures of life and experience—are neither necessarily true nor real, but instead encode a visuality of mythmaking that is today collectivized in the daily consumption of mass media images.[9] In contrast to the first, in which a laborious, studied effect of quasi-scientific observation is applied, the frenzy of mass media photography speaks less to the specificity of the photographic image as a carrier of meaning native to a singular subject, but to a whole eschatology of the industry, what Walter Benjamin called an *image world*.[10] The photographic meaning of Africa is buffeted—perhaps we should say sandwiched—between these two points of view. In Africa, photography has carried the fragmented rumors of existence and mythmaking to another level. In particular, a type of photographic practice has repeatedly staged a veritable phantasmagoria. The manner in which photography frames the African body makes the body appear peculiarly defamiliarized, if not altogether monstrous. To survey these photographic images—in newspapers, on television, in film documentaries and magazines—is to encounter an atlas of disorder. One is immediately struck by the uniformity of the pictorial focus, namely, a resolute commitment to images of entropy. Though such a focus may not perturb most observers of the global photographic industry, the images are clearly at odds with those being made by a large number of African practitioners.[11] Not discounting the censor's black marker, take any number of images published in an African newspaper or magazine and compare them to those that appear in Europe and the United States. The dissonance is striking.

The gap between these two photographic discourses points us to a historical disjunction in the relationship between photography and Africa.[12] This relationship is both rich and troubling. From the earliest recorded history of the photographic encounter, Africa has made for a fascinating and elusive subject, at once strange, intoxicating, carnal, primitive, wild, luminous.[13] At first the desire to record the exotic, mysterious beauty of the black continent may have provided the incentive to invent a kind of sport in which a hunter-like figure wielding congeries of instruments stalks a game-like subject—suspended between an abyss of indeterminacy and plenitude—waiting to be literally captured. This early phase of the photographic sport (dominated by ethnographers, prospectors, speculators, prosecutors of the colonial enterprise) yielded a huge archive of visual tropes about Africa that have persisted in the popular imagination. Today hunter and game remain more or less the same, except that the result has become not only outlandish but also has acquired a quality of myth impossible to dislodge from the real. In this latter phase, Africa has been transformed into a wasteland of the bizarre and outrageous.

No other cultural landscape has had a more problematic association with the photographic medium: its apparatus, various industries, orders of knowledge, and hierarchies of power. As already mentioned, the act of photographing Africa has often been bound up with a certain conflict of vision: between how Africans see their world and how others see that world. In a way, this is a clash of lenses, a struggle to locate and represent Africa by two committed but disparate sensibilities—one intensely absorbed in its social and cultural world, the other passing through it, fleetingly, on one assignment or another. The latter sensibility has come to represent specters that haunt Africa. It is constituted around an accumulation of myths. This photographic sensibility works on assumptions based not so much on what it sees but on a preordained, fragmented, and internalized view of the world Africans seem to occupy. This view feeds a phantom essence and releases it as a ready-made canon of fascination and repulsion. The image of Africa that I am describing, and which has overwhelmed every other pictorial value, has been produced as much from processes of estrangement as from positions of engagement.

A Vampiric Machine

Consider, for example, the work of Peter Beard, the socialite and expatriate American photographer who has spent more than forty years living and photographing in Kenya. What is immediately evident in Beard's work is its utter ambivalence toward Kenyans. His photographic pastiches of wild, Edenic Africa and the cultivated languor of settler lifestyle, published in American fashion magazines and glossy coffee-table books, give us a glimpse into a troubled image machine. Beard's photographs, in which graceful and unpredictable animals and Africans are commingled in a disjointed colonial fantasy, perfectly express the ethos of the vampiric machine and its primitivizing capacities. Beard appears simultaneously close to and distant from his subjects; the sleight of hand that permits this form of visualization is the simple trick of the telescopic lens, a tool of surveillance that enables the photographer to feign a kind of intimacy, even if the real intent is to remain untouched by that artificial proximity. The telescopic lens allows the photographic hunter to act as both ethnographer and surveyor, the more to underscore the cultural distinctions between himself and his subject. This distance is placed at the liminal point of the dichotomy of spatial and temporal relations. It exposes a civilizational gap and at the same time eschews any kind of empathy in social relations. What I am describing here ought to be familiar to us, since it is not at all different from the ideology that supports the geopolitics of North and South relations.

To make sense of the spatial formatting (distance and closeness) and temporal remoteness at the core of Beard's photographic values, one may turn to the rich research that has been initiated in anthropology. In his remarkable book *Time and the Other: How Anthropology Makes Its Object*, Johannes Fabian

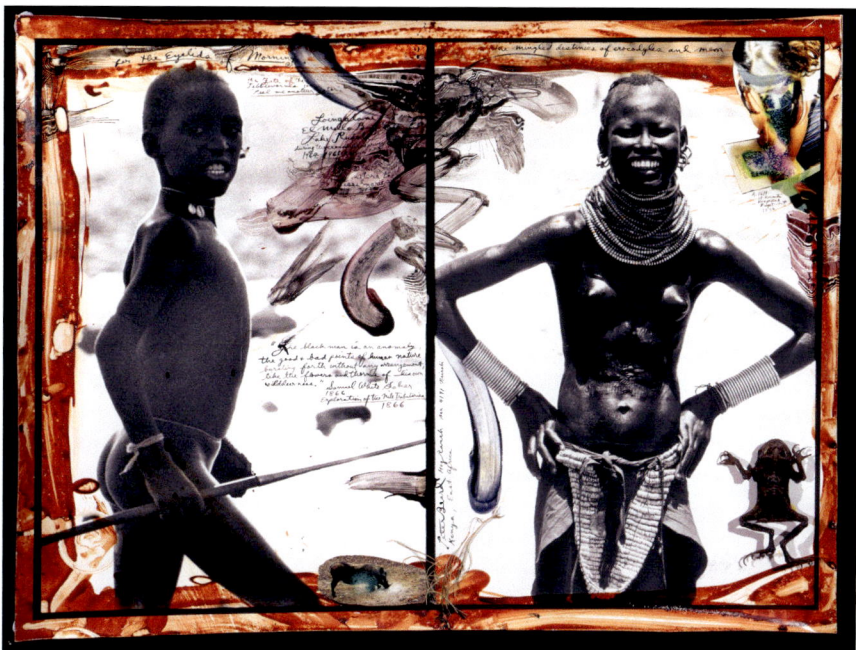

15.1 Peter Beard, *Living Sculptures at Lakeside, Ferguson's Gulf, Lake Rudolf,* for *Eyelids of Morning, the Mingled Destinies of Crocodiles and Men,* 1968. © Estate of Peter Beard. Courtesy of Peter Beard Studio.

explains this phenomenological separation: "When modern anthropology began to *construct* its other in terms of topoi implying distance, difference, and opposition, its intent was above all, but at least also, to construct ordered Space and Time—a cosmos—for Western society to inhabit, rather than 'understanding other cultures.'"[14] According to Fabian, at the root of the separation of Self and Other is the severance of temporal connection, to circumvent and deny coevalness.[15] The denial of coevalness is usually based on the principle that even if the Self and Other share space, they may not share the same time; in other words, there is no intersubjective link between them. This lack offers one explanation for the dichotomy that has been a principal problem in modernity between the idea of the modern and primitive, civilized and savage, developed and underdeveloped, and ultimately Self and Other.

Photography reflexively encodes these orders of civility and lack of civility in its approaches to the Other. Photography, which is an art about time, inverts the structure of time in order to create an unnatural temporality that it does not wish to share or coexist in with the Other. However, Fabian observes, "To recognize Intersubjective Time would seem to preclude any sort of distancing almost by definition. After all, phenomenologists tried to demonstrate with their analyses that social interaction presupposes intersubjectivity, which in turn is inconceivable without assuming that the participants involved are coeval, i.e., share the same time."[16] In Beard's photographs, human qualities of the subjects are placed at the zero degree of recognition, the more to focus on the exotic potentials of both man and animal. What we experience—looking at the pictures—is an anthropological machine at work, in which the qualities of man (the African) are always embedded in the environment of the animal.[17] Beard's photographs thus exemplify the problems of coevalness in the documentation of life and people in Africa by Western photographers. The collages that constitute his primary technique of display play off the contrast between man and animal. The images are usually torn, painted, colored, and pieced together pell-mell to create a dizzying agglomeration of bodies, objects, landscapes, and animals. Consequently, there is never a settled point at which Africa is not photographically coextensive with the carefully organized jumble of images, much like the chaos one is subtly meant to perceive in its social reality. This is the sphere of photographic meaning that must be engaged and cleared away in any project concerned with photography and Africa.

If it has been impossible to write about photography and Africa without drawing attention to the vampiric machine—which has been mostly a history of the Western photographic relationship to Africa—it is partially because this photographic archive and its apparatus have remained largely intact and their capacity for mischief undiminished.[18] The reason is simple: Western photographers have the broadest access to distribution systems and reach far more of the global public because of the Western control of global media and institutions of visual and archival modernity. Consequently, photographic depictions of Africa in the global media are shaped primarily by the subjectivity of Western photographers, many of whom wield a controlling influence over visual meaning.[19] But beyond professionals, what of the amateur photographer on a backpacking trip through Africa? Consider another example: a European tourist comes on a group of women sitting in their stalls in a West African market (say, Mali or Senegal) and, seeing them in their resplendent attire, has an overwhelming desire to photograph them. He politely asks their permission, the women good-naturedly decline, but he persists. The question is, Why would anyone want to photograph people with whom there is mutual estrangement? What would be the nature and final outcome of this transaction? The photographic sport between hunter and game often assumes the features of a low-intensity courtship, blurring the boundary between assent and violation, license and exploitation.

A good part of the research for this project was spent observing such encounters and pondering the meaning of the photographic sport. As the research progressed, a clear fact emerged—the touristic eye has entered a new era of conflict with Africans who no longer enjoy the unsolicited attention of the lens. We can see in this conflict the emergence of new measures toward the eradication of the touristic eye. Yet, at the same time, the invasive aspect of photography needs to be balanced by the common fact of praxis (artistic or otherwise) within which photography is continuously staged in Africa. To get to this story, which is the result of my research, we would still need to account for the mass media industry and the pixilated remainders that make up its photographic archive.

Suffocation of Images

It is a shocking photograph. The tremor it set off on the first viewing remains palpable, a blunt-edged blow to conscience and the humanitarian conceit.[20] Kevin Carter's photograph of an emaciated, exhausted, naked child crouched on the ground—his/her head bowed down like a supplicant—in the dusty, rutted landscape of Sudan is as iconic as it is disturbing. The child is surrounded by an eerie silence, the outlines of a straw bivouac barely visible in the background. The nakedness of the solitary figure is rendered all the starker by two ornaments attached to his/her body: a heavy white bead necklace that weighs down the fragile neck and a white hospital tag—as if marked like a statistic—still intact around the skeletal right wrist. Published on the front page of the *New York Times* on March 26, 1993, this picture accompanied a story of the mass exodus of families driven from their homes by famine and a stubborn drought that engulfed and laid waste to formerly productive farmlands. Carter's photograph is distressing not only because of the suffering it records, but also because it is an image with little meaning.[21]

The photograph is also an emblem, registering how the world links Africa to the precariousness of life: hunger, disease, civil strife, genocidal madness, debt, anomie. It encapsulates and seems to feed an intractable addiction—the fascination with Africa's ostensibly futile struggle to slip the clutches of a perpetual nightmare. The photograph therefore serves

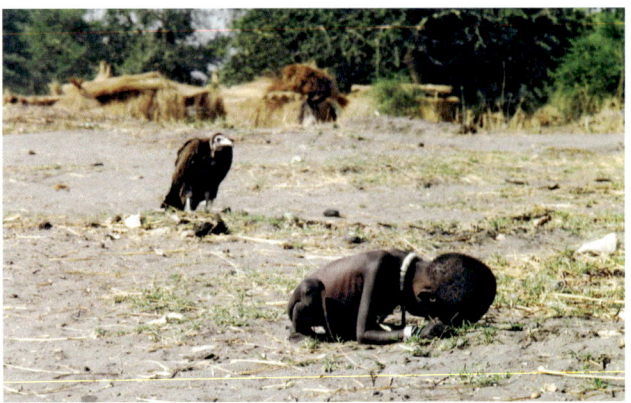

15.2 Kevin Carter, *Famine in Sudan, Vulture Watching Starving Child, 1st March 1993*, 1993. Photograph. © Kevin Carter/Sygma via Getty Images.

the function of a double image: it depicts, on the one hand, the actuality of the child's predicament, his/her utter helplessness and inability to reach the feeding center, and, on the other, the persistent image of Africa as "the land of motionless substance and of the blinding . . . and tragic disorder of creation."[22] This disorder is often organized into a visual spectrum from where the image begins its journey into inscription. One tragic event, such as a famine, is illuminated, and from this a deductive perspective is drawn, a specificity accrues into a generality. An image repertoire is developed. Every photograph of Africa created in this mode repeats the same appropriation of singular scenes as stand-ins for a larger collective scene, turning the practice of photography into a mythology factory. Every image exists under the aegis of a particular typology: there is the grotesque, the despot; the fetid shantytown that is the very picture of disorganized geometry; the dank, frightful hospital scene crowded with patients dying from diseases not yet known to science; the wild, undisturbed beauty of primeval forests full of animals. All of which signify and represent one and the same thing: Africa. A condemnation to be born stoically until the next Live Aid or Live 8, or whatever indignity Bob Geldof and his fellow miracle workers can muster to rattle the tin can of mercy for an unfortunate people and place.

"In a framework in which every word [or image] spoken is spoken in a context of urgency—the urgency of ignorance—it is only possible to take the path from sense to reason in the opposite direction by saturating the words, resorting to an excess . . . provoking a suffocation of images."[23] On the day that Live 8, the follow-up to Live Aid from twenty years earlier, opened in London's Hyde Park, Geldof reenacted that scene of excess via a slide presentation of the 1984 Ethiopian famine. Projected in slow motion across several gigantic screens in the capacious park were photographic images of an emaciated child collapsed like a sack of shredded cloth in the arms of a delirious-looking mother while a dense nest of flies played havoc on the child's gaping mouth. Was that child alive or dead? The answer to that question was the raison d'être of the presentation. Geldof showed us the motion picture of the Samaritan's plot in which are gathered a horde of hollow-eyed people who stare at us with sickening desperation, pleading literally for their lives, to be saved. Then, along with pop singer Madonna, he introduced a ravishing young woman, none other than the dying child seen earlier in the arms of her mother, now healthy and whole, rescued by the nutrient-rich gruel of the humanitarian industry. We were informed that she is studying to become, of all things, an agricultural engineer in her country.

Viewing this media spectacle within the stated reason of the concert, debt relief for African nations, one had the distinct impression of this woman being delivered twice, first from the clutches of starvation and death, then to the thunderous applause of the vast crowd gathered at Hyde Park in a secular crusade in which Sir Bob, in the role of miracle worker, literally brings the dead back to life before our eyes.[24]

Documentary Heroism

Cynicism aside, Live Aid, the original musical charity event, came about because of responses to the harrowing documentary photographs and television footage of the Ethiopian famine. This makes the whole photographic setup of the media in Africa a paradox. On the one hand, it directs our attention to serious deficits around issues of human survival; at the same time, it seems incapable of imagining any other kind of situation outside of despair. Live Aid and its myriad offspring participate in the reproduction of these photographic practices. By all counts, it was a noble act. But it is not insignificant that Geldof returned to global prominence, after a failed career as a "rock star," through the recording and concert he organized for the unfortunate famine victims. That this single event also spawned a profitable career that is part humanitarian theater, part jejune pedantry on behalf of Africa, tells us something about the capacity of images to transform lives. Not least because one can notice in the staging of Live 8 a certain sense of opportunism more than obligation. To connect the photographic misery of the 1984 famine to debt relief plays to the worst excesses of documentary heroism, which was on full display on the screens in the park.[25]

Looking back to the media experience of the Ethiopian famine sheds light on how we should read Carter's photograph of the Sudanese child, whose fate no one knows anything about today. (Perhaps a future concert will inform us whether he/she survived or perished, whether an enterprising white knight made it to the refugee camp in time to smite the agents of apocalypse that perpetually amplify the African dependency complex. For in the morality play in which documentary heroism participates, Africans are always at risk and white Europeans are forever there to deliver them.) It is no ordinary photograph. The skeletal hulk of the abandoned child fills the picture plane, as a corpulent vulture waits patiently in the background. Something beyond pity accompanied the experience of this image. The child came to represent more than a statistic—he/she was, literally, carrion. This devastating starkness tore at and touched the core of our humanitarian impulse. As an African, I felt a combination of shame and anger, disgust and outrage, at that scandal of a picture. And it brought back haunting memories of my own experience nearly forty years earlier in the infernal refugee camps where many Biafran children were abandoned to disease, despair, and death in a brutal civil war. British photographer Don McCullin documented many scenes from the wretched ruins of the Biafran dream of self-determination. Among them are images which essayed the hollow, blank stares of pitiful children reduced to zombies by hunger. Looking at McCullin's images, I count myself lucky to have survived the harrowing experience but also to have escaped from the picturesque capture of the news reporter's autistic lens. These images raise serious issues about the nature of photography, representation, and the ethics of media reporting in Africa. Their proliferation numbs the mind, to the point of glaucoma. We stop seeing the image; the heroism of the photographer becomes paramount. More importantly, I am concerned with the violence such images do to the collective African body. Central to the questions raised by images of calamity, beyond the immediate sorrow of witnessing dreadful scenes of the emptying of African life, is the relationship between photographer and subject. This question loomed large in the reception and discussions of Carter's Sudanese child. What is the photographer's ethical responsibility to the vulnerable subject? Is a living corpse, such as the image of the Sudanese child suggests, capable of being a proper subject? Can photography itself breathe life into this lifeless body in order to win it recognition as to be counted among the living? In short, can Carter's picture confer on this nameless child the status of personhood? These questions are raised here not only in relation to the image but in recognition of a broader debate directed at reaching an equilibrium between pictorial concern and violence in representation.

Problems of Anomie in Documentary Practices

Over the years, the indignant voices of Africans have grown to a crescendo, contesting the negative representations of Africa in the media. Achille Mbembe, who has frequently engaged this subject in great detail, writes about two concerns: "One is the burden of arbitrariness involved in seizing from the world and putting to death what has previously been decreed to be nothing, an empty figure. The other is the way the negated subject deprived of power, pushed even farther away, to the other side, behind the existing world, out of the world, takes on himself or herself the act of his or her own destruction and prolongs his/her own crucifixion."[26]

So, what does it take for the African body to evade participation in the grotesque ceremonies of self-crucifixion, to avoid becoming a humiliated empty figure? Here is a paradox—is it possible to turn away from the kind of wrenching scenes drawn for the global public by Carter et al. of people at risk, in situations of travail and discomfort, marooned in a crepuscular indeterminacy, deprived of both agency and visibility? There are no easy answers. However, to address these questions requires an acknowledgment that pictures of African suffering are preferred by the media; stories in the *New York Times*, for example, never depict Africa or Africans in normal, ordinary situations. Today it is Darfur and Niger, tomorrow it might be the plight of slum dwellers in Nairobi.[27] These are the kinds of stories and pictures that are rewarded, the ones that condemn many a photojournalist to the vicious cycle of media martyrdom and heroism. Carter would win the Pulitzer and other accolades and awards for his "gutsy" photograph, which in turn spurred a fierce debate about the photographer's obligation to his subject. So, what is the responsibility of the image hunter? What we see frequently is the problem of anomie in documentary photography vis-à-vis Africa. For Carter, who was born in South Africa and knew such images firsthand as picture editor of the *Mail and Guardian* in Johannesburg and as a member of the gang of four nicknamed the "Bang Bang Club," a darker emotional ravaging accompanied the making of the kind of images that turned him into a star among the elite corps of disaster and war photographers.[28] The force was centrifugal. Unable to cope with the demands of his simultaneous celebrity and vilification, the fragile photographer was drawn into a psychological maelstrom.[29]

Seeing: Beyond Pathology

In beginning this essay thus, I wanted to force from the outset a recognition of the contradictory forms of photographic practice in Africa. I want us not so much to look away from images such as Carter's—or an eerily similar photograph shot by James Nachtwey in Baidoa, Somalia, of another child abandoned on the roadside, in a similar pose of prostration, his/her feeble wrist marked by a white tag—as to demand from them more answers than the simplistic ones to which we have become accustomed. I want us to direct attention to the multiple ways of representing African life and space, to enunciate forms of visual practice that open us up to the facts that we not only share the same space but also the same time. In other words, I am speaking about visual practices that recognize coevalness, that reach beyond the stock images that have endured until now as the iconography of the "abandoned" continent.

In light of this exhibition inquiry, how might the photographic apparatus—that is, any digital or mechanical duplicating instrument—engage the continent's vast and complex visual world without resorting to the clichéd metaphors of the media's horror index? This inquiry is as much about photography as it is about representation. Wherever and whenever photography engages Africa, it invents a pathology of spectrality and transience. Each pathology in turn invents its own panacea: pity, infantilization, paternalism, or the reanimation of the grotesque. It could be said that photography's greatest accomplishment is the vast encyclopedia of cures that have followed each of its forays into the continent. Whether we are witnessing visual splendor or astounding civil disorder, Live Aid and other charity events will always be on the near horizon to intercede. This exhibition is not about any of that. It is not about disorder. Nor is it about the collapse of civility, nor genocidal wars. It is not a recapitulation of pathologies.

This exhibition is in part devised to ask pertinent questions about the role of images in the public narratives of the African self and spaces within a changing global image ecology. It is not centered on a specific dispute, nor is its critique simplistic. The exhibition comprises discreet, modest, and forceful propositions on how to look at Africa, how artists work with the tool of photography to trace the arc of a different social reality that is both deliberately pictorial and narrative in approach and at the same time questions the historical dependence on narratives of anomie. African artists and photographers are looking at the unfolding drama of contemporary life and experience in Africa with a fine-tuned alertness. They are examining and analyzing the dizzying processes of spatial transformation, massive transition, and social adaptation that make up the varied realities of diverse groups: urban and rural, formal and informal communities. The artists' penetrating insight provides the remarkable story of this project.

Each of the artists has either taken up a problematic or focused attention on social subjects. For instance, a number of artists explore the interstices of urban communities undergoing transformation, while others use very simple mechanisms of portraiture to spotlight the self-expression of individuals portrayed or deploy the artifice of fashion stylization to draw out values of individual identity. Overall, the works assembled here aid us in examining a different context of image making that is as African in its aesthetic intentions as in its ethical concerns. Given the prevailing, antiphotogenic gaze of these artists, the exhibition most certainly denies the viewer the violent spectacle of deprivation and depravity that has constituted the signature visual image of Africa. In fact, the works evidence a subtle yet substantive critique of such images. Not because there is no deprivation or depravity in contemporary Africa, but because the metaphors of violence and poverty cheapen our understanding of the cultural context. The paradox is that images of suffering—which function as a sort of shorthand for neither looking properly nor seeing Africans in normal human terms—do not ameliorate the disasters which they purportedly engage. On the contrary, they have compounded and skewed the photographic imperatives of a mediatized fascination with the continent's "abnormality" as the primal scene of global media's masochist pleasure, its unrelenting horror vacui. This is why quite often what the viewer encounters in the works produced by artists and photographers in this exhibition is a kind of antiphotogenic and antispectacular approach to making images.

Part Two: Contemporary African Art and Globalization

To properly situate the large group of works presented here, one must consider the place of contemporary African art within the global context. Until the early 1990s, contemporary African artists, though not completely unknown, were relatively unfamiliar to the international public. Although African artists had been exhibiting in international venues for the better part of the post–World War II period (for instance, the South African Ernest Mancoba, who was a founding member of the avant-garde group COBRA), many of them remained marginal in the discussions and exhibitions of modern and contemporary art. These were centered in the United States and western

Europe, due partly to the Cold War, and partly to certain forms of cultural nationalism that became prevalent as a consequence of the two ideological blocs.[30] Even so, the United States and western Europe were not the exclusive spaces for the negotiation of contemporary international art.[31] Other accounts emerged during the postwar period, albeit without the same kind of infrastructural support enjoyed by western European and American artists.[32] These other accounts existed either in the shadow of the Euro-American network or were completely peripheral to the art historical machinery that defined the key terms of all advanced art production. Despite this, the political and social changes engendered by national liberation movements and the ideological conditions in the communist bloc profoundly affected various institutions, cultural developments, and sensibilities of postwar artistic practice.[33] As I have argued elsewhere, during the tumultuous years of decolonization, African artists, along with those working in the Global South—Latin America, Asia, Australia—as well as diasporic artists in the West, were laying the groundwork for broader cultural forums which recently have fostered an incipient global artistic discourse.[34] Much of the writing about the development of contemporary art has remained mute about the degree to which the reconfiguration of the institutions of old colonial empires has reshaped the forums of both global politics and art. We are only slowly awakening to this realization, to the sociopolitical and aesthetic dynamics that shaped the art of this period both in the communist bloc and in the Non-Aligned states.[35] The work of artists within these cultural and political spheres was characterized by socio-ideological and nationalist perspectives and has become the focus of new historiographies of mid-twentieth-century modernity that have begun to sketch a more complex topography of contemporary art. Contemporary African art emerged at the juncture of these changes in the international public sphere and civil society and participated in the evolution of what is today the global art circuit.[36]

Nevertheless, until recently it was commonplace in the reception of contemporary African art to assign to its varied and multiple practices an anomalous status within the international mainstream. It seemed that a hardened stance of inattention, coupled with intellectual timidity, would fix the work of African artists in the registers of the functional and kitsch, or authentic and inauthentic.[37] While the work of contemporary African artists has begun to be evaluated and analyzed outside of these registers, much remains to be done.[38] Different perspectives on contemporary African art have informed recent exhibitions across the world, in Africa, Europe, North America, and Japan. These exhibitions have coincided with major adjustments within the field of art history. The training of younger art historians working as specialists outside of the traditional Western focus has played a significant role in reorienting the curatorial and academic analysis of contemporary art and expanded the canon in an entirely new direction.

One reason for these changes is geopolitical in nature. As globalization spreads, it also exposes the fault lines of knowledge circuits that for such a long period remained Eurocentric. As well, important pedagogical and aesthetic issues arise that are not easily resolved by methods of evaluation traditionally used for European and American art. For one, the contexts of the global public sphere and international civil society are today radically different; they have been affected by large-scale shifts in perception and experience. Art and culture are no less affected by the structural, political, economic, cultural, and technological changes that are today driving geopolitical relationships. In the past half century, we have witnessed the critical reorganization of the procedures of art; and the proliferation of the forms, methods, as well as the displays of contemporary art. These changes have occurred in concert with the sweeping rearrangements produced by globalization.[39] By the same token, institutions and audiences of contemporary art have had to constantly renegotiate their relationship to different forms of artistic modernity, and the same for contemporary art's frames of reception.

African artists work at the nexus of these dynamic processes. Like all cultural production across the global stage today, their work is illuminated by the historical conditions which produced modernity and globalization.[40] Even if globalization portends a narrowing of the ethnocentric separation that formed part of the foundation of modern art, we must remain wary of the progressive model of development often ascribed to modernity as an occasion for the encounter with advanced artistic models. We should equally recognize that many aspects of modernity, especially colonialism, oversaw the dismantling and denigration of the artistic canons of colonized societies, and as such bear witness to the disappearance of a vital archive of modern culture. This is the universe where the artistic models of Euro-American modernity and African modernity cross. Contemporary African art emerged out of various national modern art movements that were developed in Africa during colonial and postcolonial periods.[41] These movements shared an awareness of each other's aesthetic and cultural goals.[42] The work of artists in this exhibition to some extent arose from or exists in response to the processes of independent state formation in Africa, along with the political desire to invent national cultures and identities. Contemporary African artists, like their counterparts in Asia, South America, and various diasporas, produce their work in critical dialogue with that of artists in western Europe and North America.[43] In the wake of globalization, their works have taken on greater significance in that they open up avenues to entirely different artistic vocabularies and cultural logics, as well as underline their specific conditions of production. This in turn has produced greater attention to the language and discourse of their varied practices. As such, contemporary African art is by no means homogeneous.

The spotlight on contemporary African art today, though unprecedented, is fully merited.[44] A strong indicator of its status is the degree to which contemporary African artists have been showcased in important international exhibitions, museums, and festivals. Equally, African cities have created institutions and exhibition venues that reflect the expanding public for their work.[45] Individual artists have been subjects of monographic surveys in museums and in important international collections in Africa, the United States, Europe, and Asia. Moreover, the academic study of African art has expanded beyond the traditional scope of historical objects. While these cannot be taken as the main index of success, they do signal the broadening intellectual and public interest in African artists' vital contributions to contemporary art. The public reception and dissemination of works by contemporary African artists; the philosophical, conceptual, formal, and cultural concerns addressed in the works; the epistemological challenges presented in the analysis of and engagement with them, all have further opened up a fertile sphere of research taken up by curators, critics, academics, and museums.

Contemporary African Art and Postcolonialism

It is not surprising, then, that much debate centers on the definition of contemporary African art. What constitutes its field of operation, identity, and language? Historically, the terms for defining the identity of African art have been generated from inside the continent.[46] These attempts have been pursued in a number of directions. One of these focuses on the parameters of cultural encounters between Africa and Europe; here the concerns of artists informed by the experiences of colonization and the reception of modernism in Africa shaped part of the *aesthetic* project of modern and contemporary African art and continue to dominate the perspectives of most Western observers.[47] Another takes up the legacy of colonialism to address the radical prioritization of African aesthetics within the discourses of postcolonialism. This is exemplified by experiments melding African forms with the materials of painterly modernism by artists such as Ben Enwonwu, Uche Okeke, Bruce Onobrakpeya, Twins Seven-Seven (all Nigeria), John N. Muafangejo (Namibia), Ibrahim El-Salahi (Sudan), and Alexander "Skunder" Boghossian (Ethiopia), to name a few prominent examples. These readings of artistic production from the critical vantage of colonialism and postcolonialism respond to the expanded forms and new paradigms of the African artistic sphere: between artist and society, community and self, nation and citizen, culture and politics. Along with this expansion in artistic and cultural priorities, there must also be an acknowledgment of the fact that contemporary African art exists both inside and outside the continent. In fact, it is unreservedly international. This inside/outside dialectic owes much to a broad range of complex postcolonial shifts, especially the increasing participation of diasporic and expatriate African artists located in the heart of European and American art centers.[48] Consequently, the postcolonial dimension of contemporary African art encompasses recognition of the diasporic and international experiences of the artists.[49] The relationship between Africa and the Western metropolis is set in dramatic tension, producing a lively relay of arguments and counterarguments, texts and countertexts, to narrate the differing social temporalities (between modern and contemporary) and cultural perspectives (between African and diasporic) that are reshaping contemporary Africa.

The paths along which African art in the twentieth century has developed are obviously more complex than the episodic sequences articulated above.[50] Nevertheless, they are useful guides in the exploration of the distinct traditions that have contributed to our understanding of the artistic paradigms that fall under the rubric of modern and contemporary art in Africa, both in the specific meanings they generate and the possibilities each offers in clarifying the goals of African artists. However, this can only be a partial view, for it takes little account of the multiplicity of aesthetic systems that exist parallel to modernist and contemporary practices in Africa that are still being negotiated by the public, scholars, and historians.[51] The sequences I have offered are principally concerned with modern and contemporary art as complementary international discourses in which African art and artists have participated in shaping and have played significant roles in their continued expansion. Whatever its identity (a slippery proposition, to say the least), contemporary African art has occurred against the backdrop of historical change. And the quest to define it has been marked both by that change and by resistance to imposing a monolithic interpretation on it.

Postcolonial Cosmopolitanism

To understand contemporary African art's resistance to a monolithic *contextual* framework is to place it at the crux of the postcolonial. It could be argued that a fundamental feature of African art today is its postcolonial identity. This identity is both local and global and has been constructed, since the nineteenth century, chiefly by urban African elites.[52] It is that identity which has called into question any essential, authentic identity that one may want attached to it. Because contemporary African art is varied and sometimes contradicts even the most stable indicators of its means and aesthetic distinctiveness, attempts to circumscribe the art of the continent inevitably run up against its dispersed practices and references, its formal and aesthetic concerns, its conceptual and historical address. The postcolonial paradigm in Africa, more than being a historical and temporal gauge by which to acquaint ourselves with political and social transformation, perhaps indicates something else: the rupture in decolonized subjectivity and how the national cultural discourse that emerged from decolonization continues to plague the conception of a singular cultural identity. In this sense, the postcolonial helps us to arrive at the cultural plurality of the continent and the inherent multiplicity of African identities. These experiences have equally shaped artistic practice. As the artists in this exhibition remind us, postcolonial identities are neither fixed geographically nor limited by ethnicity. They range widely in their geographic locations and geopolitical formations—from continental to diasporic—and are diffused through temporal networks that defy locality and self, community and nation. Whether the artists live and work in Africa or elsewhere, one essential characteristic that unites them is the cosmopolitan nature of each of their localities. I mean *cosmopolitan* in the sense of the worldview of the artists, not in the narrow sense of the urban categories usually deployed to analyze it. As such, the quest for an essential contemporary African art immediately confronts the limit placed on such an essentializing process by the multiplicity of contemporary African discursive formations. The task of *Snap Judgments*, therefore, is a dialectical one. The exhibition is keenly aware of the limitations of place (Africa) as its organizing framework. Yet it enthusiastically deploys it to give substance to the ethical positions from which the artists address their audiences, and also to foreground the multiplicity of identities, discursive formations, and itineraries each artist taps or constructs in his/her quest to map the diffused lines of contemporary global culture.

So far, I have sketched an outline of issues and questions often posed for the public understanding of contemporary African art, which has been in wide international circulation for over forty years.[53] Let us now turn to a specific aesthetic formation within that field. Photography has been a remarkably dynamic, creatively sophisticated, and artistically important component of African visual culture for over a century.[54] But the recognition of African photographers and the unique visual language they have developed has come quite late. Until recently, works of African photographers have not been examined within the history of photography or, for that matter, contemporary African art.[55] For the American public, the first major attempt to do so was *In/Sight: African Photographers, 1940 to the Present*, an exhibition held at the Guggenheim Museum in 1996, for which I was a cocurator.[56] A decade later, I have again taken up the subject of photography, this time in recognition of the fact that it has become a vital tool and source of imagery for many artists. In short, a major medium in contemporary African art. While preparing the present exhibition, I was concerned with one fundamental question, namely, What was the governing rhetoric of the works in *In/Sight*, and how does it differ in the works created in the decade since?

While *In/Sight* clearly established the centrality of photography in African visual culture, the work of the photographers who emerged from it also expanded the general history of the medium. An observer of that earlier exhibition, and many shows that came in its wake, would have noticed the preponderance of portrait photography (so-called studio photography), which encompassed the classic modernist styles seen in the work of Seydou Keïta, Malick Sidibé, Mama Casset, and Cornélius Yao Augustt Azaglo; the conceptual, performative, and self-reflexive photography of Samuel Fosso and Rotimi Fani-Kayode; and the documentary style that has been the hallmark of South African photography.[57]

Today a different approach rules the utilization of photography—and its correlates: video, film, and digital technology—in the practices of African artists. What is clear in this new body of work is that contemporary African artists and photographers have responded to the expansion of photographic media in everyday life in much the same way as artists everywhere else.

Snap Judgments is conceived as a vehicle to investigate the recent trajectories in photographic practice by contemporary African artists and photographers and the analytical judgments and interpretations they bring

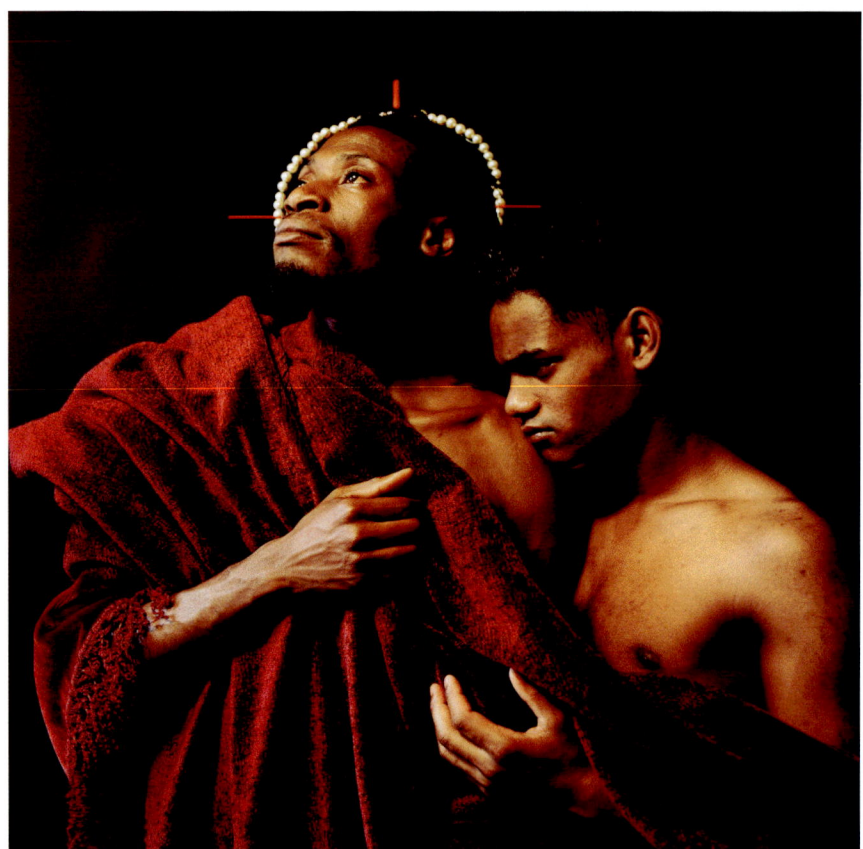

15.3 Rotimi Fani-Kayode, *Every Moment Counts (Ecstatic Antibodies)*, 1989. C-type print on archival paper, 124×124 cm. © Rotimi Fani-Kayode. Courtesy of Autograph, London.

to bear on the conditions and experiences of contemporary Africa. Naturally, there are continuities between the exhibition of a decade ago and the present one, not least because a number of artists in the first once again appear here. But the significant shift highlighted in *Snap Judgments* is the privileging of the investigative, conceptual, and archival potential of the photographic medium. Here photography has been adapted as a probing tool; it is as much a medium of witnessing as it is an analytical one. Consequently, over the past ten years, an analytical, postdocumentary photographic work oriented around the artists' heightened sense of observation has emerged more strongly.

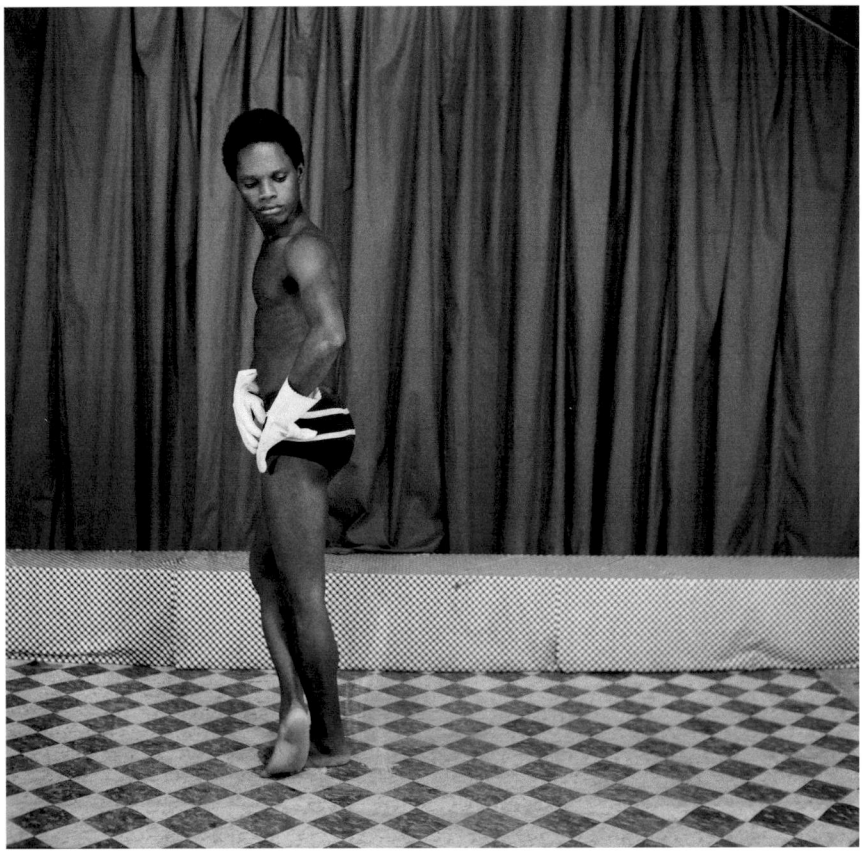

15.4 Samuel Fosso, *Untitled*, from the *70's Lifestyle* series, 1975–78. Gelatin silver print, 100×100 cm. Courtesy of Jean Marc Patras, Paris.

Portraiture, Modernity, and the Dialectical Image

A distinguishing feature of the recent reception of African photographic production is the tendency to elide the boundary between modern and contemporary works. Modern African photography, exemplified by studio portraiture though by no means limited to it, tended to be highly organized formal studies of cultures and individuals in transition. Some of the images are so stylized that they recall court portraits (Keïta), while others are more casual and revel in their very quotidianness (Sidibé). The powerful Senegalese school in Dakar and Saint-Louis (Casset, Meïssa Gaye, Mix Gueye, and others); the work of the Bamako photographers (Keïta, Hamadou Bocoum,

Abdourahmane Sakaly, and Sidibé); the politically charged works of South African photographers (Peter Magubane, Jürgen Schadeberg, David Goldblatt, Santu Mofokeng); the modernism of Sunmi Smart-Cole and J. D. Okhai Ojeikere in Nigeria; the crepuscular images of Ricardo Rangel in Mozambique; Augustt Azaglo's severe identity-card-format portraits in Côte d'Ivoire; and a number of Maghrebian photographers such as Van Leo in Cairo and Armenian-Ethiopian court photographers in Addis Ababa suggest an evolving history of modern photography in Africa.

Most modern African portrait photography constitutes an attempt at straightforward depiction of a social self, more specifically, the African self. In these portraits, beginning in the late nineteenth century, the point of view is always direct and always centered on the subject, unlike colonial photography, which usually imaged the African subject as a specimen of some exotic investigation.[58] To make this distinction between colonial images of Africans and portrayals of Africans by African photographers assists in clearing away the confusion that often attends discussions of modernity in African visual production. Such discussions tend to interpret modernity in Africa as part of the great bequest made by colonialism. This is the case only if one subscribes to the belief that "[European] colonization cohesively binds the diverse, often antagonistic, collective memories of many African cultures."[59] But, in fact, colonial institutions tried to bring these antagonistic memories into a single experience of modernity by "offering and imposing the desirability of its own memory," subtending in the process the desirability of African memory, whereby "[European] colonization promises a vision of progressive enrichment to the colonized."[60]

Whether or not modern African photographers intentionally constituted their work in response to colonial imagery, we must see it in light of their privileging of African memories. The portraits speak to us not just from the dichotomy of colonizer and colonized; they engage us in searching out positions of an African imaginary. At the same time, they reveal African involvement in a rich cultural exchange with more than European modernity, by drawing our attention to the deep roots of Islamic modernity in Africa. Most critics minimize this dialectical relationship between African and other modernities. But we see it very clearly in the portraits of Keïta.[61] We see it as well in the reflexive extension of this dialectic in the contemporary self-portraits of Fosso and later Fani-Kayode and Oladélé Bamgboyé.

In Keïta's images, a controlled, formalist approach to portraiture is often overlaid with allegorical props drawn from different cultural spaces—African, Islamic, European—to further agitate the field of photographic play.

Keïta's work emerged at that moment when the colonial establishment and its various bureaucracies, institutions, and large governmental apparatus disposed toward restricting the subjectivity of Africans through the rules of the *mission civilisatrice* were facing relentless resistance. This resistance aimed at the transformation and rehabilitation of African subjectivity. The thousands of men, women, and children who paraded before Keïta's camera from 1948 to 1962 represent a visual archive of this resistance and transformation. They did so with clear, unvarnished awareness of their grounding as subjects in a social milieu that is African in every sense. They were signaling and projecting their own singularity, as well as enunciating aesthetic values of African beauty previously denied them by the primitivizing apparatus of colonial ethnography. So, to look at Keïta's portraits of the urban inhabitants of Bamako is to witness the near disappearance of colonial subjectivity. Critics tend to view Keïta's subjects and their petit bourgeois attachments to Western fetish objects—cars, bicycles, motorcycles, radios, telephones, pens, among other props that made up the visual environment of his studio— as enacting through the portrait photographs their sense of inclusion in Western (read: colonial) modernity. This reading is incorrect on a number of levels.[62] First, it ignores the privileged standing of an African aesthetic in relation to fashion, stylization, gait, and pose in the representations and self-styling of the sitters.[63] Second, it disregards the exchange between African and Islamic modernity. Finally, never properly addressed is the fact that the privileging of other modes of subjectivity—ideals of beauty, concepts of leisure, the preponderance of non-European fashion—signifies a critique of how colonial subjectivity sought to replace African memories with its own. Beyond all this, and despite the intractable nature of Afro-pessimism, African visual practice has always contested the attenuated views of Africa and its collective memories. Here photography has proven a particularly rich tool in the debate.

Part Three: The Analytical Impulse in Contemporary African Photography

Snap Judgments proposes that the paradigmatic shift from colonial and Western documentary photography in Africa to modern and contemporary African photography is captured in the attempt by African photographers and artists to reestablish the priority of an extant African visual archive. Yet the transformation of the languages of modern and contemporary African photography contains instances of continuity and discontinuity. These are visible

15.5 (*this page*)
Seydou Keïta,
Untitled, 1957–59.
Gelatin silver print,
35.5×25.5 cm. © Sey-
dou Keïta/SKPEAC.
Courtesy of Jean Pi-
gozzi Collection of
African Art, Geneva.

15.6 (*opposite*)
Malick Sidibé,
*Nuit de Noel (Happy
Club)*, 1963/2008.
Gelatin silver print,
92.25×96.52 cm.
© Malick Sidibé.
Courtesy of the artist
and Jack Shainman
Gallery, New York.

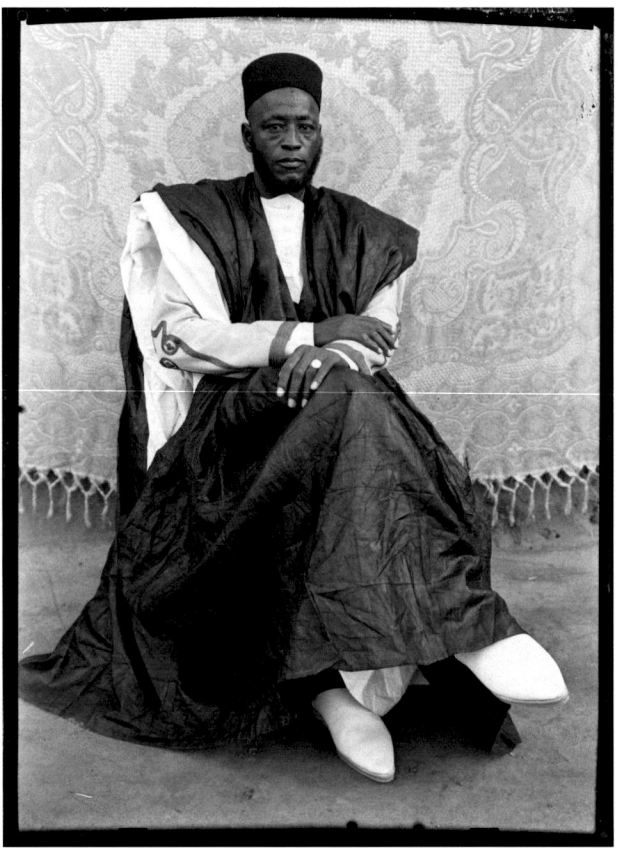

in modern African photography's subtle reinscription of the identity of
the African self, and in contemporary photography's move from depiction
to observation. The shifts I am addressing can be explored in terms of the
dialogue between the dialectical (modern) and analytical (contemporary)
photographic modes of African practitioners. Sidibé's recent work captures
this dynamic most succinctly, in a single corpus.

Though his work is still organized within the system of studio
portraiture—the dialectical structure par excellence—he has recently employed a serial, conceptual aesthetic, particularly in his studies of the eroti-
cism of Malian women. Unlike his documentary work of the 1960s and
1970s, and studio portraits which were mainly commissions, he has shifted
to a sustained analytical mode of looking that previously played little or no
role in his approach to portraiture. Fosso, on the other hand, did not have
to make such a leap in his work, which remains resolutely contemporary.

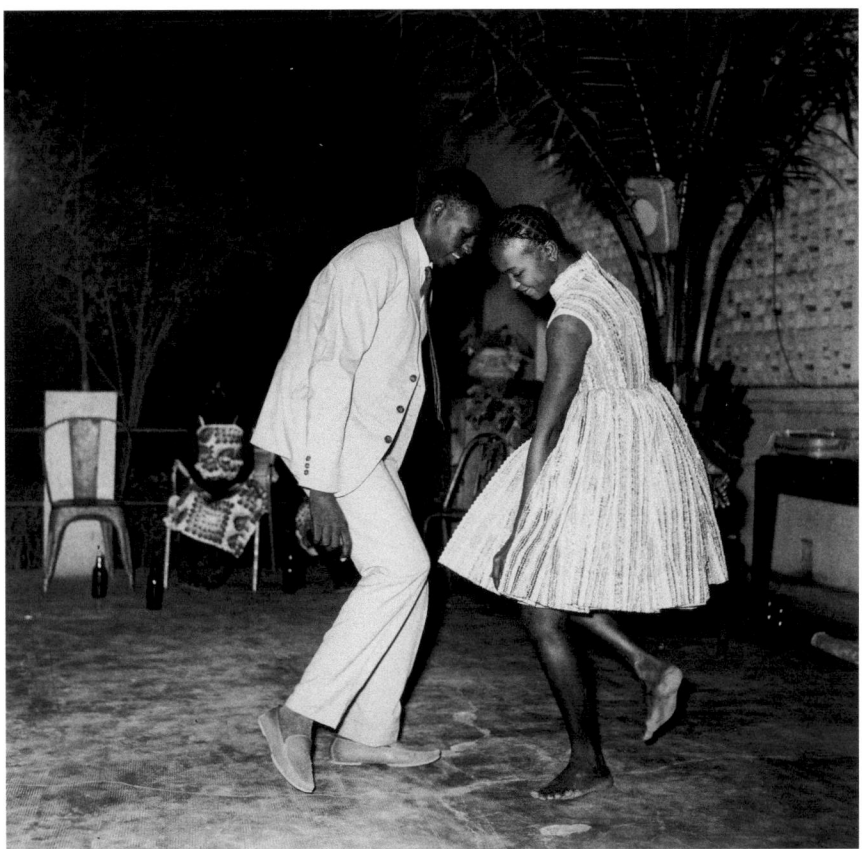

In fact, he has expanded the simple repertoire in which he transformed his studio (after hours) into a performance theater for his self-portraits. His work today involves more complex doppelgangers.

As stated above, recent photography has become increasingly documentary—therefore reflexive—and analytical.[64] And partly because of this change in emphasis, from the individual subject to society at large, it may also appear that contemporary African photography is deliberately antagonistic to the notion that photography should be deployed principally within the register of a purely mnemonic and identity-based function. Another point to be made about younger artists and photographers is that their work deviates radically from Sidibé's, for example, in that they draw exclusively from conceptual approaches common in contemporary art at large. Consequently, the new position the artists adopt engages broader spheres of interest such as landscape, urban studies, performance, portraiture, and documentary, differing from earlier approaches used in African photography. The self-reflexive uses of portraiture in the works of Bamgboyé, Fani-Kayode, Tracey Rose, and Berni Searle extend and reroute more traditional forms to document people's conceptions of themselves and their place in society. Fosso provides the critical conceptual and historical bridge between this self-reflexive mode and earlier paradigms of studio photography, particularly in the way he uses the self-portrait as a tool for examining postcolonial identity. Here photography has been transformed into a discursive method for addressing and questioning issues of gender and sexuality (Fosso, Bamgboyé, Rotimi-Kayode) or race and gender (Rose, Searle) or gender (Angèle Etoundi Essamba).

Antiphotogenic and the Eradication of the Touristic Gaze

Throughout this essay, we have been tracking the apparatus of the photographic sport, stalking its object of fascination and elements of its deformed verisimilitude. In the course of this argument, we have underlined the fact that this large apparatus and its supporting systems of production, distribution, dissemination, and mythology exist as part of the institutions of colonial modernity. We also addressed the degree to which African photographers from the late nineteenth to the latter half of the twentieth century invented a counterimaginary, aiming through the dialectical image to oppose the anthropological machinery of colonial power. The conventions of portraiture these photographers inaugurated—as diverse as the subjects who appear in the photographs—provide the critical basis of a reverse representation. In the wake of these developments emerged a different iconography of the African self, one at odds with that of colonial modernity. Contemporary African photography extends this dialectic. This photography focuses not just on individuals through social representation, but also on social environments, on networks of shared relations and coevalness, on the events of the self, on spatial practices. Some works are both documentary and social. Others are rooted in performance. But they are never predisposed exclusively to ideology, nor do they reproduce pathology. They are fundamentally analytical. One important marker of the various approaches is the antiphotogenic lens that many of the photographers deploy. If the lens of Western photojournalism or nature photography often pictures Africa as a photogenic, exotic, intoxicating bundle of color, nature, and decay, these artists and photographers permit the viewer to see a different kind of image: Africa as a living, dynamic, changing substance. What may appear to the Western lens as photographable may not have the same appeal to a photographer living and working in West Africa.[65]

The challenge to the photogenic lens may pivot on attempts by artists to redirect the roaming lens of the touristic gaze. In short, it seeks nothing less than the eradication of that gaze. Several artists address this question of tourism and the photogenic in a number of subtle and symbolic ways. In *Chambres Maliennes* (2001–2), rather than the bustling colorful city of Bamako, where he lives, Mohamed Camara focuses on the private, intimate spaces of his friends, those spaces which the lens of tourism rarely seeks or can access.

Camara's work is casual. The characteristic banality of his low-tech photographs lends them the quality of a snapshot. The intimacy of the works conveys their authenticity as recordings of daily experience. This may not elevate Camara's central concern—which is about how young people like him live normal lives in Africa—to the media's attention, because there is simply no "story" there. But his images have a complicated emotional immediacy and at the same time appear utterly ambivalent about their own status. On the other hand, if Camara does not photograph his own environment in a touristic manner, he certainly approaches the cultural rituals of Europe the way an African tourist might. In the series of photographs presented in *Snap Judgments*, he seems to have reversed the touristic gaze, aiming it squarely at the rituals of white Christmas through a form of performance employing the kitsch props (lights, snow, etc.) associated with it.

Maha Maamoun—as an artist and as a member of the Contemporary Image Collective in Cairo—has been a careful and critical interrogator of the intersection of tourism and the photogenic in her depiction of the Egyptian urban scene. The *Cairoscapes* series (2001–3) posits the fast-paced flow of the crowd, albeit as isolated and solitary figures. In the elongated horizontal format of the photographs, what is first registered is the sense of the image in motion, of bodies and gestures trapped in a freeze-frame of temporal suspension in which figuration dissolves into floral patterns (some of which may appear to the eye like designs for tablecloths or bedspreads) and the street and traffic float by like blurs and abstractions. These images project a different sensibility of the cacophonic bazaar of the African/Islamic city. Rather than focusing on the ubiquitous crowd, Maamoun's antitouristic pictures construct an imaginary domain "in which relationships between city, figure, and nature . . . converge to suggest a new terrain."[66] Close inspection might infer that they are fictive, but I do not think this is the point. More important is the evident defamiliarization that indicates layers of repression subtly unpeeled and exposed. As benign as these images may appear, there is something about their mild opacity that slightly deranges the mise-en-scène.

To apprehend the touristic imagination, we need to conduct an autopsy on its images, an act which corresponds to Maamoun's reorganized beach scene. As the image suggests, tourism and travel are the establishing shots of a troubled relationship between near and far, familiar and unfamiliar, native and tourist. In the eighteenth century, the Grand Tour (which bequeathed to us the word *tourism*) was an opportunity to broaden the traveler's horizon. Ultimately, it supported a habit of consumption: to seize and possess a slice of the world. Tourism gives the traveler the illusion of worldliness, the fleeting security of cosmopolitanism. But because the touristic imagination is famished and voracious, it feeds a habit and often makes for the manufacture of fraudulent transactions. This is especially the case with contemporary travel in the form of the packaged tour, which promises round-the-clock experience. Invented at the moment when bourgeois consciousness emerged from the development of capitalism, tourism closely follows those changes in modernity that profoundly unsettled social relations between places and peoples. With the proliferation of cameras, the touristic experience has literally expanded into surveillance. Perhaps it is possible to understand why, in so-called exotic places, tourism is a blind spot of photography. The tourist with a camera is today the ultimate figure of derision, especially in the aggressivity of his quest for images. This locates the tension proper to the wild hallucinations common to the touristic consumption of otherness. The camera grants remote access but obliterates knowledge. It deracinates all that it documents. The touristic image can be cached as a souvenir of poor pictorial judgment, because it purports to offer an innocent account of what it did not quite see.

The kind of encounter which this type of tourism implies is at the heart of how certain contemporary images of Africa have been produced and circulated. Theo Eshetu, in his pulsating, color-saturated, and hallucinatory film *Blood Is Not Fresh Water* (1997), began with a return to Ethiopia, the home of his family, to make a video about himself, his father, and his grandfather. The initial trip for this video then turned into the making of another one: *Trip to Mount Zuqualla* (2005). The video is divided into three contiguous images, two of which mirror each other on the flanks of the projection. In the center is a cut, an image different from the mirrored flanks that functions like an anchor and divides the two repeated images on the left and right corners of the projection. This device not only stretches the narrative of the video, it also distorts its spatial and temporal pace. The result is a video that has a dense imaginative visuality and mnemonic richness. Eshetu's video exemplifies the complications that arise at the intersection of diaspora and nation, between home and exile, postcolonial and postnational identities. In his extended meditation on the annual Coptic religious pilgrimage to Mount Zuqualla, we are placed at the center of a conundrum. Is a returning son a native or outsider? Is his lens that of a visitor, a tourist absorbed in the scintillating ornamentation and serene beauty of the landscape, or is he one of the celebrants who have made this journey of faith and memory? Is there a difference between Eshetu's desire to reroot and reroute himself and that of the indigenous population who have no need to be reintegrated into their own memories?[67] If so, how does it reveal this difference? Eshetu's photographic and videographic reverse journey confounds, precisely because it allows us to question the image maker's intent without passing judgment on it. However, what changes the dynamic in Eshetu's "intimate outsider" status in this quasi-ethnographic video is how he implicates himself in the narrative.[68] He is neither distant from the scenes he depicts nor remote from the celebrants: there is a complex entanglement between Eshetu and the subjects which allows us, the viewers, to assume that he has opted for subject status as well. In fact, in the long-format version of the video, this is made explicit in the interactions between Eshetu and his grandfather, and by his constant foregrounding of the notion that while the journey to Mount Zuqualla may be about faith to the celebrants, for him it is also about memory. Recognizing this makes possible a reading of the video and the photographs as critically posttouristic documents.

Passionate Bodies

Despite the initial use of the camera to present the view of the Other's baseness and moral debility, to merge his human traits with those of the non-human, the portrait photograph undermined the clinical and ideological instrumentality that beset photography the moment it touched this body. Portraiture has played a central and significant role in delineating the expressive and representational codes of modern and contemporary African photography, not least because it revealed the disjuncture between African and colonial memories. African photography transformed the instrumentality of the camera and engulfed the anthropological machine in a fiery conflagration. It registered the inscription of a figure that can no longer be subtracted from the human, excluded from the modern, or disfigured as uncivilized. The advent of postcolonialism further revealed the chasm between these memories. Postcolonialism not only rerouted the given discourse of the body politic in colonial Africa, it equally explored the cultural politics of that body after decolonization. In so doing, it illuminated the tension that demarcates cultural identity and self-representation, race and identity, gender and sexuality, masculinity and femininity. The narratives of the body and subjectivity, in the different guises in which they have appeared in recent years, obviate the primitivist codes embedded in ethnographic knowledge. If identity is understood to be underpinned by biology, it is equally underwritten by politics. The imperatives of the two always require negotiation. One can address identity in the works of the artists here by foregrounding the immediacy projected through the body's physical presence and not by some primitivist essence.

As I have been arguing, the photograph initially was a corrosive object when it touched the African body. Postcolonialism opened up another avenue by which we can explore the facts of that body in representation. Let us describe them as passionate bodies; bodies without limits, that are not circumscribed. The procedure of self-mapping in the performance-driven photographs and videos of Doa Aly is a recent example of the critical analysis artists have been pursuing about the self and gender. Aly's elegant thwarting of the body to achieve the supple pose and gesture of the ballet dancer is a rigorous test and reinvention of the docile body. In *48 Ballet Classes* (2005), Aly subjects her body to a slow process of transformation, working with a ballet master to achieve her goal. Each lesson of the progression is recorded, spanning more than a month. Here the camera is a tracking instrument as well as an observant eye. This self-surgery is equally apparent in Bamgboyé's autoerotic performances before the camera. In his photographs, the camera is literally inhabited and used as a drawing tool, creating a palimpsest of forms, objects, body parts, and movement. The densely overlaid images suggest an effect of temporal and spatial derangement, a shifting away from the rationalist view of portraiture as a vehicle of disclosure. Instead, Bamgboyé's dramatic layered photographs are physical objects that project into the viewer's space, splitting the space of encounter between the concrete formation of the studio and the imaginary domain of desire and fantasy. Such series as *Arise* (1991/1997) and *Celebrate* (1994) exploit these possibilities, giving way to both a theoretically complicated representation and an aesthetically powerful set of propositions. In *Arise*, the body as a physical specimen carves out a figurative, sculptural presence, while foregrounding a psychosexual tension that recalls Fani-Kayode's portfolio *Bodies of Experience* (1988).[69]

Tracey Rose, from the very inception of her career, has used photography as a companion to her explorations of identity, race, gender, and sexuality. Rose's allegories of miscegenation, sexual and racial difference, and feminist interrogations of gender are produced as tableaux vivants of that which is both deeply ontological and political in apartheid and post-apartheid culture. Her recent series *Lucie's Fur* (2003–4) is elliptically centered on the Eve-like figure discovered in Ethiopia and christened as the first woman. At the same time, *Lucie's Fur* conflates this figure with that of the archangel Lucifer, "the condemned angel of light" who was expelled from paradise for challenging god. The series draws from and twists biblical and literary narratives and archaeological and scientific research into human origin, the discovery of sexuality, and sexual desire in the Garden of Eden. However, the story of the first man and woman has been modified in this account: rather than Adam and Eve, the couple are two black gay lovers named Adam and Yves, who may have been introduced by Rose as a commentary on homophobia. Filmed and photographed like a movie, in the studio and on location in Johannesburg, this series, by far Rose's most complex and accomplished body of work, enlarges the arena of auto-performance that has long informed her radical production. It draws from a series of surrealist tropes: dream sequences, allegory, the destabilization of the signifier, and the transformation of cultural symbols in order to deform their meaning. These tableaux announce the interplay between relations of gender, origin, religious belief, mythology, and fantasy.

By the same token, the fashion photographic shot, which in a sense represents another order of performance, extends the dialectical form of portraiture explored throughout this essay. Andrew Dosunmu and Nontsikelelo "Lolo" Veleko take different approaches to elucidating the depth of desire which fashion disturbs. Dosunmu's images are primarily shot for fashion magazines. He is interested in the physicality of female sexuality, yet his models are not objects of his projection. In fact, unlike in most fashion photography, Dosunmu keeps fantasy at a minimum, focusing instead on his models not as characters but as subjects. There is a vérité approach in all his work, a kind of fashion documentary that collapses the boundary between the street and the studio. And because he often works on location and uses nonprofessionals as models, Dosunmu's photographs underline the ideological conditions of the fashion system and transform our understanding of it. Veleko, on the other hand, is a scavenger of individuality, a hunter of cool and street fashion. She is entirely interested in individuals and thus scours the streets to find the subjects of the photographic encounter. She is partial to subjects who express themselves through their social camouflage, by what they wear, the manner in which they present themselves to others and to themselves. These subjects are often young, fashion-conscious, urban black South Africans living in Johannesburg. As such, we can read these pictures as both explorations and celebrations of postapartheid identity. In these street portraits, the subjects are approached directly, frontally. Their open stances indicate a sense of ease in relation to the photographer, which might suggest to observers a form of social and ethical transaction between photographer and photographed. This is the nature of the dialectical and analytical image. The subject is never an object already predetermined, a priori, by a discourse.

Time Zones/Ruins of Memory

Contemporary African photography has so far led us to a juncture, to the point of a double negotiation. This is the divide between African and colonial memories. Today these memories return as ruins, as collapsed time zones: mementos of disturbed relations, for colonial subjectivity may never be completely vanquished. Even if decolonization proposed a liberation from colonial subjectivity toward "African modes of self-writing," it was never, in any case, a complete rupture.[70] Artists such as Allan deSouza, Zarina Bhimji, Otobong Nkanga, Fatou Kandé Senghor, Kay Hassan, Moshekwa Langa, and Yto Barrada have drawn from this tension, fashioning works that investigate those disturbed relations. In their individual works, a careful forensic approach searches through the remainders of the colonial and postcolonial past to question the emancipatory philosophy and utopianism of decolonization. Each of their projects in this exhibition takes up an archaeology of institutional, personal, social, and economic space which leads us to the edge of disenchantment and ennui.

Allan deSouza's series *The Lost Pictures* (2004) is a special case in point. The source of these images is the family album, that technological archive which, since the invention of photography, has never ceased confronting us with death, with disappearance, with the apparition of life. The images in *The Lost Pictures* were summoned on such an occasion: the death of the artist's mother. It was as if something that held him tethered to the flimsiest connection had broken, setting him adrift on "a feeling of an undoing, of dislocation in time, in place, as well as memory and imagination."[71] But what led to these feelings, beyond the grief we experience on loss of a close family member? It was the rediscovery of an archive, the family archive.

[Jacques] Derrida, examining [Sigmund] Freud's archive, tells us a story of Freud's receipt of the gift of his lineage when his father gave him a Torah that had previously belonged to Freud's grandfather. The gift had come leather bound: a new binding ordered by his father. It is as if the gift were presented with new skin, an opening toward identity. Derrida writes that the archive as a "science, in its very movement, can only consist in a transformation of the techniques of archivization, of printing, of inscription, of reproduction, of formalization, of ciphering, and of translating marks."[72]

The nine photographs that make up *The Lost Pictures* succinctly represent the procedures in Derrida's description of the archival imperative. The images are worn and eaten around the edges, as if by a biting melancholic fervor. This was achieved by subjecting them first to a slow process of accretion, then decay, erasure, evanescence, and reproduction. DeSouza began by collecting printed images of slides shot by his father in the mid-1960s in Nairobi, Kenya (before the family's emigration to England and the ensuing scattering that drove his mother to Portugal). These consist of pictures of Allan and his siblings, mother, and the entire family in various contexts (on the beach, sidewalk, visiting a railway exhibition). By taping the printed slides on heavily trafficked areas (the bathroom sink, shower, kitchen counter) around his house in Los Angeles, he invested them with the power of both fetish and talisman, even as he deliberately destroyed them, letting the leavings, dust, and acid of daily existence settle on them and wear them away. He lived with the images, literally, drawing from them a kind of sustenance, and at the same time subjecting them to a punishing disregard, as if wrestling with his own past. This past is entangled in a web of mnemonic, geographic, imaginary, and phantasmatic narratives. The images open up deSouza's meditation on the loss of his mother and the rupture of familial bonds and therefore can be understood as an expression of mourning.[73] But this loss, while looming large over the expansive field of the artist's memory, also enunciates his ambivalence toward the idea of a fixed home, of a place in the world that can be returned to physically. In this way, deSouza directs us toward that malady of modern existence: exile, diaspora, dislocation; to the confused itinerary of Indian diasporic communities, from South Asia to East Africa, Europe, and the United States, such has been the trajectory of the deSouza family.

Like deSouza, Zarina Bhimji is a member of the diasporic Indian community of East Africa, many of whom followed colonial trade as migrant labor, arriving on the continent at the end of the nineteenth century. Her family, who settled in Uganda and witnessed the decolonization process and independence in 1962, were expelled from the country along with other Asians by the regime of Idi Amin in 1972.[74] The expulsion marks another juncture in the series of uprootings and displacements that have remained palpable for all contemporary subjects. Again, like deSouza, Bhimji's return to Uganda was precipitated by the death of her father. But unlike him, her intent is not to blunt memory but to rouse it. Interspersing images of architecture, landscape, and objects, the photographs are vivid documentary records—from prison interiors to the ruins of the Entebbe airport—showing the unfinished aspects of her Ugandan past. At the same time, they defy the documentary reflex, for they are neither news nor purely information, made to be viewed as evidence. Embedded deep within the reflective surface of the images is the kind of disturbance that is almost imperceptible to the eye unless it is directed. But if these works are intimately connected to death, are they to be read then as works of mourning?[75] What is the object/subject of mourning: the disappeared world of the Asian community? Or their disconnection from a land, a home? Bhimji's work forces the viewer to interrogate the assumptions of documentary. Her work is located in the interstices of questions concerned with memory and in the archival reproduction of the history connected to that memory. She wants her archaeology of the Ugandan past—which she has been exploring since 1998 through film and photography—to function as historical reckoning, where "history serves the present" because, according to her, "what is not recorded does not exist."[76] The photographs in this exhibition draw from the twin legacies of colonialism and the unfulfilled promise of the postcolonial moment to further animate the photographic discourse of African modernity. Bhimji's intent is one of insistence, to carve into the withered tree a trace of her own account, to inscribe the memory and violence of expulsion, and to recuperate, even if fleetingly, a gesture of homecoming.

In a different register, Zwelethu Mthethwa's magisterial rendition of landscape and the alienation of labor in his sugarcane series (*Untitled*, 2003) strikes a critical balance between portraiture and landscape. It clearly draws from Dutch genre painting, in which everyday life is represented with little heroic fanfare. Despite the seemingly quotidian quality of Mthethwa's portraits, it is obvious that, though the formal style of the work has art historical precedents, it is not about the ordinary life of workers in the field. His take on landscape, portraiture, and social class is reminiscent of Thomas Gainsborough's famous eighteenth-century painting *Mr and Mrs Andrews* (1750), which belongs to a genre known as the *conversation piece*. The painting depicts the Andrews estate with the owners inserted in it. The typical English landscape painting of the eighteenth century was connected to the social representation of aristocracy and the landed gentry. The portraits often included inside the landscape are of a piece not only with the representation but the actuality of their ownership and therefore were expressive of the portrait subjects' social stature. It is important to make this distinction because Mthethwa's portrait of the cane workers inverts the moral codes (work ethic) and the process of identification (social stature) respectively associated with Dutch and English genre painting. On the contrary, his is an interrogation of a political landscape and its supporting economic system; namely, the imbrication of global capitalism in the postapartheid landscape. These men who stare at us like medieval warriors, dressed in the field-worker's garb, holding on to their primitive machetes, appear before us in regal defiance of their solitary fate as alienated labor, trapped in servitude to multinational capitalism. In a more recent series, Mthethwa focused on the mining industry in South Africa. As in previous works, such as the portraits of displaced workers living in "informal settlements" (née shantytowns) and the sugarcane series, Mthethwa, like August Sander, is developing a kind of photographic typology, often placing his subjects in their own surroundings. This approach has less to do with the dramatic spectacle of the ramshackle environments in which his subjects live and more with applying a stringent realism to his pictures. This realism requires a rendering of the subjects in their own environments, not the ones they would have wished for, but the actuality of their circumstances, the dignity of their grounding in their own space. Yet the aim is not to achieve some fictional authenticity. In this sense, the sugarcane series is especially apposite, because in it Mthethwa addresses the very instability of portraiture and identity.

The increased adoption of photography as a mode of working and method of analysis converges at the point where Western documentary and photojournalistic practices have always been dominant. It would appear from research to date that nineteenth-century African photography was initially uninterested in the recording or documentation of the African landscape. This lacuna is surprising. Excepting the work of David Goldblatt, the absence of landscape as a subject of historical and pictorial interest has not been remedied in modern and contemporary art. However, recently a number of artists have taken on the task of reinvesting landscape with a particular sense of urgent and historical sensitivity. In such works, landscape serves as a vehicle for understanding trauma or social alienation. Otobong Nkanga's work is resolutely centered in the postcolonial moment. Her recent ongoing projects *Emptied Remains* (2004–5) and *Things Have Fallen* (2004–5)

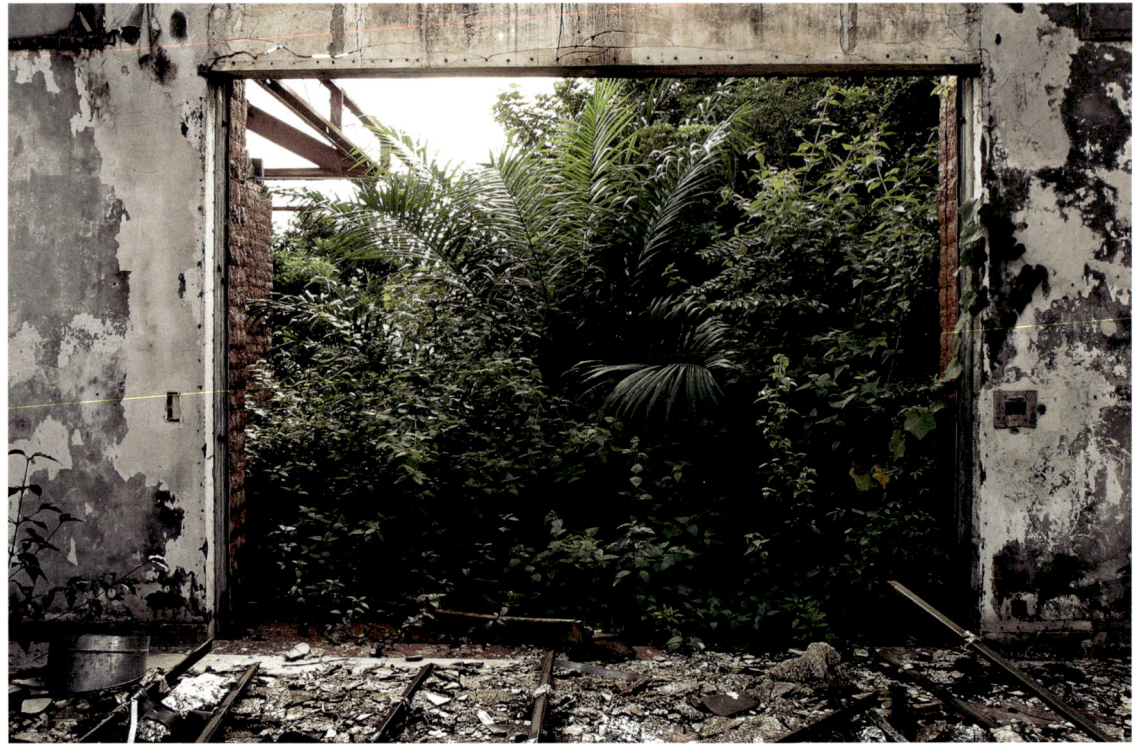

15.7 Otobong Nkanga, *Things Have Fallen I*, 2004–5. C-print on photographic paper mounted on dibond, 60×90 cm. Courtesy of the artist.

are photographic analyses of the psychological and phenomenological experience of land and landscape. In the former, Nkanga is interested in the spatial, physical attributes of the built environment, in the forms, objects, and other embedded structures that define the relationship between nature and culture. In the latter, she trawls the Nigerian, Dutch, and German countryside to record the convergence of the ruin and the picturesque, picturing the landscape as a series of disturbed, interrupted movements of development and stasis. These emptied remains address the collapse of time and space, opening them up within the mnemonic framework of loss, mourning, and melancholy.

If Nkanga photographs around loss and soft-edged dystopias, around remains and absences, addressing disturbances where nature struggles with human development, Moshekwa Langa, in his *Untitled* (2005) photographs, illuminates sites of recovery and recollection. Langa's silent photographs record the wounds of absence to memory. His focus is on domestic space and the accoutrements that dot its interior and exterior spaces. Each of these images suggests and projects the fundamental relationship between what Avishai Margalit calls the "ethics of memory" and a palpability that makes place and space more than an illusion or fantasy, hence the necessity of transforming the fatal ennui often associated with memory.[77] Photographed over a brief vacation in the Northern Province, in a rural area of South Africa where he grew up, these images of domestic scenes and still lifes are simple mementos that paradoxically efface the author's relationship to place, but at the same time reestablish the priority and necessity of a distance from one's own memories. There is no mark of homecoming in these light-filled, poetic essays on time and longing, where distance imperils connection, leading to Paul Gilroy's "postcolonial melancholia."[78]

Like Langa's enigmatic vacant sites, Nkanga's emptied remains, Bhimji's haunted landscapes, and deSouza's erased pictures, Fatou Kandé Senghor, in her work *Palais de Justice*, opens up another consideration of postcolonial melancholia. The series of photographs and accompanying video, called *Room 12*, shot in the ruins of the Palais de Justice, examine a farcical piece of colonial architecture within the postcolonial present of Senegal. A fake neoclassical structure set in a ring of similar buildings (including the presidential palace and national assembly), the Palais de Justice mimics the elusive grandeur of French colonialism in Africa. It is especially apt that this particular building, structurally unstable and now abandoned, served as a space for the administration of justice—with its various courts—and denial of the same in the prison cells that dot its interior. Senghor's archaeology of the Palais de Justice reveals its utter inappropriateness within the national ideology of the Senegalese, a Potemkin structure that stands as a monument to French colonialism. As Senghor shows in the forty-eight photographs, this is the ground in which to explore the memory now hidden behind the curve of a vanishing colonial fantasy.

Not every instance in which the artists explore memory collapses into melancholia. Lamia Naji's work is vitally concerned with foregrounding the spaces and rituals of her native Morocco. In the ironically titled *Couleurs Primaires* (2005), Naji blends a noir sensibility and a poetic documentary style in a series of black-and-white photographs recording a Muslim feast and spiritual ritual. Using stop-motion and intercutting techniques, she transformed the photographic stills into a fast-paced energetic video, whose staccato editing format gives the projected image a sense of frenzy. Photographed both close up and from a distance—including aerial shots—*Couleurs Primaires* offers glimpses of architecture, crowds, and solitary figures of celebrants in rapture or in various states of celebration. Rather than working with the false opposition between tradition and modernity, Naji (in collaboration with a Spanish composer) has wed the syncopation of Gnawa music to the abbreviated computer-driven beats of urban trance tracks. In this hybridization, Naji appears to aim at exploring the combined spiritual and social dimensions of Sufism and contemporary youth culture. Her sonic and visual elaborations of the mysticism of Sufism in Gnawa music and contemporary trance compositions point to the intersection of religious and secular subjectivity, tradition and modernity, in the contemporary experiences of Morocco, while extending its reach beyond the borders of the Muslim world. Here it is not a question of separate time zones but a relation of temporal structures that is the fundamental subject of the work.

There is visual pleasure in the allegories of desire and excess that define the orientalist kitsch of Lara Baladi's work. Baladi rarely uses the camera in the traditional sense; instead, she works like an archaeologist. But rather than excavate, she accumulates, samples, and plunders the vast digital archive (television and cell phone images, Japanese manga, digital files from the internet and other file-sharing sources) and analog files that exist today in such profusion. She expropriates images from the relentless traffic of photographic and pictographic media and internet industry and remixes them to form a new pictorial content. Consequently, her work contains an element of compositional frenzy in which multiple images, cultural settings, symbols of sentimentality, stereotypes, sexuality, gender, identity, vulgarity, and excess are intermingled and collapsed.

Chronicles of the City

A large section of *Snap Judgments* brings together studies of urban sites, as narratives and chronicles of the city. Each project addresses modes of urban living and the changes that shape the postcolonial metropolis. Depth of Field (DOF), a loose collective of six photographers residing in Lagos, Nigeria, adopts the attitude of a social geographer to investigate the layers of living arrangements in which informality and formality converge. Each of DOF's works, which reveal an increasingly documentary practice, is developed based on themes that emerge from the group's weekly meetings. From these meetings assignments are drawn by individual members who then work autonomously to develop an essay. At the conclusion of the assignment, the members meet again to discuss and analyze their output, as well as the photographic value of the work, its social and artistic relevance. Since its founding, DOF has generally focused on examining urban narratives around Lagos, the vast megalopolis, searching for the city's identity within its contours and meandering neighborhoods. To the unstudied eye, the pictures appear impressionistic, like casual tourist snapshots, as if taken on the fly. But this is because the methodology of documentation is more like a digest than a purely formal study. The huge compendium of images DOF has built so far has the quality of a wide-ranging and interpretive archive. No one picture can capture the vitality and multiplicity of the city.[79] Each image contains a story, and each story incubates another one. This archive is built around exploration of the most recognizable physical, social, and economic features of Lagos, some of which take on an almost iconic quality—its bus ranks, markets, nightlife on the beach, churches, traffic, street trading, its expanding skyline. While the images may lend themselves to the genre of touristic myth, they are anything but, since one intention of the group is to detach their approach from the picturesque study that has made Lagos the latest photographic cliché of the Third World city.

Cairo is the context of Randa Shaath's recent photographic investigation. Shaath has worked as a photojournalist for *Al Ahram Weekly* covering diverse subjects and issues across Egypt. Over the past decade, however, she has turned her attention to the cultural milieu of the Cairene artistic community, documenting its intimate environments and making portraits of actors, dancers, musicians, theater professionals, filmmakers, writers, and artists. The profoundly cosmopolitan character of the Islamic world's great intellectual and cultural crossroads gradually unfolds in Shaath's portraits. In a related but socially divergent body of work, Shaath photographed the city's architectural spaces. But rather than the classic images of monumental architecture, wide boulevards, chic neighborhoods, and middle-class haunts, she has turned her lens on another part of the city, one that is almost invisible from the street but nonetheless comprises a massive community of informal and perhaps illegal homes constructed on the rooftops of Cairo's high-rise buildings. These concealed arboreal dwellings essentially constitute a kind of "other" city. Shaath's photographic view is not panoramic. Her pictures are discreet compositions of parts and wholes, of domestic and communal spaces. There is something oneiric in these images, not least because some of the nocturnal ones lend the entire constructivist ensemble a poetic quality that belies the precariousness of the structures, which are contrasted against the solidity of the buildings dotting the jagged skyline. Yet, despite their makeshift character, there is a sense of permanence to this ur-city. I recall the solitary silence I once experienced while visiting an artist living in a small two-room flat on top of one of these buildings. Nothing about the setting appeared transitory. It was home. Shaath conveys this sense of permanence by focusing not only on the architecture but the active life of the inhabitants. Her aerial shots taken from rooftops across the city reveal the creative adaptation that Cairo's urban inhabitants have made out of their circumstances. The images unfold another reality of the city invisible from street level, showing us a new kind of urbanism, a spectacular rethinking of the rooftop as a platform of new urban community.

Hala Elkoussy's *Peripherals* (2004) provides a counterpoint to Shaath's alternate reading of Cairo, a dense city teeming with life and subjectivities. Rather than the urban core, *Peripherals* focuses on the codes of a second wave of modernity and modernization that is rapidly changing the relationship between center and periphery, fracturing the contained balance between formality and informality that characterizes a new urbanism with a distancing, sterile, vaguely modern architecture sprouting on the edge. Elkoussy insists that this group of images not function like fetishized, tastefully framed commodity objects. Staged as mock tourist wallpaper, she envisions their presentation much like a backdrop, an urban mise-en-scène. She explores the underlying vulgarity of images such as these, which project fantasies of place without revealing the fictions nestled within them. Here the wallpaper suggests certain kitschy elements of the tourist posters which invite an illusion bigger and more saturated than the reality they claim to represent. Elkoussy photographs these new urban developments, many of which remain unfinished or are already abandoned, to unmask the contradiction between the desire for Western modernity and the resolute attempt to include a vernacular modernity in the future of the city. At the core of this series of images is a subtle critical stance toward the fever of expansion and modernization that has overtaken most of the developing world.

The city as exploding megalopolis is not the locus of Yto Barrada's photographic and filmic concern; rather, it is its emptying, its slow evisceration and asphyxiation. Barrada's ongoing project *A Life Full of Holes: The Strait Project*, begun in 1998, is a critical meditation on migrancy, immigration, asylum, labor, and the illicit business of human trafficking centered in the Strait of Gibraltar, the narrow causeway linking Morocco and Spain, Africa and Europe. But more than economic determinism drives this investigation. The riskiness of attempts to cross the strait is succinctly captured in Barrada's examination of the root meanings of the word *strait*, which in French and Arabic translations "combine[s] the sense of narrowness and distress."[80]

As thousands of young men and women, without opportunity in the bleak economic conditions produced by globalization in the South, place themselves on the precarious threshold of illegality, becoming clandestine, facing deportation or lengthy detention in asylum camps throughout Europe, their desperation is unfolding a catastrophic human rights problem. The plight of these "economic immigrants" and the ensuing political and ethical tensions illuminate the core idea to which this project is addressed, namely, the biopolitical issue of the refugee problem. Refugees have become the limit figures of the new millennium. And the fact that the refugee problem is framed within an economic rationale exposes the philosophical and juridical ambiguity that surrounds the exclusion of North African immigration from the universal legal protections generally accorded refugees and people in distress. Barrada's project hinges on this aporia. She pursues the question of violence inherent in the risk of entrusting one's life, hopes, and dreams to the ability to reach the other place, to not touch the bottom of the sea but to reach the other shore. She wants to puncture the silence that surrounds the discussion of the daily tragedies of immigration: "I try to expose the metonymic character of the Strait through a series of images that reveal the tension—that restlessly animates the streets of my hometown—between its allegorical nature and immediate, harsh reality. My work attempts, in part, to exorcise the unspoken violence of other people's departures. I, too, left Tangier, for more than ten years; by moving back, I have placed myself amidst the violence of homecoming. There are no *flâneurs* here, and no innocent bystanders."[81] Poetic, photographically dense, intellectually powerful, the elliptical narratives and methodological precision of *The Strait Project* are the photographic equivalent of a surgical scalpel, used to slice open the belly of an open secret, to lay it bare and force a confrontation with one of the biggest problems of the twenty-first century: the refugee.

Shifts in urban subjectivity, questions of mobility and migration, are recurring motifs in the work of Kay Hassan and Guy Tillim. Like the strait in Morocco, the cities of South Africa have become new and complex spaces in which African social agency and sense of hospitality are currently being tested. Since the end of apartheid, the relatively modern and affluent economy, sophisticated amenities, services, and Western efficiency of South Africa have attracted new immigrants from other African countries seeking opportunity. This flood of immigrants has opened a debate on access to the country and exposed a painful conflict at the root of which cities like Johannesburg have to renegotiate old issues of inclusion and exclusion, involving social classes, racial groups, and communities. Under apartheid,

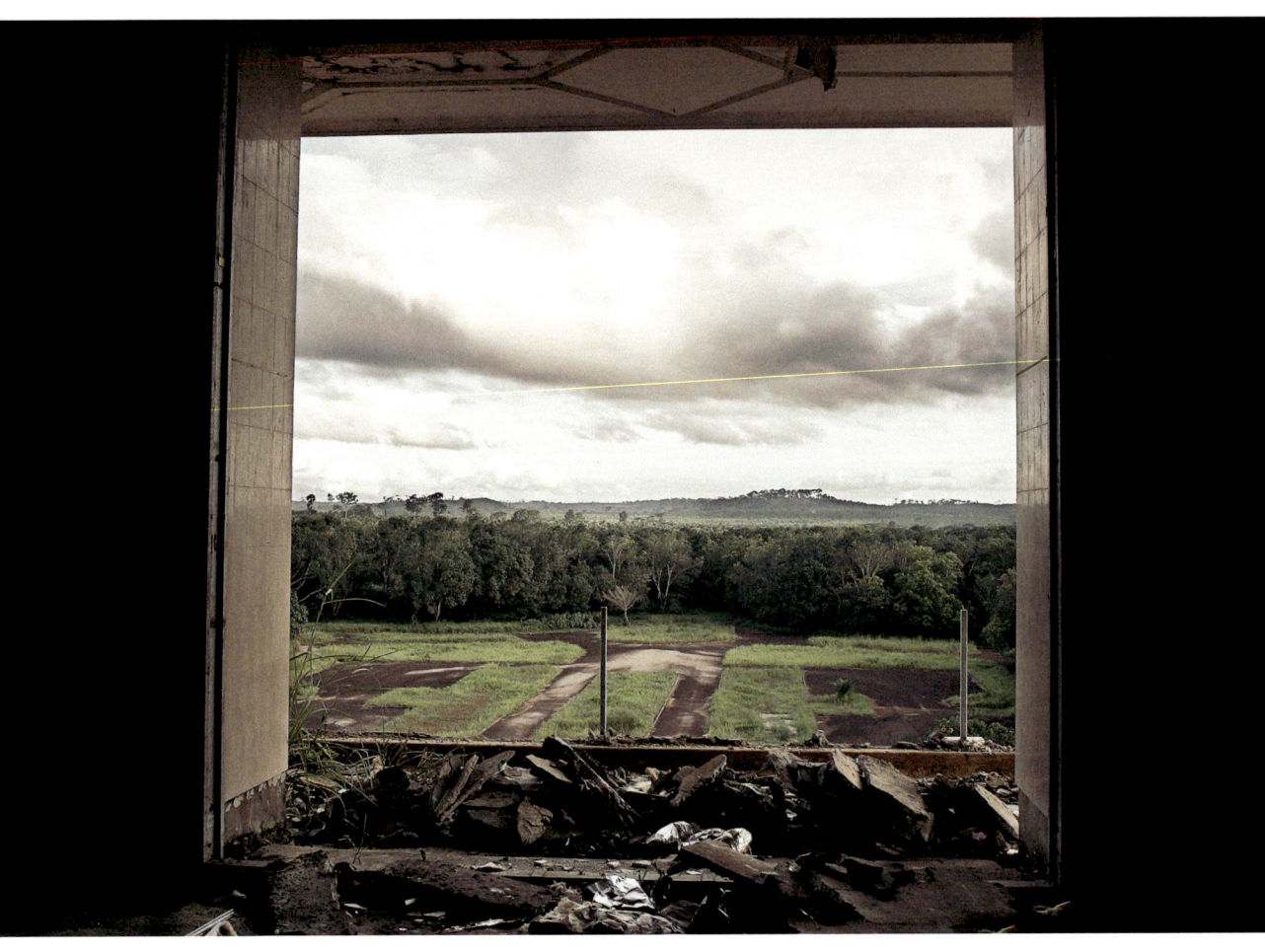

15.8 Guy Tillim, *Reception Room at Mobutu's Looted Palace at Gbadolite*, 2002–3. Archival pigment ink on 300g cotton paper, edition of 5+2 AP, diptych, image size 47.5×73 cm each. © Guy Tillim. Courtesy of Stevenson Gallery, Cape Town, Johannesburg, Amsterdam.

deplorable living conditions, brutal evictions, and spatial marginalization and invisibility were the standard tools of social deracination employed by the paranoiac state security apparatus. The city was off-limits to entire categories of people and therefore served in its organization a repressive function.

To understand the projects by Tillim and Hassan for this exhibition requires a renewed acquaintance with apartheid's social engineering, but also how the terms of urban existence have been turned on their head with the frightening influx of people seeking jobs, housing, and access. Tillim's *Jo'burg* series (2004) is located at the epicenter of the city's unique modernist downtown, which within ten years was transformed from a pretense as a cosmopolitan neighborhood inhabited by whites into a ghetto now populated mostly by blacks, immigrants, and masses of the urban poor. This section of the city represents an epic of deliberate neglect and abandonment, forcing the inhabitants to live in a kind of survivalist archipelago with little official recognition. Tillim's work on this part of the city is a sustained essay on post-apartheid Johannesburg. There is a sense of erased distance between photographer and photographed. Yet this proximity does not seem to trouble the relations of power between Tillim and the nearly incarcerated denizens of his recordings. With its gritty realism and disturbing ennui, the images that comprise this body of work (produced over the course of five months when Tillim moved into one of the grungy tenements that make up the sprawling complex of high-rises in the city's downtown) expose the fault lines of an oncoming battle between speculative real estate and tenancy rights. Sometimes the scenes are photographed the way a photojournalist would (which is what Tillim has been for two decades), as battlegrounds between competing moral and political systems. In others, the images are shot from angles that blur the line between voyeurism and pictorialism. Yet this series offers a clear vantage into the unique spatial changes that are occurring everywhere as new populations enter into settled communities and bring with them their own claims to space and identity.

A recurring issue in the work of Kay Hassan centers around questions of labor, migration, and sovereignty. Hassan has worked in diverse media—photography, film, video—and until recently was known chiefly for the large-scale installations of paper collages he made in the mid-1990s. The new work presented in *Snap Judgments* incorporates found images, Hassan's growing archive of discarded Polaroid negatives taken by self-employed street photographers. He collects these negatives by the hundreds, seeing in them another form of portraiture. Unlike deSouza's *Lost Pictures*, Hassan's could be seen as engendering a form of recovery, though the images are still very much situated between found and lost. These images, in which subjects share part of the four-panel negative, are remnants of documentation photographs that migrants require in order to procure identity cards. Continuing his work on apartheid's topographical grid and its legislation of access to the city, its laws of spatial exclusion, its transformation into a zone that lies between legality and illegality—a separation marked by the pernicious mechanism of the *dompas* (identity books required of all black Africans)—Hassan obliquely speculates, in his assessment of the growing demand for identity cards, on an emerging order of bureaucratic control over urban citizens. Over the past several years, he has continuously visited the offices of South African Home Affairs, where internal and foreign migrants come to seek papers, searching for a legal framework in which to reinvent themselves and thereby secure a space in the city.

James Muriuki, Sada Tangara, Boubacar Touré Mandémory, Michael Tsegaye, and Mamadou Gomis also study the shifting context of the city between formal and informal, official and unofficial narratives of urban life, architecture, public transport, and the fleeting presences that inhabit the postcolonial city. Tangara's *Le grand sommeil* (The big sleep, 1998–2003) is a disturbing essay on the nocturnal living arrangements of street children in Dakar. Himself a former street child, his photographs are taken at close-up, revealing the vulnerability of the young boys, who move in packs and sleep in clusters, huddled together in street corners, abandoned cars, and makeshift crevices. This is an empathetic view into the intractable problems of postcolonial urban life. In the same vein of photographic archaeology, Mamadou Gomis presents yet a different view of Dakar. Like Sylvia Plachy in New York's *Village Voice*, he employs the pages of the independent newspaper *Le Journal* to produce a deceptively simple series of urban stories, teasing out the division between *le quartier* and *centre de ville* and foregrounding through his pictorial testimonies the changing cycle of daily experience in Dakar. His work is perhaps the most methodical example of an ongoing chronicle, a shifting, dispersed group of images that never consolidate into a typology. The growing archive of images, which appear six days a week, is classic photojournalism. But it also constitutes both an iteration of a new form of self-writing and a view of the role of images in the development of African public narratives.

Over the past two years, James Muriuki has documented a range of economic and cultural scenes around Nairobi. Because the city is the gateway to the safari and vacation economy of Kenya, he is interested in the transitional spaces occupied by Kenyans. In the past, he produced a series of performance-based images of himself in his small apartment. These images were always taken after hours, upon return from work. The apartment functioned as a transitional space, between work, the street, and home, both a place of refuge and a vessel for experimentation with a different structure of being and contemporary identity. Likewise, his recent project is focused on another transitional space, the zone made up of bus terminals, taxi ranks, and other modes of transportation on which the majority of the city's in-habitants and workers depend. This recent body of work is composed of cin-ematic digital images photographed at night, at the point when the massive labor force that commutes daily into the center of Nairobi begins its exodus to the outlying towns on the margins of the city. Muriuki embeds himself like a phantom in the midst of the commuters or at a slight distance from them, focusing on the transitional relationship between himself, his subjects, and the city. The juxtaposition of the vibrant and colorful neon-rigged buses against the soft, glowing Oz-like lights of Nairobi's sparkling towers creates a contrast of forms that is at once exuberant and mysterious.

Most of the artists in this exhibition have made a shift to photography from other media such as painting. To be sure, photography has become the common tool of contemporary art. Michael Tsegaye, a former painter, sees in photography a new opportunity to compose a painterly investigation of the intimate private spaces of homes in the old quarters of Addis Ababa, as well as a lyrical interpretation of the languorous flow of the city at large. His photography has a distinct compositional formality and is organized the way a painter would work on isolated effects within an overall frame. The resulting images are dense and layered with material, forms, color, and chiaroscuro, careful translations of mood and detachment, light and shadow. The direct sense of seeing recorded in these spaces is ultimately not docu-mentary. Rather, it draws largely from tropes of painterly modernism, which distinguishes Tsegaye's work from the hard-edged urban analysis that is to be found in other works in the exhibition.

Boubacar Touré Mandémory, a veteran reporter based in Dakar, photographs with an aggressive and desensitizing lens. The weird angles of his compositions invest ordinary scenes of fleeting urban life with a surreal sense of disturbance. As with his angles, so his sense of color, timing, and detachment. The quirky movement of Mandémory's method calls on view-ers to mimic his angle of vision, to see the whirling world, the vertiginous motion of the street at the same point of contact as the photographer. These are motion pictures, in a literal sense. All forms in Mandémory's work are in motion, disenchanted, agitated, restless, torn from their immediate docu-mentary referent. These are photographs of a different kind of substance: both psychic and corporeal, haptic and retinal, real and derealized.

Jo Ractliffe, one of the most accomplished and underrated photog-raphers of her generation, continues to experiment with multiple modes of picture making. From her earliest work in the mid-1980s to her current im-ages, each of her projects can be seen as little dramas in which the subjectivity of the artist is fully registered in the resulting work. The conceptual premise of Ractliffe's work is always in her attempt to grapple with and undermine the apparatus, to use the vulnerability of the technology to her advantage. In a now-classic work, *Shooting Diana* (1995), she employed a plastic Diana camera to shoot haunting scenes of urban decrepitude. And in another, *Vlak-plaas* (1999), she used a toy camera to visit a landscape of a horrific apartheid crime, producing a continuous strip of uninterrupted images as if the camera were performing a slow pan across the landscape. We all remember Walter Benjamin's insight about [Eugène] Atget's photographs resembling crime scenes. This work, as well as the photographs in the exhibition, is shot like a drive-by shooting, literally through the scene of a crime, from the point of view of a traveler moving through and between moments of analysis and documentation. And again, the painterly, vertiginous spaces Ractliffe achieves here are accomplished with a dismantled and reconfigured toy camera, creating a fuzzy filmstrip effect of forms, structures, and street scenes.

Rather than crisis, Romuald Hazoumè and Zohra Bensemra each approach their photographic targets as witnesses to an unfolding but constantly changing drama, the making of possibility in cities ravaged by economic malaise and political violence. Both artists eschew the paradigm of victim photography common in contemporary photojournalism. Rather, they use their knowledge of the cities in their respective countries (Benin and Algeria) as guides to document the transformations taking place within each context. Hazoumè's take on the lucrative business of petrol smuggling by small-time traders shuttling between towns that line the borders of Benin and Nigeria is as lyrical as it is dispassionate. Working in the same manner he has employed as a sculptor, Hazoumè records, like sculptural propositions, the precarious but formally alluring plastic vessels used by the smugglers to ferry their contraband liquid. His compositions assume the quality of small monuments. He exploits the formal qualities of the devices tied to motorcycles, on bicycles, or lugged on top of the head—to create images of balletic grace. Bensemra, on the other hand, works from the perspective of an implicated photojournalist in her lengthy documentation of the violence precipitated by the civil war in her native Algeria, emphasizing the everyday lives and experiences of women against the backdrop of political bloodshed. A photographer for Reuters, Bensemra, in the images she has made around Algerian cities, particularly Algiers, permits herself to lose the vaunted neutrality photojournalists are supposed to bring to their assignment: "I am not suffering from acute patriotism, or from excessive professionalism. It is just that my heart is suffused with love for my country. My life is shaped by its joys, its disappointments, its fortunes and misfortunes. I have constantly had to fight with myself to remain neutral in my work, to be but an eyewitness."[82] She not only underscores the way her work implicates her, she also wants to use it to address what are for her the most pressing questions, as an Algerian and a woman living between two kinds of violation. Her work on Algeria is meant "to explain my relationship with my country—to talk about my Algeria. It was intended to show that it is difficult to remain neutral when it is one's very flesh that is being slashed. The goal was also to say that Algeria, in the same way as a woman who is marginalized because she is different from others, is striving to find a solution to its problems, on its own. The country is learning to be strong and to weather all sorts of storms."[83]

The photographs of Omar D. (Daoud) consist of close-up portraits of Algerians that dwell on the existential attributes of the subject's face. The portraits are not studies of character and do not so much objectify the sitters as underline the traumatic experiences that are permanently etched on their faces. The faces, then, become landscapes, or atlases of events that have shaped the contours of the individual but, paradoxically, do not quite divulge the emotional disturbance that threatens to burst the surface. A particularly charged portrait shows the face of a young blind man whose eyes seem to have been violently removed. Of all the portraits (including those of men and women with ancient, wrinkled faces), this image is the most direct, the one that seeks a correlation between an event and its distillation in an individual. Omar D.'s portraits are therefore not isolated from the cultural environment. They are not autonomous images of individuality. They may be read as ciphers of social trauma, in environments that lie at the intersection of public and private space, and as indictments of the spectacular conflict that has riven the nation: between secularists and fundamentalists, nationalism and religious insurgency.

In all the changes occurring in Africa today, the foregoing should be taken as signposts for understanding the photographic event as such, whether as an indexical trace or documentary account, but always as an instance for enacting a new position in the map of contemporary Africa within global culture. Toward this end, inhabitants of African cities have not remained just another specimen of photographic speculation on the limits of existence, the withering away of life from the ravages of industrial-scale diseases. The individuals have become subjects literally bearing witness to their own existence, counteracting the constant reports about their imminent disappearance. In Luis Basto's work, portraiture is the means used to signal this desire. However, Basto's images produce a subtle agitation in the images of the photographed individuals shown looking directly at the camera. Taciturn and enigmatic, the portrayed look into the camera with a sort of placid detachment or mild disregard. The frontal directness of Basto's documentary portraits of ordinary people on the streets of Maputo illuminates the boundary between the photographer and the photographed, extending his exploration of subjects and their everyday environments into a space of ethical negotiation.

Infernal Machines and Institutions of Modernity

Another area of concern takes up the question of secular institutions of modernity such as the museum, prison, and factory. Hentie van der Merwe's *Trappings* (2002–3) comprises photographs of starched, formal military uniforms confined in the Museum of Military History in Cape Town, which unfold a spectral shadow that overhangs South Africa's transition from apartheid to postapartheid democracy, from colonial to postcolonial institutions. Photographed in a soft, slightly unfocused manner, van der Merwe's hazy photographs of empty suits hover before the viewer like apparitions, suggesting both surrogate bodies and the erased corporeality of masculine sexuality. The ceremonial pageantry of the military's sense of esprit de corps gives way to the seedy violence of its machinery, its system of apartheid repression. Here the array of types and ranks comprise a collective portrait of the institution.

If the military is an institution of discipline and restraint, the prison represents the obverse: the space of the disciplined. Like the clinical vitrines in which van der Merwe's ceremonial uniforms are incarcerated, the prison stands for the brutal reality of human incarceration and denial of freedom, a despairing and dispiriting infernal machine. Mikhael Subotzky's *Die Vier Hoeke* (2004–5) is a sober and at times aesthetically paradoxical documentary project. The detailed examination of the prison complex is analytically powerful and at the same time calls attention, through the panoramic sweep of the camera, to the dreadful spectacle of the panoptic society, its regulative mechanisms, its hellish scenes of trauma, its disembodiment of the human character. Witness, for instance, the grotesque autopsy scene of a young prisoner who immolated himself in his cell, or the humiliation that accompanies the strip search of prisoners. In this body of work, which grew out of his BFA thesis at the University of Cape Town, Subotzky's picturing of the Pollsmoor and Voorberg prison complexes outside Cape Town and the groups and gangs that make up their tight-knit communities opens up those spaces concealed from public scrutiny to reveal them as sites of infamy. The pictures are documents of an infernal encounter, a descent into a netherworld of forgotten men who live out their lives in conditions of daily humiliation, rituals of masculinity, psychosexual tension, camaraderie, racial antagonism, and the search for justice.

Like the prison, the factory depersonalizes and eviscerates, radically disembodying and methodically stripping the worker down to a statistic. The factory serves a repressive function of instrumental efficiency. It represents a regulative and disciplinary space in which the personality of men and women is organized according to the logic of hierarchization: between the factory foreman and worker, man and machine, personhood and its absence. If the prison evokes, according to Michel Foucault, scenes of discipline and punishment, the factory as one of the most important inventions of modernity is not far behind. In it, the worth of a person is calculated according to the iron law of industrial science: on profit. It is all this and more that Ali Chraïbi, in his investigation of the factory, has sought to illuminate. However, it is not the factory as an isolating, overwhelming machine that he has recorded, but the very human scale of industrial production. Consequently, in his extended documentation, the machine is relegated to the background, while the workers occupy the central space of the photographic inquiry. Mingling the empathy of portraiture and the detachment directed at picturing machines, Chraïbi, like Subotzky, permits the viewer no programmatic ordering of industrial production. The men look out of the frames and at the viewer. And here we can look back in a gesture of reciprocity, in a double articulation of identification and subjectification.

The photographic projects described here represent experiments and therefore new initiatives in the artistic exploration of different dimensions of the African imaginary and African spaces. The selection of works for *Snap Judgments* was guided by a desire to highlight what, in my view, constitutes a new position in the expanding lexicon of contemporary African art. The emphasis in this case is on works and ideas that maintain a rigorous analytical perspective in photographic examinations of Africa in the twenty-first century. Most of the works (with the exception of Bamgboyé's *Arise*) were produced within the past five years, and many others were made in the past year or commissioned specifically for the exhibition. In laying out my reasons for selecting these works and artists, I should like to say that my perspective is to be read as insistently partial, yet it should also be understood as a declaration of direction without a fixed horizon.

The key task of *Snap Judgments* is to create a space for critical conversation between the artists and their ideas, to reveal their intersections and to illuminate the context and conditions of production that make up the space of contemporary African photography and artistic practices. In *Snap Judgments*, this conversation has enabled an elaboration of the conceptual methods that drive the procedures of the artists. While none of the artists explicitly address the terrain of Afro-pessimism, there is little doubt that their works register a subtle deviation from its pathology, and the dystopia associated with it. This could be understood as a repudiation of Afro-pessimism's obsession with obsolescence and entropy common to the media's view of Africa. The artists and photographers whose works are collected under the rubric of this exhibition are active in their response to the conditions of modernity and globalization and the impact each has had on African experience. But they are not inventing new fictions and mythologies. Rather, they are formulating new visions of the African present in all its heterogeneity and multiplicity: with neither heroes nor villains. The African worldview presented in this crop of images is not total. Neither is it always explicitly referential. These are pictures, to be sure, but also systems of meaning, ways of confounding and interrogating historical certitudes of the truth of the photographic mark, and of the exhibition's principal subject: the African postcolonial condition.

NOTES

1   See Léopold Sédar Senghor, *Négritude et humanisme* (Paris: Seuil, 1964). The Negritude movement, especially the version adopted by one of its principal founders, the philosopher, poet, and statesman Léopold Sédar Senghor, could be reread today as an attempt to restage colonial pessimism about Africa. But while Senghor's theory of Negritude may have unwittingly perpetuated certain prejudices about Africa by articulating the difference between Africa and Europe as the opposition between feeling (Africa) and reason (European), he was primarily vested in delineating an African ethic of which Africans should and could be proud, even if some of the values were anathema to how modern Africans actually thought of themselves.

2   For critical responses to Afro-pessimism, see Chinua Achebe, *Hopes and Impediments: Selected Essays* (New York: Anchor Books, 1988), especially the essay "An Image of Africa: Racism in Conrad's *Heart of Darkness*," 1–20; and Chinua Achebe, *Home and Exile* (Oxford: Oxford University Press, 2000); see also Ngũgĩ wa Thiong'o, *Decolonising the Mind: The Politics of Language*

in African Literature (London: James Currey; Nairobi: Heinemann, 1986); and, most famously, Frantz Fanon, *Black Skin, White Masks* (New York: Grove, 1967).

3   See Manthia Diawara, *In Search of Africa* (Cambridge, MA: Harvard University Press, 1998); Kwame Anthony Appiah, *In My Father's House: Africa in the Philosophy of Culture* (New York: Oxford University Press, 1992); and Achille Mbembe, *On the Postcolony* (Berkeley: University of California Press, 2001).

4   [*Ed. note:* George Wilhelm Frederick Hegel, *The Philosophy of History* (1892) (New York: Dover Publications, 1956), 99.]

5   [*Ed. note:* V. S. Naipaul, "The Crocodiles of Yamoussoukro," in *Finding the Center: Two Narratives* (New York: Alfred A. Knopf, 1984), 73–176. First published in the *New Yorker*, May 6, 1954, 52–119.]

6   See V. Y. Mudimbe, *The Invention of Africa: Gnosis, Philosophy, and the Order of Knowledge* (Bloomington: Indiana University Press, 1988); and V. Y. Mudimbe, *The Idea of Africa* (Bloomington: Indiana University Press, 1994).

7   In 1931 the French ethnographer and surrealist Michel Leiris embarked on a long trip as the secretary of the Dakar-Djibouti *expedition*. What resulted was not just the collection of objects and other material plundered from Africa through the course of the expedition, but a book, *L'Afrique fantôme* (1934), comprising Leiris's work during the trip. The tradition of writing and conjuring Africa from which Leiris's book emerged is long and distinguished. Joseph Conrad's *Heart of Darkness* belongs to this tradition, as does Arthur Rimbaud's retirement to Abyssinia (Ethiopia) and André Gide's *Voyage au Congo* (1927) and *Retour du Tchad* (1928). The point is that a long literature by eminent figures makes up the intellectual and visual imaginary of our exploration of Afro-pessimism.

8   In a recent edition of CNN, I saw an advertisement produced by the Nigerian Tourist Board flash across the screen touting the beauty of the people, the cultural dynamism of the cities, and the natural landscape. South Africa has used various contexts to promote itself to the world. No doubt, many African countries know the damage done their self-image and should engage the negative representations that have proved problematic to their conception of themselves.

9   See Roland Barthes, *Mythologies* (New York: Noonday, 1972). The study which Barthes initiated in this book is partly based on the specific examples of certain phenomena of postwar mass culture and popular entertainment, but guiding this examination is the attempt to understand how myth is rooted in language. In "Myth Today," a section of this fascinating book, Barthes defined myth as "a type of speech"; the conditions of this speech are what give it utility, in other words, "as a system of communication, that it is a message." He calls this message: signification, a

way to communicate a message about something as basic as a car to the description of the cultural effect it has on the public perception of transportation. Consider, then, the nature of the myth embedded within the message of Afro-pessimism, and the manner in which it amplifies what is quite secondary to the African condition, and we can understand the powerful and affective nature of myth, being as it is a translation of something quite apart from its actual content.

10 Walter Benjamin, "Little History of Photography," in *Selected Writings*, vol. 2, *1927–1934*, ed. Michael W. Jennings and Marcus Paul Bullock (Cambridge, MA: Belknap Press of Harvard University Press, 1999), 507–30.

11 A good example in this exhibition is the daily photograph published by Mamadou Gomis in the Dakar-based newspaper *Le Journal*.

12 Compare, for instance, Gomis's photographs to the examples in the September 2005 *National Geographic* special issue on Africa.

13 Leni Riefenstahl, *The Last of the Nuba* [1973] (New York: Harper and Row, 1974) is one of the great examples of this photographic discourse. See also the photographic industry Carol Beckwith and Angela Fisher have built around the powerful visual seductiveness of "tribal" African ceremonies.

14 Johannes Fabian, *Time and the Other: How Anthropology Makes Its Object* (New York: Columbia University Press, 1983), 111–12. Italics added.

15 Fabian, *Time and the Other*, 38.

16 Fabian, *Time and the Other*, 30.

17 See Giorgio Agamben, *The Open: Man and Animal* (Stanford, CA: Stanford University Press, 2004).

18 I use *archive* here in the sense employed by Jacques Derrida, in which relation to knowledge and authority is placed at the service of an interpretive, institutionalized function. Derrida noted that "a science of the archive must include the theory of this institutionalization, that is to say, the theory both of the law which begins by inscribing itself there and the right which authorizes it." *Archive Fever: A Freudian Impression* (Chicago: University of Chicago Press, 1996), 4.

19 Over the course of two weeks, as this essay was in progress, I randomly followed stories and images of Africa in my current hometown's newspaper, the *New York Times*. Each day a new story appeared about Africa, either as text or image. On Sunday, October, 23, 2005, Nicholas Kristof, writing on the op-ed page, had this to say about his visit to a hospital in Zinder, Niger: "When I walked into the maternity hospital here, I wished President Bush was with me. A 37-year-old woman was lying on a stretcher, groaning from labor pains and wracked by convulsions. She was losing her eyesight and seemed about to slip into a coma from eclampsia, a complication of pregnancy that kills 50,000 women a year in the developing world.

Beneath her, cockroaches skittered across the floor." On November 1, a story about deforestation in Malawi was published by Michael Wines, along with a black-and-white photograph by Jeffrey Barbee on page A3, showing a group of people seemingly logging wood for firewood; in the same edition, the oil giant ExxonMobil ran an advertisement about malaria in a nameless African country with a color photograph of a group of schoolchildren looking directly at the reader. On November 2, a front-page story by Michael Wines with the headline "Drought Deepens Poverty, Starving More Africans" was accompanied by a color photograph by Jeffrey Barbee of a group of men buying corn from a shopkeeper. The emphasis of the stories makes all the more clear how readers ought to understand Africa and what makes for a compelling narrative about this vast continent.

20   See Susan Sontag, *Regarding the Pain of Others* (New York: Farrar, Straus and Giroux, 2003), for an extensive analysis of the relationship between photography and humanitarianism.

21   On November 6, 2005, the *New York Times* published an extensive story on prison conditions in Africa. What makes this article fascinating is how the accompanying images by João Silva completely overshadowed the dire conditions under which the prison inmates live. The online version of the story included a slide version of the arresting images, many of which, as photographs, are indeed stunning.

22   Mbembe, *On the Postcolony*, 176.

23   Mbembe, *On the Postcolony*, 176.

24   The rock star Bono, lead singer of the Irish band U2, has since supplanted Geldof as patron saint of African debt relief and the antipoverty campaign.

25   Paris-based Brazilian photographer Sebastião Salgado is today the undisputed master of documentary heroism. The saturated dark and silvery tones of his prints monumentalize misery and turn terrible images of suffering into carefully executed pietàs, as if the struggle within the photographer's imagination is to both render the reality and transcend that reality in the name of art. A good contrast to the kind of documentary heroism often found in works such as Salgado's and even those of Gilles Peress can be observed in the work of Kenyan/American photographer Fazal Sheikh, whose practice involves making photographs in disaster areas as the first signs of normalcy begin to creep back into the lives of traumatized populations such as refugees.

26   Mbembe, *On the Postcolony*, 173–74.

27   CNN has recently been advertising its new anchor Anderson Cooper as a rising star of reporting from such disaster zones as Niger, Rwanda, and New Orleans.

28   The Bang Bang Club comprised Carter, João Silva, Ken Oosterbroek, and Greg Marinovich. Silva and Marinovich, the surviving members of this unofficial club, continue to contribute reportage to newspapers and magazines all over the world. They also recently published a memoir of the group.

29   At the height of the firestorm ignited by the publication of the photograph, in which many questioned the photographer's motives and condemned his detachment from the child, Carter, who was already suffering from depression and stress, committed suicide.

30   See Serge Guilbaut, *How New York Stole the Idea of Modern Art: Abstract Expressionism, Freedom, and the Cold War* (Chicago: University of Chicago Press, 1983).

31   In the 1960s and all through the 1980s, many African artists and filmmakers, notably Ousmane Sembène and Abderrahmane Sissako, trained in the academies of the communist bloc in the Soviet Union and Cuba. Many exhibited their work throughout much of eastern Europe, as well as in countries of the Non-Aligned Movement.

32   For example, in Nigeria a lively scene of contemporary art and writing was organized by the Mbari Club in Ibadan in the late 1950s.

33   See Geeta Kapur's excellent book *When Was Modernism: Essays on Contemporary Cultural Practice in India* (New Delhi: Tulika, 2000) on the development of Indian modern art and the relationship between vanguard artistic propositions and progressive political movements.

34   See Okwui Enwezor, ed., *The Short Century: Independence and Liberation Movements in Africa, 1945–1994* (Munich: Prestel and Museum Villa Stuck, 2001).

35   The 1955 meeting of the Non-Aligned states held in Bandung, Indonesia, under the auspices of Sukarno, was a dialectical political response to the bipolar division that characterized the capitalist and communist dichotomy that shaped much of the Cold War. The Bandung Conference marked a watershed moment in its radical response to American and Soviet hegemony and articulated an alternative perspective of twentieth-century modernity that remains a model of balance, solidarity against aggression, and support of the right of self-determination. Artists and writers were immensely influenced by the propositions of nonhegemonic international relations spelled out by the Non-Aligned states. In attendance during this historic conference were [Josip Broz] Tito (Yugoslavia), [Gamal Abdel] Nasser (Egypt), [Kwame] Nkrumah (Ghana), and [Jawaharlal] Nehru (India). See Richard Wright, *The Color Curtain: A Report on the Bandung Conference* (Cleveland: World Publishing, 1956).

36   See Chika Okeke's careful analysis of contemporary Nigerian art: "Nigerian Art in the Independence Decade, 1957–1967" (PhD diss., Emory

University, 2004); see also Clementine Deliss, ed., *Seven Stories about Modern Art in Africa* (New York: Flammarion, 1995). Rasheed Araeen's *Third Text* remains one of the most vital intellectual platforms where a countertheory of the contemporary has been developed. The journal not only exemplified this theoretical position in its name, it did so in recognition that the struggle is as much a cultural as ideological and historical issue.

37   In spite of his best efforts and intentions, Jean-Hubert Martin's *Magiciens de la terre* (1989) created an impression of a hierarchy of artistic forms within which the work of contemporary African artists could be understood; this hierarchy encompassed two tracks of practice, one authentic (meaning developed outside any influence of Western academic style and therefore more properly African) and the other inauthentic (based on a Western academic style that was read as largely derivative). It may appear too late in the day to reprise these arguments, but I do so here in light of the critical amnesia that tends to accompany exhibition surveys such as the present one.

38   Certainly, seeing the work of Yinka Shonibare (Nigeria), Malick Sidibé (Mali), William Kentridge (South Africa), and Chéri Samba (Republic of Congo) in the reinstalled permanent exhibition galleries of the Museum of Modern Art, New York, seems like a reflection on, and acknowledgment by the museum's curators of, the expanded spaces of contemporary art. In fact, this reinstallation, organized by Klaus Biesenbach, seems to me one of the most comprehensive attempts yet by a major museum to look at contemporary art through a decidedly global lens. Other artists in the galleries include Marina Abramović (Serbia), Ilya and Emilia Kabakov (Russia), and Waltercio Caldas (Brazil), among others.

39   Notwithstanding the complaints of many New York critics, the spread of biennials has had a salutary effect on access to works by artists who live and work in places other than the Western world. It has also opened curators, museums, and historians to new possibilities of artistic production.

40   It is worth emphasizing that colonialism and imperialism cannot be dissociated from the projects that led to the rise of modernity and globalization. Each of these come together in the far-reaching study of the development of capitalism that encapsulates what the eminent historian Fernand Braudel called the *longue durée* in his three-volume study *Civilization and Capitalism, 15th–18th Century* (Berkeley: University of California Press, 1992).

41   *Seven Stories about Modern Art in Africa,* an exhibition organized by the Whitechapel Art Gallery in London in 1995, explored the vital link between modern African art, artists, and institutions of postcolonial nationalism under which many artists sought to develop autonomy from Western artistic practices.

42 See Elizabeth Harney, *In Senghor's Shadow: Art, Politics, and the Avant-Garde in Senegal, 1960–1995* (Durham, NC: Duke University Press, 2004). Harney's book is an excellent and significant example of the new art history that has recently begun to address the distinct discursive, intellectual, and political developments instrumental to the emerging scholarship that shaped both modern and contemporary art in a broad sense, but also Africa in particular.

43 It is noteworthy that despite the recent integration of eastern European countries into the European Union, the art scenes of western and eastern Europe remain largely separated, though increasingly many artists from the East are being recognized in the more developed economies of the West.

44 Simon Njami's very successful and dynamic exhibition of contemporary African art, *Africa Remix: Contemporary Art of a Continent*, which has been touring European venues such as the *Museum Kunstpalast*, Düsseldorf; Hayward Gallery, London; Centre Pompidou, Paris; and Mori Art Museum, Tokyo, is a great recent example; another is *Fault Lines: Contemporary African Art and Shifting Landscapes*, curated by Gilane Tawadros for the Venice Biennale in 2003.

45 The development of new spaces of reception for contemporary art in Africa has been central to the expansion and critical positioning of the work of African artists both within and outside the continent. Institutions such as the Cairo and Dakar biennials, the Bamako photography biennial, Cape Town Month of Photography, and, before it closed, the Johannesburg Biennale have been central to animating a critical discursive space for understanding the role of photography in the changing views of African art.

46 The body of writing generated by African artists in the first half of the twentieth century has been essential to the historical projects concerned with addressing questions of modern and contemporary art in Africa. Critical essays such as Aina Onabolu's *Discourse on Art*, published in pamphlet form in 1920 in Lagos, as well as manifestos by varying groups in Egypt, South Africa, and Nigeria, are part of this trajectory. The various schools of art with which academic practices were developed spawned several distinct positions—particularly in the 1950s—on which modern and contemporary art has been elaborated in African countries. Some of the prominent ones include the École de Dakar in Senegal; the Uli art movement in Nsukka, Nigeria; the Crystalist artists of the Khartoum School in Sudan; the Oshogbo artists of Nigeria; and the Polly Street Art Centre in Johannesburg. All developed distinct artistic paradigms that remain important benchmarks in their respective countries.

47 The writings of expatriate European historians such as William Fagg, Ulli Beier, Kenneth Murray, Margaret Trowell, Pierre Delafosse, and Frank

McEwen represent some of the scholarship that can be summed up as "encounter" historiography.

48   The first great attempt to fully address the diasporic question in cultural terms was the First World Festival of Negro Arts, organized under the patronage of the Senegalese president, poet, and philosopher Léopold Sédar Senghor in 1966 in Dakar. The festival spanned the broad aesthetic and cultural connections between African artists and artists of African descent from Europe, the Caribbean, South America, the United States, and Canada. Recent exhibitions in the United States and Europe have explored the dimension of diasporic and expatriate practices of African artists: *A Fiction of Authenticity: Contemporary Africa Abroad*, curated by Shannon Fitzgerald and Tumelo Mosaka at the Contemporary Art Museum, St. Louis; and *Looking Both Ways: Art of the Contemporary African Diaspora*, curated by Laurie Ann Farrell at the Museum for African Art, New York. Salah Hassan and Olu Oguibe's *Authentic/Excentric* inaugurated the first African pavilion at the Venice Biennale in 2001 with artists from Africa and the diaspora. Hassan continued exploring this link at the Dakar Biennale in 2004 with three diasporic artists: David Hammons, Pamela Zee, and María Magdalena Campos-Pons.

49   See recent monographs on the works of the Nigerian painter Uzo Egonu, Senegalese painter Iba Ndiaye, Gerard Sekoto, and Ernest Mancoba: Olu Oguibe, *Uzo Egonu: An African Artist in the West* (London: Kala, 1995); Okwui Enwezor and Franz-W. Kaiser, *Iba Ndiaye: Peintre entre continents: Vous avez dit "primitif"?/Iba Ndiaye: Painter between Continents: Primtive? Says Who?* (Paris: A. Biro, 2002); N. Chabani Manganyi, *A Black Man Called Sekoto* (Johannesburg: Witwatersrand University Press, 1996); and Elza Miles, *Lifeline Out of Africa: The Art of Ernest Mancoba* (Cape Town: Human et Rousseau, 1994).

50   Spheres of contemporary African art can be further delineated to accommodate the vast and aesthetically vigorous practices of vernacular artists, commercial artists, artisans, and craft producers.

51   A wonderful example of the intertextual possibilities of the visual and iconographic exploration between traditional African forms and contemporary uses of those forms is provided by the Nsukka group of artists, who, in the 1970s and 1980s, devoted their research to applying the aesthetic forms of traditional Igbo women, the mural form of Uli, to new contemporary painting and sculptural inventions. While many of these dialectical paintings and sculptures have not been entirely successful, often appearing merely a stylistic hybrid of the magnificent open compositions of the Uli, they have nevertheless injected an important theoretical and aesthetic reconsideration of the positions being developed by African artists independent of any international artistic style. See Simon Ottenberg, *New Traditions from Nigeria: Seven Artists of the Nsukka Group*

(Washington, DC: Smithsonian Institution Press in association with the National Museum of African Art, 1997).

52 After decolonization, most of these elites, which comprise the main actors within the political, economic, and cultural class of the postcolonial state, were derisively labeled a comprador class by 1970s Marxist critics.

53 Ulli Beier's 1969 exhibition *Contemporary African Art* at Camden Arts Centre, London, marked one of the first instances in which contemporary African art as such was curated with the express intention of exploring its international position and scope. See the accompanying catalog, *Contemporary African Art* (London: Studio International, 1970). It was also the first concerted attempt to bring together the most significant work by East, West, North, and Southern African artists under the rubric of one exhibition. With over ninety artists, the scope and ambition of this exhibition remain unprecedented.

54 There has been historical confusion as to when photography became entrenched as an artistic form within contemporary African art. One problem of art history is the interpretation of art through chronology, through attempts to pinpoint the moment when an important shift occurred in artistic development. Because limited research has so far been undertaken with regard to how frequently photography has been included in contemporary African art exhibitions, there has been the erroneous perception that it first occurred in the 1991 exhibition *Africa Explores*, organized by the Center for African Art in New York. One can make the argument that the studio represents an informal exhibition space, and therefore offers the foundational instance for public participation in photographic exhibitions in that the public (whether or not as clients) have always visited these studios to see the newest styles each photographer was producing. However, in the more formal terms which art history tends to privilege, we can certainly indicate that as early as 1960, photography has been a part of contemporary African art. The Nigerian photographer Dotun Okubanjo (b. 1928), who studied at the Ealing School of Photography in London (1957–60), had his first exhibition in London in 1960, titled *Black and White Studies*. A review of it, with several full-page illustrations, was published in *West African Review* 31, no. 392 (July 1960), n.p. Upon his return to Nigeria, Okubanjo organized the First International Photographic Exhibition in Lagos in 1961 and exhibited his own work in a group exhibition, *Some Nigerian Artists*, at Mbari Gallery, Ibadan, in 1962.

55 For example, when the work of the great Malian portrait photographer Seydou Keïta was presented in New York in *Africa Explores*, an exhibition organized in 1991 by Susan Vogel at the Center for African Art, the prints displayed in the exhibition were designated as the work of an unknown photographer, even though Keïta's stamp was clearly visible in the published prints in the catalog. It is hard to fathom the reason for this

omission of the photographer's name and hence the invalidation of his authorship. One answer may lie in the challenge photographic practices by Africans presented to the Western museum's interest in seeing African art as the work of anonymous authors. The question raised by the exhibition therefore is not only about the proper place of photography within African visual history, but, most importantly, about the relationship between artistic practice and authorship as conventionally understood in Western terms. See Susan Vogel, *Africa Explores: 20th Century African Art* (New York: Center for African Art, 1991), 160–61.

56 Before this, a number of exhibitions in Europe, and most notably the 1994 Bamako photography biennial, had begun a concerted examination of photographic practices in Africa. Exhibitions such as *Self Evident* (1995) at Ikon Gallery, Birmingham, repositioned the work of African photographers within the terms of contemporary exhibition practices. A seminal moment in this contemporary formation is the founding of the photographic agency/collective Autograph Association of Black Photographers in London in 1986 under the leadership of the Nigerian artist Rotimi Fani-Kayode, who went on to produce some of the most important photographic works to be made in England in the past twenty-five years.

57 Because of the depredations of apartheid, the documentary style became the dominant photographic genre in South Africa. Photography was consistently used in the service of news reportage and in the ideological struggle between the apartheid state and its opponents.

58 See Okwui Enwezor, "Life and Afterlife in Benin: Photography in the Service of Ethnographic Realism," in *Life and Afterlife in Benin*, edited by Alex Van Gelder (London: Phaidon, 2005), 6–15; see also Michael Stevenson and Michael Graham-Stewart, *Surviving the Lens: Photographic Studies of South and East African People, 1870-1920* (Vlaeberg, South Africa: Fernwood, 2001).

59 Mudimbe, *Idea of Africa*, 129.

60 Mudimbe, *Idea of Africa*, 129.

61 For an excellent interpretation of Keïta's portraiture, see Elizabeth Bigham, "Issues of Authorship in the Portrait Photographs of Seydou Keïta," *African Arts* 32, no. 1 (Spring 1999): 56–67.

62 See Manthia Diawara, "Talk of the Town," *Artforum* 36, no. 6 (February 1998): 64–72; and Andre Magnin, *Seydou Keïta* (Zurich: Scalo, 1997).

63 See Michelle Lamunière, *You Look Beautiful like That: The Portrait Photographs of Seydou Keïta and Malick Sidibé* (Cambridge, MA: Harvard University Art Museums; New Haven, CT: Yale University Press, 2001).

64 My use of the term *documentary* here for the work of artists and photographers under discussion is limited to the conceptual frame of the term

as a tool of documentation and analysis, as a method of foregrounding a field and object of investigation, rather than the general understanding of *documentary* as a style of journalism for presenting facts.

65 Alioune Bâ, a photographer based in Bamako, made this point in conversation with me during my visit to Mali in summer 2005. When asked why he and other Malian photographers seem uninterested in exploring the colorful images that make up the vibrant street culture of Bamako, he responded that they did not find such images beautiful or noteworthy, that they, in fact, try to avoid any kind of representation that might appeal to Western curators and could therefore isolate or limit the range of the photographers' interests. Moreover, it would be absurd, he stated, to photograph this kind of image because it is a ready-made cliché available on postcards. He added that many photographers have chosen to photograph fragments of nonrecognizable objects or make what may appear to some eyes as hackneyed lyrical compositions as a way of resisting the photogenic object or subject. Above all, these photographers did not want to become another Keïta or Sidibé. Bâ's candor would be echoed by Boubacar Touré Mandémory in Dakar and a host of other artists and photographers throughout my travel. Their observations opened for me a new insight into the discursive framework in which the photographers have grounded their work.

66 Artist's statement sent to author, 2005.

67 I use the notions of rooting and routing in the sense employed by James Clifford as occasions for thinking about place and displacement, as moments of grounding and diaspora. See James Clifford, *Routes: Travel and Translation in the Late Twentieth Century* (Cambridge, MA: Harvard University Press, 1997).

68 The phrase *intimate outsider* has been used by Susan Vogel to describe the legitimacy of the outsider perspective of ethnographic knowledge of non-Western cultures. She suggests that an intimate outsider is one who has gained the trust of the community, who, although an outsider, is often received as a member or confidant of the community being studied. There is obviously an ethical issue surrounding the ethnographer's self-identification with the Other in this way, which raises afresh the critical issue of photographic study of other cultures where negotiation of knowledge is as much about access as about privilege and power. See Vogel, *Africa Explores*.

69 See Mark Sealy and Jean Loup Pivin, eds., *Rotimi Fani-Kayode and Alex Hirst* (Paris: Revue Noire, 1996).

70 See Achille Mbembe, "African Modes of Self-Writing," *Public Culture* 14, no. 1 (Winter 2002): 239–73.

71 Allan deSouza, "Recovering Vision," in *Allan deSouza: The Lost Pictures* (New York: Talwar Gallery, 2005), 11–14.

72   Derrida, *Archive Fever*, 15.

73   See Freud's essay "Mourning and Melancholia," in *The Standard Edition of the Complete Psychological Works of Sigmund Freud*, vol. 14 (London: Hogarth, 1957), 237–58.

74   Willy Mukasa, reporting about the expulsion order of President Idi Amin in Uganda in *Argus* on August 10, 1972, wrote, "Asians holding British passports and nationals of India, Pakistan and Bangladesh—except those in essential occupations—will have to leave Uganda within three months. This final order came yesterday from the president, General Idi Amin, who told a press conference at the command Port, Kampala, that he had signed a decree to this effect, which came into force from August 9."

75   See Jacques Derrida, *The Work of Mourning* (Chicago: University of Chicago Press, 2001).

76   Zarina Bhimji, artist's proposal for the film *Out of Blue* for Documenta11 [to Owkui Enwezor, 2001].

77   See Avishai Margalit, *Ethics of Memory* (Cambridge, MA: Harvard University Press, 2002).

78   See Paul Gilroy, *Postcolonial Melancholia* (New York: Columbia University Press, 2004).

79   See Rem Koolhaas, "Fragments of a Lecture on Lagos," in *Under Siege: Four African Cities*, edited by Okwui Enwezor, Carlos Basualdo, Ute Meta Bauer, Susanne Ghez, Sarat Maharaj, Mark Nash, and Octavio Zaya (Ostfildern-Ruit, Germany: Hatje Cantz, 2002), 173–83; and Rem Koolhaas and Pierre Belanger, eds., *Lagos Handbook, or, A Brief Description of What May Be the Most Radical Urban Condition on the Planet* (Cambridge, MA: Harvard University Graduate School of Design, 2000).

80   Yto Barrada, *A Life Full of Holes: The Strait Project* (London: Autograph, 2005), 56.

81   Barrada, *Life Full of Holes*, 4.

82   Artist's statement sent to the author.

83   Artist's statement sent to the author.

Bibliography

Published Writings of Okwui Enwezor

Compiled by Ilhan Ozan

This bibliography lists all Okwui Enwezor's published texts from 1994 to 2022. It encompasses his writings across different publication platforms, from art magazines and journals to exhibition catalogs and academic books. The few volumes that he edited but to which he did not contribute a text are not included. Writings are listed in the order published: first by year, then by month or season. Those with only a year of publication are listed first. Those with the same date are alphabetized by author name (with coauthored works alphabetized by the second author's last name) and then by title. Some of the entries include bracketed question marks [?], indicating that the relevant detail has not been found. All entries have been checked against the corresponding physical publications except those that are marked as a provisional entry with an asterisk (*). These entries were listed in Enwezor's personal cv, but neither a physical copy nor a digital record has been found. The compiler would be grateful for information about these or other entries. Please contact Ilhan Ozan at ilhan.ozan@nyu.edu.

1994

Enwezor, Okwui. "The Skoto Gallery of Contemporary African Art." *African Profiles International*, June–July 1994: 38–39.

Enwezor, Okwui. "Artefacts of Memory: The Sculptures of Leonardo Drew." *Nka: Journal of Contemporary African Art*, no. 1 (Fall/Winter 1994): 47–49.

Enwezor, Okwui. "'Fusion: West African Artists at the Venice Biennale.'" *Nka: Journal of Contemporary African Art*, no. 1 (Fall/Winter 1994): 56–59.

Enwezor, Okwui. "Redrawing the Boundaries: Towards a New African Art Discourse." *Nka: Journal of Contemporary African Art*, no. 1 (Fall/Winter 1994): 3–7.

Enwezor, Okwui. "Vortex #3." *Africa World Review*, no. [?] (Winter 1994): [??].*

1995

Enwezor, Okwui. *The Gift: Sculptures by Bright Bimpong and Tom Otterness*. New York: Skoto Gallery, January 1995. Exhibition brochure.

Enwezor, Okwui, and Salah M. Hassan. "New Visions: Recent Works by Six African Artists." In *New Visions: Recent Works by Six African Artists*, edited by Okwui Enwezor and Salah M. Hassan, 3–7. Eatonville, FL: Zora Neale Hurston National Museum of Fine Arts, 1995.

Enwezor, Okwui. "From the Editor." *Nka: Journal of Contemporary African Art*, no. 2 (Spring/Summer 1995): 7.

Enwezor, Okwui. "The Inverted Sign." *Nka: Journal of Contemporary African Art*, no. 2 (Spring/Summer 1995): 44–49.

Enwezor, Okwui. "Toyce Anderson—Critical Interventions: Beyond Abjection." *Nka: Journal of Contemporary African Art*, no. 2 (Spring/Summer 1995): 70–71.

Enwezor, Okwui, David Hammons, Bill Hutson, Al Loving, Stanley Whitney, David Henderson, Jameel Moondoc, et al. "Forum: African American Artists on Issues of Museums and Representation of African American Art." *Nka: Journal of Contemporary African Art*, no. 2 (Spring/Summer 1995): 34–41.

Enwezor, Okwui, interviewer. "Ouattara: Beyond Shamanism." Interview with Ouattara. *Nka: Journal of Contemporary African Art*, no. 2 (Spring/Summer 1995): 25–29.

Enwezor, Okwui. "Sculptor: Helen Evans Ramsaran." *African Profiles International*, May 1995: 50.

Enwezor, Okwui. "The Body in Question: Whose Body? 'Black Male: Representations of Masculinity in Contemporary American Art.'" *Third Text* 9, no. 31 (June 1995): 67–70.

Enwezor, Okwui. *Modern Life: A Continuously Elaborated Task*. Newark, NJ: Aljira, a Center for Contemporary Art; Newark, NJ: Newark Museum, September 1995.* Exhibition brochure.

Enwezor, Okwui. "Bright Bimpong: Recent Sculptures." *Atlántica: Internacional Revista de las Artes*, no. 11 (Autumn 1995): 179–82.

Enwezor, Okwui. "From the Editor." *Nka: Journal of Contemporary African Art*, no. 3 (Fall/Winter 1995): 9.

Enwezor, Okwui. "Between Worlds: Postmodernism and African Artists in the Western Metropolis." *Atlántica: Internacional Revista de las Artes*, no. 12 (Winter 1995–96): 119–33. Also published in *Reading the Contemporary: African Art from Theory to the Marketplace*, edited by Olu Oguibe and Okwui Enwezor, 245–75. London: Institute for International Visual Arts; Cambridge, MA: MIT Press, 1999.

Enwezor, Okwui. "A Critical Presence: *Drum* Magazine in Context." In *In/Sight: African Photographers, 1940 to the Present*, 179–91. New York: H. N. Abrams for the Solomon R. Guggenheim Museum, 1996. Also published in *Modern Art in Africa, Asia and Latin America: An Introduction to Global Modernisms*, edited by Elaine O'Brien, Everlyn Nicodemus, Melissa Chiu, Benjamin Genocchio, Mary K. Coffey, and Roberto Tejada, 58–62. Chichester, UK: Wiley-Blackwell, 2012.

Enwezor, Okwui. "Foreword: Note from the Edge of Nation." In *Art in South Africa: The Future Present*, edited by Sue Williamson and Ashraf Jamal, n.p. Cape Town: David Philip, 1996.

Enwezor, Okwui. "In Transit." In *Interzones: A Work in Progress*, edited by Anders Michelson and Octavio Zaya, 61–67. Copenhagen: Kunstforeningen; Uppsala: Uppsala Konstmuseum, 1996.

Enwezor, Okwui. "Strike a Pose: The Moffie's Brave World." In *Interzones: A Work in Progress*, edited by Anders Michelson and Octavio Zaya, 68–69. Copenhagen: Kunstforeningen; Uppsala: Uppsala Konstmuseum, 1996.

Enwezor, Okwui. "Writing inside the Hyphen." *Index on Censorship* 25, no. 3 (1996): 161–65.

Enwezor, Okwui, and Octavio Zaya. "Colonial Imaginary, Tropes of Disruption: History, Culture, and Representation in the Works of African Photographers." In *In/Sight: African Photographers, 1940 to the Present*, edited by Octavio Zaya, Clare Bell, Olu Oguibe, and Okwui Enwezor, 17–47. New York: Solomon R. Guggenheim Museum, 1996. Distributed by H. N. Abrams. Also published as "Negritude, Pan-Africanism, and Postcolonial African Identity: African Portrait Photography." In *Modern Art in Africa, Asia and Latin America: An Introduction to Global Modernisms*, edited by Elaine O'Brien, Everlyn Nicodemus, Melissa Chiu, Benjamin Genocchio, Mary K. Coffey, and Roberto Tejada, 49–57. Chichester, UK: Wiley-Blackwell, 2012.

Enwezor, Okwui. "Occupied Territories: Power, Access and African Art." *Frieze*, no. 26 (January–February 1996): 37–41. Also published in *Glendora Review: African Quarterly on the Arts* 1, no. 3 (1996): 29–34.

Enwezor, Okwui, and Octavio Zaya. "Moving In: Eight Contemporary African Artists." *Flash Art International*, no. 186 (January–February 1996): 84–89.

Enwezor, Okwui. "The Ruined City: Desolation, Rapture, and Georges Adéagbo." *Nka: Journal of Contemporary African Art*, no. 4 (Spring 1996): 14–17.

Enwezor, Okwui, and Olu Oguibe, interviewers. "Frank Bowling: A Conversation." Interview with Frank Bowling. *Nka: Journal of Contemporary African Art*, no. 4 (Spring 1996): 18–23, 72.

Enwezor, Okwui. "Ellen Gallagher." *Frieze*, no. 28 (May 1996): 74–75.

Enwezor, Okwui, and Octavio Zaya. "African Edge: African Art at Home and Abroad." *Flash Art International*, no. 188 (May–June 1996): 75.

Enwezor, Okwui. "Social Grace: The Work of Lorna Simpson." *Third Text* 10, no. 35 (Summer 1996): 43–58.

Enwezor, Okwui, and Octavio Zaya. "Bringing Africa into Focus: A Photo Essay." *American Visions: The Magazine of Afro-American Culture* 11, no. 3 (June–July 1996): 14–18.

Enwezor, Okwui, and Ian Berry. "Project: Madame Costello's Ball." *Nka: Journal of Contemporary African Art*, no. 5 (Fall 1996): 38–39.

Enwezor, Okwui. "Art on My Mind." *Nka: Journal of Contemporary African Art*, no. 5 (Fall/Winter 1996): 66–67. Also published as "A Necessary Icon?" *International Review of African American Art*, no. [?] (Spring 1996): [??].*

Enwezor, Okwui. "FNB Vita Art Now." *Frieze*, no. 30 (September–October 1996): 84.

Enwezor, Okwui. "Antoinette Murdoch." *Frieze*, no. 31 (November–December 1996): 80–81.

1997

Enwezor, Okwui. "Introduction: Travel Notes, Living, Working, and Travelling in a Restless World." In *Trade Routes: History and Geography; 2nd Johannesburg Biennale*, edited by Matthew de Bord and Roy Bester, 7–12. Johannesburg: Greater Johannesburg Metropolitan Council, 1997. Also excerpted in *Networks*, edited by Lars Bang Larsen, 122–24. Cambridge, MA: MIT Press, 2014.

Enwezor, Okwui. "Neglected Artform or Poor Relation? The Importance of Printmaking in Africa." In *Contemporary South African Art: The Gencor Collection*, edited by Kendell Geers, 65–79. Johannesburg: Jonathan Ball, 1997.

Enwezor, Okwui. "Okwui Enwezor—Interview." Interview by Pat Binder and Gerhard Haupt. Universes-in-Universe, July 5, 1997. http://universes-in-universe. de/car/africus/e_enwez.htm. Also published in *Trade Routes Revisited: A Project Marking the 15th Anniversary of the Second Johannesburg Biennale—1997–2012*, edited by Joost Bosland and Sophie Perryer, 18–20. Cape Town: Stevenson, 2012.

Enwezor, Okwui. "A Question of Place: Revisions, Reassessments, Diaspora." In *Transforming the Crown: African, Asian, and Caribbean Artists in Britain, 1966–1996*, edited by Mora J. Beauchamp-Byrd and Franklin Sirmans, 80–88. New York: Franklin H. Williams Caribbean Cultural Center/African Diaspora Institute, 1997. Also published in *Unpacking Europe: Towards a Critical Reading*, edited by Salah Hassan and Iftikhar Dadi, 234–43. Rotterdam: Museum Boijmans Van Beuningen; Rotterdam: NAi, 2001.

Enwezor, Okwui. "Basquiat." *Frieze*, no. 32 (January–February 1997): 82–83.

Enwezor, Okwui. "Inclusion/Exclusion: Art in the Age of Global Migration and Postcolonialism." *Frieze*, no. 33 (March–April 1997): 89–90.

Enwezor, Okwui. "Spiral Village." *Frieze*, no. 34 (May 1997): 82–83.

Enwezor, Okwui. "Gabriel Orozco: Infinite Silences." *Atlántica: Internacional Revista de las Artes*, no. 17 (Summer 1997): 136–47.

Enwezor, Okwui. "The Joke Is on You: The Work of Yinka Shonibare." *Nka: Journal of Contemporary African Art*, no. 6–7 (Summer/Fall 1997): 10–11. Also published as "Yinka Shonibare: The Joke Is on You." *Flash Art International*, no. 197 (November–December 1997): 96–97.

Enwezor, Okwui, interviewer. "A Conversation with Catherine David." Interview with Catherine David. *Siksi: The Nordic Art Review* 12, no. 3 (Autumn 1997): [??].*

Enwezor, Okwui. "Reframing the Black Subject: Ideology and Fantasy in Contemporary South African Representation." *Third Text* 11, no. 40 (Autumn 1997): 21–40. Also published in *Reading the Contemporary: African Art from Theory to the Marketplace*, edited by Olu Oguibe and Okwui Enwezor, 376–99. London: Institute for International Visual Arts; Cambridge, MA: MIT Press, 1999. Also excerpted in *Changing States: Contemporary Art and Ideas in an Era of Globalisation*, edited by Gilane Tawadros, 82–87. London: Institute of International Visual Arts, 2004.

1998

Enwezor, Okwui. "Between Locality and Worldliness." In *Cross/ing: Time, Space, Movement*, edited by Melissa Ho, 57–63. Santa Monica, CA: Smart Art, 1998. A revised version is also included in Okwui Enwezor, Mónica Amor, Gao Minglu, Oscar Ho, Kobena Mercer, and Irit Rogoff. "Liminalities: Discussions on the Global and the Local." *Art Journal* 57, no. 4 (Winter 1998): 28–50.

Enwezor, Okwui. "Collision of Worlds." In *The Archive of Development*, edited by Annette W. Balkema and Henk Slager, 71–76. Lier and Boog 13. Amsterdam: Rodopi, 1998.

Enwezor, Okwui. "A Few Notes on Tracey Rose's Quiet Subversion." In *Guarene Arte 98*, [??]. Turin: Fondazione Sandretto Re Rebaudengo per l'Arte and Neos Edizioni, 1998.*

Enwezor, Okwui. "Impressive Perversity." In *Cinco continentes y una ciudad*, edited by Marta Palau, 45–56. Mexico City: Gobierno del Distrito Federal, 1998.

Enwezor, Okwui. "Moments of Violence." In *The Edge of Awareness*, edited by Adelina von Furstenberg, 84–87. Milan: Edizioni Charta, 1998.

Enwezor, Okwui. "Remembrance of Things Past: Memory and the Archive." In *Democracy's Images: Photography and Visual Art after Apartheid*, edited by Jan-Erik Lundstrom and Katarina Pierre, 23–27. Umeå, Sweden: BildMuseet, 1998. A revised version is also published in *Trauma and Memory*, edited by Franz Kaltenbeck and Peter Weibel, 19–34. Vienna: Passagen Verlag, 2000.

Enwezor, Okwui. "William Kentridge." In *Cream: Contemporary Art in Culture*, 372–76. London: Phaidon, 1998.

Enwezor, Okwui, and Santu Mofokeng. "Black Photo Album/Look at Me: 1890–1950." In "Memory," special issue, *Grand Street*, no. 64 (Spring 1998): 152–58.

Enwezor, Okwui. "Swords Drawn: William Kentridge." *Frieze*, no. 39 (March–April 1998): 66–69. Also published in *William Kentridge*, edited by Carolyn Christov-Bakargiev, 188–89. Brussels: Société des Expositions du Palais des Beaux-Arts de Bruxelles in association with Kunstverein München and Neue Galerie Graz, 1998.

Enwezor, Okwui. "Harlem on My Mind: Rhapsodies in Black: Art of the Harlem Renaissance." *Nka: Journal of Contemporary African Art*, no. 8 (Spring/Summer 1998): 58–61.

Enwezor, Okwui. "The Second Johannesburg Biennale." Interview by Carol Becker. *Art Journal* 57, no. 2 (Summer 1998): 101–7.

Enwezor, Okwui. "Dak'Art: The 4th Dakar Biennale." *Frieze*, no. 42 (September–October 1998): 95–96.

Enwezor, Okwui, interviewer. "Truth and Responsibility: A Conversation with William Kentridge." Interview with William Kentridge. *Parkett* 54 (1998/99): 165–70.

1999

Enwezor, Okwui. "Haptic Visions: The Films of Steve McQueen." In *Steve McQueen*, edited by Gerrie van Noord, 37–50. London: Institute of Contemporary Arts in collaboration with the Kunsthalle Zürich, 1999. Distributed by D.A.P./Distributed Art Publishers.

Enwezor, Okwui. "Mirror's Edge." In *Mirror's Edge*, edited by Okwui Enwezor, Jan-Erik Lundström, and Johan Sjöström, 12–24. Umeå, Sweden: BildMuseet, 1999.

Enwezor, Okwui. "Tricking the Mind: The Work of Yinka Shonibare." In *Yinka Shonibare—Dressing Down*, edited by Elizabeth Ann McGregor and Alessandro Vincentelli, 8–19. Birmingham: Ikon Gallery; Oslo: Henie Onstad Kunstsenter, 1999. Also published in *Authentic Ex-centric: Conceptualism in Contemporary African Art*, edited by Salah M. Hassan and Olu Oguibe, 214–27. Ithaca, NY: Forum for African Arts, 2001. Also published in *Yinka Shonibare*, edited by Christine Y. Kim, 15–24. New York: Studio Museum in Harlem, 2002.

Enwezor, Okwui. "Where, What, Who, When: A Few Notes on 'African' Conceptualism." In *Global Conceptualism: Points of Origin, 1950s–1980s*, edited by Philomena Mariani, 108–17. New York: Queens Museum of Art, 1999. Also published in *Authentic Ex-centric: Conceptualism in Contemporary African Art*, edited by Salah M. Hassan and Olu Oguibe, 72–83. Ithaca, NY: Forum for African Arts, 2001.

Enwezor, Okwui, and Olu Oguibe. Introduction to *Reading the Contemporary: African Art from Theory to the Marketplace*, edited by Olu Oguibe and Okwui Enwezor, 9–14. London: Institute for International Visual Arts; Cambridge, MA: MIT Press, 1999.

2000

Enwezor, Okwui, interviewer. "Interview." Interview with Thomas Hirschhorn. In *Jumbo Spoons and Big Cake*, edited by James Rondeau and Susanne Ghez, 26–35. Chicago: Art Institute of Chicago and the Renaissance Society at the University of Chicago, 2000. Also excerpted in *The Archive*, edited by Charles Merewether, 117–20. London: Whitechapel Gallery; Cambridge, MA: MIT Press, 2006.

Enwezor, Okwui, interviewer. "Between Mask and Fantasy. Interview with Iké Udé." In *Beyond Decorum: The Photography of Iké Udé*, edited by Mark H. C. Besirre and Lauri Firstenberg, 70–73. Cambridge, MA: MIT Press; Portland, Maine: Institute of Contemporary Art at Maine College of Art, 2000.

2001

Enwezor, Okwui, interviewer. "Matter and Consciousness: An Insistent Gaze from a Not Disinterested Photographer." Interview with David Goldblatt. In *Fifty-One Years: David Goldblatt*, 13–43. Barcelona: EDITORIAL ACTAR and MACBA, 2001.

Enwezor, Okwui. "The Nostalgic Curator: Art Exhibitions at the Limits of Art History." In *Remarks on Interventive Tendencies*, edited by Henrik Plenge Jakobsen, Lars Bang Larsen, and Superflex, 26–57. Copenhagen: Danish Contemporary Art Foundation; Copenhagen: Borgens Forlag, 2001.

Enwezor, Okwui. "Phases of Monument: Liisa Roberts' Sidewalk." *Parkett* 61 (2001): 177–81.

Enwezor, Okwui. "The Short Century: Independence and Liberation Movements in Africa, 1945–1994: An Introduction." In *The Short Century: Independence and Liberation Movements in Africa, 1945–1994*, edited by Okwui Enwezor, 10–16. Munich, London, and New York: Prestel; Munich: Museum Villa Stuck, 2001. Excerpted as "Le Socialisme Africain/African Socialism." In *Georges Adéagbo: Archaeology of Motivations—Rewriting History*, edited by Silvia Eiblmayr, 88–89. Ostfildern-Ruit, Germany: Hatje Cantz, 2001.

Enwezor, Okwui. "Trickster Urbanism: The Architectural Simulations of Bodys Isek Kingelez." In *Bodys Isek Kingelez*, edited by Yilmaz Dziewior, 90–94. Ostfildern-Ruit, Germany: Hatje Cantz; Hamburg: Kunstverein Hamburg, 2001.

Enwezor, Okwui. "Without Origin: Chris Sauter's *Graft*." In *Chris Sauter 99.3*, n.p. San Antonio, TX: ArtPace, 2001.

Enwezor, Okwui, and Olu Oguibe. "Lagos: 1955–1970." In *Century City: Art and Culture in the Modern Metropolis*, edited by Iwona Blazwick, 42–69. London: Tate, 2001.

Enwezor, Okwui, interviewer. "'Elsewhere': A Conversation with Thelma Golden." Interview with Thelma Golden. *Nka: Journal of Contemporary African Art*, no. 13–14 (Spring/Summer 2001): 26–33.

Enwezor, Okwui. "Afterimages: Stan Douglas' Le Détroit and Comments on Other Works." *Nka: Journal of Contemporary African Art*, no. 15 (Fall/Winter 2001): 18–25.

2002

Enwezor, Okwui. "The Black Box." In *Documenta11_Platform5 (Exhibition)*, edited by Okwui Enwezor, Carlos Basualdo, Ute Meta Bauer, Susanne Ghez, Sarat Maharaj, Mark Nash, and Octavio Zaya, 42–55. Ostfildern-Ruit, Germany: Hatje Cantz, 2002.

Enwezor, Okwui. Introduction. With Carlos Basualdo, Ute Meta Bauer, Susanne Ghez, Sarat Maharaj, Mark Nash, and Octavio Zaya. In *Documenta11_Platform1 (Democracy Unrealized)*, edited by Okwui Enwezor, Carlos Basualdo, Ute Meta Bauer, Susanne Ghez, Sarat Maharaj, Mark Nash, and Octavio Zaya, 13–17. Ostfildern-Ruit, Germany: Hatje Cantz, 2002.

Enwezor, Okwui. Introduction. With Carlos Basualdo, Ute Meta Bauer, Susanne Ghez, Sarat Maharaj, Mark Nash, and Octavio Zaya. In *Documenta11_Platform2 (Experiments with Truth)*, edited by Okwui Enwezor, Carlos Basualdo, Ute Meta Bauer, Susanne Ghez, Sarat Maharaj, Mark Nash, and Octavio Zaya, 13–17. Ostfildern-Ruit, Germany: Hatje Cantz, 2002.

Enwezor, Okwui. Introduction. With Carlos Basualdo, Ute Meta Bauer, Susanne Ghez, Sarat Maharaj, Mark Nash, and Octavio Zaya. In *Documenta11_Platform4 (Under Siege: Four African Cities, Freetown, Johannesburg, Kinshasa, Lagos)*, edited by Okwui Enwezor, Carlos Basualdo, Ute Meta Bauer, Susanne Ghez, Sarat Maharaj, Mark Nash, and Octavio Zaya, 13–20. Ostfildern-Ruit, Germany: Hatje Cantz, 2002.

Enwezor, Okwui. "Mega-exhibitions and the Antinomies of a Transnational Global Form." Lecture at Humboldt University in Berlin, December 4, 2001. Published as *Grossausstellungen und die Antinomien einer transnationalen globalen Form*. Edited by Gottfried Boehm and Horst Bredekamp. Berliner Thyssen-Vorlesung zur Ikonologie der Gegenwart 1. Munich: Wilhelm Fink Verlag, 2002. Also published in *Manifesta Journal*, no. 2 (Winter 2003/Spring 2004): 94–119. Also published in *Documents*, no. 23 (Spring 2004): 2–19. Also published in *Other Cities, Other Worlds: Urban Imaginaries in a Globalizing Age*, edited by Andreas Huyssen, 147–80. Durham, NC: Duke University Press, 2008. Also published in *The Biennial Reader: An Anthology on Large-Scale Perennial Exhibitions of Contemporary Art*, edited by Elena Filipovic, Marieke van Hal, and Solveig Øvstebo, 426–45. Bergen, Norway: Bergen Kunsthall; Ostfildern-Ruit, Germany: Hatje Cantz, 2010.

Enwezor, Okwui. Preface. With Boris Groys, Hans Georg Knapp, and Ulrich Podewils. In *Documenta11_Platform1 (Democracy Unrealized)*, edited by Okwui Enwezor, Carlos Basualdo, Ute Meta Bauer, Susanne Ghez, Sarat Maharaj, Mark Nash, and Octavio Zaya, 9–11. Ostfildern-Ruit, Germany: Hatje Cantz, 2002.

Enwezor, Okwui. Preface. With Adebayo Olukoshi and Heiko Sievers. In *Documenta11_Platform4 (Under Siege: Four African Cities, Freetown, Johannesburg, Kinshasa, Lagos)*, edited by Okwui Enwezor, Carlos Basualdo, Ute Meta Bauer, Susanne Ghez, Sarat Maharaj, Mark Nash, and Octavio Zaya, 9–11. Ostfildern-Ruit, Germany: Hatje Cantz, 2002.

Enwezor, Okwui. Preface. With Els van der Plas and Alka Pande. In *Documenta11_Platform2 (Experiments with Truth)*, edited by Okwui Enwezor, Carlos Basualdo, Ute Meta Bauer, Susanne Ghez, Sarat Maharaj, Mark Nash, and Octavio Zaya, 9–11. Ostfildern-Ruit, Germany: Hatje Cantz, 2002.

Enwezor, Okwui. Preface to *Documenta11_Platform5 (Exhibition)*, edited by Okwui Enwezor, Carlos Basualdo, Ute Meta Bauer, Susanne Ghez, Sarat Maharaj, Mark Nash, and Octavio Zaya, 40. Ostfildern-Ruit, Germany: Hatje Cantz, 2002.

Enwezor, Okwui, and Franz-W. Kaiser. *Iba Ndiaye: Peintre entre continents—vous avez dit "primitif"? / Iba Ndiaye: Painter between Continents—Primitive? Says Who?* Paris: A. Biro, 2002.

Enwezor, Okwui. "A Conversation with Okwui Enwezor." Interview by Carol Becker. *Art Journal* 61, no. 2 (Summer 2002): 8–27.

2003

Enwezor, Okwui. "Interview: Okwui Enwezor." Interview by Anna Detheridge. In *Global Village: The 1960s*, edited by Stéphane Aquin, Diane Charbonneu, and Anna Detheridge, 110–14. Montreal: Museum of Fine Arts; Gent: Snoeck, 2003.

Enwezor, Okwui. Introduction. With Carlos Basualdo, Ute Meta Bauer, Susanne Ghez, Sarat Maharaj, Mark Nash, and Octavio Zaya. In *Documenta11_Platform3 (Creolité and Creolization)*, edited by Okwui Enwezor, Carlos Basualdo, Ute Meta Bauer, Susanne Ghez, Sarat Maharaj, Mark Nash, and Octavio Zaya, 13–16. Ostfildern-Ruit, Germany: Hatje Cantz, 2003. Also excerpted as "Créolité and Creolization, 2002." In *Appropriation*, edited by David Evans, 137–38. London: Whitechapel Gallery; Cambridge, MA: MIT Press, 2009.

Enwezor, Okwui. "Kay Hassan's Post-apartheid Gambit." In *Kay Hassan*, edited by Bernhard Fibicher, 6–16. Bern: Kunsthalle Bern, 2003.

Enwezor, Okwui. Preface to *Documenta11_Platform3 (Creolité and Creolization)*, edited by Okwui Enwezor, Carlos Basualdo, Ute Meta Bauer, Susanne Ghez, Sarat Maharaj, Mark Nash, and Octavio Zaya, 9–11. Ostfildern-Ruit, Germany: Hatje Cantz, 2003.

Enwezor, Okwui. "The Production of Social Space as Artwork: Protocols of Community in the Work of Le Groupe Amos and Huit Facettes." In *A Fiction of Authenticity: Contemporary Africa Abroad*, edited by Shannon Fitzgerald, 52–69. St. Louis, MO: Contemporary Art Museum St. Louis, 2003. Also published in *Collectivism after Modernism: The Art of Social Imagination after 1945*, edited by Blake Stimson and Gregory Sholette, 223–51. Minneapolis: University of Minnesota Press, 2007. Also excerpted as "Production of Social Space as Artwork, 2007." In *Practice*, edited by Marcus Boon and Gabriel Levine, 106–8. London: Whitechapel Gallery; Cambridge, MA: MIT Press, 2018. Also excerpted as "Huit Façettes, 2007." In *The Rural*, edited by Myvillages, 191–96. London: Whitechapel Gallery; Cambridge, MA: MIT Press, 2019.

Enwezor, Okwui. "Terminal Modernity: Rem Koolhaas's Discourse on Entropy." In *What Is OMA? Considering Rem Koolhaas and the Office for Metropolitan Architecture*, edited by Véronique Patteeuw, 103–19. Rotterdam: NAi, 2003.

Enwezor, Okwui, interviewer. "Yinka Shonibare: Of Hedonism, Masquerade, Carnivalesque and Power—the Art of Yinka Shonibare." Interview with Yinka Shonibare. In *Looking Both Ways: Art of the Contemporary African Diaspora*, edited by Laurie Ann Farrell, 163–77. New York: Museum for African Art; Gent: Snoeck, 2003.

Enwezor, Okwui. "The Postcolonial Constellation: Contemporary Art in a State of Permanent Transition." *Research in African Literatures* 34, no. 4 (Winter 2003): 57–82. A shorter version is published in *Antinomies of Art and Culture: Modernity, Postmodernity, Contemporaneity*, edited by Terry Smith, Okwui Enwezor, and Nancy Condee, 207–34. Durham, NC: Duke University Press, 2008. Also published in *The Visual Culture Reader*, edited by Nicholas Mirzoeff, 552–69. 3rd ed. London: Routledge, 2013.

Enwezor, Okwui, Tim Griffin, James Meyer, Francesco Bonami, Catherine David, Hans-Ulrich Obrist, Martha Rosler, and Yinka Shonibare. "Global Tendencies: Globalism and the Large-Scale Exhibition." *Artforum* 42, no. 3 (November 2003): 152–63.

2004

Enwezor, Okwui. "The Artist as Producer in Times of Crisis." In *Malmö Art Academy Yearbook* 2004, [??]. Lund: Lund University, Sweden, 2004.* Also published in *Empires, Ruins, + Networks*, edited by Scott McQuire and Nikos Papastergiadis, 11–51. London: Rivers Oram; Melbourne: Melbourne University Publishing, 2005.

Enwezor, Okwui. "David Goldblatt: Photography without Event." In *Citigroup Photography Prize, 2004*, edited by Lisa Le Feuvre, 58–60. London: Photographers' Gallery, 2004.

Enwezor, Okwui. "Documentary/Vérité: Bio-Politics, Human Rights and the Figure of 'Truth' in Contemporary Art." *Australian and New Zealand Journal of Art* 5, no. 1 (2004): 11–42. Also excerpted in *Experiments with Truth*, edited by Mark Nash, 97–103. Philadelphia: Fabric Workshop and Museum, 2005. Also published in *The Green Room: Reconsidering the Documentary and Contemporary Art*, edited by Maria Lind and Hito Steyerl, 62–102. Berlin: Sternberg; Annandale-on-the-Hudson: Center for Curatorial Studies and Hessel Museum of Art, 2008.

Enwezor, Okwui. "The Enigma of the Rainbow Nation: Contemporary South African Art at the Crossroads of History." In *Personal Affects: Power and Poetics in Contemporary South African Art*, edited by Sophie Perryer, 23–43. New York: Museum for African Art; Cape Town: Spier, 2004. Also excerpted in *Jane Alexander: Surveys (from the Cape of Good Hope)*, edited by Pep Subirós, 172–73. New York: Museum for African Art; Barcelona: ACTAR, 2011.

Enwezor, Okwui. "Popular Theatre, Photography, and Difference." In *Samuel Fosso*, edited by Maria Francesca Bonetti and Guido Schlinkert, 14–19. Milan: 5 Continents; Rome: Istituto Centrale per la Grafica, 2004.

Enwezor, Okwui, interviewer. "The Paulding Avenue Trilogy: Interview with Thomas Allen Harris." *Nka: Journal of Contemporary African Art*, no. 19 (Summer 2004): 20–25.

2005

Enwezor, Okwui. "Life and Afterlife in Benin: Photography in the Service of Ethnographic Realism." In *Life and Afterlife in Benin*, edited by Alex Van Gelder, 6–15. London: Phaidon, 2005.

Enwezor, Okwui, interviewer. "On the Nature of Vision and Visuality in the Landscape of South Africa: William Kentridge Speaks with Okwui Enwezor." *FYI* (San Francisco Art Institute), no. 1 (May 2005): 19–20.

2006

Enwezor, Okwui. Introduction to *The Unhomely: Phantom Scenes in Global Society*, edited by Okwui Enwezor, 12–16. Seville: Fundación Bienal Internacional de Arte Contemporáneo de Sevilla, 2006.

Enwezor, Okwui. "Narrative in the Photographic Work of Ahlam Shibli." In *Ahlam Shibli: Trackers*, edited by Adam Szymczyk, 23–30. Cologne: Verlag der Buchhandlung Walther König; Basel: Kunsthalle Basel, 2006.

Enwezor, Okwui. "Popular Sovereignty and Public Scape: David Adjaye's Architecture of Immanence." In *David Adjaye: Making Public Buildings—Specificity, Customization, Imbrication*, edited by Peter Allison, 8–12. London: Thames and Hudson, 2006.

Enwezor, Okwui. "Rapport des Forces: African Comics and Their Publics." In *African Comics*, edited by Samir S. Patel, 17–19. New York: Studio Museum in Harlem, 2006.

Enwezor, Okwui. "Repetition and Differentiation: Lorna Simpson's Iconography of the Racial Sublime." In *Lorna Simpson*, 102–30. New York: Harry N. Abrams in association with the American Federation of Arts, 2006. Also excerpted as "The American Sublime and the Racial Self, 2006." In *The Sublime*, edited by Simon Morley, 193–97. London: Whitechapel Gallery; Cambridge, MA: MIT Press, 2010.

Enwezor, Okwui. "Snap Judgments: New Positions in Contemporary African Photography." In *Snap Judgments: New Positions in Contemporary African Photography*, edited by Okwui Enwezor, 10–45. New York: International Center of Photography; Göttingen, Germany: Steidl, 2006.

Enwezor, Okwui. "Tebbit's Ghost." In *The Manifesta Decade: Debates on Contemporary Art Exhibitions and Biennials in Post-wall Europe*, edited by Barbara Vanderlinden and Elena Filipovic, 175–86. Cambridge, MA: MIT Press; Brussels: Roomade, 2006.

Enwezor, Okwui. "Schools of Thought: Keeping One Step Ahead: Art Schools in a Global Context." *Frieze*, no. 101 (September 2006): 142.

Enwezor, Okwui. "Best of 2006." *Artforum* 45, no. 4 (December 2006): 296–97.

2007

Enwezor, Okwui. "Coalition Building: Black Audio Film Collective and Trans-national Post-colonialism." In *The Ghosts of Songs: The Film Art of the Black Audio Film Collective, 1982–1998*, edited by Kodwo Eshun and Anjalika Sagar, 106–23. Liverpool: Liverpool University Press, 2007.

Enwezor, Okwui. "Contemporary Art's Civilizational Gap." In *Not Only Possible, but Also Necessary: Optimism in the Age of Global War; 10th International Istanbul Biennial*, edited by İlkay Baliç Ayvaz, 384–90. Istanbul: Istanbul Foundation for Culture and Arts, 2007.

Enwezor, Okwui. "Curating beyond the Canon: Okwui Enwezor Interviewed by Paul O'Neill." In *Curating Subjects*, edited by Paul O'Neill, 109–22. London: Open Editions, 2007.

Enwezor, Okwui. "The Diasporic Imagination: The Memory Works of María Magdalena Campos-Pons." In *María Magdalena Campos-Pons: Everything Is Separated by Water*, edited by Lisa D. Freiman, 64–89. Indianapolis: Indianapolis Museum of Art in association with Yale University Press (New Haven, CT), 2007.

Enwezor, Okwui. "Forms of Arrangement/Engagement: Josephine Meckseper's Display of Political Pop." In *Josephine Meckseper*, edited by Marion Ackermann, 48–54. Ostfildern-Ruit, Germany: Hatje Cantz, 2007.

Enwezor, Okwui. "Place-Making or in the 'Wrong Place': Contemporary Art and the Postcolonial Condition." In *Lyon Biennial 2007: 00s—the History of a Decade That Has Not Yet Been Named*, edited by Stéphanie Moisdon and Hans Ulrich Obrist, 209–25. Zurich: JRP/Ringier; Dijon: Les presses du reel, 2007. Also published in *Diaspora, Memory, Place: David Hammons, Maria Magdalena Campos-Pons, Pamela Z*, edited by Salah M. Hassan and Cheryl Finley, 106–29. Munich: Prestel, 2008. An abridged version is also published in *Former West: Art and the Contemporary after 1989*, edited by Maria Hlavajova and Simon Sheikh, 47–57. Utrecht: BAK, basis voor actuele kunst; Cambridge, MA: MIT Press, 2016.

Enwezor, Okwui. "History Lessons." *Artforum* 46, no. 1 (September 2007): 382–86.

Enwezor, Okwui, interviewer. "Photography in the Shadow of Death: A Conversation with Touhami Ennadre." Interview with Touhami Ennadre. *Nka: Journal of Contemporary African Art*, no. 21 (Fall 2007): 10–23.

Enwezor, Okwui. "Best of 2007." *Artforum* 46, no. 4 (December 2007): 316–17.

2008

Enwezor, Okwui, interviewer. *James Casebere Speaks with Okwui Enwezor*. Interview with James Casebere. Madrid: La Fábrica and Fundación Telefónica, 2008.

Enwezor, Okwui. "Archive Fever: Photography between History and the Monument." In *Archive Fever: Uses of the Document in Contemporary Art*, edited by Okwui Enwezor, 11–51. New York: International Center of Photography; Göttingen, Germany: Steidl, 2008. Also excerpted as "Documents into

Monuments: Archives as Meditations on Time, 2008." In *Memory*, edited by Ian Farr, 133–36. London: Whitechapel Gallery; Cambridge, MA: MIT Press, 2012.

Enwezor, Okwui. "Exodus of the Dogs." In *Jo Ractliffe: Terreno Ocupado*, 84–89. Johannesburg: Warren Siebrits, 2008. Also published in *Nka: Journal of Contemporary African Art*, no. 25 (Winter 2009): 78–95.

Enwezor, Okwui. "The Indeterminate Structure of Things Now: Notes on Contemporary South African Photography." In *Home Lands—Land Marks: Contemporary Art from South Africa*, edited by Tamar Garb, 28–39. London: Haunch of Venison, 2008.

Enwezor, Okwui. "On the Politics of Disaggregation: Notes on Cildo Meireles's Insertions into Ideological Circuits." In *Cildo Meireles*, edited by Guy Brett, 68–73. London: Tate; New York: D.A.P./Distributed Art Publishers, 2008.

Enwezor, Okwui. "The Politics of Spectacle." In *The 7th Gwangju Biennale*, edited by Okwui Enwezor, 10–39. Gwangju: Gwangju Biennale Foundation, 2008.

Enwezor, Okwui. "Questionnaire: In What Ways Have Artists, Academics, and Cultural Institutions Responded to the U.S.-Led Invasion and Occupation of Iraq?" *October*, no. 123 (Winter 2008): 41–44.

Enwezor, Okwui. "(Un)Civil Engineering: William Kentridge's Allegorical Landscapes." In *William Kentridge: Tapestries*, edited by Carlos Basualdo, 87–95. Philadelphia: Philadelphia Museum of Art in association with Yale University Press, 2008.

Enwezor, Okwui, Terry Smith, and Nancy Condee. Preface to *Antinomies of Art and Culture: Modernity, Postmodernity, Contemporaneity*, edited by Terry Smith, Okwui Enwezor, and Nancy Condee, xiii–xvi. Durham, NC: Duke University Press, 2008.

Enwezor, Okwui, Jessica Morgan, and Francesco Bonami. "C'est Triste Venise (Jessica Morgan, Francesco Bonami, and Okwui Enwezor Reply to Robert Storr)." *Artforum* 46, no. 6 (February 2008): 50–56.

Enwezor, Okwui. "Best of 2008." *Artforum* 47, no. 4 (December 2008): 258–59.

Enwezor, Okwui. "Curating the World." Interview by Rex Butler. *Australian and New Zealand Journal of Art* 9, nos. 1–2 (2008/9): 14–21.

2009

Enwezor, Okwui. "Better Lives, Marginal Selves: Framing the Current Reception of Contemporary South African Art." In *South African Art Now*, edited by Sue Williamson, 16–21. New York: Harper Collins, 2009.

Enwezor, Okwui. "A Lapse of Memory: Allegory in the Work of Fiona Tan." In *Fiona Tan: Rise and Fall*, edited by Bruce Grenville, 78–89. Vancouver: Vancouver Art Gallery, 2009. Also published in *Fiona Tan: Ellipsis*, edited by Hiromi Kurosawa, 122–31. Tokyo: Nitto Shoin Honsha; Kanazawa: 21st Century Museum of Contemporary Art, 2013.

Enwezor, Okwui. "Modernity and Postcolonial Ambivalence." In *Altermodern: Tate Triennial*, edited by Nicolas Bourriaud, 25–40. London: Tate, 2009. Also published in *South Atlantic Quarterly* 109, no. 3 (Summer 2010): 595–620.

Enwezor, Okwui. "Shattering the Mirror of Tradition: Chris Ofili's Triumph of Painting at the 50th Venice Biennale." In *Chris Ofili*, 142–56. New York: Rizzoli, 2009.

Enwezor, Okwui, and Chika Okeke-Agulu. *Contemporary African Art since 1980*. Bologna: Damiani, 2009.

Enwezor, Okwui. "Okwui Enwezor." Interview by Carolee Thea. In *On Curating: Interviews with Ten International Curators*, edited by Carolee Thea and Thomas Micchelli, 48–57. New York: D.A.P./Distributed Art Publishers, 2009.

Enwezor, Okwui. "Questionnaire on 'the Contemporary.'" *October*, no. 130 (Fall 2009): 33–40.

Enwezor, Okwui. "Reckoning with Empire." *Artforum* 48, no. 2 (October 2009): 175–77.

Enwezor, Okwui. "Best of 2009." *Artforum* 48, no. 4 (December 2009): 172–73.

2010

Enwezor, Okwui. "Between Apparatus and Subjectivity: Carlos Garaicoa's Post-utopian Architecture." In *Carlos Garaicoa: Overlapping*, edited by Mary Cremin, 16–21. Dublin: Irish Museum of Modern Art, 2010. Distributed by Edizioni Charta (Milan).

Enwezor, Okwui. "Documentary's Discursive Spaces." In *Berlin Documentary Forum 1: New Practices across Disciplines*, edited by Hila Peleg and Bert Rebhandl, 9–15. Berlin: Haus der Kulturen der Welt, 2010.

Enwezor, Okwui. "Events of the Self: Portraiture and Social Identity—A Conceptual Framework." In *Contemporary African Photography from the Walther Collection: Events of the Self Portraiture and Social Identity*, edited by Okwui Enwezor, 23–28. Burlafingen, Germany: Walther Collection; Göttingen, Germany: Steidl, 2010.

Enwezor, Okwui. "Excessive Exposure: The Polaroid Portraits of Lyle Ashton Harris." In *Lyle Ashton Harris, Excessive Exposure: The Complete Chocolate Portraits*, 1–34. New York: Gregory R. Miller, 2010.

Enwezor, Okwui. "Gesture, Pose, Mimesis: Seydou Keïta's Portraits." In *Contemporary African Photography from the Walther Collection: Events of the Self Portraiture and Social Identity*, edited by Okwui Enwezor, 31–33. Burlafingen, Germany: Walther Collection; Göttingen, Germany: Steidl, 2010.

Enwezor, Okwui. "Idolatry of the False: Portraiture and Mass Consciousness in Candice Breitz's Video Portraits." In *The Scripted Life: Candice Breitz*, edited by Yilmaz Dziewior, 33–41. Bregenz, Austria: Kunsthaus Bregenz, 2010.

Enwezor, Okwui. "Photography after the End of Documentary Realism: Zwelethu Mthethwa's Color Photographs." In *Zwelethu Mthethwa*, edited by Isolde Brielmaier, 100–115. New York: Aperture, 2010.

Enwezor, Okwui. "The Subversion of Realism: Likeness, Resemblance and Invented Lives in Lynette Yiadom-Boakye's Post-portrait Paintings." In *Lynette Yiadom-Boakye: Any Number of Preoccupations*, 16–31. New York: Studio Museum in Harlem, 2010.

Enwezor, Okwui. "The Vexations and Pleasures of Colour: Chris Ofili's 'Afromuses' and the Dialectic of Painting." In *Chris Ofili*, edited by Judith Nesbitt, 64–77. London: Tate, 2010. Distributed in the United States and Canada by Harry N. Abrams.

Enwezor, Okwui. "Weird Beauty: Ritual Violence and Archaeology of Mass Media in Wangechi Mutu's Work." In *Wangechi Mutu, Artist of the Year 2010: My Dirty Little Heaven*, edited by Friedhelm Hütte and Christina März, 26–35. Ostfildern-Ruit, Germany: Hatje Cantz, 2010.

Enwezor, Okwui. "What Is It? The Image between Documentary and Near Documentary." In *The Storyteller*, edited by Claire Gilman and Margaret Sundell, 73–82. New York: Independent Curators International; Zurich: JRP/Ringier, 2010.

Enwezor, Okwui, and David Adjaye. "Framing and Reformatting: A Conversation between Okwui Enwezor and David Adjaye." In *David Adjaye's Geo-Graphics: A Map of Art Practices in Africa, Past and Present*, edited by Emiliano Battista, Anne Marie Bouttiaux, Koyo Kouoh, and Nicola Setari, 369–78. Brussels: BOZAR Expo/Center for Fine Arts; Milan: Silvana Editoriale, 2010.

2011

Enwezor, Okwui. "Decolonizing Architecture (DAAR): In Conversation with Okwui Enwezor." Interview with DAAR collective. In *Sharjah Biennial 10: Plot for a Biennial*, edited by Ghalya Saadawi, 277–80. Sharjah: Sharjah Art Foundation, 2011. Also published as "Decolonization: In Conversation with Okwui Enwezor." In *Permanent Temporariness*, edited by Sandi Hilal and Alessandro Petti, 139–40. Stockholm: Art and Theory, 2018.

Enwezor, Okwui. "Friend, Enemy, Neighbour, Stranger: Proximity and the Crisis of Hospitality in an African City." In *Adjaye Africa Architecture: A Photographic Survey of Metropolitan Architecture*, edited by Peter Allison, 384–89. London: Thames and Hudson, 2011.

Enwezor, Okwui. "Images of Radical Will: Santu Mofokeng's Photographic Ambivalence." In *Chasing Shadows, Santu Mofokeng: Thirty Years of Photographic Essays*, edited by Corinne Diserens, 37–44. Munich: Prestel, 2011.

Enwezor, Okwui. "Overview of the Year 1989." In *Defining Contemporary Art: 25 Years in 200 Pivotal Artworks*, 52–57. London: Phaidon, 2011.

Enwezor, Okwui. "A Radiant Conflagration: (H'reg) On Burning and the Subjectivity of Photography in Yto Barrada's Work." In *Yto Barrada, Artist of the Year 2011: Riffs*, 21–32. Ostfildern-Ruit, Germany: Hatje Cantz, 2011.

Enwezor, Okwui. "Social Mirrors: On the Dialectic of the Abstract and Figural in Ken Lum's Work." In *Ken Lum*, edited by Grant Arnold, 60–92. Vancouver: Douglas and McIntyre and Vancouver Art Gallery, 2011.

Enwezor, Okwui. "Text, Subtext, Intertext: Painting, Language, and Signifying in the Work of Glenn Ligon." In *Glenn Ligon: AMERICA*, 51–63. New York: Whitney Museum of American Art, 2011. Distributed by Yale University Press.

Enwezor, Okwui, and James Casebere. "Photography and the Illusion of History: Conversation with James Casebere and Okwui Enwezor." In *James Casebere: Works 1975–2010*, edited by Okwui Enwezor, 17–52. Bologna: Damiani, 2011.

Enwezor, Okwui, Craig Garrett, Bob Nickas, Connie Butler, Daniel Birnbaum, Suzanne Cotter, Massimiliano Gioni, Bice Curiger, and Hans Ulrich Obrist. "Round-Table Discussion." In *Defining Contemporary Art: 25 Years in 200 Pivotal Artworks*, 455–65. London: Phaidon, 2011.

Enwezor, Okwui, interviewer. "Cartographies of Uneven Exchange: The Fluidity of Sculptural Form—El Anatsui in Conversation with Okwui Enwezor." Interview with El Anatsui. *Nka: Journal of Contemporary African Art*, no. 28 (Spring 2011): 96–105.

Enwezor, Okwui. "Spring Rain: On Ai Weiwei and Sharjah Biennial." *Artforum* 49, no. 10 (Summer 2011): 75–76.

2012

Enwezor, Okwui. "2012: Reflections." In *Trade Routes Revisited: A Project Marking the 15th Anniversary of the Second Johannesburg Biennale—1997–2012*, edited by Joost Bosland and Sophie Perryer, 11–17. Cape Town: Stevenson, 2012.

Enwezor, Okwui. "Alfredo Jaar's Art of Illumination." In *Alfredo Jaar: The Sound of Silence*, 18–29. Paris: Galerie Kamel Mennour, 2012.

Enwezor, Okwui, interviewer. "Art History and Its Discontents: Reconfiguring the Museum's Permanent Collection—Conversation with Catherine Grenier." Interview with Catherine Grenier. *Le Journal de la Triennale: Forest of Signs* 5 (2012): 40–45.

Enwezor, Okwui, interviewer. "Bright Light of the Maelstrom—Okwui Enwezor Interviews Cedric Nunn." In *Cedric Nunn: Call and Response*, edited by Ralf-Peter Seippel, 20–25. Ostfildern-Ruit, Germany: Hatje Cantz; Johannesburg: Fourthwall, 2012.

Enwezor, Okwui. "The Conditions of Spectrality and Spectatorship in Thomas Ruff's Photographs." In *Thomas Ruff: Works, 1979–2011*, 9–19. Munich: Schirmer/Mosel, 2012.

Enwezor, Okwui. "El Anatsui: A Ceaseless Search for Form." *Parkett* 90 (2012): 34–39.

Enwezor, Okwui. Foreword to *Sculptural Acts*, edited by Patrizia Dander and Julienne Lorz, 9–10. Ostfildern-Ruit, Germany: Hatje Cantz; Munich: Haus der Kunst, 2012.

Enwezor, Okwui. "From Screen to Space: Projection and Reanimation in the Early Work of Steve McQueen." In *Steve McQueen: Works, 1993-2012*, 20-35. Basel: Laurenz Foundation, Schaulager Basel; Heidelberg: Kehrer, 2012.

Enwezor, Okwui, interviewer. "Gary Simmons in Conversation with Okwui Enwezor." Interview with Gary Simmons. In *Gary Simmons: Paradise*, edited by Alexander Ferrando and Manuela Mozo, 5-16. Bologna: Damiani, 2012.

Enwezor, Okwui. "Great Big Ears: ECM—a Cultural Archaeology—Notes toward an Exhibition." In *ECM: A Cultural Archaeology*, edited by Okwui Enwezor and Markus Müller, 30-50. Munich: Prestel and Haus der Kunst, 2012.

Enwezor, Okwui. Introduction to *Intense Proximity: An Anthology of the Near and the Far*, edited by Okwui Enwezor with Mélanie Bouteloup, Abdellah Karroum, Émilie Renard, and Claire Staebler, 11-14. Paris: Centre national des arts plastiques and Artlys, 2012.

Enwezor, Okwui. "Intense Proximity: Concerning the Disappearance of Distance." In *Intense Proximity: An Anthology of the Near and the Far*, edited by Okwui Enwezor with Mélanie Bouteloup, Abdellah Karroum, Émilie Renard, and Claire Staebler, 18-34. Paris: Centre national des arts plastiques and Artlys, 2012.

Enwezor, Okwui. "Locus Agonistes—Sites of Struggles." In *Meeting Points 6: Contemporary Art Festival from the Arab World*, 4-11. Berlin: Haus der Kulturen der Welt, 2012.

Enwezor, Okwui. "Topographies of Critical Practice: Exhibitions as Place and Site." *Le Journal de la Triennale: Forest of Signs* 5 (2012): 3-7.

2013

Enwezor, Okwui. "Architecture That Can Truly Be Owned by the People—Okwui Enwezor in Conversation with Andres Lepik." Interview by Andres Lepik. In *Afritecture: Building Social Change*, edited by Andres Lepik, 60-68. Ostfildern-Ruit, Germany: Hatje Cantz, 2013.

Enwezor, Okwui. "The Death of the African Archive and the Birth of the Museum: Considering Meschac Gaba's Museum of Contemporary African Art." In *Meschac Gaba: Museum of Contemporary African Art*, edited by Kerryn Greenberg, 29-49. London: Tate, 2013. Also published in *Museum and Archive on the Move: Changing Cultural Institutions in the Digital Era*, edited by Oliver Grau, Wendy Coones, and Viola Rühse, 132-47. Berlin: De Gruyter, 2017.

Enwezor, Okwui. "Foreword." In *Kendell Geers, 1988-2012*, edited by Clive Kellner, 7-9. Munich: Prestel and Haus der Kunst, 2013.

Enwezor, Okwui, moderator. "On the Aesthetic and Political Language of Art: A Conversation between Kendell Geers and William Kentridge. Moderated by Okwui Enwezor." In *Kendell Geers, 1988-2012*, edited by Clive Kellner, 94-107. Munich: Prestel and Haus der Kunst, 2013.

Enwezor, Okwui. "Rise and Fall of Apartheid: Photography and the Bureaucracy of Everyday Life." In *Rise and Fall of Apartheid: Photography and the Bureaucracy of*

Everyday Life, edited by Okwui Enwezor and Rory Bester, 20–45. Munich: Prestel, 2013.

Enwezor, Okwui. "Chinua Achebe: 1930–2013." *Artforum* 51, no. 10 (Summer 2013): 77–78.

Enwezor, Okwui. "Predicaments of Culture—Venice 2013." *Artforum* 52, no. 1 (September 2013): 326–29.

Enwezor, Okwui. "From the Editor." *Nka: Journal of Contemporary African Art*, no. 33 (Fall 2013): 4–6.

Enwezor, Okwui. "Best of 2013." *Artforum* 52, no. 4 (December 2013): 204–5.

2014

Enwezor, Okwui. "Contingency, Porosity, and the Nomadic Imagination: Notes on the Art of Pascale Marthine Tayou." In *Pascale Marthine Tayou: I Love You*, edited by Yilmaz Dziewior, 24–35. Bregenz, Austria: Kunsthaus Bregenz; Cologne: Verlag der Buchhandlung Walther Konig, 2014.

Enwezor, Okwui. Foreword to *Matthew Barney: River of Fundament*, edited by Louise Neri, 227–31. Munich: Haus der Kunst; New York: Skira Rizzoli, 2014.

Enwezor, Okwui. "Modernity and Its Discontents." In *Kerry James Marshall: Painting and Other Stuff*, edited by Nav Haq, 167–75. Antwerp: Ludion, 2014.

Enwezor, Okwui. "Photography and the Archive: 1980–2013." In *Photography: The Contemporary Era, 1981–2013*, edited by Walter Guadagnini, 88–107. Milan, Italy: Skira, 2014.

Enwezor, Okwui. "Portals and Processions: Matthew Barney's *River of Fundament*." In *Matthew Barney: River of Fundament*, edited by Louise Neri, 232–53. Munich: Haus der Kunst; New York: Skira Rizzoli, 2014.

Enwezor, Okwui, interviewer. "These Weary Territories: A Conversation between Matthew Barney and Okwui Enwezor." Interview with Matthew Barney. *Modern Painters*, April 2014, 64–73.

Enwezor, Okwui, Salah M. Hassan, and Chika Okeke-Agulu. "*Nka* at 20." *Nka: Journal of Contemporary African Art*, no. 35 (Fall 2014): 4–5.

2015

Enwezor, Okwui. "Folds of the Self: Hanne Darboven and the Quest for Universal Knowledge." In *Hanne Darboven: Enlightenment—Time Histories, a Retrospective*, edited by Okwui Enwezor and Rein Wolfs, 170–82. Munich: Prestel; Munich: Haus der Kunst, 2015.

Enwezor, Okwui. Foreword to *Anri Sala: The Present Moment*, edited by Patrizia Dander, 11–13. Cologne: Walther König; Munich: Haus der Kunst, 2015.

Enwezor, Okwui. "Gestures of Affiliation." In *David Adjaye: Form, Heft, Material*, edited by Okwui Enwezor and Zoë Ryan, 165–87. Chicago: Art Institute of Chicago, 2015. Distributed by Yale University Press.

Enwezor, Okwui. "The State of Things." In *La Biennale di Venezia, 56th International Art Exhibition: All the World's Futures*, edited by Okwui Enwezor, 16–21. Venice: Marsilio Editori, 2015.

Enwezor, Okwui, and Zoë Ryan. Introduction to *David Adjaye: Form, Heft, Material*, edited by Okwui Enwezor and Zoë Ryan, 16–19. Chicago: Art Institute of Chicago, 2015. Distributed by Yale University Press.

Enwezor, Okwui, and Terry Smith. "World Platforms, Exhibiting Adjacency, and the Surplus Value of Art." In Terry Smith, *Talking Contemporary Curating*, 85–113. New York: Independent Curators International, 2015.

Enwezor, Okwui. "Okwui Enwezor Talks with Michelle Kuo about the 56th Venice Biennale." Interview by Michelle Kuo. *Artforum* 53, no. 9 (May 2015): 85–90.

Enwezor, Okwui. "Workers' Playtime: Marx, Theater and the 56th Biennale." Interview by Massimiliano Gioni. *artpress*, no. 422 Suppl. (May 2015): 9–11.

2016

Enwezor, Okwui. "Director's Foreword." In *James Casebere: Fugitive*, edited by Okwui Enwezor, 6–8. Munich: Prestel; Munich: Haus der Kunst, 2016.

Enwezor, Okwui. "Director's Foreword." In *Postwar: Art between the Pacific and the Atlantic, 1945–1965*, edited by Okwui Enwezor, Katy Siegel, and Ulrich Wilmes, 13–15. Munich: Prestel and Haus der Kunst, 2016.

Enwezor, Okwui. "Fugitive States: James Casebere's Political Economy of Spatial Illusion." In *James Casebere: Fugitive*, edited by Okwui Enwezor, 10–21. Munich: Prestel; Munich: Haus der Kunst, 2016.

Enwezor, Okwui, interviewer. "Georg Baselitz in Conversation with Okwui Enwezor." Interview with Georg Baselitz. In *Georg Baselitz: Jumping over My Shadow*, edited by Ealan Wingate and Stefan Ratibor, 12–39. New York: Gagosian Gallery, 2016.

Enwezor, Okwui. "The Judgment of Art: Postwar and Artistic Worldliness." In *Postwar: Art between the Pacific and the Atlantic, 1945–1965*, edited by Okwui Enwezor, Katy Siegel, and Ulrich Wilmes, 20–41. Munich: Prestel; Munich: Haus der Kunst, 2016.

Enwezor, Okwui, interviewer. "Okwui Enwezor in Conversation with Sarah Sze." Interview with Sarah Sze. In *Sarah Sze*, 7–37. London: Phaidon, 2016.

Enwezor, Okwui, Chika Okeke-Agulu, and Salah M. Hassan. "Ramez Elias: In Memoriam (1958–2016)." *Nka: Journal of Contemporary African Art*, nos. 38–39 (November 2016): 5.

2017

Enwezor, Okwui, interviewer. "Conversation." Interview with Mohamed Bourouissa. In *Mohamed Bourouissa*, edited by Emma-Charlotte Gobry-Laurencin, 6–14. Paris: Kamel Mennour; Philadelphia: Barnes Foundation, 2017.

Enwezor, Okwui, interviewer. "Making Pictures: A Conversation with Thomas Struth." Interview with Thomas Struth. In *Thomas Struth*, edited by Thomas Weski and Ulrich Wilmes, 299–311. New York: D.A.P./Distributed Art Publishers, 2017.

Enwezor, Okwui. "Mappa Mundi: Frank Bowling's Cognitive Abstraction." In *Frank Bowling: Mappa Mundi*, edited by Okwui Enwezor, 16–45. Munich: Prestel; Munich: Haus der Kunst, 2017.

Enwezor, Okwui, interviewer. "Semantics of the Moving Image—Okwui Enwezor in Conversation with Theo Eshetu." Interview with Theo Eshetu. In *Theo Eshetu: The Body Electric*, edited by Ariane Beyn and Theo Eshetu, 83–94. Berlin: Sternberg, 2017.

Enwezor, Okwui, interviewer. "A Time of Reckoning: Contemporary South African Art—Okwui Enwezor in Conversation with Sue Williamson." Interview with Sue Williamson. In *Being There: South Africa, a Contemporary Scene*, edited by Suzanne Pagé and Angeline Scherf, 27–36. Paris: Fondation Louis Vuitton; Paris: Éditions Dilecta, 2017.

2018

Enwezor, Okwui. "Andy Warhol and the Painting of Catastrophe." In *Andy Warhol: From A to B and Back Again*, edited by Donna De Salvo, 34–41. New York: Whitney Museum of American Art, 2018. Distributed by Yale University Press.

Enwezor, Okwui. "Cologne/Kinshasa: The Parodic Critiques and Social Satires of Jörg Immendorff and Chéri Samba's Realism." In *Jörg Immendorff: For All Beloved in the World*, edited by Ulrich Wilmes, 3–15. Cologne: Verlag der Buchhandlung Walther König, 2018.

Enwezor, Okwui. "Corners, Fields, Portals: Haunted Spaces of the Black Imagination." In *Jason Moran*, edited by Adrienne Edwards, 97–111. Minneapolis: Walker Art Center, 2018.

Enwezor, Okwui. "El Gran Espectáculo: Jean-Michel Basquiat, Modernity, Modernism." In *Jean-Michel Basquiat*, edited by Dieter Buchhart in collaboration with Anna Karina Hofbauer, 34–53. Paris: Fondation Louis Vuitton; Paris: Éditions Gallimard, 2018.

Enwezor, Okwui. "Katharina Grosse's Festival of Form." In *Katharina Grosse*, edited by Louise Neri, 12–31. New York: Gagosian; New York: Rizzoli, 2018.

Enwezor, Okwui. "The Wreck of Utopia: Alienation and Disalienation in John Akomfrah's Postcolonial Cinema." In *John Akomfrah: Signs of Empire*, edited by Thea Ballard and Dana Kopel, 82–91. New York: New Museum, 2018.

2019

Enwezor, Okwui. "Landings: Okwui Enwezor in Conversation with Massimiliano Gioni." Interview by Massimiliano Gioni. In *Nari Ward: We the People*, edited by Gary Carrion-Murayari, Massimiliano Gioni, and Helga Christoffersen, 74–81. New York: Phaidon in association with the New Museum, 2019.

2020

Enwezor, Okwui. "Grief and Grievance: Art and Mourning in America." In *Grief and Grievance: Art and Mourning in America*, 7. London: Phaidon in association with the New Museum, 2020.

Enwezor, Okwui, interviewer. "The Invention of the Artist as a Young Photographer: Samuel Fosso in Conversation with Okwui Enwezor." Interview with Samuel Fosso. In *Samuel Fosso, Autoportrait*, edited by Okwui Enwezor, 10–21. Göttingen, Germany: Steidl; Burlafingen, Germany: Walther Collection, 2020. French edition: Paris: Maison européenne de la photographie, 2021.

2022

Enwezor, Okwui, and Chika Okeke-Agulu. *El Anatsui: The Reinvention of Sculpture*. Bologna: Damiani, 2022.

Index

Page references in *italics* indicate figures. OE is Okwui Enwezor.